THE ARREST CONVENTIONS: INTERNATIONAL ENFORCEMENT OF MARITIME CLAIMS

The Arrest Conventions, signed in 1952 and 1999, play a fundamental role in the worldwide enforcement of maritime claims. Arrest of ships is one of the most distinctive features of international maritime law. It provides a powerful, efficient and effective means of enforcing maritime claims in rem, obtaining sufficient asset security and preserving property pending substantive proceedings. Ship arrest is, however, also a draconian power that cuts across property rights and can cause considerable commercial harm to shipowning interests. This book provides thematic and comparative analysis from leading international commentators on the most significant legal and policy issues, including practical problems arising from the Arrest Convention texts, as well as the direct implementation or indirect 'translation' of the Arrest Conventions into domestic legal systems. It critically analyses the political and historical development of the Conventions, explores the key concepts underpinning the Arrest Convention frameworks and considers the future of ship arrest.

The Arrest Conventions

International Enforcement of Maritime Claims

Edited by
Paul Myburgh

• HART •
OXFORD • LONDON • NEW YORK • NEW DELHI • SYDNEY

HART PUBLISHING

Bloomsbury Publishing Plc

Kemp House, Chawley Park, Cumnor Hill, Oxford, OX2 9PH, UK

HART PUBLISHING, the Hart/Stag logo, BLOOMSBURY and the Diana logo are trademarks of Bloomsbury Publishing Plc

First published in Great Britain 2019

A catalogue record for this book is available from the British Library.

Library of Congress Cataloging-in-Publication data

Names: Myburgh, Paul, editor.

Title: The arrest conventions : international enforcement of maritime claims / edited by Paul Myburgh.

Description: Chicago : Hart Publishing, 2019. | Includes bibliographical references and index.

Identifiers: LCCN 2019021089 (print) | LCCN 2019022040 (ebook) | ISBN 9781509928293 (EPub) | ISBN 9781509928309 (hardback)

Subjects: LCSH: Arrest of ships. | Maritime law. | BISAC: LAW / Commercial / International Trade.

Classification: LCC K1188.A7 (ebook) | LCC K1188.A7 A76 2019 (print) | DDC 343.09/6—dc23

LC record available at https://lccn.loc.gov/2019021089

ISBN: HB: 978-1-50992-830-9
ePDF: 978-1-50992-828-6
ePub: 978-1-50992-829-3

Typeset by Compuscript Ltd, Shannon

PREFACE

Like many ship arrests, the writing and editing of this book has involved the co-ordinated, concerted and occasionally frantic efforts of a number of different parties spread across the world.

I am very grateful to my friends and colleagues in the Centre for Maritime Law at the Faculty of Law of the National University of Singapore for their assistance and support in organising and hosting the colloquium on the Arrest Conventions 1952 and 1999 at the National University of Singapore that resulted in this book. In particular, I would like to thank Stephen Girvin for suggesting the theme of the colloquium and for his sage advice throughout; Rowena Goh and Jothi Bhavani d/o Panchasaram for their exceptional organisation of all aspects of the colloquium; and Luci Carey for keeping meticulous notes of the debates and discussions during the colloquium. The Centre for Maritime Law and I would also like to acknowledge the generous funding assistance provided by the Singapore Ministry of Law through its NUS Law Vision Project that enabled the colloquium to take place.

Finally, many thanks to all the contributors to this book, to Roberta Bassi and Rosamund Jubber of Hart Publishing and to Claire Banyard for making the entire editing process immeasurably more convenient and enjoyable than the average ship arrest.

Paul Myburgh
Singapore
Waitangi Day
6 February 2019

TABLE OF CONTENTS

LIST OF CONTRIBUTORS

Justice Belinda ANG
A Judge of the Supreme Court of Singapore

Assoc Prof Graham BRADFIELD
Associate Professor, Faculty of Law, University of Cape Town
An Attorney of the High Court of South Africa

Prof Martin DAVIES
Admiralty Law Institute Professor of Maritime Law, Tulane University School of Law
Director, Tulane Maritime Law Center

Dr Henning JESSEN
Associate Professor of Maritime Law and Policy, World Maritime University, Malmö, Sweden

Prof Kate LEWINS
Professor of Law, Murdoch University, Australia
Academic Fellow, Centre for Maritime Law, Faculty of Law, National University of Singapore
A Barrister and Solicitor of the Supreme Court of Western Australia and High Court of Australia

Nathanael LIN
An Advocate and Solicitor of the Supreme Court of Singapore
Group In-House Counsel, Ocean Tankers (Pte) Ltd

Dr Bevan MARTEN
Senior Lecturer in Law, Faculty of Law, Victoria University of Wellington
A Barrister and Solicitor of the High Court of New Zealand
Partner, Izard Weston, Wellington

Assoc Prof Paul MYBURGH
Deputy Director, Centre for Maritime Law, Faculty of Law, National University of Singapore
An Advocate of the High Court of South Africa

Justice Steven RARES
A Judge of the Federal Court of Australia and an Additional Judge of the Supreme Court of the Australian Capital Territory

Dr George THEOCHARIDIS
Professor of Maritime Law and Policy, World Maritime University, Malmö, Sweden

Prof D Rhidian THOMAS
Emeritus Professor of Maritime Law and Founder Director of the Institute of International Shipping and Trade Law, College of Law, Swansea University, Wales, UK

TOH Kian Sing SC
Senior Counsel, An Advocate and Solicitor of the Supreme Court of Singapore
Adjunct Faculty, Faculty of Law, Singapore Management University

Dr Anton P TRICHARDT
A Barrister of the Supreme Court, Victoria, Australia
Adjunct Associate Professor of the University of New South Wales

Prof Michael TSIMPLIS
Professor of Law, School of Law, City University of Hong Kong

Dr Yingying ZOU
Academic Fellow, Centre for Maritime Law, Faculty of Law, National University of Singapore
A Qualified Attorney-at-Law of the People's Republic of China
General Counsel of China Merchants Energy Shipping Co Ltd

TABLE OF CASES

Australia

Belgium

Canada

China

European Union

Germany

Greece

Hong Kong SAR

India

Ireland

Italy

Malaysia

Netherlands

New Zealand

Singapore

South Africa

United Kingdom

United Nations

United States of America

TABLE OF LEGISLATION

Australia

Canada

China

European Union

Germany

Greece

Hong Kong SAR

India

Ireland

Malaysia

Netherlands

New Zealand

Nigeria

Philippines

Singapore

South Africa

South Korea

Spain

United Kingdom

United States of America

TABLE OF INTERNATIONAL INSTRUMENTS

Introduction

Dr Lushington famously observed in *The Volant*[1] that ship arrest offers 'the greatest security for obtaining substantial justice in furnishing a security for prompt and immediate payment'. This quotation encapsulates several of the major themes explored in this book: the use (and abuse) of ship arrest as a means for maritime creditors to obtain security over highly mobile assets in whichever port they may find them; the need for maritime courts to use their potentially draconian powers of ship arrest wisely to achieve 'substantial justice' for both maritime claimants and defendant shipowners; and the efficacy and efficiency of the ship arrest regime in the enforcement of international maritime claims.

This book examines the two major international instruments dealing with ship arrest – the Arrest Conventions 1952[2] and 1999[3] – and their implementation and utilisation in domestic legal systems. It begins and ends with Chapters 1 and 13 providing a broad overview of international ship arrest. Prof Rhidian Thomas introduces the subject by analysing the concept of ship arrest and its development under both the Arrest Conventions and English admiralty jurisdiction and practice, and critically evaluates the availability, fairness and proportionality of ship arrest as an appropriate remedy for the enforcement of maritime claims. Prof Martin Davies surveys the future of ship arrest, concluding that the system is likely to survive future developments largely unchanged, but that the issue of how maritime courts treat corporate ownership structures of ships that put these security assets out of the reach of maritime creditors is in need of re-examination.

Chapters 2–6 provide more specific analyses of fundamental concepts that underpin the Arrest Conventions, or issues that have caused ongoing problems in this area. Assoc Prof Graham Bradfield analyses the arrest of associated ships (ships not owned by the defendant but associated through criteria of common control) with particular reference to the innovative South African reforms in this regard and the failed attempt to introduce the concept of associated ship arrest into the Arrest Convention 1999. This theme of arresting surrogate or associated ships is addressed in several of the chapters, and goes to the heart of the policy tensions that exist between broadening out the potential security asset base to assist maritime creditors, whilst avoiding undue interruption of international trade and achieving a just and commercially sensible result. Dr Anton Trichardt explores in depth the concept of ship arrest as providing security in and of itself, as well as the use of so-called 'security arrests'; both in the sense of the arrest of ships and their retention as security

[1] *The Volant* (1842) 1 Wm Rob 383, 387, 166 ER 616, 618. His dictum – if accurately reported – on the non-availability of a maritime lien for damage claims (ibid) did not, however, win favour with the Privy Council in *The Bold Buccleugh* (1851) 7 Moo PC 267, 283–84, 13 ER 884, 890 (PC).

[2] International Convention Relating to the Arrest of Sea-going Ships (adopted 10 May 1952, entered into force 24 February 1956) 439 UNTS 193.

[3] International Convention on the Arrest of Ships (adopted 12 March 1999, entered into force 14 September 2011) 2797 UNTS 3.

where there is a stay of proceedings in favour of a foreign forum selection clause, and in the more radical sense of the stand-alone security arrest allowed for in the South African legislation. Justice Steven Rares then examines the circumstances in which a maritime court may decline to exercise its jurisdiction following arrest: either because of a refusal to recognise and enforce foreign maritime claims; or on discretionary procedural or substantive grounds. Prof Kate Lewins dissects the vexed question of rearrest and multiple ship arrests which, once again, goes to Dr Lushington's remark about providing 'substantial justice' to the claimant without over-reaching and intruding unnecessarily on the property rights of the defendant shipowner. This theme is reinforced by Toh Kian Sing SC and Nathanael Lin, who discuss the issue of wrongful arrest of ships and related issues, such as the provision of counter-security by maritime claimants.

Chapters 7–9 provide contextual analyses of the Arrest Conventions and ship arrest. Assoc Prof Paul Myburgh examines the private international law (conflict of laws) issues thrown up by the institution and practice of international ship arrest and the lack of guidance on these issues provided by the Arrest Conventions. Prof Michael Tsimplis discusses the potential use of ship arrest and other regimes of detention and seizure of ships to address environmental liability claims, and the problems of adapting a twentieth-century international liability regime focused on commerce and property to twenty-first century concerns about sustainability and environmental pollution. Justice Belinda Ang explores from a Singapore perspective the palpable tensions that exist between the international ship arrest and cross-border insolvency regimes, with both regimes having very different agendas regarding the treatment and ranking of secured and general creditors and the resolution of claims arising from the failures of multinational shipping corporations. Needless to say, this is an issue that has risen to considerable prominence in recent years in the wake of the global financial crisis (or crises) and the collapse of major international shipping players.

Finally, Chapters 10–12 explore the theme of translating the Arrest Conventions into different domestic legal regimes. As Prof Francesco Berlingieri has pointed out, there are 'various degrees of uniformity in maritime law and various ways of reaching it'[4] – or, one might add, not reaching it. Drs Henning Jessen and George Theocharidis discuss issues surrounding the translation and implementation of the Arrest Conventions in Civil Law jurisdictions in Europe (with a particular emphasis on Germany and Greece) and in the context of the European Union. Dr Yingying Zou provides an insight into the transposition of the major elements of the Arrest Convention 1999 into the domestic legal regime of the People's Republic of China. Dr Bevan Marten explores the variety of ways in which different Anglo-Common Law jurisdictions have adopted or adapted the Arrest Conventions, either directly or indirectly through the machinery of the British Empire and later the Commonwealth.

Although all of the above chapters and topics have been organised thematically to provide the reader with a coherent overall picture of the Arrest Conventions and their role in the enforcement of international maritime claims, one of the strengths of this edited collection is that it brings to bear a broad range of different perspectives on the topic of ship arrest from highly experienced and expert academics, legal practitioners and judges

[4] Francesco Berlingieri, 'Uniformity in Maritime Law and Implementation of International Conventions' (1987) 18 *J Mar L & Com* 317.

from different jurisdictions. The reader will find in these pages articulate, independent and sometimes conflicting arguments regarding the pressing issues and problems surrounding international ship arrest. How does one deal with different ownership structures of ships, especially one-ship companies? Should the surrogate ship arrest concept be extended to cover seizure of associated ships or even non-maritime assets of the defendant? What are the appropriate roles of insolvency law and ship arrest law when the defendant shipowning company fails? What is the appropriate balance of convenience and justice between the conflicting rights and interests of creditors and financiers, the defendant shipowner and other involved third parties? And, given the transnational nature of the shipping industry, how should different foreign rights, commercial expectations and claims be dealt with justly and sensibly by the forum arresti? These different voices and views echo the stimulating and animated debates and discussions that followed the presentation of the contributors' draft papers at the colloquium held at the National University of Singapore that gave rise to this book, and provide proof of the illuminating and enduring value of conversations between academics, legal practitioners and judges – pilgrims all 'on the endless road to unattainable perfection'.[5]

[5] *Spiliada Maritime Corp v Cansulex Ltd* [1987] AC 460, 488 B–C (Lord Goff).

1

Ship Arrest – Issues of Availability, Fairness and Proportionality

RHIDIAN THOMAS*

I. Ship Arrest – An Introductory Overview

A. Introduction

Ship arrest is as familiar a phenomenon in maritime law and practice as any other that might be identified. It is one of the distinguishing hallmarks of the subject, as the judiciary is only too ready to declare.[1] Yet, like so many common and familiar topics, it can become surprisingly elusive and obscure when there is a pause to analyse the phenomenon closely. Exposed to the beam of the spotlight it may become distinctly hazy.

Ship arrest is consistently highlighted as a point of difference when compared to other forms of legal process and lauded as placing maritime claimants in litigation in a favourable position, enjoying privileges not available to other categories of claimant, relating primarily to questions of jurisdiction and pre-judgment security.[2] The gaze of those who adopt this viewpoint is invariably inclined to the peculiar hazards confronting maritime claimants, compelled to pursue claims in an international environment and often confronting shipowners and operators seeking to evade justice or ready accessibility of their persons or property by strategically taking advantage of the vast global oceanic and terrestrial stage on which they ply their trade. The availability of ship arrest, it is contended, enables them to counter these potential difficulties.[3]

There is, of course, some truth in this analysis, but it is also the case that in the contemporary world the potential difficulties confronting maritime claimants are substantially less

* Emeritus Professor of Maritime Law and Founder Director of the Institute of International Shipping and Trade Law, College of Law, Swansea University, Wales, UK.

[1] To provide a recent example: in *Stolt Kestrel BV v Sener Petrol Denizcilik Ticaret AS (The Stolt Kestrel and The Niyazi S)* [2015] EWCA Civ 1035, [2016] 1 Lloyd's Rep 125 [21] Tomlinson LJ considered the right to arrest to be 'the unique feature' of the admiralty jurisdiction.

[2] Considered in text at n 73ff below.

[3] *Natwest Markets plc (Formerly known as the Royal Bank of Scotland plc) v Stallion Eight Shipping Co SA (The MV Alkyon)* [2018] EWHC 2033 (Admlty), [2018] 2 Lloyd's Rep 601 [55] (Teare J): 'Given that ships are mobile assets that may be within the jurisdiction for only a short period of time such a right may well be essential to a claimant obtaining justice.'

than in bygone times and are not much different, if at all, from the difficulties confronting international litigants generally. The world has changed radically since the late eighteenth and nineteenth centuries when sea transport was the sole significant mode of international transport and the engine driving the growth in international trade, and when international communications were precarious and rudimentary. The multi-layered globalisation of modern trade, transport, communications and associated legal, insurance, finance and other services have rendered international litigation and jurisprudence commonplace, with the position and circumstances of the various categories of international claimants materially uniform. In the words of Lord Sumption, '[l]itigation between residents of different states is a routine incident of modern commercial life'.[4] It is also the case that the position of international litigants generally is much more favourable than that of their predecessors. This is not to say that there are not particular problems associated with international litigation, particularly when compared with domestic litigation, but the problems are of a common nature and confront international claimants generally. Therefore, any special pleading on account of maritime litigants must be carefully considered and not accepted as a matter of course.

Ship arrest is a process confined to courts with jurisdiction over identified maritime claims. In the Common Law tradition it is associated with the Admiralty Court and its jurisdiction:[5] in other legal traditions the position is less distinct and may be associated with any of the ordinary civil courts with jurisdiction over maritime claims. The governing law is that of the court which orders the arrest, the lex fori or lex fori arresti, and only a ship within the territorial jurisdiction of the arresting court may be arrested.[6] An arrest may be made for many purposes but its most significant consequences relate to questions of jurisdiction and security for the underlying substantive claim.[7] In contemporary practice ship arrest is viewed predominantly as a device for obtaining security for the claim. There is a common benefit in this because it also provides the means by which owners can avoid the commercial disruption caused by an arrest by providing substitute security.[8] The reality is that, even when the power to arrest exists, rarely is it exercised because predominantly parties agree on the provision of substitute security.[9]

The arrest of a ship results in the detention of property owned or operated by a legal or natural person (predominantly the former), with the consequence that the owner or operator is denied the commercial use and benefit of the ship, at least temporarily. The process necessarily involves the risk of inflicting a detriment and the position is compounded by the fact that this occurs before the question of liability in relation to the underpinning substantive claim has been determined. In its nature, therefore, it is an exceptional process. It could

[4] *Abela v Baadarani* [2013] UKSC 44, [2013] 1 WLR 2043 [53].

[5] For modern texts see Nigel Meeson and John A Kimbell, *Admiralty Jurisdiction and Practice*, 5th edn (Abingdon, Informa Law from Routledge, 2018); Sarah C Derrington and James M Turner, *The Law and Practice of Admiralty Matters*, 2nd edn (Oxford, OUP, 2016). For older texts which continue to have significant relevance, see Robert Griffith Williams, Gainsford Bruce et al, *Jurisdiction and Practice of the English Courts in Admiralty Actions and Appeals*, 3rd edn (London, Sweet & Maxwell, 1902); Edward Stanley Roscoe et al, *The Admiralty Jurisdiction and Practice of the High Court of Justice*, 5th edn (London, Stevens & Sons, 1931).

[6] See text at n 92ff below.

[7] Considered in the text at n 73ff below.

[8] See text at n 79ff below.

[9] *The MV Alkyon* (n 3) [15] (Teare J).

readily be perceived as being in conflict with human rights, the basic notion of the right to peaceful enjoyment of property in a civilised liberal society, or, alternatively, as being a disproportionate process. But this is not to say that such a process may not in particular circumstances be justified and recognised as legally valid. There may be just cause, to be confined to situations when the process takes the support of public policy and is administered fairly with due and proper regard to the competing interests of the parties. This is an aspect of ship arrest which appears not to have caused significant disquiet and consequently it has received little attention in the research literature. It is, nonetheless, a theme that underpins this Chapter.[10]

The ship arrest process gives rise to many legal issues and uncertainties, many of which are discussed and analysed by other contributors to this book. The thesis I wish to pursue relates to questions of the availability of the arrest process, and associated issues of fairness and proportionality in the way the arrest process functions. I do not query the validity of the existence of a right to arrest ships – the process is too well established to entertain such a radical position – only the extent of its availability and the way the power is exercised. In developing this thesis I take into account the international Conventions relating to ship arrest and the English admiralty jurisdiction, as the United Kingdom provides an example of an arrest-friendly State. The procedure and practice relating to ship arrest may vary significantly between States and there is a broad and imprecise tendency to group some as 'arrest-friendly' States, as compared to other States that adopt a more restrictive approach.

B. The Evolution of International Jurisprudence

The law and practice of ship arrest in contemporary jurisprudence is a mix of national and international Convention law, the latter based primarily on the International Convention Relating to the Arrest of Sea-Going Ships 1952 (Arrest Convention 1952)[11] and to a lesser extent the International Convention on Arrest of Ships 1999 (Arrest Convention 1999).[12] The Arrest Convention 1952 has received broad support and has been a significant influence on the development of an international law of ship arrest.[13] The object underlying the Arrest Convention 1999 was to develop the international law still further by clarifying the law and responding to identified omissions and limitations in the Arrest Convention 1952.[14] It has been, however, much less successful than its predecessor and has received little international support.[15]

[10] See Part II below.

[11] International Convention Relating to the Arrest of Sea-going Ships (adopted 10 May 1952, entered into force 24 February 1956) 439 UNTS 193.

[12] International Convention on the Arrest of Ships (adopted 12 March 1999, entered into force 14 September 2011) 2797 UNTS 3. For a comprehensive analysis of the Arrest Conventions, see Francesco Berlingieri, *Berlingieri on Arrest of Ships*, 6th edn (Abingdon, Informa Law from Routledge, 2017) vol 1 (on the Arrest Convention 1952) and vol 2 (on the Arrest Convention 1999).

[13] The Arrest Convention 1952, which entered into force on 24 February 1956, has been ratified by 71 States and influenced the development of the law in many more.

[14] Berlingieri (n 12) vol 2 ch 1.

[15] The Arrest Convention 1999 entered into force on 14 September 2011 and has been ratified by 11 States, of which Spain is probably the most significant in the context of shipping. It has also significantly influenced the national laws of China and India: on which see further chs 11 and 12.

The law of ship arrest has a close relationship with the subject of maritime liens because the latter represents a distinct source of the power to arrest ships, with its own distinctive characteristics. The power to arrest follows the ship even into the hands of a bona fide purchaser without notice.[16] The subject of maritime liens has also attracted a distinct cluster of unifying international Conventions which have only enjoyed minimal success.[17] Both Arrest Conventions make it expressly clear that they do not create any maritime liens[18] and the Arrest Convention 1999 also expressly recognises the power of arrest in association with claims in the nature of maritime liens.[19]

Both Arrest Conventions are restricted to the arrest of ships and constructed on a synthesis of two preceding legal traditions, the Common Law, with its specialist strand of admiralty law and procedure,[20] and the Civil Law.[21]

Under admiralty law ship arrest is an incident of the claim in rem served on the ship in respect of which the legal question or claim arose and which in turn invokes the jurisdiction in rem of the Admiralty Court.[22] The arrest of the ship is thereafter achieved by the execution of a warrant of arrest against the ship.[23] Nonetheless, service of the claim form alone is sufficient to invoke the admiralty jurisdiction in rem.[24] Concurrently with the jurisdiction in rem the Admiralty Court also possesses a jurisdiction in personam.[25] When the latter is invoked the Admiralty Court conducts itself in the same way as litigation in other senior courts. When the in rem jurisdiction is invoked it conducts itself in an exceptional way, at least initially, which is not replicated in any other senior court. Its jurisdiction in rem is established by process against property, predominantly the ship.[26] Prior to the Arrest Convention 1952 the power to arrest a ship was restricted to a claim within the admiralty jurisdiction as it then existed[27] and to the ship in connection with which the claim arose.[28]

[16] See generally D Rhidian Thomas, *Maritime Liens*, British Shipping Laws 14 (Stevens & Sons, London, 1980); William Tetley and Robert C Wilkins, *Maritime Liens and Claims* 2nd edn (Montreal, International Shipping Publications Blais, 1998); DC Jackson, *Enforcement of Maritime Claims* (London, LLP, 2005); Anton P Trichardt, *Maritime Liens and the Conflict of Laws*, Transactions of the Centre for Business Law 47 (Bloemfontein, University of the Free State, 2011).

[17] International Convention for the Unification of Certain Rules Relating to Maritime Liens and Mortgages (adopted 10 April 1926, entered into force 2 June 1931) 120 LNTS 187; International Convention for the Unification of Certain Rules relating to Maritime Liens and Mortgages (adopted 27 May 1967, not yet in force): see UNCITRAL, *Register of Texts of Conventions and Other Instruments concerning International Trade Law* (UN, New York, 1973) vol II 179; International Convention on Maritime Liens and Mortgages (adopted 6 May 1993, entered into force 5 September 2004) 2276 UNTS 39.

[18] Arrest Convention 1952, art 9; Arrest Convention 1999, art 9.

[19] Article 3(1)(e).

[20] On which see generally Meeson and Kimbell (n 5); Derrington and Turner (n 5).

[21] The distinction between the two traditions was not always as clear as it may be perceived to be today. In its early history the common law possessed a Civilian strand from which developed the modern Admiralty Court and jurisdiction. See Arthur Browne, *A Compendious View of the Civil Law and the Law of the Admiralty* (London, J Butterworth, 1802); FL Wiswall, *The Development of Admiralty Jurisdiction and Practice since 1800* (Cambridge, CUP, 1970).

[22] Senior Courts Act 1981 (UK), ss 20–24.

[23] The procedure is considered in greater detail in the text at n 134ff below.

[24] The current procedure dates back to reforms introduced by the Supreme Court Judicature Acts 1873–75 which introduced the requirement of a writ in rem (now described as a claim form in rem).

[25] Senior Courts Act 1981 (UK), s 21(1).

[26] It is also possible for cargo and freight to be arrested in particular circumstances.

[27] It was set out in the Supreme Court of Judicature (Consolidation) Act 1925 (UK), s 22.

[28] *The Beldis* [1936] P 51.

This was the concept of admiralty jurisdiction inherited by other jurisdictions which were party to the English common law.[29]

The pre-1952 position was very different in the development of the Civilian legal tradition where nothing comparable to the admiralty jurisdiction in rem existed. Maritime and commercial codes emerged but the associated disputes were allocated to the general civil courts. There was also no specific concept of 'ship arrest' but there did emerge the concept of 'saisie conservatoire'.[30] This is a conservatory right applicable generally in litigation, in respect to all categories of claimants and claims, and property. Broadly stated, it provides the means of protecting the continued availability of assets of the defendant to ensure the fruitful discharge of any future judgment obtained in favour of the claimant. The precise nature of the right and procedure applicable may vary between different jurisdictions but the essential purpose has a common thread. In litigation, where the claim was against a shipowner, it provided a procedure for the pre-judgment detention of any ship or ships owned by the shipowner as security for any successful future claim. Beyond the nature of the remedy, its reach over the property of a defendant shipowner was much less restrictive than the one-ship arrest procedure under the admiralty jurisdiction. Other ships, even multiple ships, could be seized.[31]

The respective positions under the Common Law admiralty jurisdiction and Civilian procedure changed with the emergence of the Arrest Convention 1952, which attempted to bridge the divide between these two very distinct historical traditions. It is immediately noticeable that the Arrest Convention 1952 does not make any express reference to jurisdiction in rem or claims in rem. It makes reference only to ship arrest and treats the subject as an independent and self-contained subject. For Civilian lawyers the format was unexceptional, but for Common Law lawyers matters were not that straightforward because the provisions of the Convention had to blend with the established admiralty jurisdiction in rem. This did cause difficulty and it is not by accident that, although the UK ratified the Arrest Convention 1952, it did not incorporate the Convention into law. Rather, it gave effect to certain of its provisions in legislation, a methodology which carries a degree of risk.[32] In the result the in rem jurisdiction survived unscathed.

The Arrest Convention 1952 limits the right of arrest to 'maritime claims' as defined in art 1.[33] This definition resembles closely the substantive jurisdiction of the Admiralty Court at that time.[34] The approach was far more significant for Civilian jurisdictions because it restricted the scope of 'saisie conservatoire' to the defined maritime claims.

Under the Arrest Convention 1952 the powers of arrest are set out in arts 3(1) and 3(4), which unfortunately are not clearly drafted and consequently give rise to many difficulties

[29] For the relationship between ship arrest and insolvency see ch 9.

[30] Observations on aspects of the comparison are made in Andrew Tettenborn, 'The Arrest Conventions: An Update Needed?' in Barış Soyer and Andrew Tettenborn (eds), *Maritime Liabilities in a Global and Regional Context* (Abingdon, Informa Law from Routledge, 2018) ch 13.

[31] See ch 10 for the position in Germany and Greece; and ch 11 for the position in China.

[32] Initially by the Administration of Justice Act 1956 (UK), Part 1. The law is now to be found in the Senior Courts Act 1981 (UK), ss 21–24.

[33] See Berlingieri (n 12) vol 1 ch 5.

[34] Defined in the Supreme Court of Judicature (Consolidation) Act 1925 (UK), s 22.

of interpretation.[35] The corresponding powers in English admiralty law are contained in the Senior Courts Act 1981 (UK), ss 21(2) and 21(4).

The primary right of arrest exists in relation to the particular ship in connection with which the claim arose, often described as the offending or particular ship, provided the liability is that of the owner or demise charterer of the ship, who continues to be owner or, in the case of a demise charterer, the demise charterer or owner, of that ship at the time of the arrest.[36] As defined, the power is in accord with the admiralty jurisdiction, save that in the latter the crucial moment the essential preconditions are to be satisfied is when the claim form is issued and not the time of the arrest.[37] Thereby is established the concept of a 'statutory lien'.[38]

More radically there is also established a right to arrest 'any other ship' owned at the time of arrest by the owner or demise charterer and subject to the conditions previously outlined.[39] The introduction of the right to arrest 'another ship' represented a significant modification of the admiralty jurisdiction, but so far as Civilian jurisdictions were concerned it amounted to a material restriction compared with former practice, particularly if the right was to be understood as an alternative right.

This extended power of arrest has given rise to many questions of interpretation. Two are of particular significance and what follows is the way they have been resolved in English admiralty law. First, is the right to arrest another ship conditional on the existence of a right to arrest the particular ship in connection with which the liability arose, or is it a wholly independent right? If the former, then the label 'sister ship arrest' is accurate; if the latter, the label is incorrect and misleading. What is permitted is an independent right to arrest 'another ship' provided the stipulated preconditions are satisfied. In English admiralty law the latter interpretation has been adopted.[40] It has at the same time been determined that only a single ship may be arrested; the power is not cumulative. In other words, it is an 'either/or' position: the claimant may arrest either the particular ship or another ship.[41]

This is a development of particular relevance to claims by third parties against charterers. In such a case it is clear that the particular chartered ship cannot be arrested because the necessary criteria are not satisfied. But the claimant may have a right to arrest 'any other ship' that the charterer may own, providing the other preconditions to the right of arrest are satisfied.[42]

The second question relates to the concept of common ownership as between the particular ship and another ship. The Arrest Conventions define this in terms of 'all the shares' in the respective ship.[43] The particular issue arises principally with regard to ships owned by different companies in a corporate group, or to analogous situations. The doctrine of distinct corporate personality defines each company as a distinct legal person

[35] See Berlingieri (n 12) vol 1 ch 11.

[36] Arrest Convention 1952, arts 3(1) and 3(4).

[37] Senior Courts Act 1981 (UK), s 21(4).

[38] *The Monica S* [1968] P 741, 768G.

[39] Arrest Convention 1952, arts 3(1) and 3(4); Senior Courts Act 1981 (UK), s 21(4).

[40] Following on from the decision of the Singapore Court of Appeal in *The Permina 108* [1976] SGCA 12, [1974–1976] SLR(R) 850.

[41] *Monte Ulia (Owners) v Banco (Owners) (The Banco)* [1971] P 137 (CA).

[42] *The Span Terza* [1982] 1 Lloyd's Rep 225; *The Tychy* [1999] 2 Lloyd's Rep 11.

[43] Article 3(2). The same is followed in the Senior Courts Act 1981 (UK), s 21(4).

and this approach has been followed, subject to some qualifications, by the Admiralty Court with the consequence that the extended right of arrest was lost.[44] This represented an attractive proposition for companies running fleets of ships and led to the management practice of operating a fleet through a number of one-ship companies.[45] Although not illegal, this could be considered a dubious and questionable practice which significantly undermines the objective of the Arrest Conventions. There has been a response by some jurisdictions. Of particular significance, South Africa has introduced the concept of 'associated ships', founded on the concept of corporate control, thereby establishing a basis for arresting 'any other ship' that transcends the strictness of the doctrine of distinct corporate personality.[46]

The Arrest Convention 1999 builds on and extends the platform established by the Arrest Convention 1952. In particular it increases the number and range of claims which fall within the Convention definition of 'maritime claims'[47] and also the availability of the arrest procedure. The powers of permissible arrest are set out in art 3 in a much clearer and more structured form than in the Arrest Convention 1952.

The arrest powers are again divided into those exercisable against the particular ship in respect of which a maritime claim has arisen and those against 'any other ship or ships'.[48]

The right to arrest the particular ship in respect of the liability of the owner or demise charterer is the same as under the Arrest Convention 1952. The particular ship may be arrested if the liability is that of the owner or demise charterer and at the time of the arrest the ship is owned by the owner or in the case of the liability of the demise charterer, by the demise charterer or as owner (if the demise charterer has so become).[49]

Very radically, with regard to the arrest of 'other ships' the Arrest Convention 1999 increases the range of possible arrests. It confers on claimants the right also to arrest 'any other ship or ships' which, at the time of arrest, is or are owned by the party liable for the maritime claim by virtue of being the owner, demise charterer, time or voyage charterer of the particular ship.[50] The provision is expressly indicated to be a cumulative right, which may be exercised up to the value of the claim.[51] In other words, it establishes multiple rights of arrest. Though the security of each ship is tied to its value, multiple ships may be arrested up to the value of the claim. This represents a very significant extension of the powers of ship arrest: it is a sharp acceleration of the policy commenced by the Arrest Convention 1952 and appears to lurch the international regime in the direction of the pre-1952 Civilian jurisdictional position, subject to the limitation imposed by the extended definition of maritime claim.

The common ownership issue continues into the Arrest Convention 1999 and it was a significant disappointment that the Convention failed to take steps to counter the drift to

[44] The issue is discussed in Meeson and Kimbell (n 5) paras 3.48–59.

[45] South African Law Reform Commission, *Report on the Review of the Law of Admiralty*, Project 32 (Pretoria, South African Law Reform Commission, 1982) para 7.3.

[46] Admiralty Jurisdiction Regulation Act No 105 of 1983 (AJRA 1983), s 3(7)(a). This development is concisely summarised in Meeson and Kimbell (n 5) paras 5.27–34 and is analysed in depth in ch 2.

[47] Discussed in the text at n 102ff below.

[48] Arrest Convention 1999, arts 3 and 5(2).

[49] ibid, arts 3(1)(a) and 3(1)(b).

[50] ibid, art 3(2).

[51] ibid, art 5(2).

one-ship companies. After a significant debate it was resolved that the matter should be governed by national law, which was not a satisfactory position in which to leave the issue.[52] Ironically, this decision would appear also to undermine the significance of the introduction of multiple arrests, which is likely to accelerate the movement into one-ship companies.[53]

This outline is sufficient to indicate that international policy is firmly in support of the availability of ship arrest and is seeking to promote its increased availability to claimants. This it seeks to achieve by increasing the range of maritime claims which are enforceable by ship arrest and giving claimants more flexible or multiple powers of arrest. The utility of the process is identified with security for the claim and the Arrest Convention 1999 takes a significant step in this direction.[54]

The Arrest Conventions 1952 and 1999 address many topics beyond those considered above, including matters of procedure, obtaining the release from arrest, rights of rearrest, protection offered to owners of arrested ships in the face of wrongful arrest and jurisdiction over underlying substantive claims. It is not proposed in this contribution to analyse these provisions, save to the extent that they are relevant to the theme developed in this contribution. Many are also analysed closely in some of the other contributions to this book.

C. Legal Nature of Ship Arrest

How ship arrest is to be characterised and understood as a legal process relating to property is an essential first step to understanding. I confine myself to a few observations on the distinction between ship arrest and other kinds of legal detentions or restraints on ships, a distinction which has a part to play in my thesis.[55]

The international Conventions provide the following definitions of ship arrest: the Arrest Convention 1952, art 1(2) provides that: '"Arrest" means the detention of a ship by judicial process to secure a maritime claim, but does not include the seizure of a ship in execution or satisfaction of a judgment.' The Arrest Convention 1999, art 1(2) provides that: '"Arrest" means any detention *or restriction on removal* of a ship by *order of a Court* to secure a maritime claim, but does not include the seizure of a ship in execution or satisfaction of a judgment *or other enforceable instrument*.'[56]

In their generality the definitions follow parallel tracks but the language in the Arrest Convention 1999 is a little more expansive.

The definitions make it clear that the Conventions are restricted to the arrest of ships and do not embrace arrest procedures relating to cargo and freight, as may exist under the admiralty jurisdiction. How the concept of 'ship' is to be understood is not defined in the Conventions and this leaves a troublesome issue unresolved.[57]

[52] An account of the debate is to be found in Berlingieri (n 12) vol 2 paras 8.70–74.
[53] Prof Martin Davies addresses the debate in ch 13.
[54] For an analysis of the conflict of law issues raised by the Arrest Conventions see ch 7.
[55] This topic is also addressed in ch 8.
[56] The italicised words indicate additions made to the definition in the Arrest Convention 1952.
[57] In English admiralty law, in this context, ship 'includes any description of vessel used in navigation and … incudes … a hovercraft': Senior Courts Act 1981 (UK), s 24(1).

Both definitions emphasise that ship arrest is a judicial remedy – not a self-help remedy. The arrest must be authorised by a court or other judicial authority and customarily is executed by an officer or representative of the court or other authority.

Both definitions define ship arrest as a process that effects the 'detention' of the arrested ship. The Arrest Convention 1999 also additionally describes it as a 'restriction on removal' of the arrested ship. It is difficult at first sight to appreciate what these words add to 'detention' which might itself be defined as a 'restriction on removal'. The object appears to be to make it clear that an arrest may be executed by the court taking possession of the arrested ship or by making an order restricting its removal out of the jurisdiction of the arresting court.[58] In the English admiralty jurisdiction an arrest is effected by the Admiralty Marshal or his deputy who thereafter has custody and control of the vessel, not title or possession.[59] This empowers him to restrict or manage the movement of the vessel. Responsibilities connected with title or arising from possession of the arrested ship continue to be borne by the owners.

The definitions are again in agreement that the primary purpose of ship arrest is to secure a maritime claim and not the execution of a judgment.[60] The definitions draw a clear distinction between security for a claim and security for a judgment. In the Arrest Convention 1999 the ambiguous words 'or other enforceable instrument' are added which it appears are intended to include a reference to an arbitral award and also instruments such as promissory notes and acknowledgment of debts which in some jurisdictions are enforceable in the same way as a judgment.[61] The sole reference to 'judgment' in the Arrest Convention 1952 is probably also open to a broad construction so as to include an arbitral award.

The distinction as between security for a claim and for a judgment is not always clear and obvious. A security for a claim is given in advance of any determination and is obliged to respond once the claim is upheld by a court or arbitral tribunal or by agreement. In admiralty proceedings the advance security is provided by the arrested ship which may be sold, and the claim or claims satisfied from the proceeds of sale. When judgment is given the arrested vessel may be sold by the court and the claim satisfied from the proceeds of sale.[62] In strictness, such security is not provided as a means of enforcing the determination, notwithstanding that it renders the determination effective. What the definitions seek to make clear is that ship arrest is not available as an independent procedure for the execution or satisfaction of a judgment by a judgment creditor. It is not one of the panoply of remedies open to judgment creditors against the assets of a judgment debtor in order to obtain the fruits of a favourable judgment or determination.

Ship arrest is also to be contrasted to the range of intervention powers that States and public and private national entities, such as governments, government departments, public authorities, customs and excise, ports, docks and harbours, may possess in relation to ships that infringe the law or otherwise are in breach of duty.[63] These powers may be described by

[58] Berlingieri (n 12) vol 2 para 4.02.

[59] *The Anna Helena* (1883) 5 Asp MLC 61.

[60] This also suggests some similarity with the concept of sequestration.

[61] Berlingieri (n 12) vol 2 para 4.07.

[62] *LD Commodities Rice Merchandising LLC v The Owners and/or Demise Charterers of the Vessel Styliani Z (The Styliani Z)* [2015] EWHC 3060 (Admlty), [2016] 1 Lloyd's Rep 395 [20] (Teare J).

[63] On the distinction between ship arrest and other forms of detention and seizure see further ch 8.

words such as capture, seizure, arrest, detention, restraint, forfeiture, confiscation, condemnation and expropriation in the relevant national legislation or other legal sources, and each may involve the detention and restriction on the movements of a ship, but they do not amount to an arrest within the meaning of the Conventions.[64]

A particular question arises as to whether the words 'or restriction on removal' in the Arrest Convention 1999 definition embrace the common law 'freezing injunction'. These injunctions are considered later in this Chapter,[65] but for present purposes it is sufficient to note that their essential purpose is the same, to secure claims although they do this in a different way, by preventing dissipation of assets prior to judgment.[66] This necessarily involves a 'restriction on removal' of assets, which may include a ship.[67] Nonetheless, they are distinguishable in many ways,[68] including on the basis of their procedural technicality. The injunction is an order of a court whereas the arrest is initiated by the claimant obtaining a warrant of arrest.[69] Whatever be the merits of the debate it is clear that under English law ship arrest and freezing injunctions are viewed as distinct and separate procedures. In the somewhat oblique words of Lord Denning MR '[the freezing injunction] enables the seizure of assets so as to preserve them for the benefit of the creditor; but not to give a charge in favour of any particular creditor'.[70]

The view taken of the nature and characterisation of freezing injunctions can probably be extended into a broad proposition to the effect that a court order restraining the disposition or movement of a ship, whether made by a domestic or foreign court, does not amount to an arrest, at least in English admiralty law. But in jurisdictions where the maritime factor is less distinctive and judicial powers more general in their characterisation the position could be less certain. So far as the Arrest Conventions are concerned, they appear to have contemplated that an arrest is the product of an order made by a court in the same territorial jurisdiction as the ship arrested, with the specific object of obtaining security for the claim and vesting jurisdiction in the arresting court.[71]

Finally, it is noteworthy that the definitions, in so far as they incorporate purpose, confine themselves to the obtaining of security. There is no reference to jurisdiction which is a significant incident of ship arrest.[72]

D. Legal Incidents of Ship Arrest

These have already been noted but the opportunity is taken in this part of the text to develop them further. The principal incidents are twofold, one relating to security for the

[64] The range of possible interventions is well illustrated by the insurance risks covered by standard war risks policies: see eg the Institute War and Strikes Clauses (Hulls-Time) 1/11/95.

[65] See text at n 163ff below.

[66] See text at n 171ff below.

[67] *The Rena K* [1979] 1 QB 377, 407.

[68] Most recently the comparison was examined in *The MV Alkyon* (n 3).

[69] *The Rena K* (n 67) 407.

[70] *Z Ltd v A-Z and AA-LL* [1982] 1 QB 558, 573 (CA).

[71] Compare Tettenborn (n 30).

[72] Arrest Convention 1952, art 7; Arrest Convention 1999, art 7.

claim and the other to jurisdiction to determine the underlying substantive claim.[73] There are further but probably less significant incidents. Ship arrest represents a useful procedure for bringing a ship into the custody of the court with respect to disputes relating to title, possession and employment.[74] It also provides an additional remedy to a mortgagee confronted by default on the part of the mortgagor.[75] These further incidents are not examined in the present context.

With regard to what has been identified as the principal incidents it is convenient to consider the matter of security first because of the interplay between security and jurisdiction.

i. Security

The arrested ship stands as security for the claim with the consequence that the ship may be sold by the court and the claim satisfied out of the proceeds of sale.[76] The process is aided by the purchaser being guaranteed a clean title.[77] In most instances the actual arrest of the ship is either avoided by the provision of satisfactory alternative security or released from arrest by the provision of such security.[78] If steps are not taken to obtain the release of a ship from arrest this may be an ominous indicator of financial difficulties and the pending insolvency of the owners.

Historically, in admiralty jurisdictions the security was given to the court in the form of bail which symbolically represented the ship and stood as substitute security.[79] In modern practice bail has fallen into disuse, although it continues to be recognised in the Arrest Convention 1952.[80] It has been replaced by security given directly to the claimant.[81] Nonetheless the court retains a supervisory jurisdiction over matters relating to the security just as it did with regard to bail.[82] The providing of security is not prejudicial to an owner; it is neither an acknowledgement of liability nor a waiver of legal entitlements.[83]

[73] *The MV Alkyon* (n 3) [14] (Teare J at first instance). See also *The Stolt Kestrel* (n 1) [12] (Tomlinson LJ) [12]; *The Styliani Z* (n 62) [20] (Teare J).

[74] Arrest Convention 1952, arts 1(1)(o), 1(1)(p) and 3(1); Arrest Convention 1999, arts 1(1)(s), 1(1)(t) and 3(1)(d).

[75] Arrest Convention 1952, arts 1(1)(q) and 3(1); Arrest Convention 1999, arts 1(1)(u) and 3(1)(c). See also the recent example provided by *The MV Alkyon* (n 3), where the mortgagee bank arrested the mortgaged vessel following an alleged breach of the loan agreement by the mortgagor owner.

[76] In special circumstances the ship may be sold before judgment (sale pendente lite): see Rhidian Thomas, 'Admiralty Sales Pendente Lite' (1998) 17 *CJQ* 409; Paul Myburgh, 'Admiralty Sales Pendent Lite: Reserve Prices and Broker Appointments' (2018) 24 *JIML* 369–75.

[77] *The Union Gold* [2013] EWHC 1696 (Admlty), [2014] 1 Lloyd's Rep 53 [5].The policy is that the court should be in a position to transfer a clean title to the purchaser, but acceptance of this policy is not necessarily universal which can cause significant difficulties. The CMI has established an International Working Group to examine the topic and is in the process of drafting a proposed International Convention on Recognition of Foreign Judicial Sales of Ships. On this and also on the possibility of private sanctioned sales see also Paul Myburgh, '"Satisfactory for its own Purposes": Private Direct Arrangements and Judicial Vessel Sales' (2016) 22 *JIML* 355–69.

[78] *The MV Alkyon* (n 3) [15] (Teare J at first instance).

[79] See Kenneth C McGuffie, *Admiralty Practice*, British Shipping Laws 1 (London, Stevens & Sons, 1964) ch 11.

[80] Articles 5 and 6.

[81] In the practice of the English Admiralty Court reference to 'bail' has been omitted from the provisions of the CPR Part 61 and related Practice Direction, presumably on the assumption that the practice has ceased to be relevant.

[82] Arrest Convention 1952, arts 5 and 6; Arrest Convention 1999, arts 4(2) and 4(6).

[83] Arrest Convention 1952, art 5; Arrest Convention 1999, art 4(3).

In modern admiralty practice the provision of security is primarily a matter to be decided *by the parties*. The security is given directly to the claimant, albeit it is not necessary for it to be given directly by the defendant owner. A valuable service provided by P&I clubs is to provide letters of undertaking to avoid or secure the release from arrest of ships owned by members.[84] Once a satisfactory and sufficient security is provided the court is obliged to release the ship from arrest.[85]

The nature and quantum of the security is in the first place to be agreed by the parties, but in the event of failure to agree the court may settle the question of what in the circumstances of the case amounts to sufficient and satisfactory security.[86] In the case of bail it was the rule that the sum paid into court could not exceed the value of the ship, it being in some sense a symbol of the ship.[87] But there is no reason why this rule should apply to security negotiated between the parties, when the claimant may be seeking security for the claim in its entirety. In the event that the owner has been compelled to acquiesce in the claimant's demand for what is subsequently determined to be excessive security, a question may rise as to who is to bear the cost of the excess, which may be determined under the court's supervisory jurisdiction.[88]

The international Conventions confirm much of the preceding analysis but also contain a surprising ambiguity. The Arrest Convention 1952 refers persistently to 'bail or other security' without defining the reference to 'other security'.[89] Is it to be taken to mean any other security of the same nature as bail, or any security even if wholly independent of bail? The drafting of the Convention, in its generality, suggests that the security is given to the court. It also speaks of security 'being furnished' without expressly stating to whom, but art 5 appears to imply that it is to the court or other appropriate judicial authority. With regard to the purpose of the security, it is stated that it is to obtain the release or prevent the arrest of a ship.[90] The generality of the provisions appear to assume that security is given to the court, although there is no expressly prescribed limit on the amount of the security that may be required.

The reference to bail is omitted from the Arrest Convention 1999: the reference is to security without qualification. Beyond referring to the 'provision' of security there is no express recognition that the security must be given to the arresting court, and the words of the Convention in their generality do not appear to support an implication to that effect. Nonetheless there are provisions which apply only when security has been given to a court.[91]

[84] This facility is discretionary and is generally considered to be dependent on the owner not being in fault under the insurance facility: see Steven J Hazelwood and David Semark, *P&I Clubs: Law and Practice*, 4th edn (London, Lloyd's List, 2010) ch 14; also Paul Myburgh, 'P&I Club Letters of Undertaking and Admiralty Arrests' (2018) 24 *JIML* 201–12. Note this facility was not available to the owners in *The MV Alkyon* (n 3) because of the nature of the claim.

[85] Arrest Convention 1952, art 5; Arrest Convention 1999, art 4(1).

[86] Arrest Convention 1952, art 5; Arrest Convention 1999, art 4(2).

[87] *The Kalamazoo* (1851) 15 Jur 885 (Dr Lushington); *The Majfrid* (1943) 77 Ll LR 127, 129.

[88] Arrest Convention 1952, art 6; Arrest Convention 1999, art 6.

[89] Articles 5 and 6.

[90] Article 5.

[91] See also text at n 100ff below.

ii. Jurisdiction

The broad rule is that the arresting court is vested with jurisdiction over the substantive claim.[92] This rule is followed in the Conventions save that in the Arrest Convention 1952 the rule applies when it is the national rule, otherwise the law of the country of arrest applies only if any one of specific criteria is satisfied.[93] The Arrest Convention 1999 additionally includes the court to which security has been given to obtain the release of the vessel[94] as vested with jurisdiction. This will usually be the arresting court, but if this is not the case and security is given and accepted by a different court, it appears to be suggested that that court also has jurisdiction.[95]

The Conventions recognise that jurisdiction may be surrendered when the parties have agreed a valid choice of jurisdiction agreement or arbitration agreement.[96] To this the Arrest Convention 1999 adds a reference to any other legal ground on which jurisdiction may be surrendered.[97] The principal example would be forum non conveniens.[98]

The underlying premise appears to be that the arrest of a ship within the territorial jurisdiction of the arresting court establishes a sufficient connection to justify the arresting court assuming jurisdiction over the underlying substantive claims, notwithstanding that in other regards the governing law, parties and the prevailing facts have little or no connection with the country in which the arresting court is located. This rule is not now as significant as in bygone times because contemporary courts have a far greater predisposition to surrender jurisdiction in appropriate circumstances. There is today a much keener sense of forum conveniens to be judged by taking into account the intention of the parties and the facts and circumstances of individual cases. The overriding object is to determine whether the dispute could be more appropriately resolved elsewhere.[99]

iii. Questions of Jurisdiction and Security

The fluid contemporary judicial approach to issues of jurisdiction raises a number of questions about the interrelationship between jurisdiction and security, about which the international Conventions are oblique and the questions as they arise may therefore have to be resolved primarily by reference to national law.

I confine myself to one issue and examine it from the perspective of the Conventions only.[100] What is the position of an arresting court, which has released the ship arrested against security provided, and which subsequently surrenders jurisdiction to another court or arbitral tribunal? Is the court obliged to release the security or may it be retained as

[92] Up to the enactment of the Supreme Court of Judicature Acts 1873–75 arrest was the principal, possibly the only, means of establishing jurisdiction: see Wiswall (n 21).

[93] Arrest Convention 1952, art 7(1); Arrest Convention 1999, art 7(1).

[94] Article 7(1).

[95] In the context of the English admiralty jurisdiction, ship arrest is but one of the ways of invoking the admiralty jurisdiction in rem. Service of a claim form in rem alone is sufficient without an attendant arrest.

[96] Arrest Convention 1952, art 7(1); Arrest Convention 1999, art 7(1).

[97] Article 7(2).

[98] This topic is addressed in ch 4.

[99] *Four Seasons Holdings Inc v Brownlie* [2017] UKSC 80, [2018] 1 WLR 192 [31] (Lord Sumption).

[100] This subject is analysed closely in ch 3.

security for the judgment of the other court or the award? In other words can the substantive jurisdiction relating to the claim and the jurisdiction in relation to the security be split?

Articles 7 of the Arrest Conventions 1952 and 1999 appear to be, in part, addressing this kind of situation but with no great clarity or coherence. Little benefit seems to be derived from analysing the drafting of each provision closely, but there is an identifiable theme. When surrendering jurisdiction the arresting court may specify a time by which the other proceedings are to be commenced. Failure to comply with this order has the result that the arresting court may release the security. This appears to imply that it has resolved to retain the security and, in the event that the other proceedings are commenced in time, the retained security remains available to secure the judgment of the other court or the award of the arbitral tribunal.

Article 2(3) of the Arrest Convention 1999 may also provide some support for the possibility of split jurisdictions. In general terms it provides that a ship may be arrested for the purpose of obtaining security notwithstanding that the substantive maritime claim is to be adjudicated in another State or is to be arbitrated. On one construction the provision could stand for nothing more than validating an arrest notwithstanding the existence of a jurisdiction or arbitration agreement, leaving it thereafter to the court to determine whether jurisdiction will be retained or surrendered. An alternative interpretation is that it justifies an arrest to obtain security even when the parties are agreed that the arresting court does have jurisdiction but proceedings are to be commenced, or may even have been commenced, in another forum.

Again arts 4(4) and 4(5) of the Arrest Convention 1999 address issues that may arise when jurisdiction is split between a court in a State Party and a court in a non-State Party. Under the former provision, where a ship is arrested in a non-State Party, but security is given in a State Party, and notwithstanding this the ship is not released, the court in the State Party shall release the security. Under the latter, if a ship is arrested in a non-State Party and security given for its release, any security provided in a State Party shall be released to the extent that the aggregate security exceeds the value of the claim or the value of the ship, whichever is the lower. This rule is subject to the proviso that the security provided in the non-party State is actually available.

The Conventions in this regard are to a degree tantalising incomplete. They lay down a number of rules without ever addressing the fundamental principle in issue and in the context of which the individual rules may be interpreted.[101]

II. Ship Arrest – Some Reservations and Proposals

A. Ship Arrest and Substantive Maritime Claims – Defining the Relationship

The issue of the availability of ship arrest is related to the wider question of the relation between ship arrest and substantive maritime claims. If a claim is within the jurisdiction of

[101] See generally Berlingieri (n 12) vol 1 ch 10; vol 2 chs 7 and 10.

an admiralty or maritime court does it also automatically follow that a right of ship arrest is, or should be, available to the claimant? There is, quite obviously, a close relationship between the two but is it, or should it be, invariably and inseverably the case? The question is posed as one of jurisdiction, not of discretion.

It appears to be the case that under the Conventions the defining relationship is based on the status of a claim as maritime. If the claim is definable as maritime then the right to arrest attaches and it is also limited to such defined claims.[102] The list of 'maritime claims' identified in the Arrest Convention 1952 is extensive and it was further extended by the Arrest Convention 1999.[103] Further claims were identified as maritime and this justified extending the list. It was a simple exercise in gap-filling. The leading commentary on the Arrest Convention 1999 declares that the additional claims were identifiable as maritime, and this justified their inclusion.[104] There was no attempt to define what rendered a claim as 'maritime'; it was considered self-evident. It is doubtful if the question of definition is that simple.

In the early law the precise ambit of the admiralty jurisdiction was frequently contested, with the underlying concern often associated with the availability of the right of arrest.[105] When the admiralty jurisdiction was eventually defined, with its terms closely following art 1 of the Arrest Convention 1952, the focus was directed primarily to the proper construction of the language defining the maritime claims.[106] In response the judiciary adopted a supportive and accommodating approach to questions of construction, which had the effect of further broadening the admiralty jurisdiction.[107]

The Admiralty Court has jurisdiction in rem and in personam, and its proceedings consequently are not necessarily dominated by the arrest procedure.[108] Ordinary inter-parties litigation may pertain. It is also the case that many, if not most, claims that are initially framed as being in rem proceed as if in the nature of in personam proceedings.[109] The two forms of proceeding may also be brought concurrently. There are further some matters which may be brought in personam only, limitation proceedings being the prime example and also claims for damage done to a ship other than by another ship.[110] And, finally, although ship arrest is widely perceived as the salient characteristic of the Admiralty Court the reality is that arrest is more frequently threatened than actually effected. Only a relatively small number of ships are actually arrested and of them only a small proportion end up being sold by order of the Court.[111]

I am inclined to question the basic premise underpinning the international Conventions that there exists an inseverable bond between maritime claims and ship arrest. Simply because a claim is considered to be maritime, and therefore justifiably included in the

[102] Arrest Convention 1952, art 2; Arrest Convention 1999, art 2(2).

[103] Precisely how this should be done was a much debated question. There were three possibilities, a closed list, a general definition, and a combined approach of both. The first was adopted. See Berlingieri (n 12) vol 2 paras 5.01–07.

[104] Berlingieri (n 12) vol 2 ch 5.

[105] See Roscoe (n 5) pt 1.

[106] The Arrest Convention 1952 was given effect to in part by the Administration of Justice Act 1956 (UK), pt 1.

[107] See Meeson and Kimbell (n 5) ch 2.

[108] Senior Courts Act 1981 (UK), s 21.

[109] See Meeson and Kimbell (n 5) ch 3.

[110] ibid, ch 8.

[111] *The MV Alkyon* (n 3) [15] (Teare J at first instance).

substantive jurisdiction of an admiralty or maritime court, is not a compellingly sufficient reason, without more, to justify the attachment of a power to arrest. To a degree the history and contemporary practice of the English Admiralty Court lends support for this view. Even in the absence of a right to arrest the parties will benefit from the expertise and experience of a specialist judge and practitioners, who will be quick to identify the issues involved in the dispute and how they may best be addressed. There can be few worse experiences than litigating a core maritime dispute before a court and judge without knowledge and experience of the relevant maritime law.[112]

Although a claim which is maritime in character may justifiably be included in the substantive jurisdiction of an admiralty or maritime court, it may also be justified to restrict the claimant to a proceeding in personam. It would, it is suggested, be rational to limit the power to arrest to circumstances where, objectively judged, the remedy served an essential and necessary purpose, taking into account the interests of justice. There may be circumstances where the very existence of power to arrest could be considered inappropriate or unjustified. In determining this question it would be relevant to enquire whether the power to arrest was the sole effective remedy available to the claimant, or were there alternative effective legal devices available to protect the claimant's interests? Would the availability of the power of arrest be a reasonable and balanced remedy, or an excessively heavy-handed and disproportionate process? And is there a danger that, in the hands of claimants, the power to arrest would encourage abusive conduct?

It is of interest to consider this argument in the context of some of the new maritime claims identified in the Arrest Convention 1999.

Contractual claims by passengers are now included without any express qualification.[113] The result is that a minor detriment or incident or inconvenience could result in the arrest of a cruise ship with several thousand passengers on board. This seems grossly disproportionate having regard to the potential impact on the passengers at large and the commercial operations of the owners. It is also unnecessary because there is no reason to believe that what may be styled ordinary claims procedures would not provide an effective remedy.

Insurers, including P&I Clubs, are for the first time given a right to arrest for unpaid premiums and calls payable by or on behalf of the owner or demise charterer.[114] This gives insurers an additional remedy, but are they not already adequately protected? They can effectively protect themselves by the terms of the insurance contract so that they do not bear any risk during the period of default. Mutual P&I underwriters will customarily also possess a lien on the insured vessel.[115] In view of the fact that the debtor has been accepted into the membership of a club, which may also be a member of the International Group of P&I Clubs, this is also some evidence to suggest that ordinary litigation may not be ineffective. The insurance world has survived for a very long time without the power to

[112] Referring the dispute to arbitration or agreeing to mediation or other form of alternative dispute resolution (ADR) may represent a way out of this particular kind of problem.

[113] Arrest Convention 1999, art 1(1)(g). Loss of life and personal injury claims are covered by the Arrest Convention 1952, art 1(1)(b) and the Arrest Convention 1999, art 1(1)(b).

[114] Arrest Convention 1999, art 1(1)(q).

[115] See eg North of England *P&I Rules 2018–19*, r 14(7), available at www.nepia.com/media/866754/PI-Rules-2018-19.pdf.

arrest and in the circumstances the right does not appear essential or necessary. It is also difficult to see any reason why maritime underwriters should stand in a different position from underwriters in non-maritime sectors of the market, who are compelled to resort to in personam litigation and the collateral protection orders that may be available to recover unpaid premiums.

Arrest is also made available for 'any dispute arising out of a contract for the sale of a ship'.[116] These contracts are invariably comprehensive and complex; and the disputes that arise about them can raise difficult issues of law and profoundly technical evidence. Nonetheless, a claimant (invariably the seller) may arrest the ship for a breach which is not repudiatory and nothing more than a breach of a minor warranty which sounds in low-level damages. This again is disproportionate and could result in abusive conduct. It would be best to allow any dispute that might arise to be determined according to the terms of the contract which the parties have agreed. And, it may be legitimately asked, why should the sale of a ship be different from the sale of an aircraft or any other transport vehicle?

Viewed collectively these extended rights of ship arrest are examples of rights which are alarmingly disproportionate or unnecessary, as the claimant is already well equipped to obtain an effective remedy. They also have the potential to encourage abusive conduct. Where claimants are placed in a position which gives them a disproportionate advantage, they may find the temptation to use the powers to their full advantage – and consequently unfairly – irresistible. In this position owners may consider, even if they dispute or doubt the merits of the claim, that they have no option but to settle the claim or provide security just to be rid of the risk of an arrest causing significant commercial disruption to their operations.

There is no doubting that all the claims considered above are capable of being considered maritime in character and the wisdom of including them in the substantive jurisdiction of an admiralty or maritime court is not being challenged. For reasons already stated there is significant potential benefit to litigants that this should be the case. What is being questioned is the wisdom of attaching the power of arrest to these claims. It is suggested that they should rather proceed in personam only, taking advantage of any protective procedures that may be available in that process. The consequence of this approach would be to limit the availability of the power of arrest. In the alternative such a policy could also be achieved by making ship arrest a discretionary remedy, which possibility is discussed later in this Chapter.

B. Widening the Powers of Arrest – Are There No Limits?

In contemporary policy the powers of arrest have been enlarged by increasing the number of maritime claims to which the powers attach, which was discussed in the preceding part of this Chapter, and also by increasing the available powers of arrest in respect of individual maritime claims.

[116] Article 1(1)(v). Disputes as to ownership and possession, and as between co-owners, are covered by both Conventions: Arrest Convention 1952, arts 1(1)(o) and 1(1)(p); Arrest Convention 1999, arts 1(1)(s) and 1(1)(t).

Under the Arrest Convention 1952, reproducing the pre-existing admiralty law, this increase does not apply to an arrest effected by a mortgagee of a ship to enforce the mortgage security and in relation to a dispute touching on the ownership or right to possession of a ship, and disputes between co-owners of a ship. In these instances only the ship in question (the particular ship) may be arrested.[117] The same position continues under the Arrest Convention 1999 save that arrest by a mortgagee is excluded.[118] This is a remarkable exclusion for it appears that under the Arrest Convention 1999 a mortgagee is given the right to arrest not only the mortgaged ship but also any other ship in the ownership of the mortgagor. This is unprincipled and may also have a detrimental impact on the capability of shipowners to raise finance against mortgage security.

The way in which arrest powers have been increased by the Arrest Conventions has previously been outlined.[119] In the Arrest Convention 1952 the claimant may arrest the ship in respect to which the clam arise or 'another' ship which satisfies prescribed preconditions. This is construed as an alternative and not a cumulative right of arrest and provides obvious advantages to claimants.[120]

The Arrest Convention 1999 attempts to move matters forward in a radical way. Beyond the particular ship, the claimant is given the right to arrest 'any other ship or ships' owned by the person liable for the maritime claim, provided such liability arose from a prescribed relationship with the particular ship.[121] The right is clearly cumulative and the right is extinguished only when the form and amount of the security provided is adequate, as measured against the claim made.[122] Although the security provided by each individual ship is limited to the value of the vessel,[123] the right to arrest multiple ships continues until cumulatively they provide security for the claim.[124] The subtitle to art 5 refers to 'multiple arrest' which very accurately refers to that which is being proposed.[125]

This is a bold provision which departs from the ethos of admiralty law and its influence on the provisions in the Arrest Convention 1952. It appears to seek to revert international Convention policy to the position of Civilian law and the availability of saisie conservatoire prior to the emergence of the Arrest Convention 1952, subject to the limitation that the provision applies to ships only.[126] It is a heavy-handed and disproportionate proposal and fails to strike a fair and reasonable balance between parties. It appears to embody an 'if it moves, shoot' policy which may have a place in a war zone but not in civil litigation. It is a zealous and blinkered commitment to the cause of claimants alone and to security as the all-consuming raison d'être of ship arrest. The fact that the Arrest Convention 1999 has failed to attract much support may, at least in part, be explained by this proposal.

[117] This was the case under admiralty law and continues to be so under the Arrest Convention 1952, art 3(1).
[118] Articles 2, 3(1)(c), 3(1)(d) and 3(1)(e).
[119] Text at n 11ff above.
[120] Articles 3(1) and 3(4).
[121] Article 3(1).
[122] Articles 3(2) and 5(2).
[123] Article 4(2).
[124] Article 5(2).
[125] The subject of multiple arrests is addressed in ch 5.
[126] See text at n 30ff above.

The irony of this provision is that it may well expedite the move to fleet management through multiple one-ship companies. This was the response to the much more limited expansion proposed by the Arrest Convention 1952.[127] Some companies resisted following the trend, but if the Arrest Convention 1999 with its provision for multiple arrests comes to prominence these companies may reassess their positions. This option would continue to be available because of the unfortunate failure by the Arrest Convention 1999 to cure the problem caused by the legal commitment to distinct corporate personality as between companies in any form of corporate group.[128] Without such reform the proposal relating to multiple arrest is probably meaningless, save in those jurisdictions which have made the necessary amendment and adopted concepts such as 'associated ship arrest' in their national law.[129]

C. A Critical Evaluation of Ship Arrest Procedure

Following the emergence of the international Conventions, the procedural law is sourced in a mix of national and Convention law.

i. Convention Law

Under the Arrest Conventions the procedure and practice relating to ship arrest are governed by the laws of Contracting States, in other words the national law of the Contracting State in which the arrest is effected, which may be labelled the lex fori or lex fori arresti.[130] It follows that arrest procedure and practice may vary significantly even as between Contracting States to the Conventions. Apart from this general statement of principle, only a few specific procedural rules are promulgated by the Arrest Conventions.

An arrest may be executed only with the authority of a court or appropriate judicial authority.[131] It is not a self-help remedy and may be executed only within the territorial sovereignty of the State in which the court or appropriate judicial authority is located. Unlike litigation in personam an arrest out of jurisdiction cannot be authorised. When a ship has been arrested the court or appropriate judicial authority shall order its release upon sufficient bail or security being furnished.[132]

The Arrest Conventions also anticipate the possible abuse of the prescribed procedure but again refer the question as to how abuse is to be defined and the possible legal responses to national law.[133]

[127] See text at n 39ff above.
[128] See text at n 52ff above.
[129] Text at n 46ff above. The issue is also addressed in chs 2 and 13.
[130] Arrest Convention 1952, art 6 (second para); Arrest Convention 1999, art 2(4).
[131] Arrest Convention 1952, art 4; Arrest Convention 1999, art 2(1).
[132] Arrest Convention 1952, art 5; Arrest Convention 1999, arts 2(1), 2(4) and 4.
[133] Arrest Convention 1952, art 6; Arrest Convention 1999, art 6. This issue is considered further in the text at n 161 below.

ii. English Admiralty Procedure

The procedure is consistent with the principles set out in the Arrest Conventions but, anticipating issues discussed later in this contribution, it is necessary to set out aspects of the procedure in some detail.

In broad outline the procedure involves two stages, the service of an in rem claim form and the execution of a warrant of arrest against the ship (or one of the ships) identified in the claim form.[134]

The in rem claim form must be in the prescribed form[135] and served on the defendant within 12 months after the date of issue.[136] It requires only 'brief details of the claim' in the 'Particulars of Claim' which may be attached or produced later.[137] There is no further requirement of substantiation save for a 'Statement of Truth' which requires the claimant or its solicitor (more probably the solicitor) to declare a subjective belief that 'the facts stated in these particulars of claim are true'.[138] Admiralty Form no ADM 1B includes notes on the kind of information required to be included in the Particulars of Claim. The claim form is declared to be against the ship and is served on the property against which the claim is brought by fixing a copy at a reasonably visible position on the outside of the property.[139]

The arrest of the vessel is made by attaching a copy of the warrant of arrest on the named ship by the Admiralty Marshal or his substitute.[140] The form of the warrant is set out in Admiralty Form ADM 9 and is valid for 12 months.[141]

The application for issue of a warrant of arrest is made by the claimant's solicitor who also undertakes personally to pay on demand all the fees and expenses of the Marshal in respect of the arrest, care and custody of the vessel while under arrest and the release of the vessel from arrest.[142] No doubt the solicitor in most cases would be funded by, or have obtained a security/guarantee from, his or her client.

The application to arrest is accompanied by a 'Declaration in support of application for warrant of arrest' set out in Admiralty Form ADM 5. This is primarily concerned with identifying the ship to be arrested, particularly if it may be a sister ship, obtaining information about beneficial ownership, and the amount of security for the claim sought by the claimant. This Declaration is again underwritten by a Statement of Truth signed by the claimant or the claimant's solicitor.

This outline of the procedure is sufficient to reveal how formalistic the process is. The claimant is required only to assert its claim and (provided the claim is within the in rem jurisdiction of the Admiralty Court and its powers to issue a warrant of arrest, and the

[134] The procedural rules are primarily sourced in the Civil Practice Rules (CPR) Part 61 and its associated Practice Direction PD 61. See HM Courts & Tribunals Service, *The Commercial Court Guide*, 10th rev edn, 2018, available at www.gov.uk/government/publications/admiralty-and-commercial-courts-guide, which incorporates the Admiralty Court Guide; see also Meeson and Kimbell (n 5) ch 4.

[135] CPR 61.3(2). The form is set out in PD 61, ADM 1.

[136] CPR 61.3(5)(b).

[137] CPR 61.3(3).

[138] This is contained in the claim form, Admiralty Form no ADM 1.

[139] PD 61 3.5.

[140] CPR 61.5 and PD 61.5(5).

[141] CPR 61.5(7). The process is the same as for the service of the claim form in rem – CPR 61.5(5).

[142] The undertaking is contained in Admiralty Form ADM 4 (Application and undertaking for arrest and custody).

necessary procedural steps and forms have been properly attended to) the court will sanction the arrest of the vessel in question. The court plays no further role than to ensure that the prescribed procedure has been properly discharged.[143] This is expressly recognised in PD 61.5(2) which provides: 'When it receives an application for arrest that complies with the rules and the practice direction the court will issue an arrest warrant'.

A party who asserts a maritime claim has effectively a right to the grant of a power to arrest the ship in question. The position of the court is limited to that of an administrative body, ensuring that the prescribed procedure has been properly followed. Beyond this the court has no authority. To the contrary, in *The Vasso*[144] the English Court of Appeal held that the issue of a warrant of arrest was discretionary, but this decision was patently in conflict with the weight of authority and in response the then Rules of Court were amended to reaffirm the traditional understanding. This was underlined by the English Court of Appeal in *The Varna*[145] confirming that the issue of a warrant of arrest was a matter of right and not of discretion. More recently the position has been affirmed by the current Admiralty Judge and the Court of Appeal.[146]

There is a right to damages for wrongful arrest, but this remedy is very narrowly defined.[147] It is limited to arrests which are made in bad faith or with such gross negligence as to imply malice.[148] It is clear that the remedy is available only in the most exceptional of circumstances.[149]

iii. A Critique of English Admiralty Procedure

A moment's reflection on the procedure of the English Admiralty Court indicates how straightforward and undemanding the procedure is, and, consequently, how potentially exposed defendant shipowners are. Even in the face of loss they are left without any remedy.[150] It is difficult to believe that what may be in issue is the judicial arrest of a working commercial vessel of great value and an interference with the ship's operations which may have a major adverse impact on the immediate contractual engagements of the ship and the wider business of the owner. The primary concern is to facilitate the arrest by requiring nothing more than adherence to the procedural formalities, which is not a demanding hurdle to negotiate.

The process is conducted wholly by the claimant and its lawyers, and the Admiralty Court, with no obligation to consult or give notice to the owner or to follow any pre-action protocol. There is no attempt made to assess whether the substantive claim justifies the adoption of the arrest procedure or is supportable by the available evidence, at least to

[143] *The MV Alkyon* (n 3).
[144] *The Andria now renamed Vasso* [1984] 1 QB 477.
[145] *The Varna* [1993] 2 Lloyd's Rep 253.
[146] See *The MV Alkyon* (n 3) (Teare J at first instance); *Stallion Eight Shipping Co SA v Natwest Markets plc (The MV Alkyon)* [2018] EWCA Civ 2760.
[147] The subject is considered in ch 6.
[148] *The MV Alkyon* (n 3) [18] (Teare J at first instance).
[149] See further text at n 155ff below.
[150] As was recognised by Colman J in *Centro Latino Americano de Commercio Exterior SA v Owners of the Ship Kommunar (The Kommunar) (No 3)* [1997] 1 Lloyd's Rep 22.

some minimum degree. The process functions on the basis of the claimant's bare untested assertions set out in standard form procedural documents. Beyond this the claimant is not required to establish a good arguable case or even an arguable case. It is true that the formal documents must be supported by a signed 'statement of truth', but this does not correct matters. The declaration applies only to the bare information contained in the documents and is no more than a subjective declaration of belief that the statements made in the documents are true.

The court has no discretion in the process. If the procedure is followed the claimant has a right to a warrant of arrest which undermines the role of the court as an instrument of justice. The applicant is not required to make a full and frank disclosure in support of the arrest, thereby assisting the court to consider whether the arrest of the vessel is just, fair and necessary in the circumstances. It is not open to the court to consider whether the claimant's position is sufficiently protected without the necessity of an arrest or if there is a risk that the owner may attempt to take steps to deny the claimant the benefit of any future judgment. Nor may the court take into account any question of proportionality between the quantum of the claim and the value of the ship at risk.

Most significantly the court does not have jurisdiction to grant a warrant of arrest subject to terms. What these terms might be would be dependent on the circumstances but of particular significance the court does not have jurisdiction to demand an undertaking that the applicant indemnify the owner for losses suffered in the event that the arrest is subsequently shown to be unjustified or unwarranted, as when, for example, the substantive claim fails. In other words, the court does not have jurisdiction to demand that the applicant provides a counter-undertaking in damages. Under present practice the expenses and losses associated with the arrest of the vessel are borne as a matter of course by the shipowner. This is in stark contrast to the way the common law courts deal with the pre-judgment detention of property.[151]

There is also in the process no element of forum conveniens. The court may grant the power to arrest notwithstanding that the underlying substantive claim has no connection with the jurisdiction of the court. This is an uncertain area of the law, but aspects of the international Conventions appear to relate to it.[152]

The present procedure suffers from grave imbalance and can be the source of injustice. In giving claimants an effective right to arrest and at the same time to ignore the consequences for defendants is anything but justice. The object of legal procedure is to strike a fair and reasonable balance between the interests of the parties, and this is effectively achieved by a refereed discretionary environment. Claimants seeking an arrest are entitled to a fair and supportive regime, and one capable of adjusting to changing circumstances, in terms of finance, professional support and immediate necessities. There will be occasions when a power to arrest to be effective must be obtained and executed with expedition, and a discretionary process is well equipped to respond to this kind of situation.

But at the same time the defendant is entitled to be protected against arbitrary, malicious, wrongful and unjustified arrests, and this can be achieved by requiring a claimant to act in good faith and on the basis of a degree of credible evidence in support of a claim and

[151] See text at n 162 below.
[152] Arrest Convention 1952, art 7; Arrest Convention 1999, arts 2(3) and 7.

application for arrest. There is nothing objectionable in these circumstances that a court should have the authority to impose conditions by which the claimant is required to abide.

There are three further anomalies that can be highlighted.

First, the Admiralty Court protects itself against the cost implications associated with the arrest of a ship, by the undertaking given by the solicitor representing the claimant to pay on demand the fees of the Marshal and all expenses associated with the arrest, care and custody, and release of the ship.[153] By contrast, no similar protection is provided to defendant shipowners.

Secondly, there is a difference in approach to security given in substitution to the ship, with regard to which the court has a supervisory jurisdiction. In the event of a failure to agree the appropriate quantum the court may intervene and determine the appropriate figure. Where excessive security is demanded and provided the court may intervene, substitute the appropriate sum and award compensation for the cost associated with the excessive security. But at the same time the court does not possess a corresponding jurisdiction to protect owners for losses suffered by an unjustified or unnecessary arrest.

Thirdly, it is recognised that the arrest process may be abused and a concept of 'wrongful arrest' has evolved and for breach of which damages may be awarded.[154] The concept, however, is defined so very narrowly that it is available only in extreme circumstances.[155] To be wrongful an arrest must be made knowing it to be unjustified or with reckless indifference whether it is unjustified.[156] It does not provide any redress where the underpinning substantive claim fails on the evidence. In the words of Teare J: 'Thus there is no right to damages in circumstances where an arresting party acts in good faith and without gross negligence, but it is later found that he had in fact no claim in rem.'[157] At the same time the experienced admiralty judge was aware of the exposed position of the defendant shipowner:

> If a shipowner is unable for some special reason to obtain a release of his vessel from arrest by putting up security he may therefore suffer a loss which he cannot recover because the circumstances of the case cannot be brought within the scope of an action for damages for wrongful arrest … And even if he does put up security he will or may incur a cost which he cannot recover for the same reason.[158]

The present procedure places owners in a precarious and vulnerable position because claimants risk little by threatening or making an arrest, whereas owners are exposed to the risk of commercial disruption and uncertain losses. In the absence of legal protection it is understandable if owners may be tempted to settle a claim, even if liability is disputed, seeing that as the more expedient or economic option. Otherwise they may decide to minimise their potential exposure to loss by providing security either to avoid the arrest or to

[153] See text at n 142 above.

[154] For an analysis of the nature of the right, see D Rhidian Thomas, 'Damages for Wrongful Arrest of Ships in the English Admiralty Jurisdiction' in D Rhidian Thomas (ed), *Liability Regimes in Contemporary Maritime Law*, (London, Informa, 2007) ch 13.

[155] The international Conventions leave this subject to national law. Article 6 of the Arrest Convention 1999 takes a broader view of wrongful arrest, including an unjustified arrest.

[156] See text at n 148 above.

[157] *The MV Alkyon* (n 3) [18].

[158] ibid [55].

obtain the release of the ship from arrest.[159] The provision of security, however, will have cost implications and will not always be available to all owners.[160]

iv. A Suggested Alternative Approach

It must be seriously questioned whether the present procedure and practice is acceptable or, even more fundamentally, if it is in keeping with principles of justice. It is conceivable that it might even amount to a breach of an owner's human rights.[161]

The protection of property rights has occupied a central position in the substantive and procedural branches of the common law. In the current context, of particular significance is the common law's fairly recent change of policy in relation to its long-held reluctance to recognise a power to seize/detain property of a defendant before judgment, even if its objective was to preserve property so that it would be available to satisfy any judgment in the event of default. At the end of the nineteenth century the suggested departure from this policy was judicially condemned as 'wrong in principle' and to be resisted even if in the circumstances of the case 'it would be highly just to make the order'.[162]

Nonetheless, the legal position became the subject of radical and decisive change in the 1970s in the context of the court's discretionary jurisdiction to grant injunctions.[163] It was held that, in appropriate circumstances, an interlocutory injunction could be granted to prevent a defendant disposing of assets prior to judgment, thereby making it judgment-proof.[164]

The injunctive remedy was initially labelled a Mareva injunction[165] but was subsequently re-labelled a freezing injunction. In the succeeding decades the injunctive remedy evolved apace, with the scope and essential underpinning principles extended and developed in the authorities. It became wider in scope so as to be available in respect of assets both within and outside the jurisdiction of the English courts.[166] As with all injunctions

[159] See text at n 79ff above.

[160] As was the case in *The MV Alkyon* (n 3).

[161] See the Universal Declaration of Human Rights (adopted 10 December 1948 UNGA Res 217 A(III) (UDHR), art 17; European Convention on Human Rights (Convention for the Protection of Human Rights and Fundamental Freedoms (adopted 4 November 1950, came into effect 3 September 1953) ETS No 005) Part II, Protocol 1 (ETS No 009), art 1 (Protection of Property). Compare *Baltic Shipping Co Ltd v Pegasus Lines SA* [1996] 3 NZLR 641, 650 where the New Zealand Court of Appeal dismissed an argument based on s 21 of the New Zealand Bill of Rights Act 1990, which provides that everyone has the right to be secure against unreasonable search or seizure, whether of the person, property, or correspondence or otherwise. McKay and Henry JJ observed: 'There is no doubt that the writ in rem and the arrest of a vessel is a very strong and effective remedy, but that does not make it unreasonable. It is a seizure by judicial process, to ensure that the ship or some alternative security is available to satisfy a claim which has still to be substantiated. It has been found expedient in international trade as giving some protection to those who give credit or who suffer damage in the course of maritime trade. If a claim is made unreasonably, in the sense of being without foundation, the defendant can always move to strike out as well as challenging jurisdiction ….'

[162] *Lister & Co v Stubbs* (1890) 45 Ch D 1, 14 (CA) (Cotton LJ). See also *Robinson v Pickering* (1881) 16 Ch D 660 (CA).

[163] The present law is to be found in the Senior Courts Act 1981 (UK), s 37.

[164] *Nippon Yusen Kaisha v Karageorgis* [1975] 1 WLR 1093 (CA); *Mareva Compania Naviera SA v International Bulkcarriers SA* [1975] 2 Lloyd's Rep 509 (CA).

[165] After the *Mareva* case cited ibid.

[166] See generally, Steven Gee, *Commercial Injunctions*, 6th edn (London, Sweet & Maxwell, 2016); Mark SW Hoyle, *The Mareva Injunction and Related Orders*, 3rd edn (London, LLP, 1997).

it operates in personam, and a party in default is punishable as being in contempt of court.[167]

This remedial development proved to be a significant reform, and a great benefit to claimants. The injunction is equally available when the assets in question are ships[168] and may be sought even when there is not a right to arrest in admiralty proceedings or as an alternative to, or in addition to, ship arrest proceedings.[169] The injunctive jurisdiction is discretionary and is now established by s 37 of the Senior Courts Act 1981 (UK). The section indicates that an injunction may be granted whenever it is just and convenient to do so, and that conditions may be attached.

The authorities indicate that an applicant for a freezing injunction must satisfy a number of requirements.

First, the applicant must establish a good arguable case in support of his claim. This is a threshold test which the applicant must establish before the court will consider that it has jurisdiction to consider the application further. It is a much lower test than the burden of proof borne by the claimant at trial and a detailed scrutiny of the facts and law is eschewed. But a modicum of supportive evidence is demanded beyond simple assertion, something 'more than barely capable of serious argument, and yet not necessarily one which the judge believes to have a better than 50% chance of success'.[170]

Secondly, there must be a sufficient or real risk of dissipation of assets.[171] Mere assertion is not sufficient. On an objective assessment of the facts there must be evidence from which the court may infer that if the injunction is not granted the defendant is likely to move or dissipate assets, which would involve a real risk that a judgment or award in favour of the claimant would remain unsatisfied.[172]

Thirdly, the claimant has the duty to make full and frank disclosure to the court. The object of the duty is to secure the integrity of court process and protect the interest of those affected by whatever order the court is invited to make. If the duty is breached any order made by the court may be set aside or its renewal refused.[173] One aspect of this duty is that the applicant must disclose all matters that are material to the application, with materiality defined broadly but subject to sensible limits.[174] The applicant would be obliged to identify crucial points for and against the application.[175]

As a condition of granting a freezing injunction it is customary for the court to require the applicant to give a cross-undertaking for damages.[176] Under the undertaking the

[167] *Z Ltd* (n 70), particularly the judgment of Eveleigh LJ.

[168] Hoyle (n 166) 34–35.

[169] *The Rena K* (n 67). See also *Clipper Maritime Co Ltd of Monrovia v Mineralimportexport* [1981] 1 WLR 1262.

[170] *Ninemia Maritime Corp v Trave Schiffahrtsgesellschaft mbH & Co KG (The Niedersachsen)* [1984] 1 All ER 398, 404 (Mustill J); affirmed [1984] 1 All ER 398, 415 (CA). See also *Finurba Corporate Finance Ltd v Sipp SA* [2011] EWCA Civ 465 [31]; *Kazakhstan Kagazy plc v Arip* [2014] EWCA Civ 381, [2014] 1 CLC 451 [25]; *Holyoake v Candy* [2016] EWHC 970 (Ch), [2016] 3 WLR 357.

[171] *The Niedersachsen* (n 170) 419 (CA) (Kerr LJ).

[172] *O'Regan v Iambic Productions Ltd* (1989) 139 NLJ 1378 (Nugee J); *Thane Investments Ltd v Tomlinson* [2003] EWCA Civ 1272; *VTB Capital plc v Nutritek International Corp* [2012] EWCA Civ 808, [2012] 2 BCLC 437.

[173] *PJSC Tatneft v Bogolyubov* [2016] EWHC 2816 (Comm), [2018] 1 WLR 5705. See also *Brink's-Mat Ltd v Elcombe* [1988] 1 WLR 1350, 1359.

[174] *Kazakhstan Kagazy plc v Zhunus (formerly Zhunussov)* [2014] EWCA Civ 74; *National Bank Trust v Yurov* [2016] EWHC 1913 (Comm).

[175] *Siporex Trade SA v Comdel Commodities Ltd* [1986] 2 Lloyd's Rep 428, 437 (Bingham J).

[176] *Third Chandris Shipping Corporation v Unimarine SA* [1979] 1 QB 645, 669 (CA) (Lord Denning MR).

applicant promises that if the court later finds that the order has caused loss to the respondent, and decides that the respondent should be compensated for that loss, the applicant will comply with any order the court may make.[177] The injunction provides 'pragmatic justice'[178] by protecting the interests of the party who is subjected to the restraining effect of the injunction but who subsequently succeeds at the trial from loss caused by the injunction.[179]

The court may also require the party applying for the injunction to demonstrate that it has the means to meet any liability under the cross-undertaking and in the case of a foreign party to place funds on deposit within the jurisdiction. The ability or otherwise of the applicant to meet its potential liability under this undertaking is taken into account in deciding whether to grant an injunction. Security may also be offered in substitution for the injunction.[180]

Notwithstanding the technical differences between ship arrest and freezing orders,[181] which have previously been commented on,[182] they are comparable in so far as they both relate to pre-judgment detention of property by legal process.[183] But one of the essential differences between them is how the risk relating to the seized property is distributed between the parties in the event of the underlying substantive claim not being successful. In the admiralty arrest procedure it is borne by the owner of the detained property; under the freezing injunction it is borne by the claimant.

It is suggested that the common law procedure relating to freezing injunctions is the more just. It sets out an exemplary procedure for holding a fair and just balance between claimants and defendants when property is seized before judgment. And it is suggested that it is the model that should be followed in the admiralty jurisdiction when considering applications to arrest. At the same time it must be recognised that the discretionary framework would have to be recast for the peculiar needs of the maritime jurisdiction, practice and claims, but this would not be a difficulty by virtue of the procedure being discretionary. Relevant consideration would include the status and circumstances of the claimant. The fact that the claimant was in a weak position in terms of financial means and access to professional assistance, such as seafarers and suppliers of goods and services,[184] would be a potentially relevant consideration. And more generally the ability of a claimant to fund a cross-undertaking in damages would be a fact capable of being taken into account.[185]

[177] *SCF Tankers Ltd (formerly known as Fiona Trust & Holding Corp) v Privalov* [2017] EWCA Civ 1877, [2018] 1 WLR 5623 [16].

[178] *Energy Venture Partners Ltd v Malabu Oil and Gas Ltd* [2014] EWCA Civ 1295, [2015] 1 WLR 2309 [54] (Tomlinson LJ).

[179] *F Hoffmann-la Roche & Co AG v Secretary of State for Trade and Industry* [1975] AC 295, 361 (Lord Diplock).

[180] *Energy Venture Partners Ltd* (n 178).

[181] *The Rena K* (n 67) 407 (Brandon J).

[182] See text at n 55ff above.

[183] *The MV Alkyon* (n 3) [44] (Teare J).

[184] The Admiralty Court has long assumed a protective responsibility towards seafarers: see Thomas (n 16) para 302.

[185] This is equally the case with regard to the freezing injunction. The court may require the applicant to demonstrate that it has the means to meet any liability that may arise under the cross-undertaking.

In the context of freezing injunctions Mann J has said:[186]

> What one has to do is to acknowledge the seriousness of the consequences of a freezing order, and the invasion of liberty that it involves (especially bearing in mind it is usually sought in a without notice application) and to reflect that in requiring proof to an appropriately high standard. Orders are not to be lightly sought and will not be granted on flimsy evidence.

If a reference to 'ship arrest' is substituted for 'freezing order' these words sum up in clear and cogent terms the philosophy which it is submitted should prevail in relation to ship arrest.

Abandoning the notion of claimant entitlement and vesting a discretionary jurisdiction in the Admiralty Court would enable the Court to regulate the availability of ship arrest to circumstances when it is both available at law and necessary and justifiable in fact. Placing a relatively minimal evidentiary burden on the applicant would require at least some evidence in support of the substantive claim to be produced, beyond a bare allegation. The claimant would also have to persuade the Court in the exercise of its discretion to order an arrest, but again this should not represent a demanding obligation. But in order to assist the Court the applicant would be obliged to make full and frank disclosure of all material facts. By virtue of the discretionary nature of the process it would be open to the Admiralty Court to attach conditions to any grant of the right to arrest, including a requirement that the claimant give a cross-undertaking for damages.

III. A Final Comment

The debate and contentions addressed in this contribution are not novel. They have attracted comment from a number of commentators over recent decades, with different shades of opinion expressed. Some take a similar approach to that developed in this Chapter, others oppose change or suggest limited reform or caution against abandoning long established practice.[187] The Comité Maritime International (CMI) has established an International Working Group to survey and examine the question of 'Liability for Wrongful Arrest'. It is currently obtaining information from national Maritime Law Associations regarding applicable law, whether counter-security is, or may be, demanded, and the legal test and standard of proof required in a wrongful ship arrest claim. It has yet to conclude its enquiry.[188]

What is evident is that there exists in national legal systems a range of different approaches to the process by which ship arrest may be obtained, the procedural and evidentiary burden borne by applicants and the obligations and powers of a court when

[186] *JSC Mezhdunarodniy Promyshlenniy Bank v Pugachev* [2014] EWHC 4336 (Ch), [2015] All ER (D) 16 [221] (Mann J).

[187] Stewart Boyd, 'Shipping Lawyers: Land Rats or Water Rats?' [1993] *LMCLQ* 317; Shane Nossal, 'Damages for the Wrongful Arrest of a Vessel' [1996] *LMCLQ* 368; DJ Cremean, 'Mala Fides and Crassa Negligentia' [1998] *LMCLQ* 9, Bernard Eder, 'Wrongful Arrest of Ships: A Time for Change' (2013) 38 *Tul Mar LJ* 115; Martin Davies, 'Wrongful Arrest of Ships: A Time for Change – A Reply to Sir Bernard Eder' (2013) 38 *Tul Mar LJ* 137; Bernard Eder, 'Wrongful Arrest of Ships: Rejoinder by the Honourable Mr Justice Eder' (2013) 38 *Tul Mar LJ* 143.

[188] On this development see also ch 6.

considering applications for arrest. Many of the States in the Common Law tradition follow the approach of the English Admiralty Court,[189] but not necessarily in all its details. In the Australian jurisdiction, for example, an arrest is wrongful if it is obtained 'unreasonably and without good cause'[190] and this approach has been followed in South Africa where the test is 'without reasonable and probable cause'.[191] In Nigeria the reference is to an arrest made on 'insufficient grounds' and in the absence of 'probable grounds'.[192]

In Civil Law jurisdictions maritime claimants are in general devoid of any special protection so that if the substantive claim fails the arrest is unreasonable,[193] but doubtlessly there may be variations. Developments in Spanish law justify particular comment because Spain is the only significant maritime jurisdiction which to date has ratified and given the force of law to the Arrest Convention 1999.[194] Under Spanish law the burden of proof borne by a claimant is very light. The mere 'allegation' of the maritime claim and of the 'arrestability' of the ship is sufficient.[195] But as a condition of granting a court order for the arrest of a ship the judge 'shall require a sufficient guarantee in every case'.[196] This requirement is mandatory. The guarantee must be given before the arrest is executed and must be sufficient to cover potential damages, losses and costs. In practice a minimum guarantee of 15 per cent of the alleged claim will be required, but this is a rough guideline and depending on the circumstances the requirement can be significantly higher. As for the nature of the guarantee, it may include cash, a bank guarantee, a comfort letter or any other acceptable form.[197]

By coincidence the whole debate has been revived in English admiralty law in the recent case of *The MV Alkyon* with both the Admiralty Court and Court of Appeal[198] approving the established law and practice. The case concerned the arrest of a mortgaged ship in an English port for an alleged breach of the loan agreement which the owner disputed. The owner further alleged that the bank had not acted in good faith and that maintaining the arrest was financially and commercially ruinous.

The owners applied for an order releasing the ship from arrest unless the bank provided a cross-undertaking in damages in the form usually given in the context of freezing orders.

[189] *Banque Worms v The Owners of the Ship or Vessel Maule (Cyprus Flag) (Formerly Known as Amer Deep)* [1995] HKCA 536, [1995] 2 HKC 769; *Armada Lines Ltd v Chaleur Fertilizers Ltd* [1997] 2 SCR 617, 148 DLR (4th) 217; *Mobil Oil New Zealand Ltd v The Ship Rangiora* [2000] 1 NZLR 49; *The Vasiliy Golovnin* [2008] SGCA 39 (CA), [2008] 4 SLR(R) 994.

[190] Admiralty Act 1988 (Cth), s 34(1)(a)(ii). See Michael Woodford, 'Damages for Wrongful Arrest: Section 34, *Admiralty Act 1988*' (2005) 19 *Maritime Law Association of Australia and New Zealand Journal* 115.

[191] AJRA 1983, s 5(4).

[192] Admiralty Jurisdiction Procedure Rules 2011, O 11 r 2.

[193] *The Vasiliy Golovnin* (n 189) [122] (Rajah JA).

[194] See the Spanish Shipping Act 14/2014 (Ley 14/2014, de 24 de julio, de Navegación Marítima) (LNM), arts 470–79. The official text of the LNM is available at www.boe.es/eli/es/l/2014/07/24/14.

[195] LNM, art 472(1): 'Para decretar el embargo preventivo de un buque por crédito marítimo que se define en el artículo 1 del Convenio Internacional sobre el Embargo Preventivo de Buques, bastará que se alegue el derecho o créditos reclamados, la causa que los motive y la embargabilidad del buque.'

[196] ibid, art 472(2): 'El juez exigirá en todo caso garantía en cantidad suficiente para responder de los daños, perjuicios y costas que puedan ocasionarse. Esta fianza podrá ser de cualquiera de las clases que reconoce el Derecho, incluido el aval bancario.'

[197] ibid: 'Una vez fijada esa garantía, que como mínimo será del 15 por ciento del importe del crédito marítimo alegado, el tribunal podrá revisar su cuantía, de oficio o a instancia de parte, en atención al porte y a las dimensiones del buque, al coste derivado de la estancia del buque en el puerto, a su precio de mercado por día, a si está o no sujeto a línea regular, a si está o no cargado, así como a sus compromisos contractuales.'

[198] *The MV Alkyon* (n 3); *The MV Alkyon* (n 146).

Under CPR Part 61.8(4) the court is obliged to release an arrested ship 'if … the court orders the release on an application made by any party'. These words clearly imply that the court has a discretion and the shipowner sought to persuade the court in the exercise of its discretion to impose the proposed condition. The admiralty judge rejected the submission essentially because it was contrary to the established practice of the Admiralty Court. On appeal the Court of Appeal considered there was no basis for interfering with the exercise of discretion by the judge, but interestingly rejected the submission that it was not in the jurisdiction of the court to impose such a condition. In other words, it was open to a judge on an application for an order to release a vessel from arrest to refuse the application subject to the claimant providing a cross-undertaking of damages. The Court left open what the wider implications of this decision might be.

The parties accepted that the position was different on an application for a warrant of arrest, where there did not exist any discretion and consequently the court had no jurisdiction to demand a cross-undertaking in damages. Nonetheless, there was an alignment between the two provisions. They were in a sense opposite sides of the same coin; it would be odd if on ordering the release of a ship the Court could act in a way which undermined the policy associated with granting the power to arrest. This had been one of the reasons given by the admiralty Judge for rejecting the application by the shipowner. Notwithstanding the opinion expressed by the Court of Appeal, it is probable that there will be an understandable judicial reluctance to exercise the discretion on an application to release a ship from arrest in the manner now made possible by the Court of Appeal. A more likely possibility is that the view expressed by the Court of Appeal may initiate a review of the Civil Procure Rules.

Apart from the specific issue before the courts, the case provided a platform for a comprehensive review of policy relating to the arrest of ships and the position of the Admiralty Court. In the process two significant aspects of the admiralty procedure have been confirmed. A claimant has the right to a warrant of arrest providing the power to arrest exists and the stipulated procedure has been properly followed. The court has no discretion in the matter and no authority to demand a cross-undertaking in damages or to attach any other condition.

The case stands as a rejection of many of the arguments developed in this contribution, but the debate is far from concluded. It is clear that there is not an international consensus on the issues discussed and it is a shame that the international Conventions are not more decisive. There is a strong conservative thread in maritime jurisprudence which allows precedents from the past to prevail in contemporary times notwithstanding radical changes in every aspect of social, political, commercial, philosophical and intellectual life. Doubtlessly judges in the Victorian age served their times well, but it may be suspected that they would not begin to comprehend the present and radically different age. Their dicta should be read in the context of their times and not allowed to obstruct the absorption of constantly evolving principles of procedural justice into maritime jurisprudence. The common law, almost as a matter of course, requires a cross-undertaking in damages from a party who obtains an interlocutory order and it is difficult to challenge justice of that position. It is the path that the procedural law relating to ship arrest should follow.[199]

[199] *The Vasiliy Golovnin* (n 189) [130] (Rajah JA).

2

Arrest of Associated Ships

GRAHAM BRADFIELD*

I. Introduction

The provisions of the International Convention Relating to the Arrest of Sea-Going Ships 1952 (the Arrest Convention 1952),[1] which permit the arrest of a ship – generally referred to as a 'sister ship' – other than the 'particular ship',[2] in circumstances where the sister ship is linked to the particular ship through common ownership,[3] were a compromise aimed at harmonising the law on ship arrests in Common Law jurisdictions with admiralty jurisdiction that permitted the arrest in rem of the particular ship only,[4] and in Civil Law legal

* Associate Professor, Faculty of Law, University of Cape Town.

[1] International Convention Relating to the Arrest of Sea-going Ships (adopted 10 May 1952, entered into force 24 February 1956) 439 UNTS 193. See generally Francesco Berlingieri, *Berlingieri on Arrest of* Ships, 6th edn (Abingdon, Informa Law from Routledge, 2017) vol 1.

[2] Arrest Convention 1952, arts 3(1)–3(2). See generally Berlingieri (n 1) vol 1 ch 12. The term 'particular ship' is used in the Arrest Convention 1952 to denote the ship against which the maritime claim arose, and will be used here in relation to the Arrest Convention 1952, the Arrest Convention 1999 (International Convention on the Arrest of Ships (adopted 12 March 1999, entered into force 14 September 2011) 2797 UNTS 3), the United Kingdom's proposal to introduce 'associated' ship arrest provisions into the Arrest Convention 1999 and the South African legislation, though its provisions refer to such ships as 'the ship concerned'.

[3] For the purposes of the Arrest Convention 1952, arts 3(1)–3(2), ownership means ownership of all the shares in the ships: Berlingieri (n 1) vol 1 para 12.07. The particular ship and sister ship do not have to be in common ownership at all times – the particular ship has to be owned at the time the claim arose, by the same person who owns the sister ship at the time its arrest is effected: ibid para 12.05. Certain claims cannot be enforced by the arrest of a sister ship. The claims excluded are those in arts 1(1)(o), 1(1)(p) and 1(1)(q) of the Arrest Convention 1952, namely claims arising out of 'disputes as to the title to or ownership of any ship', 'disputes between co-owners of any ship as to ownership, possession, employment or earnings' and 'mortgage or hypothecation of any ship'. The rationale for excluding these claims was that they bear a legal relationship to the particular ship that differs from other claims: ibid para 12.21. The Arrest Convention 1952 also makes provision for the arrest as sister ships of those ships owned at the time the arrest was effected by the person who was the demise charterer of the particular ship at the time a claim arose for which the demise charterer, and not the owner, was liable: Arrest Convention 1952, art 3(4). Article 3(4) applies to any instance in which a person other than the registered owner of a ship is liable in respect of a maritime claim relating to that ship, which will include charterers not by demise: ibid para 12.06.

[4] Berlingieri (n 1) vol 1 para 12.01. This was the position in South Africa regarding the action in rem before the commencement of its Admiralty Jurisdiction Regulation Act 105 of 1983 (AJRA 1983). Gys Hofmeyr, *Admiralty Jurisdiction Law and Practice in South Africa*, 2nd edn (Cape Town, Juta & Co, 2012) ch IV pt IX.1. For the history of admiralty jurisdiction in South Africa, see ibid ch I; South African Law Reform Commission, *Report on the Review of the Law of Admiralty* Project 32 (Pretoria, South African Law Reform Commission, 1982) (SALRC Report); DJ Shaw, *Admiralty Jurisdiction and Practice in South Africa* (Cape Town, Juta & Co, 1986) ch 1; Malcolm John David Wallis, *The Associated Ship and South African Admiralty Jurisdiction* (Cape Town, Siber Ink, 2010) ch 2; John Hare, *Shipping Law & Admiralty Jurisdiction in South Africa*, 2 edn (Kenwyn, Juta, 2009) ch 1.

systems that permitted arrest or attachment of any property owned by the person allegedly liable for the claim sought to be enforced.[5]

Despite the success of the Arrest Convention 1952,[6] it is generally recognised that its sister-ship provisions proved inadequate to deal with the phenomenon of single-ship companies that proliferated in the later part of the twentieth century.[7] Ships owned by separate companies, even if operated as a fleet, did not qualify as sister ships because they were not owned by the same person.[8]

South Africa did not accede to the Arrest Convention 1952.[9] When South Africa enacted the AJRA 1983,[10] unfettered by the Convention and mindful of the inadequacy of the Convention's sister-ship arrest provisions in the face of single-ship companies,[11] it implemented its own associated-ship arrest provisions that were then unique in extending the range of ships other than the particular ship that could be arrested in rem beyond those

[5] Berlingieri (n 1) vol 1 para 12.01. See too *Monte Ulia (Owners) v Banco (Owners) (The Banco)* [1971] P 137, 151 (CA); *The Eschersheim* [1976] 1 Lloyd's Rep 1, 5 (HL); *MV Heavy Metal: Belfry Marine Ltd v Palm Base Maritime SDN BHD* 1999 (3) SA 1083, 1096F (SCA); *MV Bavarian Trader: Pancoast Trading SA v Orient Shipping Rotterdam BV* 2010 (4) SA 369 [18] (KZD); Wallis (n 4) 59; Shaw (n 4) 35–36; Hare (n 4) §2-2.6.1.

[6] See Berlingieri (n 1) vol 1 ch 2.

[7] See ibid vol 2 para 11. It has been suggested that the practice of establishing one-ship companies was as a result of the introduction of these sister-ship arrest provisions. See, among others, SALC Report (n 4) para 7.3; Shaw (n 4) 36; H Staniland and JS McLennan, 'The Arrest of an Associated Ship' (1985) 102 *SALJ* 148; H Staniland, 'The Implementation of the Admiralty Jurisdiction Regulation Act in South Africa' [1985] *LMCLQ* 462, 468; Hofmeyr (n 4) ch IV pt IX.2; Sarah C Derrington and James M Turner, *The Law and Practice of Admiralty Matters*, 2nd edn (Oxford, OUP, 2016) para 5.27; P Glover, 'Sister Ship Arrest and the Application of the Doctrine of Attachment in Australia: A Jurisdictional Comparative Analysis in the Wake of the 1952 Arrest Convention' (2008) *Australia and New Zealand Maritime Law Journal* 99, 110. The point has been made, however, that it is 'highly debateable' that the practice of establishing single-ship companies resulted from the adoption of the sister-ship provisions in the Arrest Convention 1952 'as the flagging out of vessels in one ship companies registered in flag of convenience states was a trend that was underway before the conclusion of the Convention, and accelerated thereafter for sound business reasons': *The Bavarian Trader* (n 5) [18]. For the historical development of single-ship companies, see Wallis (n 4) 64–66. See further ch 13.

[8] Arrest Convention 1952, art 3(1). See Staniland, 'Implementation' (n 7) 468.

[9] South Africa is not a signatory to either the Arrest Convention 1952 or the Arrest Convention 1999. For the possible reasons for South Africa not having acceded to the Arrest Convention 1952, see *The Bavarian Trader* (n 5) [18]; Wallis (n 4) 60. By the time the Arrest Convention 1999 came into force, the features of South Africa's admiralty jurisdiction that did not conform with elements of the Convention were well-entrenched enough to preclude consideration of their being sacrificed in the interests of international uniformity.

[10] Admiralty Jurisdiction Regulation Act 105 of 1983 (assented to on 8 September 1983, commenced on 1 November 1983). The AJRA 1983 was amended significantly in 1992 by the Admiralty Jurisdiction Regulation Amendment Act 87 of 1992. The AJRA 1983 is supplemented by the Rules Regulating the Conduct of the Admiralty Proceedings of the Several Provincial and Local Divisions of the Supreme Court of South Africa (Admiralty Rules), published in GN R571 *Government Gazette* 17926, 18 April 1997 (as corrected by GN R655 *Government Gazette* 17968, 2 May 1997). Proceedings in admiralty are also governed by the Uniform Rules of Court applicable in the High Court, save for those excluded by Admiralty Rule 24 and subject to the provisions of the Admiralty Rules.

[11] See SALC Report (n 4) para 7.3; *Euromarine International of Mauren v The Ship Berg* 1986 (2) SA 700, 712A–B (A); *The Heavy Metal* (SCA) (n 5) 1096F; *MV Cape Courage: Bulkship Union SA v Qannas Shipping Co Ltd* 2010 (1) SA 53 [22] (SCA); *MV Silver Star: Owners of the MV Silver Star v Hilane Ltd* 2015 (2) SA 331 [13] (SCA); Wallis (n 4) 41–43; Hofmeyr (n 4) ch IV pt IX.1; Hare (n 4) §2-2.6.1; Staniland 'Implementation' (n 7) 467–68; Malcolm Wallis, 'The Associated Ship Jurisdiction in South Africa: Choice Assorted or Only One Bite at the Cherry?' [2000] *LMCLQ* 132, 136. Although single-ship companies are presented as the paradigm problem, they are but one manifestation of a more general difficulty in ascertaining and proving ownership in complex ownership structures deployed in shipping, as in other offshore tax and corporate planning, 'to hide beneficial ownership through the interposition of nominee directors and offshore companies and trusts': *MV Ivory Tirupati: MV Ivory Tirupati v Badan Urusan Logistik (aka Bulog)* 2002 (2) SA 407, 415D–E (C).

linked to the particular ship through ownership to those linked through common control of the shipowning companies.[12] The unique facet of these provisions has been characterised as providing for 'statutory veil piercing' of shipowning companies.[13]

These provisions were among the features of South Africa's legislation that were described at the time as 'novel, unusual and at times far-reaching'.[14] They were indeed all of these things, in permitting the arrest of a ship to enforce a claim that, the associated-ship arrest provisions aside, need have no connection with the particular ship and in doing so against a shipowner that was not liable for the claim.[15] Some 36 years on they remain unique,[16] and have earned South Africa a reputation in shipping circles as an 'arrest-friendly' jurisdiction.[17]

At the Diplomatic Conference convened in Geneva to consider revision of the Arrest Convention 1952,[18] the United Kingdom delegation tabled a proposal to substitute the sister-ship arrest provision – essentially retained in the Draft Articles presented to the Conference for discussion and debate[19] – with one providing for the arrest of associated ships.[20] The concern prompting the UK proposal was that the use of the concept of ownership might not provide sufficient flexibility to implement such provisions, and therefore restrict the scope of the provisions' ability to deal with the phenomenon of single-ship companies, preventing Member States' attempts to deal with the problem through their national laws, specifically those relating to piercing the corporate veil.[21] The UK proposal addressed this concern by providing expressly for the arrest of associated ships and adding 'control' as a basis for association between ships to provide the necessary flexibility, but for the rest leaving it to national laws to determine the meaning of 'control' and what connection between the person liable on the claim and the ship targeted for arrest would justify arrest if the person liable for the claim was not the owner of that ship.[22]

Although it found some support, the UK proposal was not adopted, essentially because of reservations about the appropriateness of dealing with what was regarded as a broader problem involving general principles of corporate and insolvency law in an international Convention dealing with a specialised area of law.[23] The general view was that a solution,

[12] AJRA, ss 3(6) and 3(7). For a comprehensive and detailed treatment of the associated-ship arrest provisions see Wallis (n 4); Hofmeyr (n 4) ch IV pt IX. See also Hare (n 4) §§2-2.6–2.7; Shaw (n 4) 35–42; Staniland, 'Implementation' (n 7); *The Bavarian Trader* (n 5) [19]; *The Silver Star* (n 11) [13].

[13] See eg *The Heavy Metal* (SCA) (n 5) 1096F; Hofmeyr (n 4) ch IV pt IX.1; Staniland, 'Implementation' (n 7) 468.

[14] See *Katagum Wholesale Commodities Co Ltd v The MV Paz* 1984 (3) SA 261, 263B (N); DB Friedman, 'Maritime Law and Practice in the Courts' (1985) 102 *SALJ* 45, 55–56; DB Friedman 'Maritime Law in the Courts after 1 November 1983' (1986) 103 *SALJ* 678; Staniland, 'Implementation' (n 7) 467; Wallis, 'The Associated Ship Jurisdiction in South Africa' (n 11).

[15] See Wallis (n 4) 61–64.

[16] See *The Heavy Metal* (SCA) (n 5) 1096I–J; *MV Heavy Metal: Belfry Marine Ltd v Palm Base Maritime SDN BHD* 1998 (4) SA 479, 490I (C); Wallis (n 4) 90; Berlingieri (n 1) vol 1 ch 13.

[17] H Staniland, '*Ex Africa Semper Aliquid Novi:* Associated Ship Arrest in South Africa' [1995] *LMCLQ* 561; J Dyason, 'South African Maritime Law – An Overview of Some Developments' (2001) 32 *J Mar L & Com* 475, 481–82.

[18] The Diplomatic Conference was that convened by the United Nations and the IMO on Arrest of Ships in Geneva from 1–12 March 1999 (Conference): Berlingieri (n 1) vol 2 ch 1.

[19] For the Draft Article, see ibid 274.

[20] ibid para 8.70.

[21] Ibid appendix IV 275, 278.

[22] ibid appendix IV 275. Cp Canada's similar proposal using 'beneficial ownership': ibid appendix IV 103 fn 33, 278.

[23] ibid para 8.71.

or solutions, would have to be found elsewhere.[24] In the result, the Arrest Convention 1999 retained the sister-ship provisions of the Arrest Convention 1952.[25]

Although the UK proposal is now a matter of history as far as the Arrest Convention 1999 is concerned, the problem it sought to address remains,[26] and, for the time being at least, the search for solutions to it will have to be directed elsewhere. Yet South Africa stands as a unique example of a jurisdiction that has implemented associated-ship arrest provisions, along the lines envisaged by the UK proposal, as a dedicated solution to the problem. It may be worthwhile reconsidering the reservations about the proposal in the light of South Africa's experience of its associated-ship arrest provisions to assess whether the reservations are borne out by that experience, and whether it is the case that solutions to the problem that single-ship companies pose for enforcement of maritime claims will have to be found elsewhere.

II. Comparison of UK Proposal and South African Provisions

A. Introduction

It is necessary for this purpose to refer to the precise wording of both the proposed article put forward by the UK delegation and the South African statutory provisions to isolate those elements of each that bear comparison, which are essentially those that deal with instances in which the person liable for the claim does not own the ship targeted for arrest, and to provide a context for understanding both the reservations expressed about the UK proposal and South Africa's experience of its statutory provisions.

B. UK Proposal

The proposed art 3(2), in revised form, read:

(a) Arrest is also permissible of any other ship which, when the arrest is effected, is:
- (i) owned by the same person who, when the maritime claim arose, was liable for the claim as owner of the ship in respect of which the claim arose,
- (ii) owned by the same person who, when the maritime claim arose, was liable for that claim as the demise charterer, time charterer or voyage charterer of the ship in respect of which the claim arose, or
- (iii) effectively controlled by a person as if that person owned the arrested ship, provided that at the time the maritime claim arose such person [is liable for that claim or][27] controlled the person liable for the claim.

[24] ibid appendix IV 272–94. Among the contributions was that of the Norwegian delegation, who pointed out that the IMO's Legal Committee were working to secure victims' accessibility to assets through the establishment of rules of strict liability coupled with mandatory insurance, particularly for passengers, pollution and wreck removal: ibid appendix IV 291.

[25] Arrest Convention 1999, art 3(2). See generally Berlingieri (n 1) vol 2. For the debate on the proposal, see the travaux préparatoires of the Arrest Convention 1999: reproduced ibid appendix IV 272–94.

[26] ibid para 8.73.

[27] At the proceedings at which the proposal was debated, the bracketed wording was added to the version of the proposal circulated in advance. See ibid Annex IV 287.

(b) In determining whether a ship is effectively controlled by a person, a court make take into account all relevant factors including, but not restricted to, whether that person is able to:
   (i) make decisions in respect of that ship,
   (ii) influence the implementation of those decisions, and
   (iii) direct the distribution of profits from the operations of that ship.

(c) If the ship is not owned by the person who is liable for the maritime claim, the question whether there is a connection between the person owning the ship and the person liable for the maritime claim such as to justify the arrest shall be decided in accordance with the law of the State in which the arrest is applied for.[28]

The UK proposal's concept of association comprised three connections, or linkages, between the ship targeted for arrest and the particular ship. The first was that of common ownership. The proposal did not differ in this respect from the sister-ship provisions of the Arrest Convention 1952.[29] The second was that dealing with charterers of the particular ship. This provided that an associated ship was one owned by the same person who, when the maritime claim arose, was liable for that claim as the demise charterer, time charterer or voyage charterer of the particular ship. This also did not differ in substance from the Arrest Convention 1952.[30] It was the third connection of common control that constituted the fundamental departure from the Arrest Convention 1952 and the Draft Articles tabled at the Conference. This formed the focus of the debate and, ultimately, the grounds for rejecting the proposal.

The provisions dealing with common control are arts 3(2)(a)(iii), 3(2)(b) and 3(2)(c). Article 3(2)(a)(iii) is the core element of the provision dealing with association through common control. It bears noting for purposes of comparison with the South African statutory provisions that art 3(2)(a)(iii) differentiates 'control' and 'effective control' and refers to 'effective control' of the ship targeted for arrest and 'control' of the 'person liable for the claim'. What was envisaged by this provision is, perhaps, best explained with reference to the two examples provided at the Conference to illustrate the new situations the proposed art 3(2)(a)(iii) was intended to cover. In the first, ship B, the ship targeted for arrest, is owned by Z Co, but the ship is effectively controlled by X, who also controls Y Co which is liable for the claim in respect of ship A, the particular ship. In the second, ship B, the ship targeted for arrest, is owned by Z Co which is controlled by X who is directly liable for the claim relating to ship A, the particular ship.

[28] ibid Annex IV 285. For the initial draft of the UK proposal see ibid Annex IV 275. The proposal in its initial form had drawn criticisms about its lack of clarity in certain respects, particularly the lack of a sufficiently precise definition of 'control', and of its guidelines indicating considerations that might weigh in determining whether a ship was effectively controlled: ibid Annex IV 278–85. This prompted the establishment of an informal working group to modify the proposal in an attempt to address these criticisms. A revised proposal was then presented for consideration by the Conference. It is this revised proposal that was the subject of debate at the Conference and that will be used for present purposes. Reference will, however, also be made to the initial proposal's guidelines as to what might indicate effective control. For ease of reference, these read (ibid 276): 'The State in which the arrest is applied for may set criteria in its national law, or provide for a case-by-case examination, for the purpose of determining whether a person owns a ship or controls a company that owns a ship. All relevant factors should be taken into account, including whether the following criteria (without regard to their order) apply in respect of the ship concerned: (a) Common or similar names; (b) Common shareholding; (c) Common management of the shipowning companies; (d) Common financing arrangements; (e) Cross-guarantees or other security between shipowning companies; and (f) Insurance on a fleet basis.'

[29] ibid Annex IV 287.

[30] ibid.

The proposed article does not define 'control', although the phrase 'as if that person owned it' points to the kind and degree of control envisaged by 'effective control'. Article 3(2)(b) supplements this provision, leaving the meaning of 'control' to national law but offering guidance as to factors that would weigh in a determination of whether a person effectively controlled a ship, without limiting the range of relevant factors that might be considered in this regard. The three criteria identified were whether that person was able to 'make decisions in respect of that ship', 'influence the implementation of those decisions' and 'direct the distribution of profits from the operation of that ship'.[31] These criteria for effective control all reinforce the indication that the nature of effective control envisaged is the type of control exercised by an owner, because they would all generally be associated with ownership.

Article 3(2)(c) deals with the situation in which the ship targeted for arrest is not owned by the person liable for the claim by leaving it to the law of the State in which the arrest is applied for to determine whether there is a linkage between the person owning the ship targeted for arrest and the person liable for the maritime claim that justifies arrest of the ship to enforce the claim. Both examples used to illustrate the situations that art 3(2)(a)(iii) was intended to cover are instances in which the ship targeted for arrest is not owned by the person liable for the claim. In each of these instances, arrest of ship B as an associated ship would be permitted only if, under the law of the forum in which the arrest was sought (the forum arresti), the relationship between the person owning the ship, Z Co, and the person liable for the claim (Y Co in the first illustration and X in the second) is such as to justify the arrest.

In effect, these provisions could be characterised as enabling or facilitative measures, providing the flexibility for Member States to implement measures to deal with the problem of single-ship companies with the addition of common control as a basis for association between ships, without prescribing those measures in the Convention text.

The UK delegation's presentation and explanation of the proposal was prefaced by remarks about its aims that bear mentioning in view of the reservations that would be expressed in the debate that followed.[32] In these prefatory remarks, it was indicated that 'association' was intended to encompass a connection by virtue of what, in English law, would be called ownership but with effective control, and extended to ships that were effectively controlled by a person who also controlled the person liable for the claim.[33] It aimed at bringing within the reach of the arrest provisions those instances in which there is a less direct relationship between that person (the controller) and the ship the controller is in effect operating.

The UK delegation was also at some pains to point out that the intention was neither to undermine the option of forming conference lines and pooling arrangements, nor to catch professional ship management organisations, agents acting on behalf of owners, banks, or other investors with minority share ownership but no element of effective control, in the net cast by the provision.[34] The proposal was rather intended to provide some protection from those who would deliberately circumvent the Convention for their own protection at the expense of legitimate claimants.[35]

[31] UK Proposal, art 3(2)(b).
[32] Berlingieri (n 1) vol 2 appendix IV 278, 286–87.
[33] ibid appendix IV 278.
[34] ibid appendix IV 278, 286.
[35] ibid appendix IV 286.

C. South African Provisions

South Africa's legislation in this regard also uses the concept of an 'associated ship' against which an action in rem, with its arrest in rem, may be brought, instead of against the particular ship.[36] South Africa's associated-ship arrest provisions define an associated ship and supplement that definition with deeming provisions.[37]

The definition of an associated ship is that it is 'a ship, other than the ship in respect of which the maritime claim arose',[38] owned, at the time when the action is commenced,[39] by the person who was the owner of the ship concerned at the time when the maritime claim arose;[40] or owned, at the time when the action is commenced, by a person who controlled the company which owned the ship concerned when the maritime claim arose;[41] or owned, at the time when the action is commenced, by a company which is controlled by a person who owned the ship concerned, or controlled the company which owned the ship concerned, when the maritime claim arose.[42] In summary, then, under the South African legislation, a ship will be an associated ship if, at the commencement of the action, it is majority owned,[43] or the company that majority owns it is controlled, by the person who, at the time the cause of action arose, majority owned the particular ship, or controlled the company that majority owned it, or chartered, or controlled the company that chartered,[44]

[36] AJRA 1983, s 3(6).

[37] ibid, ss 3(7)(a), 3(7)(b) and 3(7)(c).

[38] The phrase 'other than the ship in respect of which the maritime claim arose' mirrors that in the Arrest Conventions 1952 and 1999. Within the context of the South African provisions, this phrase in combination with the wording 'instead of the ship concerned' in s 3(6) has been interpreted as precluding the arrest of the particular ship as an associated ship. See *The Bavarian Trader* (n 5) [1], [19]; Hofmeyr (n 4) ch IV pt IX.12. For the anomalous situations to which this interpretation may give rise, see *The Bavarian Trader* (n 5) [21].

[39] As with the Arrest Conventions 1952 and 1999 and the UK proposal, the inquiries as to ownership or control of the particular ship and the ship targeted for arrest as an associated ship respectively are at two different points in time. *The Heavy Metal* (SCA) (n 5) 1098E–99A; 1109G–10A. The relevant time for determining ownership or control of the shipowning company of the particular ship is when the claim arose, which accords with the timing in the Arrest Conventions and the UK proposal. For the interpretation of the phrase 'when the claim arose' in this context, see *The Cape Courage* (n 11) [23]. For criticism of this judgment on this issue, see Wallis (n 4) 173–84. For a defence of this decision, see Hofmeyr (n 4) ch IV pt IX.8–11. See too *The F Elephant: Gulf Sheba Shipping Ltd v The F Elephant* 2012 (3) SA 633 [19] (WCC). Cp *Laemthong International Lines Co Ltd v BPS Shipping Ltd* (1997) 190 CLR 181 (HCA). The relevant time for determining ownership or control of the shipowning company of the associated ship under the South African legislation is also when the action commences, which differs from that in the Arrest Conventions and the UK proposal, in which the relevant time is when the arrest of the sister or associated ship is effected. The AJRA 1983 defines when the action commences: see s 1(2), analysed in the recent case of *MV Seaspan Grouse: Seaspan Holdco 1 Ltd v MS Mare Traveller Schiffarhts GmbH* (376/18) [2019] ZASCA 02 (1 February 2019).

[40] AJRA 1983, s 3(7)(a)(i).

[41] ibid s 3(7)(a)(ii).

[42] ibid s 3(7)(a)(iii). Although not directly relevant, it seems worth noting the claims excluded from the associated-ship arrest provisions under South Africa law are more limited than those in the Arrest Conventions and the UK proposal. They are restricted to claims 'for, arising out of or relating to any mortgage, hypothecation, right of retention, pledge or other charge on or of a ship, and any bottomry or *respondentia* bond': ibid s 3(6) read with s 1(1)(d). They do not, after the 1992 amendments to the Act, exclude claims relating to ownership and possession.

[43] That majority ownership suffices follows from the deeming provisions supplementing the definition of ownership: see ibid s 3(7)(b)(i).

[44] The inclusion of charterers in this summary follows from the provision supplementing the definition of 'associated ship' deeming charterers to be owners of the particular ship in respect of claims for which they, and not the owner, are alleged to be liable for the purposes of the associated-ship arrest provisions: AJRA 1983, s 3(7)(c); Shaw (n 4) 40–41. All the deeming provision does is to place a charterer's unpaid creditor in exactly the same position in relation to the defaulting charterer as an owner's unpaid creditor would be in relation to the defaulting owner: *The Silver Star* (n 11) [16], [18].

the particular ship. Of the two provisions supplementing this definition, only the one relating to 'control' is relevant. It deems a person to control a company 'if that person has the power, directly or indirectly, to control the company'.[45]

For purposes of comparison of these provisions with the UK proposal, two general points bear mention. The first is that the South African provisions are consistent both in their use of the term 'control', and in relating control to shipowning companies; whereas the UK proposal refers to control of the person liable for the maritime claim, and effective control of the ship targeted for arrest. Nothing much turns on this for present purposes and therefore the reasons for these differences do not matter, other than to say that the UK proposal's different kinds or degrees of control may have contributed, at least in part, to the reservations about the lack of a more precise definition of the word 'control'. The second point to make is that under the South African provisions 'control' is of the shipowning companies of the ship targeted for arrest and the particular ship respectively; as opposed to the UK proposal's combination of 'effective control' of the ship targeted for arrest and 'control' of the person liable on the debt as a basis for establishing association. This may, of course, also encompass control of shipowning companies as juristic persons, and where it does the comparison between the UK proposal and the South African provisions is direct.

The only further point to make is that the two examples used to illustrate the situations covered by the UK proposal's extension of the sister ship arrest provisions would equally be covered by the South African provisions establishing association on the basis of common control.

D. Elements for Comparison

It is the South African legislation's provision for association through common control, or an element of control through various combinations of ownership and control that bears comparison with the UK proposal, insofar as its common control elements envisaged disregard of the separate legal personality of companies.[46]

III. Reservations about the UK Proposal in Light of the South African Experience

A. Introduction

While the UK proposal garnered support, in some instances qualified, from a few countries, most delegations at the Conference were not in favour of it, with their reservations centring on those aspects of the UK proposal relating to association that went beyond ownership and chartering arrangements.[47] The primary concerns in this regard seemed to be: first, the

[45] AJRA 1983, s 3(7)(b)(ii). The other provision stipulates that 'a company includes any other juristic person and any body of persons, irrespective of whether or not any interest therein consists of shares': ibid s 3(7)(b)(iii).
[46] Wallis (n 4) ch 7.
[47] Berlingieri (n 1) vol 2 para 8.71.

lack of a sufficiently precise definition of the terms 'effective control' and 'control';[48] and a related concern expressed by some, which was not given much prominence in the debate, but which is nonetheless of considerable practical importance, about the difficulties of proving the facts necessary to establish control, particularly in the relatively short time frame in which this would generally have to be done.[49] A second primary concern was that the problem that the UK proposal aimed to address was a more general issue involving principles of corporate and insolvency law; and that it was therefore inappropriate to deal with it in an international Convention on a specialised area of maritime law.[50] A third, related concern was that leaving the meaning of the term 'control' and the issue of 'whether there is a connection between the person owning the ship and the person liable for the maritime claim such as to justify the arrest' to be determined by the law of the forum arresti would be likely to lead to an additional layer, or layers, of divergent approaches that would undermine the objective of international uniformity.[51] A cluster of other concerns were raised, such as that piercing the corporate veil of shipowning companies would adversely affect maritime trade and only protect the interests of certain groups; that the growth of single-ship companies is well justified; and that the creation of one-ship companies is not motivated by a desire to circumvent the Arrest Convention 1952's sister-ship arrest provisions; but all of these seem related to the primary concerns outlined above.

Given these reservations expressed at the Conference about the appropriateness of dealing with a more general problem in corporate and insolvency law by implementing, or at least facilitating the implementation of, measures directed specifically at shipowning companies, and about leaving elements of the solution to national law, South Africa presents an example of what might follow from doing precisely this. The South African experience with its associated-ship arrest provisions may provide a basis for reconsidering the reservations concerning the UK proposal's common control elements.

B. Meaning of 'Control'

Although the reservations were related, a sensible point of departure for consideration of these reservations in light of South Africa's experience of its associated-ship arrest provisions seems to be the meaning of 'control'.

The starting point for this analysis is the deeming provisions supplementing the definition of an associated ship,[52] the most important of which is that deeming a person to control a company if that person has the 'power to control, whether directly or indirectly, the company'.[53] What is clear from this deeming provision is that 'control' is seen in terms of a power to be exercised in relation to the shipowning company,[54] but neither

[48] ibid para 8.71, appendix IV 278–82, 291.
[49] ibid appendix IV 279 (Denmark), 281 (Sri Lanka), 283 (ICS).
[50] ibid para 8.71.
[51] UK Proposal, art 3(2)(c).
[52] AJRA 1983, ss 3(7)(b) and 3(7)(c).
[53] ibid s 3(7)(b)(ii). This provision is supplemented by an expansive definition of a company that includes 'any other juristic person and any body of persons, irrespective of whether or not any interest therein consists of shares': see ibid s 3(7)(b)(iii).
[54] *The Heavy Metal* (SCA) (n 5) 1105I.

the term 'power' nor 'control' is defined in the legislation. It therefore fell to the courts to interpret these terms in context.

Very soon after the introduction of the associated-ship arrest provisions in the AJRA 1983, the South African courts were called upon to interpret the word 'control'. It is now settled in South African law that control of the shipowning company in this context means control of its 'assets and destiny', such as would be exercised by a majority shareholder, and not mere day-to-day control of its management and administration'.[55] South Africa's experience therefore demonstrates the importance of a more precise definition of the term 'control' and bears out to some extent the concern expressed at the Conference about the lack of a precise definition of the term in the UK proposal. The meaning of 'control' was, however, settled from the outset with relatively little difficulty by the South African courts. Their interpretation of 'control' would seem to address adequately the concerns, raised in relation to the UK proposal, that the lack of a more precise definition of the term control might result in persons who could be considered to control the ship on grounds such as being in physical possession of the ship or responsible for its day-to-day operations being caught in the net cast by the provisions. The relative ease with which this issue was resolved in South African law may have something to do with the fact that the South African provisions use the word 'control' consistently, as opposed to differentiating between 'control' and 'effective control', and moreover use the term consistently in relation to shipowning companies, as opposed to the UK proposal's use of 'control' in relation to the person liable for the maritime claim and 'effective control' in relation to the ship to be targeted for arrest. The South African provisions also perhaps distinguish ownership and control more clearly, whereas the UK proposal's use of 'effective' control may have been susceptible to being interpreted as embracing issues of ownership of ships, perhaps specifically notions of 'beneficial ownership', as well as control of shipowning companies.[56] The Conference delegates' reservations about the lack of a sufficiently precise definition of the word 'control' in the UK proposal may therefore have had some foundation.

The meaning attributed to the term 'control' by the South African courts has precluded association between ships being established merely on such grounds that their shipowning companies have the same directors;[57] or that the ships are under the same management

[55] See *EE Sharp & Sons Ltd v MV Nefeli 1984 (3) SA 325, 326I–27A (C)*; *Transgroup Shipping SA (Pty) Ltd v Owners of MV Kyoju Maru* 1984 (4) SA 210, 215H–I (D); *East Cross Sea Transport Inc v Elgin Brown & Hamer (Pty) Ltd* 1992 (1) SA 102, 107D–E (D); *The Kadirga 5 (No 1): JA Chapman & Co Ltd v Kadirga Denizcilik ve Ticaret AS Shipping Cases of South Africa* C12, C14E (N); *The Heavy Metal* (SCA) (n 5) 1106A; *SY Sandokan: Owner of the SY Sandokan v Liverpool & London Steamship Protection & Indemnity Association Ltd* 2001 (3) SA 824, 826J–27A (D); *International Marine Transport SA v MV Le Cong* 2005 JDR 1366 [7] (SCA); *The Silver Star* (n 11) [40]; Wallis (n 4) ch 7; Hofmeyr (n 4) ch IV pt IX.15; Hare (n 4) §2-2.6.3; Staniland, '*Ex Africa Semper Aliquid Novi*' (n 17) 563–5. It is accepted that majority shareholding is not the only way in which a company can be controlled and that control of a company may be exercised by persons other than the majority shareholders, eg where voting rights are not determined by ownership or control of the majority of the shares. See *Zygos Corp v Salen Rederierna AB* 1985 (2) SA 486, 489B–D (C); *National Iranian Tanker Co v The Pericles* 1995 (1) SA 475, 485B–C (A); *Dole Fresh Fruit International Ltd v MV Kapetan Leonidas* 1995 (3) SA 112, 119E–G (A).

[56] Berlingieri (n 1) vol 2 appendix IV 278. For examples of reservations expressed about the use of 'beneficial ownership' see ibid 278 (Netherlands), 279 (Denmark, Russian Federation), 280 (France), 281 (Sri Lanka). For the two senses in which the term 'beneficial ownership' might be understood in South African law, namely in a narrow sense in the context of trusts, and in a broader economic sense, see Wallis (n 4) 54.

[57] See *The Heavy Metal* (SCA) (n 5) 492D–E.

company,[58] or have the same agents, among others. This goes some way to addressing concerns such as those expressed in the debate on the UK proposal that the term 'control' was difficult to define and that, without a more precise definition, its use as a basis for establishing association between ships might catch professional ship management organisations or agents acting on behalf of owners in the net cast by the provision.[59] Although the meaning attributed to 'control' in this context precludes a finding of association merely on the basis of one or more of these grounds, particularly considered in isolation, combinations and permutations of these grounds have been relied on as indicators of common control of shipowning companies from which an inference of common control sufficient to establish association may be drawn.[60]

C. 'Power to Control Directly or Indirectly'

Allied to the concerns about the meaning of 'control' already dealt with, is the meaning of the South African provision deeming a person to control a company if that person has 'power, directly or indirectly, to control the company',[61] the interpretation of which has produced a result which is unlikely to have occurred to those who raised concerns about the meaning of control. The deeming provision makes it clear that control is conceived of as a power, but the phrase 'power … to control' is not circumscribed and could mean either the power to manage the day-to-day operations of the company or to determine its direction and fate. It has been held, however, that 'where these vest in different hands it is the latter [meaning] the legislature had in mind when referring to power and hence to control'.[62]

The interpretation of the phrase 'power, directly or indirectly, to control' in the deeming provision arose squarely for determination in the *Heavy Metal* case.[63] In this case, the ship arrested as an associated ship was, at the relevant time, owned by a company whose registered majority shareholder was also the registered majority shareholder of the company owning the particular ship at the time the claim arose. This would have provided the basis for association were it not for the fact that the identified majority shareholder claimed to be merely a nominee shareholder, holding his shares in each of the two companies for two different principals. The further complication was that the majority shareholder initially claimed to be legally constrained not to disclose the identities of either of the persons on whose behalf he held the shares in the respective companies. He later claimed to have been authorised to identify the principal on whose behalf he held the shares in one of the companies, but was not authorised to identify his other principal, although he swore under oath that it was not the same person. These facts, coupled with the majority shareholder's evidence, raised the issue of whether it had been proved that the majority shareholder, or some other person, had the 'power, directly or indirectly, to control' the two shipowning

[58] *The Kyoju Maru* (n 55) 215H–I; *Hasselbacher Papier Import and Export v MV Stravroula* 1987 (1) SA 75 (C) 78H.
[59] Berlingieri (n 1) vol 2 appendix IV 278, 282–83, 286, 289.
[60] See eg *The Nefeli* (n 55) 327A; *The Ivory Tirupati* (n 11) 413F–414I; *The Silver Star* (n 11) [41]–[53].
[61] AJRA 1983, s 3(7)(b)(ii).
[62] *The Heavy Metal* (SCA) (n 5) 1105I–06B, 1112G–H; Hofmeyr (n 4) ch IV pt IX.14.
[63] *The Heavy Metal* (SCA) (n 5).

companies so that the deeming provision was triggered, from which it would follow that the ships were associated.[64] On the interpretation of this provision, the five-judge bench split three to two.[65]

All five judges were in agreement that the provision was to be interpreted as identifying two forms or manifestations of power to control – direct and indirect.[66] The majority equated direct control with control in law and indirect control with control in fact.[67] The majority considered direct control, or control in law, of a company to lie in the hands of the registered shareholder holding a majority of the shares in the company, irrespective of whether the majority shareholder held the shares as a nominee; and indirect control, or control in fact, to lie in the hands of the principal on whose behalf the majority shareholder held the shares.[68] Since the majority shareholder denied that he held the shares in each company on behalf of the same principal, it could not be established that the same person had the power to control both companies indirectly. It was therefore necessary for the Court to confront the issue of whether the provision was to be interpreted as also permitting association on the basis of a common majority nominee shareholder as the person having direct control of both shipowning companies. It was over this issue that the Court split, with the majority holding that the provision had to be interpreted as allowing a creditor to rely on either direct or indirect control to establish an association between the ships, because the purpose of the legislation was to assist creditors in enforcing their claims. Since it had been proved that the respective shipowning companies had the same majority registered shareholder, direct common control had been established and the ships were therefore associated.[69]

In contrast, the minority considered that the legislation's purpose was to identify the single repository of what has been variously described as the 'actual', 'real', or 'true' power of control of the respective companies, which would reside with a majority shareholder only where that shareholder held the shares as principal; but would instead lie in the hands of the person on whose behalf the shares were held where the majority shareholder held the shares as nominee.[70] In the latter instance, the provision was not to be interpreted as giving a claimant a choice as to whether to rely on either direct or indirect control. As Marais JA put it in his minority dissenting judgement on the interpretation of the provision:

> As I see it, the provision does not give the claimant a choice as to which of the two it best suits him to have regarded as having the power to control the company. The purpose of the provision is not to create a fiction which could place innocent third parties in jeopardy of having their ships arrested to secure payment of claims brought against persons or ships of whose existence they were quite oblivious. That would be tantamount to naked confiscation without compensation – a purpose

[64] *The Heavy Metal* (SCA) (n 5) 1093E.

[65] On the overall outcome of the appeal, the Court split 4–1. Marias JA, in the minority on the interpretation of the deeming provision, dismissed the appeal and upheld the arrest on other grounds.

[66] It has been pointed out that the section is perfectly susceptible of the more sensible construction that it is concerned with the identification of a single repository of power to control, variously referred to as 'actual', 'real' or 'true' power, and that such control may be directly or indirectly exercised. See Wallis (n 4) 206–22; Hofmeyr (n 4) ch IV pt IX.19.

[67] *The Heavy Metal* (SCA) (n 5) 1106C–E.

[68] See Marais JA's criticism of the majority's equation of indirect control with control in fact: ibid 1113A–F.

[69] ibid 1106I–07B, 1107F–G.

[70] ibid 1104B–G, 1111I–13F.

which one shies away from attributing to the Legislature unless that is unmistakably what it intended. Its purpose is to allow a claimant to pierce the veil of apparent or ostensible power to control a company and so reveal the identity of the real holder of power to control the company.[71]

The majority's rather dismissive attitude to this consequence of their decision was that it was 'the direct and foreseeable consequence of a ship-owner choosing to operate behind a cloak of secrecy', and that it was 'precisely for this reason, because the creditor is at such a disadvantage in tracing assets of his debtor, that the subsection was worded as it is'.[72] Marais JA responded robustly:

> I cannot subscribe to the proposition that, if the interpretation of the provision favoured by [the majority] should result in a third party who has no connection whatsoever with the guilty ship other than that he happened unwittingly to use as his nominee to hold shares in his ship-owning company a person who also holds as a nominee all the shares in the company which owns the guilty ship, losing his company's ship, that is his fault for 'choosing to operate behind a cloak of secrecy.' There is nothing inherently immoral, unethical, or reprehensible in nominee shareholdings. The reasons why they may be resorted to in good faith are legion and the interpretation to be given to the provision cannot be grounded upon an assumption that there must always be some or other disreputable purpose lurking behind their use.[73]

The majority judgment exposes a fundamental difference between the South African associated-ship arrest provisions and the principles applied in South Africa's general corporation law. In the latter, determination of the source of control of a company is directed at locating actual or real control;[74] and, where control lies with shareholding, the real control is considered to be the control exercised by the 'actual' or 'beneficial' holder of the shares, whether that person holds the shares as registered holder or through a nominee. The result of the majority's broad interpretation of the associated-ship provisions is that, even if two companies have no commercial connections whatsoever, the vessels owned by them could be held to be associated merely because they have the same nominee shareholder, visiting shipowning companies with liability for debts, for the creation and payment of which they otherwise would bear no legal responsibility.[75]

This decision has drawn widespread criticism, particularly directed at its interpretation of the provisions as permitting reliance on either direct or indirect control where these two forms of control lie in different hands.[76] The general view is that the minority judges' interpretation of the associated-ship provision is correct, namely that the provision is concerned with identifying a single repository of power,[77] but recognises that such power may be exercised in two ways, either directly, where the registered majority shareholder holds its shares as principal, or indirectly, where the registered majority shareholder holds the shares for or

[71] ibid 1111E–G. See too, Hofmeyr (n 4) ch IV pt IX.23; Wallis (n 4) 186–93.

[72] *The Heavy Metal* (SCA) (n 5) 1107G–H.

[73] ibid 1112H–J.

[74] ibid 1102B–04A. Cp Companies Act 71 of 2008, s 1 'holding company', read with ss 2(2)(a) and 3(1)(a).

[75] On the far-reaching consequences of the majority's interpretation of this provision, see Hofmeyr (n 4) ch IV pt IX.19.

[76] For detailed and persuasive criticism of the majority judgment, see Wallis (n 4) 206–22; Hofmeyr (n 4) ch IV pt IX.17–24. See too Hare (n 4) §2-2.6.3; Graham Bradfield, 'Guilt by Association in South African Admiralty Law' [2005] *LMCLQ* 234, 234–40.

[77] Wallis (n 4) 192.

on behalf of the actual holder of the shares, exercising its votes as registered shareholder in accordance with its principal's mandate.

This decision has prompted a proposed amendment of the South African associated-ship provision aimed at clarifying that what is required to establish an association between ships is a common, single repository of 'actual' or 'real' power to control the respective ship-owning companies. Decisions such as this lend support to the concerns raised in relation to the UK proposal that leaving the issue of the meaning of 'control' as a basis for establishing an association between ships to national laws to determine might result not only in divergent approaches developing among jurisdictions, but also in doctrinal tensions and contradictions between general corporate law principles and maritime law principles within jurisdictions.

D. Difficulties of Proving Association through Common Control

Related to the reservation about the meaning of control, is the concern about the difficulties of establishing common control within the time constraints that generally operate in ship arrests, and the associated costs of doing so.[78]

Under South African law, the burden of proving association is on the arresting creditor, and proof of association is, even at the arrest stage, on a balance of probabilities.[79] The difficulty that confronts arresting creditors seeking to establish association through common control is in establishing the source of control,[80] and gathering evidence of control of shipowning companies is made difficult by inaccessible or opaque company registers and information about shareholding being treated as confidential.[81]

While some attempts have been made to enlist the aid of statutory provisions and court rules to inspect documents and records in the hands of the shipowner or obtain discovery of what evidence of control there may be, the courts have resisted such attempts in interlocutory application proceedings to establish the court's jurisdiction, particularly if these attempts smack of 'fishing expeditions'.[82] It has been held, for example, that 'it would not be right to order discovery in the Micawber-like hope that something would turn up'.[83] It has also been held that there is no justification for allowing discovery under the Admiralty Rules unless there 'are reasonable grounds for doubting the correctness of the allegations concerned', because to do so would 'come perilously close to reversing the onus in matters like this; for it would, in effect, cast an onus on the applicant to disprove that the ships in question were associated ships'.[84]

Some relief from these difficulties is afforded by statutory provisions that permit courts to admit as evidence statements that would otherwise be inadmissible as being in the nature of hearsay evidence. The weight to be attached to that evidence lies in the discretion of the court.[85]

[78] Berlingieri (n 1) vol 2 appendix IV 279, 281–82, 290.

[79] *Bocimar NV v Kotor Overseas Shipping Ltd* 1994 (2) SA 563, 581B–C (A); *The Silver Star* (n 11) [46]–[55].

[80] See Wallis (n 4) 222–28.

[81] ibid 126. For detail on these difficulties see *The Silver Star* (n 11) [39]; Wallis (n 4) 292.

[82] AJRA 1983, s 5(5); Admiralty Proceedings Rules 15 and 25, and Uniform Rule of Court 35; *The MV Urgup: Owners of the MV Urgup v Western Bulk Carriers (Australia) (Pty) Ltd* 1999 (3) SA 500 (C).

[83] *The Kyoju Maru* (n 55) 217E–F.

[84] *East Cross Sea Transport Inc* (n 55) 109D–E.

[85] AJRA 1983, ss 6(3), 6(4); *Cargo Laden on Board the Thalassini Avgi v The Dimitris* 1989 (3) SA 820, 842G–H (A).

In many cases, however, reliance has to be placed on an inference of common control drawn from indicators of such common control. These include common directors of the shipowning companies;[86] common ship management;[87] ship names that indicate some connection between the ships;[88] and a range of other factors, including cross-guarantees, or other security between the shipowning companies,[89] insurance on a fleet basis,[90] foreign proceedings in which one company's control of another was not denied,[91] and even statements on company websites and in trade journals indicating control of companies.[92] These resonate with the initial UK proposal's guidelines as to the factors that might be considered in the determination of whether a ship was controlled,[93] but, as was pointed out in the debate on the UK proposal, these factors considered individually do not necessarily indicate 'effective' control in the sense envisaged by the proposal.[94] In the South African context of proving common control on a balance of probabilities, these indicators have seldom been relied on individually. Almost invariably, reliance is placed on some combination or permutation of these indicators as the basis for an inference of common control, but even in such instances the courts have generally been circumspect in relying on these.[95]

In application proceedings to set aside the arrest of an associated ship on the basis that the ship is not associated with the particular ship or that such association has not been proved, courts may be faced with denials of association and disputes of fact that are difficult for the arresting party to deal with. The difficulty of resolving these disputes of fact is exacerbated by the courts' reluctance to refer these disputes to the hearing of oral evidence on the grounds that to do so draws the defendant into the forum at the preliminary stage of proceedings to establish whether the court may exercise jurisdiction in the main dispute, or disputes.[96] Without resort to oral evidence, such responses have to be resolved on the papers and, in these instances, there are evidentiary rules that assist arresting creditors. For example, in the face of compelling circumstantial evidence adduced by the arresting creditor, courts may reject denials of common control where these are clearly untenable, far-fetched or limited; where there is a refusal to reveal the allegedly associated ship's ownership structures;[97] or on the basis that the papers do not raise genuine disputes of fact.[98]

Nevertheless, some associated ship arrest applications have foundered on the treacherous rocks of discharging the burden of proving association,[99] which lends credence to those concerns expressed in respect of the UK proposal about the difficulties of proving control.[100] While the reservations about the difficulties of proving association through common control may have some foundation in the South African experience of its associated-ship

[86] *The Nefeli* (n 55) 327A–C; *The Heavy Metal* (C) (n 16) 492D–E.

[87] *The Nefeli* (n 55) 327B.

[88] *East Cross Sea Transport Inc* (n 55) 107D–F; *The Ivory Tirupati* (n 11) 413G–I.

[89] *The Silver Star* (n 11) [43], [53]; *MV Bulk Joyance: Elstead Ltd v MV Bulk Joyance* 2014 (5) SA 414, [41]–[44] (KZD).

[90] *The Kadirga 5 (No 1)* (n 55); Hofmeyr (n 4) ch IV pt IX.45.

[91] *The Bulk Joyance* (n 89) [17].

[92] ibid.

[93] For the text of the UK delegation's initial proposal see n 28 above.

[94] Berlingieri (n 1) vol 2 appendix IV 282–83.

[95] See eg *The Bulk Joyance* (n 89) [41]–[44].

[96] See *Zygos Corp* (n 55); Hofmeyr (n 4) ch IV pt IX.44–46.

[97] *The Heavy Metal* (SCA) (n 5) 1107I, 1114A–15G, cp 1100H–I.

[98] ibid 1107J–08G, 1113J–15H; *The Ivory Tirupati* (n 11) 415D–I; *The Silver Star* (n 11) [54]. See generally Hofmeyr (n 4) ch IV pt IX.47.

[99] See eg *The Kyoju Maru* (n 55); *The Kapetan Leonidas* (n 55); *The Bulk Joyance* (n 89).

[100] Cp J Dyason (n 17) 481.

provisions, the hurdles confronting an arresting creditor are not insurmountable. The concerns expressed by delegations at the Conference that implementing associated-ship provisions might hold out 'false hope' to maritime creditors because of evidentiary difficulties are not borne out by South Africa's experience.[101]

E. Disregarding the Separate Legal Personality of Shipowning Companies

i. Introduction

The reservations expressed about elements of the UK proposal that countenanced piercing the corporate veil of shipowning companies could be considered as resolving themselves into two separate but related concerns. The first was that the single-ship company problem these provisions aimed to address was a more general issue not confined to shipowning companies, and that it would therefore be better dealt with under general principles of corporate and insolvency law.[102] This view seemed to predominate in the debate about the UK proposal, without perhaps exploring more fully whether there might not be justification for singling out these particular corporate structures for differential treatment. The second reservation was that, even if it were to be accepted that the problem should be addressed in a specialist Convention dealing with ship arrest, to do so on the basis suggested by the UK proposal of enabling Member States to implement national measures to deal with the problem would inevitably lead to divergent approaches, undermining the fundamental objective of the Convention to achieve international uniformity regarding ship arrest.[103]

In light of these reservations, South Africa's experience of those elements of its associated-ship arrest provisions that extend association to a connection through common control of shipowning companies bears separate consideration as the only example of just such measures.[104]

ii. Departure from General Principles of Company Law

Before dealing with possible justifications for the particular treatment of shipowning companies it is as well to consider how that treatment differs from the approach to disregarding the separate legal personality of companies generally in South Africa.

a. Departure

The provisions South Africa implemented that provided for association through common control of shipowning companies have been characterised as 'statutory veil piercing' provisions.[105] Where ships are associated through common control, or an element of

[101] Berlingieri (n 1) vol 2 appendix IV 281, 283.
[102] ibid para 8.72.
[103] ibid para 8.71.
[104] *The Heavy Metal* (SCA) (n 5) 1096I–J; *The Heavy Metal* (C) (n 16) 490I–91A; Staniland, 'Implementation' (n 7) 468; Staniland '*Ex Africa Semper Aliquid Novi*' (n 17) 571.
[105] See *The Heavy Metal* (SCA) (n 5) 1098J; Hofmeyr (n 4) ch IV pt IX.1.

common control, the proceedings against the associated ship entail claiming from the associated shipowning company payment of a debt owed by another entity – the shipowning company or the company chartering the particular ship. It is generally considered that this disregards the separate legal personalities of the companies, both in effectively treating the debt of the company owning or chartering the particular ship as that of the controller, and in effectively treating the assets of the company owning the associated ship as that of the controller, and therefore available for satisfaction of the controller's debt.[106] The fact that this is almost invariably masked by the provision of security to avoid the ship's arrest, or to obtain the release of the arrested ship, does not change this as a matter of legal principle.

Furthermore, the South African associated-ship arrest provisions permit, as a matter of course, the lifting of the corporate veil of such companies once common control – which may consist of nothing more than a common majority shareholding in each of the shipowning companies – is established. This is a significant departure from the general approach to corporate veil-piercing in South African law.[107] While it may not be possible to define with accuracy the instances in which the corporate veil will be disregarded under principles of South Africa's corporate law,[108] it is clear that corporate veil-piercing is a discretionary remedy, permitted in exceptional circumstances only,[109] and then only if it is proved that the corporate structure is a mere façade involving an element of fraud, there is other improper conduct amounting to an abuse of the corporate form or there is a failure to maintain the distinct separate identity of the company from that of its members.[110]

In contrast, in the case of the arrest of an associated ship based on common control of the respective shipowning companies, all that needs to be proved for the corporate veils to be disregarded is the fact of common control. Corporate veil-piercing will then follow automatically, without scope for the exercise of any discretion on the part of the court in this regard. The South African associated-ship arrest provisions do not differentiate between legitimate uses of corporate structures as vehicles for ship ownership and their use to

[106] Cp Hofmeyr (n 4) ch IV pt IX.23; Wallis (n 4) 63.

[107] Until the commencement of South African's Companies Act 71 of 2008, the principles on which the separate legal personality of companies was based were to be found almost exclusively in its common law. South Africa's Companies Act 71 of 2008 introduced a specific section permitting courts to declare a company 'to be deemed not to be a juristic person in respect of any right, obligation or liability of the company or of a shareholder of the company' on the grounds 'that the incorporation of the company, any use of the company, or any act by or on behalf of the company, constitutes an unconscionable abuse of the juristic personality of the company as a separate entity': Companies Act 71 of 2008, s 20(9). It has been held that this provision is 'supplemental to the common law, rather than substitutive': *Ex parte Gore and others NNO* 2013 (2) SA 382 [34] (WCC); *City Capital SA Property Holdings Ltd v Chavonnes Badenhorst St Clair Cooper* 2018 (4) SA 71 [30] (SCA). See generally, Farouk Cassim et al, *Contemporary Company Law*, 2nd edn (Claremont, Juta, 2012) 41–65.

[108] See *Cape Pacific Ltd v Lubner Controlling Investments (Pty) Ltd* 1995 (4) SA 790, 802–03 (A); *Ex parte Gore* (n 107) [28]; Cassim (n 107) 41–42; Wallis (n 4) 70. For the instances in which the courts have been prepared to pierce the corporate veil, see Cassim (n 107) 43–46.

[109] *Cape Pacific Ltd* (n 108) 803A–H, in which the Court held that there was no general discretion to pierce or disregard the corporate veil. The discretion is to be exercised only if the pre-conditions are present and the tests referred to are satisfied. See also ibid 819–21; *Hülse-Reutter v Gödde* 2001 (4) SA 1336 (SCA); Cassim (n 107) 42; Wallis (n 4) 70.

[110] See *Shipping Corp of India v Evdomon* 1994 (1) SA 550, 556 (SCA); *Cape Pacific Ltd* (n 108); *Hülse-Reutter* (n 109); Wallis (n 4) 69. The provisions of s 20(9) of the Companies Act 71 of 2008 may well broaden the bases on which the separate legal personality of companies may be disregarded: *Ex parte Gore* (n 107) [33]. This approach accords with that in many other jurisdictions. For the approaches to disregarding the separate personality of companies in certain other countries see Berlingieri (n 1) vol 1 appendix IV 285–89.

deliberately evade liability for their own protection at the expense of legitimate claimants. The reason for the use of the corporate structure is irrelevant. All that matters is the fact of common control of the respective shipowning companies.

The fact that the South African associated-ship arrest provisions do not take into consideration the reasons for the use of a particular corporate ownership structure, or focus on whether the shipowning company is set up as a single-ship company, could be regarded as evidence that the provisions are based on the premise that corporate ownership structures for ships are invariably improper,[111] and that all shipowning companies are mere façades concealing the identity of the 'true' debtor. The provisions ignore, or dismiss, the fact that the corporate structure is generally regarded as a lawful mechanism for the limitation of risk in commercial enterprise and may well have been used by a shipowning company for a range of legitimate purposes. To disregard the separate existence of such corporate structures merely on the basis of common control, or an inference of common control, without any consideration of the purpose, or purposes, behind establishing the companies or company groups, and without the exercise of any judicial discretion as to whether particular circumstances justify the piercing of the corporate veil, amounts to a significant erosion of the principle of the separate corporate entity as a legitimate vehicle for the management of commercial risks.[112] In effect, these provisions indiscriminately treat every such structure as a stratagem to avoid paying creditors' debts and, in so doing, mete out differential treatment to shipowning companies as compared with companies more generally. In not considering the reasons for establishing a particular ship ownership structure in this form, and in discriminating against shipowning companies generally, the provisions might be regarded as an overly blunt and broad instrument to deal with the specific problem of single-ship companies. The result is that these provisions can be, and may have been, invoked against perfectly respectable groups of companies that are not constituted as one-ship companies for any dishonest purpose.[113]

In sum, the South African associated-ship provisions amount to a 'wholesale departure from fundamental principles of company law',[114] and, as such, require a justification for their differential treatment of all shipowning companies. It has been argued that reliance on the concept of corporate veil-piercing as a justification for these provisions is misplaced.[115] This raises the question: are these provisions merely expedient,[116] or can a principled justification be found for them?

b. Justification

Since South Africa adopted such expansive associated-ship arrest measures, it was clearly of the view that the problem single-ship companies posed for maritime creditors warranted a solution; and that this solution could not be left to be dealt with under general principles of corporate law. The fundamental difference in approach to disregarding the separate legal

[111] Bradfield 'Guilt by Association' (n 76) 234–40. Cp Wallis (n 4) 72 fn 92.
[112] Wallis (n 4) 73.
[113] ibid 74.
[114] ibid 73.
[115] ibid.
[116] ibid 74.

personality of shipowning companies was consciously adopted on policy grounds with the enactment of South Africa's associated-ship arrest provisions,[117] even if the justification for introducing the provisions may not have been fully explored at the time. The reason generally given for their introduction was simply the proliferation of the practice of forming one-ship companies, particularly in the second half of the twentieth century,[118] and 'that the ship concerned often presents an elusive or transient target that may be deliberately kept out of the jurisdiction of the claimant or may pass through it only briefly'.[119] Their purpose has been stated to be 'to make liability for a maritime claim, or the loss from such a claim, fall where it belonged by virtue of common ownership of ships or common control of shipowning companies'.[120] These reasons for the introduction of the provisions and statements of their purposes may hint at a justification for them, but would probably not be regarded as providing a fully articulated and persuasive justification.

The example of the associated ship concept in South African admiralty law has not been followed by other jurisdictions that introduced or reformed their national admiralty legislation after the enactment of the AJRA 1983.[121] So, for example, the Australian Law Reform Commission recognised that the introduction of some form of corporate veil-piercing provision would be advantageous for local interests but ultimately rejected the idea, deciding, in the interests of consistency, to leave the issue of whether the corporate veil of the shipowning company should be disregarded to be dealt with as an exceptional discretionary remedy to be granted according to the relevant general principles of Australian corporation and insolvency law.[122] It is also clear from contributions during the Conference debate on the UK proposal that the predominant view was that the problem the proposal sought to address was of a more general nature, such that there was no justification for a differential treatment of all shipowning companies.

Although a justification for the distinctive nature of the South African associated-ship arrest provisions might not have been fully explored at the time of their introduction, there have fairly recently been indications that the question of their legitimacy and suitability may be revisited, both because of (perhaps faint) indicators of political pressure to remove them emanating from South Africa's major trading partners,[123] and in the context of the South African Government's initiatives to develop its maritime sector.[124]

Wallis has advanced a fully articulated and carefully reasoned justification for the South African associated-ship arrest provisions.[125] Constraints of space mean that only the main

[117] House of Assembly Debates (Hansard), 11 August 1983, col 11172.

[118] See *The Nefeli* (n 55) 326H.

[119] See Staniland '*Ex Africa Semper Aliquid Novi*' (n 17) 571. For the 'ship concerned', see above n 2.

[120] *The Berg* (n 11) 712A-B; *The Silver Star* (n 11) [40]; Hofmeyr (n 4) ch IV pt IX.1.

[121] See Berlingieri (n 1) vol 1 ch 13. Cp Wallis (n 4) 73.

[122] Australian Law Reform Commission, *Civil Admiralty Jurisdiction* (ALRC 33, 1986) paras 138–41. Cp Australia's support for the UK proposal: Berlingieri (n 1) vol 2 appendix IV 293. See also *Shagang Shipping Co Ltd v Ship Bulk Peace as Surrogate for the Ship Dong-A Astrea* [2014] FCAFC 48 [50].

[123] See keynote address delivered by Malcolm Wallis at the 2012 Annual Conference of the Maritime Law Association of South Africa (14 September 2012) 7, available at www.mlasa.co.za/wp-content/uploads/2012/10/Malcolm-Wallis.14-th-September-2012.pdf.

[124] See the policy objective to review the associated ship provisions in line with the Comprehensive Maritime Transport Policy: Department of Transport, *Comprehensive Maritime Transport Policy (CMTP) for South Africa* (May 2017), available at www.transport.gov.za/documents/11623/44313/MaritimeTransportPolicyMay2017FINAL.pdf/4fc1b8b8-37d3-4ad0-8862-313a6637104c.

[125] See Wallis (n 4) 74–90.

points can be addressed in this Chapter. Wallis' argument is that the provisions should be seen as designed to deal with groups of closely-held private companies comprising a series of single-ship subsidiary companies ultimately controlled by a single holding company. The provisions respond to this structure by treating the debts of the subsidiaries as the debts of the group and the assets of the subsidiaries as the assets of the group, thus disregarding the single-ship ownership structure for the limited purpose of securing payment of debts. The formulation of Wallis' justification for this particular treatment of shipowning company groups draws on the four features of the problem which he argues the South African associated-ship provisions are designed to solve: (1) privately-held companies; (2) structured as a group; (3) comprising single-ship companies; and (4) the nature of the particular asset held by these companies.

Features (1) and (2) can be dealt with briefly because they are not peculiar to shipowning companies, although they provide a necessary foundation for Wallis' justification. In relation to the companies in the group being privately-held companies, Wallis argues that recognising separate legal personality for artificial entities and limiting their liability created a more efficient way of managing large associations of persons engaged in business and provided stakeholders with the security of knowing that the risk to which they were exposed would not extend beyond their investment in the business. This was designed to attract investment from a wide range of investors drawn from the public at large.[126] It was evident from early on that these purposes were not served in the case of privately-held companies, which did not generally involve a large membership, and did not seek investment from the public at large.[127] Furthermore, in the case of company groups, even though they may generally be constituted for legitimate purposes,[128] it is, at least in some circumstances, difficult to see why each company within the group should enjoy the benefit of separate personality with limited liability, as distinct from the company group as a whole.[129] These are, of course, issues of corporate law generally and not peculiar to shipowning companies, but these problems have justified legislative intervention – albeit limited and perhaps inadequate – aimed at special treatment of company groups.[130]

Building on these considerations, which are not particular to shipowning companies, Wallis argues that the distinctive nature of the problem in the maritime context may be found in the remaining two features: the single-ship company ownership structure; and the nature of the ship as an asset owned in this manner. What is singular about these group structures for shipping operations, justifying differential treatment, is essentially their use of the separate personality of the single-ship subsidiaries to partition *assets*, rather than segregating *operations*, which generally remain unified for the whole fleet, as evidenced by single management companies, cross-guarantees, fleet insurance and other indicators.[131]

Furthermore, the assets thus partitioned are highly mobile internationally and can be redeployed very quickly on different trade routes beyond the reach of their creditors.[132]

[126] ibid 75–77.
[127] ibid 76.
[128] See eg RP Austin, 'Corporate Groups' in CEF Rickett and RB Grantham (eds), *Corporate Personality in the 20th Century* (Oxford, Hart Publishing, 1998) 71, 73–74.
[129] See Wallis (n 4) 77–78.
[130] ibid 78.
[131] ibid 79–83.
[132] ibid 83.

The combination of these two features sets such shipping operations apart and has undesirable economic consequences for the creditors of these operations. With its distinctive structure of single-ship companies, this basis for conducting shipping operations constitutes an 'opportunistic exploitation' of separate corporate personality with limited liability for purposes other than those for which it was originally intended.[133] It is this exploitation that provides a legitimate basis for legislative intervention to impose particular treatment on such ship ownership structures to deal with the undesirable consequences for maritime creditors that follow from it.[134] Wallis argues that, because the particular context of maritime litigation may exacerbate a more general problem already existing in the field of company law, the South African associated-ship arrest provisions constitute a legitimate response to this 'perceived exorbitant and opportunistic use of the benefits of corporate form'.[135]

Wallis characterises the treatment of such ownership structures as differing from veil-piercing provisions that either hold the members of a company liable for the company debts or treat the company assets as those of a member available to member's creditors for recovery of debts owed to them. Wallis sees the difference as lying in the treatment of company groups. He argues that the effect of South Africa's associated-ship arrest provisions is that all assets of the company group, albeit segregated in single-ship subsidiary companies within the group, are made available for satisfaction of the group's debts. He points out that even then, under South African law, these assets are available to creditors seeking to enforce claims against, or prove claims against the fund formed by the sale of, the associated ship, only after claims that lie directly against the ship as the particular ship have been satisfied.[136] In effect, the ships making up the fleet are treated as being owned in common, and strict legal ownership by separate companies is disregarded, save where the priority of claims is concerned.

Wallis makes the further point, often lost sight of, that disregarding the corporate veil in the context of associated ships is for a specific purpose, in this case to secure the payment of debts,[137] and does not otherwise affect the status of such companies as separate legal entities. It therefore does not undermine the use of such ownership structures, which remain intact to serve other legitimate purposes.[138] It poses no obstacle to the use of such group corporate structures and the option to use them remains available for shipowners.

iii. Reservations

South Africa's solution to the single-ship company problem and its experience implementing and interpreting its associated-ship arrest provisions, together with the justification for the differential treatment of shipowning companies that the solution involves, gives pause for thought about whether the reservations expressed about the UK proposal were well founded.

[133] ibid 87.
[134] ibid 86–9.
[135] ibid 89. Cp Francesco Berlingieri, '1952 Arrest Convention Revisited' [2005] *LMCLQ* 327, 336.
[136] See AJRA 1983, s 11(11). The effect of this provision is to subordinate the claims against the ship as an associated ship to the claims against the ship as particular ship. See generally, Hofmeyr (n 4) ch X pt V.5–11.
[137] Wallis (n 4) 86.
[138] ibid 86. Cp Berlingieri (n 1) vol 2 appendix IV 282.

Ultimately, any response to the single-ship company issue will be heavily influenced by the high level of international mobility of ships, which is directly relevant to the purposes of the Arrest Conventions.[139] However, the Arrest Conventions do not address consequences that legal systems around the world attach to companies.[140] It is not appropriate that they should do so, and it is for each jurisdiction to address the problem in its domestic law.[141] Given the combination of these two singular features of the problem, it may not have been inappropriate, as the UK proposal sought to do, to attempt to facilitate broader access to ships to arrest under the Arrest Convention 1999, but to leave the legal consequences attaching to different corporate shipowning structures to be determined by national systems of corporate law.

As regards the concern that implementation of measures in national law to deal with the problem might result in divergent approaches in different jurisdictions, thus undermining international uniformity, South Africa's associated-ship arrest provisions certainly depart from the approach to disregarding the separate legal personality of companies under its general principles of corporate law but, in this, show no more than divergences within the jurisdiction. Without any other jurisdictions having implemented measures to deal with this problem, there is no basis for an assessment of the potential degree of divergence between countries. Even if other countries were to introduce comparable measures, any additional divergences that developed might not significantly exacerbate the differences in approach that already exist to corporate veil-piercing in general corporate and insolvency law in jurisdictions around the world.[142]

As to the concern about generating a particular solution to what was regarded as a more general problem, while a closer consideration of the South African experience of its provisions and a more fully articulated and carefully reasoned justification such as that outlined above might have benefitted the Conference debate on the UK proposal, it seems unlikely, given the views expressed by various countries during the debate, that these would have allayed their concerns or altered the outcome. Ultimately, South Africa's decision to take the route of differential treatment of shipowning companies was informed by policy considerations essentially concerned with the balance to be struck between the interests of maritime creditors, on the one hand, and shipowners and allied parties, on the other. South Africa's prioritisation of these interests is clear. Its associated-ship arrest provisions favour, as they were intended to, maritime creditors over shipowning interests.[143]

Even if other jurisdictions were to implement provisions permitting associated-ship arrests, it seems unlikely that most, or even many, of them would regard the balance struck by South Africa's associated-ship provisions as appropriately even-handed. As is conceded by Wallis, the particular balance struck between these interests in different jurisdictions will depend on how these interests are arrayed, or perhaps more precisely on the relative influence that particular interest groups wield. These are bound to differ from country to country.[144]

[139] Wallis (n 4) 83.
[140] ibid 83–84.
[141] ibid 84.
[142] A review of jurisdictions' approaches indicate that marked differences exist. See Berlingieri (n 1) vol 1 paras 13.01–64.
[143] *The Heavy Metal* (SCA) (n 5) 1106I; Wallis, 'The Associated Ship Jurisdiction in South Africa' (n 11) 137.
[144] Wallis (n 4) 84.

In this regard, the argument against the UK proposal – that the broader interests of maritime trade would be best served by not treating shipowning companies differently from any other companies – perhaps strikes the balance too far in the opposite direction, focusing on the concerns of shipowning and related interests and subordinating the interests of maritime creditors in being paid what they are owed.[145] It could equally be argued that the maritime industry's overall interests would be better served by 'a system that encourages and supports payment of debts'.[146]

IV. Conclusions

As the only jurisdiction that has implemented statutory provisions permitting the arrest of associated ships on the basis of common control of shipowning companies, South Africa's experience of putting these provisions into practice does lend some weight to concerns raised about the UK proposal.

As regards the reservations about a lack of precise definition of 'control' and the danger that associated-ship provisions might ensnare professional ship managers or those shipowners with pooling arrangements, the South African experience indicates that the concern about a precise definition of 'control' was well founded. It was one of the first issues to arise for determination by the courts after the implementation of the provisions, which indicates the importance of clarity about what control is envisaged by the term. South Africa's experience has, however, also demonstrated that whatever difficulties there may have been in defining the terms this was not as big an obstacle as those concerned about this issue might have predicted. By comparison, South Africa's experience of the difficulties of proving common control gives credence to the concerns raised at the Conference about these evidentiary difficulties and their associated costs; and suggests that these concerns should have deserved more prominence than they appear to have been given. These difficulties of proof have, however, also not proved to be insurmountable, but they remain an issue of concern.[147]

The South African provisions, both in themselves and in their interpretation, mark significant departures from general principles of corporate law. The interpretation of the phrase 'power to control, directly or indirectly' that had the result of allowing an association between ships to be established on nominal or apparent common control is a vivid illustration of the problematic divergences that can develop. South Africa's provisions extending association beyond common ownership to common control of shipowning companies represent a further departure from common law principles of corporate veil-piercing, and a significant erosion of the value of separate corporate personality with limited liability.

South Africa's provisions have, however, succeeded, in some measure at least, in solving the problem that one-ship companies pose for maritime creditors seeking to enforce their claims. They have made it easier for maritime creditors to enforce their claims, benefiting not only local interests – the usual justification for their adoption and retention – but also

[145] ibid 86, 89.
[146] ibid 89.
[147] See Wallis' keynote address (n 123) 9. Cp *The Bulk Joyance* (n 89) [41].

foreign interests, affording all maritime creditors opportunities to enforce, or at least secure, their claims that they do not enjoy elsewhere.[148] In so doing, these provisions have contributed, together with the 'stand-alone' security arrest provisions,[149] both separately and in combination, to South Africa's reputation as a creditor-friendly and arrest-friendly jurisdiction. South Africa's outlier status in this regard certainly undermines international uniformity in the area of ship arrests and its reputation as a creditor-friendly and arrest-friendly venue may well attract forum shopping.

Nevertheless, at the international level the problem single-ship companies pose for maritime creditors remains. A justification for differential treatment of these corporate ship ownership structures such as that outlined above, suggests that, despite the grounds on which the UK proposal was ultimately rejected, it may not have been inappropriate to grasp the nettle and deal with the problem in the context of the Arrest Convention 1999. This is not necessarily to suggest that the problem should have been solved wholly within the four corners of the Convention text, but it could have been dealt with along the enabling or facilitating lines of the UK proposal.

As things currently stand under the Arrest Convention 1952 and, with the UK proposal not having been adopted, the Arrest Convention 1999, even if a Member State were to be persuaded of the value of implementing associated-ship arrest provisions, such implementation would entail that State having to denounce the Arrest Convention to which it was a party. This Member States would be unlikely to do, given the long hard route travelled to achieve uniformity through these Conventions.[150]

For the time being, other avenues may have to be explored to find solutions for the problem. South Africa will continue its voyage alone,[151] although how long it continues on its current course may depend on whether the South African Government sees the national interest being better served by the repeal of the associated-ship arrest provisions.

[148] See Wallis, 'The Associated Ship Jurisdiction in South Africa' (n 11).

[149] AJRA 1983, s 5(3). Hare (n 4) §2-2.8.1. See further ch 3.

[150] Wallis (n 4) 90.

[151] ibid.

3

Arrest as Security and Security Arrest

ANTON P TRICHARDT*

I. Introduction

Maritime parties are peripatetic and their assets are often transitory.[1] Ships move freely all over the world. The ship, invariably the main asset, 'may be here today and gone tomorrow, not to return for an indefinite period, perhaps never'.[2] Worse yet, as the ship sails so does the debtor. The frustrated maritime creditor, 'much like Evangeline, the poor Acadian girl separated from her lover, is tragically left to roam the shores awaiting the debtor's next arrival'.[3]

It is therefore unsurprising that courts and legislators have recognised this pressure on maritime creditors and the need for pre-litigation or pre-judgment security to enable enforcement of claims and recovery of debt. Maritime law has developed its own particular system of security,[4] combined with its own method of enforcement of that security, to deal with difficulties unique to the nautical world.[5] The resultant maritime security regime is governed, not by the strict and technical rules of the general law, but rather by procedures and remedies tempered by equitable principles and taking into account the usages and necessities of trade.[6] The maritime security regime is

> diverse, but broadly harmonious … providing for the enforcement of maritime claims by a number of procedural mechanisms. That harmony is not, however, uniformity. Important differences underlie different national legal systems, even though the basic purpose and result of the security

* Barrister (Melbourne), Adjunct Associate Professor UNSW, FCIArb, BIur LLB (Pretoria), MALS (Chicago-Kent), MLM (UNSW), PhD (UWA), PhD (UNSW). My thanks to Alexandra Osborne for her assistance in preparing this chapter and to the Document Services Unit, UNSW Library, as well as Bronwyn Betts for assistance in obtaining research material.

[1] See *Aqua Stoli Shipping Ltd v Gardner Smith Pty Ltd* 460 F3d 434, 443 (2nd Cir 2006).

[2] See *Polar Shipping Ltd v Oriental Shipping Corporation* 680 F2d 627, 637 (9th Cir 1982); *Atlasnavios Navegacao LDA v The Ship Xin Tai Hai (No 2)* [2012] FCA 1497, (2012) 215 FCR 265 [98]; *Holt Cargo Systems Inc v ABC Containerline NV (Trustees of)* [2001] SCC 90, [2001] 3 SCR 97 [25].

[3] See *Schiffahrtsgesellschaft Leonardt & Co v A Bottacchi SA De Navegacion* 732 F2d 1543, 1548 (11th Cir 1984), quoting Henry Wadsworth Longfellow, *Evangeline, A Tale of Acadie* (1843).

[4] Maritime securities have been prevalent from the very conception of international maritime law: see William Tetley, *International Maritime and Admiralty Law* (Montreal, Éditions Yvon Blais, 2002) 473–75; Don Soutar, 'Ship Arrest in the USA and Various Jurisdictions – A Discussion' in Giorgio Berlingieri (ed), *Scrittii in Onore di Francesco Berlingieri* (Genoa, Il Diritto Marittimo, 2010) 942. However, the precise historical origin and development of the arrest of ships is not entirely clear: see Chiara E Tuo, 'Arrest of Vessels' in Jürgen Basedow et al (eds), *Encyclopaedia of Private International Law* (Cheltenham, Edward Elgar Publications, 2017) 132.

[5] See W Tetley, 'Security Rights for Maritime Claims' in K Dobnig and K Zweigert (eds), *International Encyclopaedia of Comparative Law* Vol 3 (Dordrecht, Martinus Nijhoff Publishers, 1981) 108; Tetley (n 4) 473.

[6] See Anton P Trichardt, *Maritime Liens and the Conflict of Laws*, Transactions of the Centre for Business Law 47 (Bloemfontein, University of the Free State, 2011) 6.

> regime is harmonious. The national regimes of different maritime nations have differences … There is also a degree of harmony in the utilisation of common legal conceptions.[7]

The maritime security regime encompasses special legislative rights, maritime liens, mortgages, statutory rights of action in rem (SRARs)[8] and contract liens.[9] The maritime security regime is based mainly on the operation of two forms of procedure:[10] first, the action in rem (an action against a thing, for example, a ship),[11] the defining feature of admiralty law in Common Law jurisdictions, by which jurisdiction against the ship, but not the owner of the ship, is founded by the presence of the ship within the court's jurisdiction, and the ship is arrested as security for the future judgment; and, secondly, the procedural remedy of conservatory attachment (saisie conservatoire)[12] used in Civil Law jurisdictions, where the action in rem is not employed or recognised, but maritime attachment[13] is used as a collateral procedure to support a claim in personam (a claim against a named natural or legal person) otherwise within the jurisdiction of the court, or a claim elsewhere, to act as security until judgment is rendered.[14]

The arrest or attachment of a ship to secure a maritime claim is a procedure widely accepted by the maritime nations of the world – indeed, it has been said that arrest 'is just as much a part of seafaring as distress, pirates and congested ports'.[15] Arrest is a recognised feature of international maritime commerce and international maritime jurisdiction. Ships, their owners and insurers are expected in the ordinary course of their business to be ready to deal with arrests arising in connection with the operation of the ship or the owner's or charterer's business.[16] Due to the intertwined relationship between the maritime security regime and the procedures for its operation, arrest is not only the main mechanism of protection, but also the security, in the enforcement of maritime claims.[17] Arrest has been referred to as 'in effect, a pre-emptive security device, available virtually on demand to someone with an arguable claim against a relevant person if the other requirements are said to be present and if the other requirements can be substantiated, if challenged'.[18]

The maritime security regime involves security on ships deriving from consensual bargains involving those who have a proprietary interest in the ship, from the operation of

[7] *The Ship Sam Hawk v Reiter Petroleum Inc* [2016] FCAFC 26, (2016) 246 FCR 337 [41].

[8] SRARs are also referred to as statutory rights in rem or statutory liens.

[9] See Tetley (n 5) 109–19.

[10] *The Sam Hawk* (n 7) [42]; James Allsop, 'Comity and Unity in Maritime Law' (2016) 47 *J Mar L & Com* 279, 292.

[11] The action in rem is not merely a procedural matter, but is rather a substantive matter which goes to the very essence of admiralty law in Anglo-Common Law jurisdictions: *Quin-Sea Fisheries Limited v Broadbill I (The)* 2013 FC 575 [15].

[12] That is, the seizure of the ship, freight or cargo before judgment. Conservatory attachment is universally applied in Continental Europe – see ch 10; *Rasu Maritima SA v Perusahaan Pertambagan Minyak Dan Gas Bumi Negara (Pertamina)* [1978] QB 644, 658.

[13] This attachment or saisie permits any of the debtor's property, including ships, to be seized and detained under judicial authority pending judgment: see William Tetley, 'Arrest, Attachment, and Related Maritime Law Procedures' (1999) 73 *Tul L Rev* 1895, 1898.

[14] ibid; and see Tetley (n 5) 123.

[15] See Vincent Michael Mayerhofer, *Arrest of Ships in Germany and South Africa* (Master's thesis, University of Cape Town, 2007) 9, quoting Hans-Jürgen Puttfarken, *Seehandelsrecht* (Verlag Recht und Wirtschaft, Heidelberg, 1997).

[16] See *Tisand Pty Ltd v Owners of the Ship MV Cape Moreton (Ex Freya)* [2005] FCAFC 68, 143 FCR 43; *Intraline Resources Sdn Bhd v Owners of the Ship or Vessel Hua Tian Long* [2008] HKCFI 397, [2008] 4 HKC 111 [49].

[17] See Verónica Ruiz Abou-Nigm, *The Arrest of Ships in Private International Law* (Oxford, Oxford University Press, 2011) 1, 2.

[18] *The Xin Tai Hai (No 2)* (n 2) [95]–[96]; *Kim v Daebo International Shipping Co Ltd* [2015] FCA 684, (2015) 232 FCR 275 [9].

general law and from the remedial enforcement of maritime claims.[19] This Chapter deals with the last source of security, namely the operation of the international maritime security regime – the securing of maritime claims by their enforcement[20] – by reference to the procedures utilised by Common Law and Civil Law jurisdictions in the context of the two Arrest Conventions,[21] and examines the effect of such procedures on the nature and scope of the security interest created by the enforcement of maritime claims. In respect of maritime securities, the two key issues are the recognition and enforcement of the security and the ranking of securities.

II. Structure of the Chapter

This Chapter is divided into four parts. The first consists of a delineation and brief discussion of the concepts relevant to the operation of the maritime security regime, and, in particular, the notion of security in maritime law. The second part comprises arrest as security. The concept of the maritime claim, which is critical to the operation of the maritime security regime, is discussed. The mechanism for the enforcement of maritime claims, arrest of ships and the creation and activation of security for maritime claims is then considered. The third part consists of a discussion of security arrest, distinguishing between retained security arrests and pure security arrests as found in South African admiralty law. The fourth part comprises the Chapter's conclusion.

III. Delineation of Maritime Security Regime Concepts

Legal security in the context of the maritime security regime is comprised of three things:

(1) the security interests[22] at the heart of the maritime security regime:[23] special legislative rights,[24] court costs and custodia legis,[25] maritime liens,[26] mortgages, SRARs and

[19] James Leslie Bain Allsop, 'Security Interests in Ships' in Malgosia Fitzmaurice et al (eds), *The IMLI Manual on International Maritime Law Vol II: Shipping Law* (Oxford, Oxford University Press, 2016) 152.

[20] The seizure and detention of ships for the purpose of executing a judgment or arbitral award are beyond the scope of this Chapter. However, see generally DC Jackson, *Enforcement of Maritime Claims* (London, LLP, 2005) para 15.63.

[21] International Convention Relating to the Arrest of Sea-going Ships (adopted 10 May 1952, entered into force 24 February 1956) 439 UNTS 193 (Arrest Convention 1952); International Convention on the Arrest of Ships (adopted 12 March 1999, entered into force 14 September 2011) 2797 UNTS 3 (Arrest Convention 1999).

[22] See Damien Laracy and Michael Ng, 'Enforcement of Maritime Claims' in Mary Thomson (ed), *Maritime Law and Practice in Hong Kong* (Hong Kong, Sweet & Maxwell, 2015) para 17.211 referring to the charge, the common law lien and the pledge as other security interests proper.

[23] The five core concepts of the regime are mentioned in the usual order of ranking. The maritime security regime may also be affected by specific legislation in various jurisdictions, eg, the personal property securities legislation in Australia, Canada, New Zealand and the United States, or by the 2001 Unidroit Convention on International Interests in Mobile Equipment: see generally Ole Böger, 'The Cape Town Convention and Proprietary Security over Ships' (2014) 19 *Unif L Rev* 24.

[24] Special legislative rights, which often grant governmental authorities rights of detention or possession, have been adopted in several jurisdictions. See generally Tetley (n 4) 476–78; William Tetley, *International Conflict of Laws: Common, Civil and Maritime* (Montreal, Blais, 1994) 538.

[25] Court costs ordinarily include the costs of the Admiralty Marshal in effecting the arrest of the ship, maintaining the ship under arrest and judicial sale. See generally Tetley (n 4) 479–81; Tetley, *International Conflict of Laws* (n 24) 538.

[26] Tetley (n 4) 481–86.

contractual liens.[27] These rights are relevant to arrest as part of the process of enforcement of maritime claims, because they provide a creditor with a right to force a sale of the ship and obtain recovery of the debt from the proceeds. In this Chapter, the focus is on maritime liens and SRARs;

(2) the physical detention of a ship and the legal restriction of an owner's right to dispose of the ship as a result of the arrest of a ship for a maritime claim;

(3) security through retention;[28] that is, pursuant to possessory liens and rights of retention – although neither security resulting from arrest nor a security interest, these provide security in the broad sense and may impact on arrest and the resulting security for maritime claims.

Although security in admiralty includes security to avoid arrest or procure release of a ship, the provision of security on a voluntary basis in the form of bail, bank guarantees, bonds or letters of undertaking from P&I Clubs[29] – thereby indirectly forming part of the maritime security regime – is beyond the scope of this Chapter.[30] Such measures are not rights, but rather substitutes for the security provided by the arrest of a ship or the security interests enforced or realised by arrest.[31]

IV. Arrest as Security

A. Maritime Claims

Maritime claims are critical to the operation of the international maritime security regime. Although the phrase 'maritime claim' has no technical meaning in, for example, English law where it simply indicates a claim which is within the admiralty jurisdiction of the High Court, the phrase is used in the Arrest Conventions 1952 and 1999 so that, in States Parties to those Conventions it is the general label delineating all the claims in relation to which a ship may be arrested under the respective convention. One of the peculiarities of the remedial enforcement of maritime claims is that its anchor is a ship as a legal security. For arrests under the Arrest Conventions, the identification of the ship that may be arrested has to be made by reference to the description of the maritime claims enumerated in art 1(1) of both Arrest Conventions.[32] They are the claims supporting the remedy that is the hallmark of

[27] Contractual liens are rights against a ship arising from contracts for the supply of goods and services to it. These rights are granted to suppliers of necessaries, repairers, stevedores and tug operators. In Anglo-Common Law jurisdictions, contractual liens give rise to SRARs, while in the United States many contractual liens are afforded the status of true maritime liens.

[28] See Tetley (n 4) 495–98.

[29] On which see Paul Myburgh, 'P&I Club Letters of Undertaking and Admiralty Arrests' [2018] 24 *JIML* 201.

[30] See David Chong Gek Sian, 'Security in Actions in Rem' (1989) 1 *S Ac L J* 81.

[31] See Laracy and Ng (n 22) paras 17.186–97.

[32] Francesco Berlingieri, 'Enforcement of Maritime Claims' in Malgosia Fitzmaurice et al (eds), *The IMLI Manual on International Maritime Law Vol II: Shipping Law* (Oxford University Press 2016) 529, 536. By its nature, a maritime claim has a strong connection with the ship: first, it arises as a result of the operation of the ship; and, secondly, the ship may become a legal security for the maritime claim. In *MFV El Shaddai: Ignacio Arocen Oxacelay v Braxton Security Services CC* 2015 (3) SA 55 (KZD) [6] it was observed that whether a claim falls within the ambit of a maritime claim depends upon whether it achieves the purpose of establishing a link between the alleged maritime claim and the ship.

maritime jurisdiction, the arrest of a ship and, in Common Law jurisdictions, the action in rem. Although the list of maritime claims in the Arrest Convention 1952 is closed, the 17 claims are drafted in a wide fashion, in the nature of broad types or classes of claims.[33] Indeed, it has prompted one commentator to observe that the exhaustive list is so long and widely framed that it places a limit in exceptional cases only – 'ter zake van een alimentasie-vordering van de ex-vrouw van de reder'![34] Similar comments can be made about the Arrest Convention 1999.

There is a list of maritime claims for the operation of the maritime security regime in every jurisdiction, which in most instances are similar to the lists in either the Arrest Convention 1952 or the Arrest Convention 1999. The notable exception is the United States. There is, however, no uniformity in the approach to the lists of maritime claims and, accordingly, the claims that constitute maritime claims.

Having regard to these various lists of maritime claims, a two-fold categorisation of the types of claims is convenient, and is even used in the domestic legislation of some jurisdictions such as Australia.[35] The first category encompasses proprietary maritime claims pertaining to the property in, or possession of, a ship. These include disputes as to the ownership or possession of the ship or ownership of shares in the ship; disputes between co-owners of a ship as to ownership, possession, employment or earnings of the ship; or claims in respect of mortgages, hypothecations or charges on a ship or any share therein.[36]

The second category comprises general maritime claims pertaining to the use of a ship. These include claims for damage done by a ship; claims relating to loss of life or personal injury; claims relating to loss of, or damage to, goods carried in a ship; claims covering agreements relating to the carriage of goods in, or to the use or hire of, a ship; claims for salvage, towage and pilotage; claims for necessaries or disbursements on account of a ship; claims covering the construction, repair or equipment of a ship; dock charges or dues; claims for wages; claims for general average; bottomry; claims for environmental damage and reinstatement; costs associated with wreck removal; marine insurance premiums; and brokerage or agency fees on maritime contracts.[37]

General maritime claims have also been divided into secured general maritime claims and unsecured general maritime claims. Secured general maritime claims are maritime claims in respect of which maritime liens are recognised, while unsecured maritime claims are all the remaining maritime claims, or the SRARs. In Australia, the status of SRARs has

[33] See José M Alcantara, 'Some Reflections Over the Brussels Convention of 1952 Relating to Arrest of Sea-Going Vessels and Its Amending Process' (1997) 26 *Ga J Intl & Comp L* 551, 553–54.

[34] Translated as: 'in respect of a maintenance claim by the ex-wife of the shipowner' – see Eric Van Hooydonk, *Tiende Blauwboek over de Herziening van het Belgisch Scheepvaartrecht: Proeve van Belgisch Scheepvaartwetboek (Privaatrecht), Scheepvaartprocesrecht* (Commissie Maritiem Recht, Antwerp, 2012) para 10.82. Virtually all claims relating to the acquisition and operation of a ship are included in the list: see Allan Philip, 'Maritime Jurisdiction in the EEC' (1977) 46 *Nordisk Tidsskrift International Ret* 113, 116.

[35] Section 4 of the Admiralty Act 1988 (Cth) (AA 1988): see generally Damien Cremean, *Admiralty Jurisdiction: Law and Practice: Australia, New Zealand, Singapore, Hong Kong and Malaysia*, 4th edn (Alexandria, The Federation Press, 2015) 10.

[36] See Sarah C Derrington and James M Turner, *The Law and Practice of Admiralty Matters* (Oxford, Oxford University Press, 2016) paras 3.01–14. The proprietary maritime claims are found in arts 1(1)(o)–(q) of the Arrest Convention 1952 and arts 1(1)(s)–(v) of the Arrest Convention 1999.

[37] Derrington and Turner (n 36) paras 5.01–88. The general maritime claims are found in arts 1(1)(a)–(n) of the Arrest Convention 1952, and arts 1(1)(a)–(r) of the Arrest Convention 1999.

been questioned and it is a live issue whether such maritime claims amount to secured claims.[38] Once filed in court, such claims are said to create a form of qualified or quasi-security.[39] However, maritime claims in respect of which maritime liens are recognised enforce a pre-existing security interest that was created at the time of the occurrence of the event from which the maritime lien arose. This is not the case with proceedings based on SRARs, where the claimant has a secured interest in respect of the maritime claim from the time of commencement of the proceeding in rem.[40] In principle, there should be no distinction between actions in rem involving maritime liens and actions in rem involving SRARs.[41] The different security consequences of a maritime claim conferring a maritime lien and a SRAR do not justify the creation of a distinction in arrest law – to do so would be to bedevil the law with fine refinements.[42]

The scope of a particular jurisdiction's domestic provisions dealing with the maritime claims in a list depends on the language used, especially the width or narrowness of the words[43] used to indicate the relationship between the person or event and the maritime aspect of the circumstances concerned,[44] and varies depending upon which claims give rise to a maritime lien.[45]

B. Arrest under the International Arrest Conventions[46]

International arrest law is both substantive and procedural. Arrest of ships in maritime law is purely a civil matter and part of private law.[47] The substantive law of ship arrest is mainly

[38] See *The Cape Moreton* (n 16); *Yakushiji v Daiichi Chuo Kisen Kaisha* [2015] FCA 1170, (2015) 333 ALR 513 [20].

[39] See *Yakushiji* (n 38) [20].

[40] See *Kim* (n 18) [12].

[41] Once a SRAR is created it is not extinguished as long as the writ in rem, the instrument of its creation, is in force: see *The Bolbina* [1993] SGHC 322, [1991] 3 SLR(R) 894 [18].

[42] See David Chong Gek Sian, 'The Spectre of Re-Arrest of a Vessel' (1986) 28 *Malaya L Rev* 102, 112.

[43] For example, 'relating to', 'concerned with', 'directly', or 'in any way whatsoever'.

[44] The basic rule in international arrest law is that the ship must be owned by the person liable for the claim; ie there has to be an in personam link. This requirement is set out, albeit impliedly, in art 3(1) of the Arrest Convention 1952, and clearly in art 3(1)(a) of the Arrest Convention 1999. There are, however, exceptions to the rule: first, art 3(1) of the Arrest Convention 1952 is stated as being subject to art 3(4) dealing with demise charterers and art 10 (clearly a misprint for art 9, which provides that '[n]othing in this Convention shall be construed as creating a right of action, which, apart from the provisions of this Convention, would not arise under the law applied by the Court which was seized of the case'); and secondly, maritime liens: see Berlingieri (n 32) 533–36. For a discussion on the in personam link requirement, see generally David Chong Gek Sian, 'In Personam Liability, Beneficial Ownership and the Action in Rem' (1994) 6 *S Ac LJ* 272; Paul Myburgh, 'Arresting the Right Ship: Procedural Theory, the In Personam Link and Conflict of Laws' in M Davies (ed), *Jurisdiction and Forum Selection in International Maritime Law: Essays in Honor of Robert Force* (The Hague, Kluwer Law, 2005) 283.

[45] See Allsop (n 19) 161. Whether a maritime claim gives rise to a maritime lien has a significant impact on the scope of operation of the maritime security regime.

[46] For a detailed discussion of the concept of 'arrest' under the Arrest Conventions, see Francesco Berlingieri, *Berlingieri on Arrest of Ships*, 6th edn (Abingdon, Informa Law from Routledge, 2017) vol 1 ch 4; vol 2 ch 4. The Arrest Conventions are uniform law, and thus usually override conflict of laws rules: see Laura Carballo Piñeiro, *International Maritime Labour Law*, Hamburg Studies on Maritime Affairs 34 (Hamburg, Springer-Verlag, 2015) para 3.4.2.

[47] Arrest of ships is to be distinguished from detention under regulatory conventions such as the International Convention for the Safety of Life at Sea (SOLAS) and the International Convention for the Prevention of Pollution from Ships (MARPOL), which fall under public law: see generally Francesco Berlingieri, *International Maritime Conventions: Vol 2* (Abingdon, Informa Law from Routledge, 2014) 202–09. On detention of ships for environmental claims see further ch 8.

governed by the Arrest Convention 1952[48] and the Arrest Convention 1999,[49] while the procedural aspect is governed by the domestic laws of the various jurisdictions.[50] The two Arrest Conventions are concerned with arrest as a provisional or conservative remedy,[51] and as a ground for jurisdiction on the merits,[52] in that they specify the claims in regard to which a ship may be arrested (maritime claims),[53] and the circumstances in which the forum arresti has jurisdiction to adjudge the merits.[54] Arrest of a ship is not a declaration on the merits of the underlying dispute. The Arrest Conventions in themselves neither regulate jurisdiction nor demarcate the scope of the jurisdiction based upon arrest; rather they limit the cases where arrest may be made and require a nexus between the ship and the cause of action. They do not create any obligation to make arrests in the instances enumerated in the lists or to enforce claims in these cases.[55] Arrest can only be lawfully made if the claim may be enforced against the arrested ship under the applicable law.[56] Ship arrest is not an extraordinary remedy akin to injunctive relief. Rather, the right to arrest is a usual and accepted process in maritime law as a means of obtaining security for a future judgment.[57] Arrest of a ship is procedural, providing a judicial remedy, but creating no new legal vested rights.[58] Arrest is the security measure that is stipulated by the Arrest Conventions in favour of a creditor with a maritime claim, and its basis represents a personal obligation of the debtor (the owner of the ship in question, the charterer or other person responsible for the claim).[59]

[48] For a discussion of the Arrest Convention 1952 see Berlingieri (n 46) vol 1; Berlingieri (n 47); Francesco Berlingieri, 'The 1952 Arrest Convention revisited' [2005] *LMCLQ* 327.

[49] For a discussion of the Arrest Convention 1999 see Berlingieri (n 46) vol 2; Tetley (n 13) 1962–72; Robert W Lynn, 'A Comment on the New International Convention on Arrest of Ships, 1999' (2001) 55 *U Miami L Rev* 453; Md Rizwanul Islam, 'The Arrest of Ship Conventions 1952 and 1999: Disappointment for Maritime Claimants' (2007) 38 *J Mar L & Com* 75; Nicholas Gaskell and Richard Shaw, 'The Arrest Convention 1999' [1999] *LMCLQ* 470.

[50] The law of each jurisdiction will determine the arrest procedure and whether one is dealing with wrongful arrest. See D Rhidian Thomas, 'Ship Arrest as a Procedural Remedy for Ship-Source Environmental Damage' (2007) 25 *Annuaire de Droit Maritime et Oceanique* 311, 312.

[51] Arrest is also referred to as an 'interim' or 'precautionary' remedy. This is apparent from art 1(1) of both Arrest Conventions which define 'arrest' as not including the 'seizure of a ship in execution or satisfaction of a judgment'.

[52] See Berlingieri (n 46) vol 1 ch 7; vol 2 ch 7; DC Jackson, 'Current English Admiralty Jurisdiction and Practice' [1982] *Acta Juridica* 5, 6.

[53] Article 1(1) of both Arrest Conventions. For a general discussion of the list of maritime claims, see Alcantara (n 33) 553–54; Berlingieri (n 46) vol 1 ch 5; vol 2 ch 5.

[54] See art 7(1) of both Arrest Conventions; Berlingieri (n 32) 530, 544–48.

[55] See Philip (n 34) 117–18. On a strict construction of the provisions of the Arrest Convention 1952 its application is restricted to ships flying the flag of a Contracting Party. However, with regard to ships flying the flag of a non-Contracting Party it is well established that, unless a State Party makes an exception to exclude ships of non-Contracting Parties, the Convention will apply according to art 8(2).

[56] eg, if the applicable domestic law does not permit enforcement of a claim against a ship unless its owner is personally liable, the fact that arrest under the Conventions may nonetheless be permitted does not mean that such an arrest will be lawful under domestic law, or that a subsequent judgment based on such an arrest will be enforceable: see Philip (n 34) 118.

[57] See, eg, *Westshore Terminals Limited Partnership v Leo Ocean SA* 2014 FC 136, (2014) 447 FTR 275 [67].

[58] See, eg, *Striebel v Sovereign Yachts (Canada) Inc* [2002] 4 FC 377 [5]; *Magnolia Ocean Shipping Corp v Soledad Maria (The)* [1982] 1 FC 205; and the note on the *Finnlines* decision of the Hof van Beroep Gent (7de Kamer, 13 April 2015) by Michel Cornette and Véronique Beeckx, 'Het Beslag op het Schip waarop de Vordering Betrekking Heft' (2015) 3 *Tijdschrift voor Internationale Handel en Transportrecht* 346, 351.

[59] See Jelena Nikčević Grdinić and Gordana Nikčević, 'Arrest of Ships – The International Conventions on Arrest of Ships' (2012) 2 *Transactions on Maritime Science* 103, 104.

The Arrest Conventions are critical to the topic of this Chapter in two respects: first, in relation to arrest as security (discussed in this Part) they define the legal nature of 'arrest' in art 1(2) of both Arrest Conventions. Secondly, they facilitate security arrests (discussed in Part V below).

The essence of the definition of 'arrest' in art 1(2) of both Arrest Conventions is that it refers to the 'detention' of a ship by judicial authority 'to secure a maritime claim'.[60] Arrest is therefore aimed at providing security for a maritime claim.[61] The word 'security' has 'no legal signification which necessarily attaches to it on all occasions … and it is to be interpreted without the embarrassment of a legal definition and simply according to the best conclusion one can make as to the real meaning of the term as it is employed'.[62] Neither the nature nor the meaning of 'arrest' is informed by the French texts of the Arrest Conventions, which refer to 'la saisie conservatoire'. The definition of 'saisie' in the French texts of the Arrest Conventions[63] differs from the English wording as to 'arrest'.[64]

The object of arrest under the Arrest Conventions is the temporary immobilisation or the physical unavailability of a ship by judicial process[65] until the underlying dispute has been determined by a competent court.[66] It means that the ship must be present in the territorial jurisdiction of the court issuing process (the forum arresti) at the time the proceeding is started.[67] Detention of the ship means that its freedom of movement is restrained so that it

[60] Article 1(2) of the Arrest Convention 1952 defines arrest as 'the detention of a ship by judicial process to secure a maritime claim, but does not include the seizure of a ship in execution or satisfaction of a judgment', while art 1(2) of the Arrest Convention 1999 similarly defines arrest as 'any detention or restriction on removal of a ship by order of a Court to secure a maritime claim, but does not include the seizure of a ship in execution or satisfaction of a judgment or other enforceable instrument'. The latter definition is wider in that other forms of pre-trial security, such as freezing orders, have been brought within the definition of arrest, and it aims to preclude the possibility of a claimant obtaining additional pre-trial security once a ship has been arrested: see 'Legal issues and Regulatory Developments' in the UNCTAD Secretariat, *Review of Maritime Transport 2011* (New York, United Nations, 2011) ch 5, 111.

[61] The Arrest Conventions do not deal with the situation where security has been offered in order to prevent arrest: Berlingieri (n 32) 544. However, in *The Anna H* [1995] 1 Lloyd's Rep 11, 21 Hobhouse LJ held that a claimant need not show that arrest is necessary to obtain security to come within the definition of 'arrest' in art 1 of the Arrest Convention 1952. Hoffman LJ pointed out (at 24) that under the Arrest Convention 1952 there is no obligation to ensure that a claimant who arrests a ship does not have sufficient security, because there is nothing in the Convention about refraining from arrest because security had been provided in advance.

[62] See *Singer v Williams* [1921] 1 AC 41, 57; *General Motors Acceptance Corp Australia v South Bank Traders Pty Ltd* [2007] HCA 19, (2007) 227 CLR 305 [20].

[63] So too, eg, the Spanish text of the Arrest Convention 1999, which refers to 'el embargo preventivo'.

[64] The definition in the Arrest Convention 1952 provides: '"Saisie" signifie l'immobilisation d'un navire avec l'autorisation de l'autorié judiciare compétente pour garantie d'une creance maritime, mais ne comprend pas la saisie d'un navire pour l'execution d'un titre', while the definition in the Arrest Convention 1999 provides: 'Par "saisie", il faut entendre toute immobilisation ou restriction au depart d'un navire en vertu d'une decision judiciaire pour garantir une creance maritime, mais non la saisie d'un navire pour exécution d'un jugement ou d'un autre instrument exécutoire.'

[65] As Thomas ((n 50) 312) points out, arrest is 'not a self-help remedy; the claimant cannot effect a citizen's arrest'. Arrest differs from seizure or capture in that the aim is to deprive the owner of the arrested ship of its possession, or at least curtail its unrestricted use, rather than to deprive it of ownership of the ship.

[66] See Ignacio Arroyo, 'Implementation of the Arrest Convention' in Norman A Martínez Gutiérrez (ed), *Serving the Rule of International Maritime Law: Essays in Honour of Professor David Joseph Attard* (London, Routledge, 2010) 363, 370; C Van Aerde, 'Article 3(1) and (4) of the Ship Arrest Convention vs Article 1 of the First Protocol to the European Convention on Human Rights' in *60 Years Brussels Arrest Convention 1952. A Critical Retrospect* (Antwerp, Belgische Vereniging voor Zeerecht, 2012) 97; Wouter Den Haerynck and Tom Van Achter, 'Scheepsbeslag is een Dwangmiddel' (2015) 2 *Tijdschrift voor Internationale Handel en Transportrecht* 143, 145; Cornette and Beeckx (n 57) 351; Grdinić and Nikčević (n 58) 105.

[67] Since the procedure governing the arrest of ships is governed and regulated by national courts, there will inevitably be variations between different jurisdictions: see Thomas (n 50) 312.

cannot be moved from the place of its arrest.[68] The purpose of the detention is to preserve or secure the physical presence of the ship, or make certain that the ship is physically present, when the creditor/claimant exercises its maritime claim. In other words, arrest under the Arrest Conventions is simply an early step ensuring physical retention of a ship under judicial authority in the judicial process of enforcing a maritime claim.[69] Ship arrest is, however, a draconian measure: it puts commercial pressure on the shipowner by depriving it of the use of its ship, which can be very disruptive and may inflict severe economic hardship on the shipowner's trade and operations.[70]

The concept of arrest in both Arrest Conventions is neutral and identical whether viewed from an Anglo-Common Law or Civil Law perspective – the security is the physical unavailability or detention of a ship under judicial authority. Arrest is a legal process by which the court allows the control and operation of a ship to be taken from the shipowner for the duration of the arrest. In this context it is confusing to view arrest as including 'arrest as a protective measure to secure payment of a maritime claim; arrest as a preventative measure to enforce maritime liens; and arrest as a provisional measure "to secure the res"',[71] because this tends to conflate the concept of arrest under the Arrest Conventions and arrest procedures governed by the domestic laws of particular jurisdictions. Generally speaking, the latter procedures differ depending on whether the jurisdiction is a Civil Law jurisdiction (where these measures are treated separately) or an Anglo-Common Law jurisdiction (where these measures are fused). The concept of arrest under the Arrest Conventions also does not cover the provisional arrest ('saisie conservatoire', 'conservatoir beslag' or 'bewarend beslag') of the Civil Law systems.[72] The common perception that the legal nature of the concept of arrest under the Arrest Conventions is that adopted in the Civil Law jurisdictions, and that this informs the meaning of arrest as security, therefore appears to be questionable.[73]

In the context of the concept of arrest in the Arrest Conventions, the security resulting from the detention of a ship does not refer to the obtaining of a legal security or a 'security interest' in a ship, in the sense of an encumbrance on, or a proprietary interest in, the ship. Arrest of a ship under the Arrest Conventions entails physical but not legal unavailability; it does not prohibit the shipowner from dealing with the ship by disposing or encumbering it.[74] It is clear from the definitions of arrest in the Arrest Conventions that they are also not concerned with the quasi-security provided by possessory liens, because such liens do not involve a judicial process under judicial authority.[75]

[68] The additional words 'or restriction on removal of a ship by order of a Court' in the definition of arrest in art 1(2) of the Arrest Convention 1999 make this clearer.

[69] See Jackson (n 20) para 15.47.

[70] *The Xin Chang Shu* [2015] SGHC 308, [2016] 1 SLR 1096 [3].

[71] Abou-Nigm (n 17) para 3.29. In practice, the protective and security functions of arrest of ships are invariably intermingled; however, although those functions are dealt with in an integrated fashion in Anglo-Common Law jurisdictions, they are kept separate in Civil Law jurisdictions.

[72] See Pelayia Yessiou-Faltsi, 'The 1952 Brussels International Convention on the Arrest of Ships for Maritime Claims and on Jurisdiction: Important Steps for the Unification of Maritime Law' (2011) 1 *Aegean Review of the Law of the Sea* 175, 177.

[73] Berlingieri (n 32) 530.

[74] Den Haerynck and Van Achter (n 66) 145–46. See also *Ballentine's Law Dictionary* (USA, LexisNexis, 2010) where 'arrest of ship' is defined as: 'A temporary detention, without design of depriving the owner of the vessel, but to liberate the ship or goods detained, or to pay the value thereof.'

[75] Den Haerynck and Van Achter (n 66) 146 draw a distinction between detention of a ship and the exercise of a right of retention in respect of a ship.

Although the concept of arrest in the Arrest Conventions is a uniform international concept, or at least a concept susceptible to an autonomous interpretation by which a uniform meaning could be applied, the domestic 'translation' of this concept and its implementation in the arrest procedures followed in different Anglo-Common Law and Civil Law jurisdictions detracts from such international uniformity.[76] The operation of the international maritime security regime depends upon both the concept of arrest and, because arrest is not automatic or self-executing, the arrest procedures used in Anglo-Common Law and Civil Law jurisdictions. While arrest facilitates the physical unavailability of a ship, the arrest procedures facilitate the legal unavailability of the ship and the realisation of the rights (or security interests) constituting the maritime security regime. It is in this latter aspect of the operation of the international maritime security regime that the differences between Common and Civil Law systems surface.

When both the physical and legal unavailability of a ship are achieved by judicial intervention (judicial process or court order) with a view to maintaining or securing a right, the result is a coercive measure.[77] It follows that arrest under the Arrest Conventions is a coercive measure.[78] Because the Arrest Conventions refer to the detention of a ship by judicial intervention to secure a maritime claim, it is apparent that the Conventions regulate neither the exercise of a right, nor the creation of a right, but rather the use of a coercive measure.[79] It is the arrest procedure followed in a particular jurisdiction that determines the exercise of the right to arrest a ship. Needless to say, a coercive measure can only be used for the benefit of someone who can assert a right. In the context of the Arrest Conventions, the rights are those relating to the maritime claims set out in the list in art 1(1), and as provided for in the domestic laws of the various jurisdictions. The relevant domestic legislation provides in principle which parties can have recourse to the coercive measure of arrest, and under what circumstances and conditions.[80] In this regard, the Common Law and Civil Law correspond – in both systems it is possible to maintain an existing right by means of the detention of a ship with the assistance of a court or an appropriate judicial authority.[81]

Generally speaking, the arrest of a ship has a tripartite function:[82]

(1) It is a form of interim or provisional remedy – this is the principal function of arrest as conceptualised in the Arrest Conventions, being the temporary physical unavailability of a ship.[83] As mentioned above, when physical unavailability is combined with the legal unavailability of a ship, whether as a result of a Civil Law conservatory attachment

[76] See chs 10, 11 and 12.

[77] Den Haerynck and Van Achter (n 66) 146. Savo Marković, 'Legislative Prospective of the Arrest of Ships in Montenegro' (2009) 21 *Promet – Traffic & Transportation* 285 expresses the effect as follows: 'The temporary measure of the arrest of ships, based on the provisional, repressive-preventative judicial protection, is put into effect before the executive title obtains the quality necessary for the compulsory execution, by virtue of prohibiting the ship to leave the port, because of the anticipation of security for legally-based, pecuniary or non-monetary demand of the claimant.'

[78] See Den Haerynck and Van Achter (n 66) 146.

[79] ibid 147.

[80] ibid.

[81] ibid.

[82] See Jackson (n 52) 6; Jackson (n 20) paras 0.1 and 15.2.

[83] See generally Jonatan Echebarria Fernández, 'Party Autonomy and Arrest of Ships from a Comparative Perspective' in Olga Fotinopoulou Basurko and José Manuel Martín Osante (eds), *New Trends in Maritime Law: Maritime Liens, Arrest of Ships, Mortgages and Forced Sale* (Cizur Menor, Thomson Reuters Aranzadi, 2017) 497.

or an Anglo-Common Law in rem proceeding, this function morphs into a coercive measure persuading the defendant shipowner to appear to defend the merits of the substantive maritime claim, because the arrested ship, or such security as is accepted in lieu, remains to satisfy any judgment on the merits.[84] This is the proper security function of arrest – the arrest is in itself a means of security.[85] It is provisional in the sense that the remedy is only available prior to judgment on the merits of the maritime claim, and cannot be used to execute the judgment.[86] The security provided is limited to the ship (or its value), or any sum lodged as security to obtain its release,[87] or in situations where a person liable for a claim is allowed to limit its liability and establishes a limitation fund.[88] Viewed from a different perspective, this is the so-called remedial or provisional aspect of maritime claims, referring to the types of remedy that are available depending on the characterisation of a claim as a maritime claim.[89]

(2) It may operate as a ground of jurisdiction over the merits of the maritime claim.[90] This is the so-called jurisdictional aspect of maritime claims,[91] referring to the fact that the character of a claim as maritime (or not) will determine or influence the court in which relief is sought and, through that, the remedies that are available.[92] The court acquires jurisdiction over the ship because it is arrested within the court's territorial jurisdiction, regardless of the domicile or accessibility for service of the person or entity liable in personam in respect of the claim.

(3) It may provide security for the maritime claim on the merits.[93] Unless the arrest is set aside or the ship is released upon the provision of security, the arrested ship continues to stand as security for the claim: it can be sold judicially and the proceeds thus realised used to pay off the creditors. It determines the extent to which a claimant becomes a preferred creditor. It is the primary method of ensuring the availability of judicial sale, which is the means of implementing the interest conferred or enforced through the action in rem. This is the security interest function of arrest (and the so-called security

[84] In other words, ensuring that there will be assets available to turn a judgment into material gain: *The Wisdom (No 2): Olam International Ltd v Legacy Navigation Ltd* 2010 *Shipping Cases of South Africa* B201, B207; Jackson (n 20) para 0.2; Nigel Meeson and John A Kimbell, *Admiralty Jurisdiction and Practice* (London, Informa, 2011) 151.

[85] Abou-Nigm (n 17) ch 6; Jackson (n 52) 11 refers to this as the 'first "security" element' of arrest. The second element goes to the extent of the security which brings into play sister or associated ship arrest, while the third element pertains to the third function of arrest, the realisation of a security interest in the ship.

[86] Jackson (n 52) 6–7.

[87] ibid 7.

[88] Where a limitation fund is established, it is not necessary to furnish alternative security in order to obtain the release of a ship; see, eg, the International Convention on Civil Liability for Oil Pollution Damage 1969, art VI; the Convention on the Limitation of Liability for Maritime Claims 1976, art 13. Obtaining a limitation decree or establishing a limitation fund is not, however, sufficient to enable a shipowner to avoid arrest: see *The Anna H* [1995] 1 Lloyd's Rep 11; Barnabas WB Reynolds and Michael N Tsimplis, *Shipowners' Limitation of Liability* (Dordrecht, Wolters Kluwer, 2012) 152.

[89] Allsop (n 19) 159; Jackson (n 20) at para 0.2.

[90] Article 7 of both Arrest Conventions.

[91] This is especially so in Common Law jurisdictions where the arrest in rem carries with it an assertion of jurisdiction to determine the merits: see Sarah Derrington, 'Ship Arrest and the Admiralty Jurisdiction of Australia and South Africa: Too Far or Not Far Enough?' (2005) 11 *JIML* 409, 410.

[92] See Abou-Nigm (n 17) ch 7; Allsop (n 19) 159.

[93] Article 1(2) of both Arrest Conventions expressly defines ship arrest as a process 'to secure a maritime claim'. See Thomas (n 50) 313 who observes that the position is less clear in the Common Law where the establishment of jurisdiction rather than security may be the paramount purpose, but that security nonetheless continues to be the foremost practical feature.

aspect of maritime claims) which refers to the creation, or the putting into operation, of a positive security interest in favour of a claimant.[94] This function or aspect pertains to 'the extent to which an unsecured maritime claimant is, or can be transformed into, a secured claimant or preferred creditor, by the operation and working out of the maritime remedy of arrest or attachment'.[95]

The importance of arrest as a method of founding jurisdiction has declined with the growing prevalence of jurisdiction and arbitration clauses as well as the simplification of service abroad and the growing willingness of courts to recognise and enforce foreign judgments. Nevertheless, the other two functions of arrest remain primordial to maritime law.[96] These three possible functions are approached differently in Common Law and Civil Law jurisdictions. Generally speaking, in the Anglo-Common Law jurisdictions there is a theoretical weakness in that domestic admiralty legislation tends to combine the three functions of arrest, while in the Civil law jurisdictions the legislation pertaining to the enforcement of maritime claims follows the logical and chronological order of the three functions.[97]

V. Security Arrest

As a result of the failure to separate the three functions of arrest – in particular, by not separating arrest as a provisional remedy from the action on the merits – Anglo-Common Law courts have been faced with the issue of security arrests.[98] The term security arrest can conveniently be categorised by reference to, and used in respect of, two related situations.[99]

The first is where a ship is arrested in the forum arresti to determine the merits of a maritime claim, but the defendant shipowner[100] subsequently obtains a stay or dismissal of proceedings in favour of arbitration or determination by a foreign forum.[101] In such circumstances, the forum arresti has a discretion whether to keep the ship under arrest or order its release, either unconditionally, or on condition that appropriate alternative security is retained. The forum arresti's involvement is limited to the determination of the stay or dismissal of the proceedings; it is not involved, directly or indirectly, with the determination of the substantive merits of the maritime claim.[102] The forum's exercise of its discretion

[94] See Jackson (n 20) para 0.2.

[95] Allsop (n 19) 160.

[96] See Thomas (n 50) 313.

[97] See Jackson (n 20) para 0.10 for a brief discussion of the historical reasons for the intermingling of the three functions in Common Law jurisdictions. See Paul Myburgh, 'Security Arrest in Singapore' (2018) 24 *JIML* 95; Paul Myburgh, 'Richard Cooper Memorial Lecture: Admiralty Law – What is it Good For?' (2009) 28 *UQLJ* 19, 37, 38 for pertinent comments about the fundamental theoretical weakness in not separating the three functions.

[98] Security arrests are apparently not an issue in Civil Law jurisdictions: see eg Wim A Timmermans, 'The Netherlands – Arrest of Vessels and Maritime Arbitration' (2013) 1 *Russian Law: Theory and Practice* 79–93.

[99] See Paul Myburgh, *Extending New Zealand's Admiralty Jurisdiction: A Modest Proposal for Reform* (Maritime Law Association of Australia and New Zealand, 2004) 50.

[100] A claimant may also apply to stay its own action: see Toh Kian Sing, 'Judicial Assistance in Maritime Arbitration: A Singapore Perspective' (2006) 18 *S Ac L J* 771, 779.

[101] See Myburgh (n 99) 50.

[102] Although retained security may come into play in the context of obtaining security for the enforcement of an award: see Toh (n 100) 771.

to retain security, and its decision regarding the quantum of the retained security, tend to involve an assessment of the risk that the defendant shipowner will default.[103] Hare argues that security arrest in this sense is based on a fiction – the claimant, having no intention of asking the arresting court to hear its maritime claim, is required to allege that its claim should be heard in the arresting court, only to have the arrest stayed and the main action ordered to a more appropriate forum.[104] This situation can be conveniently referred to as a retained security arrest.

The second situation involves a pure security arrest, in that the ship is arrested in the forum arresti merely to obtain security, or additional security, for a maritime claim to be determined in another forum.[105] In this situation no fiction is necessary. The claimant may openly allege that it has no intention of seeking determination of its maritime claim from the arresting court. It does not have to arrest 'on the humbug of averring that the claim should be heard in the arresting court, only to have the arrest stayed and the main action ordered to a more appropriate forum'.[106] In other words, it is clear to all involved that the assistance of the local forum is merely sought to retain and preserve a security interest, to be called upon once the claimant has obtained its arbitral award or judgment from a foreign forum.[107] In this scenario, the role of the local forum is clearly limited to servicing the security aspect of the foreign arbitration or litigation.

A. Retained Security Arrest

As discussed, in Anglo-Common Law jurisdictions the three functions of arrest have not been kept separate. In particular, the initial conflation between arrest and the action in rem, and the resultant failure to separate out arrest as a provisional measure and jurisdiction on the merits of the maritime claim, has caused some difficulty in relation to retained security arrests.[108]

Historically, the position in Anglo-Common Law jurisdictions[109] was that, where the court was initially seized of in rem jurisdiction through the initiation of an action in rem only to have the action frozen through a stay in proceedings, the stay operated to dispossess the Admiralty Court of in rem jurisdiction and power to order or maintain an arrest.[110] In *The Rena K*,[111] where a ship was arrested and security provided in relation to a cargo claim arising under a bill of lading which incorporated a charterparty arbitration clause,

[103] Myburgh (n 99) 51.

[104] See John Hare, *Shipping Law and Admiralty Jurisdiction in South Africa*, 2nd edn (Cape Town, Juta, 2009) 118; John Hare, 'Shopping for the Best Admiralty Bargain' in Martin Davies (ed), *Jurisdiction and Forum Selection in International Maritime Law: Essays in Honor of Robert Force* (Dordrecht, Kluwer Law International, 2005) 137, 161.

[105] See Myburgh (n 99) 52.

[106] See Hare, *Shipping Law* (n 104) 118; Hare, 'Shopping' (n 104) 161.

[107] See Myburgh (n 99) 52.

[108] Similar issues have arisen in respect of stays granted due to foreign choice of forum agreements and the application of the forum non conveniens doctrine: see Jackson (n 20) paras 15.84–85.

[109] See *Frontier International Shipping Corp v The Tavros* [2000] 2 FC 427 [5]–[11].

[110] See Mark West, 'Arbitrations, Admiralty Actions in Rem and the Arrest of Ships in the Hong Kong SAR: In the Twilight of *The Indian Grace (No 2)*?' [2002] *LMCLQ* 259, 262; *The Athene* (1922) 11 Ll L Rep 6; *The Fehmarn* [1958] 1 WLR 159; *The Cap Bon* [1967] 1 Lloyd's Rep 543.

[111] *The Rena K* [1979] 1 QB 377.

Brandon J stayed proceedings and held that he could not impose terms such as security being retained as a precondition for the stay. The stay, not being final, could later be removed for good cause, in which case the action could still proceed. Brandon J also held that the Court only had jurisdiction to keep the ship under arrest to provide security for a judgment or settlement in the action, and lacked jurisdiction to maintain the arrest to provide the claimant with security for a subsequent arbitration award.[112] However, the Court was not obliged to release the ship from arrest, or release the security already given to secure its release.[113]

A shift in the English courts' approach to the issue occurred in *The Andria now renamed Vasso*,[114] when Robert Goff LJ held that the English Admiralty Court had jurisdiction to arrest or maintain an arrest of a ship when the purpose of the arrest was simply to obtain security for a foreign arbitral award. The mere fact that there was an arbitration clause did not preclude a claimant from instituting an action in rem against a ship.[115] The Court did not, however, express any view on the soundness of the *Rena K* principle that,

> where it is shown by the plaintiff that an arbitral award in his favour is unlikely to be satisfied by the defendant, the security available in the action in rem may be ordered to stand so that, if the plaintiff may have thereafter to pursue the action in rem (possibly using an unsatisfied arbitration award for the purpose of an issue estoppel) the security will remain available in that action.[116]

Unless the situation fell within the *Rena K* principle, the Court could not order security for an arbitral award.[117]

Building on the judicial creativity of Robert Goff LJ, the issue of retained security was finally addressed by legislative reform through the enactment of s 26 of the Civil Jurisdiction and Judgments Act 1982 (UK) (CJJA 1982).[118] In *The Bazias 3, The Bazias 4*, the English Court of Appeal considered the impact of that legislation on the *Rena K* principle and held that it disposed of the disadvantages or limitations of that principle.[119] The effect of s 26 of the CJJA 1982 is to stay admiralty proceedings in favour of foreign arbitration and grant courts the power to order the retention of any security, or the provision of alternative security, to satisfy an eventual arbitral award. Section 26 is a procedural mechanism and

[112] ibid 389.

[113] The Judge, however, qualified this by saying that there should be an unconditional release of the security if the distinct probability was that the stay of the proceeding in favour of arbitration would be final: ibid 400, 403.

[114] *The Andria now renamed Vasso* [1984] 1 QB 477, 488.

[115] See *The Andria* (n 114); *The Evmar* [1989] SGHC 40, [1989] 1 SLR(R) 433 [10].

[116] See *The Tuyuti* [1984] 1 QB 838, 845–46, 850 where Robert Goff LJ held that the principle was well-founded. The *Rena K* principle has been followed in other Anglo-Commonwealth jurisdictions: see eg *Raukura Moana Fisheries Ltd v The Ship Irina Zharkikh* [2001] 2 NZLR 801; *Nanisivik Mines Ltd v FCRS Shipping Ltd* [1994] 2 FC 662, (1994) 77 FTR 285; *Dongnam Oil & Fats Co v Chemex Ltd* 2004 FC 1732.

[117] See *The Evmar* (n 115) [23]; *The Xin Chang Shu* (n 70) [51].

[118] Section 26(1)(a) applies where a ship is still under arrest, whereas s 26(1)(b) applies where security has been given to prevent arrest of the ship or to obtain her release: see Jackson (n 20) para 15.87; Jeremy M Joseph, 'Ship Arrest as Security for Arbitration Claims' [2001] 1 *The Malayan Law Journal* 37.

[119] *The Bazias 3, The Bazias 4* [1993] QB 673, 681. The disadvantage of the principle in *The Rena K* was that much time was taken up at the early stages of every dispute in determining on affidavit evidence whether a foreign arbitral award was likely to be satisfied by the defendant shipowner: see also West (n 110) 263–64.

does not expressly state that arrest of a ship is allowed solely for the purpose of obtaining security for an arbitration award. In *The World Star*,[120] however, that was what happened. Sheen J decided that, since the case fell procedurally within the ambit of s 26, the Court could order the retention of the ship as security for the satisfaction of the arbitral award under s 26(1)(a) of the CJJA 1982.[121] Recently, in *Sam Purpose AS v Transnav Purpose Navigation Ltd*,[122] after a detailed review of the authorities and a consideration of the Arrest Convention 1952, the Court adopted the statement of principle provided by Jonathan Hirst QC in *Kallang Shipping SA Panama v AXA Assurances Senegal (The Kallang) (No 2)*[123] to the effect that

> the English Court will not restrain a party to an English arbitration clause from arresting a vessel in another jurisdiction where the sole purpose of the arrest is to obtain reasonable security for the claim to be arbitrated or litigated in England. Section 11 of the Arbitration Act 1996 also assumes that a Claimant can properly arrest a vessel in order to obtain security for an arbitration claim. The precise basis on which the Court acts – construction of the arbitration clause or discretion – is not authoritatively established but the general approach is clear enough. Where, however, the Claimant's actions go beyond simply seeking reasonable security for the arbitration proceedings, there is a breach of the arbitration clause which the English Court will restrain.[124]

Thus in England a claimant may institute an action in rem simply to obtain security for foreign arbitration or litigation. By virtue of the legislative reforms, the proceedings may be stayed and the ship (or equivalent security) retained under arrest.[125]

Other Anglo-Common Law jurisdictions have enacted similar legislation. For example, in Australia, s 29 of the Admiralty Act 1988 (Cth) (AA 1988) allows a claimant to take advantage of the extra-territorial nature of the admiralty jurisdiction to obtain security for a maritime claim elsewhere, even where there is no territorial connection with the dispute.[126] Where a court has made an order under s 29 it may make appropriate interim orders in relation to the ship. A party to a proceeding stayed under s 29 who subsequently

[120] *The World Star* [1986] 2 Lloyd's Rep 274. See also *Atlantic Lines & Navigation Co v The Didymi* [1985] 1 FC 240; *Pictou Industries Ltd v Secunda Marine Services Ltd* (1984) 78 FTR 78; *Frontier International Shipping Corp* (n 109); *Cyber Sea Technologies Inc v Underwater Harvester Remotely Operated Vehicle, Serial No UHROV-101* [2003] 1 FC 569; *The ICL Raja Mahendra* [1998] SGHC 419, [1998] 2 SLR(R) 922 [21]–[22]; Toh (n 100) 777.

[121] See also *The Jalamatsya* [1987] 2 Lloyd's Rep 164. In *Ispat Industries Ltd v Western Bulk Pte Ltd* [2011] EWHC 93 (Comm) [46] Teare J held that ancillary applications for security are not a breach of an arbitration clause provided there is no attempt to have the merits of the dispute heard other than by the agreed arbitral tribunal.

[122] *Sam Purpose AS v Transnav Purpose Navigation Ltd* [2017] EWHC 719 (Comm), [2017] 2 Lloyd's Rep 50 [24].

[123] *Kallang Shipping SA Panama v AXA Assurances Senegal (The Kallang) (No 2)* [2008] EWHC 2761 (Comm), [2009] 1 Lloyd's Rep 124.

[124] ibid [78]. See also *Ispat Industries Ltd* (n 121) [46].

[125] Jackson (n 20) para 15.44: 'Provided a claimant may obtain a stay, the division of security and substance may be attained – although only through divorce of the initial union. So, while initial separation has still not been attained, the method of suit is not now being allowed to create an artificial mandatory link between security and merits jurisdiction.'

[126] This section is relevantly similar to s 26 of the CJJA 1982. See *Allonah Pty Ltd v The Ship Amanda N* (1989) 21 FCR 60, 63; *Pan Australia Shipping Pty Ltd v The Ship Comandate (No 2)* [2006] FCA 1112, (2006) 234 ALR 483 [46]; Martin Davies, 'Maritime Law, the Epitome of Transnational Legal Authority' in Günther Handl et al (eds), *Beyond Territoriality: Transnational Legal Authority in the Age of Globalization* (Leiden, Martinus Nijhoff Publishers, 2012) 327, 330–31.

obtains an award or judgment in its favour may apply under s 29(5) to the court for an enforcement order.[127]

In Singapore, s 7(1) of the International Arbitration Act[128] (IAA) similarly provides that the court has the power to order that 'the property arrested be retained as security for the satisfaction of any award made on the arbitration' or that 'equivalent security' be provided.[129] As Steven Chong J pointed out in *The Xin Chang Shu*,[130] s 7(1) supplants the common law requirement that the arresting party must prove that the defendant would not be able to satisfy any eventual arbitration award.

Where a mandatory stay of an action is ordered pursuant to s 6 of the IAA,[131] security provided to avoid an arrest or to procure the release of an arrested ship may be retained in satisfaction of any arbitration award,[132] irrespective of whether the arbitration is taking place in Singapore or elsewhere.[133] Section 7 of the IAA reflects a distinction between the choice of forum for determination of the merits of the dispute and the right to security under the Singapore High Court (Admiralty Jurisdiction) Act (cap 123). The latter can still be invoked despite the existence of an arbitration agreement. The section 'effectively does away with the *Rena K* test'.[134]

Unlike the United Kingdom, Australia and South Africa, Singapore does not have a statutory provision explicitly providing for security arrests for foreign litigation (as opposed to foreign arbitration). In *DSA Consultancy (FZC) v The Eurohope*,[135] the Singapore High Court recently held that it was an abuse of process to commence an action in rem in Singapore for the purpose of arresting a ship in order to obtain security in aid of foreign court proceedings.[136] The purpose of arrest in an action in Singapore is to provide security in respect of the action in Singapore, and no other. The action in rem is a mode of exercising the admiralty jurisdiction conferred on the Singapore High Court by s 3(1) of the High Court (Admiralty Jurisdiction) Act. That jurisdiction

[127] See generally Cremean (n 35) 141. Section 4(3)(u) of the AA 1988 allows for the enforcement of an arbitral award within the Australian admiralty jurisdiction.

[128] International Arbitration Act (cap 143A, 2002 rev edn) which is similar to s 26 of the CJJA 1982. See Toh (n 100) 778; Toh Kian Sing, *Admiralty Law and Practice* 3rd edn (Singapore, LexisNexis, 2017) 608–10; Robert Merkin and Johanna Hjalmarsson, *Singapore Arbitration Legislation Annotated* (Abingdon, Informa Law from Routledge, 2016) 41–43. The application under s 7 is ancillary to an application for a stay: see *The Hilal I* [2000] SGHC 268, [2000] 3 SLR(R) 886.

[129] The position is similar to that in the UK: see Leng Sun Chan, 'Amendments to the Singapore International Arbitration Act' (2010) 76 *Arbitration* 200, 202.

[130] *The Xin Chang Shu* (n 70) [52].

[131] See *The Engedi* [2010] SGHC 95, [2010] 3 SLR 409. Under s 7 of the IAA, the Court can only order security to cover an arbitration award when it orders a stay of the proceeding before it. The order for a stay is distinct from the order retaining the ship under arrest. It does not follow from the granting of a stay that the ship must be released or must remain under arrest: see *The Sunwind* [1998] SGHC 420, [1998] 2 SLR(R) 929 [15].

[132] Section 7 of the IAA provides a discretionary power that is ancillary to an application under s 6: *The Hilal I* (n 128) [10], [13]–[14].

[133] See *Swift-Fortune Ltd v Magnifica Marine SA* [2006] SGCA 42, [2007] 1 SLR(R) 629; *Front Carriers Ltd v Atlantic & Orient Shipping Corp* [2006] SGHC 127, [2006] 3 SLR(R) 854. Thus, the statutory power can be exercised in aid of a foreign arbitration to ensure that there is security against which a potential award can be enforced. Section 7(1)(b) of the IAA empowers a court to order that alternative security be furnished for the satisfaction of the arbitral award.

[134] *Front Carriers* (n 133) [28].

[135] *The Eurohope* [2017] SGHC 218, [2017] 5 SLR 934, discussed in Myburgh 'Security Arrest in Singapore' (n 97).

[136] *The Eurohope* (n 135) [30].

is to 'hear and determine' maritime questions and claims set out in s 3(1)(a)–(r) of that Act.[137] Moreover, the bail form specifically covers only a judgment in or settlement of the action.[138] The court was of the view that legislative intervention along the lines of s 7 of the IAA would therefore be required before security arrests in the context of foreign litigation could be allowed.

In 2011, Malaysia passed the Arbitration Amendment Act widening the Courts' admiralty jurisdiction in the context of arbitral proceedings. If a claimant meets the maritime claim criteria for in rem proceedings,[139] the Court may stay proceedings and order the retention of the ship arrested or order that alternative equivalent security be provided to stand as security for the satisfaction of any local or foreign arbitral award.[140] However, it is not possible to arrest a ship as security in aid of foreign court proceedings.[141]

In Hong Kong, it was held in *The Britannia*[142] that, in the absence of statutory authority, the threshold test set out in *The Rena K* remained determinative as to whether a ship could be arrested in the face of an arbitration or foreign jurisdiction clause. Moreover, pursuant to s 20(6) of the Arbitration Ordinance (HK) (cap 602) and s 12B(6A) of the High Court Ordinance (HK) (cap 4), when a ship has been arrested, a court will stay the admiralty proceedings in rem in favour of arbitration pursuant to the terms of an arbitration agreement, and may impose a condition that the ship, bail or other security in the admiralty proceeding stands as security for the satisfaction of any arbitral award.

In *The Alas*[143] the Hong Kong Court of First Instance was faced with the question of what happens if a claimant first obtains a foreign arbitral award on a maritime claim and later seeks to arrest a relevant ship pursuant to that award. The Court rejected submissions that *The Rena K* was no longer good law in light of *Republic of India v India Steamship Co Ltd (No 2) (The Indian Grace)*,[144] and that arrest was not available for what was effectively an action to enforce the foreign arbitral award.[145] In *The Alas*, because the claim was pleaded with reference to the underlying maritime cause of action[146] rather than the unsatisfied foreign arbitral award, the Court was able to sustain the fiction that the arrest was for the

[137] ibid [25].
[138] ibid [26].
[139] Section 24(b) of the Malaysian Courts of Judicature Act 1964 provides that the admiralty jurisdiction of the Malaysian High Court is the same as that provided for under s 20(2) read with s 21(2)–(4) of the Senior Courts Act 1981 (UK). A ship can be arrested whether within port limits or outside port limits provided it is in Malaysian territorial waters.
[140] See s 10 read with s 11 of the Arbitration Act 2005.
[141] See *Asia Pacific Parcel Tankers Pte Ltd v The Owners of the Ship or Vessel Normar Splendour* [2001] 4 MLJ 245.
[142] *Dalmor Shipping Co Ltd v Kan's Maritime Corp (The Brittania)* [1997] HKCFI 305; [1998] 1 HKC 221. The Court concluded that the test in *The Rena K* was both logical and jurisprudentially sound and remained adamant that, provided it could be established that in all probability the stay in proceedings would be lifted, the Admiralty Court was possessed of the jurisdiction to order or maintain arrest of a ship as security for an unsatisfied award or judgment.
[143] *Handytankers KS v Owners and/or Demise Charterers of Alas subsequently renamed as Kombos* [2014] HKCFI 1281, [2014] 6 HKC 239. See also Poomintr Sooksripaisarnkit, 'Ship Arrest in Hong Kong Despite an Arbitration Award?' (2015) 21 *JIML* 94.
[144] *Republic of India v India Steamship Co Ltd (No 2) (The Indian Grace)* [1998] AC 878.
[145] *The Alas* (n 143) [13]–[17], [24]. The Court declined to follow *The Chong Bong* [1997] HKCFI 306, [1997] 3 HKC 579 and *The Bumbesti* [2000] QB 559: see Toh (n 100) 781–86 for a discussion of these decisions.
[146] That is, the claim was pleaded as a breach of the charterparty under s 12A(2)(h) of the High Court Ordinance (cap 4) (HK).

purposes of determining a de novo maritime claim, rather than enforcing a foreign award. The application for leave to appeal was decisively dismissed.[147]

In India, the Full Bench of the Bombay High Court in *JS Ocean Liner LLC v MV Golden Progress*[148] had to decide between two earlier conflicting decisions[149] on whether retained security arrests were available in support of arbitration. The Full Bench held that, since there was nothing in the Indian statutes that excluded the use of the admiralty jurisdiction to arrest a ship as security for future or pending arbitrations, the Court could allow it.[150] The Court relied on arts 2 and 7 of the Arrest Convention 1999, which is considered to be part of Indian law, to hold that security arrests are allowed in the context of arbitration. The current consensus in India seems to be that security arrests are permissible where a foreign decree is involved or where the ship is owned by a foreigner, to avoid loss of security in the case of non-reciprocity or unlawful acts on the part of the shipowner. This position does not seem to have been affected by the recent passage of the Admiralty (Jurisdiction and Settlement of Maritime Claims) Act 2017. Although that Act does not reproduce art 7 of the Arrest Convention 1999, the Bombay High Court held that there is nothing in the Act that precludes security arrest in support of foreign arbitration and the application of the principles underpinning art 7 of the Arrest Convention 1999 as part of Indian common law.[151]

Despite the fact that several Anglo-Common Law jurisdictions have adopted specific statutory provisions to deal with the retained security issue, the *Rena K* principle has not entirely lost its significance. It is still relevant in at least two instances. First, a claimant may have to fall back on the common law where the local statute giving courts power to order or retain security does not apply due to some technicality; for example, where the arbitration clause provides for 'either litigation or arbitration', or where the local legislation applies only to agreements that are required to be referred to arbitration.[152] Secondly, the *Rena K* principle is still applicable in jurisdictions where there is no statute dealing with the retained security issue. In New Zealand, the Arbitration Act 1996 has not been amended to clarify the right to retention of security in the context of a stay of in rem proceedings pending arbitration. Currently, the New Zealand courts have endorsed the *Rena K* approach.[153] The existence of an arbitration clause will therefore not preclude the bringing of an in rem action. Where a court grants a stay on the basis of such a clause, it retains a discretion as to whether to retain security.[154]

[147] *Handytankers KS v The Owners and/or Demise Charterers of the Ship or Vessel M/V Alas Subsequently Renamed as Kombos (The Alas)* [2015] HKCA 691, [2015] 6 HKC 557. For a discussion, see Sooksripaisarnkit (n 143) 94; Poomintr Sooksripaisarnkit, 'Recent Admiralty Decisions in Hong Kong – Are the Courts Ready to Deviate from Their English Predecessors?' (2016) 30 *Australia & New Zealand Maritime Law Journal* 134.

[148] *JS Ocean Liner LLC v MV Golden Progress* 2007(2) ARB LR 104 (Bom).

[149] *Islamic Republic of Iran Shipping Lines v MV Mehrab* AIR 2002 Bom 517 and *Blue Diamond Freight Pvt Ltd v MV Indurva Valley and Inspat Industries Ltd v MV Thor Orchid* 2004 (5) Bom CR 409.

[150] See Dyutimoy Mukherjee, Arka Majumdar and Anunoy Basu, 'Ship Arrest in India' (2007) 13 *JIML* 289, 296.

[151] *Siem Offshore Redri AS v Altus Uber* 2018 (6) ABR 361. See further ch 12.

[152] See *The Dai Yun Shan* [1992] SGHC 51, [1992] 1 SLR(R) 461; *Dalian Hualiang Enterprise Group Co Ltd v Louis Dreyfus Asia Pte Ltd* [2005] SGHC 161, [2005] 4 SLR(R) 646; *Tjong Very Sumito v Antig Investments Pte Ltd* [2009] 4 SLR(R) 732; David Chong Gek Sian, 'Agreements to Refer Disputes to Arbitration' [1993] *Sing JLS* 261.

[153] See *Marine Expeditions Inc v The Ship Akademik Shokalskiy* [1995] 2 NZLR 743; *The Irina Zharkikh* (n 116).

[154] See KFT Stolberger, 'New Zealand' in Christian Breitzke et al (eds), *Maritime Law Handbook* (Alpen aan den Rijn, Wolters Kluwer, updated June 2015) part 1 para 3.3.4.

In sum, retained security arrest, in one form or another, is now generally available in all jurisdictions in support of arbitration, and in most jurisdictions (with the notable exceptions of Singapore and Malaysia) in support of litigation.

B. Pure Security Arrest

i. Assisting the 'Wandering Litigants of the World'[155]

In addition to providing for actions in personam and in rem to enforce a maritime claim in South Africa,[156] the Admiralty Jurisdiction Regulation Act 1983 (AJRA 1983) provides in s 5(3)(a) that a South African court in the exercise of its admiralty jurisdiction may order the arrest of any property solely to provide security for a claim that is the subject of arbitration or other proceedings, contemplated, pending or under way, whether in South Africa or elsewhere, and whether or not the claim is subject to South African law.[157] Section 5(3)(a) provides radical relief that is not extended in other comparable jurisdictions. It is within the scope of both art 7(2) of the Arrest Convention 1952 and art 2(3) of the Arrest Convention 1999. Pure security arrest is

> the ultimate recognition of the comity of admiralty jurisdictions, for it seeks to give efficacy to arbitration awards and judgments more properly granted elsewhere than South Africa, even though the claim and its resolution have no link to South Africa other than the presence within the jurisdiction of an executable asset. The purpose of the security arrest is to bring the res, and not the person of the defendant, before the court.[158]

ii. Security Arrests and Actions In Rem

The two proceedings are fundamentally distinct and have different consequences.[159] In *MV Zlatni Piasatzi: Frozen Foods International Ltd v Kudu Holdings (Pty) Ltd*[160] it was held that a proceeding to obtain an order for security arrest operates in rem,[161] but its purpose, unlike an in rem arrest, is to obtain security in pursuing a maritime claim in

[155] See Hilton Staniland, 'Is the Admiralty Court to be Turned into a Court of Convenience for the Wandering Litigants of the World?' (1986) 103 *SALJ* 9. Section 5(3) of the AJRA 1983 was initially received with concern by many shipowners and their P&I Clubs and with delight by many charterers and cargo underwriters. There was also some judicial scepticism. These concerns have proved to be unwarranted: see *Katagum Wholesale Commodities Co Ltd v The MV Paz* 1984 (3) SA 261 (N). As Gys Hofmeyr, *Admiralty Jurisdiction: Law and Practice in South Africa* 2nd edn (Cape Town, Juta, 2012) 172 observes, these remarks overlook the fact that the admiralty creditor is frequently forced to be a 'wandering litigant' because of the need to pursue the ship to obtain satisfaction for its claim; and that admiralty courts have for this reason always extended their jurisdiction to a lesser or greater extent to accommodate foreign litigants and causes.

[156] See *MV Iran Dastghayb: Islamic Republic of Iran Shipping Lines v Terra Marine SA* 2010 (6) SA 493 (SCA).

[157] See *Babel Shipping Co Ltd v Grapsas t/a Nuova Travel; Babel Shipping Co Ltd v Zeba Maritime Co Ltd; The Rosario Del Mar* 1995 (1) SA 716, 719–20 (C) for a guide on how to interpret the provision.

[158] See Hare, *Shipping Law* (n 104) 118; Hare, 'Shopping' (n 104) 161.

[159] See Malcolm John David Wallis, *The Associated Ship and South African Admiralty Jurisdiction* (Cape Town, Siber Ink, 2010) 306.

[160] *MV Zlatni Piasatzi: Frozen Foods International Ltd v Kudu Holdings (Pty) Ltd* 1997 (2) SA 569, 574 (C).

[161] Wallis (n 159) 309, 310 opines that it is inappropriate to speak of a security arrest as a proceeding in rem or as a proceeding in personam, at least in so far as those expressions are usually understood.

another jurisdiction or before an arbitral tribunal, almost invariably foreign.[162] The security arrest proceeding has also been described as a 'stand-alone' proceeding unconnected with any other proceeding before a South African court.[163]

iii. Scope of Security Arrests

Section 5(3) of the AJRA 1983 is broadly worded. Its scope has been clarified and interpreted in accordance with common-sense and the international ship arrest framework provided for in the Arrest Conventions to address concerns raised over pure security arrest and to ensure that the South African courts grant security appropriately and do not exercise an overreaching or exorbitant jurisdiction.

The essential prerequisites for a security arrest are largely settled. The applicant must satisfy the court:[164]

(a) on the prima facie standard of proof[165] that:
  - (i) it has a case on the merits of the maritime claim for which security is sought based upon facts, which if proved, would give rise to that cause of action;[166] and
  - (ii) the forum in which that claim has been, or is to be, enforced has jurisdiction to hear the matter;[167] and

(b) on a balance of probability[168] that:
  - (i) it has a maritime claim as defined by the AJRA 1983; and
  - (ii) its maritime claim is enforceable at South African law (or would be enforceable in South Africa but for arbitration or other unsecured court proceedings) by an

[162] *The Petriana: Trade Sky Inc v Lofty Ltd* 1993 *Shipping Cases of South Africa* B91, B93: 'Section 5(3) makes it clear that the purpose of the arrest is to provide for security and not to found jurisdiction for, nor initiate, an action in rem, nor to confirm jurisdiction for the purposes other than an action in personam.'

[163] See *MV Rizcun Trader (4): MV Rizcun Trader v Manley Appledore Shipping Ltd* 2000 (3) SA 776, 785 (C).

[164] See Hare, *Shipping Law* (n 104) 119. Once an applicant satisfies these requirements it is entitled to an order under s 5(3): see *MV La Pampa: Louis Dreyfus Armateurs SNC v Tor Shipping* 2006 (3) SA 441, 448 (D).

[165] That is, the applicant need only show that there is evidence which, if accepted, will establish a cause of action: see *Cargo Laden & Latterly Laden on Board the MV Thalassini Avgi v MV Dimitris (The Dimitris)* 1989 (3) SA 820 (A); *The Almerinda: Sweetlip Navigation Inc v MV Almerinda* 1994 *Shipping Cases of South Africa* B1, B3; Hilton Staniland, 'Admiralty Law' 1994 *Annual Survey of South African Law* 637, 645–46. Where the applicant seeks to arrest an associated ship for security, however, it has to establish the association between the guilty ship and the associated ship on a balance of probabilities: see *Bocimar NV v Kotor Overseas Shipping Ltd* 1994 (2) SA 563, 581 (SCA); *The Akademik Fyodorov: Government of the Russian Federation v Marine Expeditions Inc* 1996 (4) SA 422 (C). Also see generally *Great River Shipping Inc v Sunnyface Marine Inc (The Great Eagle (No 2))* 1992 (4) SA 313, 316 (C).

[166] It is only where it is clear that the claimant has no action, or cannot succeed, that this requirement will not be met: see generally John Dyason, 'Security Arrests in South Africa' [1990] *LMCLQ* 9. In *MT Tigr: Owners of the MT Tigr v Transnet t/a Portnet (Bouygues Offshore SA & another intervening)* 1998 (3) SA 861, 868–71 (SCA), the Supreme Court of Appeal stated that in certain circumstances the prima facie requirement may be relaxed. See also *MV Heavy Metal: Belfry Marine Ltd v Palm Base Maritime SDN BHD* 2000 (1) SA 286 (C); *Farocean Marine (Pty) Ltd v Malacca Holdings Ltd* 2005 (1) SA 428, 437–38 (SCA).

[167] Further evidence may be required if it seems likely that the foreign forum will decline to exercise jurisdiction or stay proceedings, but the South African court considering the security arrest application should not involve itself with questions such as whether the foreign forum would grant a stay based on the parties' agreement or perhaps forum non conveniens: see *The Dimitris* (n 165) 831–32.

[168] This standard was applied as a matter of policy, given that the arrest of a ship, for whatever purpose, has potential damaging consequences for many relevant parties: see Hare, *Shipping Law* (n 104) 121.

action in personam against the owner of the property to be arrested or by an action in rem against such property, including, where appropriate, an associated ship;[169] and

(iii) the property to be arrested has neither been arrested before nor has security already been given for the same claim of the same claimant; and

(iv) it has a genuine and reasonable need[170] for security for its claim.[171]

Section 5(3)(a) of the AJRA 1983 stipulates that only a court exercising admiralty jurisdiction may grant a security arrest.[172] Where the application is made ex parte, as it usually is,[173] the applicant must disclose every circumstance that may influence the court in deciding whether to order the arrest, and any failure to make proper disclosure may lead the court to exercise its discretion to set aside the arrest.[174]

Although s 5(3)(a) of the AJRA 1983 uses the permissive word 'may', the South African courts have consistently regarded their discretion as fettered to the extent that the applicant is entitled to a security arrest once the prerequisites are met, unless the respondent places countervailing evidence[175] before the court of sufficient weight to persuade the court not to grant the order.[176] A respondent alleging that it will not receive a fair hearing in the contemplated proceedings bears a heavy onus to be discharged by proving its assertion with positive and cogent evidence.[177]

'Property' that may be subjected to a security arrest under s 5(3)(a) of the AJRA 1983 is not restricted to the specific maritime property enumerated in s 3(5) of the AJRA 1983 that may be arrested in rem.[178] This means that incorporeal property,[179] including incorporeal rights to bank accounts,[180] bunkers or freight, may be arrested for security. An associated

[169] See *Euromarine International of Mauren v The Ship Berg* 1984 (4) SA 647 (N); *Euromarine International of Mauren v The Ship Berg* 1986 (2) SA 700, 708 (A); *The Wisdom (No 2)* (n 84) B206.

[170] The applicant must allege and explain why it needs security; the extent to which, if at all, its claim is already secured; and why security cannot be obtained in other proceedings: *The Paz* (n 155) 268; *The Dimitris* (n 165) 832; *The Wisdom C: United Enterprises Corporation v STX Pan Ocean Company Limited* 2008 *Shipping Cases of South Africa* B380; *Asiatic Shipping Services Inc v Elgina Marine Company Ltd* 2009 (1) SA 246 (SCA); *The Ever Growth: Green Africa Shipping (Pty) Ltd v Hifu Electronic Trading CC* 2003 *Shipping Cases of South Africa* B251, B253–54; *Fino Maritime SA v Shipping Corp of India Ltd* [2008] 3 All SA 285 (D); *The Akademik Fyodorov* (n 165) 449–50. There can be no proof by inference unless there are objective facts from which to draw the inference: *P&O Nedlloyd v United African Lines (Pty) Ltd* 2003 *Shipping Cases of South Africa* B258, B265.

[171] The necessity of security must be established on a balance of probabilities: see *Bocimar NV* (n 165) 580–581; Hare, *Shipping Law* (n 104) 120.

[172] See *Devonia Shipping Ltd v MV Luis (Yeoman Shipping Co Ltd Intervening)* 1994 (2) SA 363, 372 (C).

[173] Hofmeyr (n 155) 181.

[174] The party relying on non-disclosure must show that there is a reasonable prospect that the court would not have ordered the security arrest if the non-disclosure had not occurred: *The Rizcun Trader (4)* (n 163) 793–94, 799 (C); *The Wisdom C* 2008 (3) SA 585 [19] (SCA).

[175] See *The Dimitris* (n 165) 833.

[176] See Hare, *Shipping Law* (n 104) 119; Hofmeyr (n 155) 180. See, however, *MV NYK Isabel, Northern Endeavour Shipping Pte Ltd v The Owners of the NYK Isabel* [2016] ZASCA 89 [43].

[177] In the absence of such countervailing evidence the court does not have a general discretion as to whether it should exercise its power to order the security arrest: *The Dimitris* (n 165) 833; *The La Pampa* (n 164).

[178] See *The Zlatni Piasatzi* (n 160) 575.

[179] See *The Arena: Oceanview Shipping Ltd v Dayra Shipping SA* 1999 *Shipping Cases of South Africa* B8.

[180] This is similar to US Rule B attachment. Hare, *Shipping Law* (n 104) 117 observes that, although the wording of s 5(3) is clear, 'this was probably a largely unintended extension of the powers of security arrest'. See also *The Almerinda* (n 165).

ship may also be arrested for security under s 5(3) of the AJRA 1983.[181] There are, however, two qualifications in respect of the property that may be arrested for security: the property must have intrinsic value[182] and must also have reasonably substantial value, because the purpose of security arrest is to provide security for a claim.[183] Once a security arrest has been made under s 5(3) of the AJRA 1983, the arrestor cannot invoke s 5(2) of the Act to top up the security obtained.[184]

Although s 5(3)(a) of the AJRA 1983 uses the term 'claim', the South African courts have consistently interpreted the section as referring to a 'maritime claim'.[185] In other words, the claim for which security is sought must be a maritime claim recognised as a cause of action in admiralty in South Africa.[186]

Section 5(3)(a) of the AJRA 1983 does not require the applicant for security arrest to have 'a genuine and reasonable need' for security for its maritime claim, but the courts have read those words into the section. The need for security depends on a consideration of the particular facts of each case. The applicant is only required to establish a genuine and reasonable apprehension that the party whose property has been arrested will not satisfy a judgment or arbitral award made in favour of the arresting party.[187]

Property arrested pursuant to s 5(3)(a) of the AJRA 1983 is held as security pending the outcome of the arbitration or other proceedings.[188] Unless the court orders otherwise, it is deemed for practical purposes to be property arrested in an action in rem to enforce a maritime claim.[189] The possibility of a security arrest where the claimant has an action in personam was introduced by an amendment to s 5(3)(a) of the AJRA 1983 in 1992.[190]

VI. Conclusion

The maritime industry is populated by transient participants: the 'assets that fire the industry's engines – ships, cargo, bunkers, bank funds and the electronic blips flying through the ether representing payments, profits and promises – are uniquely mobile, fungible,

[181] See *The Dimitris* (n 165) 830; *Euromarine International of Mauren v The Berg* 1984 (4) SA 647 (N); *Hasselbacher Papier Import & Export (Body Corporate) v MV Stavroula* 1987 (1) SA 75 (C).

[182] See *The Almerinda* (n 165): application to arrest a claim for security failed as the claim had no intrinsic value and did not constitute 'property' for the purposes of s 5(3)(a).

[183] See *Bocimar NV* (n 165) 581; *The Ever Growth* (n 170).

[184] *The Zlatni Piasatzi* (n 160).

[185] See *The Rosario Del Mar* (n 157). The only aberration is Msimang J's decision in *The Atlantic Spirit* 2003 *Shipping Cases of South Africa* B191, where it was held that it was sufficient to show (by implication, prima facie) that the claim was justiciable in the foreign forum even if it were not proved that the claim would be enforceable in South African law. Hare, *Shipping Law* (n 104) 119 points out that the correctness of Msimang J's ruling is doubted.

[186] However, a security arrest may be obtained even though the court may have declined to exercise its jurisdiction or stay proceedings, had the action to enforce that maritime claim been instituted in the jurisdiction: *The Paz* (n 170) 267.

[187] See generally *The Zygos No 1* 1984 (4) SA 444, 457 (C); *The Dimitris* (n 165) 831–33; *Bocimar NV* (n 165) 578; *Owner of the MV Maritime Prosperity v Owner of the MV Lash Atlantico* 1996 (1) SA 22, 27 (SCA); *MV Gladiator: Samsun Corp t/a Samsun Line Corp v Silver Cape Shipping Ltd, Malta* 2007 (2) SA 401 (D); *Asiatic Shipping Services Inc* (n 170).

[188] Section 5(3)(aA) of the AJRA 1983.

[189] Section 5(3)(b) of the AJRA 1983. See *MV Alam Tenggiri Golden Seabird Maritime Inc v Alam Tenggiri Sdn Bhd* 2001 (4) SA 1329, 1333 (SCA); Hofmeyr (n 155) 183.

[190] See *National Iranian Tanker Co v The Pericles* 1995 (1) SA 475 (A); *Associated Marine Engineers (Pty) Ltd v Foroya Banki PF* 1994 (4) SA 676 (C).

transferable, and easily depleted.'[191] The need to provide litigants with interim or provisional relief pending the determination of the main proceedings is widely recognised by all legal systems.[192] Arrest as security and security arrest are legal responses to the problems triggered by these impermanent participants. Since creditors tend to pursue their maritime claims by means of ship arrest, a country's ship arrest laws are of significance to international maritime traders in their consideration of forum selection when enforcing claims arising from their international trade arrangements.[193]

Although arrest has different functions, which are treated differently in Anglo-Common Law and Civil Law jurisdictions, they are all interconnected. In practice, despite the differences in arrest procedures, ship arrest, a practical procedural device, achieves the objective of the international maritime security regime: it provides financial security for maritime claims with a view to rendering justice in accordance with substantive law.[194] Nowadays, although maritime commerce is still international and maritime assets are still transitory, a maritime creditor armed with the remedies of ship arrest, maritime attachment, retained security arrest or pure security arrest need no longer be frustrated like Evangeline, the poor Acadian girl referred to at the beginning of this Chapter.

If one is to enhance the securing of maritime claims to facilitate their enforcement, and to discourage forum shopping in admiralty, a solution may be the worldwide acceptance of the practice of security arrest, more particularly in its pure sense. It makes sense to allow

> a competent maritime jurisdiction to arrest a vessel then situated within its own jurisdiction solely (and indeed openly) to provide security for a claim to be pursued in another jurisdiction. This is, after all, often what motivates a court to stay a matter on grounds of forum non conveniens.[195]

It is a waste of time and money to have to pursue a maritime claim in the forum arresti to obtain a ship arrest, only to have that arrest stayed and the main action ordered to a more appropriate forum. The parties and the court generally know that what an arresting claimant is after is security, and that the claimant has only come to the forum arresti because the asset is currently within that jurisdiction.[196] Why would one wish to

> perpetuate a fiction and draw the arresting court into tedious and expensive arguments of forum non conveniens[197] when even the 1952 Arrest Convention recognises that an arrest may be made where the arresting court has no jurisdiction to decide upon the merits, yet allows security to stand.[198]

[191] Cheryl A Morris, 'Maritime Seizures: Not Just Ships – Maritime Seizures of Cargo, Freight, Fuel and Other Tangible and Intangible Items' (2006–7) 19 *University of San Francisco Maritime Law Journal* 69, 70.

[192] See George D Theocharidis, 'Jurisdiction for Provisional Relief under the Brussels Convention in the Maritime Context' (2002) 55 *Revue Hellénique de Droit International* 453.

[193] See Jimmy Ng, 'How Closely does the Chinese Law of Ship Arrest Resemble International Maritime Practice and the Ship Arrest Conventions?' (2006) 12 *JIML* 337.

[194] See generally the Indian Supreme Court's observations in *MV Elisabeth v Harwan Investment & Trading Pvt Ltd* 1993 AIR 1993 SC 1014, 1993 Supp (2) SCC 433.

[195] Hare, 'Shopping' (n 104) 161.

[196] ibid.

[197] See DW Robertson, 'Forum Non Conveniens in America and England: A Rather Fantastic Fiction' (1987) 103 *LQR* 390. Jonathan Hill and Adeline Chong, *International Commercial Disputes: Commercial Conflict of Laws in English Courts* 4th edn (Oxford, Hart Publishing, 2010) 315 aptly observe that the 'theoretical attractions of the doctrine of forum non conveniens are bought at a price – namely, uncertainty, delay and expense – which has to be paid by litigants. It is arguable that the doctrine costs more than its worth'.

[198] Hare, 'Shopping' (n 104) 161.

This question has even more significance in light of art 2(3) of the Arrest Convention 1999.

The widespread adoption of a pure security arrest provision by other jurisdictions would be beneficial to, and would enhance, the international effectiveness of the securing and enforcement of maritime claims. Although it is not suggested that there should be an indiscriminate adoption of the South African security arrest provision, it may serve as a useful guide. The South African security arrest jurisdiction has gone from strength to strength and has been well canvassed by legal commentators and in judicial pronouncements over the past three decades or so. Indeed, it might be argued that, '[a]s with most heresies, vigorous usage appears to have rendered it unremarkable, even orthodox'.[199]

[199] Myburgh (n 99) 53.

4

Declining Jurisdiction Following Arrest

STEVEN RARES*

I. Introduction

The power of a court exercising admiralty or maritime jurisdiction (a maritime court) to arrest a ship is both an expression of sovereignty and an essential remedy for international trade and commerce. The scope or extent of the power, however, varies among maritime States because of the lack of international consensus as to which maritime claims, maritime liens and ship mortgages should be recognised as universally enforceable. And, as the title of this Chapter portends, in certain circumstances, maritime courts will decline to exercise their power to arrest, or continue the arrest of, a ship.

The occasion for a maritime court to exercise its jurisdiction to arrest a ship is often the product of several adventitious circumstances. First, the ship must enter, or be about to enter, the court's jurisdictional reach. Secondly, the ship itself, the events giving rise to the claim and the parties to the controversy may have no connection at all to the forum other than the transitory presence there of the ship. Thirdly, the law governing the resolution of the dispute may be, and indeed, is likely to be, foreign. Each of these factors can enliven the question whether a maritime court should continue to exercise its jurisdiction to arrest the ship.

The two principal reasons why a maritime court will decline to exercise its jurisdiction to arrest, or continue the arrest of, a ship are that: first, the claim asserted by the arresting party is found on judicial examination not to be justiciable under the relevant national law; or secondly, although the claim is justiciable under that national law, the court will exercise a judicial discretion not to deal with the claim having regard to all of the circumstances. I propose to discuss each of these alternative bases in turn, principally drawing on the concepts in the Convention Relating to the Arrest of Sea-going Ships 1952 (the Arrest Convention 1952)[1] and the International Convention on the Arrest of Ships 1999 (the Arrest Convention 1999).[2]

* A Judge of the Federal Court of Australia and an additional Judge of the Supreme Court of the Australian Capital Territory. The author is currently a national convening Judge and New South Wales registry convening Judge for the Admiralty and Maritime National Practice Area and a member of the Comité Maritime International's International Working Group on Offshore Activities. The author acknowledges the assistance of his associates, Jack Coles and Georgia Allen, in the preparation and revision of this paper. Any errors are the author's alone.

[1] International Convention Relating to the Arrest of Sea-going Ships (adopted 10 May 1952, entered into force 24 February 1956) 439 UNTS 193.

[2] International Convention on the Arrest of Ships (adopted 12 March 1999, entered into force 14 September 2011) 2797 UNTS 3.

Strictly speaking, at least in the Common Law system, a court ordinarily does not have power to 'decline jurisdiction'. If a court has jurisdiction in a matter, it is seized of a controversy or dispute between parties that requires resolution according to law. The court must resolve the controversy exercising the authority of the State by the law of which it is constituted and determine the rights in issue.[3] A court will have jurisdiction to arrest a ship only if that court's national system of law gives the court the legal authority to do so in exercise of its judicial power as an instrument of government. The judiciary is the third arm of government in the Westminster system that informs the governmental structure of most Common Law States, where the other two arms are, obviously, the legislature and the executive or administration.

Judges do not have the luxury of choosing whether they wish to decide a case. The jurisdiction of a court is inextricably connected to its judicial power. A well-known, but not exhaustive, explanation of judicial power is that given by the first Chief Justice of Australia, Sir Samuel Griffith, as follows:[4]

> [T]he power which every sovereign authority must of necessity have to decide controversies between its subjects, or between itself and its subjects, whether the rights relate to life, liberty or property. The exercise of this power does not begin until some tribunal which has power to give a binding and authoritative decision (whether subject to appeal or not) is called upon to take action.

I have approached the topic of declining jurisdiction following arrest as referring to circumstances that a court would take into account in deciding whether: first, when the ex parte arrest of a ship is later challenged, the arresting party had failed to prove jurisdictional preconditions or facts necessary to give the court the authority to hear and determine the controversy concerning the claim that the party advanced to justify the arrest; or secondly, where the requisite jurisdictional preconditions or facts do exist, there is some legally cognisable reason why the court should exercise a discretion not to hear and determine the claim.

II. When an Arrest is Not within Jurisdiction

As explained by Professor Francesco Berlingieri in his work *Berlingieri on Arrest of Ships*,[5] the Arrest Convention 1952 marked the culmination of attempts initiated by the Comité Maritime International at its 1930 Conference in Antwerp to formulate an agreed instrument on the arrest of ships. Each of the Arrest Conventions 1952 and 1999 define 'arrest' similarly in art 1(2), but with some variation, to mean in effect any detention of a ship by a court to secure a maritime claim other than the seizure of a ship to enforce or satisfy a pre-existing judgment. The Arrest Convention 1999 broadened the list of maritime claims for

[3] See *Australian Securities & Investments Commission v Edensor Nominees Pty Ltd* [2001] HCA 1, (2001) 204 CLR 559 [2] (Gleeson CJ, Gaudron and Gummow JJ).

[4] *Huddart Parker & Co Pty Ltd v Moorehead* [1909] HCA 36, 8 CLR 330, 357. The Privy Council in *Shell Co of Australia Ltd v Federal Commissioner of Taxation* [1931] AC 275, 295–296, (1930) 44 CLR 530, 542–543 (Viscount Sankey LC, Viscount Dunedin, Lords Blanesburgh and Russell of Killowen and Anglin CJ) said that Sir Samuel Griffith's exposition was 'one of the best definitions' of judicial power.

[5] Francesco Berlingieri, *Berlingieri on Arrest of Ships*, 6th edn (Abingdon, Informa Law from Routledge, 2017) vol 1 paras 1.01–20.

which an arrest can be made and extended the class of persons, other than the owner of the ship, in respect of whose conduct or dealings a right to arrest could be exercised.

The list of 17 maritime claims in art 1(1) of the Arrest Convention 1952 foreshadowed the adoption of a common core of legislative provisions in, at least, the United Kingdom, Canada, New Zealand and Australia that expressly created or confirmed the categories of maritime claims that were within the respective in rem jurisdictions of those countries' maritime courts.[6] These include claims within art 1(1)(k), namely, a claim arising out of 'goods or materials wherever supplied to a ship for her operation or maintenance'. In countries that follow the jurisdictional theory of the Commercial Instruments and Maritime Liens Act[7] (US Liens Act), a claim based on such a supply can be used to found the arrest of a ship to enforce a statutory maritime lien, even though the contract for the supply did not involve the ship's owners or master as a party.[8]

Even then, the number of express categories varies from jurisdiction to jurisdiction. Australia's Parliament recognised in the Admiralty Act 1988 (Cth) four categories of proprietary maritime claims, including claims relating to a mortgage of a ship or shares in a ship[9] and 21 categories of general maritime claim[10] including categories that overlap with the separate statutory right to proceed in rem on a maritime lien for salvage,[11] damage done by a ship,[12] master's or crew member's wages[13] and master's disbursements.[14]

However, the Act did not define or identify all categories of maritime liens, including foreign maritime liens, that could be enforced in an action in rem in Australia under s 15(1). This is because the Australian Law Reform Commission in its 1986 report, *Civil Admiralty Jurisdiction* (ALRC Report), on which the Act was based, considered that this was best left to the courts.[15] The Commission chose not to define maritime liens in detail because of uncertainties in the then existing Australian and international law.[16]

[6] Australian Law Reform Commission, *Civil Admiralty Jurisdiction* (ALRC 33, 1986) (ALRC Report) paras 145–48.

[7] 46 USC §§ 31341–43. Canada also provides ship suppliers with a statutory maritime lien through the Marine Liability Act 2001 (SC 2001 c 6), s 139, discussed in Paul Myburgh, 'The Ship Supplier's Lien: Taking a (Maple) Leaf Out of the Canadian Statute Book?' [2010] *Asia Pacific Law Review* 279. See, eg, *Comfact Corp v Hull 717 (The)* 2012 FC 1161, (2012) 355 DLR (4th) 107; *Comfact Corp v Hull 717* (The) [2013] FCA 93; *Canpotex Shipping Services Ltd v Marine Petrobulk Ltd* 2015 FC 1108; *ING Bank NV v Canpotex Shipping Services Ltd* 2017 FCA 47; *Canpotex Shipping Services Ltd v Marine Petrobulk Ltd* 2018 FC 957.

[8] The same reasoning applies to claims under art 1(l) of the Arrest Convention 1999.

[9] Section 4(2).

[10] Section 4(3).

[11] Sections 4(3)(g) and 15(2)(a).

[12] Sections 4(3)(a) and 15(2)(b).

[13] Sections 4(3)(t) and 15(2)(c).

[14] Sections 4(3)(r) and 15(2)(d).

[15] ALRC Report (n 6) paras 122–23, 274.

[16] Section 15 provides:

15 Right to proceed *in rem* on maritime liens etc.

(1) A proceeding on a maritime lien or other charge in respect of a ship or other property subject to the lien or charge may be commenced as an action *in rem* against the ship or property.

(2) A reference in subsection (1) to a maritime lien includes a reference to a lien for:

(a) salvage;
(b) damage done by a ship;
(c) wages of the master, or of a member of the crew, of a ship; or
(d) master's disbursements.

The Arrest Conventions 1952 and 1999 recognised in art 9 the lack of international consensus on the recognition and enforcement of maritime liens by expressly leaving that topic well alone. I will explore the issue of maritime liens below when discussing the recent decision of the Full Court of the Federal Court of Australia in *The Ship Sam Hawk v Reiter Petroleum Inc.*[17]

Thus, national laws identify and, to a greater or lesser extent, define categories of maritime claims, including maritime liens, that can support an action, akin to the Common Law action in rem or the Civil Law process of maritime attachment, for the arrest of a ship. However, a maritime court must decide whether the claim asserted justifies the exercise of the power to arrest a ship when a shipowner[18] challenges the court's jurisdiction to do so.

Very often a challenge to the arrest of a ship will be the occasion for a maritime court to decide whether it had jurisdiction to make the arrest. A challenge to jurisdiction requires the arresting party, first, to prove the underlying facts that give the maritime court its jurisdiction and, secondly, to satisfy the court that its claim falls within a category of maritime claim, or is a maritime lien, that the law of the forum or lex fori can entertain. There usually will be a nexus between the plaintiff who arrests a ship on a maritime claim, although not necessarily on a maritime lien, and its owners that is encapsulated in the Australian Admiralty Act's definition in s 3(1) of 'relevant person', namely '*relevant person*, in relation to a maritime claim, means a person who would be liable on the claim in a proceeding commenced in an action *in personam*'.

In *The Owners of The Ship Shin Kobe Maru v Empire Shipping Company Inc*[19] the High Court of Australia held that the plaintiff has the onus of establishing that the court has jurisdiction where the defendant challenges an arrest of a ship. Their Honours held:

> Where jurisdiction depends on particular facts or a particular state of affairs, a challenge to jurisdiction can only be resisted by establishing the facts on which it depends. And, of course, they must be established on the balance of probabilities in the light of all the evidence advanced in the proceedings held to determine whether there is jurisdiction.

The question of jurisdiction must be answered by reference to the nature of the plaintiff's claim as put forward, without reference to the further issue of whether that claim is likely to succeed.[20]

Thus, the issue of whether someone is a relevant person for the purpose of establishing jurisdiction to arrest a ship will often turn on the nature of the claim, not its strength.

[17] *The Ship Sam Hawk v Reiter Petroleum Inc* [2016] FCAFC 26, (2016) 246 FCR 337.

[18] Or demise charterer, whom I will include generally in the expression 'owners' when referring in this Chapter to a challenge to an arrest brought by a shipowner or owners.

[19] *The Owners of The Ship Shin Kobe Maru v Empire Shipping Company Inc* [1994] HCA 54, (1994) 181 CLR 404, 426 (Mason CJ, Brennan, Deane, Dawson, Toohey, Gaudron and McHugh JJ). See too *The Ship Hako Endeavour v Programmed Total Marine Services Pty Ltd* [2013] FCAFC 21, (2013) 211 FCR 369 [37]–[42] (Rares J), [135]–[136] (Buchanan J), Siopis J agreeing with both judgments at [1]; *The Sam Hawk* (n 17) [189] (Allsop CJ and Edelman J), [247] (Kenny and Besanko JJ), [296] (Rares J). See also *The Bunga Melati 5* [2012] SGCA 46, [2012] 4 SLR 546; Koo Zhi Xuan, 'Navigating the Contours of Admiralty Jurisdiction' [2013] *LMCLQ* 290.

[20] *The Owners of the Motor Vessel Iran Amanat v KMP Coastal Oil Pte Ltd* [1999] HCA 11, (1999) 196 CLR 130 [18]–[20] (Gleeson CJ, McHugh, Gummow, Kirby and Hayne JJ).

Lord Diplock explained this concept, in relation to the Arrest Convention 1952 and the then United Kingdom legislation in *The Eschersheim*,[21] saying:

> It is clear that to be liable to arrest a ship must not only be the property of the defendant to the action but must also be identifiable as the ship in connection with which the claim made in the action arose (or a sister ship of that ship). *The nature of the 'connection' between the ship and the claim must have been intended to be the same as is expressed in the corresponding phrase in the Convention 'the particular ship in respect of which the maritime claim arose.' One must therefore look at the description of each of the maritime claims included in the list in order to identify the particular ship in respect of which a claim of that description could arise.* (emphasis added)

In other words, a maritime court will have jurisdiction only if the plaintiff establishes a sufficient nexus between the ship and the alleged in personam liability of the relevant person on that maritime claim as asserted. The question of jurisdictional fact is whether the relevant person *could* be found liable, at a trial, on the plaintiff's claim as it is put forward against that person. Of course, where the plaintiff's claim in rem is on a maritime lien, then the identity of the relevant person may be irrelevant. That is because a maritime lien is a privilege or claim upon a ship to be carried into effect by legal process, irrespective of whether the ownership or possession of the ship has changed between the circumstance creating the lien and the invocation of the court's jurisdiction over the ship.[22]

Not all disputed issues of jurisdictional fact are apt to, or will, be decided on a challenge to jurisdiction. Indeed, the ultimate question of whether the plaintiff can establish the merits of the factual basis of the asserted maritime claim is necessarily an issue that can only be determined at a substantive trial. If the facts, as proved at trial, result in a verdict or judgment in favour of the ship or of the relevant person or other defendant, then, in some cases, the maritime court will also decide that it lacked jurisdiction, not just because the plaintiff's claim failed on the merits, but because on a considered examination of the facts and law the claim was not one that, properly characterised, could have legitimately triggered the jurisdiction to arrest the ship in the first place.

The English approach, that is mirrored in jurisdictions such as Australia and Singapore, uses a two-stage statutory test of jurisdiction in creating a right to proceed in rem on maritime claims for owners' or demise charterers' liabilities, as well as claims against a sister or surrogate ship. That test requires the plaintiff to prove that the relevant person had a particular relationship with the arrested ship, or sister or surrogate ship, both at the time of the events giving rise to the asserted cause of action and at the time when the proceeding is commenced.[23] In Australia, the relevant person: first, has to have been, when the cause of action arose, the owner or charterer of, or in possession or control of, the ship; and secondly, has to be, at the time when the proceeding is commenced, the owner, demise charterer or owner of the targeted surrogate (or sister) ship,[24] depending on the particular statutory proceeding in rem that the plaintiff asserts.

[21] *The Eschersheim* [1976] 1 Lloyd's Rep 1, 7 (HL) (Lords Simon of Glaisdale, Kilbrandon, Salmon and Edmund-Davies agreeing).

[22] *Harmer v Bell (The Bold Buccleugh)* (1851) 7 Moo PC 267, 13 ER 884; see too *Stainbank v Fenning* (1851) 11 CB 51, 88–9, 138 ER 389, 403–4 (Jervis CJ).

[23] See, eg, ss 17, 18 and 19 of the Admiralty Act 1988 (Cth).

[24] ibid.

For example, in the Australian case of *The Iran Amanat*[25] the issue was whether the relevant person was a party to the contract for the supply of bunkers to sister ships of the ship that had been arrested. The High Court of Australia held that that dispute was concerned with the conditional question that the definition of 'relevant person' raised, namely whether the person 'would be liable' on the plaintiff's claim which was an issue for trial. Gleeson CJ, McHugh, Gummow, Kirby and Hayne JJ said of the double connection required of the relevant person:[26]

> [P]ars (a) and (b) are concerned with facts that may need to be established, whereas the liability to which the definition of 'relevant person' refers is hypothetical. *The difference between the conditional nature of the inquiry raised by the definition of 'relevant person' and the unconditional nature of the inquiry raised by pars (a) and (b) is important.* (emphasis added)

It follows that not every challenge to jurisdiction can, or should, be decided at a preliminary stage. That is because a person, self-evidently, will not be a 'relevant person' if, after a trial on contested issues of fact as to liability, it is established that he, she or it was not in fact liable on the maritime claim alleged. In a preliminary jurisdictional challenge, the 'unconditional nature of the inquiry' that the court is usually concerned to identify is whether the plaintiff's claim, as formulated, identifies a relevant person who, in fact, had the nexus or connection with the arrested ship at each of the time: (1) when the cause of action arose; and (2) when the proceeding in rem commenced. Ordinarily, the next inquiry is the conditional one, whether that person falls within the description of a person who, because of the identified nexus with the ship, is someone who would be liable in an action in personam.[27]

I do not propose to give a comprehensive overview of the approach taken in jurisdictions other than Australia as to the law and practice for determining whether an arrest should be set aside or refused. Nonetheless, some recent non-Australian Common Law cases may throw light on this for the purposes of discussion.

The Singapore Court of Appeal took a similar approach in *The Chem Orchid*.[28] However, the Court held that, in Singapore, a defendant could choose to challenge jurisdiction on an interlocutory or final basis and that, if the defendant took the former option by relying only on affidavit evidence, any finding of jurisdiction 'will necessarily be *prima facie* non-conclusive'.[29]

The position may be different in the United States of America. There, the US Liens Act creates: first, maritime liens for what the common law treats as the supply of necessaries; and secondly, a rebuttable presumption that, when contracting for the supply of necessaries to a ship, a wide range of persons, including time or voyage charterers and their agents, have authority to bind its owners and effect a maritime lien over that ship. Jurisdictional challenges there appear to proceed on applications for summary judgment. These applications are determined using the standard set by the Supreme Court of the United States in

[25] *The Iran Amanat* (n 20) [17]–[22]; and for the Full Court of the Federal Court of Australia decision, see *KMP Coastal Oil Pty Ltd v The Owners of Motor Vessel Iran Amanat* [1997] FCA 483, (1997) 75 FCR 78, 83–6.

[26] *The Iran Amanat* (n 20) [18].

[27] This is the explanation that I gave in *The Hako Endeavour* (n 19) [40]–[41].

[28] *The Chem Orchid* [2016] SGCA 4, [2016] 2 SLR 50 [44]–[47], [48] (Sundaresh Menon CJ, Chao Hick Tin and Andrew Phang Boon Leon JJA, Judith Prakash and Quentin Loh JJ; Chao Hick Tin JA delivering the grounds of decision of the Court).

[29] ibid [48].

Celotex Corp v Catrett,[30] that summary judgment is appropriate only if 'there is no genuine issue as to any material fact and that the moving party is entitled to a judgment as a matter of law'.[31]

Recently, the United States Fifth Circuit Court of Appeals followed decisions of its own, the Fourth[32] and the Ninth[33] Circuits, and distinguished a decision of the Second Circuit[34] as 'alone … arguably contrary'.[35] The Fifth Circuit Court of Appeals said that its jurisprudence 'unabashedly enforced, against a non-party to the contract, a maritime lien for vessel insurance, which was created under the auspices of a choice of law clause'.[36] It held that the maritime lien was effective against the owner, just as much as a subsequent owner, despite 'the third party's lack of knowledge and failure to acquiesce in the creation of the debt'.[37]

As the necessarily incomplete discussion above illustrates, each national maritime court will approach the resolution of challenges to its jurisdiction in arrest cases by having regard to its relevant statute law and unwritten or common law rules. The factors that can come into play in that context include the legal rules for interpreting both the written law of the forum and ascertaining, as well as applying, any applicable foreign law relevant to the particular dispute.

III. Characterising or Classifying a Foreign Maritime Claim in the Forum

From time to time an issue of principle will arise in the forum arresti as to how its substantive law will characterise or classify circumstances or dealings that have occurred outside the forum and that have a particular legal significance under the law of the place (lex loci) or governing the circumstances (lex causae) where they happened or the law chosen by the parties to the dealings as the governing or proper law.

In an open common law judicial field, when a novel question arises as to how the courts should determine a legal rule to govern the outcome of an unprecedented factual scenario, a judge must ultimately make a policy decision that selects from a range of potential legal rules and outcomes a result that he or she considers best does justice according to law. In making such a policy choice, the judge will often examine the history and context of the existing legal rules that apply to the resolution of issues that are relevantly analogous or instructive to the solution of the problem at hand.

In doing so, an important consideration is that the selection of a solution must be as harmonious as possible with the forum's contextual legal rules, including statute law, that apply in similar cases. After all, one aspect of the rule of law is its aspiration that like cases should be decided consistently and that everyone is equal before the law. Nonetheless, anyone

[30] *Celotex Corp v Catrett* 477 US 317, 322 (1986).

[31] See too, eg, *World Fuel Services Singapore Pte Ltd v Bulk Juliana M/V* 822 F 3d 766, 770 (5th Cir 2016).

[32] *Triton Marine Fuels Ltd v M/V Pacific Chukotka* 575 F 3d 409, 414 (4th Cir 2009).

[33] *Trans-Tec Asia v M/V Harmony Container* 518 F 3d 1120, 1127–28 (9th Cir 2008).

[34] *Rainbow Line Inc v M/V Tequila* 480 F 2d 1024 (2nd Cir 1973).

[35] *The Bulk Juliana* (n 31) 773.

[36] ibid, citing *London & Liverpool SS Protection and Indemnity Ass'n v Queen of Leman M/V* 296 F 3d 350, 354–55 (5th Cir 2002).

[37] *The Bulk Juliana* (n 31) 773.

familiar with the common law process of precedent readily understands that, from time to time, a legal rule develops in a particular area that may appear, at least to some reasonable persons, to be arbitrary itself, or to produce arbitrary or unfair outcomes.

The problem for the maritime court of the forum arresti is to identify the way in which, under its private international law rules, it must classify and give effect to the parties' rights that arose from their interaction or dealings that took place outside the forum either in, or governed by, another polity's laws or on the high seas. There is a reasonable likelihood of uncertainty in the ready identification of the law that governs any particular international maritime commercial dealing. That is because, in contractual disputes for supplies of necessaries, each party often will have its own standard form of invoice or order that contains boilerplate conditions including a clause that excludes the conditions proposed by the other party to the dealings. This leads to what Lord Denning MR described, with his characteristic elegance, as a 'battle of forms',[38] a phrase echoed by Chief Judge Richard Posner[39] who suggested that the 'battle of forms in this case takes the form of something very like a badminton game'.[40]

Each party's standard form usually will include choice of law and submission to jurisdiction clauses, and equally usually those will propose different applicable laws and jurisdictions for those purposes. Frequently, the actual contract will be made in a third jurisdiction and, if one of the contracting parties is a time or voyage charterer, will not involve, directly, the owners of the ship to which the necessaries are supplied.

The United States courts give a generous operation to contracts that provide for that nation's laws, and, in particular, its maritime liens, to apply to the supply of necessaries. Necessaries suppliers will not be shy in propounding their standard forms or other contractual terms in a way that will seek to apply a maritime lien to a ship to which they provide goods or services in whatever location in the world it might happen to be. So, if the necessaries suppliers, or other parties, whose contract or standard form includes the choice of United States law or the US Liens Act, plays the last shot and wins the battle of forms in creating a contract, the question for the court of the forum is whether, and if so how, that choice of law affects the winner's right to arrest the ship.

At the risk of being parochial, in *The Sam Hawk*,[41] a Full Court of five judges of the Federal Court of Australia, on which I sat, recently had to consider whether Australian law would recognise and enforce a foreign maritime lien that would not have existed had the relevant events occurred in the forum. If the lien were capable of recognition under Australian law, the arrest of the ship would have been sustained; whereas, if – as the Court held in overturning the primary judge – it were not, the arrest had to be set aside.

The reason why the case is germane to the topic of this Chapter, is that the question whether the Court had jurisdiction to arrest the *Sam Hawk* could be decided only after the Court considered: first, the factual context, including what national law or laws actually governed the parties' rights; secondly, the Australian private international law rules that applied in those circumstances; and thirdly, how, applying the governing law so ascertained,

[38] *Butler Machine Tool Co Ltd v Ex-Cell-O Corporation (England) Ltd* [1979] 1 WLR 401, 402E.

[39] *Northrop Corporation v Litronic Industries* 29 F 3d 1173, 1175 (7th Cir 1994).

[40] ibid. See also Giesela Rühl, 'The Battle of the Forms: Comparative and Economic Observations' (2003) 24 *University of Pennsylvania Journal of International Economic Law* 189.

[41] *The Sam Hawk* (n 17), discussed in Martin Davies, 'Recognition of Foreign Maritime Liens' [2017] *LMCLQ* 206; Mohammud Jaamae Hafeez-Baig, 'A Novel Approach to Foreign Maritime Liens' (2017) 133 *LQR* 378; Michael Douglas, 'Characterisation of a Foreign Maritime Lien by the Lex Fori' (2017) 17 *OUCLJ* 152.

Australian law should characterise and to what, if any, extent it should give effect to, those legal relationships in the forum.

The issue of whether the US Liens Act created a maritime lien cognisable in Australia arose in *The Sam Hawk*[42] in the following factual scenario. Egyptian Bulk Carriers Inc had time chartered the Hong Kong-flagged ship from its owners on terms that required, as is usual, the charterer, at its expense, to bunker the ship during the term of the charter. The charterparty did not authorise the charterer to contract for necessaries on behalf of the owners or to bind the *Sam Hawk* with a maritime lien for necessaries.

In late 2013, the charterers arranged with a Canadian bunker supplier, Reiter Petroleum Inc, to bunker the ship when it called at Istanbul in Turkey. Before bunkering occurred, the ship's master issued a 'no liability' notice to the initial bunker supply subcontractor and the shipping agent at Istanbul that stated that the owners did not accept liability to pay for bunkers, which was the responsibility of the named charterer. After this, Reiter issued a revised quote that the charterer accepted and, on 7 December 2013, the *Sam Hawk* received the bunkers. The revised quote stated that it was subject to Reiter's standard terms and conditions, which included one clause requiring any contract to be construed according to the law of Canada. However, that clause was itself subject to cl 7 that provided that Reiter was entitled to assert a lien wherever it found the ship and that the law of the United States would apply to determine the existence of any maritime lien regardless of the court in which proceedings were instituted.[43]

Needless to say, the charterer failed to pay for the bunkers. In May 2014, Reiter wrote to the owners informing them of this and seeking their assistance in persuading the charterers to honour their payment obligations. About 11 months after the bunker supply at Istanbul, Reiter filed a writ in rem in the Federal Court of Australia on which the *Sam Hawk* was arrested. The writ made two claims, namely, that Reiter had, first, a maritime lien[44] and, secondly, a general maritime claim for necessaries supplied to the ship,[45] on the basis that the owners were a relevant person who would be liable were the action commenced in personam.[46]

The Full Court summarily dismissed the latter claim, as having no reasonable prospect of success, because there was no evidence that the owners in any way had held the charterer out as having authority to bind them in a contract.[47] All five judges held that the owners were not a party to, or bound by, the contract between the bunker supplier and the charterer. We held that parties who had no interest in a ship could not create a maritime lien in rem in relation to the ship that would bind it or its owners in respect of either a ship flagged, or events that occurred, in a jurisdiction, the law of neither of which created such a lien of the kind that the US Liens Act and its analogues do.[48]

Apart from the bunker supply contract, nothing about the bunker supply in Turkey connected the *Sam Hawk* or its owners, first, to the United States or its laws and, secondly,

[42] *The Sam Hawk* (n 17).

[43] ibid [13]–[19] (Allsop CJ and Edelman J), [194]–[198] (Kenny and Besanko JJ) and see too [294]–[295] (Rares J).

[44] Under s 15 of the Admiralty Act 1988 (Cth).

[45] Under ss 17 and 4(3)(m) of the Admiralty Act 1988 (Cth).

[46] *The Sam Hawk* (n 17) [20]–[22].

[47] ibid [32]–[35] (Allsop CJ and Edelman J), [270]–[274] (Kenny and Besanko JJ), [291] (Rares J).

[48] ibid [181]–[186] (Allsop CJ and Edelman J), [257]–[259] (Kenny and Besanko JJ), [296]–[303] (Rares J).

to the necessaries suppliers, that is, Reiter. In substance, the necessaries suppliers claimed that a shipowner willingly allowed a time charterer to create a maritime lien over its ship, even though all persons involved (owner, time charterer and necessaries suppliers) knew, both at the time that the bunker supply contract was made and at the place of supply, that the charterer had no proprietary rights over the ship but rather had the obligation to bunker it for the duration of the charterparty.[49]

In other words, the necessaries suppliers were seeking to appropriate the ship – being the property of a third party, the owners – as security for payment of the charterer's debt, without the owners' knowledge or agreement, based on a contract between the necessaries suppliers and the charterer. Both parties to that contract knew, or in the necessaries supplier's case, at least would have thought it highly likely, that the charterparty prohibited the charterer from creating any liability on behalf of the owners or any lien over the ship and that, at best, it was speculative whether a maritime lien could arise outside a nation in which the US Liens Act or an analogue applied as a statute governing the transaction.

Accordingly, both parties to the bunkering contract were seeking, without the owners' knowledge or authority, to convert or arrogate the owners' property in the ship, for their own private interests, as security for the charterers' personal liability. A sense of commercial morality in respect of such behaviour outside jurisdictions where the US Liens Act and its analogues apply seems to have been bypassed, perhaps because it is sanctioned by such legislation. Indeed, the underlying case theory for a necessaries supplier's claim that arises from a supply in a jurisdiction in which the US Liens Act or an analogue does not have the force of law, might well have been characterised by Sir Humphrey Appleby, of the television series *Yes Minister*, as 'courageous'.[50]

This brings me to the more legally interesting issue in the *Sam Hawk*[51] appeal, namely the hitherto unanswered question of whether Australian law should recognise and enforce a foreign maritime lien that had no counterpart in domestic law. The Full Court was confronted by two legal systems of civilised democracies that placed persons in frequently experienced commercial situations in radically different positions. Thus, whatever solution the Court adopted on the question of whether Australian law should or should not decline jurisdiction to recognise and enforce an *in rem* claim that asserted a foreign maritime lien, inevitably, the choice would produce an outcome discordant with that offered by the legal system whose solution to the same situation would be different, were its entire facts to occur wholly within the one forum.

It is necessary to determine what private international law rules should govern the identification of a right that arises under a foreign law as the lex causae and then to ascertain whether and how that right can be enforced in the forum. In *The Sam Hawk*[52] Kenny and Besanko JJ jointly, and I separately, discussed this issue in obiter dicta. In contrast,

[49] I said this ibid at [298], which was the common basis on which all five judges rejected the claim.

[50] Sir Humphrey Appleby, GCB, KBE, MVO, MA (Oxon), a fictional character from the British television series *Yes Minister* and *Yes Prime Minister*, was originally played by the actor Sir Nigel Hawthorne. Sir Humphrey was wont to describe any Minister's plans that he viewed as wrong-headed and dangerous, and thus wished to thwart, as being 'very brave' or 'courageous' decisions, whereupon the Minister would usually abandon them immediately. See generally Graham McCann, *A Very Courageous Decision: The Inside Story of Yes Minister* (Islington, Aurum Press Ltd, 2014).

[51] *The Sam Hawk* (n 17).

[52] ibid [242], [275] [292]–[293], [304].

Allsop CJ and Edelman J decided, as one of their rationes decidendi, that Australian law would not recognise a foreign maritime lien.[53] They followed the approach of the majority of the Privy Council[54] in *Bankers Trust International Ltd v Todd Shipyards Corporation (The Halcyon Isle)*.[55] Moreover, Kenny and Besanko JJ, without deciding the issue, said that they favoured the same approach.[56] I favoured the view that[57]

> Australian choice of law principles for both contract and tort claims ordinarily require the *lex loci* or *lex causae* to be used to classify the substance of the particular claim. Accordingly, a claim on a maritime lien that is properly so characterised under the law of the place where it attached, ordinarily, will be maintainable under s 15(1) of the *Admiralty Act* even though no such maritime lien would attach if the same events had occurred in Australia.

All five judges considered, like both the majority and minority[58] in *The Halcyon Isle*,[59] that the unusually ambiguous reasoning of Bankes, Scrutton and Atkin LJJ in *The Colorado*,[60] like the curate's egg, was good in part and supported their respective conclusions.

The result of the preference of Kenny and Besanko JJ for the approach in the reasons of Allsop CJ and Edelman J, is likely to be that Australian law will classify a claim to proceed in rem on a maritime lien under s 15 of the Admiralty Act as follows. First, the asserted foreign right must be characterised, usually by the lex fori, to determine whether it is properly described as a 'maritime lien'. Ordinarily, this characterisation process will have regard to the priority that the law of the forum would apply to a claim asserting a local right of the same nature as the foreign right.[61] Allsop CJ and Edelman J regarded their analysis as being consistent with that contemplated in the Australian Law Reform Commission Report[62] on which the Admiralty Act 1988 (Cth) is based.

Their Honours reasoned that a key consequence of the recognition of a maritime lien by the lex fori is the priority that the law of the forum gives it in ranking of claims. Accordingly, they reasoned it would not be appropriate to 'decouple' the analysis of the category of legal right that the law of the forum had to characterise from the remedy that the forum would accord to such a right.[63] They said that s 15 of the Admiralty Act did not evince a legislative intention or reflect a policy purpose 'that a new maritime lien without priority should be recognised'. Allsop CJ and Edelman J quoted the following passage from the ALRC 33 report:[64]

> [T]he consequences of recognising a foreign maritime lien (for example for goods supplied to a ship) where the equivalent local claim does not give rise to a lien is to give the foreign claimant priority over the local one, even where the foreign law's classification of the claim as a lien is out of line with any international consensus on the scope of liens.

[53] ibid [91]–[92].
[54] Lords Diplock, Elwyn-Jones and Lane.
[55] *Bankers Trust International Ltd v Todd Shipyards Corporation (The Halcyon Isle)* [1981] AC 221, discussed in Steven Rares, 'Maritime Liens, *Renvoi* and Conflicts of Law: The Far from *Halcyon Isle*' [2014] *LMCLQ* 183.
[56] *The Sam Hawk* (n 17) [287].
[57] ibid [430].
[58] Lords Salmon and Scarman.
[59] *The Halcyon Isle* (n 55).
[60] *The Colorado* [1923] P 102 (CA).
[61] *The Sam Hawk* (n 17) [99], [282]–[283].
[62] ALRC 33 (n 6).
[63] *The Sam Hawk* (n 17) [99].
[64] ALRC 33 (n 6) para 123; *The Sam Hawk* (n 17) [99].

Their Honours concluded that:[65]

> Because the characterisation of a right as a maritime lien involves consideration of the nature of the foreign rights *and* the priority consequence of those rights, it is necessary when characterising the foreign rights to consider the circumstances in which those rights arose. Those circumstances are essential to determine whether the foreign rights are the same as, or analogous to, those rights which would be a maritime lien in Australia which would be given the priority of a maritime lien.

Allsop CJ and Edelman J, together with Kenny and Besanko JJ, reasoned that the priority rules of the lex fori were matters of substance, rather than procedure. Therefore, they held that the appropriate analytical process for categorising a foreign law right in the forum involved two steps: first, ascertaining the nature of that right under the lex causae to see whether it is the same as, or analogous to, a local right; and secondly, characterising that right by reference to Australian law, including its place in the forum's priority rules.[66]

Importantly, in *The Halcyon Isle*[67] both the majority and minority had proceeded on the principle that, because it related to the remedy to be enforced, the ranking of priorities was a matter of procedure, rather than substance, and was therefore determined by the lex fori. Allsop CJ and Edelman J followed the ultimate decision of the majority in *The Halcyon Isle*[68] that a foreign right should be recognised by reference to the lex causae but classified and characterised by reference to its legal effect under the lex fori, although the event might have occurred elsewhere, and then applying the priorities rules of the forum.[69] However, their Honours held, having regard to modern Australian choice of law principles, that Lord Diplock's reasoning had been incorrect when his Lordship described a system of priorities as a matter of procedure, rather than of substance.[70] Their Honours said[71] that this followed from the application of conflicts principles elucidated by the High Court of Australia in *John Pfeiffer Pty Ltd v Rogerson*[72] and *Regie Nationale des Usines Renault SA v Zhang*.[73]

The selection of a choice of law rule for these purposes is one on which I like to think, as the sole voice to the contrary, reasonable minds might differ. In my wilderness, I considered that Australian choice of law rules, against the historical international background that I traced to the early 17th century, favoured the recognition and enforcement of a foreign maritime lien by Australian courts in a proceeding in rem. I regarded as a sound guide what Holt LCJ said at the turn of the 18th century as to why a foreign maritime lien should be recognised:[74]

> *No master of a ship can have credit abroad but upon the security by hypothecation*, and shall we hinder the Court of Admiralty from giving remedy, when we can give none ourselves? *It will be*

[65] *The Sam Hawk* (n 17) [101]; and see [282] (Kenny and Besanko JJ).

[66] ibid [102]–[106], [286].

[67] *The Halcyon Isle* (n 55) 230A-B (Lord Diplock), 244A-C (Lords Salmon and Scarman).

[68] ibid.

[69] *The Sam Hawk* (n 17) [180]–[188].

[70] ibid [160] and see too [286] where Kenny and Besanko JJ agreed on this point.

[71] ibid [103], [105], [134], [159].

[72] *John Pfeiffer Pty Ltd v Rogerson* [2000] HCA 36, 203 CLR 503 [99] (Gleeson CJ, Gaudron, McHugh, Gummow and Hayne JJ).

[73] *Regie Nationale des Usines Renault SA v Zhang* [2002] HCA 10, 210 CLR 491 [34], [66] (Gleeson CJ, Gaudron, McHugh, Gummow and Hayne JJ).

[74] *Johnson v Shippen* (1703) 2 Ld Raym 982, 983, 92 ER 154, 155.

the greatest prejudice to trade that can be, to grant a prohibition in this case. Indeed if a ship be hypothecated here in England before the voyage begin, that is not a matter within the jurisdiction of the Court of Admiralty, for it is a contract made here, and the owners can give security to perform the contract. (emphasis added; footnotes omitted)

Our historical analyses in *The Sam Hawk*[75] showed – if more proof were needed than was evident in the failures, over the years, of Conventions on maritime liens and ship mortgages to attract sufficient ratifications by States Parties to give them general acceptance[76] – that the recognition and enforcement of foreign maritime liens is a subject-matter that has bedevilled international trade and commerce for centuries.

IV. Discretionary Reasons for Declining Jurisdiction Following Arrest

The structure of the 1952 and 1999 Arrest Conventions is to create the right to arrest in respect of particular categories of maritime claim. In the preceding discussion I have dealt with the situation where the nature of the claim as asserted, as opposed to whether the facts necessary to prove the claim itself, when judicially examined, did not meet the jurisdictional criteria for such a claim.

In contrast, there are also occasions when a claim possesses all the formal characteristics to justify the invocation of Common Law in rem jurisdiction or Civilian maritime attachment, yet the circumstances lead to the court ordering the ship to be released from arrest. I propose to discuss four situations in which it may be appropriate for a court to exercise its discretion to decline jurisdiction following arrest – first, where the arresting party has failed in his, her or its duty to make a full disclosure of all material facts on the ex parte application when causing the ship to be arrested; secondly, where there is an arbitration agreement warranting a stay; thirdly, where the ship, its owners or demise charterers seek a stay on forum non conveniens grounds; and fourthly, where a stay is in place or sought because the owners are insolvent.

A. Non-Disclosure

Each maritime court will have its own rules dealing with the formal requirements that must be satisfied to support the issue of an arrest warrant or other similar court process. Some of those formal requirements concern what the person applying for the arrest must disclose to the court or court officer responsible for issuing the warrant.

In Australia, the Admiralty Rules 1988 (Cth) require a party applying for an arrest to disclose specific matters,[77] including matters of which the party is aware, that could affect

[75] *The Sam Hawk* (n 17).

[76] The Convention on Maritime Liens and Mortgages 1967 has never entered into force. The Conventions on Maritime Liens and Mortgages 1926 and 1993 have not been widely ratified by Civil Law countries and have been shunned by Common Law countries altogether. For more details, see comitemaritime.org/publications-documents/status-of-conventions/.

[77] Admiralty Rules 1988 (Cth), rr 39, 39A and 40.

the safety of the Marshal, master, crew or any other person or ship or other property in, or in relation to, the arrest or custody of the ship, or which relate to the risk of pollution by or from the ship,[78] the existence of relevant caveats against arrest or any payment into court including any that has had the effect of creating a stay or the filing of a bail bond.[79]

In *Altasnavios Navegacao LDA v The Ship Xin Tai Hai (No 2)*[80] I discussed disclosure requirements and the different obligations of the party seeking the issue of an arrest warrant in Australia, England, Hong Kong and Singapore.[81] I found that nothing in the Admiralty Rules or otherwise required the party seeking the issue of a warrant to disclose to the Registrar, as the person responsible for issuing it, more than the information specified in the relevant rule,[82] provided that, if the person became aware that evidence or other material originally placed before the Registrar in applying for the issue of the warrant was incorrect, or no longer correct, the person will have a duty forthwith to place the new matter fully and frankly before the Registrar.[83] That is because in Australia, there is no discretion provided in the Rules as to whether a warrant should issue, no doubt because the ALRC 33 report said: 'Arrest is a legal remedy available as of right; the Mareva injunction is equitable and discretionary.'[84]

In contrast, in both Hong Kong and Singapore, the power to issue an arrest warrant is discretionary. The courts in each of those jurisdictions require plaintiffs to make full and frank disclosure of all material facts in making applications for the issue of a warrant. In Hong Kong, the English Rules applicable when *The Andria now renamed Vasso*[85] was decided also operated in the then British Territory and, unsurprisingly, the Hong Kong Court of Appeal followed that decision in *Sin Hua Enterprise Co Ltd v The Owners of the Motor Ship 'Harima'*.[86] The Singapore Court of Appeal[87] took a similar view of the discretionary power to issue an arrest warrant in O 70 r 4(1) of the Rules of Court.[88]

As I also wrote in *The Xin Tai Hai (No 2)*:[89]

> The treatment of the circumstances in which a ship may be arrested has varied in England in the last 30 years. In *The Andria now renamed Vasso*,[90] Waller, Slade and Robert Goff LJJ held that it was axiomatic that, in *ex parte* proceedings seeking the issue of an arrest warrant, the plaintiff had a duty to make full and frank disclosure of all material facts known to it. That was because under the then form of O 75 r 5(1) of the *Rules of the Supreme Court 1965* (Eng) (RSC) the power to order an arrest was discretionary, not mandatory and the Court's exercise of its power could be affected

[78] ibid, r 39A.
[79] ibid, r 40 and the affidavit to support application for arrest warrant in Form 13 prescribed by the Rules.
[80] *Altasnavios Navegacao LDA v The Ship Xin Tai Hai (No 2)* [2012] FCA 1497, 215 FCR 265 [61]–[105].
[81] ibid [72]–[74].
[82] Admiralty Rules 1988 (Cth), r 40.
[83] *The Xin Tai Hai (No 2)* (n 80) [88]–[89], [91]–[92].
[84] ALRC 33 (n 6) para 245.
[85] *The Andria now renamed Vasso* [1984] QB 477.
[86] *Sin Hua Enterprise Co Ltd v The Owners of the Motor Ship Harima* [1987] HKCA 284, [1987] HKLR 770, 772D–73B.
[87] *The Rainbow Spring* [2003] SGCA 31, [2003] 3 SLR(R) 362 [32]; *The Vasiliy Golovnin* [2008] SGCA 39 (CA), [2008] 4 SLR 994 [83]–[84]; see also Toh Kian Sing, *Admiralty Law and Practice*, 3rd edn (LexisNexis, Singapore 2017) 190–98; Eugene Cheng Jiankai, 'Fulfilling the Duty of Full and Frank Disclosure in Arrest of Ships – Identifying, Consolidating and Presenting Material Facts' (2017) 29 *S Ac LJ* 317.
[88] Cap 332 r 5, 1997 rev edn (Sing).
[89] *The Xin Tai Hai (No 2)* (n 80) [72]–[73].
[90] *The Andria* (n 85) 491G–92B.

by the manner in which, or the purpose for which, the plaintiff had proceeded. In *The Stephan J*[91] Sheen J followed, without referring to it, the principle in *The Vasso*,[92] requiring full and frank disclosure in an application for an arrest warrant.

As a result of that decision, RSC O 75 r 5 was amended in 1986 to provide for the issue of an arrest warrant as of right, so that it was no longer a discretionary remedy: *The Varna*[93] per Scott LJ with whom Rose LJ agreed. Their Lordships held that, as a consequence, the issue of the warrant now being as of right, the requirement for full and frank disclosure mandated by the decision in *The Vasso*[94] was not engaged. The current position in England now appears to be the same as that in the early twentieth century described in *Halsbury's Laws of England*[95] where the editors (Lord Merrivale P, Langton J and H Gordon Willmer) said that the warrant was usually issued as of course unless a caveat against arrest were entered.[96]

B. Arbitration

Articles 7(2) and (3) of the 1952 Arrest Convention and arts 7(1), (2) and (3) of the 1999 Arrest Convention provide that, where the parties have agreed to submit the dispute to the jurisdiction of a court of another State or to arbitration, the court of the forum can retain any security or bail provided to obtain the release of the ship to abide, and if necessary satisfy, any judgment in those other proceedings or any award in the arbitration. This policy is reflected in s 29 of the Admiralty Act 1988 (Cth) and its international analogues.[97]

Those provisions enable the local courts to hold parties to a maritime dispute to their prior agreement to a foreign forum selection mechanism for either judicial or arbitral resolution of their disputes, while allowing a party who would otherwise have a justiciable claim in the local jurisdiction to obtain appropriate security there. That ensures that, if the foreign proceedings or arbitration results in the party's favour, there will be funds held as security in the court of the forum to satisfy the judgment or award.[98]

This power gives the arresting court an important discretion to enable it to hold parties to their bargains. Moreover, soon after the adoption of the 1952 Arrest Convention, the significance of international arbitration came to be cemented by the now widely adopted Convention on the Recognition and Enforcement of Foreign Arbitral Awards 1958, known as the New York Convention.[99] That Convention is now complemented by the 1985 UNCITRAL Model Law on International Commercial Arbitration,[100] both of which, substantially, have force of law in Australia,[101] and at least one of which has

[91] *The Stephan J* [1985] 2 Lloyd's Rep 344, 346.
[92] *The Andria* (n 85).
[93] *The Varna* [1993] 2 Lloyd's Rep 253, 255–256.
[94] *The Andria* (n 85).
[95] *Halsbury's Laws of England*, 2nd edn (London, Butterworth, 1931) vol 1 para 160.
[96] ibid para 165; see also *In re Aro Co Ltd* [1980] Ch 196, 206A (Stephenson, Brandon and Brightman LJJ).
[97] See ch 3; Berlingieri (n 5) vol 1 paras 16.67–88 (1952 Arrest Convention); Steven Rares, 'Australia's Sea Change: Towards Developing a Comprehensive System of Admiralty and Maritime Dispute Resolution for Twenty-First Century Trade in the Asia-Pacific Region' (2008) 30 *Australian Bar Review* 242.
[98] See ch 3 for a detailed discussion of the various forms of security arrest.
[99] Convention on the Recognition and Enforcement of Foreign Arbitral Awards (adopted 10 June 1958, entered into force 7 June 1959) 330 UNTS 3.
[100] See www.uncitral.org/uncitral/en/uncitral_texts/arbitration/1985Model_arbitration.html.
[101] Pursuant to the International Arbitration Act 1974 (Cth).

effect in most maritime nations. The significance to trade and commerce of those two international mechanisms for the recognition and enforcement of arbitration agreements and awards cannot be gainsaid. After an arrest to obtain security, for an arbitration, it is legitimate for the court later to release the ship so that the ship and arbitration can both proceed.

C. Forum Non Conveniens

Quite apart from the situation of a contractual forum selection clause or arbitration agreement justifying a stay under art 7 of the 1952 and 1999 Arrest Conventions, the circumstances in a particular case may call for a stay of proceedings in the local forum based on its principles for dealing with the appropriateness of hearing the dispute in one jurisdiction rather than another. These considerations can also arise when a proceeding is already pending in another jurisdiction – lis alibi pendens.[102] As is well known, the legal tests greatly vary on which different national legal regimes will stay proceedings based on what, for convenience at the expense of accuracy, I will call forum non conveniens grounds.

Since Lord Goff of Chieveley's foundational speech in *Spiliada Maritime Corp v Cansulex Ltd*,[103] English law has applied a principle of ascertaining 'the forum in which the case can be suitably tried for the interests of all the parties and for the ends of justice' to determine whether to stay domestic proceedings when the courts of another forum are available. In contrast, Australian law, since *Voth v Manildra Flour Mills Pty Ltd*,[104] requires that a stay only be granted if the local court is a clearly inappropriate forum. That test does not contemplate a comparison between jurisdictions or court systems. However, the court can take account of whether the effect of continuation of the local proceedings on the defendant would be oppressive or vexatious.

Where parallel proceedings have been brought in a local and a foreign court, Australian law considers that prima facie it is vexatious and oppressive to bring proceedings concerning the same issues in different countries that have jurisdiction in respect of the matter.[105]

One factor that Australian law has accepted as relevant to determining whether a stay of proceedings is appropriate in a case of lis alibi pendens is a consideration of which is the natural and obvious forum for the hearing of the controversy.[106]

[102] See William Tetley, *International Conflict of Laws: Common, Civil and Maritime* (Montreal, Blais, 1994) 796–99.

[103] *Spiliada Maritime Corp v Cansulex Ltd* [1987] AC 460, 480G; and see *VTB Capital plc v Nutritek International Corp* [2013] 2 AC 337 [12] (Lord Mance JSC), [80] (Lord Neuberger of Abbotsbury PSC), [156] (Lord Wilson JSC).

[104] *Voth v Manildra Flour Mills Pty Ltd* [1990] HCA 55, 171 CLR 538, 554, 558–59, 564 (Mason CJ, Deane, Dawson and Gaudron JJ) – I summarised the principles more fully in *The Xin Tai Hai (No 2)* (n 80) [108]–[110].

[105] *Henry v Henry* [1996] HCA 51, 185 CLR 571, 590–91 (Dawson, Gaudron, McHugh and Gummow JJ); *The Xin Tai Hai (No 2)* (n 80) [112]–[113]; *CMA CGM SA v Ship Chou Shan* [2014] FCA 74 [110]–[111], [129], [150]–[152] (McKerracher J); affirmed *CMA CGM SA v The Ship Chou Shan* [2014] FCAFC 90, 224 FCR 384 (Allsop CJ, Besanko and Pagone JJ).

[106] *The Chou Shan* [2014] FCAFC 90, 224 FCR 384 [62]–[63]: see too the discussion in M Davies and A Dickey, *Shipping Law*, 4th edn (Pyrmont, Thomson Reuters, 2016) para 16.250.

D. Cross-Border Insolvency

The recent collapse of several large shipping groups has illustrated the impact of globalisation on the traditional remedies available to persons with rights to proceed in rem on maritime liens and maritime claims.[107] In times past, as the 1952 and 1999 Arrest Conventions recognised, a person claiming to have a maritime lien or maritime claim could seek to arrest a ship in the territorial waters of any country into which it had sailed. The claim would then be heard and determined in the forum arresti, regardless of the solvency or corporate group structure of its owners. The local maritime court had plenary jurisdiction to sell the ship by judicial sale and in doing so would clean its hull of all maritime liens and other claims.[108] The proceeds of sale would be distributed to creditors or claimants in order of priority determined under the local law, irrespective of the shipowners' financial position, or if they were insolvent, the position in the owners' country of incorporation or centre of main interests.

However, in the late 20th century the reach of multinational corporations and groups spread. Their impact was particularly evident when recessions occurred. The international consequences of a multinational's economic collapse manifested in the impracticality and capriciousness of using only local assets of the corporation to pay local creditors in a forum and then return any surplus to the place where the company was incorporated or where the group-holding company was. That could lead to vastly different distributions to creditors of the insolvent multinational company depending on the particular country in which its assets, debts or creditors happened to be.

This led eventually to the development of the Model Law on Cross-Border Insolvency by the United Nations Commission on International Trade Law (UNCITRAL).[109] The Model Law appears largely to have been based on the European Union Convention on Insolvency Proceedings done at Brussels on 23 November 1995, which was in the process of adoption during the drafting process for the Model Law.[110]

The preamble to the Model Law states that its purpose is to provide effective mechanisms for dealing with cross-border insolvencies and to promote, among other objects, fair and efficient administration of cross-border insolvencies that protects the interests of all creditors and other interested persons, including the debtor, and protection and maximisation of

[107] On which see further ch 9; Lia Athanassiou, *Maritime Cross-Border Insolvency: Under the European Insolvency Regulation and the UNCITRAL Model Law* (Abingdon, Informa Law, 2017); Mohammud Jaamae Hafeez-Baig, 'Navigating the Waters between Admiralty and Cross-Border Insolvency: A Comparison of the Australian, German and French Positions' [2018] *LMCLQ* 97; Steven Rares, 'Ship Arrests, Maritime Liens and Cross-Border Insolvency' [2018] *LMCLQ* 398.

[108] See generally Lief Bleyen, *Judicial Sales of Ships: A Comparative Study*, Hamburg Studies on Maritime Affairs 36 (Hamburg, Springer International Publishing, 2016).

[109] Given the force of law in Australia by s 6 of the Cross-Border Insolvency Act 2008 (Cth), in South Korea by the Debtor Rehabilitation and Bankruptcy Act, and adopted in ch 15 of the United States of America's Bankruptcy Code in Title 11 of its United States Code.

[110] European Union Convention on Insolvency Proceedings 1995 (1996) 35 ILM 1223, superseded by the Insolvency Regulation (Regulation (EU) 2015/848 of the European Parliament and of the Council of 20 May 2015 on insolvency proceedings [2015] OJ L141/19). Compare *Ackers v Saad Investments Company Ltd (in official liquidation)* [2010] FCA 1221, 190 FCR 285; *Re Eurofood IFSC Ltd* [2006] Ch 508; *Re Bear Stearns High-Grade Structured Credit Strategies Master Fund Ltd (in prov liq)* 389 BR 325 (SD NY 2008).

the value of the debtor's assets.[111] The Model Law provides a straightforward structure for the local forum to recognise, under art 17, a foreign insolvency proceeding such as liquidations, receiverships, bankruptcies or debtor in possession reconstruction procedures, along the lines of ch 11 bankruptcies in the United States Bankruptcy Code.[112]

Recognition is a two-step process. First, the person authorised by law to administer the insolvent's estate in a foreign jurisdiction, called a foreign representative,[113] must apply under art 15 for the local court to recognise the foreign proceeding, which is either a foreign main, or non-main, proceeding. The former is a proceeding in the place where the debtor has its centre of main interests;[114] while the latter is a proceeding in another jurisdiction where the debtor has an establishment, being, in effect, a place of real and non-transitional economic activity involving individuals and goods or services.[115]

Once a foreign representative makes an application for recognition of a foreign proceeding, art 19 provides for the local forum to grant provisional relief, if it is urgently needed, to protect the assets of the debtor or the interests of the creditors including, relevantly, staying execution against the debtor's assets.[116] Frequently, the foreign representative in cases involving shipping groups also obtains provisional relief in the nature of a general stay preventing the commencement or continuation of proceedings concerning the debtor's assets, rights, obligations or liabilities (as contemplated on an order for recognition of a foreign main proceeding under art 20(1)(a) or a foreign proceeding under art 21(1)(a)). However, art 22 requires the court in granting or denying relief, relevantly, under art 19, to be satisfied that the interests of all interested persons, including the creditors and the debtor, are adequately protected.

Very often, foreign representatives of collapsed shipping groups bring recognition proceedings before commercial or insolvency judges with no experience of maritime law or its remedies and obtain court orders staying commencement or continuation of proceedings, in the language of art 20(1)(a), 'concerning the debtor's assets'. An application to arrest a ship is a proceeding that concerns the ship, which is one of the debtor's assets, and thus prima facie falls within the ambit of art 20(1)(a). An admiralty arrest can be, and often is, forestalled by such an order. The ship is considered to be a person and is the only defendant in proceedings in rem until the relevant person appears, at least in countries like Australia, where the personification theory still applies,[117] notwithstanding the position in England following the decision of *The Indian Grace*.[118]

The Federal Court of Australia, being a national court with general jurisdiction over both maritime and insolvency matters, has addressed this situation by requiring applications under the Model Law for recognition of foreign proceedings to be made to specialist judges assigned to its Admiralty and Maritime National Practice Area. The Court's practice in such cases is to modify the stay order by providing that any application to arrest a ship owned or chartered by the debtor brought by a person claiming to hold a security interest in

[111] Preamble, paras (c) and (d).
[112] Which has analogues in both South Korea and Japan.
[113] Article 2(d).
[114] See *Ackers* (n 110).
[115] Articles 2(a)–(c), 2(f).
[116] Article 19(1)(a).
[117] *Comandate Marine Corp v Pan Australia Shipping Pty Ltd* [2006] FCAFC 192, 157 FCR 45.
[118] *Republic of India v India Steamship Co Ltd (No 2) (The Indian Grace)* [1998] AC 878.

it be made to a judge of the Court. Drawing attention to the reasons for those orders and to the earlier decision in *Yu v STX Pan Ocean Co Ltd (South Korea)*,[119] Allsop CJ in *Yakushiji v Daiichi Chuo Kisen Kaisha*[120] explained the purpose of this qualification to what would otherwise be a general stay preventing any arrest as follows:

> [T]he protection given by the orders to a shipping company should not be seen as necessarily defeating proper maritime claims that are lien claims, and the question of the status of any claims that are lien claims (as well as the status of any claims that are 'quasi lien claims', to which I have referred), would need to be resolved in any litigation unless the matter were agreed. It would be wrong to make orders now that would forestall any vindication by such claimants against the interests of the rehabilitation. Likewise, it would be wrong to prevent the rehabilitation being supported by the Act on the mere possibility of the existence of these claims.

Allsop CJ's reference to 'quasi lien claims' included maritime claims against a ship in a proceeding in rem filed in the Court before the making of the recognition order, not being maritime liens, about which his Honour said there was a live issue.[121] Even where a ship has not yet been arrested, and may not yet have entered the local forum's waters, English and Australian cases[122] have held that the creditor, on commencing a proceeding in rem, becomes a secured creditor and, then, is not subject to automatic legislative stays preventing an unsecured creditor from commencing or continuing proceedings, once an order for sequestration or winding up is made.[123]

In one sense, the preceding discussion is more focused on asserting, rather than declining, jurisdiction and doing so before, rather than after, arrest. Nonetheless, the discussion is pertinent to considering orders in relation to: first, the continuation of proceedings in an action in rem on a maritime lien or maritime claim that have been commenced, but in which no arrest has been made when a recognition order under the Model Law takes effect; and secondly, the commencement or continuation of proceedings for such a claim after a recognition order is made.

In such situations, a court may have to strike balances between competing public policies reflected in statutes conferring rights to proceed in rem, on the one hand; and providing for the orderly administration in another jurisdiction of a debtor's affairs under the Model Law, on the other. There will be cases where, as I suggested in *Hur v Samsun Logix Corp*,[124] the interests of justice require that an unpaid ship's crew be entitled immediately to enforce their maritime lien over the ship because:[125]

> The fact that they are unpaid and are on a ship from which, if penniless, they cannot escape is a very good reason to ensure that however else the automatic stay in Art 20(2) of the *Model Law* operates, claims to such maritime liens are protected and immediately enforceable without

[119] *Yu v STX Pan Ocean Co Ltd (South Korea)* [2013] FCA 680, 223 FCR 1889 (Buchanan J).

[120] *Yakushiji v Daiichi Chuo Kisen Kaisha* [2015] FCA 1170, (2015) 333 ALR 513 [21].

[121] ibid [20].

[122] *In re Aro Co Ltd* [1980] Ch 196 (Stephenson, Brandon and Brightman LJJ); *Tisand Pty Ltd v Owners of the Ship MV Cape Moreton (Ex Freya)* [2005] FCAFC 68, 143 FCR 43 (Ryan and Allsop JJ); *Programmed Total Marine Services Pty Ltd v Ship Hako Endeavour* [2014] FCAFC 134, 229 FCR 563 [22] (Allsop CJ with whom on this point Rares J agreed at [37]); *Kim v Daebo International Shipping Co Ltd* [2015] FCA 684, 232 FCR 275 [8] (Rares J).

[123] See, eg, s 471B of the Corporations Act 2001 (Cth).

[124] *Hur v Samsun Logix Corp* [2015] FCA 1154, 238 FCR 483 [31]–[33].

[125] ibid [33].

> any requirement for prior leave to be sought. If the stay in Art 20(2) were construed to preclude members of a ship's unpaid crew from exercising their maritime lien by arresting or attaching the ship when she reached port, the consequence might be the *de facto* forced labour or enslavement of the crew until the ship finally reached the crew's or ship's home port.

On the other hand, as in cases involving arrests to seek security for an arbitration, it may be appropriate for the maritime court to obtain security before releasing a ship from arrest, but to require the plaintiff to prove, such as by filing a proof of debt, the claimed liability in the jurisdiction where the foreign main proceeding is located so that all creditors in the same class might be treated equally, if the circumstances warrant doing so.

In the end, whether a local court should decline jurisdiction after arrest (or beforehand) in cases where a recognition order has been made under the Model Law, is a matter that probably needs to be approached, at least for common lawyers, on a case by case basis, while principles are developed after careful thought and experience.

V. Conclusion

A Chapter on this topic, inevitably, cannot be comprehensive because each maritime State has its own distinct system of laws affecting arrests, even if those laws are enacted against the background provided by the 1952 or 1999 Arrest Conventions. Jurisdictional twists are as many as factual turns. That is because we are dealing with the almost infinite variety of factual and legal circumstances that human ingenuity or incompetence can produce. The most that can be said at the moment is that the future in this area looks a lot like it may involve some uncharted waters.

5

Rearrests and Multiple Arrests of Ships

KATE LEWINS*

I. Introduction

In England and its former colonies, ship arrest[1] is an interim procedure overseen by courts exercising admiralty jurisdiction. It is available only for in rem claims.[2] The arrest on an in rem claim also gives the court the jurisdiction to hear the merits of the underlying dispute. To secure the claim against what is often the only asset in the jurisdiction, the claimant[3] is entitled to call upon the aid of the court to arrest the ship whilst the ship is within the jurisdiction of the court.

The courts recognise that ship arrest is a drastic remedy and must not be permitted to become an instrument of oppression.[4] To that end, in Anglo-Common Law jurisdictions it has been a long-standing rule that, once a ship has been arrested and released on provision of alternative security, it will be protected from rearrest in respect of the same claim.[5] However, courts exercising admiralty jurisdiction retained a discretion to permit rearrest, where it was fair to the claimant and not oppressive to the shipowner.

In contrast, the traditional position in Civil Law countries was that ships can be attached as part of remedies generally available to obtain pre-judgment security for a claim,[6] whether or not that claim was of a maritime nature.[7] The assets liable to attachment were not limited to the ship, nor was the claimant limited to attaching a single asset.[8] The attachment did not necessarily give the court jurisdiction over the underlying dispute.[9] The arresting party could be required to give security for any claim by the shipowner for wrongful arrest.[10]

* Professor of Law, Murdoch University, Australia; Academic Fellow, Centre for Maritime Law, National University of Singapore.

[1] Whilst acknowledging that cargo and freight can also be liable to arrest, for the sake of brevity, this Chapter will speak only of ships.

[2] In rem claims were originally limited to those claims founded on maritime liens but later expanded by statute to certain other types of claims: DC Jackson, *Enforcement of Maritime Claims* 4th edn (London, LLP, 2005) para 15.2.

[3] For the sake of consistency, 'claimant' is used throughout this Chapter, even if a particular jurisdiction may refer to that party by some other term.

[4] *The Vasiliy Golovnin* [2008] SGCA 39, [2008] 4 SLR 994 [51] (Rajah JA).

[5] *The Wild Ranger* (1863) Br & L 84, 167 ER 310.

[6] D Rhidian Thomas, 'Damages for Wrongful Arrest of Ships in the English Admiralty Jurisdiction' in D Rhidian Thomas (ed), *Liability Regimes in Contemporary Maritime Law* (London, Informa, UK 2007) ch 13 para 13.19.

[7] Francesco Berlingieri, *Berlingieri on Arrest of Ships*, 6th edn (Abingdon, Informa Law from Routledge, 2017) vol 1 para 1.11. Also, Civil Law countries recognise a broader right to damages for wrongful arrest: ibid.

[8] Richard Shaw, 'Securing the Enforcement of Awards and Judgments' (2001) 1 *Shipping & Trade Law* 3 (1 January 2001) 9.

[9] ibid.

[10] ibid.

In the interests of harmonisation of the law concerning arrest of ships as an interim measure[11] an international compromise was struck, resulting in the International Convention Relating to the Arrest of Sea-Going Ships 1952 (the Arrest Convention 1952).[12] Relevantly, the Arrest Convention 1952:

(1) enshrined the common law notion that a claimant could generally arrest a ship to obtain security only once, with rearrest only permitted where the security for the earlier arrest has been discharged, or for other 'good cause';[13]
(2) confined the rights of arrest to a defined list of maritime claims;[14]
(3) expanded the pool of ships liable to be arrested for the claim to include other ships in the same ownership (the sister ship provisions).[15]

The Arrest Convention 1952 has been widely accepted.[16] In addition to those States that are parties to the Convention, other States have sought to align their laws with the international arrest regime it created. Because the international ship arrest regime interacts with local law, one might say there is a harmony of approach rather than uniformity. How individual countries regulate the possibility of rearrest is a good example of this. Whilst the general attitude to rearrest might align with the Arrest Convention 1952, the domestic approaches of countries vary quite considerably. Some domestic statutes prescribe the circumstances in which rearrest will be permitted, while other jurisdictions have enacted a 'one ship, one arrest' rule whilst leaving the possibility of rearrest to the court's discretion. As we shall see, this variation is apparent even amongst Anglo-Common Law countries.

The International Convention on Arrest of Ships 1999 (the Arrest Convention 1999)[17] has an updated rearrest provision. The words of general discretion to permit rearrest found in the Arrest Convention 1952 ('with good cause') have been replaced with a list of specific circumstances where rearrest will be permissible. The Arrest Convention 1999 also authorises multiple arrests for one maritime claim up to the total value of the claim. Although in force, the Arrest Convention 1999 has not yet received widespread acceptance.[18] The provisions permitting multiple arrest have proved an anathema to most Common Law countries. However, multiple arrest is useful because:

> Where a shipping line or group is in financial difficulties with a number of creditors pursuing a limited range of assets not every attempt to enforce a claim will succeed nor will every arrest of a vessel give rise to payment or the provision of security for the claim.[19]

[11] Berlingieri (n 7) vol 1 para 1.12. The Arrest Convention 1952 expressly does not apply to post-judgment claims: see art 1(2).

[12] International Convention Relating to the Arrest of Sea-going Ships (adopted 10 May 1952, entered into force 24 February 1956) 439 UNTS 193.

[13] Article 3(3).

[14] Article 1.

[15] Article 3(1).

[16] There are currently around 70 parties to the Arrest Convention 1952. Further details are available online at comitemaritime.org/publications-documents/status-of-conventions/.

[17] International Convention on the Arrest of Ships (adopted 12 March 1999, entered into force 14 September 2011) 2797 UNTS 3.

[18] The Arrest Convention 1999 entered into force on 14 September 2011. It currently has 11 parties: comitemaritime.org/publications-documents/status-of-conventions/.

[19] Malcolm John David Wallis, *The Associated Ship and South African Admiralty Jurisdiction* (Cape Town, Siber Ink, 2010) 230.

This Chapter will examine the means by which the Arrest Conventions 1952 and 1999, and the domestic laws of certain countries, regulate the exceptions to the 'one ship, one arrest' rule. This Chapter begins by examining the origins of the traditional common law rule alongside the court's broad discretion to allow rearrest exceptionally. It will then outline the rearrest provisions in the Arrest Convention 1952, which, to a large extent, have adopted the Common Law position. It will then briefly consider the domestic legal approaches to rearrest of several Anglo-Common Law countries, which differ despite their shared backdrop of common law: the orthodox Common Law position (England); the codifier (Australia); and the reformer (South Africa). Of particular interest is the question – how has each jurisdiction chosen to manage the exceptions to the rule? Is it by way of broad judicial discretion or statute? And what are the benefits of each approach? In closing, the Chapter will briefly discuss the Arrest Convention 1999.

II. Common Law Rule Prior to the Arrest Convention 1952 – 'One Ship, One Arrest'

Upon the arrest of a ship in admiralty proceedings, the owner either provides alternative security[20] to ensure the arrest is lifted, or abandons the ship to be sold by the court.[21] Once security for the claim has been provided, the courts will not permit the claimant to 'harass' the debtor by means of further arrests of the ship.[22] In those circumstances, rearrest of the same ship by the claimant would ordinarily be viewed as vexatious and oppressive and an abuse of the court's process.

As was said by Dr Lushington in *The Wild Ranger*: 'Now bail given for a ship in any action is a substitute for the ship; and whenever bail is given the ship is wholly released from the cause of action, and cannot be arrested again for that cause of action.'[23] To put it another way, the shipowner has, by posting security, 'purchased her freedom from arrest'.[24] To quote Dr Lushington again, this time in *The Kalamazoo*:

> [I]t is perfectly competent to take bail to the full value, but the effect of taking bail is to release the ship in the action altogether. It would be perfectly absurd to contend that you could arrest a ship, take bail to any amount, and afterwards arrest her again for the same cause of action. The bail represents the ship, and when the ship is once released upon bail she is altogether released from the action.[25]

[20] Such as bail, a guarantee or a P&I club letter of undertaking. As to the last, see generally Paul Myburgh, 'P&I Club Letters of Undertaking and Admiralty Arrests' [2018] 24 *JIML* 201. See also *FSL-9 PTE Ltd v Norwegian Hull Club (FSL New York)* [2016] EWHC 1091 (Comm), [2017] Lloyd's Rep Plus 18. Claimants sought an increase in security where the letter provided 'liberty to apply … if the security sum is reasonably deemed insufficient to adequately secure owners' reasonable claims'. The court held this did not give the claimant a right to apply to the court for an increase, but rather permitted a rearrest to obtain additional security.

[21] A court sale provides a fund against which the arresting party's claim can be satisfied, once other claims ranking higher in priority have been paid. Sarah C Derrington and James M Turner, *The Law and Practice of Admiralty Matters*, 2nd ed (Oxford, OUP, 2016) 12.

[22] See Wallis (n 19) 247.

[23] *The Wild Ranger* (n 5) 87, 312.

[24] A phrase used by Sheen J in *The Despina GK* [1983] QB 214.

[25] *The Kalamazoo* (1851) 15 Jur 885.

However, the broad rule against rearrest was bound up in qualifications and exceptions, and through the exercise of judicial discretion the rule could be cast aside if justice required it.

At common law the tripwire of the rule was only triggered in certain circumstances. The prohibition was generally effective where both proceedings were brought in rem[26] on the same claim by the same claimant, usually to increase the amount of security available for the original proceedings.[27] If the first arrest warrant had been issued but not served before the ship sailed, that would not 'count' in terms of the rule, and courts would permit the issue of a second arrest warrant.[28] In early cases the court would only look to see if there was a previous arrest in its own jurisdiction,[29] although increasingly the English courts exercised jurisdiction 'founded on international comity'.[30] However, that respect for comity would only extend so far – it was not uncommon for the English courts to find that an earlier foreign attachment effected on a ship under Civil Law was insufficiently in rem in nature to prevent the English courts from effecting a later ship arrest.[31]

Even where there had been an earlier arrest, the admiralty courts might still permit rearrest in accordance with their 'broad discretion' to permit rearrest as a question of

[26] The rule was not triggered if there had been an earlier in personam action in a jurisdiction that permitted pre-trial arrest – see *The Bold Buccleugh* (1851) 7 Moo PC 267, 13 ER 884 (PC): unsuccessful in rem proceedings in England, followed by in personam proceedings, arrestment of the ship in Scotland and provision of security. Once released, the ship sailed again for England and was (re)arrested pursuant to an English in rem writ, at which point the Scottish proceedings were abandoned. The defendant owners protested, claiming lis alibi pendens at the time of the second arrest. At first instance (*The Bold Buccleugh* (1850) 3 W Rob 220, 166 ER 944) Dr Lushington permitted the English proceedings to stand. It was the claimant's right to abandon its action in Scotland and proceed in England. It would have been imprudent to discontinue the Scottish proceedings without knowing whether the ship would return to England to be arrested. The claimants arrested her on the first opportunity and withdrew the action in Scotland at the earliest possible time (229, 948). On appeal the Privy Council found a different route, holding that, because the Scottish and English proceedings were of a different type (one in personam and the other in rem), 'the pendency of the one cannot be pleaded in suspension of the other' (286, 891). See also *The Rena K* [1979] 1 QB 377 in which it was decided that a cause of action in rem does not merge in a judgment in personam and remains available to the extent the judgment remains unsatisfied.

[27] See eg *The Point Breeze* [1928] PD 135, where the defendant shipowners put up a bail bond of £3,500 to avoid arrest. After the judgment on liability and drydocking revealed more damage, the claimants realised the bail bond would be insufficient to meet their costs. The vessel was rearrested, and an additional undertaking given under protest. The defendant shipowner then applied for that second bail amount to be discharged. It was held that a second arrest of the ship to 'top up' the security amount was impermissible. A different issue is whether, and in what circumstances, a second arrest can be used to enforce a judgment or arbitral award that has already been obtained. As the Arrest Convention 1952 and Arrest Convention 1999 explicitly do not apply to in rem actions to enforce a judgment (art 1(2)), it is strictly speaking outside the scope of this Chapter, but see amongst others *The Rena K* (n 26); *The Daien Maru No 18* [1984] SGHC 43, [1983–1984] SLR(R) 787; *Republic of India v India Steamship Co Ltd (No 2) (The Indian Grace)* [1998] AC 878; *Handytankers KS v Owners and/or Demise Charterers of Alas subsequently renamed as Kombos* [2014] HKCFI 1281, [2014] 6 HKC 239; *Handytankers KS v The Owners and/or Demise Charterers of the Ship or Vessel M/V Alas Subsequently Renamed as Kombos (The Alas)* [2015] HKCA 691, [2015] 6 HKC 557. Notably, some jurisdictions such as Australia and South Africa now explicitly permit the use of admiralty proceedings in rem to enforce directly a judgment or award (see eg Admiralty Act 1988 (Cth), ss 4(2)(c) and 4(3)(u); Admiralty Jurisdiction Regulation Act 1983 (SA), s 1(1)(aa)).

[28] For example, the rule against rearrest was not triggered where the first arrest warrant had been issued but not served, being thwarted by the sailing of the vessel: *The Bold Buccleugh* (PC) (n 26).

[29] See the first instance decision in *The Bold Buccleugh* (n 26); overturned on other grounds.

[30] *The City of Mecca* (1879) 5 PD 28, although on appeal the civil proceedings were found not to be in rem: see *The City of Mecca* (1881) 6 PD 106 (CA).

[31] *The Bold Buccleugh* (PC) (n 26); *The City of Mecca* (CA) (n 30); but see *Castrique v Imrie* (1870) LR 4 HL 414.

admiralty procedure.[32] This discretion recognised that not every rearrest would be an abuse of process – indeed, rearrest might be necessary to ensure 'full justice'.[33] A second arrest might be permitted, for example, if there had been an earlier arrest but no security had been given, or where the security given had proved defective in some way (perhaps due to insolvency of the guarantor).[34] The existence of this 'broad discretion' to permit rearrest caused a Canadian court to refuse to declare a maritime lien extinguished by the provision of security.[35] As the purpose of ship arrest is to obtain security *and* a submission to the jurisdiction of the court on the merits, a court can permit a rearrest even though security has been posted, where the shipowner refuses to acknowledge the jurisdiction of the court.[36]

The general rule would ordinarily operate to prevent a rearrest merely to 'top up' the security amount already obtained by an earlier arrest.[37] However, the courts have occasionally exercised a discretion to permit 'top-up' rearrests. In *The Hero*, the court permitted the discharge of arrest and rearrest where a clerical mistake led to the setting of bail too low. In allowing the rearrest, Dr Lushington said:

> I am of opinion that where application to increase the amount of the action is made before judgment has been pronounced, the Court has power to direct measures to be taken to do full justice to the plaintiff.[38]

In summary, although the general rule was that a ship could be arrested only once in relation to any claim, the English admiralty courts have long recognised an equitable discretion to allow rearrest. This required the judge to weigh up the merits of any rearrest application, considering what was required to achieve 'full justice' for the claimant, against whether the rearrest was vexatious and oppressive to the defendant. It would seem that 'full justice' encapsulated claimants' rights to true and substantial security, as well as shipowners' submission to the jurisdiction of the court. The discretion has been described as 'broad' and 'pragmatic'.[39]

Of course, such a broad discretion has both advantages and disadvantages. The obvious advantages are flexibility, equity and the ability to tailor a solution to individual circumstances. Such a broad mandate, though, renders the court's conclusion less predictable in any given case; it also lessens the ability of an appellate court to review the decision. Despite that, reviewing the case law shows that the admiralty courts are keen to look to earlier cases for guidance on the exercise of the discretion. Such guidance is not always easy to obtain, given the long history of admiralty cases and the often urgent nature of admiralty matters concerning ship arrest.

[32] *The Ruta* [2000] 1 Lloyd's Rep 359, 366 (Steel J).

[33] *The Hero* (1865) Br & L 447, 167 ER 436 (Dr Lushington).

[34] See *The Ruta* (n 32) 365 (Steel J citing *The City of Mecca* (1879) 5 PD 28; *Westminster Bank Ltd v West of England Steamship Owners' Protection & Indemnity Association Ltd* (1933) 46 Ll LR 101).

[35] *The Birchglen* [1990] 3 FC 301, 36 FTR 92. After a collision, in rem proceedings were issued. The insurers of the relevant tugs provided a letter of guarantee. The tug owners wished to sell them and applied for a declaration that they were, in effect, unencumbered by a maritime lien because of the provision of security. The judge refused to grant that declaration. If the security were to prove deficient in the future, the court might permit a rearrest.

[36] *The Prinsengracht* [1993] 1 Lloyd's Rep 41.

[37] *The Kalamazoo* (n 25).

[38] *The Hero* (n 33).

[39] Steel J in *The Ruta* (n 32) 366 (citing *The Birchglen* (n 35)).

III. The Arrest Convention 1952

The Arrest Convention 1952 sought to achieve international uniformity in respect to the arrest of ships. It largely preserved and consolidated the rule against rearrest that had developed in English common law. It usurped, and therefore constrained, the more liberal Civil Law notions of attachment as they applied to ships.

A. Rearrest Provisions

Article 3 of the Arrest Convention 1952 enshrined the common law notion that only one ship is to be arrested and security is only to be given once in relation to the same maritime claim by the same claimant. The key provision is art 3(3):

> *A ship shall not be arrested, nor shall bail or other security be given more than once* in any one or more of the jurisdictions of any of the contracting States *in respect of the same maritime claim by the same claimant* and, if a ship has been arrested in any one of such jurisdictions, or bail or other security has been given in such jurisdiction either to release the ship or to avoid a threatened arrest *any subsequent arrest* of the ship or of any ship in the same ownership by the same claimant for the same maritime claim *shall be set aside*, and the ship released by the Court or other appropriate judicial authority of that State, *unless* the claimant can satisfy the Court or other appropriate judicial authority that *the bail or other security had been finally released before the subsequent arrest or that there is other good cause for maintaining that arrest.* (emphasis added)

Importantly for the shipowner, the Arrest Convention 1952 extends this protection to the shipowner, not only in the original jurisdiction where arrest took place, but also in any other State Party to the Convention. This is a critical plank of the Arrest Convention 1952, ensuring that all ships owned by a shipowner, who has responded to the requirements to provide security in order to secure release, should be free from further arrest in any State Party.

B. Exceptions to the Rule against Rearrest

Article 3(3) contains two exceptions[40] to the rule against rearrest:

(1) where the bail or other security obtained in the first arrest has been finally released before the second arrest; and
(2) where the claimant can satisfy the court that there is 'other good cause' for maintaining the arrest.

[40] There has been concern that these exceptions, as drafted, may operate only once a second arrest has already occurred and may therefore not cover the situation where a claimant is applying to the court for a second arrest warrant: Francesco Berlingieri, 'The 1952 Arrest Convention Revisited' (2005) *LMCLQ* 327, 337. However, international Conventions are to be interpreted 'unconstrained by technical rules … but on broad principles of acceptation': *James Buchanan & Co Ltd v Babco Forwarding & Shipping (UK) Ltd* [1978] AC 141, 152 (Lord Wilberforce). In my view, art 3(3) should not be interpreted overly narrowly and technically: the question of principle (and the mischief to be avoided) remains the same regardless of whether the court is dealing with an application for a second arrest warrant or an actual second arrest.

i. Security has been Finally Released

The Arrest Convention 1952 permits a second arrest where the first arrest has been set aside or[41] security has been discharged.[42] These are straightforward examples where the claimant no longer has the comfort of security for its outstanding claim. It has been said that the reason for discharge is irrelevant and the discharge of the security may be due to the decision of the claimant.[43] This exception reflected English case law at the time.[44]

ii. Other Good Cause

As Berlingieri explains,[45] the drafters were particularly concerned with situations where the security had not been discharged but had been rendered parlous – whether by insolvency of the bailor or guarantor, or by some other reason beyond the control of the claimant (such as a sudden depreciation in currency).[46] The drafters accepted the likelihood that the generality of the exception would lead to different conclusions in different countries.[47] Thus, the wording leaves State Parties with plenty of room to determine what would constitute 'good cause' in their own jurisdictions. Either the legislature might direct the courts via statute, or they could leave the question of 'good cause' to the courts' discretion. Some domestic examples will be considered shortly.

C. Can a Different Ship be Arrested the Second Time?

The Arrest Convention 1952 enshrines the general rule that only one ship is to be arrested for one claim, whilst anticipating that the arrested ship might need to be rearrested in certain circumstances. However, the Convention also increased the pool of ships potentially amenable to arrest.[48] The Convention allows the claimant to arrest either the offending ship or another ship in the same ownership at the time the maritime claim arose (sister ships).[49] Whilst designed to benefit maritime claimants,[50] the possibility of arresting

[41] See Berlingieri (n 7) vol 1 paras 15.10–11, discussing the differences between the English and French texts of art 3(3). The English text says: 'if a ship has been arrested *or* bail or other security has been given' (emphasis added). The French text uses 'et' (and).

[42] Assuming that the dispute is still on foot and no judgment has been entered. For example, if the first arrest was discharged because that ship was not answerable on the claim, the court may permit a second arrest of another ship. In *The Stephan J* [1985] 2 Lloyd's Rep 344, Sheen J permitted a second arrest by the claimant after the first arrest on a ship mistakenly thought to be a sister or surrogate ship had been set aside and the security discharged. The key factor is whether the earlier security has been discharged, as envisaged by the Arrest Convention 1952.

[43] See Berlingieri (n 7) vol 1 para 15.12.

[44] Whether the English legislation giving effect to the 1952 Convention can be regarded as having that effect is discussed below at Part IV A i.

[45] Berlingieri (n 7) vol 1 para 15.13 ff, particularly paras 15.21–34.

[46] ibid, paras 15.01–02. Note that the British Association, who proposed the wording of the exception, doubted that a sudden depreciation in currency would be considered to be a 'good reason' for a second arrest in England.

[47] ibid, para 15.01 n 3.

[48] At least for a time: the widespread adoption of one-ship companies and other imaginative corporate arrangements has blunted the effectiveness of the surrogate ship provisions. South Africa's associated ship jurisdiction is discussed in depth in ch 2.

[49] Article 3(1).

[50] At least before the ubiquitous adoption of one-ship companies.

a surrogate ship creates difficulties in assessing the exceptions to the 'one arrest' rule. If the first arrest has been rendered a nullity then the situation is clear – it is as if the first arrest never occurred.[51] However, sometimes the situation is not so straightforward. If the ship originally arrested (the *Black Cat*) is liable to rearrest (because the security offered after the first arrest proves insufficient, for example) can a surrogate ship (the *White Dog*) be arrested in its stead? It is, of course, up to the claimant whether to choose to arrest the surrogate or wait for the original ship to re-enter the jurisdiction.[52] What about if the *White Dog* is the only ship susceptible to arrest? Either way, more than one ship will have been arrested for the claim because both ships, the *Black Cat* and the *White Dog*, have been arrested at different times.

The sister ship provisions have created blossoming complexity. Did the Arrest Convention 1952 intend the carving out of an exception to the one ship rule, allowing a second arrest of a different ship for the same claim? Where the first arrest was in some respect a nullity, the answer would be yes. But other situations are rather less clear-cut:[53]

(1) If the first arrest did not result in sufficient security because the claim exceeds the value of any one ship owned by the shipowner, can a claimant use a second arrest of a sister ship under the Arrest Convention 1952 to secure its claim? According to Berlingieri, the answer is yes: examples he gives include where the value of the ship is less than the claim against it, or where the ship is to be sold but it is clear that the proceeds of sale will not meet the claims of all claimants.[54] However, such an interpretation requires a most generous reading of the 'other good cause' exception. It is not entirely clear to what extent courts – at least in Common Law jurisdictions – would agree.[55] Allowing a second arrest in those circumstances would amount to a 'top-up' arrest – and moreover, a multiple arrest – rather than a substitute arrest under the 'one arrest' rule.
(2) A related scenario is where the claimant is the arresting party for the first arrest, but a higher-ranked secured creditor sweeps the pool on judicial sale. The claimant thereafter seeks to arrest a second ship. It is clear that justice has not been done to the claimant. But there may be other objections. If the claimant's claim has been ranked for distribution after judicial sale, did it have the benefit of court order or a judgment against the proceeds arising from an in rem proceeding? This will undoubtedly raise questions of res judicata for any new proceedings in rem.[56]
(3) Assume the claimant is the holder of a maritime lien. If the claimant first participates in the distribution of proceeds of the judicial sale of an earlier arrest of a surrogate ship on the basis of a statutory right of action in rem, may it still proceed on its maritime lien against the relevant ship for any outstanding amount? Does it make any difference if it was the arresting party in the earlier arrest, or if the arrest was instigated by another claimant? Here, once again, the claimant swims in murky waters: would those proceedings raise issues of res judicata?

[51] *The Silver Athens (No 2)* [1986] 2 Lloyd's Rep 583.
[52] Which would be desirable if the claim is one that gives rise to a maritime lien.
[53] These examples are inspired by the learned discussion in Wallis (n 19) ch 8.
[54] Berlingieri (n 7) vol 1 para 15.21.
[55] Although the domestic statutes may constrain a liberal view in any event. See the discussion of this issue in the South African case of *MV Fortune 22: Owners of the MC Fortune 22 v Keppel Corp Ltd* 1999 SA 162 (C) at text accompanying n 141 below.
[56] Discussed again in Part IV(C) below.

(4) What if the claimant had merely participated as an intervenor in a distribution of proceeds consequent on a judicial sale of one ship by another party, and came away empty-handed (or short-changed)? Can it then arrest a sister ship for its claim? Technically, the claimant has not actually arrested a ship or obtained security for the claim.

These questions concerning the interplay of the exceptions to rearrest and surrogate ships are difficult but surprisingly it appears that they rarely trouble the courts. Perhaps the reason for this is the proliferation of one-ship companies: it is rare to find a 'sister' to arrest.[57] Another reason why such questions do not appear frequently is that, where the unpaid maritime claimant is simply one of many clamouring creditors, the shipowner may well be facing insolvency. In that situation, the cross-border insolvency regime may be in play.[58] However, it may be that these questions emerge more than we know: as decisions on rearrest are interlocutory in nature, they have traditionally been heard in chambers rather than in open court and may thus go unreported.

Regardless of how frequently these questions may arise, the fact is that it is likely that court responses differ from jurisdiction to jurisdiction. This is symptomatic of the degree to which domestic law and local practice are involved in determining questions of rearrest, even for States that are parties to the Arrest Convention 1952. While these types of scenarios are more clearly governed by the Arrest Convention 1999 – which permits both rearrest and the arrest of multiple ships to obtain security for one claim – the slow uptake of that Convention means the Arrest Convention 1952 still represents the status quo in many parts of the world.

The Arrest Convention 1952 provides that a second arrest can follow where security has been finally released or 'for other good cause'. One might think that countries whose laws grant the courts a broad discretion when to permit a rearrest (or further arrest of another ship) would be able to respond to the many possible rearrest scenarios more adroitly. It is interesting to ponder how different jurisdictions manage this discretion. In one camp are States that are parties to the Arrest Convention 1952 or claim to be sympathetic with it. Even within that camp there is a degree of variation. How have they interpreted the Convention's rather open wording: what constitutes 'good cause' for maintaining a rearrest? And what of other jurisdictions that are not parties to the Arrest Convention 1952 and have chosen a different path? Space dictates that only a few jurisdictions can be selected here as examples, and the discussion must necessarily be brief.

IV. Comparing Domestic Approaches

A. The Orthodox Position: England

We have already considered English common law. It is relevant because of its long history as a centre of admiralty and maritime law but also because its former colonies

[57] See comments by the UK delegation to the Diplomatic Conference negotiating the Arrest Convention 1999 (Document 188/3/ADD.2, [10]–[12] extracted at Berlingieri (n 7) vol 2 appendix IV 274–75: 'Article 3(1) of the 1952 Convention provides for the arrest of "sister" ships … Since 1952, the stratagem of the single ship company has proliferated. As a result, few ships have "sisters" within the meaning of the 1952 Convention. The only option available to many claimants, therefore, is to arrest the particular ship in respect of which the maritime claim arises. The balance that the 1952 Convention sought to strike has tilted in favour of the shipowner.'

[58] England, Australia and South Africa have all given effect to the UNCITRAL Model Law on Cross-Border Insolvency: see further ch 9.

continue, to various degrees, to follow its lead in this area. For example (and at the risk of overgeneralising) the law relating to rearrest in Singapore[59] and New Zealand[60] bears a general resemblance to that in England (even though neither jurisdiction is a State Party to the Arrest Convention 1952). As we have seen, English law was the genesis of the 'one ship, one arrest' rule in the Arrest Convention 1952.

England is a party to the Arrest Convention 1952. It implemented the Convention by paraphrasing its effect in domestic legislation, initially in the Administration of Justice Act 1956 (UK) (AJA 1956).[61] The English legislation has been the subject of criticism.[62] As Lane J put it in the first instance decision of *The Banco*: 'There is no attempt in the Administration of Justice Act, 1956 … to give an exact reproduction of what was agreed at the convention of 1952 … . [N]owhere in the preamble … or elsewhere … is there found a reference to the convention.'[63]

The AJA 1956 did not explicitly deal with ship arrest or rearrest and its provisions were strikingly different to the Arrest Convention 1952.[64] The relevant provision of the AJA 1956 was s 3(4):

> In the case of any such claim as is mentioned in paragraphs (d) to (r) of subsection (1) of section one of this Act, being a claim arising in connection with a ship, where the person who would be liable on the claim in an action in personam was, when the cause of action arose, the owner or

[59] Singapore is not a party to the Arrest Convention 1952. However, its original enactment of the Courts (Admiralty Jurisdiction) Ordinance 1961 (Cap 123) was in substantially the same terms as the AJA 1956 and was designed to bring the law in Singapore into line with the provisions of Part 1 of the AJA 1956. See Steven Chong, 'Charting our Own Courses: the Australia, New Zealand and Singapore Journeys in Maritime Law' (2016) 30 *Australian & New Zealand Maritime Law Journal* 1, 4. For a description of the legislative history of Singapore's admiralty jurisdiction, see *The Vinalines Pioneer* [2015] SGHC 278, [2016] 1 SLR 44 [14]–[17] (Belinda Ang J). Case law broadly follows the English position. *Monte Ulia (Owners) v Banco (Owners) (The Banco)* [1971] P 137 has been accepted in Singapore, such that this provision is said to permit the arrest of one ship only: *The Brunei 602* [1984] SGCA 4, [1983–1984] SLR 306. In *Equatorial Marine Fuel Management Services Pte Ltd v The Bunga Melati 5* [2010] SGHC 193 [103] it was held, consistent with *The Kommunar No 2* [1997] 1 Lloyd's Rep 8, that the 'one ship, one claim' principle enunciated in the legislation does not extend to foreign proceedings. Of course, the Singapore courts are content to depart from English authority should they consider it appropriate: see eg *The Daien Maru No 18* (n 27). There is no mention of rearrest in the Rules of Court nor the court's Practice Directions. Consistent with the English position, the Singaporean courts exercise a broad discretion when it comes to rearrest. It has been held that on an application for a 'second arrest' the arresting party must show it is not an abuse of the arrest process: 'In short, the court will want to know whether it is oppressive and vexatious to re-arrest.' See *The Eagle Prestige* [2010] SGHC 93, [2010] 3 SLR 294 [77] (Belinda Ang J).

[60] New Zealand is not a party to the Arrest Convention 1952. As regards rearrest, s 5(2)(b) of the Admiralty Act 1973 (NZ) is based upon the AJA 1956. The Admiralty Rules provide that the warrant of arrest is to be issued against one ship only: High Court Rules 2016, r 25.34. While rearrest is not mentioned in the Rules, it was held in *Det Norske Veritas AS v The Ship Clarabelle* [2002] NZCA 129, [2002] 3 NZLR 52 that the Court may order rearrest pursuant to the general power to give directions on matters not specified by the Rules: see the High Court Rules 2016, r 25.4.

[61] At the time of the AJA 1956 the UK had not formally ratified the Arrest Convention 1952. For a discussion of some of the difficulties with the AJA 1956 as an implementation measure of the Convention, see *The Cap Bon* [1967] 1 Lloyd's Rep 543; *The Golden Trader* [1975] QB 348.

[62] See Jackson (n 2) paras 0.23–26, 0.34–36, 15.40.

[63] *The Banco* (n 59) 141–42 (Lane J). This same criticism can be levelled against the replacement of the AJA 1956, the Supreme Court Act 1981 (UK) (later renamed the Senior Courts Act 1981 (UK) (the SCA 1981).

[64] There has been some debate as to whether the Arrest Convention 1952 has the force of law in England and discussion about the extent to which regard should be had to the Convention in interpreting the English legislation: eg *The Nordglimt* [1988] QB 183; *The Po* [1991] 2 Lloyd's Rep 206 (CA); *The Tjaskemolen (now named Visvliet) (No 2)* [1997] 2 Lloyd's Rep 476. These issues are put to one side, along with the related questions about the effect of EU Conventions and Regulations as to jurisdiction and enforcement.

charterer of, or in possession or in control of, the ship, the Admiralty jurisdiction of the High Court … may (whether the claim gives rise to a maritime lien on the ship or not) be invoked by an action in rem against –

(a) *that ship*, if at the time when the action is brought it is beneficially owned as respects all the shares therein by that person; or

(b) *any other ship* which, at the time when the action is brought, is beneficially owned as aforesaid. (emphasis added)

In what might be described as a masterful example of succinct drafting, it was held in *The Banco*[65] that the prohibition of the arrest of more than one ship spelled out in art 3(3) of the Arrest Convention 1952 is found in the use of the singular noun – 'ship' – and the disjunctive 'or' between paras (a) and (b). In that case, the claimant had issued writs in rem and served warrants of arrest on the offending ship as well as the six surrogate ships in relation to the one maritime claim. The defendant protested. At first instance, Lane J found that, as the AJA 1956 intended to implement the Convention, it was appropriate to consult the Convention in the face of ambiguity. The subsection should be interpreted to mean that the claimant could arrest only one of the defendant's ships. The service of the writs and arrests on the six sister ships were set aside. The Court of Appeal affirmed that interpretation.[66]

i. Senior Courts Act 1981 (SCA 1981)

The admiralty jurisdiction of the courts of England and Wales is now set out in the SCA 1981. Section 21(4) of the SCA 1981 is broadly equivalent to s 3(4) of the AJA 1956. A new s 21(8) enshrined the decision in *The Banco*:[67]

> Where, as regards any such claim as is mentioned in section 20(2)(e) to (r), a ship has been served with a writ or arrested in an action in rem brought to enforce that claim, no other ship may be served with a writ or arrested in that or any other action in rem brought to enforce that claim; but this subsection does not prevent the issue, in respect of any one such claim, of a writ naming more than one ship or of two or more writs each naming a different ship.

Despite the redraft, s 21(8) does not closely align to the provisions of the Arrest Convention 1952. Unlike the Convention, there is no mention of security; yet it is widely accepted that the intent of the Arrest Convention 1952 was to prohibit further arrest whether the ship had been arrested and proper security obtained.[68] Instead, s 21(8) rules out a second arrest where there has been a ship 'served with a writ or arrested'. Taken literally, this provision would appear to prohibit a second arrest even if no security had been forthcoming from the first arrest.

[65] *The Banco* (n 59).

[66] ibid 151 (Lord Denning MR). The question was raised about the registry practice of permitting one writ in rem to be issued that named multiple ships as defendants. Lord Denning, with whom Megaw LJ agreed, considered that the practice was acceptable because the jurisdiction of the court was not invoked until service upon the ship. The writ itself could be served on only one ship, and only that one ship arrested. As a result, the security for the claim was limited to the value of the single arrested ship.

[67] As observed by Sheen J in *The Stephan J* (n 42) 346.

[68] Berlingieri (n 7) vol 1 paras 15.01–03.

In two decisions Sheen J clarified the operation of s 21(8) in these situations. In *The Stephan J*[69] His Honour observed:

> Subsection 8 of s21 of the Act was introduced to deal with the question raised in *The Banco* … The purpose is to make it quite clear that the plaintiff whose claim is within that part of the jurisdiction of the High Court which can be invoked by an action in rem, can arrest only one ship, either the offending ship or another ship in the same ownership, in accordance with the [Arrest Convention 1952] … in my judgment sub-s. 8 of s. 21 cannot be interpreted in isolation. It must be interpreted in conjunction with sub-s. 4 of the same section.

It was held that the subsection had to be read: 'Where … a ship [against which an action in rem may be brought] has been served with a writ or arrested in an action *in rem* brought to enforce that claim …'.[70] Therefore, where the first arrest has been mistakenly carried out on the wrong ship (which is not available to be arrested because it is not in the same ownership), it cannot be an 'arrest' under s 21(4). As a result, when the correct ship is then arrested, that arrest will not offend s 21(8).

In the *Silver Athens (No 2)* the defendant shipowner argued that the wording of s 21(8) would prohibit a further arrest after the first arrest was discharged, even though the security from the first arrest had been returned. Sheen J gave this argument short shrift, holding that s 21(8) was 'not designed to deal' with that situation:

> The parties are effectively in the position they would have been in if the ship had not been arrested. The principle that when a ship is once released upon bail she is altogether released from that action and thereafter the bail represents the ship does not apply when the arrest has been set aside and the bail released. This was recognized in the [Arrest Convention 1952].[71]
>
> It was recognized in the Arrest Convention that a ship might be rearrested if the bail or other security had been released before the subsequent arrest. There is nothing in [the SCA 1981] that prevents a second arrest if the first has been set aside. The first arrest must thereafter be treated as a nullity.[72]

This common-sense approach of Sheen J led to a result that was undoubtedly just, and it did shelve the restrictions apparent on a literal reading of the provision in favour of the more general words of the Arrest Convention 1952 (and, indeed, the position under English law prior to the Convention).

In yet another example of the misalignment between s 21 of the SCA 1981 and the Arrest Convention 1952, in *The Kommunar (No 2)*[73] Coleman J concluded that s 21(8) was intended to apply only to proceedings in English courts. Considering the whole of s 21, the Judge held that the language addressed matters of English procedure and made no mention of overseas proceedings. Therefore, it only prohibited rearrest in England where there had been a prior arrest in England. As a result, the Judge concluded that the fact the claimant

[69] *The Stephan J* (n 42).

[70] ibid 346.

[71] *The Silver Athens (No 2)* (n 51) 584.

[72] ibid 585. The first arrest had been set aside on the basis of the compulsory stay required by reason of s 1 of the Arbitration Act 1975 (UK). The court ordered that claimant was entitled to have the stay on proceedings lifted to allow the arrest to obtain security for the claim; that being the case the Judge ordered that prior security given to the court be retained as security for any award made in the arbitration.

[73] *The Kommunar (No 2)* (n 59).

participated in a distribution of proceeds in earlier proceedings in South Africa did not have the effect of barring the proceedings before the English court.[74]

It has been said of the English admiralty court that on matters of rearrest 'the judges adopt a pragmatic approach, guided by what would be fair and just in the circumstances.'[75] As Jackson has noted, s 21(8) is 'not to be seen as implementing the more flexible but wide prohibition on rearrest in the *Arrest Convention* Article 3(3).'[76]

ii. Rules of Court (CPR 61)

In Common Law jurisdictions, because ship arrest is treated as a procedural remedy, the admiralty jurisdiction of the courts is generally prescribed by a combination of statute, court rules and practice directions. Rules of court and practice directions are easier to amend than statutes. Currently, Part 61 of the Civil Procedure Rules deals with admiralty claims.[77] CPR 61.6 outlines the court's broad discretion regarding security and rearrest:

> **Security in claim in rem**
>
> (1) This rule applies if, in a claim in rem, security has been given to –
>   (a) obtain the release of property under arrest; or
>   (b) prevent the arrest of property.
>
> (2) The court may order that the –
>   (a) amount of security be reduced and may stay the claim until the order is complied with; or
>   (b) claimant may arrest or re-arrest the property proceeded against to obtain further security.
>
> (3) The court may not make an order under paragraph (2)(b) if the total security to be provided would exceed the value of the property at the time –
>   (a) of the original arrest; or
>   (b) security was first given (if the property was not arrested).

This provision extends beyond the strict ambit of s 21(8) of the SCA 1981. For example, it would appear to support a rearrest to obtain 'top-up' security up to the total value of the property at the time of the original arrest. Say a ship is valued at £1 million and the

[74] ibid 20.

[75] Aleka Mandaraka-Sheppard, *Modern Maritime Law, Volume 1: Jurisdiction and Risks*, 3rd edn (Abingdon, Informa Law from Routledge, 2013) ch 5 para 2.5.5. See also *The Italy II* [1987] 2 Lloyd's Rep 162, 163, where Sheen J made it clear that if a ship has been languishing under arrest and the claimant has not progressed proceedings, he would be minded to release the ship from arrest and look unfavourably upon any application to rearrest. In *The Prinsengracht* (n 36) the claimant had issued but not served a writ in rem when the defendant shipowner volunteered to provide a bail bond to avoid arrest. Having submitted the bail bond, the defendant refused to submit to the jurisdiction of the court and claimed the arrest to secure jurisdiction, later that day, was invalid. The argument was that once bail has been posted, the ship is released from the action and cannot be arrested. Sheen J refused the shipowner's motion. First, the filing of bail had been submission to the jurisdiction of the court in any event (at 48). Alternatively, the question of arrest after bail is to be viewed in the light of whether the arrest is oppressive and vexatious. Here, his Honour held 'if … bail could be given without submitting to the jurisdiction and it remains necessary for the plaintiff to arrest the ship that arrest cannot be unlawful' (at 47).

[76] Jackson (n 2) para 15.55.

[77] For a broader introduction to CPR 61, see Michael Tsimplis and Nicholas Gaskell, 'Admiralty Claims and the New CPR Part 61' [2002] *LMCLQ* 520.

shipowner originally gives security for a claim to the tune of £500,000 but that amount turns out to be overly modest.[78] This rule says that the claimant may apply for a further arrest of 'the property proceeded against' for 'further' security under CPR 61.6(2)(b). The use of the words 'the property proceeded against' appears to rule out a second arrest of a sister ship. However, as subordinate legislation the rules must be interpreted consistently with the governing statute and long-standing authority. As we have seen, the courts are tasked to exercise this discretion in a manner avoiding oppression or unfairness.[79] For example, if the shipowner had taken deliberate steps to undermine the value of the security originally given,[80] a sudden drop in currency has affected the original security,[81] the value of the claim is higher than originally estimated at the time of the first arrest,[82] or the court registrar had set the original security amount too low,[83] a rearrest should be justifiable under the Arrest Convention 1952 and CPR 61.6, even if it does not comfortably fit the wording of the SCA 1981.

iii. 'Good Cause'?

In which circumstances will the English courts consider there to be 'good cause' to permit a second arrest in England? As we have seen, the statutory framework as interpreted by the courts mean that the court will consider whether the second arrest is an abuse of process, or whether the interests of justice support the second arrest.

The strength of such a broad discretion is that the judge may take into account a broad range of factors arising in the particular case. While prior cases may provide guidance, the discretionary nature of the remedy means that the courts are not firmly shackled to earlier decisions:

(1) *Security obtained upon the first arrest of the ship has turned out to be defective (eg guarantor insolvent).* The English courts have indicated their willingness to exercise a discretion to permit a rearrest to obtain security in this instance.[84] It is commonly referred to as a sufficient ground to exercise the discretion to allow a rearrest.[85] It would fall within CPR 61.6.
(2) *Error (eg mistake in quantum of claim inserted in original arrest warrant).* The discretion envisaged in CPR 61.6(2) would appear to permit this, subject to the cap in

[78] Such as where the security has proven to be too little given an unexpected blowout in costs, or even where the cost of repairs was greater than anticipated at the time of the earlier arrest.

[79] Steel J said as much in *The Ruta* (n 32) 366.

[80] *The Arctic Star*, The Times, 5 February 1985.

[81] Another situation envisaged by the participants at the Conference, although the English contingent doubted that this would be sufficient to justify rearrest in England: see n 46 above.

[82] An example given by Berlingieri relates to a collision claim: if more extensive damage to the claimant's ship is subsequently uncovered during drydocking than was apparent at the time of the initial arrest, that might be viewed as a 'good cause' for permitting a second arrest to enable security for the additional amount: Berlingieri (n 7), vol 1 para 15.14.

[83] *The Clarabelle* (n 60).

[84] See Steel J in *The Ruta* (n 32) 365, citing *The City of Mecca* (1879) 5 PD 28 and *Westminster Bank Ltd* (n 32).

[85] Berlingieri (n 7), vol 1 para 15.14.

CPR 61.6(3).[86] The 19th-century case of *The Hero*[87] permitted the first arrest to be discharged and the ship rearrested for the higher amount in such circumstances. There is no indication that the courts would rule any differently now.

(3) *First arrest was released due to insufficient evidence to support maintaining the arrest.* According to *The Tjaskemolen (now named Visvliet) (No 2)*[88] the simple question will be whether the second arrest of the vessel is vexatious or oppressive. The Judge ruled that the claimants should not be in a better position as a result of a second arrest and permitted the second arrest subject to the provision of counter-security by the claimant.

(4) *Using a rearrest to 'top up' security amount obtained on arrest of offending ship.* The usual application of the 'one arrest' rule would prevent a top-up arrest (at least where the second arrest is prior to judgment). However, given the discretion in CPR 61.6 to allow additional arrest for 'further' security, it would appear that a court could permit a rearrest if justice required it.[89]

(5) *In rem arrest followed by post-judgment arrest.* The Arrest Convention 1952 (and the Arrest Convention 1999, for that matter) applies only to pre-judgment ship arrest. Therefore, if an arresting party sought to rearrest by way of execution of a judgment, the Convention-based rule against rearrest would not be offended. For individual countries though, other complications can arise: this topic raises vexed issues around merger of judgments,[90] recognition of foreign proceedings under English law, the survival of maritime liens and, indeed, the very nature of in rem proceedings.[91] The resultant tangled web may be slowly teasing out,[92] but in any event it lies outside the ambit of this Chapter.

iv. Traditional Approach: Summary

The Arrest Convention 1952's permissive phrase 'any good cause' gives maximum flexibility to the States who are party to it. While English law imposes a rule against rearrest, English admiralty courts nonetheless retain a broad discretion to grant rearrest (or permit a rearrest to stand). Their overarching concern is to strive to reach a result that is in the interests of justice. As befits a broad discretion, it gives the court great flexibility in responding to the particular facts before it. In that balancing process, the court is informed by (but, as the question is a matter is discretion, not bound by) earlier decisions of the court. The court

[86] Compare *LD Commodities Rice Merchandising LLC v The Owners and/or Demise Charterers of the Vessel Styliani Z (The Styliani Z)* [2015] EWHC 3060 (Admlty), [2016] 1 Lloyd's Rep 395 for an error in procedure in the issue of the wrong court form (in personam rather than in rem), where the Judge had to weigh up whether to remedy the error by the claimant's solicitor or let it lie (which would mean that the merits of the claim would never be considered and the defendant would receive an unexpected windfall): see [48].

[87] *The Hero* (n 33).

[88] *The Tjaskemolen* (n 64) 476.

[89] See eg *The Clarabelle* (n 60).

[90] See *The Alletta* (1974) 1 Lloyd's Rep 40, which held that a judgment creditor could not pursue an in rem action after obtaining a judgment in England, as the underlying cause of action had merged with the judgment; but see *The Daien Maru No 18* (n 27). However, in rem proceedings have been permitted where a judgment creditor had obtained a foreign judgment: *The Despina GK* (n 24).

[91] See *The Indian Grace (No 2)* (n 27).

[92] Tsimplis and Gaskell (n 77) 526–27.

looks to assess whether the arresting party is seeking to overreach its advantage, or whether the arresting party finds itself without sound security through no fault of its own. In some circumstances, the court may be able to disregard the first arrest as a mistake, despite the arresting party acting in good faith.

Given the breadth of this judicial discretion and the extent of the detailed rules, exceptions and limitations that have been introduced in the SCA 1981 and CPR 61, one may wonder whether English domestic admiralty practice truly complies with the broad 'rule plus exception' framework of the Arrest Convention 1952. Perhaps a more realistic description of the English position is that the courts will consider what can reasonably be done to secure the claimant's claim without subjecting the shipowner to undue harassment.

There have long been calls for England to adopt a fresh approach to its admiralty jurisdiction by means of a comprehensive admiralty code explicitly dealing with matters such as interim remedies and security.[93] If England ever decided to ratify the Arrest Convention 1999, that opportunity would present itself.

B. The Codifier: Australia

Australia has trod some way along the codifying path. Australia is not a party to the Arrest Convention 1952. Nonetheless, the Admiralty Act 1988 (Cth) (AA 1988) was intended to bring Australia's laws more closely into line with the generally accepted international principles of that Convention. However, as a non-signatory, Australia was free to clarify or modify aspects as it considered necessary.

The Australian Law Reform Commission (ALRC) released its report entitled *Civil Admiralty Jurisdiction* (ALRC Report) in 1986.[94] The AA 1988 reflects almost entirely the form recommended by the ALRC.[95] The AA 1988 accepts Australia's status as a user of shipping services rather than a shipowning country.[96] The ALRC Report acknowledged the importance of international uniformity, but also recognised the 'conspicuous lack of uniformity' in many areas of maritime law.[97] It aimed to strike a balance between following the English legislation and seeking to clarify and simplify the law, whilst stopping short of complete codification.[98]

i. *Maintaining the General 'One Arrest, One Ship' Rule*

The ALRC Report recommended a continuation of the rule that only one ship should be arrested for a single cause of action, in line with the Arrest Convention 1952 and the

[93] Jackson (n 2) paras 0.26, 0.33.

[94] Australian Law Reform Commission, *Civil Admiralty Jurisdiction* (ALRC 33, 1986).

[95] In *Patrick Stevedores No 2 Pty Ltd v MV Skulptor Konenkov* (1996) 64 FCR 223, 239F Sheppard J stated 'it is not only permissible, but essential, to look at what the Law Reform Commission has said about particular provisions in the bill and thus the Act and about the reasons for the absence from the bill of other provisions which, on a different view of matters, might have been included'.

[96] ALRC Report (n 94) para 93.

[97] In particular, the wholesale expansion of in rem arrest was to be discouraged because there was no guarantee that countries abroad to recognise judicial sales under the Australian law as providing clear title to the ship, and this was of utmost importance: see ibid para 94.

[98] ibid para 95.

English position.[99] Further, it noted that, if a rearrest should be necessary, as a rule the same ship should be rearrested. However, it suggested that limited exceptions should be created to permit the arrest of a second, different ship where:

(1) the first arrest had been set aside;
(2) the second ship was the particular ship liable on a maritime lien claim that had not yet been extinguished; or
(3) where the first arrested ship had broken arrest.[100]

Accordingly, the AA 1988 provides proceedings for a maritime claim may only be commenced against one ship,[101] then explicitly sets out the limited exceptions to the 'one ship' rule. The relevant provision is section 20:

> **Service on and arrest of only one ship**
>
> (1) Where service of initiating process in a proceeding commenced as mentioned in section 15, 17, 18 or 19 has been effected on a ship, service of initiating process in the proceeding shall not be effected on any other ship unless the service on the first-mentioned ship has been set aside or the proceeding, so far as it relates to that ship, has been discontinued, dismissed or struck out.
>
> (2) Where service of initiating process in a proceeding commenced as mentioned in section 15, 17, 18 or 19 has been effected on a ship, service of initiating process in some other proceeding on the same claim commenced as mentioned in any of those sections shall not be effected on any other ship unless the first-mentioned proceeding has been discontinued, dismissed or struck out.
>
> (3) Where a ship has been arrested in a proceeding commenced as mentioned in section 15, 17, 18 or 19, no other ship shall be arrested in the proceeding unless the first-mentioned ship:
>
> (a) was invalidly arrested and has been released from arrest; or
> (b) was unlawfully removed from the custody of the Marshal and the Marshal has not regained custody of the ship.
>
> (4) Where:
>
> (a) a person has a claim that is both:
>
> (i) a claim on a maritime lien or other charge; and
> (ii) a general maritime claim;
>
> in respect of a ship; and
>
> (b) the person has commenced a proceeding under section 19 against a surrogate ship; subsection (3) does not prevent the arrest of the first-mentioned ship in a proceeding on the maritime lien or other charge if the amount recovered by the person in the proceeding commenced under section 19 is less than the amount of the claim on the maritime lien or other charge.

[99] The ALRC noted that, while there might be rare occasions where the security provided from one arrest would not be sufficient to satisfy the claimant's claim, many procedural questions need to be resolved if a second ship was able to be arrested. While noting that the 'draft revision of the 1952 Convention' (which would later become the Arrest Convention 1999) did contain a provision on multiple arrest, it was considered premature to introduce such a provision until it was definitively accepted at international level: see ibid para 210.

[100] ibid para 212.

[101] ibid; see s 20(1)–(2). The arrest process is set out in Part IV of the Admiralty Rules 1988.

Section 20 permits a second arrest on a *different* ship where:

(1) the first ship had been invalidly arrested and then released (for example, because the wrong ship was arrested);[102]
(2) the ship the subject of the first arrest has left the custody of the Marshal without permission;[103] and
(3) where a claimant holding a maritime lien proceeds first against a surrogate ship but seeks to proceed against the relevant ship for any outstanding claim.[104]

In the first two instances, the AA 1988 regards the first arrest as deficient or defective.

The AA 1988 also seeks to deal with the difficult question of whether a claimant can arrest in rem and then rearrest to enforce a judgment. Rule 43(4) of the Admiralty Rules 1988 permits a claimant to arrest a ship either before or after judgment. This abrogates the principle in *The Alletta*,[105] which the ALRC considered undesirable.[106] This statutory abrogation of the merger doctrine is consistent with another useful extension, namely the inclusion of enforcement of a judgment[107] or award[108] as itself a head of jurisdiction under the AA 1988. Australia also permits security obtained under arrest proceedings to be held for claims heard elsewhere, whether in arbitration or judicial proceedings.[109]

Australia has chosen to permit a remedy for damages for wrongful arrest.[110] By that means, a party who rearrests a vessel without leave of the court may be liable to the shipowner in damages. Given that the rule against rearrest only operates where the original arrest was in Australia, this is a weapon of rather limited effect, but it exists, nonetheless.

In relation to 'one ship one arrest' and multiple arrest, the AA 1988 largely follows the traditional English common law position but manages to lay out the permutations and exceptions while smoothing out some of the more troublesome kinks.

One aspect that continues to trouble admiralty courts is the extent to which previous foreign proceedings in rem should be taken into account. In *Patrick Stevedores No 2 Ltd v Proceeds of Sale of the Vessel MV Skulptor Konenkov* it was held that the words 'initiating process in a proceeding', when used to refer to earlier proceedings in ss 20(1) and 20(2), apply only to initiating processes issued in Australia.[111] The Judge admitted he found the decision difficult, particularly as there appeared to be no authority on point, and the matter had not been dealt with in the ALRC Report. Ultimately, his Honour concluded that Parliament had not intended the Act to have international operation because Parliament had not provided for the obvious difficulties that would arise from construing the Act in that way.[112] The result was that a claimant who had already shared in the proceeds of sale after a different party caused a surrogate ship to be arrested in Canada was permitted to bring a separate

[102] As later confirmed by Sheen J in *The Silver Athens (No 2)* (n 51) 585; and *The Stephan J* (n 42).
[103] Section 20(3) of the AA 1988.
[104] ALRC Report (n 94) para 212. See s 20(4) of the AA 1988. The Act does not have the effect to create a new cause of action or a new maritime lien or charge: see s 6.
[105] See discussion at n 90 above.
[106] ALRC Report (n 94) para 213.
[107] Section 4(2)(c).
[108] Section 4(3)(u).
[109] Section 29.
[110] Section 34; and see art 6 of the Arrest Convention 1952. On wrongful arrest see further ch 6.
[111] *Patrick Stevedores No 2 Pty Ltd v The Proceeds of Sale of the Vessel MV Skulptor Konenkov* (1997) 75 FCR 47.
[112] ibid 53–56.

claim in Australia against the proceeds of sale of another ship in the same ownership. Over 20 years have now passed since that decision, and it appears the precise point has not been raised in Australia again.[113]

ii. Rearrest of the Ship

Section 21 of the 1998 Act deals with the circumstance where the first arrest was valid, but for some reason the arresting party wishes to rearrest the same ship in the same proceedings on the same claim.

As regards the circumstances sufficient to justify a rearrest, the ALRC preferred to specify the main exceptions to the rule whilst leaving the court with a general discretion to permit rearrest in other situations.[114] The ALRC was concerned about providing only specified exceptions to the rule without providing the courts with a general discretion:

> The main advantage of such an approach [stipulating explicit exceptions to the rule] is that it would remove any lingering uncertainty on the right to re-arrest, and clarify its extent. The main disadvantage would be a loss of flexibility, including the danger of not anticipating all possible circumstances in which re-arrest should be permitted. It is better to leave a court with a discretion whether to permit re-arrest (and confer the power to impose conditions on the right to re-arrest) while specifying the most important of the grounds on which re-arrest is likely to be permitted.[115]

Accordingly, the AA 1998 provides in s 21:

> **Re-arrest**
>
> (1) A ship or other property arrested in a proceeding on a maritime claim may not be re-arrested in the proceeding in relation to the claim unless the court so orders, whether because default has been made in the performance of a guarantee or undertaking given to procure the release of the ship or property from the earlier arrest or for some other sufficient reason.
>
> (2) An order under subsection (1) may be made subject to such conditions as are just. (emphasis added)

Conditions imposed under s 21(2) may include, for example, the provision of counter-security by the claimant.

iii. Exercising the Discretion to Grant a Rearrest

There have been very few cases that have required the application of s 21 of the AA 1988. Although s 21 explicitly deals with situations where the first arrest was valid but there has

113 In a fluke of timing the English Commercial Court came to much the same conclusion concerning the English provisions about a week later: see *The Kommunar (No 2)* (n 59). In Australia, a non-Convention country, this is one thing; however, it is quite another in the United Kingdom, given that it is a party to the Arrest Convention 1952. The 1952 Convention requires parties to recognise arrest proceedings at least in relation to other State Parties: see art 3(3). Also see the discussion of *The Fortune 22* (n 55) at text accompanying n 141 below.

114 ALRC Report (n 94) para 211. The ALRC adapted the approach of the 1985 Comité Maritime International (CMI) Draft Revision of the Arrest Convention 1952, which sets out specific exceptions to the 'one arrest' rule. The 1985 CMI Revision provision on rearrest was hardly changed in the Arrest Convention 1999 provision. See Berlingieri (n 7) vol 2 appendix IV; and see discussion in Part V below.

115 ALRC Report (n 94) para 211.

been a failure of security, it would certainly also extend (under the 'sufficient reason' wording) to a situation where the first arrest had been discharged or struck out.[116]

In *Laemthong International Lines Co Ltd v BPS Shipping*[117] the respondent had arrested a surrogate ship, the *Laemthong Pride*. No security was forthcoming. Instead, an application was brought on behalf of the ship seeking its release from arrest. The applicant disputed the right to proceed against that ship as a surrogate ship on various grounds, including that the ship was not in fact a surrogate of the relevant ship at the time of commencement of proceedings. The trial Judge granted the application and discharged the arrest warrant, telling the respondent it could reapply if more information became available. A few days later, the respondent, armed with more information to bolster its argument as to the surrogate status of the ship, applied for a rearrest of the *Laemthong Pride* under s 21. It was agreed that the trial Judge had a discretion to order rearrest under s 21.[118] The Judge took the view that the respondent needed to establish a 'strong argument' that the court had jurisdiction. The Judge considered that this threshold had been met, and permission to rearrest was granted. The applicant appealed, arguing that key documents were inadmissible, and jurisdiction had not been established. The Court of Appeal gave leave to appeal because the trial Judge had applied the wrong test as to the requisite burden of proof. The respondent needed only to establish jurisdiction on the balance of probabilities.[119] However, the Court of Appeal ultimately agreed with the trial Judge that the respondent ought to be given leave to rearrest.[120]

iv. Summary

In almost all cases concerning pre-judgment rearrest, the Australian regime would lead to the same result as the current English law. However, in contrast to the English position, the solution is apparent from the legislation itself. In certain circumstances, a first arrest can be ignored. There is discretion to allow rearrest even where there has been a valid first arrest. The statute requires an arresting party to seek leave from the court to rearrest ahead of time rather than generating extra costs and wasted time by leaving the issue to a later application to have the rearrest set aside.

Even allowing for my familiarity bias, the Australian approach has much to recommend it. As noted by Crawford: 'The legislation thus resolves most of the issues in relation to multiple arrest and rearrest on its face, saving litigants from the need to refer to some complex and confused case law.'[121] This must also be beneficial given that most matters concerning arrest, release and rearrest are conducted under significant time pressure.

[116] Compare the wording of s 20(1) of the AA 1988, which explicitly envisages that a different vessel could be the subject of a second arrest in such circumstances. It would be illogical for the same vessel not to be susceptible to rearrest in the same circumstances, not to mention out of alignment with the pre-Convention English maritime cases.

[117] *Laemthong International Lines Co Ltd v BPS Shipping* (1995) 5 NTLR 59.

[118] ibid 67.

[119] ibid 71 (Mildren J, with whom Thomas J agreed. Angel J also dismissed the appeal).

[120] The case proceeded to the High Court of Australia on other grounds: see *Laemthong International Lines Co Ltd v BPS Shipping* [1997] HCA 55, (1997) 190 CLR 181.

[121] James Crawford 'The Australian Admiralty Act: Project and Practice' [1997] *LMCLQ* 519, 534.

C. The Reformer: South Africa

South Africa is not a party to the Arrest Convention 1952. South Africa inherited English maritime law while a British colony.[122] Prior to reform in the 1980s, the state of admiralty jurisdiction was most unsatisfactory. The Supreme Court of South Africa was effectively 'two courts',[123] one applying English admiralty law and the other applying Roman-Dutch common law.[124] Shortly after the South African Law Reform Commission completed its *Report on the Review of the Law of Admiralty* in 1982 (SALRC Report),[125] reforming legislation was passed in the form of the Admiralty Jurisdiction Regulation Act 1983 (SA) (AJRA 1983).

The AJRA 1983 is known for its 'novel, unusual and at times far reaching provisions';[126] particularly its extended list of maritime claims, its 'associated ship' provisions,[127] its codification of priorities and the ability to obtain security for claims to be heard elsewhere.[128] Also notable is the ability to attach property in an admiralty claim in personam to found jurisdiction.[129]

When South Africa was considering reform in the early 1980s, it had regard to contemporary political manoeuvrings within the CMI. The CMI at that stage was in the throes of developing a Convention to replace the Arrest Convention 1952. That replacement would become the Arrest Convention 1999, which would permit multiple arrests. The AJRA 1983 was therefore 'ahead of its time' in permitting rearrest or multiple arrest where the original security proved to be inadequate and additional security was required. However, the AJRA 1983 maintained the provision requiring there to be an arrest of only 'one ship'.

i. *'One Arrest' Rule v Multiple Arrests*

The relevant provisions can be found in ss 3 and 5. Section 3 contains the following provisions:

> 3(6) … an action in rem, other than such an action in respect of a maritime claim … may be brought by the arrest of an associated ship instead of the ship in respect of which the maritime claim arose. …
>
> 3(8) Property shall not be arrested and security therefor shall not be given more than once in respect of the same maritime claim by the same claimant.

Notably, s 3 contains neither explicit exceptions nor an express acknowledgement of judicial discretion. As we shall see shortly, this has created difficulties.

[122] For a detailed explanation see the South African Law Reform Commission, *Report on the Review of the Law of Admiralty*, Project 32 (Pretoria, SALRC, 1982) para 3.

[123] ibid para 3.9

[124] The English admiralty law was to be applied as the law stood in 1891, and according to the jurisdiction of the English admiralty courts at that time: see ibid.

[125] The SALRC Report unfortunately does not capture or set out in detail the discussions and consultations that occurred prior to its release. However, at 17 pages, one has to admire its brevity. In contrast, the ALRC Report is some 259 pages long.

[126] See *Katagum Wholesale Commodities v The MV Paz* 1984 (3) SA 261, 263B (N) (Friedman J); Malcolm Wallis, 'The Associated Ship Jurisdiction in South Africa; Choice Assorted or Only One Bite at the Cherry?' [2000] *LMCLQ* 132, 136.

[127] On which see ch 2.

[128] On which see ch 3.

[129] See the AJRA 1983, s 4(4); and see eg *The Alina II* [2010] ZAWCHC 503.

It has been held that for the prohibition in s 3(8) to be enlivened, there must have been an arrest[130] and security must have been provided.[131] Therefore, this provision does not prevent an arrest when an earlier arrest has been set aside. In *Great River Shipping Inc v Sunnyface Marine Ltd*[132] an arrest obtained ex parte was set aside on the basis that the applicant had not made out a prima facie case as to the underlying cause of action. The applicant returned sometime later with supplementary evidence and a second arrest was obtained. The question was whether this second arrest offended s 3(8). It was held that it did not:

> [W]here an arrest ... is set aside by reason of a want of one or other of the legal requisites of a valid arrest (such as the absence of a prima facie case) then in my view s3(8) does not prejudice a further arrest provided such legal requisites are present on the later occasion.[133]

Nor will s 3(8) prevent an arrest by way of execution of a judgment where there has been an earlier in rem security arrest. Enforcement of a judgment or arbitration award is a direct ground for exercising in rem jurisdiction under the AJRA 1983.[134] In *The Ivory Tirupati*[135] the Supreme Court of Appeal rejected an argument that s 3(8) would prevent an arrest to enforce a judgment when security had already been given to release the claim. The first claim was the underlying claim for damage to cargo; the second a claim to recover the judgment debt created by the judgment given in respect of the first underlying claim: they were therefore distinct heads of maritime claim under the AJRA 1983.

However, s 3(8) has proved problematic in respect of rearrest. Section 3(8) itself contains no explicit discretion to permit a rearrest of the same ship (or a second arrest on a different ship for that matter). This reflects the early English legislation. As we have seen, the English courts held that there was such a discretion. The English view is now bolstered by the exception recognised by the Arrest Convention 1952, to which England is obliged to give effect. Although the AJRA 1983 is clearly inspired by the English provisions and therefore, by extension, the Arrest Convention 1952, as a non-party to that Convention South Africa is not obliged to interpret the AJRA 1983 with due regard to the Convention.[136]

There is no doubt that the courts maintain a general discretion to prevent an abuse of their own process.[137] However, the absence of an explicit discretion to allow rearrest in appropriate circumstances seems to sit uncomfortably with the otherwise

[130] Actual or deemed, in terms of the AJRA 1983, s 3(10). Under s 3(10) property is deemed to have been arrested where security or an undertaking has been given to prevent arrest. This disposes of any argument that a claimant can arrest the ship or property when security has already been given to prevent arrest.

[131] *Great River Shipping Inc v Sunnyface Marine Ltd (The Great Eagle)* 1992 (2) SA 87, 91 (C).

[132] See ibid generally.

[133] ibid 89: cited and applied in *United Enterprises Corp v STX Pan Ocean Co Ltd* [2007] ZAWCHC 12, 2008 (1) SA 665 (C).

[134] The definition of 'maritime claim' in s 1(aa) of the AJRA 1983 includes 'any judgment or arbitration award relating to a maritime claim, whether given or made in the Republic or elsewhere'.

[135] *The Ivory Tirupati* [2002] ZASCA 155, [2003] 1 All SA 55 (SCA).

[136] The Bill apparently contained a provision allowing judges to take cognisance of laws in other maritime States as well as provisions of international Conventions: see Alan Rycroft, 'Changes in South African Admiralty Jurisdiction' [1984] *LMCLQ* 417, 418. This was not included in the Act as promulgated.

[137] Eg *The Alina II* (n 129).

broadminded legislation. Malcolm Wallis argues that s 3(8) must be read with s 5(2)(d).[138] That subsection reads:

> 5(2) A court may in the exercise of its admiralty jurisdiction –
>
> (a) …
> (b) order any person to give security for costs or for any claim;
> (c) order that any arrest or attachment made or to be made or that anything done or to be done in terms of this Act or any order of the court be subject to such conditions as to the court appears just, whether as to the furnishing of security, the liability for costs, expenses, loss or damage caused, or likely to be caused otherwise;
> (d) *notwithstanding the provisions of section 3(8), order that*, in addition to property already arrested or attached, *further property be arrested or attached in order to provide additional security for any claim*, and order that any security given be increased, reduced or discharged, subject to such conditions as to the court appears just.[139] (emphasis added).

Along the lines of the binary 'rule plus exception' approach of the Arrest Convention 1952, one might view s 3(8) as constituting the 'rule', and s 5(2)(d) as permitting exceptions at the court's discretion. However, one must be careful not to take this argument too far, because the AJRA 1983 was not intended to replicate the Arrest Convention 1952 and is more progressive in many respects. Further, s 5(2) permits the arrest or attachment of 'further' property to provide 'additional security for any claim'. Those words, on their face, would appear to permit the arrest or attachment of a second, different ship to obtain further security.[140]

The relationship between the two provisions was tested in the case of *The Fortune 22*.[141] In that case, the claimant arrested the relevant ship in Hong Kong. The ship was abandoned to the claim; no security was posted. The ship was sold by the court, but the claimant was left empty-handed after higher-ranked creditors swept the pool. The claimant had obtained default judgment, but only after the ship was sold.[142] The claimant then effected a second arrest of an associated ship in South Africa. The Court held that this was impermissible. The claimant could arrest an associated ship 'instead of'[143] the relevant ship, but not one and then the other.[144] While s 5(2)(d) explicitly permits further arrest to increase the amount of security, the Judge noted that the claimant had not brought the claim under that subsection.[145] In other words, the Court took the view that s 3(8) dictated that the claimant

[138] See Wallis (n 19) ch 8 and Wallis (n 126).

[139] The provision was slightly different when first enacted: 'order that any security given be increased, reduced or discharged subject to such conditions as to the court appears just and, for the purpose of an increase of security, authorise the arrest of property notwithstanding the provisions of section 3(8)': see Rycroft (n 136) 427.

[140] But the security sought in an action in rem can only amount to the value of the res, and s 5(2) does not permit 'topping up' to the full amount of the claim: *MV Zlatni Piasatzi: Frozen Foods International Ltd v Kudu Holdings (Pty) Ltd* 1997 (2) SA 569, 576–77 (C).

[141] *The Fortune 22* (n 55).

[142] The significance of this was that the judgment could not be relied upon in arresting another associated ship. See Wallis (n 19) 256.

[143] Section 3(6) provides: 'an action *in rem* … may be brought by the arrest of an associated ship *instead of* the ship in respect of which the maritime claim arose.' (emphasis added)

[144] *The Fortune 22* (n 55) 163.

[145] ibid 166.

had one shot in the locker and had it had been fired in Hong Kong. The decision was the subject of an appeal but settled before the appeal could be heard.

Malcolm Wallis argues stridently and persuasively that the decision is wrong.[146] One strand of his comprehensive argument is that ss 3(8) and 5(2)(d) must be read together; that section 5(2)(d) is, in effect, the section that permits a court to exercise a discretion to allow a further arrest. Another strand of his argument is that the provision was only intended to operate where the first arrest also took place in South Africa.[147] He says that the ARJA 1983 can and should be construed to permit either a rearrest or a second arrest of a different ship in circumstances where security for that claim has not been forthcoming[148] (particularly where the sale of a vessel in a foreign jurisdiction has not led to satisfaction of the debt,[149] as occurred in *The Fortune 22*). Indeed, the underlying purpose of the 'special' jurisdiction enacted in South Africa would otherwise be thwarted:[150]

> [W]here a claim is unsecured … there is no reason in the language of the legislation or in reasons of principle and policy to prevent the creditor from pursuing each and every vessel that is available to be arrested, whether the ship concerned, or an associated ship.

However, *The Fortune 22* has been followed, albeit only by another first instance decision. In the case of *The Multi Diamond*,[151] the relevant ship, the *Marios*, was first arrested in Poland and released on provision of a letter of undertaking. However, the guarantor became insolvent and the security therefore failed. An associated ship, the *Multi Diamond*, was then arrested in South Africa for the same claim. The Court set aside that arrest, relying on *The Fortune 22*.

The Fortune 22 may well be an example of a hard case making bad law. If the original arrest had taken place in South Africa, not Hong Kong, might the claimant have sought a further arrest under s 5(2)(d)? The lack of security for the claim would surely entitle the claimant to arrest 'further property'. Alternatively, if the claimant had obtained judgment in Hong Kong prior to that court selling the ship, the claimant would have been able to enforce the judgment in separate in rem proceedings against an associated ship in South Africa.[152] *The Fortune 22* gives precedence to the 'one ship' rule rather than the overall purpose of the AJRA 1983, namely 'the purpose of promoting the ability of creditors to recover maritime claims'.[153]

Whilst not directly on point, the recent case of *The NYK Isabel*[154] might be a useful bellwether of the approach of the Supreme Court of Appeal of South Africa to the powers and discretion of the admiralty courts under section 5(2). Wallis JA's judgment, with whom

[146] See Wallis (n 126); Wallis (n 19) ch 8.

[147] Wallis (n 19) 244. This argument is similar to the one that was successful in *Patrick Stevedores* (n 111).

[148] Wallis (n 19) 262.

[149] ibid 241: Wallis argues that s 3(8) does not have extra-territorial reach and should be interpreted as applicable only to arrests taking place in South Africa.

[150] Wallis (n 19) 262.

[151] *Tabora Navigation Co Ltd v Sucden M (Moscow) Co Ltd (The Multi Diamond)* (High Court (Durban and Coastal Local Division), 31 March 2000) 98 (Hugo J).

[152] Compare *The Ivory Tirupati* (n 135).

[153] *MV NYK Isabel: Northern Endeavour Shipping Pte Ltd v The Owners of the NYK Isabel* [2016] ZASCA 89 [29] (Wallis JA).

[154] ibid.

the other judges concurred, warned against the discretions contained s 5(2) being 'unduly circumscribed'.[155] His Honour approved of the approach of Friedman J in *The Paz*:[156]

> [This] discretion is an unfettered judicial discretion which falls to be exercised up on a consideration of all relevant facts and circumstances. To endeavour to categorise or catalogue those facts or circumstances … is not only undesirable but is fraught with obvious dangers.

Wallis JA went on to say:

> The Act is a special statute dealing with maritime matters and is directed at meeting the needs of the shipping industry in enforcing maritime claims. It provides the court with very extensive powers to deal with maritime cases … .[157]
>
> [T]he provisions of the Act should be given a generous interpretation consistent with its manifest purpose of assisting maritime claimants to enforce maritime claims … . There is, however, a need for balance when court exercise the expansive powers of arrest and attachment embodied in the Act … . Sections 5(2)(b) and (c) give courts the means to balance the interests of claimant and defendant by ordering countersecurity in appropriate cases and attaching conditions to orders of arrest or attachment.[158]

ii. Summary

At the time of the introduction of the AJRA 1983, one commentator said that South African admiralty jurisdiction had been freed from its 'timewarp'.[159] However, given the decision in *The Fortune 22*, one might ponder whether South Africa is doing the timewarp again. South Africa's law of arrest is so liberal that adherence to the 'one ship' rule – at least as currently interpreted – appears seriously out of step. The right to claim top-up security by way of multiple arrests is more constrained than some commentators would like.[160] Legislative amendment would provide the clearest guidance; failing that, the South African Supreme Court of Appeal will no doubt critically revisit *The Fortune 22* decision when the opportunity arises.

V. The Arrest Convention 1999

The Arrest Convention 1999 came into force on 14 September 2011 after 10 parties ratified the instrument.[161] However, it has yet to be widely accepted amongst maritime nations. The process of negotiation and compromise surrounding the Arrest Convention 1999 is the

[155] ibid [43].
[156] *The Paz* (n 126) 264A–C.
[157] *The NYK Isabel* (n 153) [44].
[158] ibid [45].
[159] Rycroft (n 136) 417.
[160] See Wallis (n 19) ch 8, particularly 251ff. 'In simple terms the purpose of the jurisdiction is to enable to creditor to obtain payment'.
[161] See n 18 above.

subject of a fascinating article by Gaskell and Shaw.[162] The provision concerning rearrests and multiple arrests is Article 5:

Right of rearrest and multiple arrest

1. Where in any State a ship has already been arrested and released or security in respect of that ship has already been provided to secure a maritime claim, that ship shall not thereafter be rearrested or arrested in respect of the same maritime claim unless:
   (a) the nature or amount of the security in respect of that ship already provided in respect of the same claim is inadequate, on condition that the aggregate amount of security may not exceed the value of the ship; or
   (b) the person who has already provided the security is not, or is unlikely to be, able to fulfil some or all of that person's obligations; or
   (c) the ship arrested or the security previously provided was released either:
      (i) upon the application or with the consent of the claimant acting on reasonable grounds, or
      (ii) because the claimant could not by taking reasonable steps prevent the release.
2. Any other ship which would otherwise be subject to arrest in respect of the same maritime claim shall not be arrested unless:
   (a) the nature or amount of the security already provided in respect of the same claim is inadequate; or
   (b) the provisions of paragraph 1 (b) or (c) of this article are applicable.
3. 'Release' for the purpose of this article shall not include any unlawful release or escape from arrest.

A. Permissible Rearrests

Article 5 sets out a number of situations where rearrest will be permissible. These largely cover situations in which the courts would probably also exercise their discretion to allow further arrest under the Arrest Convention 1952:[163]

(1) Article 5(1)(b) enshrines the uncontroversial exception that such a rearrest is available where the guarantor is rendered insolvent;
(2) Article 5(1)(c) permits rearrest where the first arrest or the security provided was released either because the claimant reasonably consented to it, or the claimant was not able to prevent the release by taking reasonable steps.[164] The concept of 'reasonableness' was not universally well received at the negotiations, and there is certainly room for interpretation and fleshing out. It does, however, give some leeway on the facts of any particular case; and
(3) Article 5(3) makes it clear that a ship that is unlawfully released or escapes arrest is not protected from rearrest. This makes explicit what caselaw has established in any event.

[162] Nicholas Gaskell and Richard Shaw, 'The Arrest Convention 1999' [1999] *LMCLQ* 470.
[163] See generally Berlingieri (n 7) vol 2 ch 9.
[164] id para 9.07–08; appendix IV. Two examples proffered by CMI were where a claimant agrees to release the ship without a guarantee due to some overwhelming commercial imperative; or where the claimant agrees to release the ship because the place of arrest is such that the arresting ship may be in danger or endanger others in the face of impending heavy weather.

B. Rearrests and Multiple Arrests to 'Top Up' Security

There are other significant changes. Article 5(1)(a) is broadly cast. It permits rearrest to top up security, up to the value of the ship, simply on the ground that the 'nature' or 'amount' of the security already provided is 'inadequate'. What exactly is meant by inadequate will presumably become clear: it will include the financial status of the guarantor, but might the amount or type of security also be inadequate? Indeed, inadequacy may only require the security to be 'insufficient'.[165] This relaxation of the Arrest Convention 1952's 'one ship, one arrest' rule is a fundamental change.

The other fundamental change is Article 5(2)(a), which permits a further 'top-up' arrest of a sister ship, and is unlimited by the value of the arrested ship. This would appear to permit serial arrests until the total claim amount has been reached. Article 5(2) permits not only a second arrest of another ship, but also appears to permit that second arrest even while the first ship remains under arrest.[166]

Overall, there are two things to note. First, and more obviously, there is a significant change in tone and an acceptance that more than one arrest may be necessary to ensure full security for the claim; and that the arrest may be of either the relevant ship or any sister ship. This represents a shift closer to the traditional Civilian position and places the emphasis firmly on the adequacy of security rather than the act of arrest. Secondly, the Arrest Convention 1999 jettisons the 'prohibition plus exception' model of the Arrest Convention 1952 and its framing of the judicial discretion to permit rearrest with reference to 'another good cause'. Instead, the Arrest Convention 1999 prefers to set out the specific categories in which it will be permissible to rearrest or effect multiple arrests. This change is important, because (not unlike the Australian legislation) it makes it much easier for the claimant to work out whether it can bring itself within those categories, rather than having to guess how a court will exercise its discretion in any given case.

The travaux préparatoires show that the new art 5 concerning rearrest and multiple arrest was controversial. Countries such as the US, Liberia and Korea were unhappy that rearrest was not maintained as an exceptional measure.[167] In any event, the recalibration to a more liberal rearrest and multiple arrest regime is unlikely to have much practical effect unless and until the Arrest Convention 1999 receives broader international acceptance.

VI. Conclusion

English courts devised the 'one arrest' rule given the drastic remedy of ship arrest.

> The arrest of a vessel is never a trifling matter. Arrest is a very powerful invasive remedy. An arrest of a ship can lead to tremendous inconvenience, financial distress and severe commercial embarrassment … . Even the briefest of delays can sometimes cause significant losses. It can also in certain instances prejudice the livelihood of the ship's crew and the commercial fortunes of the shipowner.[168]

[165] See Gaskell and Shaw (n 162) 481.
[166] See Berlingieri (n 7) vol 2 para 9.09.
[167] ibid, appendix IV. Liberia has since acceded to the Convention.
[168] *The Vasiliy Golovnin* (n 4) [51] (Rajah JA).

An admiralty court is keenly aware that it must ensure that a claimant's right to arrest the ship does not become an instrument of oppression. However, even the earliest English cases showed that there needed to be some leeway to ensure the balancing of the scales of justice. The courts exercised a broad power to permit rearrest if it was necessary to do justice between the parties, and various exceptions were created. Unfortunately, the English traditional approach does not lead to predictable outcomes and litigation has often been required to settle the matter. By contrast, the Australian model has shown that articulating the types of situations when rearrest will be permitted, or when a discretion may be exercised, is both feasible and beneficial. This is consistent with the most recent model adopted at an international level, with the Arrest Convention 1999 provisions stipulating, first, the grounds which will not constitute a rearrest; secondly, the circumstances where rearrest is permissible; and finally, going one step further to permit additional arrests where security is inadequate.

6

Wrongful Arrest of Ships

TOH KIAN SING* AND NATHANAEL LIN‡

I. Introduction

Liability for wrongful arrest of ships, or more accurately the threshold for liability for wrongful arrest of ships, has always been a contentious issue, with Common Law and Civil Law countries sharply divided in their views on this topic. An early draft of what became the Arrest Convention 1952[1] contained the following provision in art 7:

> In case an unjustified arrest is released, the arrestor shall be condemned to pay the cost of the security provided in order to release the ship. In case the unjustified arrest has been effected in bad faith, the arrestor may also be condemned to pay the damages caused by the arrest to all persons having an interest in the ship or in the cargo.

This draft provision was strongly opposed by the British delegation, because it clashed with the established common law test for wrongful arrest set out by the Privy Council in *The Evangelismos*, which provided that damages for wrongful ship arrest might only be obtained 'where there is either *mala fides* or that *crassa negligentia* which implies malice'.[2] The Comité Maritime International (CMI), convinced that, 'if the draft Convention will provide too hard sanctions, it will clash against the irreducible opposition of British interests', jettisoned the draft provision,[3] replacing it instead with what is now art 6 of the Arrest Convention 1952, which leaves all issues of damages for wrongful arrest to 'the law of the Contracting State in whose jurisdiction the arrest was made or applied for'.

The inevitable result of the inability to find a compromise between Common Law and Civil Law interests in drafting the Arrest Convention 1952 is that the issue remained to be determined by domestic law rather than the international ship arrest regime. Although the drafters of the Arrest Convention 1999[4] grasped this nettle a little less gingerly,

* Senior Counsel, Advocate and Solicitor of the Supreme Court of Singapore; Adjunct Faculty, Faculty of Law, Singapore Management University.

‡ Advocate and Solicitor of the Supreme Court of Singapore; Group In-House Counsel, Ocean Tankers (Pte) Ltd.

[1] International Convention Relating to the Arrest of Sea-going Ships (adopted 10 May 1952, entered into force 24 February 1956) 439 UNTS 193.

[2] *The Evangelismos* (1858) Moo PC 352, 359, 14 ER 945, 948 (PC). See Francesco Berlingieri, *Berlingieri on Arrest of Ships*, 6th edn (Abingdon, Informa Law from Routledge, 2017) vol 1 paras 1.08, 18.01.

[3] Berlingieri (n 2) vol 1 para 1.08 fn 24.

[4] International Convention on the Arrest of Ships (adopted 12 March 1999, entered into force 14 September 2011) 2797 UNTS 3.

by providing in art 6 of the Arrest Convention 1999 that courts have jurisdiction to impose counter-security on claimants as a condition of allowing or maintaining ship arrest, and have jurisdiction to determine liability for wrongful arrest, this essentially restates the inherent jurisdiction of most admiralty courts.[5] The question of substantive liability for wrongful arrest was still left to be determined by the lex fori of the State where arrest was effected.[6]

Given that both Arrest Conventions 1952 and 1999 ultimately leave the issue of liability for wrongful ship arrest to the lex fori of the State in which the arrest has taken place, this Chapter will focus on domestic law, and in particular on the development of the test for liability for wrongful ship arrests by the Singapore courts. The Chapter will conclude with a brief discussion of the CMI International Working Group (IWG) on liability for wrongful ship arrest.

II. Wrongful Arrest in Singapore

The threshold which a defendant shipowner has to cross in order to obtain damages for wrongful arrest has long been thought to be high, so much so that the protection that a shipowner gets from a wrongful arrest claim is often more illusory than real. As a result, some Commonwealth jurisdictions have lowered the bar for wrongful arrest through legislative reform. So, for example, in Australia, s 34(1) of the Admiralty Act 1988 (Cth) now provides that:[7]

> Where, in relation to a proceeding commenced under this Act:
>
> (a) a party unreasonably and without good cause:
>
> (i) demands excessive security in relation to the proceeding; or
>
> (ii) obtains the arrest of a ship or other property under this Act; or
>
> (b) a party or other person unreasonably and without good cause fails to give a consent required under this Act for the release from arrest of a ship or other property;

[5] Berlingieri (n 2) vol 2 para 11.02. For this reason, the Canadian delegation argued that the provision should be deleted as otiose.

[6] ibid paras 11.01ff. Although in force, the Arrest Convention 1999 does not enjoy widespread support and has therefore had relatively little impact on wrongful ship arrest issues. However, see s 11(1) of the Indian Admiralty (Jurisdiction and Settlement of Maritime Claims) Act 2017, which is based on art 6 of the Arrest Convention 1999:

> The High Court may, as a condition of arrest of a vessel, or for permitting an arrest already effected to be maintained, impose upon the claimant who seeks to arrest or who has procured the arrest of the vessel, an obligation to provide an unconditional undertaking to pay such sums of money as damages or such security of a kind for an amount and upon such terms as may be determined by the High Court, for any loss or damage which may be incurred by the defendant as a result of the arrest, and for which the claimant may be found liable, including but not restricted to the following, namely:—
>
> (a) the arrest having been wrongful or unjustified; or
>
> (b) excessive security having been demanded and provided.

[7] See the Australian Law Reform Commission, Civil Admiralty Jurisdiction (ALRC 33, 1986) paras 301ff; Shane Nossal, 'Damages for the Wrongful Arrest of a Vessel' [1996] *LMCLQ* 368; Michael Woodford, 'Damages for Wrongful Arrest: Section 34, *Admiralty Act 1988*' (2005) 19 *Maritime Law Association of Australia and New Zealand Journal* 115; *Delaware North Marine Experience Pty Ltd v The Ship Eye-Spy* [2017] FCA 708, [2017] 2 Lloyd's Rep 463 [292].

> the party or person is liable in damages to a party to the proceeding, or to a person who has an interest in the ship or property, being a party or person who has suffered loss or damage as a direct result.

Section 5(4) of the South African Admiralty Jurisdiction Regulation Act 1983[8] is framed in similar terms, providing that:

> Any person who makes an excessive claim or requires excessive security or without reasonable and probable cause obtains the arrest of property or an order of court, shall be liable to any person suffering loss or damage as a result thereof for that loss or damage.

Singapore has not gone down a similar path of legislative reform. The Singapore courts have instead adapted a long-established common law test for wrongful arrest by giving it a fresh interpretation, such that (if the recent first-instance decisions applying it are anything to go by) it now has renewed vigour in according the necessary protection to shipowners.

A. *The Vasiliy Golovnin*: Reinterpretation of the *Evangelismos* Test

The test for wrongful arrest at common law may be traced back to the high (and apparently difficult to satisfy) threshold test laid down in *The Evangelismos*.[9] This case involved a damage claim brought by the owners of the British brig *Hind* against the Greek brig *Evangelismos* arising from a collision at the mouth of the river Thames. The claimants failed to establish their case against the *Evangelismos*, and the action was dismissed with costs, but without damages.[10] The owner of the *Evangelismos*, Antonius Xenos, appealed to the Privy Council, claiming that he was entitled to both costs and damages for the injury sustained by the detention and demurrage of the ship while under arrest. The Privy Council dismissed his appeal on the basis that the arrest of the *Evangelismos* had been in good faith. In doing so, the Privy Council made the following famous observations:[11]

> Undoubtedly there may be cases in which there is either *mala fides*, or that *crassa negligentia*, which implies malice, which would justify a Court of Admiralty giving damages, as in an action brought at Common law damages may be obtained. …
>
> The real question in this case … comes to this: is there, or is there not, reason to say that the action was so unwarrantably brought, or brought with so little colour, so little foundation, that it rather implies malice on the part of the Plaintiff, or that gross negligence which is equivalent to it?

For ease of exposition, the two paragraphs cited above will be referred to throughout this Chapter as the first and second paragraphs respectively.

[8] The Act also broadens out the heads of South African admiralty jurisdiction to cover any actions for damages for local or foreign wrongful arrests: see s 1(1)(bb) covering 'wrongful or malicious proceedings in respect of or involving any property referred to in section 3(5), or the wrongful or malicious arrest, attachment or detention of any such property, wherever any such proceedings, arrest, attachment or detention took place, and whether in the Republic or elsewhere, and any loss or damage contemplated in section 5(4)'.

[9] *The Evangelismos* (n 2).

[10] The first instance decision by Dr Lushington in the High Court of Admiralty is reported ibid 352–55, 945–46.

[11] ibid 359, 948.

The *Evangelismos* test, as encapsulated by the first paragraph, has been applied on various occasions by Singapore courts. Successful claims for wrongful arrest, as a matter of Singapore law, were relatively few, which has led some commentators to opine that the process of arrest may be abused with impunity.[12] It was commonly understood that to satisfy the first paragraph of the *Evangelismos* test, the shipowner would have to demonstrate actual malice, or gross negligence amounting to malice or *crassa negligentia*.[13] Therefore, the *Evangelismos* threshold was thought to be exceptionally hard to satisfy.

In *The Vasiliy Golovnin*,[14] the Singapore Court of Appeal traced the historical root of the abovementioned test to the fact that, when *The Evangelismos* was decided, the admiralty jurisdiction of the court could only properly be invoked by the arrest of the vessel, as opposed to avoiding arrest by providing substitute security. A high threshold for wrongful arrest, analogous to the tort of malicious prosecution, was deemed necessary to protect plaintiffs who were unable to prove their claims on a balance of probabilities from liability for damages. In that historical context, the high threshold adopted in *The Evangelismos*[15] is unsurprising, as malice and a lack of reasonable or probable cause are two essential elements of the tort of malicious prosecution.[16] In his historical survey VK Rajah JA referred to various decisions of the English Admiralty Court, including *The Victor*,[17] *The Cheshire Witch*,[18] *The Cathcart*[19] and *The Mary Jane*,[20] all of which had uniformly held that damages could be recovered as a result of a wrongful detention only if there was evidence of *mala fides* or *crassa negligentia*.[21]

In the twentieth century, there was academic and judicial disquiet about the evidential difficulty which the *Evangelismos* test demanded. Proving actual malice calls for evidence of subjective intent of *mala fides* on the part of the arresting party which, in an interlocutory setting, is always going to be difficult to demonstrate from affidavit evidence. The criterion of *crassa negligentia* is ostensibly easier to satisfy but only ever so slightly. The 'grossness' of the negligence, amounting to malice, still calls for very clear evidence, which is again a tall order in an interlocutory setting.

[12] See eg the ALRC Report (n 7) para 301; Nossal (n 7). VK Rajah JA put the perceived difficulty aptly in *The Vasiliy Golovnin* [2008] SGCA 39, [2008] 4 SLR(R) 994 [120]: 'Aside from deterring deserving shipowners from pursuing wrongful arrest claims, the difficulties in making out such claims have also given rise to some concerns that an arrest may be procured with impunity on insubstantial grounds so long as there is no malice or gross negligence … . This is because the *Evangelismos* test is so plaintiff-oriented that the risk of having to pay damages, even if the arrest turns out to be unjustified, is so minimal that the plaintiff hardly ever needs to be concerned about it.'

[13] The *Evangelismos* test has not always been restated consistently: so eg in *The Strathnaver* (1875) 1 App Cas 58, 67 the Privy Council reformulated the test as being one of '*mala fides* or malicious negligence'. See Nossal (n 7) 373.

[14] *The Vasiliy Golovnin* (n 12). See generally Toh Kian Sing, *Admiralty Law and Practice*, 3rd edn (Singapore, LexisNexis, 2017) 205ff for a comprehensive survey of wrongful arrest in Singapore.

[15] *The Evangelismos* (n 2).

[16] *The Vasiliy Golovnin* (n 12) [124]. See also *The Walter D Wallet* [1893] P 202, 205–7; *The Ohm Mariana ex Peony* [1992] SGHC 57, [1992] 1 SLR(R) 556 [48].

[17] *The Victor* (1860) Lush 72, 167 ER 38.

[18] *The Cheshire Witch* (1864) Br & L 362, 167 ER 402.

[19] *The Cathcart* (1867) LR 1 A&E 314.

[20] *The Mary Jane* (1869) LR 2 A&E 345.

[21] *The Vasiliy Golovnin* (n 12) [114]–[115].

Colman J's influential decision in *The Kommunar (No 3)*[22] explains that the *Evangelismos* test essentially envisages two types of cases where damages for wrongful arrest may be awarded:

> Firstly, there are cases of mala fides, which must be taken to mean those cases where on the primary evidence the arresting party has no honest belief in his entitlement to arrest the vessel. Secondly, there are those cases in which objectively there is so little basis for the arrest that it may be inferred that the arresting party did not believe in his entitlement to arrest the vessel or acted without any serious regard to whether there were adequate grounds for the arrest of the vessel. It is, as I understand the judgment [in *The Evangelismos*], in the latter sense that such phrases as 'crassa negligentia' and 'gross negligence' are used and are described as implying malice or being equivalent to it. The reference at the end of the passage from the judgment just cited to there being circumstances which afforded grounds for believing that the arrested ship was the one that had been in collision suggests that if on the evidence there is a genuine but understandable mistake as to the identity of the vessel, that will not amount to crassa negligentia. Taking the judgment as a whole, it would not appear that mere absence of reasonable care to ascertain entitlement to arrest the vessel would necessarily amount to ['crassa negligentia'] in the sense there used.

This restatement of the *Evangelismos* test by Colman J was subsequently referred to approvingly by the English Court of Appeal in *Gulf Azov Shipping Co Ltd v Idisi*[23] as an 'exposition of the modern law'. In *The Vasiliy Golovnin*[24] VK Rajah JA refers to Colman J's restatement as a 'modern formulation' of the *Evangelismos* test and notes that it, together with the traditional formulation, was cited with approval by Karthigesu JA in *The Kiku Pacific*.[25] The significance of Colman J's reformulation of the *Evangelismos* test in *The Kommunar (No 3)*,[26] it may be argued, lies in bringing within the ambit of *crassa negligentia* an arrest that has 'little basis'; that is, an arrest where the plaintiff did not genuinely believe in its entitlement to do so, or in which it acted without any serious regard as to the adequacy of its grounds to arrest. Colman J did not elaborate on what considerations should go into this exercise and, in particular, whether a plaintiff whose claim is completely unmeritorious may be said to have acted with such gross negligence as to amount to malice.[27]

There is another dimension to the easing of the *Evangelismos* test. Since the enactment of the Supreme Court of Judicature Acts 1873–75 (UK) admiralty proceedings have been commenced by the issue of an admiralty writ in rem (as opposed to an arrest), and the admiralty jurisdiction may be invoked either by service of the writ or the warrant of arrest. The historical rationale for the traditional strict *Evangelismos* test based on the tort of malicious prosecution may therefore be said to have lost its relevance.[28]

[22] *Centro Latino Americano de Commercio Exterior SA v Owners of the Ship Kommunar (The Kommunar) (No 3)* [1997] 1 Lloyd's Rep 22, 30.

[23] *Gulf Azov Shipping Co Ltd v Idisi* [2001] 1 Lloyd's Rep 727, 735.

[24] *The Vasiliy Golovnin* (n 12) [117].

[25] *The Kiku Pacific* [1999] SGCA 9, [1999] 2 SLR(R) 91 [14], [17].

[26] *The Kommunar (No 3)* (n 22).

[27] In this regard see VK Rajah JA in *The Vasiliy Golovnin* (n 12) [120]: one of the perceived problems with the *Evangelismos* test is 'that an arrest may be procured with impunity on insubstantial grounds so long as there is no malice or gross negligence'.

[28] See Nossal (n 7) 376–77.

In an attempt to mitigate the high threshold of the *Evangelismos* test, which has arguably become 'conceptually anachronistic'[29] and a serious obstacle to the recovery of losses by an aggrieved shipowner, VK Rajah JA, after an extensive review of the case law and statutory regimes in other jurisdictions, placed his emphasis on the second paragraph; that is, the part of the *Evangelismos* test which poses the question whether 'the action was so unwarrantably brought, or brought with so little colour, or so little foundation' that it implies malice or gross negligence on the plaintiff's part. In his Honour's words:[30]

> Reverting to the proper application of the *Evangelismos* test, we note that in many of the cases that have applied the test, the courts have always placed emphasis on the first part of the Rt Hon T Pemberton Leigh's famous passage at 359 (ie, '[u]ndoubtedly there *may* be cases in which there is either *mala fides*, or that *crassa negligentia*, which implies malice, which would justify a Court of Admiralty giving damages, as in an action brought at Common law damages may be obtained' [emphasis added]), focusing on the words *mala fides* and *crassa negligentia* … . A plain reading of that part merely suggests that he was of the view that, in cases involving *mala fides* or *crassa negligentia*, damages would naturally be awarded, especially given that he had used the word 'may' at the start of the statement. It appears that the real focus of the test (if any) he had in mind is that found in the second part of his passage which begins with the opening words '[t]he *real question* in this case … comes to this' [emphasis added], viz, whether 'the action was so unwarrantably brought, or brought with so little colour, or so little foundation' that it implies malice or gross negligence on the plaintiff's part.
>
> In most cases, the fact that the *in rem* action (together with the arrest) was 'so unwarrantably brought, or brought with so little colour, or so little foundation' would probably mean that there has been *mala fides* or *crassa negligentia* on the part of the plaintiff. The two may perhaps be said to be plainly apparent in most cases where the facts are clear, but we are of the view that where the focus or emphasis lies during the inquiry may prove to be determinative in other more difficult cases where it is hard to put a finger as to whether there is or there is no *mala fides* or *crassa negligentia* on the part of the plaintiff, but where it is clear that the arrest was wholly unwarranted in the circumstances at the time when the arrest was sought. Focusing on the first part of the passage … would mean that the inquiry would be both an objective and a subjective one into the plaintiff's state of mind at the time of the arrest as there would be a need to establish if the plaintiff had a genuine and honest belief that the arrest was legitimate then. On the other hand, if the focus is on the second part of the passage, this would mean a more objective inquiry into the circumstances prevailing and the evidence available at the time of the arrest, so as to determine if the action and the arrest were so unwarrantably brought, or brought with so little colour, or so little foundation, as to imply that they were brought with malice or gross negligence. The answer to this question may also, depending on the facts of the case, lead to an objective finding of the subjective intention of the plaintiff at the time of the arrest. In situations involving the more difficult cases as mentioned above, this approach could prove determinative as to whether damages should be awarded to the shipowner. In our view, this is indeed the correct approach, and the inquiry of wrongful arrest should be focused on the question of whether the action and the arrest were so unwarrantably brought, or brought with so little colour, or so little foundation, as to imply malice or gross negligence on the plaintiff's part.

Several observations may be made in connection with this reinterpretation of the *Evangelismos* test. First, it introduces a greater degree of objectivity into the test of malice

[29] *The Vasiliy Golovnin* (n 12) [126].
[30] ibid [136]–[137].

or gross negligence (*crassa negligentia*). The court is invited to conduct an objective analysis into the evidence and circumstances prevailing at the time of the arrest, from which it may make a finding on the plaintiff's intent in bringing about the arrest. Secondly, in considering whether the action is so 'unwarrantably brought' or 'brought with so little colour', (to borrow Pemberton B's words),[31] the enquiry is not limited to the plaintiff's motive in bringing the arrest. A multi-factorial approach is necessary, one in which even the substance of the underlying claim (or more accurately, the relative lack of it) does not avoid scrutiny. This may well tilt the balance in favour of the shipowner in the borderline cases to which VK Rajah JA alluded. Thirdly, this reinterpretation of the *Evangelismos* test came about against a backdrop of judicial concern that the previously understood formulation of the *Evangelismos* test afforded shipowners too little protection. In reformulating the test to meet modern concerns, there was a clear judicial intent to guard against ship arrest brought on the back of speculative claims that do not stand up to even minimal scrutiny.

In practice, it is often not difficult to identify those ship arrests that are brought with little or no foundation or justification. A plaintiff with no right to arrest or a flimsy right to arrest (whether because of a lack of admiralty jurisdiction or because the right to arrest has been lost) may try to conjure up such a right. A plaintiff with a completely baseless claim may try to misrepresent the facts to give them a more palatable look when applying for a warrant of arrest. A plaintiff may arrest a vessel, not so much because it is seeking pre-judgment security for a genuine claim, but to pressurise the defendant shipowner into entering a settlement agreement, or simply because the plaintiff believes that, immediately after the arrest, the action can be stayed in favour of arbitration, where its claim may receive a more sympathetic reception.

The Dilmun Fulmar[32] is perhaps a classic example of such a situation. In this case a shipyard entered into a repair contract with the former owner of the vessel. The former owner failed to pay for the repairs. The shipyard arrested the vessel. The parties entered into a settlement agreement that was personally guaranteed by the former owner's director. The vessel was subsequently sold. The former owner defaulted on the settlement agreement. Despite the change in ownership, the shipyard rearrested the vessel, arguing that the settlement agreement allowed it to revive its original claim in the event of non-payment of any instalments, and it was therefore entitled to rearrest the vessel. Belinda Ang J described the shipyard's arguments as 'tissue paper thin' and 'wholly illusory'[33] and held that the rearrest of the ship was in bad faith and an abuse of the court process.[34]

On the facts of *The Vasiliy Golovnin*,[35] the Singapore Court of Appeal found that the bank had wrongfully arrested the vessel. In coming to its decision to award the shipowner damages for wrongful arrest, the Court paid special regard to three pertinent facts. To begin with, the Court found that the plaintiff had unreasonably persisted in arresting a sister ship in Singapore even after the same claim had already been disposed of overseas in the

[31] *The Evangelismos* (n 2) 359, 948.
[32] *The Dilmun Fulmar* [2003] SGHC 270, [2004] 1 SLR(R) 140.
[33] ibid [14].
[34] ibid [17].
[35] *The Vasiliy Golovnin* (n 12).

Lomé court – and, in particular, in circumstances where the Lomé court had already ruled that sufficient security had been furnished for the plaintiff's claim.[36]

Secondly, the Court affirmed the High Court's decision to strike out the plaintiff's claim for breach of the contract contained in, or evidenced by, the bills of lading.[37] The defendant shipowner had discharged the cargo shipped under the bills of lading in accordance with an order issued by the Lomé court.[38] The plaintiff's attempt to justify the arrest in Singapore to obtain security for its alleged claims for loss and damage to the cargo was also held to be insufficient, given that a P&I club undertaking had already been furnished for exactly the same claims.[39]

Finally, the Court held that the plaintiff had failed to comply with its duty of full and frank disclosure in applying for the warrant of arrest.[40] In particular, the plaintiff had failed to disclose that it had previously arrested a sister ship in Lomé for the same claim, which arrest had been set aside by the Lomé court at a contested hearing.[41] The plaintiff had not appealed against the decision of the Lomé court, and had instead proceeded to arrest another vessel in Singapore for the same claim.[42] The plaintiff had also failed to disclose the fact that the bills of lading had been switched to change the port of discharge from Lomé to Douala – without which the defendant shipowner would, in fact, have performed the terms of the contract of carriage by delivering the cargo at Lomé.[43]

B. Post-*Vasiliy Golovnin* Decisions on Wrongful Arrest

Since the decision of *The Vasiliy Golovnin*[44] in 2008, Singapore courts have on two occasions shown that they are prepared in appropriate cases to delve into the merits of the arresting plaintiff's claim and determine summarily whether a case for implying malice may be made out. Where such summary determination is not possible at the interlocutory stage, the Singapore courts have held that it is still open to a defendant shipowner to pursue a counter-claim for damages for wrongful arrest at trial. In each of these two decisions a claim for wrongful arrest was made out at the first instance.

i. The STX Mumbai

The STX Mumbai[45] featured an application to strike out the plaintiff's claim, as well as the usual prayer to set aside the warrant of arrest. In this case, the plaintiff bunker supplier had arrested the vessel, the *STX Mumbai*, to obtain security for its claim arising from an unpaid invoice in relation to the supply of bunkers. The plaintiff alleged that an entity,

[36] ibid [141].
[37] ibid [78], [146].
[38] ibid [74].
[39] ibid [78].
[40] ibid [141].
[41] ibid [97]–[100].
[42] ibid [144].
[43] ibid [121], [147].
[44] *The Vasiliy Golovnin* (n 12).
[45] *The STX Mumbai* [2014] SGHC 122, [2014] 3 SLR 1116.

STX Corporation, had entered into a bunker supply contract as agent for the defendant, the registered owner of the *STX Mumbai*.

The plaintiff argued that the insolvency of STX Pan Ocean Pte Ltd (STX Pan Ocean), an entity related to the defendant, and the financial difficulties facing the STX group of companies, of which the defendant STX Corporation was a part, led it to believe that the defendant would not be able to pay for the price of the bunkers, and was therefore in repudiatory breach of the bunker supply agreement.[46] The plaintiff's alternative argument was that the insolvency of STX Pan Ocean gave rise to an anticipatory breach of the payment obligation under the bunker supply agreement, thereby entitling the plaintiff to treat the bunker supply agreement as discharged.[47]

The defendant argued that it had no contractual relationship with the plaintiff, as the bunkers had been ordered through a chain of bunker supply contracts with various parties.[48] The defendant further argued that no valid cause of action existed at the time that the writ of summons was issued and the *STX Mumbai* was arrested on 14 March 2013.[49] Furthermore, as a matter of law, the insolvency of STX Pan Ocean could not amount to anticipatory breach.[50]

The Singapore High Court agreed with the defendant's arguments and struck out the claim on the ground of legal unsustainability, in that the plaintiff did not have a proper and valid cause of action when the writ was filed.[51] Having struck out the claim, the Singapore High Court proceeded to consider whether bad faith could be imputed to the plaintiff as a result of commencing an action without a valid cause of action.[52]

Belinda Ang J held that the second limb of the *Evangelismos* test involved an objective finding of the plaintiff's subjective intention as to whether or not it believed in its entitlement to arrest.[53] On the facts of the case, Belinda Ang J held that the plaintiff's attempt to send the defendant a letter of demand via email after office hours calling for immediate payment on the same day was designed to 'set the stage for an imminent arrest', given the vessel's scheduled call at Singapore the very next day.[54] That email 'appeared perfunctory given its timing' and the 'tight deadline was designed to achieve and create a semblance of refusal to pay as amounting to repudiation that was clearly artificial'.[55] In the circumstances, Belinda Ang J held that the defendant had succeeded in its claim for wrongful arrest damages.

While the Singapore Court of Appeal allowed the appeal against the Singapore High Court's decision on the striking out point, and by extension, the finding of wrongful arrest, the Court nevertheless also delved into the merits of the case in considering whether the claim for wrongful arrest could be made out on the present evidence before the Court

[46] ibid [5].
[47] ibid.
[48] ibid [16].
[49] ibid.
[50] ibid [17].
[51] ibid [75].
[52] ibid [79]–[83].
[53] ibid [78].
[54] ibid [79].
[55] ibid.

(that is, at an interlocutory hearing, based on affidavit evidence).[56] In so concluding, the Singapore Court of Appeal placed significant emphasis on the fact that the High Court's decision to strike out the claim had been overturned.[57] In particular, the Court of Appeal considered that there was no conclusive evidence to determine, at this summary stage, that STX Pan Ocean's insolvency did, in fact, render performance of the contract impossible.[58] Nevertheless, more evidence could still emerge during the proceedings which might well point towards a finding that the arrest was the result of either bad faith or gross negligence.[59] The question of damages for wrongful arrest was thus reserved to the trial judge, to be considered at trial.[60]

ii. The Xin Chang Shu

In *The Xin Chang Shu*[61] the plaintiff arrested a vessel for unpaid bunkers on the premise that an intermediary (OW Singapore) was the shipowner's agent when the documentary evidence pointed overwhelmingly to two back-to-back bunker supply contracts. The claim was struck out as being legally and factually unsustainable. In addition to applying to strike out the claim, the shipowner also sought damages for wrongful arrest against the plaintiff. The shipowner's claim for wrongful arrest succeeded and much of the judgment of Steven Chong J pertained to his Honour's conclusion in this regard.[62] Perhaps as a foretaste of what was to come, Steven Chong J made the following statement in the opening paragraphs of his judgment:[63]

> The law on wrongful arrest was developed to protect shipowners against malicious arrests or arrests brought with 'so little colour' or 'so little foundation' that implies malice on the part of the arresting party.
>
> Proof of actual malice is often difficult to establish, especially at the interlocutory stage, where most applications for wrongful arrest are pursued. However, the malice threshold can be satisfied by inference in circumstances where the case is so hopelessly bereft of merit that it warrants a finding that the claim is seriously lacking in 'colour' or 'foundation'.
>
> Ship arrest is an extremely draconian remedy. It can be very disruptive and may inflict severe economic hardship on the shipowner's trade and operations. In order for the protection against this draconian measure to be meaningful and effective, the judicial threshold should not be set too high so as to render the right to damages practically illusory.
>
> In appropriate cases, where the threshold has been crossed, the court should express its opprobrium towards the arresting party's conduct by ordering it to be accountable for the damages occasioned by its wrongful arrest. Indeed, our courts have in a number of cases held the arresting party accountable for wrongful arrest.

[56] *The STX Mumbai* [2015] SGCA 35, [2015] 5 SLR 1 [95]. See also *The Vinalines Pioneer* [2015] SGHC 278, [2016] 1 SLR 448 [109] (Belinda Ang J) where the High Court's determination of the claim for wrongful arrest was postponed pending determination of all the applications to set aside the warrant of arrest.

[57] *The STX Mumbai* (n 45) [95].

[58] ibid [79], [85]–[86].

[59] ibid [95].

[60] ibid.

[61] *The Xin Chang Shu* [2015] SGHC 308, [2016] 1 SLR 1096.

[62] See also *The Xin Chang Shu* [2016] SGHC 93, [2016] 3 SLR 1195 (appeal to the Singapore Court of Appeal dismissed on procedural grounds).

[63] *The Xin Chang Shu* (n 61) [1]–[4].

The above excerpt underscores and reaffirms the point made in *The Vasiliy Golovnin*,[64] which is that a balance must be struck between the competing interests of admiralty plaintiffs and defendant shipowners in deploying the draconian remedy of an arrest. It signals that the balance in Singapore admiralty law will in future tilt towards affording more protection to defendant shipowners to prevent any abuse of the ship arrest remedy. This, as suggested above, is achieved through the reinterpretation of the *Evangelismos* test in *The Vasiliy Golovnin*,[65] which calls for an examination of whether the arrest is made without basis, foundation or substance as to enable a court to impute malice. The latter exercise, as the judgment of Steven Chong J in *The Xin Chang Shu*[66] makes clear, extends to arrests for claims that are 'hopelessly bereft of merit'.[67] The connection between a totally hopeless claim and an abusive arrest is not difficult to draw.

If a plaintiff knows that its claim is totally hopeless and tries to recharacterise its claim as something else to make it more palatable and relies on that recharacterised claim to mount an ex parte application for a warrant of arrest, then, in appropriate cases, particularly where there is also material non-disclosure in the course of that ex parte application, a court may be prepared to say that the line has been crossed. Lest the point be misunderstood, this approach does not open the floodgates for judicial scrutiny into the merits of a claim for the purposes of finding wrongful arrest. In this regard, a weak claim, or one that may be defeated, is not the same as a hopeless claim. There is a line which can be drawn, and courts are used to drawing that line.

The decision in *The Xin Chang Shu*[68] is also not authority for the proposition that, where there is a totally hopeless claim, that will without more render the arrest wrongful. If a claim is seriously wanting in merits, or there are potential defences that may deliver a knock-out blow to that claim, the plaintiff is obliged to disclose those deficiencies or defences when applying for a warrant of arrest. If in its application for a warrant of arrest the plaintiff knows its claim is hopeless or sweeps deficiencies or defences under the carpet, and puts forward a different, contrived claim before a court, then that court will be more prepared to make the necessary finding of malice. Indeed, it may rhetorically be asked, if a finding of wrongful arrest is not made in such a situation, how much more egregious must the conduct of the plaintiff be before such a finding of wrongful arrest is made?

It is respectfully submitted that *The Xin Chang Shu*[69] was decided with these considerations in mind. The Court found that the plaintiff's completely unfounded claim, and its attempts to make out the agency premise in the affidavit supporting its warrant of arrest application and in the hearing of its ex parte application, without addressing fundamental weaknesses in its case, had crossed the malice threshold in that the claim had 'so little foundation' and 'there was at least reckless non-disclosure of material facts'.[70]

[64] *The Vasiliy Golovnin* (n 12).

[65] ibid.

[66] *The Xin Chang Shu* (n 61).

[67] Looking at the merits in the context of a wrongful arrest is not novel. In the inquiry of whether an arrest is malicious, courts do conclude if the wrongful arrest is fundamentally flawed: see eg *Ocean Gain Shipping Pte Ltd v Owner and/or Charterer of Demise of Vessel Dong Nai Registered at Haiphong Port, Vietnam (The Dong Nai)* [1996] 4 MLJ 454.

[68] *The Xin Chang Shu* (n 61).

[69] Ibid.

[70] ibid [86].

In other words, the Court in *The Xin Chang Shu*[71] awarded damages for wrongful arrest on two closely related grounds: the first was the complete or hopeless lack of merit in the arresting plaintiff's claim, which makes the claim and the arrest one with little or no foundation; and the second was the material inexcusable non-disclosure both in the affidavit supporting the warrant of arrest application and in the course of the ex parte hearing of that application. In considering this issue, the Court, following the previous Singapore Court of Appeal decision of *The Kiku Pacific*,[72] held that malice should not be inferred simply because there is no reasonable or probable cause for an arrest.[73] Something more is required: that the claim must have been brought with so little colour or foundation that implies malice.[74] Such a determination is, ultimately, a matter of judgement and can only be determined on the facts of each case.[75]

In that regard, the Court held that special attention should be paid to what the arresting party knew or must have known at the time of the arrest.[76] If, based on the information available, a court finds that the arresting party knew or must have known that it had no reasonable or probable cause to arrest the vessel, a court may be justified in awarding damages for wrongful arrest. Conversely, if a court arrives at the finding that the arresting party had no reasonable or probable cause to arrest the vessel after a legal analysis of the jurisdictional basis of the claim or based on documents or information which were not available to the arresting party at the time of arrest, such a finding may not be a sufficient basis for the award of damages for wrongful arrest.[77]

On the facts of the case before the Court, the Singapore High Court held that the arresting party had sought to give the Court the false appearance that the defendant had authorised OW Singapore to order the bunkers on its behalf.[78] In its initial letter of demand, the plaintiff did not assert any such alleged agency, choosing instead to premise its claim on the basis of an alleged lien. There was also no communication between the defendant and OW Singapore prior to the supply of the bunkers itself. In fact, the plaintiff had known that its invoice had never been sent to the defendant prior to its letter of demand.[79] More pertinently, the parties' respective contracts with their counterparties contained different terms, not least, differences in price, payment terms and interest.[80] Such facts were known to the plaintiff: in attempting to paint a picture of agency, the plaintiff was attempting to bring a claim which it knew or ought to have known was based on a false foundation.[81]

The second ground on which damages for wrongful arrest were awarded in *The Xin Chang Shu*[82] was that of the plaintiff's material non-disclosure. In that regard, in an attempt to establish some link between itself and the defendant, the plaintiff alleged that

[71] *The Xin Chang Shu* (n 61).
[72] *The Kiku Pacific* (n 25).
[73] *The Xin Chang Shu* (n 61) [32].
[74] ibid.
[75] ibid [38], [42].
[76] ibid [39], [60].
[77] ibid [39].
[78] ibid [61].
[79] ibid [62], [66].
[80] ibid [68].
[81] ibid [83].
[82] *The Xin Chang Shu* (n 61).

the defendant's agent had provided 'details ... on the commercial aspects' of the bunker supply.[83] Yet such details emanated from the plaintiff.[84] In fact, there was no evidence that the defendant was even aware of OW Singapore's involvement in the transaction.[85] The Singapore High Court held that there was no legal or factual foundation for the plaintiff's case of agency, and that the plaintiff knew or at least must have known as such at the time of arrest.[86]

Both *The STX Mumbai*[87] and *The Xin Chang Shu*[88] demonstrate the Singapore courts' willingness to delve into the merits of a claim as part of the process of determining whether to award damages for wrongful arrest.[89]

It may be argued that on the facts of *The STX Mumbai*[90] and *The Xin Chang Shu*,[91] the arresting plaintiff had sought to present the facts and/or evidence in an unfair or grossly inaccurate manner in its bid to obtain the warrant of arrest. So, in *The STX Mumbai*,[92] the plaintiff attempted to engineer a repudiatory breach by sending a letter of demand, after office hours, demanding immediate repayment. In *The Xin Chang Shu*,[93] the plaintiff purported to build a case based on agency, ignoring, amongst other things, the fact that the defendant had not even been aware of the plaintiff's involvement in the transaction until receipt of the plaintiff's letter of demand. The respective High Court judgments in both cases demonstrate that Singapore courts will not tolerate such attempts to fashion an arrest based on inherently unsustainable claims.

Even where a court is not able to make a finding of wrongful arrest at the interlocutory stage, the Singapore courts have observed that it is still open to defendants to bring a counter-claim for wrongful arrest at trial.[94] The ability to raise wrongful arrest as a counter-claim at the trial is potentially another useful tool. What cannot be revealed in an interlocutory application can be unmasked by the process of specific discovery, interrogatories and, of course, cross-examination of witnesses at trial. An admiralty plaintiff (and its advisers) who may be tempted to take a punt, will now have to think beyond surviving an interlocutory challenge to the propriety of the arrest.

The Vasiliy Golovnin[95] has not been applied outside Singapore, in so far as the wrongful arrest issue is concerned.[96] Indeed, apart from a single Hong Kong decision, which is discussed below, there appear to have been no recent reported decisions handed down by

[83] ibid [74].
[84] ibid [77].
[85] ibid [78].
[86] ibid [82], [83], [89].
[87] *The STX Mumbai* (n 45).
[88] *The Xin Chang Shu* (n 61).
[89] Although it must be noted that the process is not confined to looking at the merits alone.
[90] *The STX Mumbai* (n 45).
[91] *The Xin Chang Shu* (n 61).
[92] *The STX Mumbai* (n 45).
[93] *The Xin Chang Shu* (n 61).
[94] *The STX Mumbai* (n 45) [95]; *The Xin Chang Shu* (n 61) [24].
[95] *The Vasiliy Golovnin* (n 12).
[96] The decision has, however, been referred to in several cases on the issue of disclosure of information in the context of ex parte applications, as well as the issue of discretion in the issue of an arrest warrant for a ship: see *Atlasnavios Navegacao LDA v The Ship Xin Tai Hai (No 2)* 2012 FCA 1497, (2012) 215 FCR 265 [74]. *The Vasiliy Golovnin* was also recently discussed in depth by the English Court of Appeal in the context of counter-security: see text at n 119 below.

Commonwealth courts that are directly on point in applying the *Evangelismos* test to alleged wrongful ship arrests.[97] So it is not entirely clear whether the Singapore approach encapsulated by the three decisions discussed above would travel well.

It is worth pointing out, however, that a fairly recent decision of the Hong Kong Court of First Instance exhibits similar judicial robustness as the Singapore cases. In *Birnam Ltd v The Owners of the Ship or Vessel Hong Ming*[98] the arresting plaintiff, Birnam, was the nominated buyer under a Memorandum of Agreement (MOU). Birnam failed to pay the requisite deposit under the MOU and sought to renegotiate terms. As part of its negotiations, Birnam asked the sellers to make the vessel available for inspection in Hong Kong. On the vessel's arrival in Hong Kong, Birnam arrested the vessel to obtain security for its claim under the original MOU.

In striking out Birnam's claim, Reyes J held that, in light of Birnam's failure to pay the requisite deposit under the original MOU, 'the stark reality is that Birnam is the wrongdoer'.[99] Reyes J went on to find that the evidence before him 'gives rise to a strong inference that the inspection requested by Birnam was merely a ruse to bring the Vessel into Hong Kong waters so it could be arrested'.[100] There was also no attempt by Birnam to disclose either the fact that a claim under an MOU for the sale and purchase of a vessel does not give rise to a right of arrest or that Birnam had itself accepted that the original MOU had been terminated.[101] Birnam's apparent failure to address its mind to either consideration gave rise to an inference that it had proceeded in a 'cavalier fashion', and that Birnam's motive in luring the vessel into Hong Kong waters amounted to 'a misuse of the arrest process'.[102]

Judicial robustness in making findings on wrongful arrest aside, there is another source of protection for shipowners as a matter of Singapore law, namely, the duty of disclosure which a plaintiff has to observe when applying for a warrant of arrest.[103] The Singapore Court of Appeal has, on two recent occasions,[104] reiterated the importance of this duty, as well as clarifying that it extends to both the contents and manner of presentation of evidence before the Court. It is seen as an important bulwark against abuse of the process of arrest and, as *The Vasiliy Golovnin*[105] and *The Xin Chang Shu*[106] amply demonstrate, serious material non-disclosure is a strong contributory factor to a finding of wrongful arrest.

[97] The Australian decisions, *Fuk Hing Steamship Co v Shagang Shipping Co Ltd* [2015] FCA 682 (discussed in Martin Davies, 'Australian Maritime Law' [2016] *IMCLY* 2–3) and *The Eye-Spy* (n 7) on s 34 of the Admiralty Act 1998 (Cth) do not deal with the substantive merits of the wrongful arrest claim.

[98] *Birnam Ltd v The Owners of the Ship or Vessel Hong Ming* [2011] HKCFI 577, [2011] 5 HKC 512.

[99] ibid [24].

[100] ibid [34].

[101] ibid [30], [31].

[102] ibid [34], [35].

[103] While this issue is strictly beyond the scope of this Chapter, the insistence on full and frank disclosure by the arresting party in its ex parte application for an arrest warrant obviously has a significant indirect impact on the balance of power between the arresting plaintiff and defendant shipowner.

[104] *The Vasiliy Golovnin* (n 12); *The Bunga Melati 5* [2012] SGCA 46, [2012] 4 SLR 546.

[105] *The Vasiliy Golovnin* (n 12).

[106] *The Xin Chang Shu* (n 61).

III. Counter-security for Ship Arrest?

Given the greater judicial readiness to accord protection to defendant shipowners, it may be wondered if additional safeguards against abuse in the process of ship arrest is necessary. In this regard, it has been suggested by Sir Bernard Eder, writing in an extrajudicial capacity, that courts should guard against the risk of wrongful arrest by requiring the plaintiff to furnish counter-security, or at least, a cross-undertaking as to damages, as in the case of a Mareva injunction or freezing order.[107] The concern underlying such a proposal is the unduly advantageous position of the arresting party who does not have to exhibit to any degree of the strength of its case at the application for the warrant of arrest, since it is entitled to an arrest of the vessel as of right; that is, it does not have to attend before a court for an ex parte hearing on its application, nor is there any duty of disclosure.[108]

This idea is not new. It was first articulated in the 'startling' decision[109] of the Canadian Federal Court of Appeal in 1995 in *Armada Lines Ltd v Chaleur Fertilizers Ltd.*[110] In this case, the Federal Court of Appeal analogised ship arrest to Mareva injunctions and held that it was therefore appropriate that plaintiffs arresting ships should provide an undertaking as to damages for wrongful arrest. The Federal Court of Appeal also awarded damages to the defendant shipowner without any evidence of *mala fides* or *crassa negligentia* on the part of the arresting party. This part of the decision was, however, overturned on appeal to the Canadian Supreme Court.[111] The Supreme Court reaffirmed the orthodox *Evangelismos* test in the following terms:[112]

> In asking this Court to depart from the *Evangelismos* rule, the respondent focused on the similarities between the maritime arrest procedure, on the one hand, and the seizure of assets pursuant to a *Mareva* injunction, on the other. And, indeed, in substance, the two orders are not dissimilar: both the admiralty arrest and the *Mareva* injunction restrain a defendant from dealing with his or her property prior to judgment. However, despite this similarity of purpose and effect, the rules surrounding the two remedies differ in certain important respects.
>
> A plaintiff who obtains a *Mareva* injunction, like a plaintiff who obtains any type of interlocutory injunctive relief, must give an undertaking to compensate the defendant for damages sustained by reason of the injunction, should the action ultimately fail. … By contrast, Rule 1003(2) of the Federal Court Rules, which governs the arrest of a ship or cargo, does not require that the plaintiff give any undertaking for damages. Furthermore, as discussed above, the common law only imposes liability for damages flowing from the arrest of property if the plaintiff acted with either mala fides or crassa negligentia.
>
> The respondent argued that the disparity between these two sets of rules operates unfairly against defendants in admiralty law actions. To remedy this unfairness, the respondent suggested

[107] See Bernard Eder, 'Wrongful Arrest of Ships: A Time for Change' (2013) 38 *Tul Mar LJ* 115; Martin Davies, 'Wrongful Arrest of Ships: A Time for Change – A Reply to Sir Bernard Eder' (2013) 38 *Tul Mar LJ* 137; Bernard Eder, 'Wrongful Arrest of Ships: Rejoinder by the Honourable Mr Justice Eder' (2013) *38 Tul Mar LJ* 143. See also Aleka Mandaraka-Sheppard, 'Wrongful Arrest of Ships: A Case for Reform' (2013) 19 *JIML* 41.

[108] *The Varna* [1993] 2 Lloyd's Rep 253.

[109] Robert Margolis, 'Damages for the Wrongful Arrest of a Vessel: The Venerable Rule Confirmed' [1998] *LMCLQ* 11, 12.

[110] *Armada Lines Ltd v Chaleur Fertilizers Ltd* [1995] 1 FC 3, 85 FTR 26.

[111] *Armada Lines Ltd v Chaleur Fertilizers Ltd* [1997] 2 SCR 617, 148 DLR (4th) 217.

[112] ibid [23]–[27].

> imposing a new rule on maritime law. Under this proposed rule, a plaintiff who effects a maritime arrest and then has his or her claim dismissed will be liable for all damages caused by the arrest. This position finds support among certain academic writers, who have criticized the *Evangelismos* rule as being out of step with modern developments in the common law. …
>
> While I have some sympathy with this argument, in my view, any such change in the law falls not to the courts, but rather to the legislature to carry out. As noted above, the rule in *The 'Evangelismos'* is of long standing. Whether it does or does not operate harshly upon defendants is a question best resolved by the legislature. As this Court said in *Rhône (The) v Peter AB Widener (The)*, [1993] 1 SCR 497, at p 531:
>
> > '… whether this regime is responsive to modern realities is a question of policy to be determined by Parliament and not the courts whose task is to interpret and give effect to the intention of Parliament.'
>
> In this regard, I note that, apparently alone among the common law jurisdictions, Australia has departed from the rule in *The 'Evangelismos'*. Section 34(1)(a)(ii) of the Australian Admiralty Act 1988, No. 34 of 1988, provides that a party may recover damages arising out of the arrest of property if the arrest was obtained 'unreasonably and without good cause'. As pointed out by counsel for the appellant, this change was effected not through judicial means, but rather by specific legislative enactment. In my opinion, any analogous change in Canadian law must originate in the legislative branch of government. For these reasons, in my view, the rule in *The 'Evangelismos'* remains good law in Canada.

This debate has resurfaced very recently in the English courts. In *Natwest Markets plc (Formerly known as the Royal Bank of Scotland plc) v Stallion Eight Shipping Co SA (The MV Alkyon)*[113] the defendant shipowner applied for an order releasing its vessel from arrest unless the claimant bank provided a cross-undertaking in damages in the form usually given in the context of freezing orders; namely, that if the court later found that the warrant of arrest had caused loss to the shipowner and decided that the shipowner should be compensated for that loss, the bank would comply with any order the court might make. The bank argued that this would be contrary to established English admiralty practice.[114] Teare J was not unsympathetic to the shipowner's argument, noting that:[115]

> In view of the size of the Bank's claim there is, notwithstanding that an inability to provide security has not been established, the potential for injustice in this case and the requested cross-undertaking in damages would serve to avoid that injustice, reduce the pressure upon the Shipowner and thereby put the parties on what was submitted to be an equal footing.

However, his Honour concluded that there was

> much to be said for the view that the requested change in practice (assuming that a court at first instance were free to bring it about) is or may be so far-reaching in its consequences that it should be a matter either for Parliament to consider (if a change in primary legislation is required or desirable) or for the Rules Committee to consider (if all that is required is a change in the rules of court) having consulted with the Admiralty and Commercial Court Users' Committee and the shipping and marine insurance industry. In this regard it is to be noted that when the Arrest Convention 1952 (which is the foundation of the present statute conferring jurisdiction in rem)

[113] *Natwest Markets plc (Formerly known as the Royal Bank of Scotland plc) v Stallion Eight Shipping Co SA (The MV Alkyon)* [2018] EWHC 2033 (Admlty), [2018] 2 Lloyd's Rep 601.

[114] ibid [7]–[8].

[115] ibid [53].

> was under consideration the UK delegate to the diplomatic conference was opposed to a suggestion that arresting courts be empowered to order security and in the event the proposal was defeated. The UK delegate said that actions for wrongful arrest are very rare in England and that 'he has never heard of any complaint in that respect' … . The Arrest Convention 1999 does contain such a provision but the UK has not ratified that Convention … .[116]
>
> Whether the balance between, on the one hand, the interests of the claimant in rem and, on the other hand, the interests of the shipowner, which has been struck by English Admiralty law and practice over the last 150 years or more remains appropriate and sufficiently 'responsive to modern realities' (the phrase used by the Supreme Court of Canada) is, in my judgment, not a matter for the court to judge but a matter for either the legislature or the Rules Committee to consider.[117]

The shipowner appealed to the English Court of Appeal.[118] The Court of Appeal canvassed the international academic literature and case law, including the decision of the Singapore Court of Appeal in *The Vasiliy Golovnin*,[119] which the Court described as 'a most valuable judgment, both for its depth of analysis and the width of its comparative law survey'.[120] The Court also noted VK Rajah JA's conclusion that any rebalancing of the *Evangelismos* test should probably occur through legislative, rather than judicial, reform.[121] The Court of Appeal differed from Teare J in finding that the Court was not strictly bound by *The Evangelismos*,[122] as that case went to damages for wrongful arrest, whereas here the issue was the Court's discretionary power to order the release of a vessel from arrest.[123] The Court therefore held that a judicial departure from the usual admiralty practice was indeed possible, but that, doubtless, 'a Court at any level would think long and hard before departing from the usual practice with regard to the release of a vessel from a maritime arrest'.[124] The Court concluded as follows:[125]

> We only part company from Teare J insofar as … he considered that the intervention of Parliament or the Rules Committee was required to alter the present position. As already indicated, we do not share that view, at least with regard to the question of any requirement for a cross-undertaking as the price of maintaining an arrest, whatever the position might be in the case of a direct challenge to the rule in *The Evangelismos* itself, given the high authority of that decision. Instead, in the present context, particularly because it concerns the discretionary power of the Court to order the release of a vessel from arrest, we are respectfully much attracted to the approach adopted by the Singapore Court of Appeal in *The Vasiliy Golovnin*, at [134] … . As envisaged by that approach, it is open to the Court itself to reconsider the position, but it should only do so if properly informed as to the views of the maritime community, including the practical ramifications of any proposed changes and the preferred route to be adopted if any such changes are decided upon. Moreover, the Court would wish to be informed of the likely consequences for this jurisdiction internationally if the *status quo* was to be altered. In short, the Court would wish and

[116] ibid.
[117] ibid [56].
[118] *Stallion Eight Shipping Co SA v Natwest Markets plc (The MV Alkyon)* [2018] EWCA Civ 2760.
[119] *The Vasiliy Golovnin* (n 12).
[120] *The MV Alkyon* (n 118) [62].
[121] ibid [68]. See too *Mobil Oil New Zealand Ltd* [2000] 1 NZLR 49 (Giles J) for a similar conclusion.
[122] *The Evangelismos* (n 2).
[123] ibid [79].
[124] ibid [81].
[125] ibid [95].

need to have a clear understanding of the industry implications of any proposed change before acceding to it. It is unnecessary to be prescriptive as to how the views of the maritime community should be obtained (whether by way of consultation or otherwise) or whether a consensus would need to be apparent – but, plainly, a case for change would be much strengthened if it could rely on significant support from the maritime community, extending much wider than the views of (even eminent) legal commentators. Additionally, it would be for the Court entertaining such a challenge to consider the impact on the rule in *The Evangelismos* of a departure from the existing practice.

It is submitted that the general approach adopted by the English Court of Appeal in *The MV Alkyon*[126] is correct. It is further submitted that imposing a requirement for counter-security or a cross-undertaking as to damages in Singapore is not necessary, both as a matter of principle and as a matter of practice, for the following two reasons. First, unlike in England,[127] a warrant of arrest in Singapore is not available as of right: it remains a discretionary remedy.[128] Furthermore, there remains on the arrestor's part the obligation of full and frank disclosure in making the ex parte application for an arrest warrant. This obligation extends to disclosing defences which deal a knock-out blow to the plaintiff's claim.[129] A breach of this obligation of full and frank disclosure may, depending on the facts of the case, result in an award of damages for wrongful arrest. Secondly, given the judicial readiness in Singapore to protect a shipowner from wrongful arrest, whether at an interlocutory stage or at trial, arresting parties and their advisers would hesitate to bring an arrest unless they are satisfied that the risk of wrongful arrest is low. Given these two safeguards, there is accordingly no real need for a further deterrent built around the provision of counter-security or a cross-undertaking as to damages.

Subjecting a plaintiff to furnish counter-security or an undertaking as to damages also poses practical difficulties. There is the question of whether an arresting party would, practically speaking, be able to furnish counter-security, whether at all or in time for the arrest. The arresting party may also not be able to obtain such counter-security before the vessel calls into port and leaves again. The decision to arrest a ship is one which may have to be taken under urgent circumstances. This is particularly the case if the vessel is only calling at port to take on bunkers, or for quick cargo operations, in which case the vessel's call at port could be a matter of mere hours.

There is the further practical question of whether a court will be able to determine whether the terms of any such counter-security afford sufficient protection to the defendant. Furthermore, if the plaintiff is unable, say because it is a special purpose entity incorporated in a tax-free haven, to satisfy any award of damages for wrongful arrest, it is unclear how requiring a mere cross-undertaking from the plaintiff would afford the defendant any further relief in the case of an impecunious plaintiff.

Seen in this light, imposing an additional requirement for counter-security or a cross-undertaking on a plaintiff seeking the issuance of a warrant of arrest could affect the attractiveness and nimbleness of the remedy of arrest as a means to obtain pre-judgment security. Proponents of such reform appear to base at least part of their argument on a

[126] *The MV Alkyon* (n 118).
[127] See *The Varna* (n 108).
[128] *The Rainbow Spring* [2003] SGCA 31, [2003] 3 SLR(R) 362 [30].
[129] See *The Eagle Prestige* [2010] SGHC 93, [2010] 3 SLR 294 [73], [84]; *The Xin Chang Shu* (n 61) [48].

change in the CPR or Rules of Court.[130] Such reform, if considered desirable, would, from a Singapore perspective, have to be legislatively driven. At this juncture, there appears to be little appetite for that.

IV. Conclusion

As we have seen, the Arrest Conventions 1952 and 1999 have not been of much assistance in developing international uniform rules regarding liability for wrongful arrest or rights to counter-security or damages. Instead, with a few statutory exceptions, the *Evangelismos* test, in one formulation or another, remains the de facto international standard in Commonwealth jurisdictions at least. As mentioned in the introduction to this Chapter, the CMI has set up an IWG to revisit the issue of whether it is possible to achieve international uniformity on the issue of liability for wrongful ship arrest. The CMI IWG has been garnering responses from national maritime law associations on the issue and aims to propose an international uniform standard set of rules, either in the form of a Protocol to the Arrest Convention 1999, or as a model law or other instrument suitable for domestic implementation.[131] It remains to be seen whether the CMI IWG will have any greater success in this regard than past international unification initiatives. There remains a 'sharp disparity' between Common Law and Civil Law jurisdictions on the issue of wrongful ship arrest. Some jurisdictions characterise the issue of damages for wrongful ship arrest as a procedural law matter, whereas others treat it as one of substantive law. There are complexities, amongst other things, regarding governing law and whether there are to be limits on recoverable damages. Accordingly, it would appear to be 'a major challenge' to reach a definition of wrongful arrest and insert it into any future international instrument.[132]

[130] See Bernard Eder, 'Wrongful Arrest of Ships: A Time for Change' (n 107) 133.

[131] See comitemaritime.org/work/liability-for-wrongful-arrest/; Giorgio Berlingieri, 'Liability for Wrongful Arrest: A Report on this Study and on the Activities of the IWG' *2015 CMI Yearbook: New York I: Documents for the Conference* 296.

[132] See *The MV Alkyon* (n 118) [70]–[75], discussing the CMI survey of national maritime law association responses and commentary by Aleka Mandaraka-Sheppard (*2015 CMI Yearbook: New York I: Documents for the Conference* 300). See further the responses of 31 countries to the questionnaire of the CMI IWG on Liability for Wrongful Arrest in comitemaritime.org/wp-content/uploads/2018/05/Table-1-Answerts-to-the-CMI-Questionnaire-per-question-and-country.pdf.

7

Conflict of Laws and the Arrest Conventions

PAUL MYBURGH*

I. Introduction

There are always 'trade-offs inherent in flattening a globe'.[1] From well before the famous Mercator projection of 1569 to over 200 subsequent attempts, including the controversial Gall–Peters projection,[2] cartographers have tried, and failed, to project the real three-dimensional world faithfully onto an artificial two-dimensional map without significant distortions of shape, distance, direction or land area. Mapping is 'never politically neutral nor socially indeterminate'.[3] Similarly, the particular projection of foreign legal rights adopted by the forum called upon to map those rights (in the context of international ship arrest, usually the forum called upon to determine preliminary jurisdiction issues, security issues or the merits of the case following arrest, which will be referred to by the shorthand of the forum arresti) in maritime conflict of laws is never ideologically neutral, and can give rise to significant distortions of foreign rights and illogical and unjust results.

Lexforism[4] is arguably particularly undesirable in the context of maritime conflict of laws, for a number of reasons. First, international shipping law disputes and international ship arrests routinely involve significant foreign elements, and therefore tend to raise complex private international law issues. Secondly, they often involve significant numbers of foreign parties with various different rights and interests in relation to the arrested ship. Thirdly, the highly mobile nature of ships and the in rem nature and territorial reach of admiralty jurisdiction in Common Law jurisdictions, as well as the Civil Law equivalents of attachment and seizure, mean that the forum arresti, and therefore the

* Deputy Director, Centre for Maritime Law, Faculty of Law, National University of Singapore. This Chapter is dedicated to the memory of Michael Marks Cohen, a dear friend who would have vehemently disagreed with much of its content.

[1] Mark S Monmonier, *Rhumb Lines and Map Wars: A Social History of the Mercator Projection* (Chicago, University of Chicago Press, 2004) 1.

[2] See generally Jeremy Crampton, 'Cartography's Defining Moment: The Peters Projection Controversy, 1974–1990' (1994) 31 *Cartographica* 16.

[3] John R Short, *Alternative Geographies* (Abingdon, Routledge, 2017) 50.

[4] On which see Michael S Green, 'Legal Realism, Lex Fori, and the Choice-of-Law Revolution' (1995) 104 *Yale LJ* 967; Lea Brilmayer, 'Rights, Fairness, and Choice of Law' (1989) 98 *Yale LJ* 1277.

lex fori arresti, may be considerably more of a lottery than in land-based proceedings with foreign elements. In certain circumstances, the mobility of ships and their amenability to arrest in every port may also facilitate a forum shopping spree. Fourthly, although the in rem nature of ship arrest and admiralty proceedings means that there are rarely enforcement issues in respect of judgments in rem, it also means that enforcement is against a very narrow and limited asset base, which heightens the stakes for competing foreign and local claims and brings priority issues into prominence. As a result of a combination of these elements, and others, it is highly undesirable for the forum arresti to adopt a parochial conflicts approach to the arrest of either foreign-flagged ships or locally-registered ships with foreign creditors.

There is, however, a radical tension in the international enforcement of maritime claims. Although it is well recognised that substantive uniformity of international maritime law is highly desirable – to the extent that international uniformity, like the historical pedigree of maritime law, has become a rather over-used and meaningless shibboleth in this area[5] – the nub (and the rub) is that maritime claims are enforced at a local level, by the forum arresti of a particular State, in accordance with its own domestic jurisdiction gateway statute and admiralty procedure – matters that have always been characterised as properly governed by the lex fori.[6] This tension between the parochialism of a procedural characterisation of maritime proceedings and the cosmopolitan nature of the shipping industry has given rise to significant conflicts problems and disparate outcomes in international ship arrest law.

Indeed, it was concerns over the practical problems caused by substantive variations between the domestic laws of ship arrest in various jurisdictions (most notably differences between Civil Law countries, where attachment of ships was typically conceived of as a general provisional, protective and security measure in both maritime and non-maritime cases, and Anglo-Common Law countries, where ship arrest of the relevant ship only was allowed in specific instances falling within tightly defined heads of admiralty jurisdiction in rem)[7] and the failure of the Maritime Liens and Mortgages Convention 1926[8] to unify the substantive law of international maritime claims that originally drove the drafters of the Arrest Convention 1952[9] to attempt to craft an instrument that would render the concept

[5] See Paul Myburgh, 'Richard Cooper Memorial Lecture: Admiralty Law – What is it Good For?' (2009) 28 *UQLJ* 19, 27ff.

[6] Laura Carballo Piñeiro, *International Maritime Labour Law*, Hamburg Studies on Maritime Affairs 34 (Berlin, Springer, 2015) 131: Private international law 'rules cannot be absolutely disregarded as none of the [Arrest Conventions] are comprehensive, for example, in the procedural rules of the provisional measure they provided for. Consequently, and also as a result of the well-known *lex fori regit processum* rule, the national law of the court responsible for making the arrest has to be resorted to, to complement their provisions'.

[7] For a summary of the historical differences and the compromises embodied in the Arrest Convention 1952, see N Gaskell and R Shaw, 'The Arrest Convention 1999' [1999] *LMCLQ* 470, 471–72; V Ruiz Abou-Nigm, *The Arrest of Ships in Private International Law* (Oxford, Oxford University Press, 2011) para 7.89. When making such comparisons between domestic legal traditions, however, it is important to bear in mind that the existence of functional equivalents with different labels may mean that these differences are not as great in practice as they seem in theory: see Martin Davies, 'In Defense of Unpopular Virtues: Personification and Ratification' (2000) 75 *Tul L Rev* 337, 403–07 (comparison of US admiralty law and the Arrest Conventions 1952 and 1999).

[8] International Convention for the Unification of certain Rules relating to Maritime Liens and Mortgages (adopted 10 April 1926, entered into force 2 June 1931) 120 LNTS 187.

[9] International Convention Relating to the Arrest of Sea-going Ships (adopted 10 May 1952, entered into force 24 February 1956) 439 UNTS 193.

of ship arrest and its availability in shipping disputes internationally uniform, or at least achieve a workable compromise between these two extremes.

This Chapter examines the success of both the Arrest Conventions 1952 and 1999[10] in achieving substantive and procedural international uniformity of ship arrest through a private international law or conflict of laws lens.[11] The exact definition of international uniformity is subject to debate, but it may be taken to mean a situation in which roughly comparable procedural and substantive results are reached by the ship arrest process in different countries, despite the use of different domestic labels for the relevant legal concepts or institutions. It should also be noted that the achievement of international uniformity does not necessarily equate to the erasure of all conflicts issues – that would be unrealistic, particularly in an area as complex and varied as international shipping law. However, the Arrest Conventions, if successful by this measure, should result in a diminution of conflict of laws problems[12] and a situation in which roughly identical or comparable substantive legal results are achieved in different maritime jurisdictions.[13]

II. Characterisation of Ship Arrest

The first step in any private international law issue, at least from an Anglo-Common Law perspective, is to characterise or classify the nature and scope of the legal problem or issue in order to identify the appropriate private international law principles or approach to be applied.[14] In relation to the most fundamental issue, that of characterising the conceptual nature of the institution of ship arrest, the Arrest Conventions offer little theoretical or practical assistance. The Arrest Convention 1952 defines arrest as meaning 'the detention of a ship by judicial process to secure a maritime claim', as well as providing negative guidance that arrest 'does not include the seizure of a ship in execution or satisfaction of a judgment'.[15] The Arrest Convention 1999 is to similar effect, defining arrest as 'any detention or restriction on removal of the ship by order of a Court to secure a maritime claim' but not including 'the seizure of a ship in execution or satisfaction of a judgement or other enforceable instrument'.[16]

The lack of a more theoretical definition of the core concept of ship arrest is unsurprising. From the travaux préparatoires of both Arrest Conventions it is obvious that

[10] International Convention on the Arrest of Ships (adopted 12 March 1999, entered into force 14 September 2011) 2797 UNTS 3.

[11] On this topic see generally Abou-Nigm (n 7).

[12] See Symeon C Symeonides, 'Private International Law: Idealism, Pragmatism, Eclecticism' (2017) 384 *Recueil des Cours* 30, 65ff. Symeonides argues that these types of Conventions, if successful, achieve conflicts minimisation through harmonisation of the 'substantive carve-out' produced by their scope of (usually) mandatory application, as opposed to the usual 'selectivist' method of private international law. The difficulty with applying this model to a field like international ship arrest, which involves significant domestic and procedural elements, is that drafters may be tempted to narrow down the scope of rules that are seen as susceptible to a 'substantive carve-out', thereby undermining the effectiveness of any resulting uniform law instrument.

[13] See generally Francesco Berlingieri, *Berlingieri on Arrest of Ships*, 6th edn (Abingdon, Informa Law from Routledge, 2017) vol 1 paras 2.01–03.

[14] C Forsyth, 'Characterisation Revisited: An Essay in the Theory and Practice of the English Conflict of Laws' (1998) 114 *LQR* 141.

[15] Article 1(2) of the Arrest Convention 1952.

[16] Article 1(2) of the Arrest Convention 1999.

the primary aim of the drafters was to promote pragmatic substantive harmonisation by describing the practical ambit of the institution of ship arrest and by attempting to bring together the disparate Common Law and Civil Law traditions of domestic ship arrest.[17] The focus of both Conventions is therefore on setting out an agreed list of substantive maritime claims for which vessels may be arrested, demarcating the required link between the liable owner or demise charterer and the ship that may be arrested, and providing for some subsequent procedural matters relating to security, release, wrongful arrest,[18] and in the case of the Arrest Convention 1999, rearrest and multiple arrest.[19]

If one were to characterise explicitly legal issues arising out of, or related to, the institution of ship arrest in private international law terms, they would seem to fall within the broad category of provisional and protective judicial measures.[20] Such measures are typically regarded in private international law as being governed by the lex fori, as they involve a mixture of court procedure, judicial administration and jurisdictional issues. It is therefore no surprise that, where they do expressly address conflicts issues, both Arrest Convention texts refer such issues exclusively to the forum arresti for determination under the lex fori. So, for example, art 6 of the Arrest Convention 1952 provides that:[21]

> All questions whether in any case the claimant is liable in damages for the arrest of a ship or for the costs of the bail or other security furnished to release or prevent the arrest of a ship, shall be determined by the law of the Contracting State in whose jurisdiction the arrest was made or applied for.
>
> The rules of procedure relating to the arrest of a ship, to the application for obtaining the authority referred to in Article 4, and to all matters of procedure which the arrest may entail, shall be governed by the law of the Contracting State in which the arrest was made or applied for.

However, one of the complications inherent in any maritime or admiralty jurisdiction (and the jurisdiction provided by the Arrest Conventions is no different) is that it is a specialist jurisdiction applicable only to certain substantive claims and subject to certain substantive connections between the liable person and the arrested ship being met. It is therefore unhelpful and artificial to characterise ship arrest in purely procedural or preliminary terms, especially when the Arrest Conventions 1952 and 1999 require an investigation into whether the substantive maritime claim on the basis of which arrest is sought falls within the ambit of the Arrest Convention,[22] and to some extent enter into issues relating to jurisdiction on the merits.[23] There is thus inevitably a conflation of substantive and procedural issues in any ship arrest situation under the Arrest Conventions. By seemingly referring all conflicts issues automatically to the lex fori arresti, the Arrest Conventions fail to given any direction on the appropriate approach to solving the preliminary substantive conflicts issues – surrounding both the existence and validity of maritime claims[24] and the

[17] See Berlingieri (n 13) vol 1 para 1.11.

[18] Although this hot potato was largely passed back to the lex fori arresti: see further ch 6; Berlingieri (n 13) vol 1 ch 18.

[19] See ch 5.

[20] So too Abou-Nigm (n 7) paras 3.24–52.

[21] Articles 2(4) and 6 of the Arrest Convention 1999 are to similar effect.

[22] Article 1(1) of the Arrest Conventions 1952 and 1999.

[23] Article 7 of the Arrest Conventions 1952 and 1999.

[24] See Piñeiro (n 6) 131–32: The 'convention provision sets out an exhaustive list of potential maritime claims, but the mere existence and validity of the claim or right depends on the law applicable to the legal relationship in question, hence on the relevant conflict rule'.

connection between liable owners or demise charterers and the ships that may be targeted for arrest – that often arise in the context of ship arrest and the forum arresti's subsequent exercise of jurisdiction on the merits. This has two unfortunate effects.

First, the procedural and practical flavour of the Arrest Conventions encourages the forum arresti to 'flatten' three-dimensional transnational shipping disputes with significant foreign elements by viewing the Arrest Conventions and/or relevant domestic legislation giving effect to the Arrest Conventions through the two-dimensional lens of the internal lex fori arresti. This lexforism encourages judicial parochialism and submerges and subsumes substantive issues that, on an application of general private international law principles outside the context of ship arrest and the vesting of admiralty jurisdiction, would generally fall to be governed by the appropriate lex causae (foreign law). As discussed above, lexforism inevitably increases the risk of disparate outcomes in different jurisdictions and undermines the Arrest Conventions' goal of achieving international uniformity.

Secondly, the emphasis placed on the application of the lex fori arresti by the Arrest Conventions, and their silence on the potential relevance of foreign law to determine substantive preliminary issues, means that they provide little in the way of guidance or support to a forum arresti that is minded to view such preliminary issues in a more three-dimensional and internationalist manner. Such courts will inevitably have to fall back on their own domestic conflicts rules for assistance. While the application of a reasoned domestic conflicts approach will often produce better results than an unthinking broad-brush application of the internal lex fori arresti, differences in domestic conflicts rules may also mean that the outcomes in such cases fall considerably short of achieving the goal of harmonisation or international uniformity.

Apart from the Arrest Conventions' emphasis on the lex fori arresti, the lack of an express requirement in either of the Arrest Conventions that their provisions, or even key concepts such as ship arrest, be interpreted autonomously,[25] allows – or perhaps even encourages – a 'homeward trend' towards reliance on, and application of, the domestic legal concepts and categories of the lex fori arresti. It is to be expected that the older Arrest Convention 1952 would not contain a specific interpretation provision mandating autonomous interpretation of its provisions, but it is perhaps surprising that this issue was not addressed by the drafters of the Arrest Convention 1999.[26]

[25] See eg art 7 of the United Nations Convention on Contracts for the International Sale of Goods (adopted 11 April 1980, entered into force on 1 January 1988) 1489 UNTS 3 (CISG), which expressly requires the CISG to be interpreted with regard 'to its international character and to the need to promote uniformity in its application and the observance of good faith in international trade'. Article 7(2) of the CISG further discourages the homeward trend to reliance on domestic law concepts by providing that '[q]uestions concerning matters governed by this Convention which are not expressly settled in it are to be settled in conformity with the general principles on which it is based or, in the absence of such principles, in conformity with the law applicable by virtue of the rules of private international law'. See generally F Diedrich, 'Maintaining Uniformity in International Uniform Law via Autonomous Interpretation' (1996) 8 *Pace International Law Review* 303.

[26] See Berlingieri (n 13) vol 2 appendix IV for the travaux préparatoires of the Arrest Convention 1999. Although there is some superficial and anecdotal discussion surrounding uniformity of interpretation (or the lack thereof) in relation to specific issues such as whether to maintain a closed list of maritime claims (184–90) and the UK proposal regarding associated ships (278ff), there is surprisingly little sophisticated or detailed analysis of the desirability of uniform international interpretation and none at all on how to achieve autonomous interpretation of the international instrument. Both Arrest Conventions must, of course, be interpreted by States Parties in accordance with the general principles contained in arts 31–33 of the Vienna Convention on the Law of Treaties (adopted 23 May 1969, entered into force on 27 January 1980) 1155 UNTS 331.

These two factors have inevitably contributed to a weakening or undermining of the international unifying effects of both Arrest Conventions. Countries have tended to decant their own domestic synonyms for ship arrest (arrestment, kvarstad, saisie conservatoire, embargo preventive etc) into the relatively empty conceptual container provided by the Arrest Conventions.[27] The result is that the Arrest Conventions, at best, serve as a superimposed public international law layer curbing the forum arresti's exercise of its jurisdiction and policing the boundaries of existing domestic ship arrest processes;[28] or, as in the case of the United Kingdom and the Arrest Convention 1952, merely provide a starting point for a relatively cosmetic restatement of the domestic admiralty jurisdiction in rem[29] – a restatement that was subsequently passed down to other Anglo-Common Law jurisdictions, whether or not they themselves ratified the Arrest Convention 1952.[30] It is therefore unsurprising that, in the Anglo-Common Law world at least, the significance of the Arrest Convention 1952 text as a source of uniform international law has been significantly diluted, with the Arrest Conventions often appearing to occupy a position more akin to a model law than to a directly binding international treaty.[31]

III. Scope of Application of the Arrest Conventions

Article 2 of the Arrest Convention 1952 provides that:

> A ship flying the flag of one of the Contracting States may be arrested in the jurisdiction of any of the Contracting States in respect of any maritime claim, but in respect of no other claim; but nothing in this Convention shall be deemed to extend or restrict any right or powers vested in any Governments or their Departments, Public Authorities, or Dock or Harbour Authorities under their existing domestic laws or regulations to arrest, detain or otherwise prevent the sailing of vessels within their jurisdiction.

[27] See also DC Jackson, *Enforcement of Maritime Claims*, 4th edn (London, Informa, 2005) para 15.15: 'In addition, the Convention recognizes any circumstances in which a domestic law permits jurisdiction on the merits. In particular, this means that those countries such as England, Scotland and the United States, which permit jurisdiction based on the availability of arrest, may become parties and maintain their domestic laws at international level.'

[28] See N Gaskell and R Shaw, 'The Arrest Convention 1999' [1999] *LMCLQ* 470, 475: 'In effect, for those from a civilian tradition which gives wide powers to seize the property of debtors, the Arrest Convention 1999 (like the Arrest Convention 1952) is really a restrictive Convention about when ships cannot be arrested, as opposed to a Convention granting new powers of seizure.'

[29] As Brandon J pointed out in *The Eschersheim* [1974] 2 Lloyd's Rep 188, 192, the Administration of Justice Act 1956 (UK) was promulgated to give effect to the Arrest Convention 1952, and ambiguous provisions in the Act should therefore be interpreted consistently with the provisions of the Convention. However, because of significant divergences between the domestic legislation and the Convention text, the latter has provided useful interpretation assistance in relatively few English cases: see eg *Gatoil International Inc v Arkwright-Boston Manufacturers Mutual Insurance Co (The Sandrina)* [1985] AC 255 (HL); *Samick Lines Co Ltd v Owners of the Antonis P Lemos (The Antonis P Lemos)* [1985] AC 711 (HL); *The River Rima* [1988] 1 WLR 758 (HL). See also *Dicey, Morris and Collins on The Conflict of Laws* 15th edn with 4th cumulative supplement (London, Sweet & Maxwell, 2017) vol 1 paras 13-009, 13-031.

[30] eg, in the Asia-Pacific region, the domestic admiralty statutes of Australia, Hong Kong, New Zealand and Singapore are all to a greater or lesser extent modelled on English law, but only Hong Kong is a party to the Arrest Convention 1952. See further ch 12.

[31] See N Gaskell and R Shaw, 'The Arrest Convention 1999' [1999] *LMCLQ* 470, 472: 'The courts have been prepared to refer to the Arrest Convention 1952, but the cases show that there have been many differences between the UK legislation and the Convention.' See also *Handytankers KS v Owners and/or Demise Charterers of Alas*

Article 8(1) of the Arrest Convention 1952 restates this principle by providing that the Convention provisions 'shall apply to any vessel flying the flag of a Contracting State in the jurisdiction of any Contracting State'. As such, art 8(1) provides reasonably clear guidance on the Arrest Convention 1952's scope of application, establishing a mandatory forum rule linked to the arrested ship's flag status and its presence within the forum arresti's territorial jurisdiction.

However, arts 8(2)–8(4) of the Arrest Convention 1952 unfortunately undermine the clarity of the Convention's scope. Article 8(2) also allows vessels flagged in non-Contracting States to be arrested in Contracting States in respect of the maritime claims enumerated in the Convention 'or of any other claim for which the law of the Contracting State permits arrest'. This provision, which sought to ensure that vessels flagged in non-Contracting States were not placed in a better position than vessels flagged in Contracting States,[32] has the effect of allowing discrimination against the former vessels, and again undermines the Convention's status as a uniform international code by allowing inconsistent domestic law principles to prevail, thereby generating potential conflicts issues.[33]

Further, art 8(3) of the Arrest Convention 1952 allows Contracting States to exclude some or all of the 'benefits of this Convention' in respect of foreign non-Contracting State governments or persons who, at the time of arrest, were not habitually resident or did not have a principal place of business in one of the Contracting States.[34] This peculiar provision, which seems to be in the nature of an informal reservation,[35] is also potentially discriminatory, illogical and productive of uncertainty and unnecessary conflicts issues.

Finally, art 8(4) of the Arrest Convention 1952 allows Contracting States to preserve existing domestic ship arrest rules 'relating to the arrest of any ship within the jurisdiction of the State of her flag by a person who has his habitual residence or principal place of business in that State'. In other words, Contracting States may operate a dual arrest system for 'international' and 'domestic' arrest cases.[36] Berlingieri has criticised this provision as one which is 'clearly influenced by the approach adopted in respect of private international law rules, but is not justified in conventions aiming at the unification of substantive rules'.[37]

subsequently renamed as Kombos [2014] HKCFI 1281, [2014] 6 HKC 239, where Ng J brushed aside an argument that s 12A(2) of the High Court Ordinance, cap 4 (HK) should be construed consistently with the definition of arrest in art 1(2) of the Arrest Convention 1952.

32 This provision was championed by the British delegation. See Berlingieri (n 13) vol 1 paras 3.30–40, appendix V 541ff.

33 As the discussion of the differing national positions on the arrest of vessels flagged in non-Contracting States in ibid paras 3.41–68 makes plain. But see W Tetley, 'Arrest, Attachment, and Related Maritime Law Procedures' (1999) 73 *Tul L Rev* 1895, 1971 for the (unargued) view that the wording of art 8(2) should have been retained in the Arrest Convention 1999.

34 Berlingieri (n 13) vol 1 paras 3.69–77.

35 Berlingieri (ibid para 3.70) describes it as a 'liberty'. Because it is not an official reservation under art 10 of the Arrest Convention 1952 it may be applied, wholly or partly, in national legislation without any official notice to the Convention depositary.

36 For a discussion of the operation of the dual domestic and international saisie conservatoire regimes in France see Tetley (n 33) 1940–49.

37 Berlingieri (n 13) vol 1 paras 3.81–86. Berlingieri also argues (ibid para 3.85) that art 8(4) of the Arrest Convention 1952 may give rise to a conflict of regimes – between the uniform Convention rules and national rules – where a ship is arrested by both domestic and foreign claimants. However, it is arguable that such proceedings would no longer fall within the ambit of art 8(4), as they would no longer be purely domestic proceedings.

While there is some force to this argument, it is not unprecedented for international maritime law Conventions to distinguish between purely domestic or internal situations and shipping issues with international elements,[38] and it might be argued that, of the three provisions under discussion, art 8(4) is the least objectionable and destructive to international uniformity.

Article 8 of the Arrest Convention 1999, by comparison, provides for a clearer, more non-discriminatory scope of application rule. Articles 8(1) and 8(2) respectively provide that the Arrest Convention 1999 is mandatorily applicable 'to any ship within the jurisdiction of any State Party, whether or not that ship is flying the flag of a State Party',[39] but is inapplicable 'to any warship, naval auxiliary or other ships owned or operated by a State and used, for the time being, only on government non-commercial service'. The only differential treatment permitted under the Arrest Convention 1999 is the application of the domestic ship arrest rules of the lex fori arresti to purely domestic cases.[40] The Arrest Convention 1999 therefore represents an advance on the Arrest Convention 1952 in achieving clarity of the scope of its intended 'substantive carve-out' and minimising conflict of laws issues surrounding its scope of application as a mandatory forum rule.[41]

IV. Jurisdiction

Article 4 of the Arrest Convention 1952 provides that only the forum arresti has the authority to arrest a ship within its territorial jurisdiction, as well as the competence to decide subsequent issues regarding provision of security and the release of the vessel.[42] Article 7(1) of the Arrest Convention 1952 further provides that the 'Courts of the country in which the arrest was made[43] shall have jurisdiction to determine the case upon its merits

[38] Compare eg arts 30(1)(a)–(c) of the International Convention on Salvage (adopted 28 April 1989, entered into force 14 July 1996) 1953 UNTS 165, which allow the exclusion by reservation of salvage on inland waters or where all interested parties to the salvage are nationals of the relevant State.

[39] States may, however, exercise an official reservation under art 10(1)(b) of the Arrest Convention 1999 to exclude the application of the Convention to ships not flying the flag of a State Party: see Berlingieri (n 13) vol 2 para 3.01, Appendix IV 351ff. This at least results in greater clarity and a more binary approach to the scope of application of the 'substantive carve-out' of uniform rules.

[40] Article 8(6) of the Arrest Convention 1999.

[41] The drafters of the Arrest Convention 1999 were acutely aware that art 8(2) of the Arrest Convention 1952 'had given rise to problems of interpretation in various jurisdictions': see Berlingieri (n 13) vol 2 para 3.01, appendix IV 347.

[42] Article 5 of the Arrest Convention 1952.

[43] This wording means that a mere threat of arrest or provision of security to avoid arrest will be insufficient to trigger jurisdiction under the Arrest Convention 1952. This is of particular practical significance in the EU context, where the Brussels I Regulation (Recast) (Regulation (EU) No 1215/2012 of the European Parliament and of the Council of 12 December 2012 on jurisdiction and the recognition and enforcement of judgments in civil and commercial matters [2012] OJ L351/20) or revised Lugano Convention (Convention on Jurisdiction and the Recognition and Enforcement of Judgments in Civil and Commercial Matters [2007] OJ L339/3) rules would otherwise override the jurisdiction provisions of the Arrest Convention 1952 where the defendant shipowner or demise charterer is domiciled in another Member or Convention State. See *The Deichland* [1990] 1 QB 361 (CA); *The Po* [1991] 2 Lloyd's Rep 206 (CA); *The Nordglimt* [1988] QB 183; *The Anna H* [1995] 1 Lloyd's Rep 11 (CA); *The Bergen* [1997] 1 Lloyd's Rep 380; *The Bergen (No 2)* [1997] 2 Lloyd's Rep 710. See further *Dicey, Morris and Collins* (n 29) vol 1 paras 11-053–56, 12-123, 13-022–33; Berlingieri (n 13) vol 1 paras 8.65–69; Abou-Nigm (n 7) paras 7.38–51.

if the domestic law of the country in which the arrest is made gives jurisdiction to such Courts', or if various other connecting factors are present, such as where the claimant has its habitual residence or principal place of business in the country of arrest or the claim arose in the country of arrest, or if the claim is of a specific type (collision, salvage or mortgage claims). It is precisely this direct and deliberate nexus between the arrest procedure and the forum arresti's subsequent jurisdiction over the substantive merits that gives rise to conflicts distortions if the Arrest Convention regime is viewed solely through a procedural and lex fori lens.

Article 7(2) of the Arrest Convention 1952 deals with the situation where the forum arresti conversely does not have jurisdictional competence to decide the claim on the merits, providing that, in such situations, any bail or security provided to procure the release of the ship will operate as security for the satisfaction of any judgment handed down by another competent court provided that foreign proceedings are brought within the requisite time.[44] Article 7(3) of the Arrest Convention 1952 also recognises the legal effect of submission of maritime disputes to foreign judicial determination or arbitration, and provides that the foreign court or arbitration tribunal 'may fix the time within which the claimant shall bring proceedings'.[45] Article 7(4) provides that the defendant may apply to the forum arresti to release the ship, bail or security held for foreign proceedings if such proceedings are not brought within the relevant period.

Article 7 of the Arrest Convention 1952 does therefore deal with fundamental issues of substantive jurisdiction, but only in very basic and binary terms,[46] and does not address the possibility of a forum arresti refusing to exercise jurisdiction on a self-denying discretionary basis, for example on an application of the doctrine of forum non conveniens.[47] That gap has now been plugged by art 7(2) of the Arrest Convention 1999, which provides that

> the Courts of the State in which an arrest has been effected, or security provided to obtain the release of the ship, may refuse to exercise that jurisdiction where that refusal is permitted by the law of that State and a Court of another State accepts jurisdiction.

Article 7(5) of the Arrest Convention 1999 also expressly confirms that, where the vessel remains under arrest or substitute security is retained in the forum arresti to support any foreign proceedings, the subsequent foreign judgment or arbitral award obtained must be recognised and enforced by the forum arresti, provided that the judgment or award was obtained in time, requirements of natural justice have been met, and recognition of the foreign judgment of award is not against public policy (ordre public).

The wording of both the Arrest Conventions 1952 and 1999 therefore seems to be broad enough to support the concept of security arrests, both in the narrower sense of the

[44] See further ch 3.

[45] The same idea is expressed – more clearly and elegantly – in art 2(3) of the Arrest Convention 1999: 'A ship may be arrested for the purpose of obtaining security notwithstanding that, by virtue of a jurisdiction clause or arbitration clause in any relevant contract, or otherwise, the maritime claim in respect of which the arrest is effected is to be adjudicated in a State other than the State where the arrest is effected, or is to be arbitrated, or is to be adjudicated subject to the law of another State.'

[46] See Abou-Nigm (n 7) para 8.29: The 'issue of ancillary jurisdiction for interim measures of protection was far from being developed at the time' of drafting of the Arrest Convention 1952.

[47] See ch 4.

traditional *Rena K* principle[48] and its subsequent statutory codifications and variations,[49] and the more radical South African stand-alone institution of 'pure' security arrest.[50]

Both Arrest Conventions recognise the legal effects of foreign choice of forum and arbitration agreements, without elaborating on how the forum arresti exercises its discretion (if any) in respect of a stay of proceedings.[51] Neither Arrest Convention, however, deals directly with the issue of lis alibi pendens.[52] The problem of concurrent arrests in rem or other parallel proceedings in respect of the same maritime claim between the same parties will therefore fall to be resolved by relevant domestic law concepts or by another applicable Convention framework.[53]

V. Liable Person Link

Article 3 of the Arrest Convention 1952 sets out (in a rather cryptic and tortuous fashion) the required link between the liable person and the arrested ship, by providing in art 3(1) for 'particular ship' or surrogate ship arrest based on ownership of the arrested ship by the liable person at the time when the maritime claim arose. Article 3(4) extends this connection to vessels in the ownership of a charterer by demise.[54] Article 3 of the Arrest Convention 1952 was then (very) freely translated into the 'relevant person' link enacted in the Administration of Justice Act 1956 (UK), which was subsequently inherited by most Anglo-Common Law jurisdictions.[55]

Article 3 of the Arrest Convention 1999 also provides – with considerably more clarity of drafting that more closely resembles the familiar 'relevant person' link in most Anglo-Common Law jurisdictions – for a connecting link between the liable person and the arrested ship for arrests of the same ship in respect of which the maritime claim arose or a surrogate ship, together with an extension to include claims against the owner, demise charterer, manager or operator of the arrested ship that are 'secured by a maritime lien which is granted or arises under the law of the State where the arrest is applied for'.[56]

[48] *The Rena K* [1979] 1 QB 377.

[49] See eg s 26(1) of the Civil Judgments and Jurisdiction Act 1982 (UK); s 7(1) of the International Arbitration Act (cap 143A, 2002 rev ed) (Singapore).

[50] Section 5(3) of the Admiralty Jurisdiction Regulation Act 105 of 1983 (South Africa). See further ch 3.

[51] Article 7(3) of the Arrest Convention 1952; art 7(1) of the Arrest Convention 1999.

[52] But see *The Nordglimt* [1987] 2 Lloyd's Rep 470, 481 (Hobhouse J) for a suggestion that there is 'indirect provision for the problem of concurrent proceedings in more than one jurisdiction or tribunal in art. 7(2) of the 1952 Convention.'

[53] In the context of the EU, this means that the Brussels I Regulation (Recast) and the revised Lugano Convention will apply: see *Dicey, Morris and Collins* (n 29) vol 1 para 11-056; *The Nordglimt* [1987] 2 Lloyd's Rep 470, 478; *The Linda* [1988] 1 Lloyd's Rep 175; Case C-406/92 *Owners of the Cargo Laden on Board the Ship Tatry v Owners of the Ship Maciej Rataj* [1994] ECR I-05439, ECLI:EU:C:1994:400. For a trenchant critique of this outcome, see A Briggs, 'The Brussels Convention Tames the Arrest Convention' [1995] *LMCLQ* 161.

[54] See Francesco Berlingieri, 'The 1952 Arrest Convention Revisited' [2005] *LMCLQ* 327, 331–37 for a summary of the problems with the drafting of art 3 of the Arrest Convention 1952.

[55] See ch 12.

[56] Article 3(1)(e) of the Arrest Convention 1999. The original wording of this provision referred to 'a maritime lien which is *recognized* under the law of the State where the arrest is applied for' (emphasis added). However, this was replaced with the final wording because of concerns that the word 'recognized' necessarily implicated the application of a particular domestic private international law rule. A suggestion from the US delegation to add a

From a conflict of laws perspective, the most fundamental issue is whether this liable person link is to be characterised as a two-dimensional procedural or three-dimensional substantive issue. In other words, is 'ownership' of a foreign-flagged vessel (or indeed the validity or legal status of a foreign demise charter relationship or ship management or operation agreement) in the context of this liable person connection merely another jurisdictional or procedural element to be determined by the lex fori arresti, or is it to be characterised as a preliminary substantive issue to be determined by the applicable foreign law (lex causae) indicated by the private international principles of the lex fori arresti?

This issue is crucial because it goes to the heart of a forum arresti's exercise of its substantive jurisdiction under the relevant Arrest Convention and may also have significant knock-on effects on the efficacy and enforceability of any subsequent judicial sale in the same proceedings. The problem is exacerbated by the fundamentally different approaches to the legal effects of registered or beneficial ship ownership in Common Law and Civil Law jurisdictions.[57] Unfortunately, the Arrest Conventions 1952 and 1999 are silent on this issue, both seeming to treat ownership as a merely factual prerequisite of arrest, without any reference to the private international law approach to be adopted on such issues as ownership of foreign-flagged vessels in the context of the liable person link.

Unsurprisingly, given this lacuna in the Arrest Conventions, domestic courts have approached this issue in different ways. Courts in some countries have characterised all the elements of the liable person connection as jurisdictional and procedural per se, or as subsumed within a broader jurisdictional and procedural category of enquiry.[58] This characterisation has inevitably resulted in an application of the lex fori arresti to determine the issue, either without any reference to the relevant foreign law which would otherwise have governed the substantive merits of such an issue[59] (in respect of disputed ownership of foreign-flagged vessels, the lex causae would be likely to be the deemed lex situs[60] or law of the place of registration of the vessel),[61] or with only an indirect enquiry as to the

statement to the effect that 'nothing in this Convention prevents any court of a State party from arresting a ship for a claim secured by a maritime lien granted or arising under foreign law' was rejected. See Berlingieri (n 13) vol 2 para 8.51, appendix IV 257, 263ff for the relevant travaux préparatoires.

[57] In general terms, Civil Law countries do not recognise the concept of beneficial ownership, and regard unregistered ownership arrangements in respect of ships as non-binding on third parties. See eg *The Andres Bonifacio* [1993] SGCA 70, [1993] 3 SLR(R) 71 [32], referring to art 573 of the Code of Commerce (Philippines); *The Halla Liberty (South Korean Flag)* [1999] HKCFI 1185, [2000] 1 HKC 659 [59]ff, referring to art 743 of the Commercial Code (South Korea).

[58] See eg *The Andres Bonifacio* (n 57) [35] and *Vostok Shipping Co Ltd v Confederation Ltd (The Kapitan Lomaev)* [2000] 1 NZLR 37, 45–46 (CA). Both courts, with respect, interpreted *The Halcyon Isle* (*Bankers Trust International Ltd v Todd Shipyards Corp* [1981] AC 221 (PC)) far too broadly as standing for the characterisation principle that all jurisdictional issues are automatically procedural.

[59] See *The Andres Bonifacio* (n 57) [47], where the Singapore Court of Appeal described submissions on the law of the Philippines, as the deemed lex situs/law of the place of registration of the ship, as 'irrelevant' in the context of s 4(4) of the High Court (Admiralty Jurisdiction) Act (cap 123, 2001 rev edn).

[60] See eg *Tisand Pty Ltd v Owners of the Ship MV Cape Moreton (Ex Freya)* [2005] FCAFC 68, 143 FCR 43 [146]: 'There seem to us to be powerful reasons for giving effect to the law of the country of register as the lex situs in relation to questions of title, property and assignment (subject, of course, to local statute and public policy). The chance location of a working merchant ship in a port within its range of sailing or on the high seas appears to introduce an element of arbitrariness to the legal analysis.'

[61] Sergio M Carbone, 'Conflits de Lois en Droit Maritime' (2010) 340 *Recueil des Cours* 63, 253: 'Citons, en particulier, l'importance de la loi du pavillon pour établir la réglementation de la propriété, la possession, les droits de garantie sur le navire, et, en outre, la publicité et les actes de leur transfert ou de leur extinction.' ('We note, in

vessel's foreign registration as part of the factual or evidential mix in determining beneficial ownership according to the lex fori arresti.[62] Courts in other countries, by comparison, have characterised the determination of disputed elements of the liable person link as a substantive preliminary issue, to be resolved on an application of the lex causae indicated by the forum arresti's private international law rules, prior to a decision as to whether the forum arresti has jurisdiction under the lex fori arresti.[63]

In my view, a strict or even a modified lex fori approach cannot be justified as it is out of step with general private international law principles regarding the ownership status of personal property, is illogical and artificial in the sense that it may produce an entirely different answer to the question of foreign ownership in the jurisdictional context as opposed to foreign ownership on the merits, and may be productive of significant injustice.[64] This injustice may manifest itself either in the arrest of a ship on an application of the lex fori arresti that does not meet the requisite ownership link under the law of the place of the ship's registration, or in the thwarting of legitimate commercial expectations where a court releases a vessel from arrest that does satisfy the liable person connection under the Convention or relevant domestic legislation on an application of the law of the place of the ship's registration, but not at the lex fori arresti.[65]

particular, the significance of the law of the ship's flag in governing the regulation of ownership, possession and security rights over ships, and, furthermore, public notice [of their registration] and acts of their transfer or of their deletion [from the register].')

[62] This is the approach adopted in England (*The Nazym Khikmet* [1996] 2 Lloyd's Rep 362 (CA)), New Zealand (*The Kapitan Lomaev* (n 58)) and the more recent Singapore cases (*The Sangwon* [1999] SGCA 82, [1999] 3 SLR(R) 919; *The Makassar Caraka Jaya Niaga III-39* [2011] 1 SLR 982; *The Min Rui* [2016] SGHC 183, [2016] 5 SLR 667, discussed in Senthil Sabapathy, 'Admiralty Jurisdiction and Beneficial Ownership: Some Unanswered Questions' (2017) 29 *S Ac LJ* 552, especially 565ff).

[63] See *The Halla Liberty* (n 57); *The Cape Moreton* (n 60). Sabapathy ((n 62) 566–67) argues – erroneously, in my view – that these two decisions are also better categorised as instances of a modified lex fori approach, in the sense that the judges in both cases ultimately 'returned home' to the lex fori after applying the lex causae to the preliminary issue of foreign ownership of the arrested vessel. Although the conflicts methodology could undoubtedly have been spelled out more clearly in both judgments, both Courts characterised the issue of ownership in terms of the lex fori *including its private international law rules*, which meant giving full substantive effect to the law of the place of the ship's registry on the ownership issue without distortion of foreign ownership rights on remapping to the lex fori, subject only to the usual exceptions involving public policy objections (eg unlawful seizure or expropriation of ships) and situations that cannot possibly be characterised as ownership even within the broader conflicts categories adopted by the lex fori arresti (eg where the lex causae has no concept of ownership or property). It is not suggested that a full lex causae approach can, or should, be divorced from the jurisdictional matrix of the forum gateway statute, but rather that preliminary issues involving ownership of foreign-flagged ships, as involving substantive foreign legal rights rather than merely jurisdictional or procedural facts: (1) should be properly referred to the appropriate governing law for a full determination of the issue; and (2) the determination of that issue by the lex causae should be afforded as much recognition and respect by the forum arresti in the context of the jurisdictional enquiry as it would be in any other context. As the Court pointed out in *The Cape Moreton* (n 60) [140] its approach is *similar to* (but not, in my view, the same as) that adopted in *The Nazym Khikmet* (n 62). See further *Korea Shipping Corp v Lord Energy SA* [2018] FCAFC 201, [2019] Lloyd's Rep Plus 17 [48]ff where the Full Court of the Federal Court of Australia overturned Rares J's finding that ownership arrangements in respect of a South Korean-flagged vessel were analogous to beneficial ownership under Australian law. The Court (Allsop CJ, Besanko and McKerracher JJ) held that Korean law did not recognise the Australian concepts of an equity of redemption or a clog on the equity of redemption: '[T]he rights and interests … under the foreign law [are] to be characterised, not altered, by reference to Australian law.' This does not, by any stretch of the imagination, suggest a modified lex fori conflicts approach.

[64] For more detailed arguments along these lines, see Paul Myburgh, 'Arresting the Right Ship: Procedural Theory, The In Personam Link and Conflict of Laws' in Martin Davies (ed), *Jurisdiction and Forum Selection in International Maritime Law: Essays in Honor of Robert Force* (The Hague, Kluwer Law International, 2005) 283ff.

[65] As, in my view, was clearly the case in *The Kapitan Lomaev* (n 58).

Certainty and uniformity of outcome is one of the main goals of both international maritime law and private international law. It therefore seems considerably less than satisfactory that a maritime creditor cannot decide whether to arrest a foreign vessel based on accurate ownership information available in the relevant public ship register, but rather has to consider variations in the private international law approaches of different domestic legal systems when deciding whether or where to arrest. This inevitably encourages confusion and unproductive forum shopping.[66]

Equally, an application of the lex fori arresti to determine all elements of the liable person connection may result in the seizure and judicial sale of a vessel that meets ownership requirements under the lex fori arresti, but not under the law of the place of the ship's registration. In such circumstances, it seems unlikely that the courts or administrative officials of the flag State will recognise or enforce the effects of any foreign judicial sale arrived at on that basis.[67]

Even the 'halfway-house' approach adopted by courts in the UK, New Zealand and latterly Singapore, whereby the lex causae is consulted to glean facts and evidence 'for a better picture' of foreign ownership, adopts a peculiarly cavalier approach to foreign ownership rights over (often substantial) commercial assets that would not pass muster in any other conflicts context, where the lex situs principle in relation to proprietary rights over property has traditionally been regarded as one of the more sacrosanct and totemic rules of private international law.[68] While paying lip service to internationalism by going on a foreign fact-finding and evidence-gathering expedition, the modified lex fori approach still ultimately forces (or not) the foreign ownership connection to fit the shape and pattern of the lex fori concept of beneficial ownership. It therefore minimises, but does not prevent, distortions when the foreign concept is mapped back onto the lex fori's categories, with the resultant potential for absurdity and injustice.

The concern that the lex fori arresti will somehow be 'supplanted' by a full application of the lex causae to determine foreign legal rights implicated in the jurisdictional context is, with respect, totally misconceived.[69] As the Federal Court of Australia pointed out in *The Cape Moreton*, the correct conflicts approach both begins and ends with the lex fori arresti.[70] The law of the place of the ship's registration is only called upon to determine the specific preliminary and incidental issue of foreign ownership, just as it would, under normal private international law rules, determine the ownership of any other foreign personal property in any other context. That enquiry into foreign law may be more difficult in some cases,

66 As Berlingieri ((n 54) 334) points out: '[I]t seems reasonable to consider that the nature and effect of registration should be governed by the law of the country where the public register is maintained. This principle is laid down, in connection with mortgages and hypothèques, by Art 2 of the 1993 Convention on Maritime Liens and Mortgages, pursuant to which not only the ranking of registered mortgages, hypothèques or charges, but also their effect in regard to third parties is determined by the law of the state of registration.'

67 In *Castrique v Imrie* (1870) LR 4 HL 414, the House of Lords held that a French court's misinterpretation of English mortgage law did not invalidate the effects of the assignment of property arising from its subsequent judicial sale of the vessel, but one wonders whether a forum at the place of registration would refuse to recognise or enforce the effects of the foreign seizure and sale of what it sees as a vessel owned by an innocent third party on the basis of a breach of public policy or the principles of natural justice.

68 See Albert A Ehrenzweig, 'Specific Principles of Private Transnational Law' (1968) 124 *Recueil des Cours* 167, 270–71.

69 *The Makassar Caraka Jaya Niaga III-39* (n 62) [9].

70 *The Cape Moreton* (n 60) [140].

but in my view the difficulties have been greatly exaggerated.[71] If the plaintiff has arrested the 'wrong ship' according to the law at the ship's place of registration, the defendant shipowner will no doubt adduce evidence disproving the liable person connection with alacrity. If the parties do not produce appropriate evidence of foreign law, the default assumption of similarity of foreign law to the lex fori, however unsatisfactory, will solve any remaining practical difficulties.

The lex causae approach to determining the elements of the liable person connection adopted by the Australian and Hong Kong courts is therefore to be preferred. Given the existing diversity of conflict approaches to this issue in domestic jurisdictions, it is particularly disappointing that the drafters of the Arrest Convention 1999, at least, did not attempt to provide any explicit guidance on a uniform conflicts approach to this issue.

VI. Foreign Maritime Liens

Article 9 of the Arrest Convention 1952 provides that:

> Nothing in this Convention shall be construed as creating a right of action, which, apart from the provisions of this Convention, would not arise under the law applied by the Court which had seisin of the case, nor as creating any maritime liens which do not exist under such law or under the Convention on Maritime Mortgages and Liens, if the latter is applicable.

This provision can be read in one of two ways. First, art 9 may be interpreted as having been intended to restrict parties to the Arrest Convention 1952 to enforcing only maritime liens recognised at the lex fori arresti or under the Maritime Liens and Mortgages Convention 1926 without regard to the rules of private international law.[72] The effect of such a restrictive interpretation would be to disallow arrests to enforce any maritime liens that are not listed under the relevant internal lex fori arresti. Alternatively, art 9 has been characterised as at least providing evidence that the drafters were leaning against recognition of foreign maritime liens under the lex causae.[73]

However, it seems unlikely that the drafters intended art 9 of the Arrest Convention 1952 to operate as a restrictive lex fori rule in the private international law sense.

[71] One is reminded here of the Somerset Maugham quote: 'The most useful thing about a principle is that it can always be sacrificed to expediency': W Somerset Maugham, *The Circle* (New York, George H Doran Co, 1921) Act 3, 67. See eg the cases cited by Toh Kian Sing, *Admiralty Law and Practice*, 3rd edn (Singapore, LexisNexis, 2017) 130 fn 134. However, the Singapore Court of Appeal's ability in *The Sangwon* (n 62) to navigate expert evidence regarding the ownership of a North Korean-flagged vessel surely provides cause for optimism rather than pessimism regarding the feasibility of an appropriate lex causae approach.

[72] See Michael Marks Cohen, 'In Defense of The Halcyon Isle' [1987] *LMCLQ* 152, 153: 'The 1952 Arrest Convention strictly limits to the parameters of forum law both the scope of an arrest remedy and the availability of a maritime lien.'

[73] See *The Ship Sam Hawk v Reiter Petroleum Inc* [2016] FCAFC 26, (2016) 246 FCR 337 [47] (Allsop CJ and Edelman J): 'Article 9 of the 1952 Arrest Convention above directs attention, for the question of existence of maritime liens in the context of an arrest (that is the jurisdiction to arrest), to the law applied by the Court which is seised of the case – that is, seised of the arrest of the ship. Such does not negate the possibility of recognising the lex causae for some purpose, such as recognition of the nature of rights, but it does tend against the notion that the lex causae will determine what is to be characterised as a maritime lien in the place of the action (the forum).' For a detailed analysis of *The Sam Hawk*, see ch 4.

Article 9 seems rather to have been drafted merely to acknowledge two different substantive sources of maritime liens, that is, the domestic law of the forum arresti or the Maritime Mortgages and Liens Convention 1926. The main message of art 9 is that it does not alter the status quo in respect of maritime liens, and, in particular, that the enumeration of maritime claims under art 1(1) of the Arrest Convention 1952 was not intended to create any new maritime liens.

In respect of the issue of recognition and enforcement of foreign maritime liens, therefore, the better view is that art 9 of the Arrest Convention 1952 is an exercise in agnosticism. The reference to maritime liens 'existing' under the lex fori arresti is broad enough to include foreign maritime liens already recognised under the private international law rules of the lex fori arresti. Further, given the emphasis of the drafters of the Arrest Conventions on substantive international uniformity rather than on technical private international law guidance, it seems highly implausible that the basic reference to 'the law applied by the Court which had seisin of the case' was intended to amount to a technical direction to the forum arresti as to how to apply (or not to apply) its own private international law rules in respect of recognition of foreign maritime liens.[74]

Article 9 of the Arrest Convention 1999 is even more succinctly and clearly agnostic, simply declaring that '[n]othing in this Convention shall be construed as creating a maritime lien'. Article 3(1)(e) of the Arrest Convention 1999, which extends the liable person link to include claims against the owner, demise charterer, manager or operator of the arrested ship that are 'secured by a maritime lien which is granted or arises under the law of the State where the arrest is applied for' is also relevant to this issue.

Although some commentators have again read art 3(1)(e) of the Arrest Convention 1999 as indicating a restrictive lex fori approach to recognition of foreign maritime liens,[75] it seems rather to have been an attempt to clarify an issue, that had arisen under art 3(4) of the Arrest Convention 1952, as to whether demise charter arrest under that provision was limited to circumstances of a maritime lien or whether the provision conveyed a wider right of demise charter arrest.[76]

The reason some commentators interpret art 3(1)(e) of the Arrest Convention 1999 as a conflicts rule is that there was significant debate amongst the delegates as to whether the word 'granted' or 'recognised' should be used in this context. The latter wording was suggested by the US delegation, specifically because of concerns that the former wording might be interpreted as mandating a restrictive internal lex fori arresti approach, thereby excluding the possibility of recognition of foreign maritime liens. Eventually, the rather meaningless compromise of 'granted or arises under' was settled upon.[77]

The travaux préparatoires of the Arrest Convention 1999 graphically illustrate the sensitivities of the delegates about not intruding on domestic private international law

[74] See Berlingieri (n 13) vol 1 appendix V 683–85.

[75] See Tetley (n 33) 1975: '[A]rrest of ships for foreign maritime liens differing from those existing under the lex fori will not be permitted (article 3(1)(e) permits arrest only for a maritime lien that is "granted or arises" under the law of the State where the arrest is applied for, rather than for any maritime lien "recognized" under that law.'

[76] *The Sam Hawk* (n 73) [45] (Allsop CJ and Edelman J): 'The 1952 and the 1999 Arrest Conventions did not deal in detail with maritime liens, other than (see Art 9 in each convention) by stating that the convention should not be construed as creating a maritime lien and in clarifying the intended limits of demise charter arrest (in Art 3(1)(e) of 1999 Arrest Convention).'

[77] See n 56 above.

approaches, or on the territory already carved out by the existing Maritime Liens and Mortgages Conventions.[78] They also demonstrate that many delegates had absolutely no understanding of the private international law issues potentially arising from the provision:[79]

> Mr Chairman I was trying to put myself in the position of a judge who in a number of years to come will have to interpret this provision and the reason why the word 'granted' or the word 'recognized' has been adopted and to be quite frank, from this debate I wouldn't be able to draw any conclusion at all because many delegates have just said that they prefer one word and not the other but I have not heard the reason for which they do prefer one word or the other one. Some delegation[s] have been very clear: they said that they want the word 'granted' because they don't want that the Court of the place of arrest [should] be able to refer to liens other than the national liens of that country. On the other hand the US delegate for example, who expressed his opinion in favour of the word 'recognized', clearly stated that it is necessary to permit also the adoption of liens recognized in other countries if the local law permits to do so. I think that we should look at the substance of this problem. It seems to me that if the decision is not to permit the Court of the place of arrest to apply liens other than the national liens you would infringe upon the private international law of that country and I wonder whether we have an interest or we have the power to do so.

The unfortunate result of this unwillingness on the part of the drafters to engage with the issue of recognition of foreign maritime liens, and indeed the fundamental conflict of laws fragmentation caused by the substantive separation of international maritime liens and mortgage rules and the international arrest regime, is that neither the Arrest Convention 1952 nor the Arrest Convention 1999 provides any useful guidance on this matter. One is therefore sucked back into the proverbial 'dismal swamp'[80] of domestic law approaches to recognition of foreign maritime liens.

These domestic law approaches generally fall into one of three broad categories:

(1) an application of the lex fori arresti, on the basis that maritime liens are to be classified as procedural rather than substantive rights, or that the issue of recognition of foreign maritime liens falls within the broad category of jurisdictional issues,[81] or that the gateways of the characterisation process at the lex fori are never going to be large or flexible enough to let in foreign rights that are not 'analogous' to local maritime liens;[82] or

[78] See n 8 above; International Convention for the Unification of Certain Rules relating to Maritime Liens and Mortgages (adopted 27 May 1967, not yet in force): see UNCITRAL, Register of Texts of Conventions and Other Instruments concerning International Trade Law (UN, New York, 1973) vol II 179; International Convention on Maritime Liens and Mortgages (adopted 6 May 1993, entered into force 5 September 2004) 2276 UNTS 39.

[79] See Berlingieri (n 13) vol 2 annex IV 266–67 (statement by CMI delegate), analysis at para 8.51.

[80] William L Prosser describing the state of conflict of laws in 'Interstate Publication' (1953) 51 *Mich L Rev* 959, 971.

[81] See eg Lord Diplock's exposition in the majority judgment of *The Halcyon Isle* (n 58); *Transol Bunker BV v MV Andrico Unity (The Andrico Unity)* [1989] ZASCA 30, 1989 (4) SA 325; *Fournier v The Ship Margaret Z* [1999] 3 NZLR 111; *Ocean Gain Shipping Pte Ltd v Owner and/or Charterer of Demise of Vessel Dong Nai Registered at Haiphong Port, Vietnam (The Dong Nai)* [1996] 4 MLJ 454.

[82] See *The Sam Hawk* (n 73) [180]–[188] (Allsop CJ and Edelman J). As Martin Davies, 'Recognition of Foreign Maritime Liens' [2017] *LMCLQ* 206, 209 pithily points out: 'This is the *Halcyon Isle* result by a different, more convoluted, route.'

(2) an application of the deemed lex situs, that is, the law of the flag/law of the place of the ship's registration, on the basis that maritime liens are substantive proprietary rights affecting vessel ownership;[83] or
(3) an application of the lex causae, in other words, the applicable foreign law on an application of the lex fori arresti's private international law rules.[84]

The issue of recognition of foreign maritime liens has spawned one of the more enduring and controversial debates in maritime conflict of laws.[85] An exhaustive restatement of the domestic conflicts debates falls outside the ambit of this Chapter. Four brief points will hopefully suffice.

First, the diversity of domestic approaches highlights the necessity to characterise conflicts issues correctly. In my view, the lex fori and deemed lex situs approaches are both flawed, in that they ask the wrong category question. The conflicts question raised by the recognition of foreign maritime liens issue is not, or should not be, 'is this foreign cause of action equivalent or analogous to a maritime lien under the lex fori or the law of the flag?' That characterisation of the issue is both parochial and pointless, in the sense that it removes the possibility of any perspective or dimension or mapping of rights other than that of the lex fori arresti or the law of the flag. It is particularly problematic, in an area of law that is supposed to be as internationalist as possible, for courts to frame the issue of recognition of foreign maritime claims in a manner that will almost inevitably result in the non-recognition of the status of any foreign rights that are 'different'. The law of the flag approach to identifying relevant foreign maritime liens is at least preferable to the lex fori approach, in the sense that it is less likely to encourage opportunistic forum shopping, and that it does not produce the ludicrous results of maritime liens disappearing and reappearing from port to port, but that is about all that can be said in support of it.[86]

In my view, the lex causae approach adopted by North American courts asks the correct category question by characterising the issue as one of the status of substantive foreign legal rights. The question therefore is 'should the forum arresti accord to the foreign cause of action the same – or at least as similar as possible – status that it enjoys under the applicable lex causae'? That question cannot sensibly be answered by reference to the lex fori or the deemed lex situs – both of those legal systems have nothing relevant or useful to say about the legal status of the relevant foreign maritime claim.[87] There is even less excuse

[83] See Abou-Nigm (n 7) para 6.74 fn 155 for discussion of the European and Scandinavian countries that have adopted this approach.

[84] See the minority approach of Lords Salmon and Scarman in *The Halcyon Isle* (n 58). The Canadian and US courts have also consistently adopted a lex causae approach, although there have been debates as to what that means and how it is to be implemented. See eg *Kent Trade & Finance Inc v J P Morgan Chase Bank* 2008 FCA 399, [2009] 4 FCR 109; *World Fuel Services Singapore Pte, Ltd v Bulk Juliana M/V* 822 F 3d 766 (5th Cir 2016).

[85] See generally Martin Davies and Kate Lewins, 'Foreign Maritime Liens: Should They be Recognised in Australian Courts?' (2002) 76 *Australian LJ* 775; Martin Davies, 'Choice of Law and US Maritime Liens' (2009) 83 *Tul L Rev* 1435; Steven Rares, 'Maritime Liens, Renvoi and Conflicts of Law: The Far from *Halcyon Isle*' [2014] *LMCLQ* 183; Anton P Trichardt, *Maritime Liens and the Conflict of Laws*, Transactions of the Centre for Business Law 47 (Bloemfontein, University of the Free State, 2011); Abou-Nigm (n 7) paras 6.26–79.

[86] But see Abou-Nigm (n 7) para 6.77.

[87] Compare *The Cape Moreton* (n 60) [146], [148] where Ryan and Allsop JJ observed that the issue of ownership of a foreign registered vessel in the context of the in personam link ought to be referred to the deemed lex situs, because the lex fori had nothing relevant to say about foreign ship registration. It is, with respect, difficult to see why the same reasoning did not apply to the issue of applying the proper law to recognition of the status of foreign maritime liens in *The Sam Hawk* (n 73).

for lexforism here than in the context of establishing the liable person link, as the issue of recognition of the status of foreign maritime lien claims should clearly not be characterised as jurisdictional or (despite Lord Diplock's best efforts)[88] procedural, and the gateway forum statute typically does not define or provide a closed list of maritime liens, thereby leaving the issue open to the judicial application of a more appropriate and principled conflicts approach.

Secondly, from the perspective of the development of conflicts scholarship, it is deeply disappointing that we do not seem to be able to escape the sterility and circularity of the procedure–substance paradigm underpinning this debate, and move towards a more realistic policy-based, or preferably rights-based, analysis of this issue.[89]

Thirdly, the amount of ink spilled on this issue would seem to be inversely proportional to the magnitude of the actual practical problem. For the most part, there is broad international agreement on the lowest common denominator of 'core' maritime liens.[90] Apart from very occasional outliers,[91] the most commonly recurring issue is whether a ship supplier's maritime lien granted under US law (and more recently Canadian law)[92] or in certain Civil Law countries[93] should be recognised by the forum arresti of another country as a maritime lien (presumably, on an application of the lex fori arresti's priority principles and policies, ranking the recognised foreign maritime lien below other 'domestically preferred' maritime liens, but ahead of ship mortgages).[94] In my view, given that

[88] See the majority approach in *The Halcyon Isle* (n 58) which classifies 'by reference to the events on which each claim was founded and giving to it the priority to which it would be entitled under the lex fori if those events had occurred within the territorial jurisdiction of the distributing court'. This objectionable fictional exercise in projection and remapping 'events' back into the forum is of the same ideological ilk as the brand of 'lexforism lite' practised in relation to the issue of foreign ownership of vessels in the jurisdictional context – it downgrades and degrades issues of foreign substantive rights to mere facts, evidence or events, presumably to make the subsequent mutilation of foreign rights on the Procrustean bed of the lex fori appear more palatable. On this score, strict lexforism is perhaps to be preferred for the honesty of its shunning of internationalism.

[89] So too *The Sam Hawk* (n 73) [158]–[161] per Allsop CJ and Edelman J, who describe the debate as a 'distraction'. With respect, however, it is difficult not to be distracted by this issue, given Lord Diplock's characterisation in *The Halcyon Isle* (n 58) at 238, 239, 241 of 'maritime lien[s] in English law as involving rights that are procedural or remedial only'. See *The Sam Hawk* (n 73) [356]ff, [373]ff for Rares J's rather more critical analysis of the majority approach in *The Halcyon Isle*.

[90] It is therefore considerably less likely in the 21st century that the lex fori will need to play a protective role in, eg, upholding a seafarers' rights to wages that is allowed under the lex fori, but not the lex causae – and if it needs to, it should arguably be on the basis that an application of the lex causae offends the forum's public policy or mandatory minimum standards, rather than by distorting the choice of law process: but see *The Sam Hawk* (n 73) [113]–[117] (Allsop CJ and Edelman J).

[91] See, eg, *Metaxas v The Galaxias* [1989] 1 FC 386, 19 FTR 108 (recognition by Canadian court of Greek maritime union's lien in respect of unpaid contributions).

[92] See Paul Myburgh, 'The Ship Supplier's Lien: Taking a (Maple) Leaf Out of the Canadian Statute Book?' (2010) 18 *Asia Pacific Law Review* 279.

[93] The Maritime Liens and Mortgages Convention 1926 (n 8), art 2(5) recognises a necessaries maritime lien in the following circumstances: 'Claims resulting from contracts entered into or acts done by the master, acting within the scope of his authority, away from the vessel's home port, where such contracts or acts are necessary for the preservation of the vessel or the continuation of its voyage, whether the master is or is not at the same time owner of the vessel, and whether the claim is his own or that of ship-chandlers, repairers, lenders, or other contractual creditors.' States Parties to the Maritime Liens and Mortgages Convention 1926 include Argentina, Belgium, Brazil, France, Italy, Turkey and Uruguay. See further Francesco Berlingieri, 'The Maritime Lien for "Necessaries" in the 1926 Brussels Convention on Maritime Liens and Mortgages' (2005) 10 *Unif L Rev* 587.

[94] The pragmatic approach to priorities adopted by Rouleau J in *The Galaxias* (n 91). See also generally Rares J's discussion of priorities in *The Sam Hawk* (n 73) [319]–[412].

foreign ship suppliers' maritime liens are hardly outlandish, unexpected or against public policy, such recognition would seem to be a small price to pay for international uniformity, giving effect to the parties' legitimate commercial expectations and respecting the autonomy of foreign parties. If anything, it might be time for Anglo-Common Law jurisdictions which do not recognise ship suppliers' maritime liens to fall in line with the rest of the world.

The two-stage process of recognising foreign maritime liens on an application of the lex causae and then ranking them according to the priority rules of the lex fori, as advocated by the minority in *The Halcyon Isle*, does not amount, as has been suggested, to a splitting or 'decoupling' of rights and remedies,[95] or to a necessary subjugation of one regime by the other.[96] The primary question is always whether the lex fori arresti will recognise the status of the foreign maritime claim at the lex causae. Only if the answer to that question is yes, does the secondary question of ranking arise. Given that the priority principles of the lex fori are typically open-ended and subject to policy considerations,[97] it hardly does the lex fori violence to accommodate the recognised foreign maritime claim in the appropriate ranking category of other maritime claims of the same or similar status. Indeed, this is consonant with the equitable and internationalist principles underpinning the ranking and distribution admiralty rules at the lex fori. Equally, given that the domestic policy of the lex fori arresti regards certain maritime claims as having a certain preferred status and others not, there is nothing particularly objectionable in ranking local and foreign maritime claims that meet the policy criteria of the lex fori arresti ahead of recognised foreign maritime claims that do not, while still recognising their status by ranking them in the appropriate category of preferred maritime claim.[98] Arguments that admitting foreign maritime claims to the distribution of the proceeds of a judicial sale will somehow distort the ranking of claims at the lex fori or unfairly cause other creditors to 'lose out',[99] are based on the logical fallacy that ranking is somehow a fixed and predetermined exercise in privilege, rather than always being subject to, and contingent upon, the prior primary decision on which maritime claims will be recognised and admitted to the ranking and distribution exercise under the lex fori arresti.[100] Equally, the 'decoupling' argument – that recognised foreign maritime liens will somehow suffer a diminution or dilution of their legal nature and status as maritime liens if the priority rules of the lex fori

[95] See eg Mohammud Jaamae Hafeez-Baig, 'A Novel Approach to Foreign Maritime Liens' (2017) 133 *LQR* 378, 383: 'One may query the extent to which it is realistic to separate the nature of the right from the effect which is given to it. On one view, any change to the effect which is given to a right is tantamount to changing the nature of the right itself.' See also *The Sam Hawk* (n 73) [80], [82], [99], [138].

[96] See also *The Sam Hawk* (n 73) [99]: 'This demonstrates a degree of intractability in using a *lex causae* to characterise the maritime lien, but accepting the *lex fori* as governing priorities. Either the former changes the latter by the act of characterisation or recognition, or the latter affects the former by refusing to give priority of a lien character to a right characterised as a maritime lien.'

[97] See *The Ruta* [2000] 1 Lloyd's Rep 359; *The Posidon* [2017] SGHC 138, [2018] 3 SLR 372.

[98] See *The Galaxias* (n 91).

[99] See eg Michael Douglas, 'Characterisation of a Foreign Maritime Lien by the Lex Fori' (2017) 17 *OUCLJ* 152, 159.

[100] It will, of course, be a different matter where the lex fori arresti's priority rules are closed or codified and do not allow the recognised foreign maritime claim to be ranked, in which case the ranking policy 'tail' of the lex fori will wag the recognition 'dog' of the lex causae.

arresti rank them lower than they would have been ranked according to the priority rules of the lex causae – while perhaps of theoretical interest, has little practical or commercial relevance. If one were to ask any foreign maritime claimant whether it would prefer the possibility of ranking and satisfaction of its recognised but 'decoupled' foreign maritime lien rights at the lex fori arresti, or the inevitable rejection and non-satisfaction of its non-recognised (but nonetheless conceptually pure and uncoupled) maritime lien rights, it is blindingly obvious what the answer would be.

Fourthly, the signal failure of the various iterations of the Maritime Liens and Mortgages Conventions,[101] and the inability or unwillingness of the drafters of both the Arrest Conventions 1952 and 1999 to engage with crucial comparative private international law issues, or to integrate meaningfully the subject matter covered by the Maritime Liens and Mortgages Conventions into the international ship arrest framework,[102] again underlines the limitations inherent in the existing international maritime law treaty-making processes and the relevant international institutions to achieve anything resembling both substantive and conflicts uniformity in this area.

VII. Other Foreign Maritime Claims

Maritime claims are defined in art 1 of the Arrest Convention 1952. As is well known, the debate over whether the Arrest Convention should be modelled on a more general statement of subject-matter jurisdiction (which would more closely accord with the North American and Civilian approaches) or an open-ended or closed list of heads of jurisdiction was finally settled in favour of a closed list of maritime claims based on the heads of jurisdiction previously allowed under English law.[103] Despite the well-founded concern that a closed list of claims is 'dangerous, for it is unlikely to be complete or, in any event, to continue to be complete in the light of new developments',[104] the drafters of the Arrest Convention 1999 also eventually opted for the compromise of a closed list of maritime claims, albeit expanded and updated.[105]

This adoption of a closed list of maritime claims (other than maritime liens)[106] in article 1(1) of both Arrest Conventions, read together with the prohibition on ship arrest

[101] See, eg, J Allsop 'Comity and Unity in Maritime Law' (2016) 47 *J Mar L & Com* 279, 295 n 41, who observes that the 'changing policy over the years can be seen in the different (and narrowing) classes of liens posited for international agreement in the maritime lien and mortgage conventions: the 1926 MLM Convention, Art. 2 (especially para. 5), the 1967 MLM Convention, Art. 4(1), and the 1993 MLM Convention, Art. 4(1)'.

[102] See Berlingieri (n 13) vol 2 appendix IV 193: 'The two Conventions should remain entirely independent.'

[103] See the Supreme Court of Judicature (Consolidation) Act 1925 (UK) (15 & 16 Geo 5 c 49); Berlingieri (n 13) vol 1 paras 5.01–03.

[104] Berlingieri (n 13) vol 1 para 5.03. See also Tetley (n 33) 1966: 'In my view, it is regrettable that an 'open-ended' list was rejected, because it would have provided greater flexibility to courts applying the Arrest Convention 1999 in future years.'

[105] See Berlingieri (n 13) vol 2 ch 5.

[106] As discussed above, however, it is clear from arts 9 of both Arrest Conventions that the issue of whether maritime claims are to be afforded the status of a maritime lien is to be left to one side: see Tetley (n 33) 1965: 'It is important, of course, not to confuse "maritime claims" with "maritime liens." In the 1952 and 1999 Arrest Conventions, "maritime claims" refers merely to claims permitting the arrest of a ship. Some "maritime claims" are "maritime liens" and some are not. Whether specific types of "maritime claims" constitute "maritime liens," which

in respect of any other maritime claims in art 2 of both Arrest Conventions, effectively polices both the substantive subject-matter and private international law boundaries of maritime claims (other than maritime liens), rendering impermissible the recognition of any other foreign maritime claim not on the list, or extension of subject-matter jurisdiction by reference to foreign law. The private international law effect of these two provisions broadly accords with the Anglo-Common Law approach to statutory rights of action in rem, which, as choses in action created under the lex fori arresti, rather than substantive proprietary rights,[107] are appropriately regulated by the lex fori arresti. It does not, of course, accommodate (or perhaps, more accurately, it entirely fails to engage with) the US conceptual approach to admiralty jurisdiction.

VIII. Recognition and Enforcement of Foreign Judgments and Awards

Both the Arrest Conventions 1952 and 1999 (the former by implication and the latter expressly) seem to sanction the enforcement of foreign judgments or arbitral awards against a previously arrested vessel or substitute security retained by the forum arresti in support of pending foreign proceedings (that is, in the context of security arrest).[108] The position is less clear in respect of post-judgment or post-arbitration award arrests designed directly to enforce prior judgments or awards. Articles 1(2) of both Arrest Conventions exclude the seizure of a ship 'in execution or satisfaction' of a judgment (or other enforceable instrument, in the case of the Arrest Convention 1999).[109] This provision, when read together with the absence of any reference to recognition or enforcement of foreign maritime claims in the list of permissible maritime claims in Article 1(1) of the Arrest Conventions, would seem to preclude this possibility.[110]

However, if a recent Hong Kong case is anything to go by, Anglo-Common Law courts at least do not seem willing to take the restrictive definition in art 1(2) of the Arrest Convention 1952 very seriously. In *The Alas*[111] the relevant vessel was arrested in Hong Kong, effectively to enforce an unsatisfied foreign arbitration award. Because previous English and Hong Kong authorities[112] had held that this was impermissible because the domestic heads of admiralty jurisdiction (modelled on the Arrest Convention 1952 list of claims in art 1(1)) did not include a direct cause of action for recognition or

follow the ship and rank before ship mortgages, or merely statutory rights in rem, which do not follow the ship and rank after the mortgage, depends on other international conventions (governing maritime liens and mortgages) and on national law.'

[107] On the debate as to whether vested statutory rights of action in rem give rise to 'quasi-secured rights', see ch 3.

[108] Article 7(2) of the Arrest Convention 1952; Art 7(5) of the Arrest Convention 1999. See ch 3.

[109] Although several countries have extended the definition of ship arrest to cover 'enforcement arrests' in their domestic legislation: on China, see ch 11; on India, see ch 12.

[110] See Berlingieri (n 13) vol 1 para 4.05: 'The purpose of the definition is to exclude from the scope of the Convention all enforcement proceedings, irrespective as to whether the seizure of a ship is effected on the basis of a judgment or any other order issued by a court.'

[111] *Handytankers KS v Owners and/or Demise Charterers of Alas subsequently renamed as Kombos* [2014] HKCFI 1281, [2014] 6 HKC 239.

[112] *The Chong Bong* [1997] HKCFI 306, [1997] 3 HKC 579 and *The Bumbesti* [2000] QB 559.

enforcement of foreign judgments and awards, the plaintiff was careful to draft its claim in terms of a de novo determination of the underlying cause of action (the defendant's breach of a charterparty).

The defendant argued that the arrest procedure was not available in these circumstances because of, inter alia, the restrictive definition of arrest in art 1(2) of the Arrest Convention 1952. The defendant therefore urged the court to construe the Hong Kong domestic admiralty statute consistently with art 1(2) of the Arrest Convention 1952.

Ng J dismissed the defendant's argument:[113]

> Regarding Mr Alder's submission that the procedure of arrest is not available once a plaintiff's claim has crystallised in an in rem judgment, it does not assist the Defendants in any way since the Plaintiff has not yet obtained in rem judgment in this action. Even that proposition of law, supported as it is by *The Alletta* [1974] 1 Lloyd's Rep 40, is of dubious weight – it was not followed by the High Court of Singapore in '*The Daien Maru No. 18*' [1986] 1 Lloyd's Rep 387 for good reasons. Arrest of a ship in an action in rem is a mere procedure the object of which is to obtain security from which the judgment can be satisfied: *The Beldis* (1936) 53 Ll L Rep 255; *The Cap Bon* [[1967] 1 Lloyd's Rep 543]. Like Thean J, I find it extremely odd that the right of security by the arrest of a vessel is available to a plaintiff who merely asserts a claim whereas it is lost when he finally obtains a judgment in the action.

While the court's dismissal of the argument may be technically correct, in the sense that art 1(2) of the Arrest Convention 1952 simply refers to 'execution or satisfaction of a judgment' as opposed to an arbitration award, it is telling that Ng J analysed the issue through an entirely domestic legal lens, despite the fact that Hong Kong is a party to the Arrest Convention 1952.

IX. Conclusions

In sum, and because academic marking habits die hard, I would award the Arrest Convention 1952 no more than a mediocre to middling pass grade for its success in achieving substantive international uniformity, especially when compared to the relative successes of star students such as the Hague-Visby Rules[114] or the CISG.[115] Despite improvements in drafting, the Arrest Convention 1999 seems unlikely to perform more successfully on that front. When assessed under the marking rubric of achieving private international law uniformity, however, both Arrest Conventions fail miserably.

As discussed above, there are various interrelated reasons for this failure. The drafters of the Arrest Convention 1952 focused on the task of substantive harmonisation without considering the private international law dimension, and therefore inevitably produced an old-fashioned two-dimensional map rather than a more useful three-dimensional globe.

[113] *The Alas* (n 111) [24]. The defendant's application for leave to appeal was dismissed in *Handytankers KS v The Owners and/or Demise Charterers of the Ship or Vessel M/V Alas Subsequently Renamed as Kombos (The Alas)* [2015] HKCA 691, [2015] 6 HKC 557, with no reference to the Arrest Convention 1952 argument.

[114] On which see generally Stephen Girvin, *Carriage of Goods by Sea*, 2nd edn (Oxford, Oxford University Press, 2011).

[115] See n 25 above.

The Arrest Convention 1999 simply updates and redraws slightly more clearly the same old two-dimensional map, with most of its existing potential for distortion.

It is not clear why private international law issues were not properly debated or addressed in the Arrest Convention 1999 at least. Some answers may be found in the peculiarities of the international Convention drafting process and the fact that the institutions and delegates behind the Arrest Conventions are specialist experts in substantive maritime law rather than private international law issues. The effect of 'Convention silos',[116] the desire not to trespass on territory already covered by the existing (and spectacularly unsuccessful) Maritime Liens and Mortgages Conventions, and concerns about inflaming domestic jurisdictional and procedural sensitivities also appear to have played a significant role.

To the limited extent that the Arrest Conventions 1952 and 1999 do appear to grapple with private international law issues, they defer by default to the forum arresti and an application of the lex fori arresti, in a manner that leaves it unclear whether this is simply meant as shorthand for describing the domestic/international law divide, or whether it is indicating or mandating a particular private international law approach. Even in the latter case, it remains unclear whether the Arrest Convention texts are referring to the lex fori arresti as internal domestic law, or whether such references are to be read as inclusive of the lex fori's private international law rules.

In the absence of any useful global wayfinding from the Arrest Conventions in this regard, private international law problems in the ship arrest context will unfortunately continue to proliferate, and will have to be navigated, as best they can be, by following the relatively inconsistent, fragmentary and outdated conflicts maps available in domestic law.

[116] See Berlingieri (n 13) vol 2 para 8.47: the avoidance of any union between the Arrest Convention and the Maritime Liens and Mortgages Conventions is down to 'the general principle … that no express reference should be made in one convention to other conventions in order to avoid that the ratification of one convention be adversely affected by the reference to another convention which a State is not willing to become a party to.'

8

Arrest, Detention and Seizure of Ships: Availability for Environmental Claims

MICHAEL TSIMPLIS*

I. Introduction

It is difficult for a claimant to get reparation for damages caused by a ship if the ship is permitted to sail away, unless security for the claim has been obtained whilst the ship was still in port. The ship, a moving and easily transferable asset, could be the only asset of a foreign company that is not directly under the jurisdiction of a court where the claim can be heard. Even with a court judgment, the enforcement against such a foreign company without other assets could be problematic. Ship arrest prohibits the ship from sailing, puts it under the custody of the court, establishes jurisdiction on the merits for the arresting court and permits judgment and enforcement, because the property is located where the judgment is granted and can be sold by the court. The shipowner can provide appropriate financial security and continue trading, but the claimant is then secured, as the security provided replaces the ship.[1]

The international legal system concerned with ship arrest is rather recent and reflects the aspiration to harmonise national laws, which have been utilising ship arrest in different ways for many years before that. The United Kingdom's system is a hybrid of the Arrest Convention 1952, pre-existing English law and innovative drafting.[2] To preserve the pre-existing system, the UK has included the Arrest Convention 1952 within the rules related to the admiralty jurisdiction of the High Court.[3]

Compared with the long history of ship arrest in national systems, environmental rights and obligations are much more recent. The first international Convention for the control of operational ship-source pollution was agreed in 1954,[4] two years after the Arrest

* Professor of Law, City University of Hong Kong. I am grateful to Mr S Papadas for his assistance in researching the sources for this article.

[1] On the security function of ship arrest see ch 3.

[2] See further ch 12.

[3] See DC Jackson, *Enforcement of Maritime Claims*, 4th edn (London, LLP, 2005) for a detailed analysis of the admiralty jurisdiction. See also Aleka Mandaraka-Sheppard, *Modern Maritime Law, Volume 1: Jurisdiction and Risks*, 3rd edn (Abingdon, Informa Law, 2013) ch 1. In addition, a significant part of the English law related to ship arrest is contained in Part 61 of the Civil Procedure Rules, the Practice Direction for admiralty claims and case law.

[4] International Convention for the Prevention of Pollution of the Sea by Oil (adopted 12 May 1954, entered into force 26 July 1958, amended in 1962 and 1969) 327 UNTS 3.

Convention 1952. However, States did not establish an international compensation regime for pollution damage for another 15 years, when the images of tankers polluting extensive areas and destroying wildlife forced them to do so.[5] It was under these conditions that the Civil Liability Convention 1969 (CLC 1969)[6] was agreed. Before the CLC 1969, pollution damage claims were based exclusively on national law (which, in England, meant claims in tort) and many of them were unsuccessful.[7] The establishment of an international pollution damage liability regime only after the international legal framework of ship arrest had been fully developed creates a number of issues with respect to the position of claimants for pollution damage. The first concerns the general availability of ship arrest as a security option for pollution damage claims and the priority status of such claims. The second concerns the inter-relationship of ship arrest with the international environmental liability conventions, namely the CLC 1969, the Civil Liability Convention 1992 (CLC 1992),[8] the Bunker Oil Pollution Convention 2001 (BOPC 2001)[9] and the Hazardous and Noxious Substances Convention 2010 (HNS 2010).[10] The third issue concerns the inter-relationship of arrest with what we will term administrative environmental liability regimes. These include cleanup for pollution under the EU Environmental Liability Directive (ELD)[11] and the Nairobi Wreck Removal Convention 2007 (WRC 2007).[12] The fourth issue is whether detention or forfeiture of a ship can be considered as an alternative in cases of environmental damage caused by a ship. This Chapter will address each question separately and will consider whether the answers to these questions are appropriate under the current normative requirements.

[5] A detailed review of the history, the well-known incidents and the political and financial conflicts involved is beyond the scope of this Chapter. The interested reader is advised to read Colin de la Rue and Charles B Anderson, *Shipping and the Environment*, 2nd edn (Abingdon, Informa Law, 2009) where a good summary of the history is provided.

[6] The International Convention on Civil Liability for Oil Pollution Damage (adopted 29 November 1969, entered into force 19 June 1975) 973 UNTS 3 establishes strict but limited liability for the shipowner, coupled with compulsory insurance and direct action against the insurer. The Protocol to the International Convention on Civil Liability for Oil Pollution Damage (adopted 19 November 1976, entered into force 8 April 1981) 1225 UNTS 356 has been used as an interim solution to increase the low limits of liability agreed within the CLC 1969.

[7] *Esso Petroleum Co Ltd v Southport Corp* [1956] AC 218, [1955] 2 Lloyd's Rep 655. One difficulty is related to the need to prove fault on the part of the tortfeasor. Another is the fact that pure economic losses are not, in general, recoverable at English law.

[8] The International Liability Convention on Civil Liability for Oil Pollution Damage 1992, as amended in 2000, was created by the modification of the 1969 CLC by the 1992 Protocol to the 1969 CLC (adopted 27 November 1992, entered into force 30 May 1996) 1956 UNTS 255: see arts 11(2) and 1(5) of the 1992 Protocol. There was also a (not too dissimilar) 1984 Protocol to the CLC 1969, which, despite being ratified by various major trading nations (eg, France, Germany and Australia), was ratified by insufficient countries for it to enter into force. Its provisions have largely been included in the CLC 1992.

[9] International Convention on Civil Liability for Bunker Oil Pollution Damage (adopted 23 March 2001, entered into force 21 November 2008), IMO Doc LEG/CONF 12/19, 23 March 2001.

[10] International Convention on Liability and Compensation for Damage in Connection with the Carriage of Hazardous and Noxious Substances by Sea (adopted 3 May 1996, not yet in force, superseded by the Protocol of 2010 to amend the International Convention on Liability and Compensation for Damage in Connection with the Carriage of Hazardous and Noxious Substances by Sea 1996 (adopted 29 April 2010, not yet in force)), IMO LEG-CONF.17/DC/1, 29 April 2010. The Protocol consists of 29 articles that significantly amend HNS 1996 in various ways. Article 2 of the 2010 Protocol requires the parties to the Protocol to give effect to HNS 1996 as amended by the Protocol. HNS 1996 read together with the 2010 Protocol form HNS 2010.

[11] Directive 2004/35/EC of the European Parliament and of the Council of 21 April 2004 on environmental liability with regard to the prevention and remedying of environmental damage [2004] OJ L143/56, which entered into force on 30 April 2004.

[12] Nairobi International Convention on the Removal of Wrecks, (adopted 18 May 2007, entered into force 14 April 2015) 46 IML 697.

II. The Availability of Arrest as a Security Option for Environmental Claims

A. The Arrest Convention 1952

Presently the International Convention Relating to the Arrest of Sea-Going Ships 1952 (the Arrest Convention 1952)[13] and the International Convention on the Arrest of Ships 1999 (the Arrest Convention 1999)[14] provide the international framework for ship arrest.[15] Both Conventions include a very similar arrangement. A list of maritime claims is specified,[16] and it is for the satisfaction of a maritime claim within this list that ship arrest becomes available.[17] The ship is not subject to arrest for any other claim. Therefore, the starting point for any inquiry regarding the availability of ship arrest for pollution damage claims must be whether such claims are contained within the list of maritime claims.

The Arrest Convention 1952 does not have a specific provision dealing with pollution damage claims. Pollution damage at that time was not an important concern, despite studies showing the toxic effects of oil on various species.[18] In order to argue for pollution damage as a maritime claim that can lead to ship arrest, an argument must be made that such damage falls under the natural meaning of the words in one or more categories of maritime claims. Indeed, there are various such categories of claims. The most likely candidates are these maritime claims under art 1(1) of the Arrest Convention 1952:

> 'Maritime claim' means a claim arising out of one or more of the following:
>
> (a) damage caused by any ship either in collision or otherwise;
> (b) loss of life or personal injury caused by any ship or occurring in connexion with the operation of any ship;
> (c) salvage;
> (d) agreement relating to the use or hire of any ship whether by charter party or otherwise;
> (e) agreement relating to the carriage of goods in any ship whether by charter party or otherwise;
> (f) loss of or damage to goods including baggage carried in any ship; …
> (k) goods or materials wherever supplied to a ship for her operation or maintenance.

Whether these headings include pollution damage depends: first, on the interpretation of the term 'arising out of';[19] and secondly, on the character of each category of claim.

[13] International Convention Relating to the Arrest of Sea-going Ships (adopted 10 May 1952, entered into force 24 February 1956) 439 UNTS 193.

[14] International Convention on the Arrest of Ships (adopted 12 March 1999, entered into force 14 September 2011) 2797 UNTS 3.

[15] Article 1(2) of the Arrest Convention 1952 describes 'arrest' as 'the detention of a ship by judicial process to secure a maritime claim, but does not include the seizure of a ship in execution or satisfaction of a judgment'. However, no equivalent definition exists in English law. See *The Anna H* [1995] 1 Lloyd's Rep 11 (CA) for the difference between the definition and the purpose of arrest under English law.

[16] Article 1 of the Arrest Conventions 1952 and 1999.

[17] Article 2 of the Arrest Conventions 1952 and 1999.

[18] See eg RW Holcomb, 'Oil in the Ecosystem', (1969) 166 *Science* 204–06 for a review of the science after the *Torrey Canyon* incident.

[19] Thus, eg, if the intention of the drafters of the Arrest Convention 1952 was that arrest was only to be available for 'the damage caused by any ship either in collision or otherwise', the term 'arising out of' would not have been necessary. Therefore, the term 'arise out of' must have been included to broaden out the meaning of the aforementioned paras. See further Francesco Berlingieri, *Berlingieri on Arrest of Ships*, 6th edn (Abingdon, Informa Law from Routledge, 2017) vol 1 para 5.08 on the meaning of 'arising out of' and 'ayant l'une des causes suivantes' in the French text.

The term 'arising out of' arguably broadens the interpretation of the otherwise closed list of claims of the Arrest Convention 1952 and permits the consideration of indirect, consequential and indemnity claims to the extent that they arise out of the relevant maritime claim. It follows that such claims may potentially include pollution damage claims. A broad interpretation of 'arising out of' for the aforementioned provisions may be capable of covering one or another type of pollution damage. For example, oil spills from cargo may give rise to claims under paras (c), (d), (e) and (f). Claims for bunker oil spills could be argued under paras (a), (c) or (k) and loss of life and personal injury from noxious and hazardous materials carried on board as cargo or for the use of the ship could be argued under para (b).

Whether such a broad interpretation is supported depends on how national courts interpret this term. The enactment of the Arrest Convention 1952 into national law then becomes important.

B. The Action In Rem

In English law the Arrest Convention 1952 has been rewritten to co-exist with the procedural requirements for in rem admiralty jurisdiction of the English courts. This resulted in 'burying arrest'[20] within the admiralty jurisdiction of the High Court provisions of the Senior Courts Act 1981 (UK) (SCA 1981) and translating it into the availability of the procedural action in rem for claims under the Admiralty jurisdiction of the High Court,[21] which bear a resemblance to the maritime claims under the Arrest Convention 1952 but are not expressed in identical terms.

In particular, the maritime claims 'arising out of' arts 1(1)(d) and 1(1)(e) of the Arrest Convention 1952 have been rewritten as 'any claim arising out of any agreement relating to the carriage of goods in a ship or to the use or hire of a ship'.[22] The opportunity to resolve the interpretation of the term 'arising out of' was presented in *The Antonis P Lemos*,[23] where the term was held to have the wider meaning of 'connected with' rather than the narrower meaning of 'arising under'.[24] The House of Lords held in this case that a claim for the negligent overloading of the ship by the master, which caused financial loss to the sub-charterer with whom the shipowner had no contract, fell under s 20(2)(h) of the SCA 1981 and thus entitled the sub-charterer to have the ship arrested.[25]

[20] Richard Shaw and Nicholas Gaskell, 'The Arrest Convention 1999' [1999] *LMCLQ* 472.

[21] SCA 1981, s 20(2).

[22] ibid, s 20(2)(h).

[23] *Samick Lines Co Ltd v Owners of the Antonis P Lemos (The Antonis P Lemos)* [1985] AC 711 (HL).

[24] Lord Brandon, who delivered the leading speech in the House of Lords, said (ibid 731): 'I am not persuaded that any one of those points singly, or any combination of them together, lead to the conclusion that the expression 'arising out of' in s. 20(2)(*h*) of the 1981 Act should be given the narrow meaning of the expression 'arising under', rather than the wider meaning of the expression 'connected with'. On the contrary, I am satisfied, on four main grounds, that the expression 'arising out of' should be given the second and wider meaning.'

[25] In *Gatoil International Inc v Arkwright-Boston Manufacturers Mutual Insurance Co (The Sandrina)* [1985] AC 255, the House of Lords recognised that the term 'relating to' – which is present in both the Arrest Convention 1952, arts 1(1)(d) and (e) and the SCA 1981, s 20(2)(h) – limits the broadness of the interpretation of the term 'arising out of'. Lord Keith said (271): 'There must in my opinion, be some reasonably direct connection with such activities. An agreement for the cancellation of a contract for the carriage of goods in a ship or for the use or hire of a ship would, I think, show a sufficiently direct connection. It is unnecessary to speculate what other cases might be covered. Each case would require to be decided on its own facts. As regards the contract of insurance founded

In *The Eschersheim*[26] the claim in rem against a negligent salvor included the shipowner's potential pollution liability to the Spanish government from the leakage of chemicals and bunker oil. The House of Lords held that the salvage contract was a contract arising out of the use of the salvor's ship and was therefore covered by s 20(2)(h) of the Administration of Justice Act 1956 (UK), the forerunner of the SCA 1981.

Thus, the English courts[27] have accepted a broad interpretation of the term 'arising out of' and have confirmed that indemnity claims for pollution damages that have been paid out can be part of an action in rem. However, the existing decisions do not clarify whether direct pollution claims can be supported by an action in rem. The answer to this question depends on whether the various heads of jurisdiction under s 20(2) of the SCA 1981 are capable of including such claims. While the legislator preserved the term 'claim arising out of', which appears in all the maritime claims under art 1(1) of the Arrest Convention 1952 in s 20(2)(h) of the SCA 1981, this is not the case for the other heads of jurisdiction.

Article 1(1)(a) of the Arrest Convention 1952 has been rewritten in 20(2)(e) of the SCA 1981 as 'any claim for damage done by a ship'.[28] This term, which does not include the 'arising out of' phrase, significantly reduces the scope of this head of jurisdiction under English law and preserves pre-existing English law. Clarke J in *The Rama*[29] said:

> The question is whether the defendants' claims are claims 'for damage done by a ship' within the meaning of s. 20(2)(e) of the Supreme Court Act, 1981. If they are, they give rise to a maritime lien, whereas, if they are not, they do not give rise to a maritime lien.[30]

The suggested equivalence of the statutory provision with the damage lien is a significant obstacle, as maritime liens were settled well before any marine pollution claims were ever considered. Its interpretation by the courts has been further restricted by requiring that the ship must have been the actual instrument that inflicted the damage. Thus, Lord Diplock in *The Eschersheim*[31] said:

> The figurative phrase 'damage done by a ship'[32] is a term of art in maritime law whose meaning is well settled by authority: see *The Vera Cruz*,[33] *Currie v. M'Knight*.[34] To fall within the phrase not

on in the instant appeal, I am of opinion that it is not connected with the carriage of goods in a ship in a sufficiently direct sense to be capable of coming within paragraph (e).'

[26] *The Eschersheim* [1976] 2 Lloyd's Rep 1 (HL).

[27] Courts in several other jurisdictions have adopted a similar approach. eg, in Australia see *Heilbrunn v Lightwood plc* [2007] FCA 1518, (2007) 164 FCR 1 [31]–[40]; *Beluga Shipping GmbH & Co v Headway Shipping Ltd (No 2)* [2008] FCA 1770 [9]–[10]; in Canada see *Margem Chartering Co Inc v Cosena, SRL* [1997] 2 FC 1001, (1997) 127 FTR 161; *Paramount Enterprises International, Inc v An Xin Jiang (The)* (1997) 147 FTR 162; in New Zealand see *Reef Shipping Co Ltd v The Ship Fua Kavenga* [1987] 1 NZLR 550; in Singapore see *The Evpo Agsa* [1992] SGHC 74, [1992] 1 SLR(R) 662; *The Indriani* [1996] SGCA 2, [1995] 2 SLR(R) 458; *The MARA* [2000] SGCA 47, [2000] 3 SLR(R) 31; *The Catur Samudra* [2010] SGHC 18, [2010] 2 SLR 518.

[28] SCA 1981, s 20(2)(e).

[29] *Berliner Bank AG v C Czarnikow Sugar Ltd (The Rama)* [1996] 2 Lloyd's Rep 281, 292. See also *The Vinalines Pioneer* [2015] SGHC 278, [2016] 1 SLR 448.

[30] *The Rama* (n 29) 292. For the definition and categories of maritime liens see *Harmer v Bell (The Bold Buccleugh)* (1851) 7 Moo PC 267, 13 ER 884 (PC).

[31] *The Eschersheim* (n 26).

[32] Brandon J in *The Eschersheim* [1974] 2 Lloyd's Rep 188, 193 traced the term 'claim for damage done by a ship' from s 7 of the Admiralty Court Act 1861 (UK) through to s 22(1)(a)(iv) of the Supreme Court of Judicature (Consolidation) Act 1925 (UK) and then to s 1(1)(d) of the Administration of Justice Act 1956 (UK).

[33] *The Vera Cruz* (1884) 9 PD 96 (CA).

[34] *Currie v M'Knight* [1897] AC 97.

> only must the damage be the direct result or natural consequence of something done by those engaged in the navigation of the ship but the ship itself must be the actual instrument by which the damage was done. The commonest cause is that of collision, which is specifically mentioned in the Convention: but physical contact between the ship and whatever object sustains the damage is not essential – a ship may negligently cause a wash by which some other vessel or property on the shore is damaged.[35]

In this case the House of Lords held that the damage caused by the beaching of the tow entitled the owners of the tow to an action in rem. The pollution liability for the spillage of the cargo and the bunker oil was considered to constitute part of the loss suffered by the ship in tow that was caused by the negligence of the salvaging ship.[36]

In *Currie v M'Knight*[37] the crew cut off the lines of another ship in order to sail away. The other ship ran aground and was damaged. This was not considered to be 'damage done by the ship'. Similarly damage on board the ship is not within the provision.[38]

The Vera Cruz[39] concerned a claim for loss of life brought by the relatives of a drowned master. The House of Lords held that a claim created by Lord Campbell's Act, which entitled the relatives to sue for the loss of life of the victim, was not 'damage done by a ship'.[40] In the Court of Appeal Bowen LJ said:[41] '"Done by a ship" means done by those in charge of a ship, with the ship as the noxious instrument', while Fry LJ observed that:[42] 'It cannot be correctly said that it is an action for damage done …, though it is for damage resulting from or arising out of damage done'. This latter statement reinforces the argument that s 20(2)(e) of the SCA 1981 is narrower than the corresponding wording of the Arrest Convention 1952.[43]

Clarke J in *The Rama*[44] considered that 'damage done by a ship' requires three criteria that must be satisfied:

1. the damage must be caused by something done by those engaged in the navigation or management of the ship in a physical sense;
2. the ship must be the actual or noxious instrument by which the damage is done; and
3. the damage must be sustained by a person or property external to the ship.[45]

35 *The Eschersheim* (n 26) 8.

36 Lord Diplock continued (ibid): 'Had the damage been caused by the beaching, there could in my view have been no question but that the *Rotesand* could properly be regarded as the actual instrument by which that damage was done. Although for my part I find this a borderline case, I do not think that the intervening failure of the appellants to take steps to avert the risk of damage, which forms the subject of the alternative grounds of negligence, prevents the *Rotesand* from remaining the actual instrument by which the damage subsequent to the beaching was done. I accordingly agree with the Court of Appeal that the shipowners' and cargo-owners' claims also fall under par. (d) of s. 1(1).'

37 *Currie v M'Knight* (n 34).

38 See *The Victoria* (1887) 12 PD 105; *The Igor* [1956] 2 Lloyd's Rep 271. See also *The Vinalines Pioneer* (n 29); but see *Nagrint v The Ship Regis* [1939] HCA 6, (1939) 61 CLR 688; *Union Steamship Co of New Zealand Ltd v Ferguson* (1969) 119 CLR 191; *Fournier v The Ship Margaret Z* [1999] 3 NZLR 111.

39 *The Vera Cruz* (n 33).

40 *The Vera Cruz (No 2)* (1884) 10 App Cas 59 (HL).

41 *The Vera Cruz* (n 33) 101.

42 Ibid 102.

43 However, this last decision concerned a purely national instrument, namely s 7 of the Admiralty Court Act 1861 (UK). The position may not be as restrictive – at least in relation to loss of life and personal injury claims – under the SCA 1981, given that the SCA 1981 is meant to give domestic effect to the Arrest Convention 1952.

44 *The Rama* (n 29) 292.

45 It could be a part of the ship: *The Minerva* [1933] P 224.

It follows that only environmental damage directly caused by a ship could fall under this provision. This may include, for example, physical damage caused to a coral reef or to the coast by a ship running aground due to negligence in navigation. However, the current interpretation accepted by the courts does not appear to be wide enough to cover cargo spills. It would be difficult to argue that the ship itself is the 'noxious instrument' in such a case. Bunker oil spills may have a better chance of being considered as falling within the term 'damage done by a ship', as bunkers can be argued to be a necessary part of the ship. A further difficulty concerns situations where the polluting ship is not at fault, but strict liability for pollution damage is imposed as a matter of regulation. Such cases would certainly seem to fall outside the criteria set in *The Rama*.[46] This creates a paradox. Pollution claims supported by strict liability – where it should in principle be easier to recover – would, under English law, not be entitled to an action in rem under s 20(2)(e) of the SCA 1981 or to security through ship arrest.

This paradox is partly resolved by s 20(5) of the SCA 1981, which extends s 20(2)(e) of the Act to 'any claim in respect of a liability incurred under the Chapter III of Part VI of the Merchant Shipping Act 1995'. This enlarges the admiralty jurisdiction of the High Court to include all persistent oil pollution claims – in essence claims under the CLC 1992 and the BOPC 2001 – as well as oil pollution from persistent oil not covered by these Conventions. While this extension of the scope of s 20(2)(e) of the SCA 1981 enables claims in rem in support of persistent oil pollution damage under these Conventions, it arguably does not do so in relation to pollution claims arising for other substances or under other legal regimes, for example liability under the ELD,[47] implemented in the United Kingdom under the Environmental Damage (Prevention and Remediation) Regulations 2009;[48] clean up liability under the Wastes Directive;[49] or liability for noxious and hazardous substances, other than persistent oil carried as cargo.

Clarke J's statement in *The Rama* to the effect that, if a claim can be classified as 'damage done by the ship', it attracts a maritime lien was based on pre-existing case law. It is unlikely that the statutory extension of s 20(2)(e) of the SCA 1981 to include pollution damage can be considered to create a corresponding expansion of the scope of the damage maritime lien so as to include oil pollution damage. This view is supported by Jackson:[50]

> Admiralty jurisdiction in respect of damage by a ship was extended to liability incurred under the Merchant Shipping (Oil Pollution) Act 1971 and any claim in respect of a liability falling on the International Oil Pollution Compensation Fund under the Merchant Shipping Act 1974. It seems hardly arguable that such claims can attract maritime liens. They create a jurisdiction over claims based on a cause of damage which is entirely new – although the ultimate effect may be similar to that caused by physical damage. Furthermore, the statutory phraseology makes it clear that the 'extension' is not through an extension of the concept of 'damage' but through the inclusion of a claim in relation to oil pollution damage within the category of claims based on damage.

[46] *The Rama* (n 29) 292.
[47] ELD (n 11).
[48] SI 2009/153.
[49] Council directive 75/442/EEC of 15 July 1975 on waste [1975] OJ L194/39; see Case C-188/07 *Commune de Mesquer v Total France SA and Total International Ltd* [2008] ECR I-04501.
[50] Jackson (n 3) para 2.77.

Nevertheless, an argument in support of such an extension can be made by noting that the supremacy of the damage maritime lien is based on considerations of public policy which demand the safeguarding of the property of other users of the sea. Arguably the only reason that the damage lien does not historically encompass pollution damage is the timing of when the notion of maritime liens was crystallised. When *The Bold Buccleugh*[51] was decided in 1851, neither national nor international environmental law was in place, because the potential of environmental damage was very low due to the nature of the cargoes being carried, the size of the ships and the use of sails and coal for propulsion. The notion that maritime liens evolve is not new. In *The Halcyon Skies*[52] Brandon J said:

> A further question arose, following the passing of the 1840 and 1861 Acts, as to whether, in cases where those Acts had enlarged the existing jurisdiction of the Court as distinct from conferring new jurisdiction, it was intended that maritime liens recognized in respect of claims under the existing jurisdiction should extend also to claims of a similar kind under the enlarged jurisdiction. [O]bservations appear to indicate that …, in such cases, the relevant maritime lien should be regarded as extending to claims under the enlarged jurisdiction. The correctness of this last view, so far as damage and salvage cases are concerned, appears to have been accepted early on, and I do not consider that it is any longer open to challenge today.

Thus, according to Brandon J's judgment, the concept of wages has been gradually extended and expanded over the years.[53] This view – that maritime liens should expand congruently with statutory extensions of admiralty jurisdiction – supports the proposition that the inclusion of pollution damage cases within s 20(2)(e) of the SCA 1981 by virtue of s 20(5) of the SCA 1981 should have a similar effect. That expansion would, however, create another peculiar anomaly in that the same type of pollution damage, when caused by persistent oil or bunker oil, would be supported by a maritime lien, but, when caused by a non-persistent oil or another chemical, would not be so supported.

The argument that international policy has shifted to the point where pollution damage claims are now of the highest importance, and should therefore attract maritime lien status, is further supported by the following observations. Article 192 of the United Nations Law of the Sea Convention 1982 (UNCLOS 1982)[54] imposes a fundamental obligation on States to protect and preserve the marine environment. This UNCLOS obligation, combined with numerous national, regional and international agreements concerned with the reduction of, and liability for, marine pollution, provide strong evidence that liability for pollution damage is a new international legal norm.

With respect to the maritime lien for seafarers' wages, David Steel J in *The Ruta*[55] supported his decision prioritising the seafarers' wages liens over the damage liens

[51] *The Bold Buccleugh* (n 30).

[52] *The Halcyon Skies* [1976] 1 Lloyd's Rep 461. This case dealt with the issue of the ambit of the wages maritime lien. It was held that, where a seafarer's employer fails to pay contributions to a pension fund, the seafarer's claim for damages was protected by a wages maritime lien or under s 1(1)(o) of the Administration of Justice Act 1956 (UK), notwithstanding the fact that the seafarer's employment was under a special contract.

[53] See *The Ever Success* [1999] 1 Lloyd's Rep 824, 828 (Clarke J).

[54] United Nations Convention on the Law of the Sea 1982 (adopted 10 December 1982, entered into force 16 November 1994) 1833 UNTS 3.

[55] *The Ruta* [2000] 1 Lloyd's Rep 359.

arising out of collisions by reference to the Maritime Liens and Mortgages Conventions 1926[56] and 1967[57] – even though the first Convention was signed but never ratified by the United Kingdom and the second Convention was never even signed by the United Kingdom. In addition, he looked at the laws of other States and referred to a survey produced by counsel stating that 80 per cent of jurisdictions provided for priority of the wages claim.[58] David Steel J used these public policy indicators to support the decision he had already reached. They therefore do not, strictly speaking, form part of the ratio decidendi of his judgment. However, the policy arguments supporting a high priority for pollution damage claims as part of the damage maritime lien are much stronger than the evidence employed for the wages lien in *The Ruta*,[59] because UNCLOS 1982 and the major pollution conventions enjoy widespread international acceptance and implementation. Permitting pollution damage claims to be treated as maritime liens would rank them above registered ship mortgages and rank and file commercial claims; a position that is unlikely to raise any eyebrows and would ensure that the polluter pays, thus internalising the costs of environmental damage into international transport and logistics costs and the prices of products transported by sea.

However, two counter-arguments exist. The first, based on art 4(2) of the Maritime Liens and Mortgages Convention 1993, is discussed below.[60] The second argument relates to the fact that CLC claims are supported by the shipowner's fund and compulsory insurance. As a consequence, it is said that they do not represent risks in need of the additional support of a maritime lien. This argument is, of course, correct for claims subject to the CLC and the BOPC. However, it leaves all other pollution claims of similar character completely unprotected. Those pollution claims that are captured by the statutory extension of s 20(2)(e) of the SCA 1981 and are defined as 'damage done by the ship' will enjoy an action in rem and the ability to arrest a ship or a sister ship under s 21(4). However, if such claims do not attract maritime lien status, they will only be paid out (if at all) after all claims by maritime lienholders and ship mortgagees, and on the same level as other commercial claims, despite the pollution clean-up costs having to be borne by the taxpayer.

Therefore, the extension of s 20(2)(e) of the SCA 1981 only partly solves the issue of the effective enforcement of pollution damage claims: first, it only deals with persistent oil pollution; and second, it does not seem to be capable of raising the priority of pollution damage claims to the level of maritime liens. As a result, all other pollution claims are presently excluded from the scope of the term 'damage done by a ship' and therefore they would not entitle the claimant to an action in rem and, consequently, to ship arrest.

We now turn to see whether any other subsection of s 20(2) of the SCA 1981 provides for an action in rem. Article 1(1)(b) of the Arrest Convention 1952, which concerns loss of life, has also been rewritten in s 20(2)(f) of the SCA 1981, without the generalising term

[56] International Convention for the Unification of Certain Rules Relating to Maritime Liens and Mortgages (adopted 10 April 1926, entered into force 2 June 1931) 120 UNTS 187.

[57] International Convention for the Unification of Certain Rules relating to Maritime Liens and Mortgages (adopted 27 May 1967, not yet in force): see UNCITRAL, *Register of Texts of Conventions and Other Instruments concerning International Trade Law* (UN, New York, 1973) vol II 179.

[58] *The Ruta* (n 55) [24]–[25].

[59] *The Ruta* (n 55).

[60] See text at n 71 below.

'any claim arising out of', and has been significantly narrowed down.[61] It can potentially include loss of life and personal injury suffered through negligence in navigation or the (mis)management of the ship, cargo or passengers. Where the escape of pollutants from a ship causes loss of life or personal injury, an action in rem is available under this section. It should be noted, though, that the wording of the provision requires a 'wrongful act, neglect or default' on the part of the tortfeasor.[62] None of the international pollution Conventions currently in force provides for liability for loss of life or personal injury. This is currently dealt with under ordinary tort law.

The HNS 2010 does provide for strict liability for loss of life and personal injury from hazardous and noxious substances on board as well as from outside the ship.[63] If the HNS 2010 comes into force, the effect of the requirement in s 20(2)(f) of the SCA 1981 of a 'wrongful act, neglect or default' for the claim to fall within the admiralty jurisdiction of the High Court will create an anomalous differentiation between HNS claims. Where fault is present, there will be liability under the HNS 2010 and an action in rem will be available, but where an HNS 2010 claim is based on strict liability and there is no fault on the part of the relevant person, an action in rem under s 20(2)(f) of the SCA 1981 is not possible. This anomaly could be avoided by amending and extending s 20(2)(f) of the SCA 1981 to include loss of life and personal injury under the HNS 2010, similar to the statutory extension of s 20(2)(e) by s 20(5) of the SCA 1981.[64] However, as with the extension of s 20(2)(e), a statutory extension of s 20(2)(f) to cover liability for HNS claims will presumably not give rise to a congruent expansion of the damage maritime lien.[65]

The original wording of art 1(1)(f) of the Arrest Convention 1952 includes the generalising term 'arising out of any claim'. This has, however, been narrowed in s 20(2)(g) of the SCA 1981 to 'any claim for loss of or damage to goods carried in a ship'.[66] However, even with the original wording it would be very challenging to accept that a marine pollution claim could fall within its ambit. This would require a strained interpretation of 'any claim arising out of' as including claims by any party who has suffered damage (resulting from contamination or otherwise) caused by the goods carried by a ship.[67] For the English

[61] Section 20(2)(f) of the SCA 1981 covers:

> any claim for loss of life or personal injury sustained in consequence of any defect in a ship or in her apparel or equipment, or in consequence of the wrongful act, neglect or default of—
>
> (i) the owners, charterers or persons in possession or control of a ship; or
> (ii) the master or crew of a ship, or any other person for whose wrongful acts, neglects or defaults the owners, charterers or persons in possession or control of a ship are responsible,
>
> being an act, neglect or default in the navigation or management of the ship, in the loading, carriage or discharge of goods on, in or from the ship, or in the embarkation, carriage or disembarkation of persons on, in or from the ship.

[62] But see *The MARA* (n 27) [20] where the Singapore Court of Appeal interpreted the Singapore equivalent of s 20(2)(f) disjunctively, allowing for the possibility of strict liability in respect of the first category of claims based on 'any defect in a ship or in her apparel or equipment'.

[63] HNS 2010, art 1(6).

[64] In addition, a similar amendment to s 20(2)(5) of the SCA 1981 will be required in order to enlarge s 20(2)(e) to cover the pollution damage aspect of claims brought under the HNS 2010.

[65] As it will not meet the requirements set out in *The Rama* (n 29).

[66] SCA 1981, s 20(2)(g).

[67] In addition to actions in rem brought by cargo claimants against the carrying ship.

provision, the suggested interpretation would mean that the term 'any claim for loss of or damage to goods carried by the ship' does not (or does not only) refer to losses suffered by the owner of the goods, but (also) to losses suffered by any other potential claimant consequentially affected by the physical loss of or damage to that cargo. There is no authority directly addressing whether this broader interpretation is possible, but it would not, in our view, be easy to support against the general structure of the Arrest Convention 1952 or the SCA 1981.

A similarly broad interpretation would be required in relation to art 1(1)(k) of the Arrest Convention 1952, rewritten under s 20(2)(m) of the SCA 1981,[68] which would potentially cover bunker and lubricating oil pollution claims. The inclusion of such claims under s 20(2)(e) via s 20(5) of the 1981 SCA, however, makes the need for such extensive interpretation completely unnecessary, and perhaps the very need to modify the scope of s 20(2)(e) via s 20(5) of the SCA 1981 can be used as an argument that the wide interpretation argued for is contradictory to the need for this inclusion.[69] It has to be admitted that the historical development of the provisions does not indicate any such intention and no such evidence is found in the travaux préparatoires of the Arrest Convention 1952.[70] However, there is nothing against it either; and, if one considers the list of claims as a negotiation between a closed and an open list, the broadening of the closed list by the use of the term 'any claim arising out of' may be seen as part of this compromise. If that argument is correct, s 20(2) of the SCA 1981 might also be argued as supporting an action in rem for a claim for pollution damage caused by bunker oil, as opposed to that caused by a cargo of persistent oil.

C. The Arrest Convention 1999

The Arrest Convention 1999 has introduced additional categories of claims to those included under the Arrest Convention 1952. The provision relevant to this discussion is art 1(1)(d), which defines as a maritime claim any claim arising out of:

> damage or threat of damage caused by the ship to the environment, coastline or related interests; measures taken to prevent, minimize, or remove such damage; compensation for such damage; costs of reasonable measures of reinstatement of the environment actually undertaken or to be undertaken; loss incurred or likely to be incurred by third parties in connection with such damage; and damage, costs, or loss of a similar nature to those identified in this subparagraph (d).

[68] SCA 1981, s 20(2)(m) covers 'any claim in respect of goods or materials supplied to a ship for her operation or maintenance'.

[69] There is another technical difficulty in that s 20(2)(m) only covers claims for goods or materials supplied 'to a ship'. In *The Alexandrea* [2002] SGHC 82, [2002] 1 SLR(R) 812 marine fuel oil supplied from the bunker tanker *Alexandrea* to the *Front Melody* was contaminated by di-methyl ester of hexabedioic acid, a chemical compound used in paint strippers. The plaintiffs commenced an in rem action against the *Alexandrea* in negligence, alleging a failure on the part of the owners of the *Alexandrea* to ensure that that the oil stemming from the *Alexandrea* was free of contaminants. Belinda Ang J set aside the writ of summons and warrant of arrest on the basis that the oil was supplied *from* the *Alexandrea* and *to* the *Front Melody*. The *Front Melody* rather than the *Alexandrea* was, therefore, the ship 'in connection with which the claim arose'.

[70] See *The Nore Challenger and the Nore Commander* [2001] 2 Lloyd's Rep 103 approving the decision in *The Edinburgh Castle* [1999] 2 Lloyd's Rep 362.

The introduction of this new provision is in itself an admission that, at the very least, the inclusion of environmental claims within the Arrest Convention 1952 headings is contestable. This provision opens the door for many environmental claims. An examination of the travaux préparatoires of the Arrest Convention 1999 reveals a number of points.

First, in earlier draft versions of this provision, attempts were made to restrict its ambit to claims arising under international environmental Conventions.[71] These efforts failed and therefore no such restriction was imposed.

A second point concerns objections raised with respect to the desirability of allowing ship arrests for claims under international environmental Conventions. It was argued that the Arrest Convention 1999 should be in line with art 4(2) of the Maritime Liens and Mortgages Convention 1993[72] which states:

> No maritime lien shall attach to a vessel to secure claims as set out in subparagraphs (b) and (e) of paragraph 1 which arise out of or result from:
>
> (a) Damage in connection with the carriage of oil or other hazardous or noxious substances by sea for which compensation is payable to the claimants pursuant to international conventions or national law providing for strict liability and compulsory insurance or other means of securing the claims; or
>
> (b) The radioactive properties or a combination of radioactive properties with toxic, explosive or other hazardous properties of nuclear fuel or of radioactive products or waste.

This argument was also rejected.[73]

The earlier draft versions of this provision referred to damage to the 'marine environment' and did not include a reference to a ship. The word 'marine' was removed to promote consistency with other IMO Conventions, but also to encompass different types and impacts of environmental damage. The inclusion of the reference 'caused by the ship' was seen as a means of differentiating environmental claims under the Arrest Convention 1999 from ordinary environmental claims.

On the basis of the earlier discussion it may be questioned whether the wording 'damage or threat of damage caused by the ship to the environment' requires that the damage must be 'caused by the ship' in the narrow sense adopted by the English courts. The answer is clearly provided by the statement of the UK delegate who said:

> I am just looking at the words that we were given for the addition at the end of the paragraph, 'arising out of the operation of the ship' and I am almost drafting as I talk, but I think we might like something, instead of that phrase from the Japanese delegation, to say simply such damage 'caused by the ship', so the ship may not actually be moving, but something is come off the ship or has arisen from the ship. If that concept is accepted, I think that this just a drafting point, for the drafting Committee, Mr. Chairman.[74]

[71] UN/IMO Diplomatic Conference on Arrest of Ships, 'Preparation and Adoption of a Convention on Arrest of Ships – Compilation of Comments and Proposals by Governments and by Intergovernmental and Non-governmental Organizations on the Draft Articles for a Convention on Arrest of Ships' (25 November 1998) UN Doc A/CONF.188/3.

[72] International Convention on Maritime Liens and Mortgages (adopted 6 May 1993, entered into force 5 September 2004) UN Doc A/CONF. 162/7, 33 ILM 353.

[73] Berlingieri (n 19) vol 2 appendix IV 198–99.

[74] ibid 202.

The provision encompasses environmental claims in tort[75] as well as claims under international Conventions. Arguably, it does not require the ship to be the 'noxious instrument', but it requires a link between the damage or threat of damage to the environment, the coastline and related interests and a specific ship. No more than this should be required. The reference to third party losses is also rather broad. In earlier draft proposals these were limited by reference to the various international environmental Conventions. The removal of this limitation means that, on the face of it, third parties suffering losses are all entitled to arrest the ship. This may in turn permit even remotely affected claimants to arrest the ship.[76]

The only known restriction on this provision is that, according to the understanding of the delegates, it does not cover loss of life or personal injury.[77]

It has to be said that the lack of a definition of 'damage to the environment' in the Arrest Convention 1999 leaves the application of this provision unclear. The deliberate removal by the drafters of the reference to the international pollution Conventions arguably means that it was intended that the term should not be confined to pollution damage as defined in the relevant Conventions. National courts will then have to decide on the breadth of this term on a case by case basis. However, the discussion in the travaux préparatoires indicates that the intention was to leave this provision as open as possible and to encompass as many environmental claims as possible.

D. Arrest in the Context of the International Environmental Liability Conventions

Our examination of whether arrest for environmental claims is something that can be supported under the Arrest Convention 1952 can be assisted by exploring the civil liability Conventions for oil pollution damage.

The CLC 1969 provides that where a shipowner constitutes a fund:

> the Court or other competent authority of any Contracting State shall order the release of any ship or other property belonging to the owner which has been arrested in respect of a claim for pollution damage arising out of that incident, and shall similarly release any bail or other security furnished to avoid such arrest.[78]

This provision was not changed by the 1992 Protocol which formed the CLC 1992. The HNS 1996 includes the same provision in art 10(1)(b), which was not affected by the 2010 Protocol which created the HNS 2010. None of these Conventions includes a definition of arrest. It is reasonable to assume that the reference to arrest must correspond to the

[75] See the USA submissions (ibid 200–01).

[76] See *Landcatch Ltd v International Oil Pollution Compensation Fund* [1999] 2 Lloyd's Rep 316; *Smith v Braer Corp* [1999] GWD 21-1023; *P&O Scottish Ferries Ltd* v *Braer Corp* [1999] 2 Lloyd's Rep 535; *Skerries Salmon Ltd v Braer Corp* [1999] SLT 1196; *Alegrete Shipping Co Inc v International Oil Pollution Compensation Fund 1971 (The Sea Empress)* [2003] 1 Lloyd's Rep 327 for litigation to resolve the extent of liability for economic losses arising from pollution damage.

[77] Berlingieri (n 19) vol 2 appendix IV 194–95. This has been provided for separately in art 1(1)(b) of the Arrest Convention 1999, which covers loss of life or personal injury generally – whether caused by hazardous and polluting activities or any other reason – 'occurring on land or on water, in direct connection with the operation of the ship'.

[78] Article VI(1)(b).

definition of arrest under the Arrest Convention 1952, which predates the environmental liability Conventions, at least for the Contracting States of the Arrest Convention 1952. Another possible explanation is that the reference to arrest is to whatever national system of ship arrest is applicable, as there are States which are not parties to the Arrest Convention 1952, but have a national system for ship arrest and have signed up to one or more of the environmental liability Conventions.

From their inception, the IMO pollution liability Conventions have acknowledged ship arrest as a possibility and have provided for the release of the relevant ship against the pollution fund instead of the normal arrest fund. This would indicate that pollution damage was considered under some laws as being included in the maritime claims leading to ship arrest. There is an alternative possible interpretation that the reference to arrest in the pollution liability Conventions is broader than that under the Arrest Convention 1952 and covers all types of ship detention. This latter interpretation is probably incorrect for the very simple reason that detention in many cases is for the purpose of preventing a harm from occurring, rather than compensating for a harm incurred, which is the objective of arrest under the civil liability provisions in the pollution liability Conventions.

E. Arrest and Pollution Damage Claims by the State

Pollution damage under the CLC 1992, the BOPC 2001 and the HNS 2010 includes a mixture of damage heads.[79] There is compensation for losses incurred from oil spills, whether suffered by private or public entities. Clean-up costs and reinstatement of environmental damage are also included, but these can be claimed exclusively by public authorities.

The WRC 2007 provides for payments for the location, marking and removal (defined as the removal of the hazard) of the relevant wreck. Hazard includes both environmental and navigational hazards.[80] The liability is imposed on the registered shipowner, and the claimant can only be a public authority. The WRC 2007 removes the shipowner's liability 'if and to the extent that liability for such costs is in conflict' with the CLC 1992, the BOPC 2001 or the 2010 HNS, provided that the relevant Convention is applicable and in force.[81]

Liability for environmental damage is, in the European Union, imposed by the ELD[82] which entered into force on 30 April 2004. The ELD imposes strict and unlimited liability on the operator of a facility (which includes shipowners)[83] for environmental damage but

[79] CLC 1992, art 1(6); BOPC 2001, art 1(9); HNS 2010, art 1(5).

[80] WRC 2007, art 1(5).

[81] ibid, art 11.

[82] See n 11 above. The ELD has been transposed to English law through the Environmental Damage (Prevention and Remediation) Regulations 2009 (n 48), which came into force on 1 March 2009.

[83] The operator is defined under the ELD, art 2(6) as 'any natural or legal, private or public person who operates or controls the occupational activity or, where this is provided for in national legislation, to whom decisive economic power over the technical functioning of such an activity has been delegated, including the holder of a permit or authorisation for such an activity or the person registering or notifying such an activity.' Shipowners may fall with the definition. In addition, owners of jetties and oil storage facilities and refineries are also subject to this definition.

does not cover loss of (human) life or damage to property. The claims are brought by public administrators,[84] not by injured parties, with the damages paid being for the remedy of the environment rather than for compensation for losses suffered by private parties.

The ELD imposes liability for preventive measures when a threat of environmental damage occurs[85] and liability for remedial actions when actual environmental damage occurs.[86] The ELD covers three types of damage: to land, to water and to protected species and natural habitats.[87] The ELD currently excludes from its application[88] damage arising from incidents covered by some of the major Conventions concerned with liability for marine pollution arising from carriage of goods by sea, namely the CLC 1992,[89] the IOPC Fund Convention 1992,[90] the BOPC 2001,[91] the HNS 2010,[92] as well as the Nuclear Material Convention 1971,[93] and their future amendments. There is a requirement that each of the Conventions is in force for the exclusion to apply. Therefore, the ELD is currently applicable to claims that will be covered by HNS 2010 if it comes into effect, as well as to any other environmental liability claims that are not covered by the specified IMO environmental liability Conventions.

Both the WRC 2007 and the ELD provide tools for EU Member States to recover from the relevant polluter. These may be described as administrative in character. They have an additional role, however: they also impose upon the relevant authority an obligation to deal with pollution damage, irrespective of whether the polluter is identifiable or can, or will, pay.

The Arrest Conventions 1952 and 1999 differ significantly in the way they treat such claims. The Arrest Convention 1952 does not cover wreck removal costs and does not have an express provision for environmental damage, especially in the form of clean-up costs and financial losses. By contrast, the Arrest Convention 1999 has a distinct category of environmental claims, which is drafted as an open-ended provision.[94] In addition, there is an express provision for wreck removal.[95]

Under English law, as explained earlier, ELD claims in general would not be considered as 'damage done by the ship', except perhaps in marginal cases, where ships have themselves physically caused environmental damage. Similarly, wreck removal liability would not give rise to an action in rem. The reason why State claims are excluded from the in rem action

[84] The competent authorities are under an obligation to act to remedy environmental damage, whether this damage is caused by a private or public entity.

[85] ELD, art 5.

[86] ibid, art 6.

[87] ibid art 2(1).

[88] ibid art 4(2), annex IV(a–d).

[89] ibid annex IV(a).

[90] ibid annex IV(b).

[91] ibid annex IV(c).

[92] ibid annex IV(c). The HNS 2010 is not yet in force.

[93] ibid annex V(e).

[94] Arrest Convention 1999, art 1(1)(d): 'and damage, costs, or loss of a similar nature to those identified in this subparagraph (d)'.

[95] ibid, art 1(1)(e): 'costs or expenses relating to the raising, removal, recovery, destruction or the rendering harmless of a ship which is sunk, wrecked, stranded or abandoned, including anything that is or has been on board such ship, and costs or expenses relating to the preservation of an abandoned ship and maintenance of its crew'.

under English law may well have to do with the availability to public authorities of statutory powers of detention and seizure that can be used to secure their claims. It is, therefore, necessary to examine how such rights are considered in terms of priority when competing with pollution damage claims. This discussion needs to start by analysing the general position for ship detention and seizure under statutory powers.

III. Detention and Seizure

Arrest under the Arrest Conventions 1952 and 1999 is a specific type of ship detention, which requires an order by a judicial authority for the purpose of securing a maritime claim.[96] Under English law arrest brings the ship under the custody of the Admiralty Marshal.

Arrest is also referred to in UNCLOS 1982 within two contexts: arrest of ships and arrest of persons onboard ships. The meaning of arrest[97] within most of the relevant UNCLOS provisions is detention by law enforcement agencies rather than by the powers of a court.

Article 28(2) of UNCLOS 1982 prohibits the coastal State from levying execution against or arresting a ship on innocent passage 'for the purpose of any civil proceedings, save only in respect of obligations or liabilities assumed or incurred by the ship itself in the course or for the purpose of its voyage through the waters of the coastal State'.[98] Within this context, the term arrest comes close to the meaning that it has within the Arrest Conventions 1952 and 1999.

Detention powers over a ship may be granted by a variety of legal instruments and are granted to various authorities.

[96] The Arrest Convention 1952 defines arrest in art 1(2) as 'the detention of a ship by judicial process to secure a maritime claim'. Thus, arrest is a category of detention, which is effected through the courts or other judicial process, and is for the purpose for providing security for what is determined as a maritime claim under the Convention. See further ch 3. The definition of arrest has been modified in art 1(2) of the Arrest Convention 1999 to mean 'any detention or restriction on removal of a ship by order of a Court to secure a maritime claim'. This brought about two changes. First, arrest now includes any other restriction on removal of a ship, thus broadening the definition; and, second, arrest requires a court order, a term that is arguably narrower than the term 'judicial process' used in art 1(2) of the Arrest Convention 1952. However, the definition in the Arrest Convention 1999 of the Court as 'any judicial authority' reduces the differences between the two Conventions. The term 'restriction on removal' includes documentary detention within the scope of the Arrest Convention 1999. This may include an order against removing a ship from the jurisdiction, such as a freezing order. However, such an order will have to be in support of a maritime claim and must be directed solely against a ship in order to fall under the definition of arrest.

[97] UNCLOS 1982, art 73 gives a coastal State powers to enforce its laws by taking various measures, including boarding and arresting a ship, to protect its sovereign rights to explore, exploit, conserve and manage the living resources in its EEZ. On the high seas every State may seize a pirate ship or aircraft (ibid, art 105). A State adversely affected by unauthorised broadcasting from the high seas may arrest any person or ship engaged in unauthorised broadcasting and seize their broadcasting apparatus (ibid, art 109). Arrest or seizure of a ship is prohibited for penal jurisdiction in matters of collision or any other incident of navigation (ibid, art 97). Arrest is also referred to in respect of hot pursuit (ibid, art 111).

[98] UNCLOS 1982, art 28(2) preserves the right of the coastal State, in accordance with its laws, to levy execution against or to arrest, for the purpose of any civil proceedings, a foreign ship lying in the territorial sea, or passing through the territorial sea after leaving internal waters.

A. Detention under International Conventions

The detention right most comparable with ship arrest, as defined under the Arrest Conventions 1952 and 1999, is granted under the powers a coastal State may exercise within its ports.[99] Such powers depend on national laws that provide for the documentary detention of the ship. This means that the ship is ordered by a State authority not to depart, although it is not in the custody of any authority. Such powers have been enhanced by powers of detention granted under art 220 of UNCLOS 1982 in the context of port State control for marine pollution. These powers include rights to interrogate, board and detain foreign ships for marine pollution violations in the territorial sea and the EEZ of the relevant coastal State.[100] States can also seize ships that have violated its laws within the territorial sea, provided they are not on innocent passage. The coastal State within its contiguous zone can further punish the infringement of its customs, fiscal, immigration or sanitary laws and regulations of its territorial sea. In addition, UNCLOS 1982 imposes an obligation[101] on the coastal State to detain unseaworthy ships that pose danger to the marine environment.

Detention rights are further detailed under the various IMO regulatory conventions dealing with operational pollution (MARPOL 73/78),[102] safety of life at sea (SOLAS)[103] and other similar instruments.[104] The aforementioned international instruments do not define detention or arrest.

Detention is defined in the IMO Procedures for Port State Control,[105] art 1.6.3 as:

> Intervention action taken by the port State when the condition of the ship or its crew does not correspond substantially with the applicable conventions to ensure that the ship will not sail until it can proceed to sea without presenting a danger to the ship or persons on board, or without presenting an unreasonable threat of harm to the marine environment.

Similarly, the EU Council Directive on Port State Control[106] defines 'detention' as 'the formal prohibition for a ship to proceed to sea due to established deficiencies which, individually or together, make the ship unseaworthy'.[107] In addition to the general prohibitive character of all arrests and detentions, such port State control detentions display a preventative dimension. Arrest under the Arrest Conventions 1952 and 1999 seeks to ensure

[99] See *Military and Paramilitary Activities in and against Nicaragua (Nicaragua v United States of America)*, (Jurisdiction and Admissibility) [1984] ICJ Rep 392.

[100] There is, however, a different threshold for triggering such powers.

[101] UNCLOS 1982, art 219.

[102] International Convention for the Prevention of Pollution from Ships (adopted 2 November 1973, entered into force 2 February 1983) 12 ILM 1319 (1973) (MARPOL 73/78), art 5, reg 8A of annex I, reg 15 of annex II, reg 8 of annex III, reg 8 of annex V, reg 10 of annex VI.

[103] International Convention for the Safety of Life at Sea (adopted 1 November 1974, entered into force 25 May 1980) 1184 UNTS 2 (SOLAS), regs I/6, I/9, I/19, XI/4.

[104] International Convention on Standards of Training, Certification and Watchkeeping for Seafarers, as Amended by the 2010 Manila Amendments to the Annex (adopted 7 July 1978, entered into force 28 April 1984) 1361 UNTS 190 (STCW 1978), art X(3), annex I reg I/4; International Convention on Load Lines (adopted 5 April 1966, entered into force 21 July 1968) 640 UNTS 133 (Load Lines Convention 1966), art 21. See also the Maritime Labour Convention (adopted 23 February 2006, entered into force 20 August 2013) 2952 UNTS I-51299 reg 2.5, standard A2.5; reg 5.2, standard A5.2.1, guideline B5.2.1.

[105] IMO Assembly, 'Procedures for Port State Control, 2017' (6 December 2017) IMO Res A.1119(30).

[106] Council Directive 2009/16/EC of 23 April 2009 on port State control [2009] OJ L131/57.

[107] ibid, art 2.15.

security for maritime claims, whereas detentions in the contexts discussed in this section also seek to prevent future damage from occurring. Thus, these two types of detention are conceptually and practically distinct from each other.

B. Detention Rights under Statutory Provisions

Detentions under the UK statutes are documentary detentions, requiring a detention order and leading to fines and penalties for the master and owner of a ship if disobeyed. The Merchant Shipping Act 1995 (UK) (the MSA 1995) provides for the detention of ships under several sections.[108] Various non-judicial authorities have such powers. Powers of detention are granted to any commissioned naval or military officer, any officer of customs and excise, and any British consular officer.[109] In addition, the receiver of wrecks can detain and sell ships for salvage liability,[110] and the harbour master can do likewise for oil spills in a harbour.[111] The provisions of s 284 of the MSA 1995 are extended to cover the detention powers in relation to breaches of the IMO Conventions[112] under the Merchant Shipping (Port State Control) Regulations 2011.[113] This is the expression of the port State control powers under UNCLOS 1982 written into national law.[114] A detention cannot be lifted until all costs and fees are paid or security is provided for them, but there is no right to sell the ship under these provisions.[115]

The Harbours Docks and Piers Clauses Act 1847 (UK) also provides for the detention of ships,[116] with some of its sections granting further powers to port authorities to sell ships.[117] Oil pollution, payment of port dues and fees, damage to the docks and harbour installations as well as wreck removal are claims for which powers to sell the ship exist in addition to those under the Arrest Convention 1952.

[108] MSA 1995, s 6 concerns an attempt to go to sea without declaring the name and the nationality of the ship to an officer for the purpose of obtaining clearance to sail. Section 7 provides for powers of seizure and detention when a ship is subject to forfeiture. Section 95 provides for the power to detain dangerously unsafe UK and foreign ships. Section 144 provides for the detention of ships in relation to discharge of oil from ships into certain UK waters. Section 226 provides powers for the detention of property liable for salvage. In this case, provision for the sale of the property by the receiver of the wrecks is provided for under s 227.

[109] ibid, s 284. Additional options are available for Northern Ireland.

[110] ibid, s 226.

[111] ibid s 144.

[112] See text at n 4ff above for the list of relevant Conventions.

[113] SI 2012/2601. The Regulations transpose the EU Council Directive on Port State Control (n 105) into English law.

[114] Thus, the Merchant Shipping (Port State Control) Regulations 2011, reg 9(2) provides for the compulsory detention for deficiencies which 'are clearly hazardous to safety, health or the environment'. Regulation 10(1) provides for powers to deny access to a ship when the detention rates for the flag State falls in the black or grey lists under the Paris MOU.

[115] ibid, reg 22.

[116] Section 40 of the Harbours Docks and Piers Clauses Act 1847 (UK) concerns detention of ships where there is a dispute between the shipowner or the goods owner and the collector of rates regarding the amount of goods shipped. Section 44 concerns payment of port fees and includes powers to sell ships in order to recover unpaid fees. Section 46 concerns rates due during arrestment or 'any distress'. The goods to which the rates relate may be detained until the judge ascertains the amount due. Finally, s 74 provides for the detention of ships for damage to docks and harbour installations. Section 75 provides for the sale of property if payment is not made.

[117] ibid, ss 44 and 75. Section 56 also provides powers to sell wrecks for wreck removal costs.

C. Forfeiture

In addition to arrest and detention a ship may be liable under the MSA 1995 to forfeiture under certain circumstances.[118] The Customs and Excise Act 1979 (UK) further provides for the forfeiture of a ship, which is or has been in UK waters and has been built or modified for the concealment of goods,[119] or from where goods have been jettisoned when it is approached for inspection.[120] None of the sections for forfeiture identified are applicable to situations where environmental damage occurs. They are exclusively linked either with the national identity of a ship or with breaches of customs and excise laws. Forfeiture requires seizure of the ship, but the alteration of title relates back to the time of the wrongful act.[121]

IV. Conflicts between Concurrent Arrest, Detention and Forfeiture

In summary, English law grants powers to:

1. enforcement authorities that can lead to the forfeiture and subsequent sale of a ship as punishment for breaches of customs and excise laws or concealment of its true nationality;
2. port authorities that can lead to the detention and sale of the ship for the payment of specific dues, fees or damages; and
3. judicial authorities that can lead to the judicial sale of the ship following an action and judgment in rem.

Conflicts may arise where such powers are exercised concurrently. For example, the ship may be arrested following an action in rem and at the same time an authority may attempt to exercise its statutory rights in order to recover a debt. The issue then is whether the detention and sale rights have priority over claims in rem. If a right of detention is exercised and the ship is sold following that detention, a second question that arises is whether what is left from the sale of the ship, after the debt owed to the authority is paid, becomes available

[118] MSA 1995, s 3(1): a non-British ship is liable to forfeiture if the owner or the master do or permit anything to be done to make the ship appear as a British ship. Section 3(4) provides that a British ship is liable to forfeiture if the master or owner attempt or permit any action attempting to conceal its nationality. In such a case, the ship can be detained or seized by any commissioned naval or military officer or any person appointed by the Secretary of State for the purposes of this section (see s 7). Where a ship or a share of a ship is transferred and as a result the ship loses the required British connection under the MSA 1995, the ship may become liable to forfeiture if the conditions in sch 1 reg 4(4) are met. Fishing vessels (s 15) and dangerous goods not properly marked (s 87) may also become liable to forfeiture.

[119] ibid, s 88.

[120] Ibid, s 89. The same applies for illegally imported goods.

[121] Lord Denning in *The Attorney-General of New Zealand v George Ortiz, Sotherby Parke Bernet & Co and Lance Entwistle* [1982] 2 Lloyd's Rep 224, 227 described English law as follows:

> 'So far as England is concerned, whenever there is legislation providing that goods are to be forfeited for one cause or another, the law has always said that the forfeiture does not take effect until the goods are seized and that the title then relates back to the cause of forfeiture. If the owner or anyone else disputes the forfeiture, there are proceedings for condemnation. After condemnation, the title is perfected and can no longer be disputed by anyone.

for the satisfaction of any action in rem. The opposite situation is also problematic: if a ship is sold by a court, would an authority with detention rights lose such rights, or be forced to enforce its rights under the forfeiture head of admiralty jurisdiction (s 20(2)(s) of the SCA 1981), which may afford its claim a lower priority?

A starting point for the discussion is the observation that rights in rem and other rights of detention and forfeiture are all statutorily determined and therefore it must be a matter of appropriate statutory interpretation to deal with conflicts arising between them. However, where a maritime lien is also in existence the discussion becomes more problematic because the lien attaches to the ship[122] and travels with it. In such a case, the additional questions are whether the statutory rights granted to the various authorities trump the maritime lien as a matter of statutory interpretation and whether, where the detention of the ship leads to its administrative sale by the authority (as opposed to a judicial sale in admiralty which confers clean title) the title conferred to a buyer is clean of existing maritime liens.

In *The Emilie Millon*[123] the port authority had a right of detention of the ship for dock dues owed and until the dues were paid. The vessel was arrested under an action in rem and sold in order to satisfy the crew's maritime lien for unpaid wages. The sale was completed by private agreement because the auction failed. At first instance, the court ordered the sale of the ship and payment of the dock dues from the proceeds of the sale. However, the Court of Appeal held that the Admiralty Court could not sell the ship without the consent of the dock authority if such sale would deprive the dock authority of its statutory right of detention. The Court of Appeal also held that the right of detention was not a right capable of being transferred to the sale fund. This latter point was doubted in *The Queen of the South*,[124] where the judge avoided the difficulty by ordering the Admiralty Marshal to pay the amount due to the port authority and recoup that from the proceeds of the ship sale as part of his expenses. In *The Sea Spray*[125] it was held that a harbour authority could sell the ship and reimburse itself from the proceeds of the sale. The action in rem available to salvors, in this case a maritime lien, was a right against the surplus.[126] In *The Blitz*[127] a ship was sold by a port authority for unpaid dues, but the mortgagee tried to enforce the mortgage by arresting the ship after it was sold. It was held that a sale of the ship for unpaid harbour dues gave to the bona fide buyer a title free from encumbrances.[128] The same holds for the sale for wreck removal costs.[129]

> That was settled in the great case of *Lockyer v Offley* (1786) 1 T.R. 252. The master of the sailing vessel *Hope* smuggled 60 gallons of brandy into London. The customs officers, a month later, seized the ship and claimed her as forfeited. Mr. Justice Willes said (at p. 260):
>
> > "It has been said that under the 24 Geo. 3, c.47, and the Excise laws, the forfeiture attaches the moment the act is done … but I think the actual property is not altered till after the seizure, though it may be before condemnation … Till the seizure of the ship, it was not certain that the officers of the Crown knew of the illicit trade carried on by the master, or whether they would take advantage of the forfeiture.'"

[122] *The Bold Buccleugh* (n 30).
[123] *The Emilie Millon* [1905] 2 KB 817 (CA). See also *The Spermina* (1923) 17 Ll L Rep 17, 52, 76, 109; *Readhead v The Admiralty Marshal* [1998] FCA 1173, (1998) 87 FCR 229.
[124] *The Queen of the South* [1968] 1 Lloyd's Rep 182.
[125] *The Sea Spray* [1907] P 133.
[126] See *The Ousel* [1957] 1 Lloyd's Rep 151.
[127] *The Blitz* [1992] 2 Lloyd's Rep 441.
[128] The Arrest Convention 1952, art 1(1)(l) classifies any claim arising out of dock charges or dues as a maritime claim; as does the SCA 1981, s 20(2)(n).
[129] *The Ousel* (n 125).

Therefore, the statutory rights granted to public authorities for the detention and sale of the ship give them priority over a claim in rem, whether the claim in rem attracts a maritime lien or is merely a statutory right of action in rem.

Claims for the forfeiture of ships and goods fall under s 20(2)(s) of the SCA 1981 and can be enforced by an action in rem and the arrest of the relevant ship.[130] The existence of the action in rem for forfeiture means that the relevant public authority has rights to the proceeds of the judicial sale. In *The Skylark*[131] the judge ordered the Admiralty Marshal to pay the import duty that ought to be paid, so that the ship's sale for a claim in rem brought by its repairers would not be delayed.

When the ship is forfeited and then sold by the Admiralty Court in a judicial sale, existing claims in rem, whether or not they enjoy maritime lien status, are extinguished and the ship is sold free of encumbrances. However, where a statute provides for the release of the forfeited ship back to its owner upon payment of a release fee, it appears that claims in rem against the forfeited vessel may be revived in certain circumstances.[132] William Young J, delivering the reasons for the decision of the Supreme Court of New Zealand in *Hartono v Ministry For Primary Industries*[133] put the position of rights in rem following the forfeiture of a ship as follows:

> The associated rights come to an end upon forfeiture. If the vessel is released to the owner, the claims revive but if the vessel is disposed of to a third party, the claims and any associated rights are extinguished. In a scheme addressed to 'relief from the effect of forfeiture on' the interests specified, there is no obvious policy reason to distinguish between maritime liens and statutory in rem claims if the effect of forfeiture on such claims is the same.[134]

Thus, detention and forfeiture rights enjoyed by public authorities are, under English law, superior to rights of arrest.[135] This position has been derived by a series of decisions prioritising the statutory rights granted to public authorities against those of private claimants. In pollution claims, the State is normally the largest claimant, but this has not been recognised in prioritising pollution claims within the international ship arrest framework of the Arrest Conventions 1952 and 1999. This is perhaps so because pollution damage claims under the IMO Conventions invariably also include losses caused to private parties.

130 SCA 1981, s 21(2).

131 *The Skylark* [1965] 2 Lloyd's Rep 250. See also *Planmarine AG v Maritime and Port Authority of Singapore* [1999] SGCA 16, [1999] 1 SLR(R) 669: Maritime and Port Authority's port dues treated as part of Admiralty Sheriff's expenses, ranking ahead of all other in rem claims.

132 See the unreported New Zealand decision of *Kareltrust v Wallace & Cooper Engineering (Lyttelton) Ltd* CA192/99, CA211/99. In this case, however, the ship's beneficial ownership changed immediately after its release back to the original owner. As the claim in question was not a maritime lien, and the writ in rem was only issued after the post-release sale of the ship, that change in ownership extinguished the statutory right of action in rem against the ship. The correctness of the reasoning in *Kareltrust* has been doubted, however, given that the Fisheries Act 1996 (NZ), s 255E(1) and its predecessors provide unequivocally that if 'any property … is forfeited to the Crown under this Act, such property … vests in the Crown absolutely and free of all encumbrances'. See Paul Myburgh, 'Shipping Law' [2001] *New Zealand Law Review* 105, 120–23; Jeremy Browne, 'The Extinction of Maritime Liens' [2003] *LMCLQ* 361, 367–68.

133 *Hartono v Ministry For Primary Industries* [2018] NZSC 17, [2018] 1 NZLR 857, discussed in Paul Myburgh, 'Fisheries, Forfeiture Relief and Admiralty' [2018] *LMCLQ* 322.

134 *Hartono* (n 132) [41].

135 See *The Sierra Nevada* (1932) 42 Ll L Rep 309 for the position in Scotland.

Where detention or forfeiture rights also entitle public authorities to an action in rem, their rights can arguably be transferred to the fund created by the judicial sale in admiralty. Without such entitlement to an action in rem, there is arguably no such option, as their statutory rights of detention do not come within the heads of admiralty jurisdiction in rem. However, the only powers of detention relevant to environmental claims are those granted to harbour masters for oil discharges in ports. These do not provide for the sale of the ship. It follows that they cannot lead to an action in rem unless they are claims for oil pollution covered by s 20(5) of the SCA 1981.

V. Conclusions

The security for environmental claims appears to be exclusively based on statutory rights developed under international Conventions for, primarily, oil pollution liability. Despite the importance of such claims in terms of financial significance and potential reputational damage to the shipping and oil industries, environmental claims are not supported by an express right of arrest under the Arrest Convention 1952. Instead, they must be argued as claims arising out of 'damage caused by any ship either in collision or otherwise' if a right to ship arrest is to be established. The introduction of environmental claims as maritime claims under the Arrest Convention 1999 within an exceptionally open list of environmental claims, independent of any reference to the existence of relevant international liability regime, significantly improves the position of environmental claims and recognises the environmental, financial and social importance of such claims. Unfortunately, however, the Arrest Convention 1999 has not enjoyed widespread support to date.

Under English law, pollution claims under the MSA 1995 are included within the admiralty jurisdiction of the High Court. The extension of the Admiralty Court's jurisdiction is achieved by extending the scope of the term 'damage done by a ship'. This statutory extension enables an action in rem for such claims and creates a halfway house between the two Arrest Conventions. However, only pollution damage claims under the specified section of the MSA 1995 permits an action in rem to be brought against the polluting ship or a sister ship. Moreover, the way in which this section is drafted means that it does not create a new maritime lien for the benefit of environmental claimants against the polluting ship. If environmental claims had given rise to a maritime lien, the insertion of the amendment to extend the admiralty heads of jurisdiction would not have been necessary in the first place. However, it is submitted that a combination of factors – including new and specific State obligations for the protection of the marine environment, the socially enhanced importance of environmental considerations within the context of sustainable development and the realisation that such damages will, in the absence of adequate security, inevitably be paid by taxpayers – suggest that securing environmental claims through a maritime lien constitutes a necessary and urgent reform to the international maritime claim enforcement framework. The consequence of assigning a maritime lien to all environmental claims would reflect the priority that should be placed on such claims over ship mortgages and other commercial claims, which attract only statutory rights of action in rem.

If this submission is correct, the priority between the existing maritime liens and a new environmental maritime lien would be fixed according to the discretion of the court.[136]

[136] *The Ruta* (n 55).

The starting point would arguably be that the new environmental maritime lien should enjoy the same priority as the existing damage lien. Because the courts examine the availability of alternative avenues of recovery in determining the priority of maritime liens, however, the existence of adequate insurance or the establishment of an appropriate fund under the CLC (or perhaps the Limitation of Liability for Maritime Claims Conventions, if the concern is bunker pollution) may result in the ranking of the environmental maritime lien being adjusted downwards. The availability of insurance or a fund may also lead to the complete satisfaction of the pollution claim which would mean that, in such a case, the traditional in rem priority would remain unaltered. However, for pollution damage for which there is no compulsory insurance or fund, and therefore no security, environmental claims should rank together with the traditional damage lien.

Authorities do have alternative means that they can employ with respect to pollution claims. These include rights of detention for oil pollution in ports. However, pollution claims by harbour authorities, as well as claims by environmental authorities for pollution, currently enjoy less protection than claims made by authorities with respect to dock dues, forfeiture of the ship and rights of recovery for wreck removal, which all apparently trump the judicial sale of a ship following a judgment in rem. This state of affairs does not make sense either legally or as a matter of public policy. It may be argued that it is purely a product of historical chronology – admiralty law and the concept of maritime liens developed in an earlier time, when there was no awareness of the significance of environmental protection as a vital component of sustainable global development. While the current system works to some extent because of the additional security provided for oil pollution damage, the absence of a general, consistent and principled legal solution for all types of environmental damage from the shipping industry creates a lacuna in the law that needs to be remedied. The polluter-pays principle dictates that States must develop the necessary liability regimes that will enable victims of environmental damage to recover.[137] International maritime Conventions provide for the availability of security for pollution damage claims through compulsory insurance and the establishment of one or more funds. The thesis of this Chapter is that, for pollution damage not covered by these international instruments, establishing a right to ship arrest for pollution claims is a necessary first step. This can be achieved in English law by adopting a provision in the SCA 1981 that reflects the more generous provision for environmental claims under the Arrest Convention 1999.

The elevation of environmental claims to the status of maritime liens or the statutory recognition of their superiority over commercial claims are further necessary improvements to the international maritime claim enforcement regime, in order to ensure that the polluter will pay. This additional step to extend the damage lien to pollution claims could then be modelled on the statutory intervention utilised to extend the maritime lien for

[137] eg, UNCLOS 1982, art 235. The European Community adopted the polluter-pays principle in 1972 in its first Environment Action Programme (EAP), thus making it part of European law. It is included in art 174 of the Treaty establishing the European Community (Amsterdam consolidated version) (art 130r of the EC Treaty (Maastricht consolidated version)). Principle 16 of the Rio Declaration on Environment and Development (12 August 1992) UN Doc A/CONF.151/26 (Vol I), Annex I (UNCED) states: 'National authorities should endeavour to promote the internalisation of environmental costs and the use of economic instruments, taking into account the approach that the polluter should, in principle, bear the cost of pollution with due regard to public interest and without distorting international trade and investment.'

wages to cover master's disbursements.[138] The relevant provision, as it currently is, states: 'The master of a ship shall have the same lien for his remuneration, and all disbursements or liabilities properly made or incurred by him on account of the ship, as a seaman has for his wages.' A similar statement enabling marine pollution damage claimants to have the same lien as claimants for damage done by a ship would arguably be sufficient to effect the necessary change.

[138] In *The Sara* (1889) LR 14 App Cas 209 (HL) it was held that the master's disbursements were not supported by a maritime lien.

9

Arrest and Cross-Border Insolvency: The Singapore Experience

BELINDA ANG*

I. Introduction

The slump in the shipping industry worldwide has seen many known names in shipping buckle under the financial strain of an exceedingly dismal business outlook. In August 2016, the world woke up to Hanjin Shipping Co Ltd (Hanjin)'s debacle.

As other big names in the shipping industry engage in corporate restructuring and reorganisation that see them retreat to concentrate on core businesses or narrower geographical areas of operation, the corporate failures of established international shipping names like Hanjin bring to the forefront Prof Rhidian Thomas' often-quoted observations in *Maritime Liens*:[1]

> The law of corporate liquidation and bankruptcy seems to have developed with little regard to the Admiralty proceeding *in rem*. Certainly it is difficult to fit the Admiralty proceedings into the legislative language of the relevant statutes which regulate the winding up of companies and bankruptcy. Yet the need for the latter to accommodate the action *in rem* and the potential conflict between the two processes is plain. A *res* may concurrently be the subject of an arrest in the Admiralty Court and an asset capable of liquidation in a company winding up or personal bankruptcy. In such a circumstance it is important for a maritime claimant to be able to ascertain whether it is the jurisdiction of the Admiralty Court or some other court which prevails and which mode of legal process is available for the satisfaction of the claim. Most ships today are operated by commercial companies, many of which are one-ship companies, and therefore in practice the inter-relationship between an action *in rem* and a winding up is likely to be of much greater importance than the relation the Admiralty proceeding bears to a bankruptcy proceeding.

* Justice of the Supreme Court of Singapore. The author is grateful to Ms Deborah Koh, a former legal associate of M/s Ang & Partners and now consultant with the Singapore Mediation Centre, and in 2016, Justices' Law Clerk, Mr Jasper Wong, for their assistance, comments and suggestions. This paper was first delivered at the Colloquium on the Arrest Conventions 1952 and 1999 on 29 November 2016. Subsequently, the Companies (Amendment) Act came into force on 23 May 2017, and the paper is updated to reflect the position in Singapore as at 24 January 2018. All views expressed are personal to the author and do not represent those of the Supreme Court of Singapore. All errors are entirely the author's own.

[1] D Rhidian Thomas, *Maritime Liens*, British Shipping Laws No 14 (London, Stevens & Sons, 1980) para 99.

Thomas' observations are still true in the twenty-first century. In a prescient way, they reflect the state of affairs between two branches of the law that serve to protect economic interests in different spheres and ways. We see the modern-day tension between the notions of universalism and territoriality, with each particular national cross-border insolvency framework adopted and adapted in response to social, cultural, political and economic policy objectives as well as the business exigencies of each state. One example is the recent legislative amendments intended to enhance Singapore's competitiveness as a forum for cross-border insolvency and debt restructuring following the Insolvency Law Review Committee's recommendation to adopt the UNCITRAL Model Law on Cross-Border Insolvency (the Model Law)[2] as well as to reform the legal corporate rescue framework. Continuing tension resides between the parallel and, at times, overlapping jurisdictions of the insolvency court and the admiralty court, which is territorial in focus by the very nature of its rules and practice.

As we already know, admiralty courts have over the centuries in the sphere of international commercial trade developed maritime law with its own body of maritime claims and rights. The list of maritime claims and rights have been extended by the International Convention Relating to the Arrest of Sea-Going Ships 1952 (the Arrest Convention 1952)[3] and the International Convention on the Arrest of Ships 1999 (the Arrest Convention 1999).[4] The admiralty jurisdiction of the Singapore court is derived from the High Court (Admiralty Jurisdiction) Act (cap 123, 2001 rev edn) (HCAJA).

A well-placed striking reminder of the importance of this branch of maritime law came from Allsop J (as he then was) who in 2007 insightfully described the space occupied by admiralty jurisdiction in modern times as

> a body of law, and the administration of a body of law, with roots in public international law, civil law, international commerce, international agreement and the law of nations. Its history is rich and its contents are vibrant and modern. It is only an arcane or obscure branch of the law to those whose legal thinking is informed exclusively by land-based human activity.[5]

A typical scenario in a cross-border insolvency is a foreign insolvency order with a moratorium order. Considerations arise as to its recognition and assistance to the foreign insolvency representative in Singapore. If recognised here, what would its effect be on the commencement or continuation of in rem proceedings against the ships of the foreign debtor and its related entities in Singapore? The position that I have taken in this Chapter is that the Singapore court is not bound to recognise the foreign insolvency proceedings under common law, and after the 2017 amendments to the Companies Act and the adoption of the Model Law as part of Singapore's insolvency law, the Singapore court does not need to stay proceedings of all types of in rem claims. Moreover, the in rem claimant

[2] See UNCITRAL Secretariat, *UNCITRAL Model Law on Cross-Border Insolvency with Guide to Enactment and Interpretation* (New York, UN, 2014).

[3] International Convention Relating to the Arrest of Sea-going Ships (adopted 10 May 1952, entered into force 24 February 1956) 439 UNTS 193.

[4] International Convention on the Arrest of Ships (adopted 12 March 1999, entered into force 14 September 2011) 2797 UNTS 3.

[5] Justice James Allsop, 'Admiralty Jurisdiction – Some Basic Considerations and Some Recent Australian Cases' (FCA) [2007] *Federal Judicial Scholarship* 5.

who has previously filed its maritime claim here may be able to proceed with the in rem action to arrest the ship in question.

In this Chapter, reference to maritime claims attracting in rem jurisdiction encompasses the traditional maritime liens like collision, salvage and wages as well as the statutory liens claims under s 3 of the HCAJA.

II. Singapore's Common Law on Cross-Border Insolvency

Before the 2017 amendments to the Companies Act, the Singapore courts could give very limited judicial co-operation to foreign courts. There was no known procedure for obtaining recognition of insolvency proceedings of foreign courts.[6] There was neither a procedure for supervising the activities of a foreign insolvency administrator, nor a procedure for the co-ordination of concurrent insolvency proceedings in Singapore and abroad.[7]

Former Chief Justice Chan Sek Keong, writing extrajudicially at a joint multinational judicial colloquium on insolvency in 2011,[8] doubted that the principle of modified universalism expressed by Lord Hoffmann in *Re HIH Casualty & General Insurance Ltd*[9] needed to be seriously considered in Singapore, given the express provisions of the Companies Act (cap 50, 2006 rev edn) where very limited co-operation can be given to foreign courts in relation to the remittance of the assets of an insolvent company.[10] Chan CJ referred to instances of limited co-operation in the past where our judges have, consistent with the local statutory insolvency regime, provided assistance as is proper to foreign courts and liquidators based on what his Honour termed 'the tradition of common law judges', which differs from the principle of modified universalism, a judge-made English common law principle, that was accepted with limitations by the Privy Council in *Singularis Holdings Ltd v PricewaterhouseCoopers*.[11] In my view, given his choice of terminology, Chan CJ must have had in mind the traditional common law ancillary liquidation doctrine that is part of the common law and has existed in Singapore alongside our statutory insolvency regime where no other statutory provision has been made. The Singapore Court of Appeal in *Beluga Chartering GmbH (in liquidation) v Beluga Projects (Singapore) Pte Ltd (in liquidation)*[12] aligned itself with Lord Scott's enunciation[13] of the traditional common law ancillary liquidation doctrine that gives the court a general power to order the remittance of realised assets to the principal place of liquidation; but does not have the power to authorise the local liquidator to ignore the statutory provisions that deprive creditors proving in a local liquidation of any vested rights under the insolvency statute or other written law.

[6] See *Singapore MLA Reply to Questionnaire* comitemaritime.org/work/cross-border-insolvencies/ (2012) 6.
[7] ibid 6–7.
[8] Chan Sek Keong, 'Cross-Border Insolvency Issues Affecting Singapore' (2011) 23 *S Ac LJ* 413 para 21.
[9] *Re HIH Casualty & General Insurance Ltd* [2008] UKHL 21, [2008] 1 WLR 852.
[10] Companies Act, s 377(3)(c).
[11] *Singularis Holdings Ltd v PricewaterhouseCoopers* [2014] UKPC 36, [2015] AC 1675.
[12] *Beluga Chartering GmbH (in liquidation) v Beluga Projects (Singapore) Pte Ltd (in liquidation)* [2014] SGCA 14, [2014] 2 SLR 815.
[13] In *Re HIH Casualty and General Insurance Ltd* (n 9).

In *Cambridge Gas Transportation Corp v Official Committee of Unsecured Creditors of Navigator Holdings plc*[14] Lord Hoffmann put forward what he described as the 'underlying principle of universality', namely, that under English common law there should be a single insolvency process, both in corporate and personal bankruptcies, whereby the English court will recognise and assist a foreign insolvency representative empowered under its local law. This single insolvency process was to obviate the need for the foreign insolvency representatives or creditors to start parallel proceedings and to give them the remedies which they would have been entitled to if the equivalent proceedings had taken place in the domestic forum.

However, from *Singularis Holdings Ltd*[15] two broad principles under English law emerge:

(1) common law ancillary liquidation starts with the winding-up of a foreign company and requires a sufficient connection with the forum; and
(2) the principle of modified universalism forms the basis of the court's common law power to assist in recognition of foreign insolvencies which is not contrary to local law and public policy.

As Lord Sumption there pointed out, the recognition of the foreign liquidator's power was no more than what he was entitled to do as a matter of private international law. Furthermore, the principle of modified universalism was founded on a public interest which was based on comity. It was in the interest of every country that companies with transnational assets and operations should be capable of being wound up on a basis that would be recognised and effective internationally.[16]

Whilst the majority of the Board in *Singularis Holdings Ltd*[17] accepted the principle of modified universalism, namely that the court has a common law power to recognise and grant assistance to foreign insolvency proceedings so far as it properly can, caution should be taken in jurisdictions where there are no statutory powers to assist foreign insolvency representatives. Notably, the principle of modified universalism is subject to local law and local public policy and the assisting court can only act within the limits of its statutory and common law powers.

The liquidator's question on appeal to the Privy Council was whether legislation may be extended by the judiciary to apply to cases where the legislature has not applied it; that the court should apply legislation, which ex hypothesi does not apply, 'as if' it applied. The Privy Council held that the Bermuda court had no common law power to assist a foreign liquidator by ordering the production of information where: (1) the Bermuda court had no power to wind up an overseas company such as Singularis; and (2) its statutory power to order production of information was limited to cases where the company had been wound up in Bermuda. The production of materials sought was not available under Cayman law because the Cayman court would have been limited to ordering production of materials belonging to Singularis. Audit working papers were not owned by Singularis and the

[14] *Cambridge Gas Transportation Corp v Official Committee of Unsecured Creditors of Navigator Holdings plc* [2006] UKPC 26, [2007] 1 AC 508.
[15] *Singularis Holdings Ltd* (n 11).
[16] ibid [12].
[17] ibid.

majority of the Board declined to exercise the common law powers of the court in favour of the liquidator.[18]

The precise limits of the court's common law powers to assist may (as the minority's views demonstrated) not be easy to define; it really depends on the assistance sought. As the majority determined, it did cover the ordering of the provision of information, this being a development of the court's established common law discovery powers. However, there were limits to the power to order provision of information. Lord Sumption referred to five limitations.[19] First, it was available only to assist the officers of the foreign court of insolvency jurisdiction. It would not, for example, be available to assist a voluntary winding-up or to enable the foreign liquidators to do something which they could not do under the law by which they were appointed. Second, it was a power of assistance. It existed for the purpose of enabling courts to surmount the problems posed by a worldwide winding-up of a company's affairs. It was therefore not available to enable the foreign liquidators to do something which they could not do under the law by which they were appointed. Third, the power was available only when it was necessary for the performance of the foreign liquidators' functions. Fourth, it had to be consistent with the substantive law and public policy of the assisting court. It was not available for obtaining material for use in actual or anticipated litigation. Finally, its exercise was conditional on the applicant being prepared to pay the third party's reasonable costs of compliance.

Returning to the 2014 decision of *Beluga Chartering GmbH*,[20] the company, Beluga Chartering GmbH, had been placed in liquidation in Germany and was wound up in Singapore under s 351(1) of the Companies Act as an unregistered foreign company. The Court of Appeal upheld the fact that Beluga Chartering was an unregistered foreign company not carrying on business in Singapore, and therefore s 377(3)(c) of the Companies Act (which provides for the ring-fencing of assets of foreign companies carrying on business in Singapore) did not apply.[21] Instead, the common law ancillary liquidation doctrine applied. The liquidation of a foreign company in Singapore was regarded as the ancillary liquidation while its liquidation in the place of its incorporation was the principal liquidation. The common law took the view that worldwide creditors of the company would be treated equally, and the court should generally direct that the liquidator in an ancillary liquidation transmit funds to the liquidator in the principal liquidation for pari passu distribution to worldwide creditors. The court, therefore, directed the Singapore liquidators to remit the realised assets of Beluga Chartering in Singapore to the German liquidator, without first satisfying the judgment debt owed to the Singapore subsidiaries.[22]

Relevant to this Chapter is the Court of Appeal's discussion of the side issue of recognition of the title of a foreign liquidator and the recognition of foreign winding-up proceedings. The observations on the side issue were premised on the existence of local litigation, assets in the jurisdiction and the absence of local liquidation in play.

First, on the recognition of a foreign liquidator, it was accepted that a liquidator of a foreign company would be recognised as the representative of the company for the

[18] ibid [19], [25], [28]–[29], [31], [33], [109]–[115].
[19] ibid [25].
[20] *Beluga Chartering GmbH* (n 12).
[21] ibid [53]–[54].
[22] Ibid [56]–[60], [100].

purposes of getting in and realising the company's worldwide assets and there would generally be no basis for a Singapore court to decline to recognise the liquidator's claim to assets belonging to the company under general principles of property law.[23]

Secondly, on the recognition of a foreign winding-up order, the Court of Appeal acknowledged that under common law rules in Singapore, the foreign winding-up order, including any foreign order to stay proceedings in the forum, would not be recognised.[24] The Court of Appeal did not consider the principle of modified universalism as articulated by Lord Hoffmann in *Re HIH Casualty & General Insurance Ltd*[25] to be a legal rule, having rather characterised it as an aspirational principle.[26] On the limitations of judicial law-making, former Master of the Rolls Lord Dyson has commented:

> An important principle is that the common law should not be developed where the courts are not equipped to decide whether the development is in the interests of justice or to define the parameters of development. … But where the court feels that it is equipped to develop the law, sometimes radically, it can and, in my view, it should be willing to do so.[27]

Nonetheless, the Court of Appeal provisionally observed that it remained open to the Singapore courts assisting the foreign liquidation proceedings through regulating the proceedings in the local forum, but this would be on a case by case basis. In other words, it is possible to grant assistance though the court's existing procedural powers, for instance, to stay a claim if Singapore was not the forum conveniens, to stay execution or attachment, to exercise discretion against grant of a garnishee order absolute, to refuse leave to serve process out of the jurisdiction or to wind up a company in Singapore. More importantly, the Court of Appeal clarified that it was permissible to commence legal proceedings against a defendant foreign company or attempt to levy execution against its assets even though insolvency proceedings have been commenced against the company in another jurisdiction. The court's response would depend on the application sought.[28]

Since Chan CJ's extrajudicial writing[29] and the Court of Appeal's decision in *Beluga Chartering GmbH*,[30] contemporary judicial attitudes here have shifted beyond the traditional common law ancillary liquidation doctrine and the appellate court's provisional observations on recognition of a foreign winding-up order. I now turn to the 'deployment' of the English's common law power to recognise and grant assistance to foreign insolvency proceedings in two local cases in 2016 – examples of how 'the product of today's buccaneer sometimes becomes tomorrow's orthodoxy',[31] finally realised by our adoption of the Model Law.

[23] ibid [86]–[88].
[24] ibid [89]–[99].
[25] *Re HIH Casualty & General Insurance Ltd* (n 9).
[26] *Beluga Chartering GmbH* (n 12) [75].
[27] The Right Honourable Lord Dyson, Singapore Academy of Law Distinguished Speaker Series Lecture 2014 – 'The Limits of the Common Law' (2015) 27 *S Ac LJ* 271 para 8.
[28] ibid [98]–[99].
[29] Chan (n 8).
[30] *Beluga Chartering GmbH* (n 12).
[31] Dyson (n 27) para 30.

A. *Re Opti-Medix Ltd (in liquidation)*[32]

In June 2016 the Singapore High Court in *Re Opti-Medix Ltd*[33] was faced with the issue of recognising a foreign liquidation in a jurisdiction other than the place of incorporation. The corporate bankruptcy orders were made by the Tokyo District Court against two companies incorporated in the British Virgin Islands. The applicant, who was the foreign liquidator, sought recognition of his appointment as bankruptcy trustee in order to ascertain, administer and dispose of assets in Singapore. The liquidator undertook to pay all debts in Singapore before remitting any funds out of Singapore. Notably, the liquidator was not appointed by the court of the place of incorporation, and thus could not rely on established principles of private international law that recognise the dissolution of foreign companies under the law of the place of incorporation. Besides, a foreign liquidator has no automatic power in relation to the property of a foreign company located in Singapore; the foreign liquidator must either: (1) be an approved Singapore insolvency practitioner, or (2) instruct an approved insolvency practitioner in Singapore to act for the foreign liquidator.

Aedit Abdullah JC (as he then was) recognised that Lord Collins in *Rubin v Eurofinance SA*[34] doubted that it was open to the courts to introduce a new basis for recognition in relation to insolvency proceedings that did not start in the place of incorporation and that such a matter should be left to the legislature. However, the judge then opined that the development of the common law should not be so constrained and in cross-border insolvency, there had been a general movement away from the traditional territorial focus of the interest of the local creditors towards a universalist approach of co-operation between jurisdictions. This co-operation between jurisdictions was a necessary part of the contemporary world to achieve the promotion and facilitation of the orderly distribution of assets, as well as the orderly resolution and dissolution of the affairs of entities being wound up.

This philosophy was reiterated in *Re Gulf Pacific Shipping Ltd (in creditors' voluntary liquidation)*.[35] The judge there adopted the differing stance of Lord Neuberger in *Singularis Holdings Ltd*,[36] who made no distinction between a foreign voluntary liquidation and a foreign compulsory liquidation involving officers of a foreign court.

In *Re Opti-Medix Ltd*[37] the judge relied on the 'centre of main interest' or COMI test, as proffered by Lord Hoffman in *Re HIH Casualty & General Insurance Ltd*,[38] as a basis for recognition at common law of the foreign insolvency proceedings. These companies had assets in Singapore bank accounts and two Singapore creditors. The liquidator sought to exercise his powers under the Japanese bankruptcy order to ascertain, administer and dispose of the companies' assets and the judge allowed his application.

Japan was the sole place where actual business was carried out, and that provided the basis for recognition of the Japanese bankruptcy order, even if Japan was not the place of incorporation of the companies. The judge said that on a common law adoption of the

[32] *Re Opti-Medix Ltd (in liquidation)* [2016] SGHC 108, [2016] 4 SLR 312.
[33] ibid.
[34] *Rubin v Eurofinance SA* [2012] UKSC 46, [2013] 1 AC 236.
[35] *Re Gulf Pacific Shipping Ltd (in creditors' voluntary liquidation)* [2016] SGHC 287 [10].
[36] *Singularis Holdings Ltd* (n 11) [149] ff.
[37] *Re Opti-Medix Ltd* (n 32) [19].
[38] *Re HIH Casualty & General Insurance Ltd* (n 9) [31].

COMI test, there need not necessarily be a presumption in favour of the registered office, as under the Model Law or EU Insolvency Regulation.[39] In any event, the judge declared that the recognition of the Tokyo order could be justified 'on practical grounds'.[40]

The judge noted the Court of Appeal's views in *Beluga Chartering GmbH*[41] that the court's power to recognise the foreign liquidator's power was a matter of private international law where no local liquidation proceedings had been initiated. A foreign liquidator properly appointed under the law of the place of incorporation would be recognised for the purposes of getting in and realising the company's assets by the Singapore court. The judge nonetheless said that he 'did not see anything in that judgment that precluded recognition of the liquidator on other grounds, such as COMI'.[42] Another noteworthy point is that the Privy Council in *Rubin*[43] was dealing with the question whether and in what circumstances an order of a foreign court in avoidance proceedings in insolvency would be recognised and enforced in England. The holding there was that the '*Dicey* rule' applied to foreign judgments in avoidance proceedings in insolvency and that, if there was to be a change to this rule, it would be a matter for the legislature.[44] The further point made in *Rubin* was that the Model Law was not designed to provide for the reciprocal enforcement of judgments and there was nothing to suggest that it applied to the recognition and enforcement of foreign judgments.[45] Nevertheless, the judge stated that Lord Collins' remarks need not concern him for *Rubin*[46] was a different case and clearly distinguishable.[47]

B. *Re Taisoo Suk (as Foreign Representative of Hanjin Shipping Co Ltd)*[48]

In September 2016 Abdullah JC was faced with an ex parte application for recognition of Hanjin's rehabilitation proceedings in Korea and restraint of all pending, contingent or fresh

[39] Regulation (EU) 2015/848 of the European Parliament and of the Council of 20 May 2015 on insolvency proceedings (recast) [2015] OJ L141/19.

[40] *Re Opti-Medix Ltd* (n 32) [26].

[41] *Beluga Chartering GmbH* (n 12) [86].

[42] *Re Opti-Medix Ltd* (n 32) [23].

[43] Rubin (n 34).

[44] ibid [7]ff, referring to AV Dicey, JHC Morris, Lawrence Collins, *Dicey, Morris and Collins on the Conflict of Laws*, 15th edn (London, Sweet & Maxwell Thomson Reuters, 2012), para 14R-054, Rule 43. Rule 43 provides that

> 'a court of a foreign country outside the United Kingdom has jurisdiction to give a judgment in personam capable of enforcement or recognition as against the person against whom it was given in the following cases:
>
> First Case — If the person against whom the judgment was given was, at the time the proceedings were instituted, present in the foreign country.
> Second Case — If the person against whom the judgment was given was claimant, or counterclaimed, in the proceedings in the foreign court.
> Third Case — If the person against whom the judgment was given, submitted to the jurisdiction of that court by voluntarily appearing in the proceedings.
> Fourth Case — If the person against whom the judgment was given, had before the commencement of the proceedings agreed, in respect of the subject matter of the proceedings, to submit to the jurisdiction of that court or of the courts of that country'. (citations omitted)

[45] *Rubin* (n 34) [24], [133]ff.

[46] *Rubin* (n 34).

[47] *Re Opti-Medix Ltd* (n 32) [21]–[22].

[48] *Re Taisoo Suk (as foreign representative of Hanjin Shipping Co Ltd)* [2016] SGHC 195, [2016] 5 SLR 787.

proceedings, enforcement or execution against assets and a stay of all present proceedings against Hanjin and its Singapore subsidiaries until 25 January 2017.[49] This time, the ex parte application to stay proceedings was made pursuant to the inherent powers of the court to make any order as may be necessary to prevent injustice or an abuse of the process of the court.[50] The applicant's reliance on a procedural rule prompted the judge rightly to remark that O 92 r 4 was often the 'first resort in dubious claims'.[51]

In urging the court to exercise its inherent powers, the applicant foreign representative of Hanjin argued that the application made was an essential part of the series of applications that Hanjin had made across the world to prevent piecemeal and haphazard resolution of the company's difficulties. Any disparate treatment would imperil Hanjin's rehabilitation and there would be a disorderly scramble amongst Hanjin's creditors to act quickly to seize or exercise their liens on vessels and containers which constituted Hanjin's principal business assets. In fact, this had already taken place in various ports of the world and the *Hanjin Rome* had already been arrested here.[52] The applicant further relied upon Hanjin's 'substantial' connections to Singapore, namely, its two Singapore incorporated subsidiaries (and their 112 employees here), which were said to have significant trade volume. Hanjin and its two subsidiaries also had assets here.

Pending the determination of an inter partes application, the court ordered:

(1) a restraint of all pending, contingent or fresh suits, actions, proceedings, against Hanjin and its subsidiaries or any enforcement or execution against any asset of Hanjin and its subsidiaries; and
(2) a stay of all present suits, action or proceedings against Hanjin and its subsidiaries.

Notably, orders (1) and (2) included any enforcement or execution against the vessels beneficially owned or chartered by Hanjin and its subsidiaries, but they were not to apply to the earlier arrest of *Hanjin Rome*; instead, liberty to apply was granted in respect of that arrest.

In granting the orders, the judge was satisfied that the Korean rehabilitation orders should be recognised and assistance rendered. He was mindful of the impact on Singapore creditors, particularly the restraint of admiralty proceedings by barring the arrests of vessels. But the judge nevertheless adopted the universalist approach. He noted that:

> the imperative for orderly rehabilitation and restructuring of a company running a global business across jurisdictions, and the need to ensure that the company's assets could be marshalled or collected for such effort, both provided sufficiently strong grounds for the exercise of the inherent powers of the court to grant the restraint and stay orders.[53]

He even stated that such recognition and assistance perhaps constituted a development of the common law in Singapore and was satisfied that this development was principled and justified.[54]

Restraining arrests of vessels belonging to the debtor and its two subsidiaries and for all types of in rem claims reflects universalism taken at its highest and goes well

[49] Hanjin's foreign representative ceased to pursue the continuation of the stay orders on 6 January 2017.
[50] Order 92 r 4 of the Rules of Court (cap 332 r 5 2014 rev edn).
[51] *Re Taisoo Suk* (n 48) [32].
[52] ADM 178 of 2016.
[53] *Re Taisoo Suk* (n 48) [32].
[54] ibid [13].

beyond the approach of several Australian decisions (which I shall examine)[55] and even the Model Law. Abdullah JC's stay order was later tested before the duty registrar when an arrest of the *Hanjin New York* was sought on 6 October 2016. The duty registrar accepted the in rem claimant's argument that the registered owner of the *Hanjin New York* was a Panamanian entity and was therefore not caught by the judge's order. The vessel was released from arrest following a settlement between the parties and proceedings have since been discontinued.

As for the nexus established by the two Singapore subsidiaries, this argument, offered as a nexus in recognition of foreign insolvency proceedings, was specifically rejected by Kannan Ramesh JC (as he then was) in *Re Pacific Andes Resources Development Ltd*:[56]

> Nexus in this context is that which enables a court to wind up a foreign company. The fact that the Subsidiaries are wholly owned by PARD does not afford a basis. Neither does the fact that they are part of PARD's business offer any foothold. The Subsidiaries are independent legal entities and the fact that they intend to present a group restructuring with a composite, inter-dependent and inter-connected restructuring plan does not have the effect of or warrant the piercing or lifting of the corporate veil such that they may be regarded as one composite entity. This, I would venture to say, is settled law.

III. The Companies (Amendment) Act 2017

In October 2016 the Companies (Amendment) Bill 2017 introduced the adoption of the Model Law and reformed Singapore's debt restructuring and corporate rescue framework (the US Chapter 11 bankruptcy regime[57] inspired refinements to Singapore's scheme of arrangement mechanism). The Bill was passed in Parliament and the amendments came into force on 23 May 2017. The Companies (Amendment) Act 2017 aligns Singapore's insolvency regime to international standards. There are five significant amendments to the Companies Act in relation to cross-border insolvencies.[58]

First, the adoption of the Model Law as the 10th Schedule to the Companies Act. The recognition of foreign insolvency proceedings under the Model Law will sit more comfortably with the concept of modified universalism as compared to the broad-brush approaches we have seen in *Re Opti-Medix Ltd*[59] and *Re Taisoo Suk*.[60]

Secondly, the scheme of arrangement or debtor-in-possession (DIP) regime was enhanced through:

(1) Rescue financing now being made available to companies in distress, for which the court can grant super priority over all other creditors;[61]

[55] See Part IV(A) below.
[56] *Re Pacific Andes Resources Development Ltd* [2016] SGHC 210, [2018] 5 SLR 125 [39].
[57] Bankruptcy Code, 11 USC, ch 11 §§ 1101–74.
[58] See Ministry of Law, 'Commencement of Legislative Amendments Relating to Debt Restructuring and Corporate Rescue in the Companies Act' (22 May 2017) available at https://www.mlaw.gov.sg/content/minlaw/en/news/press-releases/commencement-of-legislative-amendments-relating-to-debt-restruct.html.
[59] *Re Opti-Medix Ltd* (n 32).
[60] *Re Taisoo Suk* (n 48).
[61] Companies Act, s 211E.

(2) Protection from law suits and other legal action through:
    (a) An automatic 30-day moratorium[62] against creditor action immediately upon the filing of an application by the debtor company, even when the restructuring proposal has not been fully worked out and there is only an intention to present a restructuring proposal as soon as practicable. The court can extend the moratorium if satisfied there are good reasons to do so;[63]
    (b) Worldwide effect of such moratoriums, provided the injuncted persons are subject to the in personam jurisdiction of the Singapore courts;[64] and
    (c) Extension of moratoriums to the debtor company's related entities.[65]

Thirdly, judicial management[66] will be made available to foreign companies,[67] and is enhanced through:

(1) Super priority for rescue financing;[68] and
(2) Relaxation of the test for judicial management. Previously, one had to show that the company was actually insolvent before a judicial management order could be made. Now, one only needs to show that it will be likely that the company will become insolvent.[69]

Fourthly, the addition of specific criteria on when the Singapore court may exercise its discretion to take jurisdiction over foreign debtors, the test now codifying whether the company has a 'substantial connection' with Singapore, and factors to determine this including whether Singapore is the centre of main interests (COMI) of the company.[70]

Fifth and finally, the abolition of the general ring-fencing rule in the winding-up of foreign companies. Ring-fencing, however, will be retained for specific financial institutions, such as banks and insurance companies.

The issue of how maritime claims are affected by these statutory changes will now be discussed. I pause to note that, whilst the Model Law's universalist approach to

[62] Available once in one 12-month period to prevent abuse through repeated filings: ibid, s 211B(9).

[63] ibid, s 211B(8).

[64] ibid, s 211B(5).

[65] ibid, s 211C.

[66] See Part VIIIA of the Companies Act. Judicial management will not be discussed in this Chapter.

[67] The Companies Act, s 227A widens the definition of 'company' to mean 'any corporation liable to be wound up under this Act' and 'property' to include 'money, goods, things in action and every description of property, whether real or personal, and whether in Singapore or elsewhere, and also obligations and every description of interest whether present or future or vested or contingent arising out of, or incidental to, property'.

[68] ibid s 227E.

[69] ibid s 227B.

[70] The Companies Act, s 351(2A) now provides:

> For the purposes of subsection (1)(d), the Court may rely on the presence of one or more of the following matters to support a determination that a foreign company has a substantial connection with Singapore:
>
> (a) Singapore is the centre of main interests of the company;
> (b) the company is carrying on business in Singapore or has a place of business in Singapore;
> (c) the company is a foreign company that is registered under Division 2 of Part XI;
> (d) the company has substantial assets in Singapore;
> (e) the company has chosen Singapore law as the law governing a loan or other transaction, or the law governing the resolution of one or more disputes arising out of or in connection with a loan or other transaction;
> (f) the company has submitted to the jurisdiction of the Court for the resolution of one or more disputes relating to a loan or other transaction.

cross-border insolvency treats multinational bankruptcy as a single process with other courts assisting the foreign main proceeding, the Model Law is procedural in character and is not intended to bring about a change to the substantive law of the recognising court. It has been said that the central purpose of insolvency proceedings is to provide a mechanism of collective execution against the property of the debtor by creditors whose rights are admitted or established; the insolvency proceedings are not to determine or establish the existence of rights.[71] The Model Law also does not deal with enforcement of foreign judgments.

IV. The In Rem Creditor in Admiralty and the Model Law's Moratoriums

Below is Singapore's amendment to art 20 of the Model Law:

Article 20. Effects of recognition of a foreign main proceeding

1. Upon recognition of a foreign proceeding that is a foreign main proceeding, subject to paragraph 2 of this Article —
   (a) commencement or continuation of individual actions or individual proceedings concerning the debtor's property, rights, obligations or liabilities is stayed;
   (b) execution against the debtor's property is stayed; and
   (c) the right to transfer, encumber or otherwise dispose of any property of the debtor is suspended.
2. The stay and suspension mentioned in paragraph 1 of this Article are —
   (a) the same in scope and effect as if the debtor had been made the subject of a winding-up order under this Act; and
   (b) subject to the same powers of the Court and the same prohibitions, limitations, exceptions and conditions as would apply under the law of Singapore in such a case, and the provisions of paragraph 1 of this Article are to be interpreted accordingly.
3. Without prejudice to paragraph 2 of this Article, the stay and suspension mentioned in paragraph 1 of this Article do not affect any right —
   (a) to take any steps to enforce security over the debtor's property;
   (b) to take any steps to repossess goods in the debtor's possession under a hire-purchase agreement (as defined in section 227AA of this Act);
   (c) exercisable under or by virtue of or in connection with 15 any written law mentioned in Article 1(3)(a) to (i); or
   (d) of a creditor to set off its claim against a claim of the debtor,
   being a right which would have been exercisable if the debtor had been made the subject of a winding-up order under this Act.
4. Paragraph 1(a) of this Article does not affect the right to —
   (a) commence individual actions or proceedings to the extent necessary to preserve a claim against the debtor; or

[71] *Cambridge Gas Transportation Corp* (n 14) [14].

(b) commence or continue any criminal proceedings or any action or proceedings by a person or body having regulatory, supervisory or investigative functions of a public nature, being an action or proceedings brought in the exercise of those functions.

5. Paragraph 1 of this Article does not affect the right to request or otherwise initiate the commencement of a proceeding under Singapore insolvency law or the right to file claims in such a proceeding.

6. In addition to and without prejudice to any powers of the Court under or by virtue of paragraph 2 of this Article, the Court may, on the application of the foreign representative or a person affected by the stay and suspension mentioned in paragraph 1 of this Article, or of its own motion, modify or terminate such stay and suspension or any part of it, either altogether or for a limited time, on such terms and conditions as the Court thinks fit.

Under the Model Law, the foreign representative of the COMI debtor will have to apply for recognition of the foreign insolvency proceedings including any urgent moratorium against the debtor's assets. The Singapore insolvency court will be bound to recognise the foreign insolvency proceedings as 'foreign proceedings'[72] if the procedure in art 15 and the conditions in art 17(1) are satisfied. Where the Singapore insolvency court recognises the foreign insolvency proceedings as a main proceeding, there is within Singapore an automatic and mandatory moratorium on all proceedings against the COMI debtor under art 20(1). Article 21, by contrast, allows the court the discretion to grant relief upon recognition of a foreign proceeding, whether a foreign main proceeding or a foreign non-main proceeding.

The important point is that the COMI debtor is not in liquidation in Singapore simply by virtue of recognition under art 17. There is (as yet) no domestic Singapore insolvency proceeding in place under the Singapore Companies Act. However, art 20(2)(a) may be interpreted as creating the fiction that the COMI debtor is to be treated as if it was in liquidation in Singapore, and this is for the purpose of assessing the scope of the art 20(1) stay (albeit for no other purpose).

What art 20(2) does is to state expressly that the scope and effects of the matters contemplated under art 20(1) depend on the exceptions or limitations of the law of the enacting state. In particular, art 20(2)(b) stipulates that the stay under art 20(1) subjects the COMI debtor to the same protection and the same disabilities as apply to a company undergoing liquidation in Singapore. As the Model Law is procedural in character and is not intended to bring about a change to the substantive law of the recognising court, the Model Law does not go beyond domestic law in interfering with security.

Article 2(j) of the Model Law defines security as 'any mortgage, charge, lien or other security'. As a matter of construction, the stay under art 20(1) effectively applies to unsecured creditors (as in the general body of creditors) because of the right granted to secured creditors under arts 20(2) and 20(3) read with art 20(1). In this sense, secured creditors, including in rem creditors, remain outside of and are unaffected by the stay under art 20(1). Equally, art 20(4)(a) enables a protective writ to be issued to preserve an in rem claim from being time-barred or from a change of ownership. It had long been established that a statutory right of action in rem cannot survive a change of ownership unless a claim form in rem has been issued prior to the change of ownership.

[72] Although not explicitly defined in art 2(h), this would include liquidation, judicial management and schemes of arrangement.

The breadth of the discretionary relief that may be granted in art 21(1)(a), that is, 'any appropriate relief' that 'concerns the debtor's property' is potentially very wide, but its meaning cannot possibly extend to barring the issuance of in rem writs against the property of the debtor's related entities. This must be so since the Model Law does not recognise group enterprises, which I will come to later.[73] Article 21(1) reads:

> Upon recognition of a foreign proceeding, whether a foreign main proceeding or a foreign non-main proceeding, where necessary to protect the property of the debtor or the interests of the creditors, the Court may, at the request of the foreign representative, grant any appropriate relief, including —
>
> (a) staying the commencement or continuation of individual actions or individual proceedings concerning the debtor's property, rights, obligations or liabilities, to the extent they have not been stayed under Article 20(1)(a);

Article 22 cautions that the courts must be satisfied that the interests of creditors, including secured creditors, are adequately protected. Ultimately, this will be at the court's discretion, bearing in mind that art 20(2) expressly preserves and gives precedence to local laws.[74]

All said, there may be considerations which are unique in a cross-border situation, and I will develop on these matters later. Suffice to say for now that an admiralty claimant who proceeds in rem is a secured claimant for purposes of consequent insolvency proceedings. If ever leave of the court is required to continue with the in rem action, the application is made under art 20(6) and the same principles governing an application under s 262(3) of the Companies Act are likely to apply. Section 262(3) reads:

> **Actions stayed on winding up order**
>
> (3) When a winding up order has been made or a provisional liquidator has been appointed, no action or proceeding shall be proceeded with or commenced against the company except —
>
> (a) by leave of the Court; and
>
> (b) in accordance with such terms as the Court imposes.

A. Australian Perspective

The Australian experience in the recognition of foreign insolvency and the right of arrest provides helpful insights. Australia implemented the Model Law via the Cross-Border Insolvency Act 2008 (Cth) (CBIA 2008). However, the CBIA 2008 is not a comprehensive international insolvency statute, and cross-reference is made to provisions in the Corporations Act 2001 (Cth) (the CA 2001) and the Bankruptcy Act 1966 (Cth).

In the Federal Court of Australia decision of *Yu v STX Pan Ocean Co Ltd (South Korea), in the matter of STX Pan Ocean Co Ltd (Receivers appointed in South Korea)*[75]

[73] See Parts VII and VIII below.

[74] Morgan J in *Fibria Celulose S/A v Pan Ocean Co Ltd* [2014] EWHC 2024 (Ch), [2014] WLR (D) 288 [108] stated he was not persuaded that 'any appropriate relief' allowed him to grant relief that would not be available in a domestic insolvency.

[75] *Yu v STX Pan Ocean Co Ltd (South Korea), in the matter of STX Pan Ocean Co Ltd (Receivers appointed in South Korea)* [2013] FCA 680, (2013) 223 FCR 189.

the Federal Court took the opportunity to clarify that Australia's adoption of the Model Law was indeed subject to the operation of local insolvency laws in their version of modified universalism.

Starting with *Yu*[76] in 2013, then *Kim v Daebo International Shipping Co Ltd*,[77] *Hur v Samsun Logix Corp*,[78] *Yakushiji v Daiichi Chuo Kisen Kaisha*[79] and *The Ship Sam Hawk v Reiter Petroleum Inc*,[80] in the insolvency context, Australian courts have distinguished between proceedings to enforce an existing security right (eg, a maritime lien) and proceedings to satisfy a judgment out of the proceeds of sale of a ship. Only the former can proceed as an action by a secured creditor within the exception allowed under s 471C of the CA 2001. Sections 471B and 471C of the CA 2001 preserve the rights of secured creditors and recognise the power of the court to grant leave to commence a proceeding or an enforcement process in appropriate circumstances:

> **471B Stay of proceedings and suspension of enforcement process**
>
> While a company is being wound up in insolvency or by the Court, or a provisional liquidator of a company is acting, a person cannot begin or proceed with:
>
> (a) a proceeding in a court against the company or in relation to property of the company; or
> (b) enforcement process in relation to such property;
>
> except with the leave of the Court and in accordance with such terms (if any) as the Court imposes.
>
> **471C Secured creditor's rights not affected**
>
> Nothing in section 471A or 471B affects a secured creditor's right to realise or otherwise deal with the security.

The question before the Full Federal Court of Australia in the *Sam Hawk*[81] was how Australian law treated a maritime lien arising under foreign law within the regime of the Admiralty Act 1988 (Cth) (the AA 1988).

Allsop CJ and Edelman J in a joint judgment held that as the owners were not party to the bunker supply contract, that contract could not create a maritime lien in relation to the vessel which binds its owners. The lex causae was not the law of the contract, but either the law of Hong Kong (where the vessel was flagged or registered), Turkey (where bunkers were supplied) or Australia (where the vessel was arrested). As there was no evidence of the former two, it was presumed they were the same as the latter, the law of the forum. However, Australian law did not recognise a maritime lien arising from the supply of necessaries, including bunkers, to a ship. Section 15 of the AA 1988 would only characterise a foreign right as a maritime lien if it was, or was closely analogous to, a maritime lien which would be recognised by Australian law. There were reasons of construction of the AA 1988, principle and policy, why Australian law should follow the long established English approach in *The Halycon Isle*.[82]

[76] ibid.
[77] *Kim v Daebo International Shipping Co Ltd* [2015] FCA 684, (2015) 232 FCR 275.
[78] *Hur v Samsun Logix Corp* [2015] FCA 1154, (2015) 238 FCR 483.
[79] *Yakushiji v Daiichi Chuo Kisen Kaisha* [2015] FCA 1170, (2015) 333 ALR 513.
[80] *The Ship Sam Hawk v Reiter Petroleum Inc* [2016] FCAFC 26, (2016) 246 FCR 337. See further ch 4.
[81] ibid.
[82] *Bankers Trust International Ltd v Todd Shipyards Corporation (The Halcyon Isle)* [1981] AC 221.

In *Yu*[83] the recognition of the Korean insolvency proceedings was fairly straightforward. The question before Buchanan J was whether 'additional orders' should be granted to supplement statutory consequences automatically arising after recognition was granted,[84] namely, whether maritime claimants should be able to exercise their in rem rights by arresting a ship in Australia. Buchanan J explained that a proceeding on a maritime lien in respect of a ship or other property subject to the lien may be commenced as an action in rem against the ship under s 15 of the AA 1988. Such a claim enforces a pre-existing security that was created at the time of the occurrence of the event from which the lien arose, unlike a proceeding in rem on a general maritime claim.[85] Rares J pointed out in *Kim*[86] that international maritime law developed by sea trading nations over millennia protect the interests of those who trade or have encounters with a peripatetic ship and those interested in the ship, which may never again call into a port of the creditor's own jurisdiction. He added that it could not be the intention of Parliament, when giving the Model Law the force of law in Australia, to 'supervene' or 'impliedly repeal' the AA 1988 in respect of maritime creditors' rights to proceed in rem on a secured or proprietary claim that pre-existed any interim or final orders recognising a foreign insolvency proceeding under arts 19 or 20 of the Model Law.[87] Thus, a person with a maritime lien is someone within s 471C of the CA 2001 and is thus excluded from an automatic stay in art 20 of the Model Law.[88]

Soon after filing his Singapore application in *Re Taisoo Suk*,[89] Mr Suk applied for recognition of Hanjin's Korean rehabilitation proceedings in New South Wales, Australia. In *Tai-Soo Suk v Hanjin Shipping Co Ltd*[90] Jagot J granted on an ex parte basis recognition of the Korean proceedings as a 'foreign main proceeding' and Mr Suk as the foreign representative as well as further consequential relief. Notably, this time the stay and suspension of enforcement and insolvency proceedings were the same as that under s 440D of the CA 2001,[91] as the Korean rehabilitation proceedings were considered to resemble most closely a voluntary administration under Pt 5.3A of the CA 2001. Article 20(2) of the Model Law was held to impose a duty on the court to identify the

[83] *Yu* (n 75).

[84] Orders under art 19 of the Model Law – relief that may be granted upon application for recognition of a foreign proceeding – had been granted, but this would cease once recognition was granted.

[85] *Yu* (n 75) [40] ff.

[86] *Kim* (n 77).

[87] ibid [14].

[88] See *Hur* (n 78) [31]–[32].

[89] *Re Taisoo Suk* (n 48).

[90] *Tai-Soo Suk v Hanjin Shipping Co Ltd* [2016] FCA 1404.

[91] Section 440D provides:

Stay of proceedings

(1) During the administration of a company, a proceeding in a court against the company or in relation to any of its property cannot be begun or proceeded with, except:

(a) with the administrator's written consent; or
(b) with the leave of the Court and in accordance with such terms (if any) as the Court imposes.

(2) Subsection (1) does not apply to:

(a) a criminal proceeding; or
(b) a prescribed proceeding.

type of proceedings under Chapter 5 of the CA 2001 which the foreign proceedings most closely resembled.[92]

Section 440D of the CA 2001 was held not to exclude actions under a maritime lien. What remains controversial is statutory claims in rem made pursuant to the AA 1988 and in rem actions that have been filed prior to insolvency. Once filed and before any stay came into effect, they are treated as a form of secured claims (or a 'quasi security' according to Allsop CJ).[93] Whether they amount to a secured claim within the meaning of s 471C of the CA 2001 is a live issue in Australia to be resolved.[94]

In *Yakushiji*[95] Japanese civil rehabilitation proceedings were recognised as the main foreign proceedings. The Japanese proceedings focused on reordering the arrangements under a number of long-term charters, excluding secured creditors. Allsop CJ made the point that the protection to a shipping company given by court orders under the Model Law should not be seen as necessarily defeating proper maritime claims that are lien claims, and the question of the status of any statutory lien (or 'quasi lien') claims would need to be resolved in litigation unless the matter were agreed.[96] He went on to observe that it would be wrong to make orders now that would forestall any vindication by such claimants against the interests of the rehabilitation. Likewise, it would be wrong to prevent the rehabilitation being supported by the CBIA 2008 on the mere possibility of the existence of these claims.[97] Academics have taken the view that this case supports the proposition that an admiralty claimant who proceeds in rem is a secured claimant for the purposes of subsequent insolvency proceedings.[98]

B. Singapore Perspective

The Singapore position of a person with a right to proceed on a maritime lien in rem under the HCAJA is expected to be the same as the position in Australia. As regards the rights of statutory in rem claimants, three Singapore decisions are instructive. First, *Lim Bock Lai v Selco (Singapore) Pte Ltd*.[99] The plaintiffs in that case had sought leave under s 262(3) of the Companies Act to continue to pursue three in rem writs for unpaid bunkers that had been filed and issued, but not served, before the commencement of winding-up proceedings. Lai Kew Chai J referred to the English Court of Appeal decision in *Re Aro Co Ltd*[100] which stated that the plaintiffs' position immediately before the presentation

[92] In *Suk v Hanjin Shipping Co Ltd* [2017] FCA 404 Jagot J vacated her previous orders protecting Hanjin's assets in Australia as Suk had failed to inform the court of a substantial change in circumstances as required by art 18 of the Model Law, namely, that on 2 February 2017 rehabilitation proceedings had been terminated and Hanjin had been declared bankrupt. Jagot J stated that Australian creditors should not be prejudiced by a contravention of the Model Law.

[93] *Yakushiji* (n 79) [20].

[94] ibid.

[95] *Yakushiji* (n 79).

[96] ibid [21].

[97] ibid.

[98] Martin Davies, 'Cross-Border Insolvency and Admiralty: A Middle Path of Reciprocal Comity' (2018) 66 *Am J Comp L* 101.

[99] *Lim Bock Lai v Selco (Singapore) Pte Ltd* [1987] SGHC 35, [1987] SLR(R) 466.

[100] *Re Aro Co Ltd* [1980] Ch 196.

of the winding-up petition of an unregistered Liberian shipping company should be tested to see if they could properly assert as against all the world that the vessel *Aro* was security for their claim, not whether they could assert that they had invoked the jurisdiction of the Admiralty Court within the meaning of s 3 of the Administration of Justice Act 1956 (UK):

> If it was correct to say, as was not challenged in the court below and is not challenged in this court, that after the issue of the writ in rem the plaintiffs could serve the writ on the *Aro*, and arrest the *Aro*, in the hands of a transferee from the liquidator and all subsequent transferees, it seems to us difficult to argue that the *Aro* was not effectively encumbered with the plaintiffs' claim.[101]

Thus, the plaintiffs in *Lim Bock Lai*[102] were considered as secured creditors and granted leave to continue their actions in rem. It was irrelevant that these plaintiffs had not invoked the jurisdiction of the admiralty court prior to the winding-up. Lai J stated that the 'issue of a writ in rem in exercise of what has been generally referred to as the statutory right of action in rem has crucial consequences which enure to the benefit of such plaintiffs. Their claims are not affected by any subsequent changes of ownership'.[103] Given their status as secured creditors, the court would ordinarily exercise its discretion to grant leave to proceed with the action.

Secondly, in the Singapore Court of Appeal decision in *The Hull 308*,[104] the in rem writ was issued *after* the petition for the winding-up of the defendant company and no prior leave of court was obtained under s 262(3) of the Companies Act. Thean J (delivering the judgment of the Court of Appeal) accepted that the plaintiffs in *Lim Bok Lai*[105] and *Re Aro Co Ltd*[106] filed their in rem writs against the ships *before* the commencement of the winding-up of the respective owners and the 'plaintiffs could at that point of time "properly assert against all the world" that the ships in question were a security for the claims respectively'.[107] Brightman LJ in *Re Aro Co Ltd*[108] described the plaintiff's right of suit in rem to be similar to those of a legal or equitable mortgagee or chargee, and such persons were entitled in appropriate circumstances to have the subject matter of the charge preserved for their benefit. However, where the plaintiffs had filed the writ in rem *after* the commencement of the winding-up of the defendant company, they could not effectively encumber the ship with their claim, and they could not be considered as secured creditors for the purpose of deciding whether the discretion under s 262(3) should be exercised in their favour.

Thirdly is another Singapore Court of Appeal decision. In *Kuo Fen Ching v Dauphin Offshore Engineering & Trading Pte Ltd*,[109] the respondent arrested the ship based on its claim for materials supplied and works and services performed on the ship. The shipowner was a company incorporated in the Netherlands Antilles. The ship was released after security

[101] ibid [10].
[102] *Lim Bock Lai* (n 99).
[103] ibid [11].
[104] *The Hull 308* [1991] SGCA 34, [1991] 2 SLR(R) 643.
[105] *Lim Bock Lai* (n 99).
[106] *Re Aro Co Ltd* (n 100).
[107] *The Hull 308* (n 104) [13].
[108] *Re Aro Co Ltd* (n 100) 207–08.
[109] *Kuo Fen Ching v Dauphin Offshore Engineering & Trading Pte Ltd* [1999] SGCA 95, [1999] 2 SLR(R) 793.

in the form of a letter of guarantee was provided by Citibank, and the appellant guarantors had provided counter-security in return for Citibank's security. In fact, the owner had been dissolved after it had entered an appearance to the action and filed its defence. The guarantors appealed against the High Court decision[110] that a judgment in rem could be entered despite the fact that the owner had been dissolved.

The High Court accepted that, once the owner entered an appearance in an admiralty action in rem, the owner was effectively the defendant in respect of the action in rem as well as the action in personam, and the two proceedings remained separate.[111] The judge also found on the facts that the repairers had a possessory lien over the vessel for unpaid charges. In addition, the arrest of the ship, before the owner was wound up, created a statutory lien in favour of the respondent on the ship. Thus, the ship remained as security for the respondent's claim and it was suitable to grant leave to proceed against the owner under s 262(3) of the Companies Act.[112]

Without expressly mentioning the inapplicability of s 262(3) of the Companies Act, the Court of Appeal agreed with the judge's finding that the in rem action continues to proceed against the res even though the real party to the action is the shipowner.[113] The Court of Appeal noted that one of the main advantages of an admiralty action in rem is that the plaintiff's claim is secured before judgment is obtained in an action in rem. More importantly, with security obtained before judgment, satisfaction of the plaintiff's claim will not be hampered by any intervening financial impecuniosity which may embarrass the shipowner.[114] Once a vessel is arrested, the ship, or the security provided in lieu of it, represents pre-judgment security and the respondent becomes a secured creditor of the owner of the vessel,[115] as held in *Re Aro Co Ltd*.[116] This entitles the plaintiff to arrest and detain the ship and, if the court adjudicates in its favour, to a judicial sale and satisfaction of its claim out of the proceeds of sale. Only in an admiralty court-ordered sale by the Sheriff is the ship sold free of all liens and encumbrances so that the purchaser takes a completely clean title.[117] A sale by the liquidator does not have this effect. Accordingly, a higher price is more likely to be realised by the Sheriff in a court-ordered sale.

Further, in cases such as *Kuo Fen Ching*,[118] where release from arrest was via security provided by a third party, a bank or a P&I Club, there is no actual claim against the insolvent company's assets, and therefore no reason why such secured claims cannot take full effect. This is especially since the interests of the insolvent company's creditors are not affected.

I mentioned earlier that the Court of Appeal in *Beluga Chartering GmbH*[119] had observed that commencement of foreign insolvency proceedings should not preclude the commencement of proceedings or the attempted execution of a judgment in Singapore. Nor should the existence of foreign insolvency proceedings stop the issuance of in rem

[110] *The Capricorn* [1998] SGHC 366, [1998] 3 SLR(R) 822.
[111] ibid [9].
[112] ibid [17].
[113] *Kuo Fen Ching* (n 97) [24].
[114] ibid [26]. See further ch 3.
[115] ibid [28].
[116] *Re Aro Co Ltd* (n 100).
[117] *Kuo Fen Ching* (n 109) [28], [32]–[33].
[118] ibid [1], [4].
[119] *Beluga Chartering GmbH* (n 12).

proceedings or arrest of the ship. Karthigesu JA stated in *Kuo Fen Ching*[120] that even the dissolution of the shipowner would not defeat the plaintiff's claim or the granting of a judgment in rem in the plaintiff's favour. To rule otherwise

> would result in an astounding loophole and defeat the purpose of the admiralty *in rem* action being a means of providing a prejudgment security for a plaintiff with a claim against the ship. This is so especially after the statutory lien has accrued against the vessel before the owners have been wound up or dissolved.[121]

In the context of Singapore admiralty law, the arrest and subsequent sale of a ship is not characterised as a process of execution. Thean J in *The Daien Maru No 18*[122] explained that an execution proceeding is to enforce a monetary judgment in personam.[123] In contrast, a judgment in rem is against the res and such a judgment can be enforced against the res by a remedy in rem. The arrest of the ship is to obtain security for the judgment. Thean J held that an in rem claimant who sued in rem and obtained a judgment for his claim can still assert that the ship is security for the judgment obtained and is therefore entitled to arrest the ship provided no bail or other guarantee has been previously put up. The right to security in the ship (enforced by an arrest of the ship) is not lost or extinguished by the merger of the claim in the judgment obtained in the action.[124] In the context of domestic insolvency proceedings, although leave of the court to proceed in the admiralty jurisdiction after a winding-up order is made is required, the right to proceed to arrest a ship should be forthcoming.

To summarise, recognition of the foreign insolvency proceedings as 'foreign main proceedings' under art (20)(a) would not affect in rem creditors' rights. The implementation of the Model Law only alters the procedure by which a Singapore court extends assistance to a foreign representative or foreign office-holder; there is no change to the content of Singapore's winding-up regime or even our private international law which applies in cross-border insolvency.[125]

Equally, there is no change to our admiralty law. In rem creditors like maritime lien holders and others whose in rem rights are derived from the HCAJA and have taken steps to file their in rem writs early enough are essentially distinguishable from the company's general body of creditors. They are regarded as secured claimants in admiralty proceedings against that one and only asset to which they must look to satisfy their claims according to admiralty's order of priorities. Admiralty creditors are thus unique in this sense. Generally, the amendments to the Companies Act should not change the status of the secured creditors in admiralty proceedings.[126] Section 262(3) applies in liquidation proceedings under Singapore's Companies Act.

Furthermore, the Model Law's moratorium is limited to the debtor's property, rights, obligations or liabilities. In this regard, first, the Model Law does not apply to

[120] *Kuo Fen Ching* (n 109).
[121] ibid [33].
[122] *The Daien Maru No 18* [1984] SGHC 43, [1983–1984] SLR(R) 787.
[123] ibid [14].
[124] ibid [16].
[125] *UNCITRAL Model Law on Cross-Border Insolvency with Guide to Enactment and Interpretation* (n 2) para 3.
[126] However, see Part V below, and in particular the discussion of s 211E.

group enterprises. There is no provision in the Model Law dealing with cross-border enterprises comprised of multiple entities. In the shipping industry, one-ship companies are commonly recognised as a legitimate way of managing business risk. This single ship ownership structure feeds into the scope of the foreign moratorium order, and an examination of the foreign order is a must. If the foreign order extends to the debtor's related entities, there is an over-reach which is contrary to the Model Law. Secondly, in so far as Singapore is concerned, the separate entity doctrine still applies in insolvencies. Hence, the single economic entity concept has no place in Singapore and again, under the Model Law, any foreign moratorium order that seeks to extend the foreign moratorium over assets of related entities in the jurisdiction is an over-reach that is contrary to Singapore law and should not be recognised. These two points are developed later.[127]

V. Section 211 Moratoriums and the In Rem Creditor in Admiralty

Where creditors' schemes of arrangement are in place, an automatic 30-day moratorium (with worldwide effect that extends to debtors' related entities, whether in Singapore or not; in other words, subsidiaries and holding companies may also apply for a moratorium)[128] kicks in. This debt restructuring regime is new. Section 211B of the Companies Act now protects companies in schemes of arrangement from legal action:

> Where a company proposes, or intends to propose, a compromise or an arrangement between the company and its creditors or any class of those creditors, the Court may, on the application of the company, make one or more of the following orders, each of which is in force for such period as the Court thinks fit: …
>
> (c) an order restraining the commencement or continuation of any proceedings (other than proceedings under this section or section 210, 211D, 211G, 211H or 212) against the company, except with the leave of the Court and subject to such terms as the Court imposes;
>
> (d) an order restraining the commencement, continuation or levying of any execution, distress or other legal process against any property of the company, except with the leave of the Court and subject to such terms as the Court imposes;
>
> (e) an order restraining the taking of any step to enforce any security over any property of the company, or to repossess any goods held by the company under any chattels leasing agreement, hire-purchase agreement or retention of title agreement, except with the leave of the Court and subject to such terms as the Court imposes;

Upon closer scrutiny, the provision may not be a bar to admiralty action for the following reasons:

(1) Section 211B(1)(c) refers to 'proceedings … against the company'[129] (seemingly the phraseology expressly tracks the language in Chapter 15 of the US Bankruptcy Code

[127] See Parts VII and VIII below.

[128] See s 211B.

[129] And similarly s 211C(1)(c).

that has been used to recognise schemes of arrangement)[130] but in rem actions are against the vessel, the asset of the company rather than the company itself;

(2) s 211B(1)(d) refers to 'levying of any execution, distress',[131] and thus the words 'other legal process' ought to be read eiusdem generis to refer to similar legal processes like garnishee proceedings. Arrest clearly falls out of this scope on the authority of *The Daien Maru No 18*;[132] and

(3) Section 211B(1)(e), while referring to 'taking of any step to enforce any security over any property of the company',[133] is restricted to chattels leasing, hire-purchase or retention of title agreements only.

Even though a debtor company can under s 211C seek an extension of the moratorium against actions over vessels owned by the debtor's related companies, the wording of s 211C gives rise to the same constraints as explained above in respect of subsections 211B(1)(c),(d) and (e).

The introduction of new rescue financing provisions in the Act (s 211E for schemes of arrangement and s 227HA for judicial management) allows the court to treat the rescue financing as part of the costs and expenses of winding-up or to grant the rescue financier priority over all other creditors' claims (preferential and unsecured debts). If super priority for rescue financing is granted under either provision, in rem claims may be affected by the definition of 'security interest' in s 211E(9) and s 227HA(10) that includes a 'lien'. This terminology encompasses liens that are contractual, statutory or derived from common law.

An attempt to obtain super priority under s 211E(1)(a) and (b) failed on the facts in *Re Attilan Group Ltd*[134] as the court held there had been insufficient evidence of reasonable efforts expended to secure financing without any super priority. Super priority disrupts the expected order of priority and the courts should be slow to grant such status unless strictly necessary.

VI. Other Issues Arising from the 2017 Amendments

While the amendments to the Companies Act contain carve-outs for specified companies[135] and certain arrangements,[136] there is currently no express carve-out for admiralty and maritime claims, similar to the position in the US and the UK. The rationale behind this is that there is no change in the law except where super priority is invoked.

Arguably, an express carve-out of in rem claims to avoid unnecessary litigation should logically follow, having regard to the special features that inure to the advantage of the

[130] See 11 USC Ch 15: Ancillary and Other Cross-Border Cases.

[131] And similarly s 211C(1)(d).

[132] *The Daien Maru No 18* (n 122).

[133] And similarly s 211C(1)(e).

[134] *Re Attilan Group Ltd* [2017] SGHC 283, [2018] 3 SLR 898.

[135] Banks and financial institutions under rules to protect consumer deposits and special purpose vehicles for approved securitisation transactions and covered bonds: see Companies (Prescribed Companies and Entities) Order 2017.

[136] Derivative transactions in relation to closeout netting: see Companies (Prescribed Arrangements) Regulations 2017.

maritime lien holder and in rem creditors with protective in rem writs. A carve-out of in rem claims as described is a matter of admiralty jurisdiction rather than discretion and provides simplicity, clarity, predictability and promotes coherence between the laws of admiralty and insolvency. There is no confusion that such rights in rem are protected from any moratorium which may arise under the main foreign proceedings. Their right of security and priority can only be enforced by maritime proceedings and not the insolvency court. There is also a close relationship between the jurisdiction to arrest and priorities of in rem claims. Both matters are governed by Singapore law as the lex fori. In principle, for such cases, there is no unfairness in further tweaking the principle of modified universalism.

I now discuss another controversial case in Singapore law, *The STX Mumbai*,[137] to reinforce the jurisdictional argument that in rem claimants are essentially outside the scope of the Model Law and the recent changes to the Companies Act. Interestingly, the group owner obtained a bankruptcy order from the Seoul Central District Court on 7 June 2013 which pre-dated the arrest of the *STX Mumbai* on 14 June 2013.[138] The point of controversy in the decision is the proposition that the foreign insolvency of a group owner could amount to an anticipatory breach to give rise to a cause of action against the registered ship owner. The jurisdictional argument here has to do with the principle of separate legal entity and the absence of provisions in the Model Law that extend to subsidiaries, affiliates and associates. In the context of admiralty jurisprudence, the separate legal entity regime is almost inextricably linked to the special purpose vehicles set up to own individual ships.

A. *The STX Mumbai*

In 2014 the arrest of the *STX Mumbai*, a casualty of the STX Pan Ocean Pte Ltd (STX Pan Ocean) collapse, challenged the application of the traditional rules of contract and company law in the context of admiralty and insolvency principles.

The respondent was the registered owner of the *STX Mumbai*. The appellant claimed the price of bunkers supplied to the vessel pursuant to a bunker supply agreement concluded by STX Corporation, acting as agent for the respondent. Three days before payment was due, the appellant, via an email after office hours, demanded immediate payment of the bunker invoices and addressed it to STX Corporation and the respondent but only sent it to STX Corporation in Seoul. No payment was received, so the very next morning the appellant issued in rem proceedings and arrested the vessel that same afternoon.[139] The vessel was released eight days later after security was provided. The demand for accelerated payment was made on the basis that the bunker supply contract had been repudiated by the respondent's anticipatory breach, namely, the respondent had evinced a clear intention to renounce the contract by refusing to comply with the letter of demand. Alternatively, with STX Pan Ocean filing for bankruptcy protection in South Korea, circumstances were such that it was impossible for the respondent to make payment on the due date. The appellant primarily relied on the poor financial health of the STX group of companies that the respondent was

[137] *The STX Mumbai* [2014] SGHC 122, [2014] 3 SLR 1116 (*The STX Mumbai* HC); *The STX Mumbai* [2015] SGCA 35, [2015] 5 SLR 1 (*The STX Mumbai* CA).

[138] See *The STX Mumbai* HC (n 137) [9]; *The STX Mumbai* CA (n 137) [14].

[139] For a discussion of the wrongful arrest aspect of this case, see ch 6.

part of, in particular, the insolvency of STX Pan Ocean, which was named as the 'group owner' of the vessel. The respondent applied to strike out the in rem action and set aside the warrant of arrest, and succeeded before the assistant registrar, whose decision was upheld on appeal to the High Court.[140]

However, a five-member Court of Appeal allowed the appellant's appeal.[141] New arguments and fresh evidence on the appellant's standard terms and conditions were adduced as the respondent's counsel did not object. The appellant submitted that, on a true interpretation of the relevant clause in its standard terms and conditions, they were in fact entitled to receive payment on the date of the arrest itself and so, in the absence of contrary evidence, it was virtually impossible for timely payment to have been made. While the crux of the appellant's case remained premised on the doctrine of anticipatory breach, the focus now shifted to the ground of impossibility of performance by the respondent.[142]

Two key issues were before the Court of Appeal. On the first, Phang JA found that it was just and fair for the doctrine of anticipatory breach to apply to both executory and executed contracts. A key consideration was the conduct of the defendant. If the defendant evinced a clear intention that it would not perform its obligations under the contract, then it was only just and fair that the plaintiff be permitted, in law, to rescind the contract or claim damages on the basis of an anticipatory breach of contract, regardless of whether the contract was executed or executory.[143]

The second issue was whether the insolvency of the 'group owner' could amount to an anticipatory breach, though insolvency, of itself, could not amount to an anticipatory breach. Phang JA held that everything would ultimately fall to be determined on the precise facts of each case. The defendant's insolvency, viewed in its proper context, might well be found to constitute an anticipatory breach.[144]

Adopting a 'practical sphere of application',[145] Phang JA found that the evidence the appellant relied on pointed to 'some plausible connection between STX Pan Ocean and the respondent' such that, at the striking out stage, it was arguable that the former's insolvency could make it impossible for the latter to make timely payments under the bunker supply contract.[146]

However, Phang JA noted that, ultimately, this would be a finding of fact by the trial judge. At this striking out stage, the appellate court was satisfied that the appellant's case as based on the insolvency of STX Pan Ocean was legally sustainable when considered in light of the factual assertions made.

VII. Legitimacy of One-Ship Companies

The Court of Appeal's decision in *The STX Mumbai*[147] presents uncertainties as the Court was willing to consider evidence pointing to a single economic entity, and in the process to

[140] *The STX Mumbai* HC (n 137) [75].
[141] *The STX Mumbai* CA (n 137) [96].
[142] ibid [4].
[143] ibid [40]–[78].
[144] ibid [79]–[89].
[145] ibid [85].
[146] ibid [86].
[147] *The STX Mumbai* CA (n 137).

side-step the traditional and fundamental one-ship company business model. The use of the single purpose entity for tax, governance or limitation of liability reasons is a legitimate way to conduct business in multiple jurisdictions as a single entity. In *The Skaw Prince*[148] the High Court stated:

> It is well known that businesses engaged in shipping set up and utilise one-ship companies within their corporate structure for the purpose of limiting liability. The device has been around and recognised by the courts as a legitimate one and the court's view has been that the court will not lift the corporate veil unless the circumstances are exceptional.[149]

One-ship companies may be incorporated in 'flag of convenience' states and centrally managed from the true place of business for fiscal or other reasons. The fact that a one-ship company is being managed by its ultimate parent is not evidence that it has no separate existence. It is quite normal for companies in a group to use inter-group finance or even a central treasury. Further, the fact that intra-group loans are interest free and unsecured is unsurprising and would not be the basis for piercing the corporate veil.[150] In *Public Prosecutor v Lew Syn Pau*[151] Sundaresh Menon JC (as he then was) held that the separate entity principle was not displaced even if the companies within a group are organised as a single economic entity.

In the admiralty court, piercing of the corporate veil is permitted only in exceptional cases where justice requires the court to do so and this is where there is cogent evidence of fraud or dishonesty, or of a nominee holding, trust or agency relationship.[152]

Nevertheless, the Court of Appeal's decision in *The STX Mumbai*[153] effectively states that, without lifting the corporate veil, evidence of the poor financial health of a group of companies, in particular, the evidence of the insolvency of the 'group owner', was sufficient to ground an assertion of anticipatory breach, namely, the inability to make good a debt, of a *separate* entity within the group. The question of when insolvency may form a basis for repudiation is now dependent on a proper appreciation of the factual matrix within which the insolvency occurs.

To some, Phang JA's decision perhaps represents judicial innovation in accepting commercial realities when dealing with the insolvency of cross-border corporate groups, a step towards achieving a global solution for cross-border corporate group insolvencies. In the Australian *Hanjin* recognition proceedings[154] Jagot J also extended her earlier prohibition of enforcement or recovery actions against the *Hanjin Milano* without leave of the court, until the determination of the recognition application. This was despite the fact that the *Hanjin Milano* was not beneficially owned by Hanjin.

The extension of moratoriums to the debtor company's related entities, namely its 'subsidiary, holding company or ultimate holding company' under s 211C appears to be

[148] *The Skaw Prince* [1994] SGHC 18, [1994] 3 SLR (R) 146.
[149] ibid [19].
[150] Aleka Mandaraka-Sheppard, *Modern Maritime Law, Volume 1: Jurisdiction and Risks*, 3rd edn (Abingdon, Informa Law from Routledge, 2013) 135.
[151] *Public Prosecutor v Lew Syn Pau* [2006] SGHC 146, [2006] 4 SLR(R) 210.
[152] Mandaraka-Sheppard (n 150) 135.
[153] *The STX Mumbai* CA (n 137).
[154] *Tai-Soo Suk* (n 90).

aligned with Phang JA's 'practical' outlook. The moratorium becomes a powerful tool in cross-border multi enterprise group restructurings. However, such liberal extensions would clearly erode the foundations upon which one-ship companies were established, with detrimental effects on the shipping industry.

VIII. Issues in Cross-Border Multiple Enterprise Group Insolvencies

One school of thought is that judicial incursion into the separate entity doctrine in fact reduces inefficiencies in the form of transaction costs in the case of multinational group insolvencies.[155] This dovetails with the universalist view that the insolvency of global multinational enterprises should be subject to a single proceeding responsible for disbursing assets to all claimants. There have been calls to look at the economic realities and to treat the multinational COMI debtor with overseas subsidiaries, associates and affiliates as one single entity. At present, there are no global laws to regulate the insolvency of such groups of corporations where one or more entities within the group are situated in different countries.

While we have global efforts to resolve cross-border insolvencies of *single* entities through the Model Law, it has no provisions to deal with cross-border enterprises comprised of multiple entities, as is typical with shipowners. The decision of *Re Taisoo Suk*[156] suffers from this over-reach.

Some countries have attempted to address these issues. In Australia, responses to group insolvency include amendments to the CA 2001 to make parent companies liable for the debts of subsidiaries in certain circumstances[157] and for group assets to be pooled[158] to pay creditors of one subsidiary where the court is 'satisfied that it was just'.[159] Similarly, New Zealand legislation allows the court to make a contribution order on broad grounds in the case of the insolvency of a related company and also provides for pooling orders in respect of insolvent related companies, where the court is satisfied that it is 'just and equitable to do so'.[160]

The United States has substantive consolidation which is driven by the courts based on the Bankruptcy Court's general powers in s 105 of the Bankruptcy Code.[161] That power is derived from an equitable background and the court is therefore guided by what is just and equitable in the circumstances.[162] The European Union Insolvency Regulation[163] addresses

[155] Sandeep Gopalan and Michael Guihot, 'Cross-Border Insolvency Law and Multinational Enterprise Groups: Judicial Innovation as an International Solution' (2016) 48 *George Washington International Law Review* 549, 555.

[156] *Re Taisoo Suk* (n 48).

[157] CA 2001, s 588V makes the holding company liable for the subsidiary's insolvent trading if the company was aware or should have been aware that the subsidiary was trading while insolvent.

[158] ibid s 579E.

[159] ibid s 579E(1).

[160] Sections 271 and 272 of the Companies Act 1993 (NZ).

[161] See 11 USC § 105(a).

[162] What the court will order is 'substantive consolidation', which is that the assets and liabilities of different entities are consolidated and treated as one entity. The consolidated assets create one fund from which all of the claims against the consolidated debtors are satisfied.

[163] Regulation (EU) 2015/848 (n 39), arts 56–77.

the issue of insolvent group of companies with group members in various member states via modest first steps in coordinating and communicating insolvencies, but has not yet taken the next step to regulate the consolidating of group insolvencies.

Whilst Phang JA opened a portal for pragmatic incursion into the separate entity doctrine, this may have been an aberration. In so far as Singapore is concerned, the separate entity doctrine still applies in insolvencies, with the likelihood that multiple courts will administer the assets of enterprises based on their locations. In *Manuchar Steel Hong Kong Ltd v Star Pacific Line Pte Ltd*[164] Lee Kim Shin JC stated that the single economic entity concept had no place in Singapore:

> If the single economic entity concept were accepted, all such one-ship companies would be considered as part of the same single economic entity with the corollary that the liability of a one-ship company may be visited on several (or all) of its other one-ship sister companies. The existence of abusive conduct becomes irrelevant because liability can be established by the mere fact of the existence of a group structure; the piercing of the corporate veil exception would not even be needed. In short, there would be no place for the survival of the one-ship companies practice and doctrine which has long existed and [been] recognised as a legitimate tool for limiting liability.[165]

Thus, the settled rule is that each entity is responsible for its own debts in insolvency proceedings, and any change is a matter for the legislature. This was most recently confirmed in *Re Zetta Jet Pte Ltd.*[166] It is arguable that the Companies Act has not attempted any such change in the new section 211C. If anything, an indirect change in the scheme of arrangement regime is in the form of the court's power to restrain proceedings against a debtor company's related entities. The purpose is to extend the scope of the moratorium available to related entities of the debtor company. There is no 'pooling of assets' as such.

It cannot be disputed that co-operation and co-ordination are important goals for any effective and successful rehabilitation proceedings. However, the doctrine of separate entity is the bedrock of corporate law. Hence, the tension between the two will have to be managed pragmatically, founded on initiatives taken outside of the Model Law. I will return to this point later.[167]

IX. COMI Debtor is Unlikely to be Admiralty's 'Beneficial Owner'

Overlaying the notion of lifting the corporate veil in order to look behind the separate entity is the other unique concept of the 'beneficial owner of all the shares in the ship' under the HCAJA. This 'beneficial owner' is usually the person who would be liable on the statutory maritime claim. In admiralty law, ownership of a ship is denoted by the concept of the owner of the shares in a ship and this is a statutory jurisdictional requirement that is important to the arrest of the relevant ship or sister ship. A statutory in rem creditor cannot ignore

[164] *Manuchar Steel Hong Kong Ltd v Star Pacific Line Pte Ltd* [2014] SGHC 181, [2014] 4 SLR 832.
[165] ibid [133].
[166] *Re Zetta Jet Pte Ltd* [2018] SGHC 16, [2018] 4 SLR 801.
[167] See Part X below.

the reality of separate corporate entities. A subsidiary company and a parent company are two separate entities and even the full control of the subsidiary by the parent company does not lead to the conclusion that the asset of the subsidiary belongs to the parent company. A right of control is insufficient to prove beneficial ownership in the shares of the ship, and despite the difficulty faced by an arresting party in cases of one-ship companies, the court will not ordinarily lift the corporate veil. The COMI debtor, through its control of the one-ship companies, is not the 'beneficial owner of all the shares in the ship'. A shareholder of a company does not have property, legal or equitable, in the assets of the company. It is not the beneficial owner of the ship, who can be a separate and distinct legal entity or person from the shareholder-owner of the company. The recognition of the insolvency of the COMI debtor should therefore not affect the status of one-ship companies. At the same time, the COMI of a shipholding company, usually flag of convenience states, will not necessarily be a jurisdiction that is competent to provide an effective liquidation of the company.

In *The Min Rui*[168] the High Court accepted that the entity registered as owner of a ship is not necessarily the beneficial owner of the ship. Whilst there is no rule in Singapore that the registered ownership of a ship is always co-extensive with beneficial ownership for the purpose of arrest under s 4(4) of the HCAJA, the ship's register is a useful starting point, and cogent evidence is needed to show that someone else is the beneficial owner within the meaning of s 4(4) of the HCAJA.

The issue of beneficial ownership is further muddied by the House of Lords decision in *Ayerst v C & K (Construction) Ltd*[169] where it was held that, by virtue of the statutory trust that comes into existence on the making of a winding-up order, a company loses all custody and control of its property, and all powers of dealing with the company's assets are transferred to the liquidator, who is bound to act in accordance with the statutory scheme in the Act. This would thwart in rem claims against assets which were the subject of insolvency.

This position has been rejected in Australia and Hong Kong. In *Federal Commissioner of Taxation v Linter Textiles Australia Ltd (in liquidation)*[170] the majority of the High Court of Australia held that

> the circumscribing or suspension by reason of the appointment of the liquidator of the exercise by the usual organs of the company of the incidents of ownership of the assets of the company does not mean that the company itself has ceased to own beneficially its assets … . Power to deal with an asset and matters of ownership or title are not interchangeable concepts.[171]

An insolvent company's assets remained under its beneficial ownership. It was only that, as a result of insolvency, the company's assets came to be 'administered' for the benefit of its creditors.

Hong Kong has yet to sign on to the Model Law. In *The Convenience Container*[172] the shipowner, Powick, had been wound up in Singapore, then four of its vessels were arrested in Hong Kong and sold by the Admiralty Court. There were in fact seven in rem actions

[168] *The Min Rui* [2016] SGHC 183, [2016] 5 SLR 667.

[169] *Ayerst v C & K (Construction) Ltd* [1976] AC 167.

[170] *Federal Commissioner of Taxation v Linter Textiles Australia Ltd (in liquidation)* [2005] HCA 20, (2005) 220 CLR 592.

[171] ibid 613 (Gleeson CJ, Gummow, Hayne, Callinan and Heydon JJ).

[172] *Rudolf A Oetker KG v The Owners and/or Demise Charterers of the Ship or Vessel Convenience Container (The Convenience Container)* [2006] HKCFI 556, [2006] 4 HKC 435.

instituted in Hong Kong after liquidation in Singapore. Powick relied on *Ayerst*[173] to argue that the winding-up of the company divested it of beneficial interest in the ships. The Hong Kong Court of Appeal,[174] agreeing with the judge at first instance, refused to set aside the in rem writs, holding that *Ayerst*[175] was distinguishable as it deal with tax statutes, which were irrelevant in this case. One of the former appeal judges who decided the case now doubts the correctness of his decision in light of the current adoption of the principle of modified universalism by the Hong Kong courts, and its obvious consequence.[176] Reyes J (as he then was) had found that beneficial ownership of the vessels remained with Powick, based on the finding that registration under the owner's name is 'virtually conclusive', but he now reflects that the 'beneficial owner' as required under the admiralty statute must entail something more than simply the ability to sell and pass good title to the vessel. Instead, the identity of the 'beneficial owner' is a question of fact determined on the totality of evidence. Given the principle of modified universalism, Powick in liquidation was possibly different from Powick as a going concern.[177]

In Singapore, a statutory trust only arises upon the making of a winding-up order, and not when a winding-up application is filed. The statutory trust does not confer beneficial or proprietary interests on the unsecured creditors, and in Lord Diplock's words in *Ayerst*:[178]

> the effect of the statute was to give to the property of a company in liquidation that essential characteristic which distinguished trust property from other property, viz., that it could not be used or disposed of by the legal owner for his own benefit, but must be used or disposed of for the benefit of other persons.[179]

Where in rem claims are concerned, the decision in *Lim Bock Lai*[180] has clearly stated that these claims are unaffected by subsequent changes in ownership once the in rem writ had been issued prior to insolvency. As I have posited earlier, the status of admiralty actions remains unchanged despite the adoption of the Model Law.

X. Communication and Co-operation in a Cross-Border Insolvency

In the single restructuring of a large single entity, Prof Martin Davies has argued that the conflict between insolvency law and admiralty law need not result in one body of law prevailing over the other. He advocates for a middle path that achieves the main goal of universalism, which means recognising the primacy of the insolvency proceedings, while also preserving the rights of maritime claimants to secure their claims by proceeding

[173] *Ayerst* (n 169).

[174] *Rudolf A Oetker KG v The Owners and/or Demise Charterers of the Ship or Vessel Convenience Container (The Convenience Container)* [2007] HKCA 305, [2007] 4 HKC 484.

[175] *Ayerst* (n 169).

[176] Anselmo Reyes, 'Cross-Border Insolvency and Shipping Companies' [2016] *LMCLQ* 517.

[177] ibid 521–22.

[178] *Ayerst* (n 169).

[179] ibid 180F, cited in *Media Development Authority of Singapore v Sculptor Finance (MD) Ireland Ltd* [2013] SGCA 58, [2014] 1 SLR 733 [52].

[180] *Lim Bock Lai* (n 99).

against the debtor's assets. This middle path is grounded on notions of comity and demands that the country where the ship is arrested under its lex fori must recognise the primacy of insolvency proceedings in the debtor's COMI. Reciprocity demands that the country of the insolvency proceedings recognise and respect the legitimacy of the admiralty arrest. Reciprocity would require the debtor's COMI to grant the admiralty claimants the same secured status in the insolvency proceedings.[181] In Singapore, there would be no need for this middle path since the view I hold is that the Model Law has no material impact on in rem claims here.

This co-operation outlined above is really not different from a group plan involving inter-related plans because of multiple companies in the restructuring. It is apposite here that I mention the initiatives of the Judicial Insolvency Network (JIN) since 2016.[182]

Whether there is a single company restructuring or a group plan where various satellite proceedings may happen, the JIN Cross-Border Co-operation Guidelines (JIN Guidelines)[183] are intended to facilitate communication and co-operation in a cross-border restructuring. If the main restructuring is in Singapore, the master restructuring plan would be developed here and the Singapore court would co-ordinate the various satellite proceedings involving the inter-related satellite plans.

These Guidelines were the fruits of JIN's inaugural meeting in Singapore in October 2016 attended by 11 judges from the Southern District of New York, Delaware, England and Wales, Australia, Bermuda, the Cayman Islands, the British Virgin Islands, Ontario, Canada, Hong Kong (as an observer) and Singapore. They cover a wide range of matters including joint case management of cross-border insolvencies, the use of protocols and even the conduct of joint hearings. In short, the JIN Guidelines are intended to help supervising courts and parties by suggesting issues that should be addressed and procedures that could be implemented to make parallel insolvency proceedings more effective.

At the time of writing, 10 of the participating courts have adopted the JIN Guidelines – the United States Bankruptcy Courts for the District of Delaware, the Southern District of New York and the Southern District of Florida, the Supreme Court of Singapore, the Supreme Court of Bermuda, the Chancery Division of England and Wales, the Eastern Caribbean Supreme Court, the Supreme Court Equity Division of New South Wales, the Seoul Bankruptcy Court and the Grand Court of the Cayman Islands.[184]

XI. Conclusion

In summary, in Singapore:

(1) the Court of Appeal decision of *Beluga Chartering GmbH*[185] states that, under common law, foreign winding-up orders (including any foreign winding-up orders to

[181] Davies (n 98).
[182] See jin-global.org.
[183] See jin-global.org/jin-guidelines.html.
[184] See ibid for a copy of the JIN Guidelines as prepared at the inaugural JIN conference in October 2016, and the versions of the JIN Guidelines adopted by the participating courts.
[185] *Beluga Chartering GmbH* (n 12).

stay proceedings in the forum) will not be recognised. However, the Singapore courts could assist foreign liquidation proceedings through the courts' existing procedural powers. This would be on a case by case basis;

(2) the enactment of the Model Law will not affect the rights of secured in rem creditors by virtue of arts 20(2) and 20(3), and protective writs may be filed by virtue of art 20(4) of the Model Law;

(3) on the current wording of the Companies Act, the enhanced scheme of arrangement regime in s 211B should not affect in rem rights;

(4) the Model Law does not deal with single economic entities like subsidiaries, associates and affiliates of the COMI debtor, so the separate entity doctrine prevails;

(5) through the co-operation envisaged by global initiatives such as the JIN network, insolvencies of cross-border single economic entities will be more efficiently and effectively handled.

From the above, it is clear that we need a definitive enactment to clarify that the legislative changes in favour of 'universalism' simply do not have any impact when ships are arrested or are capable of arrest within Singapore's jurisdiction. The tension is palpable – the amendments to the Companies Act favour the rescue of businesses in distress over creditors, contradicting the body of maritime law that protects in rem creditors in the interests of commerce. This is unsurprising since the maritime law that governs international maritime commerce and credit has existed long before 'universalism' emerged in cross-border insolvency. The expectations of shipowners, traders and others in the industry need to be protected for harmonious conduct of international trade and commerce.

10

National Translations of the Arrest Conventions: European Civil Law Jurisdictions

HENNING JESSEN* AND GEORGE THEOCHARIDIS‡

I. Introduction

Focusing on the codified Civil Law approach of most continental European countries, this Chapter discusses ship arrest as a means of attaching property and conserving the status quo for creditors until the merits of the case are heard. General reference will be made to the recently updated German procedural law, as well as to the legal position in Greece. We will focus more specifically on the question of how conservative measures – that is, the institution of ship arrest proceedings – achieve a 'freezing' of assets (that is, the protection and preservation of the status quo) in these European jurisdictions, and how this relates to the subsequent case on the merits. The Chapter concludes with a short discussion of whether traditional Civil Law systems may in future also allow 'Mareva-like' freezing injunctions as an alternative possible means of attachment.

II. Competition between European Civil Law Jurisdictions for Ship Arrests

The European map of the foundation of jurisdiction relating to ship arrest is fragmented and, as such, comparable to other inadequately unified areas of international maritime law. Only certain questions relating to the arrest of ships have been unified by the applicable Conventions. About 20 European countries (this figure includes non-EU states like Norway and Common Law jurisdictions like the United Kingdom) have ratified the International

* Associate Professor of Maritime Law and Policy, World Maritime University, Malmö, Sweden. Unless otherwise stated, English translations of all German sources are by the author.

‡ Professor of Maritime Law and Policy, World Maritime University, Malmö, Sweden. Joint Rapporteur of the CMI International Working Group on Liability for Wrongful Arrest. Unless otherwise stated, English translations of all Greek sources are by the author.

Convention Relating to the Arrest of Sea-Going Ships 1952 (Arrest Convention 1952),[1] which is the primary international instrument in this area. Four EU members (Bulgaria, Estonia, Latvia and Spain) and one non-EU country (Albania) have ratified the International Convention on the Arrest of Ships 1999 (Arrest Convention 1999),[2] which has in practice not resulted in the successful substitution of its predecessor.[3]

Both Arrest Conventions refer the issue of jurisdiction for the adjudication of the case on its merits to the court of the State in which the ship arrest has been effected and security provided by the shipowner to obtain the release of the ship (in other words, the forum arresti: see art 7 in both Arrest Conventions).[4] Further, an understanding of ship arrest almost always necessitates practical knowledge and familiarisation with the domestic laws of the individual arresting State, to be able to answer further questions relating to the mechanics of arrest proceedings. As a consequence, even though more than 50 years have passed since the Arrest Convention 1952 was adopted, there is still vast potential for comparative legal research. For example, the details of the possible liability of a creditor for wrongful arrest (see art 6 in both Arrest Conventions)[5] are still exclusively subject to domestic private law and are currently the subject of new attempts by the Comité Maritime International (CMI) to try to find an international uniform standard on this issue.[6]

It is of particular comparative legal interest to evaluate how a recently updated national legal system (which continues to adhere to the Arrest Convention 1952) has translated the uniform rules on ship arrest into its domestic legal approach to ship arrest proceedings. Generally, apart from aspects of modernisation, legal reforms should always seek to remedy identified weaknesses, pitfalls, loopholes (in other words, lacunae) and obstacles for practice. A good example of this type of reform is to be found in Germany, which – like Turkey and Belgium – has recently reformed its formerly outdated domestic maritime law in a fairly holistic manner. The impact of the reform of German maritime law of 2013 also extends to the applicable procedural rules for ship arrest under German law.[7] This reform

[1] International Convention Relating to the Arrest of Sea-going Ships (adopted 10 May 1952, entered into force 24 February 1956) 439 UNTS 193. The Arrest Convention 1952 was drafted by the Comité Maritime International after several debates held in consecutive Conferences. It was finally approved in 1952 at a Diplomatic Conference held in Brussels with 13 votes in favour. Out of the rich academic literature on the Arrest Convention 1952 see, indicatively, Francesco Berlingieri, *Berlingieri on Arrest of Ships*, 6th edn (Abingdon, Informa Law from Routledge, 2017) vol 1; Antoine M Antapassis, *I Symbasi tou 1952 gia tin Syntiritiki Katasxesi Plion/The Convention of 1952 Relating to the Arrest of Ships* (Athens, Sakkoulas, 1988).

[2] International Convention on the Arrest of Ships (adopted 12 March 1999, entered into force 14 September 2011) 2797 UNTS 3. For an overview of the Arrest Convention 1999 regime, see Nicholas Gaskell and Richard Shaw, 'The Arrest Convention 1999' [1999] LMCLQ 470; Berlingieri (n 1) vol 2.

[3] At the time of writing, the Arrest Convention 1999 has only 11 parties. For the official ratification status of both Arrest Conventions, see the United Nations Treaty Collection at treaties.un.org.

[4] Art 7 of the Arrest Convention 1952 reads: 'The Courts of the country in which the arrest was made shall have jurisdiction to determine the case upon its merits if the domestic law of the country in which the arrest is made gives jurisdiction to such Courts', while art 7 of the Arrest Convention 1999 reads: 'The Courts of the State in which an arrest has been effected or security provided to obtain the release of the ship shall have jurisdiction to determine the case upon its merits.'

[5] See Frank Smeele, 'Liability for Wrongful Arrest of Ships from a Civil Law Perspective' in D Rhidian Thomas (ed), *Liability Regimes in Contemporary Maritime Law* (London, Informa UK, 2007) 261. See further ch 6.

[6] See the work of the CMI International Working Group on Liability for Wrongful Arrest at comitemaritime.org/work/liability-for-wrongful-arrest; *Stallion Eight Shipping Co SA v Natwest Markets Plc* [2018] EWCA Civ 2760 [70]–[76].

[7] For good English summaries of this reform, see Beate Czerwenka, 'The Proposal for a Reform of German Maritime Law' in Jürgen Basedow et al (eds), *The Hamburg Lectures on Maritime Affairs 2009 & 2010*,

was fast-tracked, with the explicit political goal of the legislator being to strengthen the German jurisdiction and its practical relevance as a legal venue in competition with other jurisdictions.[8] Ship arrest law is definitely an arena for (sometimes intense) legal competition between countries.[9] Specifically, the recent amendments to domestic ship arrest laws may serve as a good practical illustration of this phenomenon. The German legislator – when amending just one specific provision of the German Code of Civil Procedure (The Zivilprozessordnung or ZPO) – explicitly referred to the motive for this reform as being Germany's existing legal competition with a neighbouring port State, the Netherlands: 'The objective of the provision is to align the legal situation with Dutch law to strengthen Germany as a legal venue.'[10]

Why was such an explicit 'comparative alignment' deemed to be necessary by the German domestic legislator, despite the existence of a long history in maritime law, including maritime arrests? First, the legislative initiative had a simple practical and economic background. Annual statistics indicated that fewer than five vessels were being arrested in all German ports, while the numbers for the major port of Rotterdam alone amounted to around 300 ship arrests per year.[11] This comparison is quite astonishing! The Dutch jurisdiction had emerged as an arrest-friendly jurisdiction (if not an 'arrest heaven') while the neighbouring German jurisdiction had dried out to become an 'arrest desert'. Secondly, the legislative reform had a procedural background. Before 2013, ship arrest in Germany was by no means automatic. German civil courts would only grant a ship arrest where the applicant was able to demonstrate a 'good reason' for arresting a ship. Thus, in order to achieve a provisional arrest for securing a later potential forced judicial sale, the creditor had to argue that, without the arrest, the enforcement of a judgment would be rendered impossible or substantially more difficult.

However, demonstrating an additional 'good reason' for requesting a court to provisionally arrest a ship is not a legal prerequisite in most jurisdictions.[12] The Arrest Convention 1952 does not unify these procedural or evidentiary aspects at all.[13]

Hamburg Studies on Maritime Affairs 23 (Berlin, Springer-Verlag, 2012) 55; Beate Czerwenka, 'The Reform of German Maritime Law' (2014) *Il Diritto Marittimo* 48.

[8] A good general example of the international marketing of a national legal venue is the regularly updated brochure 'Law Made in Germany', which is available at www.lawmadeingermany.de.

[9] See, eg, Liz McMahon, 'Competing Jurisdictions', *Lloyd's List*, 16 December 2011 (quoting Norton Rose partner Roger Heward: '[T]here is no doubt some jurisdictions are more efficient at dealing with claims than others. The best tend to be common law jurisdictions based on English law, such as the UK, Gibraltar, Singapore, Hong Kong, Australia, New Zealand and Canada. The Netherlands also deals with arrests swiftly and competently.' Recall too Lord Denning's (in)famous statement in *The Atlantic Star* [1973] 1 QB 364, 382: 'You may call this "forum-shopping" if you please, but if the forum is England, it is a good place to shop in, both for the quality of the goods and the speed of the service.'

[10] See BT-Drs 17/10309 (12 July 2012) 143 (available at dipbt.bundestag.de/dip21/btd/17/103/1710309.pdf) for an explanation of the motives of the German legislator for its proposed reform of German maritime law, which includes the draft law of the reform as it was later passed by the German Parliament.

[11] See Smeele (n 5) 263.

[12] By comparison, according to art 682 of the Greek Code of Civil Procedure (the Greek CCP), the applicant is required to submit evidence pending litigation or prior to a hearing of the main proceedings in respect of the cause of action, the necessity of ship arrest, and the 'urgency' of the situation, which is presumed if the ship flies a foreign (that is, a non-Greek) flag: see George Theocharidis, 'Jurisdiction for Provisional Relief under the Brussels Convention in Maritime Context' [2002] *Revue Hellénique de Droit International* 453, 476–80.

[13] Rather, art 6(2) of the Arrest Convention 1952 provides that the 'rules of procedure relating to the arrest of a ship, to the application for obtaining the authority [to arrest the ship], and to all matters of procedure which the arrest may entail, shall be governed by the law of the Contracting State in which the arrest was made or applied for.'

Article 1(4) of the Arrest Convention 1952 merely requires that the claimant 'alleges' (for example, by filing an affidavit) that a maritime claim as listed in art 1(1) of the Arrest Convention 1952 prima facie exists in its favour.

For decades, however, German courts insisted on applying the stringent domestic requirements of the German Code of Civil Procedure,[14] thus making ship arrest in Germany a comparatively difficult task. This choice represented a considerable burden, in particular, in comparison to neighbouring port State jurisdictions (even though it was held to be sufficient to create a 'good reason' for ship arrest if a judgment had to be enforced abroad where reciprocity was not guaranteed).[15] As a consequence, older German case law provides several examples of failed ship arrests in which applications had not been granted, ultimately, because the 'good reason' requirement had not been met to the satisfaction of the national civil court.[16] For example, no arrests would be allowed against a shipowner running a regular scheduled liner service calling repeatedly at German ports,[17] regardless of the flag that was being utilised by its vessels. Furthermore, requests to arrest a ship had been unsuccessful before German courts when the application was primarily based on the fact that the owner was a 'letter box company' (while the company owned several vessels, thus not representing one of the notorious 'single-ship companies').[18] In sum, it was still technically possible to arrest a ship in a German port, but this had dwindled into a rare phenomenon, rather than being normal practice.

After the reform of German maritime law in 2013, the procedural situation has completely changed, while the real impact on ship arrest practice still remains to be evaluated. The general rule remains unchanged. There is a right to arrest any kind of asset owned by the debtor, wherever there is the concern that, without such arrest, the enforcement of a judgment would be frustrated or would be significantly more difficult. However, a completely new additional provision now states that 'no grounds for a writ of seizure need be submitted, if the seizure is being implemented solely by way of securing the compulsory enforcement against a ship'.[19] It is very important to understand that this explicit clarification and exception relates exclusively to ships. It simply aims to facilitate possible ship arrests in German ports. If an applicant seeks to arrest other maritime-related assets (for example, bunkers, freight, receivables or cargo), the requirement for demonstrating 'good reasons' (or 'grounds for a writ of seizure', according to the official translation) still applies, as was

[14] An English translation of the most current version of the relevant ZPO provisions is available online at www.gesetze-im-internet.de/englisch_zpo/englisch_zpo.html#p3424.

[15] The pre-reform legal situation is extensively discussed by Rolf Herber in his first edition of *Seehandelsrecht: Systematische Darstellung* (Berlin, de Gruyter, 1999), 120–23.

[16] For references to this case law, see Klaus Ramming, 'Der Arrest von Schiffen' (2014) 2 *Recht der Transportwirtschaft* 177, 179 fns 15–18.

[17] Christopher Hill et al, *Arrest of Ships: Volume 1: England and Wales, The Federal Republic of Germany, Japan, The United States* (London, Lloyd's of London Press, 1985) 54.

[18] See Higher Regional Court of Hamburg NJW, 1990, 1425; see generally Dieter Rabe, 'Nochmals: Die Arrestierung eines ausländischen Seeschiffes' (2001) 24 *Transportrecht* 185, 187.

[19] Obviously, the German legislator was influenced by the wording of art 728 read in conjunction with art 711 of the Dutch Wetboek van Burgerlijke Rechtsvordering: see already earlier on this particular aspect Herber (n 15) 126. The updated German text of § 917(2), second sentence, of the ZPO now reads as follows: 'Eines Arrestgrundes bedarf es nicht, wenn der Arrest nur zur Sicherung der Zwangsvollstreckung in ein Schiff stattfindet.' Notably, the German term 'arrest' has been translated by the translation services of the German Ministry of Justice with the term 'seizure'. For details see also Ramming (n 16) 181.

the case prior to the 2013 amendment.[20] As a result, the German legislator has completely deleted the requirement for a 'good reason' – but only in relation to the arrest of ships.[21] For all other assets (maritime or non-maritime) the general rule still applies that a creditor must establish sufficient legal grounds and 'it is to be deemed sufficient grounds for a writ of seizure to be issued if the judgment would have to be enforced abroad and reciprocity has not been granted'.[22]

Regardless of the 2013 reform, in the wake of the insolvency of the Korean shipping giant Hanjin in 2016, the busy German port of Hamburg was one of three ports around the globe (together with Los Angeles and Singapore) which was designated as a 'safe haven' or 'base port' for Hanjin vessels.[23] In these three ports, Hanjin was obviously guaranteed legal protection from vessel seizures, which allowed its ships to discharge their cargo without risk of arrest by creditors seeking outstanding payments. However, the real reason behind this strategic move was not primarily related to the legal framework for ship arrest in Germany. Rather, it needs to be traced back to the protective provisions offered by domestic insolvency law.[24]

III. The Basics of Arrest Procedures in European Civil Law Systems

In Civil Law systems, the initiation of a ship arrest procedure will not deviate substantially from that in Common Law jurisdictions. The procedure will begin with an application for ship arrest, usually lodged with the competent court by a lawyer. This court will generally be the court with local jurisdiction for the port in which the ship is berthing, unless main proceedings on the merits between the applicant and the shipowner have been entertained in another jurisdiction. In this situation, an inland court may decide on the application for provisional arrest. Its interim relief jurisdiction will usually be concurrent with the

[20] This can be a challenge, in particular, for physical bunker suppliers, who might have no contractual nexus with the shipowner on which to base their claim. Under Greek law, however, such a problem would not occur if the bunkers had been ordered by the ship operator (eg, the bareboat or demise charterer), because art 106(b) of the Greek Code of Private Maritime Law would make the ship itself liable for such claim: see Ioannis Rokas and George Theocharidis, *Naftiko Dikaio/Maritime Law* (Athens, Sakkoulas, 2015) 70–73.

[21] See Czerwenka, '*The Reform of German Maritime Law*' (n 7) 66. The pre-reform German text of § 917(2) ZPO did not include any explicit reference to a ship at all. Rather, the second sentence referred broadly to the 1968 Brussels and 1988 Lugano Conventions (both on jurisdiction and the enforcement of judgments in civil and commercial matters). The provision stated that it would not be sufficient for a creditor to establish a 'reason for arrest' if enforcement would be possible under both Conventions. The (now deleted) sentence read as follows: '(2) Dies gilt nicht, wenn das Urteil nach dem Übereinkommen vom 27. September 1968 über die gerichtliche Zuständigkeit und die Vollstreckung gerichtlicher Entscheidungen in Zivil- und Handelssachen und den Beitrittsübereinkommen dazu oder dem Übereinkommen vom 16. September 1988 über die gerichtliche Zuständigkeit und die Vollstreckung gerichtlicher Entscheidungen in Zivil- und Handelssachen vollstreckt werden müßte.'

[22] The official translation of the first sentence of § 917(2) ZPO, as available at www.gesetze-im-internet.de/englisch_zpo/englisch_zpo.html#p3424.

[23] Wei Zhe Tan, 'South Korea names Hanjin "Safe Haven" Ports' *Lloyd's List*, 6 September 2016: 'Hamburg in Germany, Los Angeles in the US and Singapore are to be the shipping line's so-called base ports, a Ministry of Strategy and Finance official told Lloyd's List. The ports have all issued stay orders or have guaranteed legal protection from vessel seizures, which allows Hanjin's ships to unload, the ministry official said.'

[24] On which see further ch 9.

jurisdiction of the court in which the ship is berthing.[25] The arrest application itself will have to be made in the official language of the court in which it has been filed, and it must be supported by prima facie evidence as to the maritime claim. The success of an arrest application generally depends on its content, as set out in detail by the arresting party. If the application contains an additional request for the prohibition of the sailing of the ship until the interim hearing,[26] it may be supplemented by a sworn affidavit of a competent manager or director of the applicant, confirming that the facts stated in the application are true.[27] Alternatively, this officer may testify as a witness before the judge, who will adjudicate the injunction, either on the same day that the application was lodged or within 24 hours of its filing.

Over the years, the civil law courts in the Netherlands have gained a particular reputation for affirming the prerequisite of prima facie evidence of a maritime claim very swiftly, thus showing an efficient, if not to say generous,[28] approach towards serving the applicant's interests.[29] But generally speaking, most Civil Law jurisdictions should be capable of rendering a decision on the application comparatively swiftly and, as a rule, in an ex parte hearing and without summoning the shipowner. The situation will be different if the shipowner files a protective writ to avoid a potential arrest order. Most Civil Law courts would then probably allow an oral hearing before issuing an arrest order.

If an arrest is granted, a Civil Law court will generally also determine an amount of security (bail), which, upon payment, will entitle the ship owner to have the arrest lifted. The amount will generally be an amount equal to the applicant's claim, plus interest and costs. In some Civil Law jurisdictions, the court may grant the measure subject to certain conditions. In particular, the execution of the provisional arrest may be conditional upon the creditor providing counter-security,[30] either in cash or by depositing a first-class bank guarantee

[25] In Greece, see art 683(4) of the Greek CCP. Equally, the revocation or amendment of the provisional arrest judgment may be realised, either by the local court, which issued the measure while the ship was berthing there, or by the court which became competent by reason of main proceedings having been entertained after filing suit on the substance of the case. However, after the hearing of the case on the merits and until the judgment is issued, only that court would have the power to revoke or amend the provisional arrest judgment (see arts 696(3) and 697 of the Greek CCP).

[26] eg, Greece offers protection to the applicant, even prior to the lodging of the application for the provisional arrest of the ship, by virtue of a remedy called an 'injunction for the prohibition of sailing' as provided for in art 691A of the Greek CCP. It is usually ordered ex parte against ships flying foreign flags, so as to prevent the hasty departure outside the jurisdiction of the Greek court: Antapassis (n 1) 203–04. Conversely, the court will refuse, almost invariably, to grant the injunction, if the ship is registered in the Greek Shipping Registry: Rokas and Theocharidis (n 20) 39. Such refusal does not prejudice the power of the court to order the provisional arrest of the Greek ship. As stated above, it may be possible that the injunction is granted ex parte, to be adjudicated the next day in inter partes proceedings after summoning the shipowner by telephone.

[27] For Germany see, eg, Ramming (n 16) 179.

[28] eg, in a judgment rendered on 9 December 2011 the Dutch Hoge Raad (Supreme Court) ruled that arrest proceedings in the Netherlands are not even restricted to sister ships in connection with which the maritime claim arose. Rather, an arrest may even extend to any ship which is the property of the debtor in a claim, provided that the claim is a maritime claim and is recoverable against the ship under national law, as applied under conflict of law rules: see *Furtrans Denizcilik Ticaret Ve Sanayi AS v Augusta Due Srl* ECLI:NL:HR:2011:BT2708, NJ 2012/243 with annotation of KF Haak, S & S 2012/24, CMI112 (9 December 2012).

[29] For details, see Smeele (n 5) 272 ff.

[30] See the current position on counter-security in 31 countries in response to the questionnaire of the CMI IWG on Liability for Wrongful Arrest in comitemaritime.org/wp-content/uploads/2018/05/Table-1-Answerts-to-the-CMI-Questionnaire-per-question-and-country.pdf.

with the court secretary.[31] The amount of counter-security required is at the discretion of the competent court and is usually based on confidential or public commercial facts (for example, the monthly charter hire could be a good commercial indicator if the vessel is time-chartered).[32]

Ultimately, in those Civil Law systems which prescribe counter-security and its deposit to be verified by the court's secretary, the sums can be quite substantial, usually ranging between 10–30 per cent of the amount claimed, although the sum required could even rise up to 100 per cent of the value of the claim.[33] This is because the guarantee is not necessarily linked to the applicant's claim. Rather, the counter-security serves the objective of safeguarding possible compensatory damage claims by the shipowner potentially resulting from a wrongful arrest. The necessity for providing counter-security will thus arise particularly in jurisdictions which have a stricter approach towards compensation for wrongful arrests.[34] Germany was (and, technically speaking, still is) among those stricter jurisdictions because it has a special provision in the ZPO on the liability of creditors for wrongful seizures.[35] The underlying legal concept is comparatively strict, because in the event a court subsequently determines that the arrest was initially unfounded, liability arises irrespective of illegality or fault on the part of the claimant. This concept differs from the approach applied in other European countries[36] (for example, in Belgium, France, Italy or Greece).[37]

However, it is presently unclear whether creditors will still be required to provide counter-security before a vessel can be arrested in a German port. To follow the 'old' procedural approach rigorously would contradict the express intention of the German legislator, who regarded Dutch law as a prototype model for ship arrests. There is no provision in the ZPO which explicitly excludes the requirement of counter-security in ship arrest applications. A discretionary case-by-case approach from the German court seems likely until the issue is authoritatively resolved. Thus, it may be anticipated that legal uncertainty surrounding counter-security may have the effect of undermining the recent reforms and may mean that we do not see a significant rise in ship arrest proceedings before German courts.

The execution of a ship arrest judgment itself may differ significantly in various Civil Law jurisdictions. In some Common Law and Civil Law jurisdictions, the execution may only be imposed if the ship has not started its voyage and is still moored within a port of the relevant jurisdiction. Equally, a ship that is ready to sail but has not sailed yet, can

[31] A letter of undertaking issued by a P&I Club may also be acceptable. However, this requires either agreement by the parties or acceptance by the local court.

[32] See generally Herber (n 15) 125; Ramming (n 16) 185.

[33] See McMahon (n 9).

[34] See ch 6.

[35] ZPO § 945 provides: 'Should the order of a seizure or an injunction prove to have been unfounded from the start, or should the measure directed be repealed …, the party that has obtained the order is under obligation to compensate the opponent for the damages that he has suffered as a result of the measure directed having been enforced, or as a result of the opponent having provided security in order to avert the enforcement or to obtain the repeal of the measure.'

[36] Smeele (n 5) 261.

[37] The Greek CCP, art 702 makes compensation for wrongful arrest conditional upon three prerequisites. First, the defendant must prove knowledge or gross negligence of the applicant about the lack of existence of the right, the protection of which was brought before the court. Secondly, the main claim must have been rejected by an unappealable judgment. Thirdly, the claimant must prove that it has suffered damage from the enforcement of the provisional judgment. It is clear from the above that success in wrongful arrest claims in Greece is exceptional.

still be arrested. In other jurisdictions[38] a ship may be provisionally arrested if it lies at anchor, or even if it has left the jurisdiction's internal waters and is sailing in territorial waters.[39]

There may be other significant differences, for example, relating to time bars. In Germany, an arrest judgment may only be executed within one month from its delivery to the applicant. The applicant has to ensure that service of the arrest judgment to the shipowner is effected, or at least applied for, within one week after the ship has been arrested and within the 30-day time limit.[40] If any of these time restrictions have not been observed, under German law the arrest will be lifted, provided the shipowner notifies the court and applies for the lifting of the arrest.[41] The arrest itself will often be executed by a judicial bailiff on a specific instruction from the applicant. Thus, for example, German courts will neither automatically execute the arrest judgment nor instruct the bailiff to do so. In contrast, the applicant/claimant has to activate the procedure.[42] The bailiff will usually inform the port authorities requesting them to prevent the vessel from sailing as long as the arrest judgment is valid. In addition, under German law, the execution of the arrest establishes an overriding statutory lien on the vessel.[43]

In contrast, Greek law prescribes a much longer 12-month time limit in respect of the enforcement of a provisional ship arrest judgment. The period starts from the moment the copy of the judgment is formally served on the shipowner or the ship's master by a judicial bailiff, instructing them to abstain from sailing. Another copy is served on the harbour authority to ensure compliance with the judgment.[44] Once these two acts are executed, the legal consequence of the material detention of the ship is perfected. If the applicant is a Greek citizen and the ship flies the Greek flag, the judgment is also served on the Ship Registrar, who records it in the relevant book. In this case, an additional legal consequence is imposed, which is the legal detention of the ship.[45] The effect of legal detention is that the shipowner cannot sell or otherwise dispose of the ship. As may be appreciated, the provisional arrest of a Greek flag vessel by a Greek citizen is considered to be a strictly domestic dispute, thus falling outside the scope of the Arrest Convention 1952.[46] Finally, the arrest is automatically lifted if the applicant fails to file the main action on the merits within a 30-day period after service of the arrest judgment on the defendant.[47]

[38] This is the position in Greece, on which see Single-Member First Instance Court of Piraeus 2716/1988 [1988] *Maritime Law Review* 293, discussed in Berlingieri (n 1) vol 1 para 7.01 fn 1.

[39] Valid jurisdiction for such enforcement could derive from art 28(3) of the United Nations Convention on the Law of the Sea 1982 (UNCLOS), which reads: 'Paragraph 2 is without prejudice to the right of a coastal State, in accordance with its laws, to levy execution against or to arrest, for the purpose of any civil proceedings, a foreign ship lying in the territorial sea, or passing through the territorial sea after leaving internal waters.'

[40] See Thomas Wanckel, 'Ship Arrest in Germany' in Felipe Arizon et al (eds), *Ship Arrests in Practice*, 11th edn (2018) www.shiparrested.com/ship-arrests-in-practice 161 (reply to question no 13).

[41] ibid.

[42] ibid.

[43] For procedural details see Ramming (n 16) 190–3.

[44] The Greek Coast Guard will order the master of the ship to hand over to the authority certain documents, which will ensure that the vessel cannot sail without them. With that act, the provisional arrest judgment is enforced in full.

[45] See art 715 Greek CCP.

[46] Regarding this distinction, see Theocharidis (n 12) 476ff, especially fn 112.

[47] See art 715(5) Greek CCP in conjunction with art 7(2) of the Arrest Convention 1952.

IV. Translating the Arrest Convention 1952 into National Law: Germany and Greece

In codified Civil Law systems, such as those found in Germany and Greece, arrest proceedings make no exception to codification. Provisional arrest law is standardised in specific parts of the relevant Codes of Civil Procedure.[48] In Germany, the Arrest Convention 1952 is directly applicable in the national legal order,[49] while in Greece, the international regime has been ratified by virtue of Legislative Decree 4570/1966.[50] Arrest proceedings are interim proceedings to secure execution levied upon the debtor's movable or immovable property once a judgment on the merits is issued. As a result, the matter in dispute is not the cause of action itself. Rather, it is the admissibility of ample security[51] for the subject-matter which is at the centre of interim proceedings. In some countries, this security may be crucial if the shipowner becomes insolvent and bankruptcy proceedings are instituted.[52]

A. The Notion of the 'Maritime Claim'

One of the objectives of both Arrest Conventions is to introduce a common understanding on the issue of which 'maritime claims' may give rise to a ship arrest. For this reason, the Arrest Convention 1952 prescribes a closed catalogue and specifies a variety of possible 'maritime claims' in arts 1(a)–(q). The Arrest Convention 1999 has updated and supplemented this list in a laudable way but there are reasons – to be highlighted below – why countries like Germany and Greece did not feel pressured to cancel the 'old' arrest regime of the Arrest Convention 1952 in favour of the 'new' regime represented by the Arrest Convention 1999.

German and Greek domestic procedural rules do not refer anywhere explicitly to claims which are specifically 'maritime'. Rather, both apply the simple and general approach that a provisional arrest, regardless of whether it pertains to a ship or another asset, may be applied for if the applicant's claim is for any kind of debt or may become a claim for a debt.[53] As a result, this may also include liability claims.[54] It is irrelevant how the claim arose (or will arise in the future) as long as the claim is already due or will become due on a

48 See §§ 916–34 and 943–45 ZPO; arts 709, 713, 715 Greek CCP.

49 Hans Jürgen Abraham; Georg Schaps, *Das Seerecht in der Bundesrepublik: Kommentar und Materialsammlung*, 4th edn (Berlin, de Gruyter, 1978), Anh § 482 Rn 2.

50 Pavlos Avrameas, To asfalistiko metro tis apagorefsis apoplou kata to n.d. 4570/1966/The Provisional Measure of Prohibiting the Sailing of the Vessel under Law Decree 4570/1966' [1999] *Epitheorisi Emporikou Dikaiou* 15–27.

51 In many States, provisional ship arrest transforms the applicant into a secured creditor, whose claim ranks ahead of other claimants from the proceeds of sale of the ship (eg, under German law, ZPO §§ 917 and 931.1–2). This does not work against maritime lien creditors though.

52 See further ch 9; Andrew Tettenborn, 'International Insolvency Law: Its Impact on the Arrest of Ships' (2017) 23 *JIML* 266; Lia Athanassiou, *Maritime Cross-Border Insolvency* (Abingdon, Informa Law from Routledge, 2017).

53 In Germany, see Hanns Prütting, Markus Gehrlein et al, *ZPO Kommentar*, 8th edn (Cologne, Hermann Luchterhand Verlag, 2016) on § 916 ZPO n 12. For Greece, see art 682 Greek CCP.

54 Wolf-Dietrich Walker and Hans Brox, *Zwangsvollstreckungsrecht* 10th edn (Berlin, Verlag Franz Vahlen, 2014) n 1495.

specific date in the future.[55] This conceptual breadth may be surprising for lawyers trained in the Common Law system, but they may be comforted by the usually stricter domestic requirements of procedural law. The breadth of the scope of application of provisional arrest is also one of the reasons why an updated list of maritime claims (as introduced by the Arrest Convention 1999) does not serve as a convincing prompt to denounce the Arrest Convention 1952 in favour of the Arrest Convention 1999.

Nevertheless, Greece explicitly insists on the fulfilment of the prerequisite of art 1(1) regarding the maritime nature of the claim if the relevant ship flies the flag of a Contracting State to the Arrest Convention 1952. As a result, the broader domestic procedural rule is displaced for reasons of public international law. With regard to Germany, there is simply not enough existing case law to confirm an identical approach. However, the Arrest Convention 1952 has been described in academic literature as representing 'merely another filter, in addition to the strict domestic procedural requirements for enforcing any kind of claim'.[56]

A restrictive approach is generally achieved, first, by the general procedural requirement for the claimant to establish a 'good reason' for arrest, as discussed in Part II above. It has to be stressed, once more, that the 2013 abolition of that procedural burden in Germany applies exclusively to vessels, but not to bunkers or removable appurtenances on a vessel, etc. As a consequence, arrest applications for 'other' assets of the shipowner have to be clearly distinguished from applications which aim at the arrest of the vessel per se. Conversely, Greek law treats the arrest of other assets belonging to the shipowner in an identical way, as the conditions that need to be met apply equally across all maritime-related assets.

Secondly, although the German approach to provisional arrest is generally broader and not necessarily maritime-related as compared to the claims encompassed by art 1 of the Arrest Convention 1952, practitioners have highlighted that no major aggravations have ever been reported. 'Maritime claims' arising against shipowners are almost always covered by the broad German understanding of any (prospective) claim for payment.[57] The result is that a claim of a marine insurance company or a classification society could – in theory – give rise to a ship arrest in a German port, even though these claims are not explicitly listed in art 1 of the Arrest Convention 1952.[58] Conversely, in the unlikely case of a creditor trying to arrest a vessel for a claim that is not at all related to the vessel and its commercial operation, the debtor-shipowner could still refer to the German ratification of the Arrest Convention 1952 and argue that an application to arrest a vessel for such a completely unrelated ('non-maritime') claim is repugnant to the German 'ordre public'. However, no such case has ever been reported in Germany. This may also be attributed to the admittedly limited number of ship arrest applications in the past years.

Additionally, there are three official German reservations on the issue of 'maritime claims' which should be taken into consideration in practice.[59] The first two reservations

[55] In Germany, see Ramming (n 16) 178. For Greece, see the wording of art 682(1) Greek CCP.
[56] Herber (n 15) 119.
[57] Wanckel (n 40) 159–60 (reply to question no 5).
[58] Ramming (n 16) 178.
[59] Pursuant to art 10 of the Arrest Convention 1952.

relate to arts 1(1)(o)[60] and 1(1)(p)[61] of the Arrest Convention 1952. For those kinds of dispute, German law applies without any restrictions. A third reservation applies in respect of art 1(1)(q)[62] of the Arrest Convention 1952. Here, for reasons of legal clarity, the German reservation invalidates the procedural exclusion established by art 3(1) of the Arrest Convention 1952. This means that a sister ship arrest, which is generally regarded as unproblematic under German law, is theoretically possible for disputes relating to the mortgage or hypothecation of any other sister ship. A sister ship arrest may thus theoretically be utilised as leverage for disputes arising out of outstanding claims relating to a mortgage or hypothec on another ship. As a matter of procedural practice, however, there is no real difference between German national law and the position adopted by the Arrest Convention 1952. This is because, ultimately, a mortgage or hypothec on a certain ship tends to grant enforcement rights only in respect of the specific vessel charged with that mortgage or hypothec.[63]

B. The Link between the 'Maritime Claim' and the Shipowner

A potential problem – which may obviously arise in many jurisdictions – emerges from the commercial exploitation of the vessel by various third-party stakeholders or as a result of complicated legal structures for the financing of the vessel. In other words, it could be a problematic issue if a creditor were to be allowed to apply for a ship arrest in relation to 'maritime claims' for which the shipowner was not a contracting party (in other words, for which it has no personal liability). As Berlingieri has stressed, art 3(4) of the Arrest Convention 1952 indicates that a ship arrest is generally permissible in respect of claims against the bareboat charterer and any other person 'liable in respect of a maritime claim relating to that ship', but nothing in that should be construed as extending the available remedies at national level.[64] Accordingly, the German view, which was expressed in a 1972 position paper of the legislator on the Arrest Convention 1952, is that art 3(4) has to be interpreted narrowly and in connection with the restrictive purpose of art 9 of the Arrest Convention 1952.[65] The same narrow interpretation is adopted in Greek law.

The resulting position is that the Arrest Convention 1952 has to be construed from a purely procedural point of view. As a result, certain substantive questions on material law are left to be determined by national law. According to the German view, amongst those

[60] 'Disputes as to the title to or ownership of any ship'.

[61] 'Disputes between co-owners of any ship as to the ownership, possession employment or earnings of that ship'.

[62] 'The mortgage or hypothecation of any ship'.

[63] Except if the bank has inserted in the loan agreement and in the deed of covenants of the mortgage a cross-collateral clause for the various ships belonging in the same group. In that case, even if one shipowning company defaults in respect of the loan, enforcement rights could be exercised on all ships of the fleet.

[64] Berlingieri, (n 1) vol 1 para 11.104: 'Article 3(4) clearly indicates that, although arrest is permissible in respect of claims against the bareboat charterer and any other person liable in respect of a maritime claim relating to the ship, the owner of the ship is not liable in respect of such claim and, therefore, it is not possible to interpret such provision as creating a right to expropriate a ship not owned by the person liable. In any event such right is excluded by article 9, reference to which is made, together with the reference to article 3(4), in article 3.1. (citations omitted)'

[65] Published on the occasion of the German ratification of the Arrest Convention 1952: see BT-Drs VI/2224 available at http://dipbt.bundestag.de/doc/btd/06/022/0602224.pdf.

non-procedural issues is the question whether a maritime claim is admissible in arrest proceedings against a person other than the shipowner. Under German law, the position regarding (maritime) claims concluded by a bareboat charterer is that a ship arrest would generally be admissible; however, only against those vessels which are, in fact, beneficially owned by that bareboat charterer, but not against vessels owned by third parties. In other words, German law strictly insists on the rule that a ship arrest will only be granted if the shipowner is personally liable for the claim.[66] Exceptionally, German national law would allow a provisional ship arrest where the claim against the bareboat charterer would be secured by a maritime lien.[67] As a consequence, a vessel may only be arrested if the claim against the bareboat or demise charterer is equipped with a maritime lien – and otherwise arguably not (assuming that the vessel is beneficially owned by another party).[68] In general, applicants may have to consider the existence of maritime liens and mortgages, because Germany has implemented the applicable international Conventions (that is, the International Conventions on Maritime Liens and Mortgages of 1967 and 1993) into its Commercial Code, without, however, ratifying those Conventions. As such, possessory maritime liens may prevail over other liens on the ship.[69]

The position is different under Greek law. As stated earlier,[70] art 106(b) of the Code of Private Maritime Law imposes liability on the ship itself in respect of claims arising out of obligations incurred by the 'ship operator'. As the bareboat or demise charterer is regarded as the 'ship operator', a creditor would be able to apply for the provisional arrest of the ship.

When it comes to (maritime) claims from the activities of time charterers or voyage charterers, the situation is less complicated. Under German law, it is not possible to arrest a vessel for maritime claims arising out of obligations incurred by a time charterer or a voyage charterer. In contrast, property that is owned by the time or voyage charterer is freely available to the creditors for provisional arrest, which will be enforced separately (for example, by arresting bunkers specifically on board a ship owned by another person). It seems that most other European Civil Law jurisdictions follow the same approach, including Greece.[71] It is, however, possible to arrest a vessel for claims arising out of obligations incurred by time or voyage charterers in at least five European Civil Law jurisdictions.[72]

Finally, art 3(2)(b) of the Arrest Convention 1999 explicitly states that claims against time charterers and voyage charterers as eligible persons may give rise to provisional arrest of the vessel, provided the vessel is owned by those persons. This shift represents another reason why the German legislator saw no necessity to ratify the Arrest Convention 1999. In any case, even after 50 years, there is truly no unified position on this legal question.

[66] Wanckel (n 40) 160 (reply to question no 7).
[67] Ramming (n 16) 179.
[68] Wanckel (n 40) 160 (reply to question no 9).
[69] ibid 160–61 (reply to question no 12). See generally Herber (n 15) 110–14.
[70] See text at n 20 above.
[71] See Rokas and Theocharidis (n 20) 139–41.
[72] Berlingieri (n 1) vol 1 paras 11.109 ff (Belgium, Portugal, Poland, Slovenia, and Spain).

C. The Link between the 'Maritime Claim' and the Particular Ship

The position of the vast majority of European Civil Law jurisdictions on so-called 'sister ship' arrest[73] is quite straightforward. Such arrests are possible both under German law and Greek law. The reason for this simple answer is that arrest proceedings relate to any kind of assets owned by the debtor and, from this perspective, ships do not represent any special category of property.[74]

V. The Impact of EU Law

A. EU Ship Arrest Judgments under the Brussels I Regulation (Recast)[75] Regime

Interim proceedings – not only relating to ships – aim to secure, primarily, the prospects of enforcement of a future judgment on the merits. This is also true for any provisional ship arrest within a European port (such as Hamburg or Piraeus) but the concept applies also for the pre-judgment attachment of other assets. So, the first critical question that emerges for a creditor is, which port could provide the necessary provisional protection in respect of the ship?

It should be recalled that many EU States had already ratified the Arrest Convention 1952 well before the negotiation for the adoption of common jurisdictional rules was on the European table. When the issue of a unified jurisdictional regime came into maturity, the European drafting committee had to take two parameters into consideration. First, the Contracting States of the Arrest Convention 1952 should remain committed to the obligations undertaken towards other non-European states. Secondly, the relationship between the two regimes should not be open to various interpretations. Instead, a conspicuous hierarchical rule should address the problem of clashing jurisdictions. Alternatively, the solution adopted by the jurisdictional regime should be compatible with that of the ship arrest regime. In this respect, the European legislators struck a perfect balance.

[73] Not referring to the identical design of ships in fleets, but rather to the arrest of two or more ships directly owned by the same shipowner (see also art 3(2) of the Arrest Convention 1952, which mentions 'shares' in the sense of ownership proportions): see Berlingieri (n 1) vol 1 para 12.07. The position is different if the ships are owned by distinct companies, the full number of shares of which companies are owned by the same person. This refers to arrest of 'associated' ships and it is achieved by piercing the corporate veil of the ship-owning companies, a legal solution not adopted by all countries: see ibid para 13.01ff; ch 2; ch 13.

[74] For the sake of completeness, the only exception applicable under German law is if the ship arrest is initiated directly to secure already existing rights of enforcement against that particular vessel – most commonly this would relate to a forced sale of a particular vessel. Such arrest proceedings may not be extended to sister ships under German law: see Ramming (n 16) 179.

[75] Regulation (EU) 1215/2012 of the European Parliament and of the Council of 12 December 2012 on Jurisdiction and the Recognition and Enforcement of Judgments in Civil and Commercial Matters (Recast), [2012] OJ L351/1 (Brussels I Regulation (Recast)).

Not only did they recognise,[76] in respect of 'particular matters',[77] the superiority of the Arrest Convention 1952 by inserting art 57[78] into the Brussels Convention,[79] but the jurisdictional base of art 24[80] was also fully compatible with that of the Arrest Convention 1952. The latter provision was inserted to ensure that interim relief, so far as it relates, ratione materiae, to a civil or commercial case, falls within the application scope of the regime, although the drafters did not wish, or did not manage, to agree on common jurisdiction grounds as in other cases.[81] It would fall outside the scope of this Chapter to examine the nature of this particular provision; however, two remarks should be noted. First, it is a reference rule and not a distinct jurisdictional ground rule, which means that Member States may offer domestic provisional measures, provided that their national procedural law confers jurisdiction to grant such relief, but not otherwise (that is, if no jurisdiction is vested in that State court by virtue of its lex fori).[82] More surprising was the finding of the European Court of Justice (now the Court of Justice of the European Union) in the *Van Uden* case[83] that national courts could even invoke exorbitant jurisdictional bases to assume jurisdiction for interim relief, subject to some qualifications. Secondly, the fact that the provision left the type[84] of provisional measures to be determined by national laws of the Member States ensured full compatibility with the jurisdictional choice adopted by the drafters of the Arrest Convention 1952. That is to say, if the national jurisdictional bases duly respected the obligations stemming from the Arrest Convention 1952, how could it ever be possible to be incompatible with the Brussels Convention choice for interim relief protection? So, regarding

[76] Official Journal of the European Communities C59/108 para 121 and C59/139 para 238 (Schlosser Report). Official Journal of the European Communities C59/59-60 (Jenard Report).

[77] Case C-406/92 *Owners of the Cargo Laden on Board the Ship Tatry v Owners of the Ship Maciej Rataj* [1994] ECR I-5461.

[78] Article 57, now art 71 of the Brussels Regulation I (Recast) reads: 'This Regulation shall not affect any conventions to which the Contracting States are or will be parties and which, in relation to particular matters, govern jurisdiction or the recognition or enforcement of judgments.' The above provision was supplemented by art 25(2) of the Accession Convention 1978 (Convention of Accession of 9 October 1978 of the Kingdom of Denmark, of Ireland and of the United Kingdom of Great Britain and Northern Ireland to the Convention on jurisdiction and enforcement of judgements in civil and commercial matters and to the Protocol on its interpretation by the Court of Justice [1978] OJ L304/1 (78/884/EEC)), which reads: 'the 1968 Convention as amended shall not prevent a court of a Contracting State which is a party to a convention on a particular matter from assuming jurisdiction in accordance with that convention, even where the defendant is domiciled in another Contracting State which is not a party to that convention.'

[79] 1968 Brussels Convention on jurisdiction and the enforcement of judgments in civil and commercial matters [1972] OJ L299/32, as amended after the accession of certain States in 1978, 1982 and 1989. Superseded by the Brussels Regulation (Council Regulation (EC) No 44/2001 of 22 December 2000 on jurisdiction and the recognition and enforcement of judgments in civil and commercial matters [2001] OJ L12/1) and more recently by the Brussels I Regulation (Recast).

[80] Article 24, now art 35 of the Brussels Regulation I (Recast), reads: 'Application may be made to the courts of a Member State for such provisional, including protective, measures as may be available under the law of that Member State, even if the courts of another Member State have jurisdiction as to the substance of the matter.'

[81] See *Ibrahim Shanker & Co v Distos Compania Naviera SA (The Siskina)* [1979] AC 210, 260 (Lord Diplock): '[B]ut as article 24 of the Convention indicates, this is a field of law in which it has not been considered necessary by member States or by the Council or Commission to embark upon a policy of harmonisation'.

[82] Case C-99/96 *Mietz v Intership Yachting Sneek BV* [1999] ECR I-02277 [40], repeating [19] of *The Van Uden* Case (see n 83 below).

[83] Case C-391/95 *Van Uden Maritime BV v KG Deco-Line* [1998] ECR I-07091 [42].

[84] Peter Kaye, *Civil Jurisdiction and Enforcement of Foreign Judgments* (Abingdon, Professional Books Ltd, 1987) 1140.

maritime claims, this means that art 35 of Brussels I Regulation (Recast) (the equivalent of art 24 of the Brussels Convention) accords priority to the national jurisdictional rule for provisional ship arrest.

At this point, it is considered appropriate to examine whether a judgment for interim relief obtained in one Contracting State can be executed in another by invoking the simple mechanism of recognition and enforcement of Chapter III of Brussels I Regulation (Recast). It is expedient to divide the analysis into the pre- and post-Brussels I Regulation periods.

The *Van Uden* case introduced new principles regarding the extraterritorial effect of provisional measures issued by Contracting States' courts. First, it was held – albeit implicitly – that a measure may have effect beyond the territorial boundaries of the court that granted it.[85] In such a case, a real connecting link must exist between the subject-matter of the measure and the jurisdiction of the court that issued the measure.[86] This has been interpreted as meaning that, for the purpose of granting interim relief, the jurisdiction of the court in which the measure will be enforced has preference over any other Contracting State's court.[87] The reason for this is that only the former court can assess the circumstances and impose restrictions to ensure restoration to the status quo ante. Furthermore, it is submitted that, based on the structure of the Brussels Convention, the recognition and enforcement[88] of the extraterritorial measure in the foreign Contracting State could be refused on the ground that there is no 'urgency', an explicit prerequisite for the granting of the provisional measure[89] in many jurisdictions (for example, Greece).[90] Last, but certainly not least, a provisional measure which interferes with absolute rights in respect of property[91] lying outside the court's jurisdiction could infringe that other state's sovereignty.

Significant changes were brought about by the introduction of the Brussels I Regulation (Recast)[92] in respect of the extraterritorial effect of judgments ordering provisional measures. First, the basic provision,[93] which conferred jurisdiction to Member State courts for interim relief according to national procedural law, remained intact. At the same time, an effort was made to limit the free mobility of provisional or protective measures issuing

[85] *Van Uden* (n 83) [38].

[86] ibid [40].

[87] Ibid [39] repeating the reasoning adopted in Case C-125/79 *Bernard Denilauler v SNC Couchet Frères* [1980] ECR 1553.

[88] On extraterritorial enforcement see Rolf Stürner, 'Das grenzübergreifende Vollstreckungsverfahren in der Europäischen Union' in Walter Gerhard et al (eds), *Festschrift für Wolfram Henckel zum 70. Geburtstag am 21. April 1995* (Berlin, de Gruyter, 1995) 863 ff.

[89] Berhard-Rudolf Heiss, *Einstweiliger Rechtsschutz im europäischen Zivilrechtsverkehr: Art. 24 EuGVÜ*, Schriften zum Prozessrecht 87 (Berlin, Duncker & Humblot, 1987) 92 ff.

[90] By virtue of art 682 Greek CCP, in urgent cases or when an imminent danger must be averted, the courts can order provisional measures for the security of a right or the temporary regulation of a situation. It is the first type of relief which is of interest in maritime cases.

[91] Such is the case with the ordering by the court of the material detention of a ship, which deals with physical possession of the ship (ie, the judgment has in rem effect).

[92] The introduction of the recast regime represents a fairly new procedural development within the EU, which applies since January 2015. Chapter III of this Regulation, which is entitled 'Recognition and Enforcement' has been revised and extended.

[93] Article 35 Brussels I Regulation (Recast).

from courts which are not vested with jurisdiction on the merits of the case.[94] Equally, care was taken to eliminate the possibility of enforcing abroad a judgment, which had been issued in proceedings without due summoning of the defendant,[95] except if the judgment was duly served prior to enforcement.[96] Subject to the above conditions and the completion of specific formalities[97] at the place of execution, prima facie, a provisional measures judgment may be enforced across all Member States by invoking the simple mechanism embodied in Chapter III of Brussels I Regulation (Recast).

The next topic for examination is the mobility of ship arrest judgments in EU waters.[98] The analysis focuses on two questions. First, is it possible to enforce a ship arrest judgment issued by a national court of the EU outside that court's territorial reach? Secondly, does the ship have to be physically present in a port situated in the jurisdiction of the court that has issued the provisional arrest, and moreover at the moment of issuing the judgment?

The Arrest Convention 1952 clearly links the forum arresti of the ship with the jurisdiction of the same forum to adjudicate the case on its merits. However, this jurisdiction on the merits cannot be assumed[99] before the ship moves into the territorial reach of the court, so that the provisional arrest will be ordered. This fundamental principle is embodied in the declaratory statement of art 4 of the Arrest Convention 1952, which prescribes that the ship may only be arrested by the court ordering the arrest. Now, since the Arrest

[94] See para 33 of the preamble: 'Where provisional, including protective, measures are ordered by a court having jurisdiction as to the substance of the matter, their free circulation should be ensured under this Regulation … Where provisional, including protective, measures are ordered by a court of a Member State not having jurisdiction as to the substance of the matter, the effect of such measures should be confined, under this Regulation, to the territory of that Member State;' and art 2(a) which provides: 'For the purposes of Chapter III, 'judgment' includes provisional, including protective, measures ordered by a court or tribunal which by virtue of this Regulation has jurisdiction as to the substance of the matter.'

[95] Such proceedings would be adversary, including ex parte applications, provided the defendant was duly summoned to appear.

[96] See para 33 of the preamble: 'However, provisional, including protective, measures which were ordered by such a court without the defendant being summoned to appear should not be recognised and enforced under this Regulation unless the judgment containing the measure is served on the defendant prior to enforcement. This should not preclude the recognition and enforcement of such measures under national law;' and art 2(a) which provides: 'It does not include a provisional, including protective, measure which is ordered by such a court or tribunal without the defendant being summoned to appear, unless the judgment containing the measure is served on the defendant prior to enforcement.'

[97] See art 42(2):

> For the purposes of enforcement in a Member State of a judgment given in another Member State ordering a provisional, including a protective, measure, the applicant shall provide the competent enforcement authority with:
>
> (a) a copy of the judgment which satisfies the conditions necessary to establish its authenticity;
> (b) the certificate issued pursuant to Article 53, containing a description of the measure and certifying that:
>
>   (i) the court has jurisdiction as to the substance of the matter;
>   (ii) the judgment is enforceable in the Member State of origin; and
>
> (c) where the measure was ordered without the defendant being summoned to appear, proof of service of the judgment.

[98] When it comes to ships and the implementation of the Brussels I Regulation (Recast), once more, courts in the Netherlands seem to be the most progressive in the EU. In fact, Dutch courts have already issued EU-wide ship arrest orders, as will be discussed later, while no case of that kind has so far been reported from the German or Greek jurisdictions.

[99] See the wording of art 7 of the Arrest Convention 1952: 'The Courts of the country in which the arrest is made shall have jurisdiction to determine the case upon its merits.'

Convention 1952 deals exclusively with the material detention[100] of a ship, no other reading could be attributed to the above provision, except that the provisional arrest should be conditional on the ship being within the territorial reach[101] of the ordering court or, exceptionally, on its imminent approach.[102] Indeed, the phraseology that a 'ship may only be arrested under the authority of a court' in art 4 of the Arrest Convention 1952 has the meaning that the provisional arrest must be ordered by the court that has power over the ship according to the above considerations. Further, the term 'arrested' does not refer to the process of enforcement, because such procedural issues would be governed by the relevant lex fori in any case, so the provision would not make sense if interpreted in this manner. Based on the above, it is safe to assume that the power of the arresting court on the ship by virtue of its 'presence' within its territorial reach is a sine qua non for the issuing of the arrest judgment according to the Arrest Convention 1952.[103]

So what is the significance of the above prerequisite in relation to the extraterritorial effect of a ship arrest judgment? Again, the matter will be explored by distinguishing between the pre- and post-Brussels I Regulation periods. Regarding the first period, it was settled in most jurisdictions that a ship arrest judgment from one Member State could not be enforced in other Member States via the simple mechanism provided by Title III of the Brussels Convention.[104] *The Van Uden* case[105] reinforced that position, reasoning that the real connecting link would exist when the forum that issued the judgment would also be called upon to enforce it. However, the option to activate the domestic mechanism for recognition and enforcement of the provisional ship arrest judgment would always be open. On the latter approach, however, a serious impediment would be the lack of 'urgency', thus exerting pressure on the applicant to file a new application for interim relief before the local court.

The position subsequent to the entry into force of the Brussels I Regulation (Recast) should be as follows: Any analysis should focus on the possibility of enforcing a ship arrest judgment with extraterritorial effect by virtue of the new provisions of the Brussels I Regulation (Recast), as the remainder of the cases would still fall under the previous regime. The amendments allegedly opened the path for the free mobility of ship arrest judgments issued in adversarial proceedings (including ex parte applications with due summoning of the defendant), provided the issuing court also has jurisdiction over the substance of the case, even if its national law would grant the provisional arrest without physical presence of the ship. The justification for this position would seem to be the necessity to regard the

[100] See art 1(2) of the Arrest Convention 1952.

[101] The term 'territorial reach' could encompass the physical presence of the ship in a port or in internal waters by anchorage, as well as the sailing in territorial waters after entering or leaving a national port. See discussion in text at n 38ff above.

[102] This is the case when the ship is expected to call at a particular port and the application is adjudicated before the ship has entered the territorial waters of that State. Conversely, as long as the ship remains outside the territorial waters, the effect of the judgment cannot be accomplished: Single-Member First Instance Court of Piraeus 2716/1988 (n 38) 293).

[103] Berlingieri (n 1) vol 1 para 7.21: 'The recognition and enforcement of a foreign order of arrest by the Court of a State party to the 1952 Convention would in fact be in conflict with article 4, pursuant to which only a court in the jurisdiction of which the arrest is made is competent.' Further, he cites (ibid fn 21) the decision in *Gie Dream Bail v Pallavicino*, Tribunale di Genoa, 21 May 2004 (2006) *Il Diritto Maritimo* 537.

[104] Theocharidis (n 12) 485.

[105] *Van Uden* (n 83).

whole of the EU as a single area within which the measure should be enforced, subject to furnishing a certificate evidencing: first, the jurisdiction of the issuing court; and second, enforceability according to the procedural law of the issuing State. In that case, purportedly, the local bailiff – or other enforcement body – where the ship is berthing should enforce the foreign judgment immediately on the ship and without intervention of the local court.

This position should not be upheld for the following reasons.[106] First, it must be recalled that, according to art 71 of the Brussels I Regulation (Recast), its provisions will not affect any Convention in relation to 'particular matters', such an instrument being the Arrest Convention 1952. According to the Schlosser Report, proper interpretation of this issue calls for certain principles to be applied.[107] First, when the issue in question is specifically dealt with by the Arrest Convention 1952, its provisions shall prevail, since the Brussels Convention provisions will be displaced. Conversely, if the Arrest Convention 1952 is silent on the matter, the Brussels Convention provisions shall apply.[108] Secondly, despite the hierarchical superiority of the Arrest Convention 1952, its provisions, when read together with the Brussels Convention,[109] should be regarded as if they were provisions of the latter.[110] But, as shown earlier, the Arrest Convention 1952 imposes the requirement of 'presence' of the ship within the jurisdiction of the forum ordering the provisional arrest. More importantly, the provisional measure, which is regulated by the Arrest Convention 1952, is the material detention of the ship and only that. It is for this reason that the Contracting States to the Arrest Convention 1952 – including those which are simultaneously Member States of the Brussels I Regulation (Recast) – are required to have replaced any national provisional measures regarding material detention of ships with the requirements of the Arrest Convention 1952. If parallel national provisional measures were to survive, those States would indirectly infringe their international law obligations under the Arrest Convention 1952. The same consequence follows, a fortiori, if those States were to grant provisional measures regarding material detention of ships according to national prerequisites which are repugnant to the conditions entrenched in the Arrest Convention 1952.

[106] Berlingieri (n 1) vol 1 para 11.104: 'Therefore, at present, the regime of Regulation 1215/2012 would not apply in case of an order of arrest issued without prior hearing'. However, he leaves open the extraterritorial effect of an arrest order, if issued inter partes or ex parte with prior summoning of the defendant shipowner.

[107] See the Schlosser Report (n 76) para 240.

[108] See ibid: 'The 1968 Convention contains the rules generally applicable in all Member States; provisions in special conventions are special rules which every State may make prevail over the 1968 Convention by becoming a party to such a convention. In so far as a special convention does not contain rules covering a particular matter the 1968 Convention applies.'

[109] See ibid: 'This is also the case where the special convention includes rules of jurisdiction which do not altogether fit the inter-connecting provisions of the various parts of the 1968 Convention, especially those governing the relationship between jurisdiction and enforcement. The overriding considerations are simplicity and clarity of the legal position. The most important consequence of this is that provisions on jurisdiction contained in special conventions are to be regarded as if they were provisions of the 1968 Convention itself, even if only one Member State is a Contracting Party to such a special convention.'

[110] This passage was approved by Lord Hobhouse in *The Anna H* [1995] Lloyd's Rep 11, 18: 'The purpose of this provision is to ensure that the relevant statutory provisions and other rules of English law shall be treated as if they are parts of the Convention which they have the effect of implementing and nothing shall turn upon the fact that in English law Conventions are not self-executing.'

Now, if the above proposition is right, art 4 of the Arrest Convention 1952 prevails over the provisions of the Brussels I Regulation (Recast),[111] in the sense that compliance with the Arrest Convention 1952 requirements amounts to a precondition for the conferral of interim jurisdiction on the national court where the ship is berthing or is otherwise within the territorial reach of the court. And this should apply regardless of whether that court has jurisdiction to determine the substance of the case.

But for the moment, let us suppose that there is no need to comply with art 4 of the Arrest Convention 1952. In such a case, a Member State court of the EU, vested with jurisdiction on the merits by virtue of, say, an exclusive jurisdiction agreement between the disputing parties, could order a ship arrest, even where the ship has not called into its ports. The applicant, after obtaining the required certificate evidencing the conditions of art 42 of the Brussels I Regulation (Recast), will then be able to instruct any bailiff in any EU Member State to enforce the material detention of the ship wherever it may be found. It should be remembered that the local enforcing body has no power to question the procedure and would be bound to enforce the measure. Certain crucial problems would emanate. First, would the local harbour authority, responsible for the due enforcement of the material detention of the ship, be bound to comply with the foreign judgment? Secondly, by virtue of art 5 of the Arrest Convention 1952, the court issuing a ship arrest judgment must include – in the absence of agreement between the parties – a proviso for the release of the ship upon sufficient bail or other security. Would compliance with this proviso be required to be verified by the issuing court or by a body where the material detention of the ship has been effected? Further, once the arrest is lifted by the issuing court, will the foreign harbour authority release the ship ex officio or with the intervention of the local court? Thirdly, it was mentioned earlier that provisional arrest accords jurisdiction on the substance of the case by virtue of art 7 of the Arrest Convention 1952 on the basis of the physical presence of the ship. Where the first court issuing the provisional judgment has jurisdiction over the merits of the dispute as forum contractus (for example, because it is specified in an exclusive jurisdiction clause in a bill of lading or charterparty), would the second court in whose territorial jurisdiction the ship is provisionally arrested on the basis of the provisional judgment of the first court, assume concurrent jurisdiction on the merits as the forum arresti? In that case, would it have power to countermand the first provisional arrest by a provisional judgment of its own? It is obvious that the replies to the above questions militate against extraterritoriality of provisional ship arrest judgments under the Brussels I Regulation (Recast) when the Arrest Convention 1952 applies.[112]

[111] In other words, by virtue of art 71 of the Brussels I Regulation (Recast), the requirements of art 4 of the Arrest Convention 1952 prevail over arts 2, 35 and 42 of the Brussels I Regulation (Recast).

[112] The situation should be different if the Arrest Convention 1952 does not 'bite' on the dispute. On 12 March 2015 the Court of Rotterdam issued a judgment in *Allegro BV v Fanty-GT AD* (ECLI:NL:RBROT:2015:3395). It involved a dispute between a Dutch owner of a barge and a Bulgarian time charterer, who allegedly failed to pay the agreed hire, causing the owner to cancel/withdraw from the lease contract and claim back his vessel. The time charter incorporated a jurisdiction clause for the resolution of disputes in favour of the Rotterdam District court. The vessel was either in Germany or Austria when the owner filed an application before the Dutch court for the conservative preservation of his rights. He also included two additional requests for the attachment of the vessel's documents (ie, its certificate of measurement and survey), and for the barge to be delivered to the Netherlands or to be held in sequestration by a third party. The Dutch court granted the conservative attachment to be enforced abroad and the attachment of the vessel's documents, but not the delivery of the barge. It is submitted that the case fell outside the scope of the Arrest Convention 1952 and, as such, the court had no restriction in granting the

Let us proceed with the examination of the validity of the above line of reasoning with a practical example. Suppose that a Greek-flagged ship, which has been time-chartered to a Dutch company, enters the territorial waters of Italy to call at the port of Genoa. The time charterer addresses a notice of protest to the shipowner for breach of the chartering agreement which has allegedly resulted in financial damage. If the charterparty includes a jurisdiction clause in favour of the court in Amsterdam, this would ensure that that court would have jurisdiction over the substance of the dispute. Further, the Dutch company files an application for the provisional arrest of the ship before the Dutch court based on domestic procedural law in conjunction with the Brussels I Regulation (Recast). The shipowner has not been summoned and fails to appear before the court. The Dutch court accepts interim jurisdiction on the basis of the domicile of the applicant and a certificate of enforceability and verification of jurisdiction as to substance is issued. By this stage, the ship is berthing at Genoa and the Dutch provisional ship arrest judgment is served on the master. At the same time, the Dutch company forwards all relevant documentation to an Italian bailiff with instructions to proceed with the material detention of the ship by virtue of the Arrest Convention 1952 and the Brussels I Regulation (Recast). Should the arrest be imposed and, if so, how could the shipowner defend its position? Based on the wording of the Brussels I Regulation (Recast), it seems that the local bailiff has no power to investigate the matter on the substance, except for the originality and the validity of the relevant enforcement documents. So, the bailiff will be bound to proceed with the material detention of the ship at the Italian port. Serious doubts, however, may be expressed about whether the Italian harbour authority has the legal power to enforce a foreign ship arrest judgment.[113] At this point, it should be stressed that maritime authorities in the EU are vested with public power, but they are not enforcement authorities for the exercise of foreign private civil or commercial rights. Therefore, the Italian harbour authority will arguably have no right or obligation to restrain

particular provisional measure. More specifically, the barge was not deemed to be a ship by the court. Presumably, this is the reason why there was no mention on the applicability of the Arrest Convention 1952. Moreover, there was no mention about the flag that the barge was flying. Also, the ownership of the barge was vested in the Dutch company, from which it could be assumed that it was registered with the Dutch Registry. The measure granted was not provisional ship arrest (ie, material detention) but a conservative preservation of rights based on the absolute right of ownership. More critical was the dismissal of the request of delivery, indicating that the Dutch court was well aware that such ruling would probably infringe the sovereignty of the foreign legal order. We have no reliable source to verify if the Dutch court's order was ever enforced abroad according to the Brussels I Regulation (Recast) and, if so, how this was done. For the above reasons, it is submitted that the particular judgment caused no 'harm' to the unified regime, which applies for provisional ship arrests under the Arrest Convention 1952. Another unreported decision with similar reasoning (discussed in Robert Hoepel and Elske Torreman, 'Amsterdam Court Authorises EU Ship Arrest Order' *International Law Office*, 12 October 2016) involved the Dutch buyer of a yacht who filed an application for the provisional arrest of a (fully paid for) yacht before the Amsterdam court because the German seller refused to deliver it. The sale and purchase agreement contained a jurisdiction clause in favour of the court in Amsterdam, which accorded jurisdiction on the merits to the Dutch court. Interestingly, it took the Dutch buyer no more than a day successfully to request from the Amsterdam court leave to have the yacht potentially arrested in no less than four EU jurisdictions (Croatia, Italy, Greece and Cyprus) where the yacht could have sailed. Ultimately, the yacht was arrested in Croatia. The Croatian enforcement body executed pre-judgment arrest without any procedural involvement of the domestic court. Again, the dispute here fell outside the scope of the Arrest Convention 1952, as it was a contractual dispute involving the sale and purchase of property rather than a maritime claim under art 1(1).

[113] It should be stressed that the provisional ship arrest judgment orders two things. First, the defendant is required to refrain from sailing; second, the competent maritime authority (usually the harbour master) is required to prohibit the departure of the vessel. It is a means of enforcement, of a similar nature to the forced seizure of property (material detention of the seized asset). It deals with an in rem proprietary right (ie possession) over the ship, which for arrest purposes is treated as immovable property in many Civil Law jurisdictions (eg Greece).

the vessel from sailing on the basis of the Dutch court's ship arrest judgment. This is one crucial reason why art 4 of the Arrest Convention 1952 prescribes the physical presence of the ship within the jurisdiction of the court ordering the ship's arrest. However, the fact that the Italian bailiff has partially enforced the Dutch court's foreign provisional measure might cause uncertainty regarding the status of the ship. To resolve this uncertainty, the Greek shipowner would have to file an application for refusal of enforcement before the court in Genoa according to the Brussels I Regulation (Recast) provisions. The ground for refusal would not be the breach of jurisdiction rules by the Dutch court issuing the judgment,[114] but rather that execution of the Dutch ship arrest judgment in Genoa contravenes Italian public order because it breaches art 4 of the Arrest Convention 1952.

B. Freezing Orders Slowly Creeping into European Civil Law Jurisdictions

Another interesting question for the future is whether other instruments will become more efficient and effective than traditional ship arrest for creditors to secure their maritime claims. Some European Civil Law jurisdictions, for example France, have for decades utilised measures that are akin to Mareva injunctions or freezing orders (saisies conservatoires).[115] In contrast, the German legal order (and Belgium, Denmark and the Baltic states) have in the past not recognised freezing orders at all;[116] and other European Civil Law jurisdictions have also adopted a rather restrictive approach towards such instruments.

Since 2004, however, asset freezing has slowly started creeping into all European Civil Law systems via European Union law. The EU Intellectual Property Rights Enforcement Directive (IPRED) represents a first singular step in this direction.[117] The key provision for possible asset freezing, art 9(2) of IPRED, states that:

> In the case of an infringement committed on a commercial scale, the Member States shall ensure that, if the injured party demonstrates circumstances likely to endanger the recovery of damages, the judicial authorities may order the precautionary seizure of the movable and immovable property of the alleged infringer, including the blocking of his/her bank accounts and other assets. To that end, the competent authorities may order the communication of bank, financial or commercial documents, or appropriate access to the relevant information.

[114] See art 45 Brussels I Regulation (Recast):

> 1. On the application of any interested party, the recognition of a judgment shall be refused:
>   (a) if such recognition is manifestly contrary to public policy (ordre public) in the Member State addressed; …
>
> 3. Without prejudice to point (e) of paragraph 1, the jurisdiction of the court of origin may not be reviewed. The test of public policy referred to in point (a) of paragraph 1 may not be applied to the rules relating to jurisdiction.

[115] See Kaye (n 84) 1144; May Lee, 'Prejudgment Attachment in England: The Mareva Injunction' (1982) 5 *Loy LA Intl & Comp L Rev* 143 (1982).

[116] See the uncompromising replies to questions no 3 and 4 of Wanckel (n 40) 159: '3. Is there any other way to arrest a ship in your jurisdiction? No.; 4. Are these alternatives e.g. saisie conservatoire or freezing order? No.'

[117] Directive 2004/48/EC of 2 June 2004 of the European Parliament and of the Council of 29 April 2004 on the enforcement of intellectual property rights, [2004] OJ L195/16.

Because of IPRED, EU Member States that did not recognize freezing orders in their national legal order were forced to implement new domestic instruments or to update their domestic laws accordingly. For some EU Members, including Germany, the real challenge was to avoid creating a new general legal right to precautionary seizure of immovable property.[118] The second sentence of art 9(2) of IPRED, which requires the creation of a domestic legal framework enabling competent authorities officially to order the communication of bank, financial or commercial documents (or appropriate access to the relevant information) was a completely new element for some EU Members, and this also explains why it took some Member States considerable time to transpose IPRED into national law.[119]

In recent years, the European Commission has identified an existing general obstacle for the European single market resulting from the fragmentation of national rules on the enforcement of debts across EU borders.[120] In fact, in 2006 the Commission had already described this area as the 'Achilles' heel' of the European Civil Judicial Area.[121] Even in the twenty-first century, creditors seeking to enforce a civil court order in another EU country are still confronted with a number of administrative burdens (above all, different procedural requirements) which entail additional costs and delays. In particular, until 2016 there was no method for enforcing a bank attachment or preservation order throughout the EU. The evolution in this area has proceeded slowly to culminate in an EU Regulation which establishes a procedure for a European Account Preservation Order (EAPO).[122] With the exception of the UK and Denmark, this Regulation came into effect throughout the EU on 18 January 2017. In contrast to a Directive, the EAPO Regulation demands no transposition into national law.

From 18 January 2017 the EAPO Regulation has enabled claimants/creditors – if domiciled in one of the 26 Participating EU Members – to make a single application to courts of the Participating States for an order which will 'freeze' funds held by a debtor/defendant in bank accounts in other Participating Member States without a further court order being required in those Member States.[123] Thus, on the one hand, there is an intra-EU geographic limitation to the EAPO Regulation. On the other hand, the EAPO Regulation represents a significant step towards overcoming procedural burdens related to different national laws.

Applications under the EAPO Regulation have some similarities with ship arrest procedures. First, they are usually made on a 'without-notice' basis to the debtor. The procedure is

[118] eg § 916(1) of the ZPO is entitled 'Claim to Seizure' and has long provided that '[s]eizure is a remedy serving to secure compulsory enforcement against movable or immovable property for a monetary claim or a claim that may evolve to become a monetary claim.'

[119] In the case of Germany, the Directive was transposed with a delay of two years.

[120] See generally www.ec.europa.eu/info/law/cross-border-cases/procedures-simplify-cross-border-cases/late-or-non-payment-debts/freezing-debtors-bank-account_en.

[121] See Commission for the European Communities, *Green Paper on Improving the Efficiency of the Enforcement of Judgments in the European Union: The Attachment of Bank Accounts*, COM/2006/0618 final, 24 October 2006.

[122] Regulation (EU) No 655/2014 of the European Parliament and of the Council of 15 May 2014 establishing a European Account Preservation Order procedure to facilitate cross-border debt recovery in civil and commercial matters [2004] OJ L189/59.

[123] For an early discussion of the Regulation see Allen & Overy, 'The New European Account Preservation Order – A Nightmare for Defendants and a Litigant's Dream?' *European Finance Litigation Review* www.allenovery.com/publications/en-gb/european-finance-litigation-review/Pages/default.aspx. See also Nicolas Kyriakides, 'The United Kingdom's Stance to the Recently Introduced European Account Preservation Order' (2014) 33 *CJQ* 375.

largely administratively formalised, thus not requiring any court hearing. The earlier IPRED has paved the legal way in the EU for creditors to be able to obtain all necessary information from banks, if needed, via competent authorities in the Member States. Secondly, EAPOs can be granted at any time during legal proceedings; thus, even before proceedings on the substantive claim have been initiated by the creditor. Thirdly, another similarity to ship arrest proceedings (at least in some jurisdictions) is the requirement for the creditor to provide counter-security (for example in the form of a security deposit or via an alternative assurance, such as a bank guarantee or a mortgage) to ensure that the debtor can be compensated at a later stage for any damage caused by the EAPO. And, as evident in the area of ship arrest as well, there are fears that the EAPO Regulation might lead to incentives for forum shopping.

However, there are also differences to ship arrest proceedings: For example, art 7(2) of the EAPO Regulation includes a requirement for a claimant to provide 'sufficient evidence' to satisfy a court that the creditor is likely to succeed on the substance of a claim. This generally resembles the 'good reason' procedural requirement that applied to ship arrest applications in Germany before 2013. As practice has shown, this requirement had proved to be a significant burden for swift ship arrests. Despite this, art 7(1) of the EAPO Regulation requires a claimant to provide 'sufficient evidence' to satisfy the court that there is an

> urgent need for a protective measure in the form of a Preservation Order because there is a real risk that, without such a measure, the subsequent enforcement of the creditor's claim against the debtor will be impeded or made substantially more difficult.

If a claimant is successful in establishing 'sufficient evidence', this could initiate proceedings against the debtor which could result in frozen assets across a maximum of 26 EU Member States. With the use of EAPO orders it will be possible effectively to paralyse businesses without debtors having had the opportunity to make representations to the court granting the order.

VI. Conclusions

On the global scale, the conditions and procedures for ship arrest can differ significantly, not only between Common Law and Civil Law jurisdictions but also even between neighbouring European Civil Law countries. Uniformity and a restrictive approach to ship arrest, the primary goals for both Arrest Conventions 1952 and 1999, have not yet been completely achieved.[124] It seems highly unlikely that those European Civil Law jurisdictions which have not yet ratified the Arrest Convention 1999 will do so in the near future. Other states (for example, the United States and Turkey) have not ratified either of the Arrest Conventions, thus adding to the existing fragmented picture regarding international ship arrest law. As a consequence, it may seem that the Arrest Convention 1999 represents a failed attempt to achieve a higher degree of uniformity. It is unfortunate that some of the more laudable reform initiatives and modernised elements of the Arrest Convention 1999 (in particular

[124] On the goal of uniformity of the Arrest Conventions see William Tetley, 'Arrest, Attachment and Related Maritime Law Procedures' (1999) 73 *Tul L Rev* 1895, 1968.

the updated list of maritime claims) could not be integrated (or retrofitted) into the more popular Arrest Convention 1952.

Until 2013, German and Dutch law provided an excellent comparative example of the extremes of different arrest jurisdictions in Europe because of their significantly differing procedural requirements. The German approach was then deliberately realigned with, and remodelled on, Dutch law to re-establish procedural competitiveness for future ship arrests. For creditors, it is often difficult to foresee whether a maritime claim will be enforced efficiently in a particular jurisdiction, especially if they are 'testing out' a ship arrest in a jurisdiction for the first time.[125] This is why, if there is a choice in the matter, arrestors are far more likely to continue to arrest vessels in ports where they have experienced cost-effective, positive and quick results in the past. Speed, efficiency and predictable procedures seem to be the key elements for successful 'arrest logistics'.[126]

According to a permissive interpretation of the latest EU jurisdictional regime set out in the Brussels I Regulation (Recast), it would seem to be possible to apply for an EU-wide ship arrest judgment (as has already happened in the Netherlands) with effect throughout EU waters, provided that the national court has indisputable jurisdiction on the merits of the case, even if the ship was not physically present in the territory of the relevant EU Member State where the court issuing the judgment is situated. However, our thesis is that this outcome should not be permitted where the Arrest Convention 1952 applies, because it would contravene art 4 of the Arrest Convention 1952, a provision of paramount significance. Of course, we are well aware that some EU national courts might be tempted to take an opposite view. This would come as an unpleasant surprise to foreign shipowners who do not regularly trade within the EU region. However, the general conditions to achieve a ship arrest in the first place will continue to depend on the procedural effectiveness and efficiency of any given national legal order, both within and outside the EU.

[125] See, eg, Robert W Lynn, 'A Comment on the New International Convention on Arrest of Ships' (1999) 55 *U Miami L Rev* 453.

[126] This term has been used in applicable German literature to describe that 'just in time' expectation – known from supply chains in logistics – that may also extend to other areas: see Manfred Quade and Stefan P Rindfleisch, 'Arrest und Zwangsversteigerung' in Henning Winter (ed), *Grundlagen der Schiffsfinanzierung* (Frankfurt, Bankakad-Verl, 2008) 809, 826.

11

National Translations of the Arrest Conventions: China

YINGYING ZOU*

I. Introduction

The People's Republic of China (the PRC) is not a contracting party to either the International Convention Relating to the Arrest of Sea-Going Ships adopted in Brussels on 10 May 1952 (the Arrest Convention 1952)[1] or the International Convention on the Arrest of Ships adopted in Geneva on 12 March 1999 (the Arrest Convention 1999).[2] Nonetheless, both Arrest Conventions, and particularly the Arrest Convention 1999, have played an important role in the evolution and development of the legal system and practice of ship arrest in China.[3] The Arrest Convention 1999 provided the main foundation for China's current statutory framework of ship arrest and its principles and provisions were amply adopted in the Special Maritime Procedure Law of the PRC (the SMPL), the primary national legislation governing ship arrest in China.[4]

II. Evolution of the System of Ship Arrest in China

China spent more than 30 years gradually establishing a judicial system of ship arrest and judicial sale. This process was consistent with the implementation of

* LLB, LLM, PhD in Law, General Counsel of China Merchants Energy Shipping Co Ltd.

[1] International Convention Relating to the Arrest of Sea-going Ships (adopted 10 May 1952, entered into force 24 February 1956) 439 UNTS 193.

[2] International Convention on the Arrest of Ships (adopted 12 March 1999, entered into force 14 September 2011) 2797 UNTS 3.

[3] The Hong Kong Special Administrative Region (SAR) of the PRC maintains its Common Law regime, and the Arrest Convention 1952 applies in the Hong Kong SAR with two reservations. For the purpose of this Chapter, all discussions of the systems, provisions and practices of the PRC or China refer to those that are being, or have been, implemented within the jurisdiction of the mainland of the PRC, unless otherwise indicated.

[4] The SMPL was adopted at the 13th Meeting of the Standing Committee of the Ninth National People's Congress and promulgated by Order No 28 of the President of the PRC on 25 December 1999. It came into effect on 1 July 2000. The original text and an English translation of the SMPL are available in Liang Zhao and Lianjun Li, *Maritime Law and Practice in China* (Abingdon, Informa Law from Routledge, 2017) Annex II. An English translation is also available online at www.npc.gov.cn/englishnpc/Law/2007-12/11/content_1383565.htm.

Deng Xiaoping's economic reform policies and the 'opening-up' of China (改革開放), which began in 1978, with far-reaching effects on Chinese society.[5]

Before this significant reform policy, ship arrest in China existed only as a process of administrative detention executed exclusively by the Chinese port authorities.[6] These detentions were in accordance with administrative regulations such as the Provisional Rules on the Inspection of Importing and Exporting Vessels, Crew, Passengers and Luggage of 1950, and the Regulations on Seaports of 1954. These administrative detentions were mainly imposed for violations of safety requirements on the vessels, failure to pay port charges, damages caused to port facilities, investigations for marine casualties, and so forth. During this period, Chinese courts either had no power to impose these types of administrative detentions, or always played an ancillary role to the Chinese port authorities, even in some special cases in relation to ship arrest for commercial disputes in the later 1970s.

However, the reform and opening-up policy of 1978 gave a vigorous boost to trade and commercial activities throughout China and significantly increased demand for the development and implementation of a comprehensive civil and commercial legal system with adequately developed substantive and procedural aspects. The implementation of the reform policy also provided practical experience to support the development of such a legal system.

A. Establishment of a Judicial Ship Arrest System and Legislation Prior to the SMPL (1979–1999)

i. Ship Arrest as a Preservation Measure in the Intermediate Courts (1979–1984)

In 1979 a trial system of property preservation was launched in China; and in 1982 the Civil Procedure Law of the PRC (for Trial Implementation) came into force. These Acts set out the judicial procedures for provisional remedies under civil law, including property preservation, which should be carried out by the people's courts of China. However, the general civil procedure rules did not yet provide any clear guidance for ship arrest.

In 1981, in an official reply to a report proposing a ship arrest procedure submitted by the High People's Court of Shanghai, the Supreme People's Court (SPC) indicated that applications for ship arrest should be submitted to an Intermediate People's Court (Intermediate Court) for court approval and that:

> When the Intermediate Court determines the necessity to arrest a ship, it shall, after consulting with the Foreign Affairs Office of the municipal government and the Port Administration, apply for the approval to the High People's Court and then to the Supreme People's Court. With an approval granted, the Intermediate Court shall serve an arrest Order to be executed by the relevant Port Superintendancy.[7]

[5] See too Xiang Minghua, *Comparative Study of Legal Systems of Ship Arrest Against the Background of Economic Globalization*, (Beijing, Law Press–China, 2013) 69–93 for a discussion of these stages of the evolutionary history of ship arrest in China.

[6] The names and functions of the port authorities in China have changed from time to time, but the core powers and responsibilities have remained the same over the years.

[7] See the SPC, Official Reply on the Procedure of Ship Arrest before the Issuance of Provisions on Ship Arrest, 1981, cited in Xiang (n 5) 80.

This Official Reply therefore conferred jurisdiction over ship arrest on Intermediate Courts, although their exercise of this jurisdiction was not independent – the process is best described as a combination of judicial and administrative execution.

This inefficient dual-approval mechanism was soon simplified by a Notice on Certain Issues of Proceedings of Sea Traffic Accident Cases with Foreign Elements issued by the SPC in December 1983. In art 3(5)(1) of this Notice the SPC stated that

> the purpose of arresting foreign Vessels by judicial process is to preserve maritime claims. Such arrest is a kind of preservation measure, and the procedures of the arrest should be in line with Article 199 of the Civil Procedure Law of PRC (for Trial Implementation).

Article 5(2) of the Notice further prescribed that issues relating to ship arrests could be decided by an Intermediate Court with the High People's Court's approval and that consultation with administrative departments would no longer be required.

Thus, the courts' exclusive jurisdiction over ship arrest for commercial claims was conferred and China's system of judicial ship arrest was established as an additional and parallel regime to the existing administrative detentions of ships executed by administrative authorities for public or administrative reasons only.

ii. Ship Arrests and Judicial Sales Executed by Maritime Courts (1984–1999)

In order to accommodate increases in international trading and shipping, China set up special Maritime Courts in 1984.[8] This heralded a new era of specialist maritime jurisdiction, including jurisdiction over ship arrests. In terms of the Decision of the Standing Committee of the National People's Congress on the Establishment of Maritime Courts in Coastal Cities,[9] these Maritime Courts would exercise exclusive jurisdiction over admiralty or maritime cases in the first instance,[10] but would not hear any other criminal or civil cases.[11] According to the Decision, ship arrest prior to the commencement of legal proceedings, as a new type of preservation measure, would be placed under the exclusive authority of the Maritime Courts. Thereafter, the process of ship arrest would be regarded as a special preservation procedure for maritime disputes rather than a general civil procedure issue. Meanwhile, legal provisions on ship arrest and judicial sales of ships developed quickly.

In January 1986 the SPC issued Detailed Rules on Ship Arrest Prior to Legal Proceedings (Arrest Rules 1986). These Arrest Rules 1986 were based on the practices of the Maritime Courts and included several references to the Arrest Convention 1952 and the

[8] The first 6 Maritime Courts were established in 1984 in Guangzhou, Shanghai, Qingdao, Tianjin, Dalian and Wuhan. Thereafter, 4 more Maritime Courts were established in Haikou (1990), Xiamen (1990), Ningbo (1992) and Beihai (1999). See further Zhao and Li (n 4) paras 18.6–7. According to arts 1 and 3(2) of the Decision, Maritime Courts are to be established in coastal port cities according to need. The establishment, designation of territorial jurisdiction, administration, alteration and abolition of Maritime Courts is determined by the SPC.

[9] Adopted at the Eighth Meeting of the Standing Committee of the Sixth National People's Congress and promulgated for implementation by Order No 20 of the President of the PRC on 14 November 1984. For an English translation of the Decision see www.npc.gov.cn/englishnpc/Law/2007-12/13/content_1383963.htm.

[10] The Higher People's Court where the Maritime Court is located has jurisdiction over appeals against the judgments and orders of the Maritime Court: art 3(3) of the Decision. This appeal is final, except for applications to the SPC for a retrial in special situations.

[11] Article 3(1) of the Decision.

Comité Maritime International (CMI)'s 1985 draft revision of the Arrest Convention 1952.[12] The Arrest Rules 1986, amongst other things, set out the list of maritime claims for which ships could be arrested, stipulated which ships could be arrested, and provided procedures for arrest and jurisdiction on the merits.

In 1987 the SPC issued Detailed Rules on Compulsory Selling-off of Arrested Ships for Liquidating Debts (Selling-Off Rules 1987). The Selling-Off Rules 1987 also referred to the Arrest Convention 1952 and the Maritime Liens and Mortgages Convention 1967.[13] It imposed a limit of 30 days for an arrest of ship prior to proceedings and detailed the procedures on notices of sale, auctions, the ranking of debts and their liquidation. These two detailed Rules provided the basic building blocks for the system of ship arrest and judicial sale in China.

However, with the development of judicial practice in the Maritime Courts, the shortcomings of the Arrest Rules 1986 and the Selling-Off Rules 1987 were revealed. For example, the demarcation of which vessels could be arrested was drafted too narrowly, there was vagueness about counter-security, and the criteria for releasing arrested vessels were unclear. In addition, with the procedural and substantive innovations brought about by the Civil Procedure Law of the PRC (Civil Procedure Law) in 1991[14] and the Maritime Code of the PRC (Maritime Code) in 1992,[15] the existing ship arrest and judicial sale rules needed to be updated.

In 1994 the Rules of Arrest of Ships by Maritime Courts Prior to Litigation Proceedings (Ship Arrest Rules 1994) and the Rules of Auction Sales of Arrested Ships by Maritime Courts for Liquidating Debts (Sales of Ship Rules 1994) therefore repealed and replaced the former 1986 and 1987 Rules. The 1994 Rules made obvious improvements on such issues as multiple arrests, the relationship between ship arrest and jurisdiction on the merits and the procedures for auction sales of ships.

Under these special rules, the Maritime Courts successfully arrested around 1,500 foreign and domestic vessels from 1984 to the first half of 1999.[16]

[12] Draft of the CMI International Sub Committee, *Draft Revision of the International Convention for the Unification of Certain Rules Relating to the Arrest of Sea-Going Ships*, Document Arrest 32/II-1985, Lisboa I, 168, reproduced in Francesco Berlingieri, *Berlingieri on the Arrest of Ships*, 6th edn (Abingdon, Informa Law from Routledge, 2017) vol 2 appendix IV 180 ff.

[13] International Convention for the Unification of Certain Rules relating to Maritime Liens and Mortgages (adopted 27 May 1967, not yet in force): see UNCITRAL, *Register of Texts of Conventions and Other Instruments concerning International Trade Law* (UN, New York, 1973) vol II 179.

[14] Civil Procedure Law of the PRC (adopted at the Fourth Session of the Seventh National People's Congress, promulgated by Order No 44 of the President of the PRC and came into effect on 9 April 1991). The Civil Procedure Law 1991 abrogated the Civil Procedure Law of the PRC (for Trial Implementation) 1982. For an English translation of the Civil Procedure Law 1991 see www.npc.gov.cn/englishnpc/Law/2007-12/12/content_1383880.htm.

[15] Maritime Code of the PRC (adopted at the 28th Meeting of the Standing Committee of the Seventh National People's Congress and promulgated by Order No 64 of the President of the PRC on 7 November 1992, came into effect on 1 July 1993). For an English translation of the Maritime Code see www.npc.gov.cn/englishnpc/Law/2007-12/12/content_1383863.htm.

[16] See Li Guoguang, *Explanatory Report on the Draft of the Special Maritime Procedure Law*, http://www.npc.gov.cn/wxzl/gongbao/2000-12/06/content_5007229.htm. Li was then Vice-Chancellor of the SPC and this explanatory report was submitted to the 11th meeting of the Standing Committee of the Ninth National Congress of the PRC on 24 August 1999 for their consideration and adoption of the Draft SMPL.

B. Judicial Procedures of Arrest and Judicial Sale of Ships under the SMPL (2000–Present)

After four years of drafting, the SMPL was promulgated by the Standing Committee of the Ninth National People's Congress in 1999 and entered into force on 1 July 2000. The SMPL provides a comprehensive system for maritime procedures and tries to match and complement the particular substantive maritime law system instituted by the Maritime Code and a series of international Conventions, such as the International Convention for Civil Liability of Oil Pollution 1969 (CLC 1969),[17] to which China is a party. The SMPL is an important supplement to the Civil Procedure Law, and in respect of particular maritime procedures, prevails over the Civil Procedure Law if there is any conflict between the two instruments.

According to Chapter III of the SMPL, 'Arrest and Auction of Ships', a ship may be arrested in order to preserve a maritime claim. Section II of this Chapter specifies the types of maritime claims in respect of which ship arrests are allowed (art 21), the scope of applications for arrest (art 22), the circumstances under which ships may be arrested (art 23), the circumstances in which rearrest of a ship is allowed (art 24), the time limits for arresting (arts 28–30) and procedures for auction of arrested ships (arts 31–43). Section III of this Chapter deals with attachment and auction of cargo carried by ships (arts 44–50). Chapter IV deals with maritime injunctions (arts 51–61)[18] and Chapter V deals with the preservation of maritime evidence (arts 62–72).[19] Chapter VI, 'Maritime Security', deals with security and counter-security involved in maritime preservation (arts 73–79).[20] In addition, art 111 in Chapter X, 'Procedure for Registration and Repayment of Debts', further provides that, after the public announcement of the Maritime Court's order relating to the compulsory auction of a ship, the creditors must apply for registration of their claims pertaining to the ship to be auctioned within the time limit as announced. Failure to do so means that the creditors' rights to obtain repayment of their debts from the proceeds of the auction are deemed to have been waived.

Unlike the Ship Arrest Rules 1994 and the Sales of Ship Rules 1994, which deal with ship arrest prior to litigation proceedings only, the SMPL established a system of arresting ships as a preservation measure that can be adopted, not only before the commencement of proceedings, but also during litigation or arbitration proceedings. In addition, ship arrest can also be utilised to enforce court judgments, arbitral awards or other legal documents.[21] In addition, unlike the Ship Arrest Rules 1994 and other past practices that set out stricter conditions for arresting foreign-flagged ships, the SMPL harmonised the conditions and procedures for arrest and auction of all ships regardless of their flags or nationalities.

[17] International Convention on Civil Liability for Oil Pollution Damage (adopted 29 November 1969, entered into force 19 June 1975) 973 UNTS 3.

[18] See further Zhao and Li (n 4) ch 21.

[19] ibid, ch 22.

[20] ibid, ch 23.

[21] Article 22 of the SMPL provides that no application may be made for the arrest of a ship on account of maritime claims other than the ones specified in art 21 of the SMPL, except for the enforcement of a judgment, an arbitration award or other legal documents.

III. The SMPL and the Arrest Convention 1999

Before the drafting of the SMPL, China had been attentive to the development and drafting of the international ship arrest Conventions and was actively involved in this process. From the early 1980s, China followed the progress of CMI's revision of the Arrest Convention 1952 closely.[22] As discussed above,[23] CMI's 1985 draft revision of the Arrest Convention 1952 was also partly adopted into China's Ship Arrest Rules 1986.

When the Joint Intergovernmental Group of Experts (JIGE)[24] – established under the auspices of the United Nations Council on Trade and Development (UNCTAD) and the International Maritime Organisation (IMO) – embarked in 1993 on researching the revision of the Arrest Convention 1952, China was active in this research and the drafting of the revision.[25] After more than five years' work, China became one of the core members of the Drafting Committee and at the UN/IMO Diplomatic Conference on Arrest of Ships held from 1–12 March 1999 for the purpose of adopting the Arrest Convention 1999, the late Mr Zhu Zengjie was elected President of the Conference.[26] At its last stage of drafting the SMPL incorporated many of the developments brought about by the Arrest Convention 1999.[27]

A. Similarities between the SMPL and the Arrest Convention 1999

i. Nature and Function of Ship Arrest

First, ship arrest is a preservation mechanism to provide security for relevant maritime claims. Under art 1(2) of the Arrest Convention 1999 'arrest' is defined as meaning 'a detention or restriction on a ship … to secure a maritime claim'. Article 12 of the SMPL is of similar effect, providing that ship arrest before or during a legal proceeding is a preservation of maritime claims, which 'means the compulsory measures taken by a Maritime Court on the application of a maritime claimant against the property of the person against whom a claim is made, for the purpose of ensuring fulfilment of the claim of the maritime claimant'. In respect of this preservation function outlined in art 12, it should be noted that arrest of the ship does not amount to bringing an action against the ship itself. In other words, Chinese law does not subscribe to the personification theory: the defendant to the action is still a person (whether a natural person or juristic entity).[28]

[22] Zhu Zengjie, 'Issues on Revision of the 1952 Convention of Ship Arrest' (1994) 5 *Annual of Chinese Maritime Law* 312, 313.

[23] See text at n 12 above.

[24] The JIGE was originally set up as a group of experts on maritime liens and mortgages and related subjects and provided the draft for the Convention on Maritime Liens and Mortgages 1993 (International Convention on Maritime Liens and Mortgages (adopted 6 May 1993, entered into force 5 September 2004) 2276 UNTS 39). With the adoption of this Convention, the UN/IMO Conference approved a resolution to reconvene the JIGE 'with a view to examining the possible review of' the Arrest Convention 1952, and that the JIGE should take a decision on the scope of the revision of the Arrest Convention 1952. See Berlingieri (n 12) vol 2 paras 1.5–10.

[25] See Zhu (n 22) 312–18.

[26] UN/IMO Diplomatic Conference of Arrest of Ships, *Final Act and International Convention on Arrest of Ships* (19 March 1999) UN Doc A/CONF.188/6 3.

[27] See Li (n 16).

[28] See Jimmy Ng, 'How Closely does the Chinese Law of Ship Arrest Resemble International Maritime Practice and the Ship Arrest Conventions?' (2006) 12 *JIML* 337, 345.

Secondly, ship arrest vests jurisdiction on the merits of the case upon the court executing the ship arrest (the forum arresti). According to art 7 of the Arrest Convention 1999, the courts of the State in which an arrest has been effected or security furnished to obtain the release of the ship have jurisdiction to determine the case upon its merits. Article 19 of the SMPL similarly provides that:

> Where legal proceedings or arbitral proceedings are not commenced in respect of a maritime dispute after execution of the preservation of a maritime claim, any party may bring an action in respect of the maritime claim in the Maritime Court that adopts measures for preservation of the maritime claim or another Maritime Court that has jurisdiction, unless a jurisdiction agreement or arbitration agreement has been reached between the parties.

Both instruments deal with the exception of the existence of a jurisdiction or arbitration agreement between the parties in the same way. In such a case, the selected court will have priority of jurisdiction.

ii. Ships May Only be Arrested for Maritime Claims

Following the principle established by the Arrest Convention 1952, art 2(2) of the Arrest Convention 1999 provides that 'a ship may only be arrested in respect of a maritime claim but in respect of no other claims'. Article 21 of the SMPL is to similar effect: 'no application for arresting a ship can be made on account of maritime claims other than those stipulated in Article 21'.

The 22 categories of maritime claims set out in art 21 of the SMPL are largely the same as those set out in art 1(1) of the Arrest Convention 1999.[29]

iii. Ship Arrest Jurisdiction Exclusively Reserved to Courts

Both Chapter III of the SMPL and art 2(1) of the Arrest Convention 1999 confer jurisdiction for ship arrest only on a court, unlike the Arrest Convention 1952, which in art 3(3) gave the power to detain a ship to a 'Court or other appropriate judicial authority of that State'.

In Chinese maritime law practice, the Maritime Court will serve the ship arrest order on the master on board to arrest the ship. Notification for ship arrest will simultaneously be sent to the port authority, Maritime Safety Administration (MSA) and border administration. Without further notification from the court ordering the release of the vessel, these authorities will not issue their administrative documents to allow the vessel to leave port. Even if a vessel is ready for sailing, that is, it has obtained approval for sailing from the above administrative authorities, the Maritime Court's arrest order may still be served to stop the ship leaving port. Where the arrested ship is registered in China, notification for ship arrest will also be sent to the Ship Registry to restrain the transfer of the ship.

[29] There are minor differences of detail, however: eg art 21(3) of the SMPL does not contain any explicit reference to special compensation under art 14 of the Salvage Convention 1989; arts 21(6) and (7) of the SMPL do not contain the wording 'whether contained in a charter party or otherwise'; art 21(12) of the SMPL does not contain a reference to containers. See further Ng (n 28) 342–44.

iv. Blending of Common Law and Civil Law

Although almost all of the countries which have adopted the Arrest Convention 1999 to date are Civil Law countries,[30] the Arrest Convention 1999 is said to represent a compromise or consolidation of the ship arrest systems to be found in both Common Law and Civil Law regimes.[31] Similarly, although the SMPL is a statute promulgated in a Civil Law regime, it is also regarded as having borrowed some of its concepts from the Common Law system of actions in rem and as being innovative, in the sense that it introduces some non-traditional mechanisms into Chinese law.

The first of these innovations is that only ships can be arrested under the SMPL for maritime claims. This is clearly modelled on the admiralty action against the ship found in Common Law regimes and differs from the general approach to preservation measures in China which, as a Civil Law regime, allows seizure of all types of the defendant's property for all classes of claims.[32]

Secondly, as discussed above,[33] ship arrest will vest substantive maritime jurisdiction on the court which orders the arrest (the forum arresti). This differs from the traditional jurisdiction rules in China, pursuant to which jurisdiction on the merits of the case usually vests in the court at the place of the defendant's domicile or the place where the casualty occurred.[34] Merely taking preservation measures will not normally confer jurisdiction over the merits on that court. In respect of maritime law and practice, art 30 of the Civil Procedure Law also vests jurisdiction in the forum arresti over particular maritime disputes. For cases involving maritime collisions or compensation for maritime damages, the court where 'the ship concerned'[35] is arrested will have jurisdiction on the merits of the case in addition to the courts located in the places where the ship(s) concerned first arrive after the collision, where the collision occurred or where the defendant is domiciled.

Another example is the possibility of ship arrest where the defendant is not yet identified. It is a general principle in China's legal procedure that claims and legal proceedings are brought against a person, and that no judicial process or preservation measure will be instituted in a case until the defendant has been identified. However, the SMPL provides an exception that, where a maritime claimant applies to arrest the ship concerned, the application is effective even if the name of the party against whom the claim is made cannot be ascertained promptly.[36] In judicial practice, the 'defendant' in the application letter can be indicated as 'the owner/bareboat charterer of the stipulated vessel' without specifying a name or address. This special arrangement is in consideration of the very real possibility of the need to arrest a ship urgently to secure a claim.

[30] However, India has implemented much of the Arrest Convention 1999 in its Admiralty (Jurisdiction and Settlement of Maritime Claims) Act 2017: see ch 12.

[31] Xiang (n 5) 57. See also Zhang Liying, *A Study on Ship Arrest and Certain Related Issues* (Beijing, Law Press–China, 2009) 20–34.

[32] See further ch 10.

[33] At Part (III)(A)(i) above.

[34] See ch II 'Jurisdiction', Section 2 'Territorial Jurisdiction' (arts 22–35) of the Civil Procedure Law.

[35] 'The ship concerned' is a term introduced by the SMPL. It is similar to the 'ship in respect of which a maritime claim is asserted' under art 3(1) of the Arrest Convention 1999, or the 'particular ship in respect of which the maritime claim arose' under art 3(1) of the Arrest Convention 1952. See Part IV(A)(i)(a) below.

[36] SMPL, art 25.

It needs to be pointed out that, although the SMPL incorporates some Common Law procedural mechanisms, there is no concept of an action in rem in China. The introduction of the above exception allowing for an unidentified defendant when filing a ship arrest application, does mean that ship arrest can fulfil another important function in practice, although the SMPL does not state this explicitly; that is, ship arrest can be utilised as a procedural stratagem to force the owner or bareboat charterer to appear and submit to the court's jurisdiction to solve the dispute.

In addition to the above, the other substantive clauses in the SMPL covering issues such as the power to arrest and the scope of arrest applications are approximately the same as their equivalents in the Arrest Convention 1999.

B. Differences between the Arrest Convention 1999 and the MPL

Nevertheless, the SMPL and other Chinese legislative instruments on ship arrest are national rules and therefore have their own particular characteristics, which differ from those of the Arrest Convention 1999:

(1) The SMPL and other Chinese legislation includes detailed provisions modifying the procedures regarding ship arrest and the release of a ship, as well as comprehensive stipulations on judicial sales of arrested ships. These are issues that the Arrest Convention 1999 leaves to national legislation (see, for example, art 2(4)), or does not even touch upon, as with judicial sales of arrested ships.

(2) Article 21 of the SMPL provides that, in addition to arresting ships for the preservation and securing of maritime claims, ships can also be arrested for enforcing judgments, arbitral awards or other legal documents, and the SMPL provisions apply equally to such 'enforcement arrests'. In contrast, the Arrest Convention 1999 explicitly excludes 'the seizure of a ship in execution or satisfaction of a judgment or other enforceable instrument' from its definition of 'arrest' in art 1(2).

(3) The SMPL made some adjustments during the process of transplanting the provisions of the Arrest Convention 1999 into Chinese law. For example, art 76 of the SMPL provides as follows:

> The amount of the security requested for preservation of a maritime claim by a maritime claimant from a person against whom the claim is made shall be equal to the amount of his credit, but shall not exceed the value of the property preserved.
>
> The amount of the security provided by a maritime claimant shall be equal to the loss the person against whom the claim is made may suffer as a result of his application. The exact amount shall be determined by the Maritime Court.

In contrast, art 4(2) of the Arrest Convention 1999 provides that the court has a discretion to determine the nature and amount of counter-security, subject only to the amount 'not exceeding the value of the arrested ship' (see also art 6). The exceptions to the prohibitions on rearrest and multiple arrests in art 24 of the SMPL and art 5 of the Arrest Convention 1999 are also slightly differently drafted. While some of these adjustments under the SMPL have been made in consideration of the special characteristics of China's domestic legal practices, others seem to have arisen from a misunderstanding of the provisions of the Arrest Convention 1999.

IV. Statutory Supplements to the SMPL

The SMPL repeals past practices in previous Rules that conflict with it.[37] Nevertheless, the SMPL does not provide guidance for procedures in all aspects of ship arrest and auctions, so the Ship Arrest Rules 1994 and the Sales of Ship Rules 1994 were important supplements to the SMPL and applied until 2015, to the extent that they did not conflict with the SMPL.

In 2003, in order to clarify the implementation of the SMPL, the SPC issued its Interpretation of the Supreme People's Court on the Application of the Special Maritime Procedure Law of the PRC (SPC Interpretation 2003).[38] The SPC Interpretation 2003 affirmed that none of the local district courts other than Maritime Courts is authorised to accept any applications for arresting vessels; if a local district court needs to arrest or sell a ship for the enforcement of a judgment or other legal document, it shall entrust the execution to the Maritime Court of the place of registry of the ship or of the place where the ship is located (art 15). Part II of the SPC Interpretation 2003, 'Preservation Measures for Maritime Claims', details the procedures of maritime preservation including that of ship arrest (arts 18–23), specifies the scope of the damages resulting from wrongful arrests (art 24), sets a 30-day limit for arresting and auctioning of a ship (art 25), allows the release of a ship if insufficient counter-security is provided by an claimant (art 26), and provides that the maintenance charges and expenses incurred while the ship is under arrest shall be deemed to have been paid for the joint interest of the creditors, and shall therefore be set aside as a first priority from the sum obtained from auction of the ship (art 28).

With new issues arising in practice that could not be resolved satisfactorily under the SMPL and its previous statutory supplements, as well as the developed principles of preservation introduced by the amended Civil Procedure Law,[39] further interpretation of or improvement to the SMPL was necessary. The SPC therefore enacted the Provisions of the Supreme People's Court on Several Issues concerning the Application of Law in the Arrest and Auction of Ships in 2015 (SPC Interpretation 2015).[40]

The SPC Interpretation 2015 aims to clarify and streamline the rules and judicial practice of ship arrest and auction sales in China. The main changes the Interpretation introduces are as follows:[41]

(1) Article 3 clarifies that, where a ship is arrested because the bareboat charterer is liable for the maritime claim, if the claimant applies for the auction of the ship concerned for the purpose of paying off the relevant debts arising from the operation of the ship

[37] The SPC, *Notice on Study, Propagating and Implementation of the Special Maritime Procedure Law* (28 February 2000) Fa [2000] No 7 (SPC).

[38] Interpretation of the Supreme People's Court on the Application of the Special Maritime Procedure Law of the PRC (adopted and promulgated at the 1259th meeting of the Adjudication Committee of the Supreme People's Court on 3 December 2002, came into force on 1 February 2003).

[39] The Civil Procedure Law was amended in 2007, 2012 and 2017.

[40] The Provisions of the Supreme People's Court on Several Issues concerning the Application of Law in the Arrest and Auction of Ships, (adopted at the 1,631st meeting of the Judicial Committee of the Supreme People's Court on 8 December 2014, issued on 28 February 2015, came into force on 1 March 2015) Fa Shi [2015] No 6. An English translation is available at enccmt.court.gov.cn/chinamaritimetrial/2016-10/26/c_59499.htm.

[41] The SPC Interpretation 2015 was accompanied by a public statement by Luo Dongchuan, who was then Division Chief of the 4th Civil Division of the SPC: see Dexter Yan, 'China Clears Way for Auction of Arrested Bareboat Charter Vessels', *Fairplay*, 27 March 2015.

by the bareboat charterer in accordance with the provisions of art 29 of the SMPL, the Maritime Court will approve such application.[42]

(2) Article 4 provides that the requirement of providing counter-security for ship arrest can be waived in respect of disputes over the employment contracts of seafarers or compensation for personal injury at sea or in navigable waters 'if both the facts and the rights and obligations of the parties are clear', in order to assist particular classes of claimants in a generally weaker bargaining or economic position.

(3) Article 6 regulates the circumstances in which counter-security may be returned to the claimant.[43]

(4) The Interpretation simplifies and enhances the efficiency of the judicial sale and auction process. For example, if the first ship auction fails, the notice period for the second auction is shortened to 7 days, in accordance with art 45 of the Auction Law,[44] instead of the 30 days provided for under art 10 of the SMPL; and if ship auctions fail twice an arrested ship can then be sold at no less than 50 per cent of its appraised value (SPC Interpretation 2015, art 13).[45]

(5) The Interpretation formulates the rules of jurisdiction in cases of realising security interests on a vessel. Article 196 of the Civil Procedure Law provides that a security interest holder or any other party entitled to request realisation of the security interest shall, in accordance with the Property Law,[46] file an application before the local people's court at the place where the property held as security is located or at the place of registration of the security interest. However, the SMPL reserves exclusive jurisdiction over vessel-related cases to Maritime Courts. In order to resolve the confusion about this issue, the Interpretation emphasises that an application for auction of a ship for realising the security interest on it shall fall under the jurisdiction of the Maritime Court where the ship attached as security is located or at the place of the ship's port of registration (art 23).

(6) The Interpretation also clarifies and closes up loopholes on some other issues, such as multiple arrests (art 2), the obligation of the shipowner and bareboat charterer to supervise the ship during the arrest (art 7), and the application of the Interpretation to ship auctions for repaying debts in enforcement procedures (art 24).

It should be pointed out that the SPC Interpretation 2015, in ending the ambiguity surrounding judicial auctions of bareboat-chartered vessels, specifically referred to

> the experiences of the 1952 International Convention for the Unification of Certain Rules Relating to the Arrest Of Sea-Going Ships and the 1999 International Convention on the Arrest of Ships. The court also referred to the maritime laws of major international shipping powers.[47]

[42] See Feifei Deng, 'New Regulations Relating to Arrest of Ships in China' (2015) 21 *JIML* 309, 310.

[43] ibid 311.

[44] Auction Law of the PRC (Adopted at the 20th Meeting of the Standing Committee of the Eighth National People's Congress and promulgated by Order No 70 of the PRC on 5 July 1996, came into effect on 1 January 1997, amended according to the Decision of the Standing Committee of the Tenth National People's Congress on Amending the Auction Law of the PRC adopted at its 11th Meeting on 28 August 2004). An English translation is available at www.npc.gov.cn/englishnpc/Law/2007-12/11/content_1383591.htm.

[45] Deng (n 42) 313.

[46] Property Law of the PRC (adopted at the Fifth Session of the Tenth National People's Congress of the PRC and promulgated by Order No 62 of the President of the PRC on 16 March 2007, came into effect on 1 October 2007). An English translation is available at www.npc.gov.cn/englishnpc/Law/2009-02/20/content_1471118.htm.

[47] Yan (n 41) reporting the public statement by Luo Dongchuan.

In addition to the above special legislation, some other Acts or regulations also form part of the legal system of ship arrest and auction sale by providing general rules or applying to certain issues in this field. The Civil Procedure Law outlines the general principles and procedures of property preservation, the Guaranty Law[48] provides general background principles dealing with security interests in the arrested ship and the Auction Law[49] provides general principles for the procedures to be followed in the auction of ships.

Together with the issuance of the SPC Interpretation 2015, the SPC published 10 Guiding Cases of Ship Arrest and Auction Adjudicated by Maritime Courts from 2000–2014. These selected cases reflect significant developments in judicial practices, or efforts by Maritime Courts to remedy deficiencies in the statutes, or other complicated substantive and procedural issues. China is not a case-law country, but the officially published guiding cases may act as guidance to courts faced with similar cases or provide valuable references to judicial practices. In 2016, the published 10 guiding maritime law cases also included a case in relation to ship arrest and ship sales.[50]

A. Interpretation and Practical Guidelines on Specific Issues

i. Ships that May be Arrested

a. 'The Ship Concerned'

'The ship concerned' is a term introduced by the SMPL. It is similar to the 'ship in respect of which a maritime claim is asserted' under art 3(1) of the Arrest Convention 1999, or the 'particular ship in respect of which the maritime claim arose' under art 3(1) of the Arrest Convention 1952.

According to art 23 of the SMPL, Maritime Courts can arrest the ship concerned in any of the following circumstances:

(1) the shipowner is liable for the maritime claim and is the owner of the ship at the time of arrest;
(2) the bareboat charterer of the ship is liable for the maritime claim and is the bareboat charterer or owner of the ship at the time of arrest;
(3) a maritime claim that gives rise to a ship mortgage or to rights of a similar nature;
(4) a maritime claim related to ownership or possession of a ship; and
(5) a maritime claim that gives rise to a maritime lien.

In spite of slight differences in wording, these provisions are similar to those found in art 3 of the Arrest Convention 1999.

If a maritime claim arises, whether in contract or in tort, the ship concerned can be arrested only if the person liable for the claim is still the owner or the bareboat charterer

[48] Guaranty Law of the PRC (adopted at the 14th Meeting of the Standing Committee of the Eighth National People's Congress and promulgated by Order No 50 of the President of the PRC on 30 June 1995), came into effect on 1 October 1995). An English translation is available at www.npc.gov.cn/englishnpc/Law/2007-12/12/content_1383719.htm.

[49] Auction Law (n 44).

[50] See www.court.gov.cn/zixun-xiangqing-42642.html.

of that ship on the execution of the arrest. For example, when a claim arises against a time or voyage charterer for unpaid charges on bunkering or other services or supplies, the ship concerned may not be arrested.

However, if a maritime claim is based on a mortgage or other rights of a similar nature, or secured by a maritime lien, or related to the ownership or possession of a ship, only the ship concerned can be arrested, regardless of whether the defendant owns or possesses the ship at the time when the claim arises or at the time of arrest.

The 10 Guiding Cases of Ship Arrest and Auction Adjudicated by Maritime Courts from 2000–2014 contain a case, *The MV Amin*, on ship arrest and auction by the ship mortgagee. In this case, the claimant, DVB Bank SE, lent money to the defendant, ISIM Amin Ltd of Malta. Both parties executed a mortgage agreement and registered the mortgage on the *MV Amin* (later renamed the *MV Amin 2*) to secure the loan. The borrower failed to repay the loan amount of more than €27 million. Therefore, in October 2013 the lender applied for the arrest of the *MV Amin 2* while the ship was anchored at Zhangzhou, a port within the jurisdiction range of Xiamen Maritime Court, requiring payment of the loan debt. The ship was successfully arrested and auctioned by the court in May 2014 as the defendant failed to provide adequate security to release the ship. In this case, the ship could not be arrested for the claim for breach of contract based upon the loan agreement, because this is not listed as a maritime claim in art 21 of the SMPL. Instead, the maritime claim arose under art 21(21) of the SMPL in respect of a 'ship mortgage or rights of a similar nature'. Therefore, strictly speaking, the *MV Amin 2* should have been arrested and auctioned for realisation of the registered security interests over the ship concerned, rather than for the payment claim on the underlying loan agreement.

b. Sister Ships

Besides the 'ship concerned', art 23(2) of the SMPL stipulates that a Maritime Court may arrest 'other ships' owned, at the time of arrest, by the shipowner, bareboat charterer, time charterer or voyage charterer who is liable for the maritime claim, except for claims related to ownership or possession of a ship. The scope of the 'other ships' that may be arrested is the same as that stipulated under art 3(2) of the Arrest Convention 1999.[51] These ships are usually regarded as 'sister ships' in China.

The scope of 'other ships' defined by the above two instruments constitute an extension of the rules laid down by arts 3(1) and 3(4) of the Arrest Convention 1952, in terms of which reference was made only to other ships owned by the owner or demise charterer of the particular ship in respect of which the maritime claim arose, who is liable for a maritime claim. This extension by the Arrest Convention 1999 and the SMPL is certainly an improvement in favour of the claimant.

However, it is still unsatisfactory for a number of reasons. First, in some maritime legal regimes it is not only shipowners and charterers who can be liable for a maritime claim – liability may extend to other parties as well. For instance, art 1(4) of the International Convention on Civil Liability for Bunker Oil Pollution Damage 2001 (BOPC 2001)[52]

[51] See also Berlingieri (n 12) vol 2 paras 8.63, 8.66.

[52] International Convention on Civil Liability for Bunker Oil Pollution Damage (adopted 23 March 2001, entered into force 21 November 2008), IMO Doc LEG/CONF 12/19, 23 March 2001.

provides that the shipowner liable for the pollution resulting from the escape or discharge of the bunker oil of the ship under art 3 includes the '[r]egistered owner, bareboat charterer, operator and manager of the ship'. In addition, we have seen an increasing number of varieties of co-operation, operation, capacity/slot sharing, volume and time contracts being used in shipping practice. These arrangements may not be easily classifiable into traditional types of ownership or charterparties. Some Maritime Courts in China have already affirmed the arrest of a sister ship owned by an operator of the ship concerned. Therefore, in the interests of the claimant, the concept of 'other ships' in art 23(2) of the SMPL should be broadened to include other ships owned by the 'shipowner, bareboat charterer, time charterer, voyage charterer, manager or operator' – or maybe even the 'capacity sharer' – who is liable for the maritime claim.

c. Associated Ships

The concept of 'associated ships' is broader than that of 'sister ships'. In terms of Chinese law, it refers to other ships that may not be under the same registered ownership as the ship concerned, but may have the same controller, beneficial owner or ultimate owner. For example, as a jurisdiction famous for its 'arrest-friendly' system of associated ships, South Africa allows the arrest, not only of traditional sister ships in common ownership, but also of associated ships controlled directly or indirectly through a common company or company group.[53] Similarly, ships under the ownership of separate state-owned entities seem to have been regarded as associated ships in France in the 1980s.[54]

There is no legal concept of 'associated ships' under the Arrest Convention 1999 or the SMPL. However, arguments supporting the arrest of ships under ultimate or indirect common control or ownership, or for piercing or lifting the corporate veil in the case of corporate ownership structures, are certainly not rare, in China or elsewhere.[55]

Article 3(2) of the Arrest Convention 1952 provides that a 'ship shall be deemed to be in the same ownership when all the shares therein are owned by the same person or persons.' Despite this, during the review of the Arrest Convention 1952, in light of the evolution in several countries of jurisprudence relating to situations in which it is permitted to pierce the corporate veil, the CMI recommended in its position paper that explicit permission should be granted to the States Parties to pierce or lift the corporate veil if this was permitted by the lex fori.[56] The UK delegation proposed that 'the arrest of a ship not owned by the person against whom the claim is asserted but it is "controlled" by such person to be permissible', and also suggested a number of factors to discern the existence of such control.[57] The UK's proposal 'gave rise to a lengthy debate' and was rejected by the great majority of delegations, including China. Most of them stated that this issue should be left for national laws or an ad hoc Convention to resolve.[58] The result is that the Arrest Convention 1999 defaulted to the 'sister ship' model of the Arrest Convention 1952 rather than expressly mandating arrest of associated ships.

[53] See further ch 2.
[54] Berlingieri (n 12) vol 1 para 13.62.
[55] See further ch 13.
[56] Berlingieri (n 12) vol 2 para 8.70ff.
[57] ibid.
[58] ibid para 8.71ff.

The domestic law of China does not expressly clarify this issue either. On examining art 23 of the SMPL, there appears to be no clear legislative intention to expand the scope of ships that may be arrested to include associated ships. However, this approach has been criticised by some Chinese academics and judges, because 'it could not resolve the rampant existence of single-ship companies, or flag of convenience ships'. Some commentators have suggested that the concept of 'shipowners' in the SMPL be extended to cover all registered owners, actual owners or beneficial owners;[59] while others have suggested that sister ships should be identified by 'reasonable criteria' taking into account both ownership and 'control' for the sake of legitimacy.[60]

Some Maritime Courts have also examined common ownership or control by an ultimate owner to determine a sister ship or have pierced or lifted the corporate veil to find the liable party. In 1999, the *MV Ice Mountain* was arrested for damage to cargo caused during its carriage. The ship was registered under the name of Ice Mountain Limited SA, a single-ship company incorporated in Panama. After the ship's arrest, the actual beneficial owner, a Chinese company, brought a suit in Qingdao and promptly provided security to secure the release of the ship.[61] However, in most cases, the Maritime Courts still adhere strictly to the literal wording of the SMPL about ownership and limit the scope of sister ships liable for arrest accordingly.

In my view, lifting the corporate veil too freely to look behind single-ship company structures to expand the scope of sister ships is undesirable. I agree with the main points of the large majority of the delegations' arguments against the UK's proposal in 1993,[62] namely:

(1) single-ship companies or special purpose vehicles are common arrangements, not only in shipping but also in other industries;
(2) the establishment of single-ship companies is based on the legal rule of corporate personality and the limited liability that flows from this doctrine;
(3) in most cases, one-ship companies are well justified for economic, financial, tax or political reasons, and are not merely artifices constructed to circumvent the arrest of sister ships;
(4) limiting maritime liability to a single ship or a single company helps to keep afloat the maritime industry, which requires significant investment of capital and is inherently highly risky;
(5) extensive applications of the doctrine of piercing the corporate veil will adversely affect maritime trade as well as crews and ship management companies; and
(6) the issue of piercing the corporate veil is a question for company law, and not a particular maritime law issue.

Even in the field of company law, piercing or lifting the corporate veil should be applied prudently. For example, in the Hong Kong case of *The Neptune*,[63] the plaintiff arrested the

[59] Xiang Minghua, 'The Values and Limitations on Ship Arrest Procedure' (2009) 2 *Journal of International Economic Law* 308, 335.

[60] Yang Weiwei and Li Zhiwen, 'On the Legitimacy of Arrest of Ships' (2013) 3 *Chinese Journal of Maritime Law* 82, 86.

[61] Cited in Xiang (n 59) 333.

[62] Berlingieri (n 12) vol 2 para 8.71.

[63] *Bakri Bunker Trading Co Ltd v The Owners of and Other Persons Interested in the Ship Neptune* [1985] HKCFI 236.

ship for unpaid bunkers supplied to other two ships owned by two separate companies. The plaintiff argued that the same person was the alter ego of the three companies and controlled them all. The plaintiff asked the High Court to lift the corporate veil on the ground of fraud to establish that the beneficial owner of the three ships was the said person. The Court held that it is necessary to provide positive evidence to prove fraud:

> In my finding there is no positive evidence that suggests fraud; what has been put forward falls more within the realms of speculation and suspicion. It follows that I would not be justified in attempting to lift the veils of incorporation of the corporations in question. Nor would it, I believe, be right or appropriate, for essentially the same reason, to order the existence of fraud to be tried as a preliminary issue …. Even if it were, it is difficult to see what additional evidence the Plaintiffs could procure or indeed what such a preliminary trial would achieve.[64]

The Court also noted that one-ship companies 'are by no means uncommon, and as a legitimate means of limiting liability, in my opinion, do not of themselves raise any inference of fraud.[65]

So, in principle, the general rule to determine a sister ship for the purpose of ship arrest in China is direct common ownership in the legal sense. However, in exceptional cases, where the form of the corporate owning structure is positively proved to be fraudulent or fictitious, or a malicious abuse of the limitation of liability of the company, the doctrine of lifting or piercing the corporate veil can be applied in order to protect the claimant or to protect the public interest. Given the views on this issue expressed in a review of national laws and jurisprudence during the revision of the Arrest Convention 1952, this seems to be the position in most other jurisdictions too.[66]

B. Rearrests and Multiple Arrests

i. *Rearrest of the Same Ship*

Rearrest in terms of Chinese law means the repeating of the arrest of the same ship for the same maritime claim after it has been released or security has been provided.[67] A ship cannot be rearrested after release under art 24 of the SMPL unless:

(1) the person against whom the claim is made fails to provide sufficient security;
(2) it is likely that the surety cannot perform the obligations under the security in full or in part; or
(3) the maritime claimant agrees, on reasonable grounds, to release the arrested ship or to return the security provided; or the maritime claimant cannot, by reasonable means, stop the release of the arrested ship or the return of the security provided.

The difference of the above exceptions in art 24 of the SMPL and those provided in art 5(1) of the Arrest Convention 1999 is that the latter instrument qualifies the first exception by

[64] ibid [28].
[65] ibid [24].
[66] Berlingieri (n 12) vol 1 para 13.06ff.
[67] See further ch 5.

including the condition 'that the aggregate amount of security may not exceed the value of the ship', whereas there is no such restriction in art 24 of SMPL. The SMPL therefore provides less clarity on the upper limit of what constitutes 'sufficient security' for rearrest of the same ship.

Article 76(1) of the SMPL provides that the 'amount of the security requested for preservation of a maritime claim by a maritime claimant from a person against whom the claim is made shall be equal to the amount of his credit, but shall not exceed the value of the property preserved'. Therefore, it may be understood that the SMPL sets two ceilings on the amount of security required for releasing an arrested ship: the first being the amount of the credit, and the second (maximum) ceiling being the value of the ship. In my view, it would be reasonable and logical to apply the ceilings in art 76(1) of the SMPL to the aggregate amount of the security to be furnished in the case of rearrest of the ship for the same maritime claim.

ii. *Multiple Arrests*

'Multiple arrests' under the Arrest Convention 1999 means the arrest of one or more of any other ships owned by the same defendant – that is, sister ships – in respect of the same maritime claim.[68] Article 5(2) of the Arrest Convention 1999 prohibits the multiple arrest of 'sister ships' for the same maritime claim, and sets out similar exceptions to those under the situation of rearrest: '(a) the nature of amount of the security already provided in respect of the same claim is inadequate; or (b) the provisions of paragraph 1 (b) or (c) of this article are applicable'; that is, the person who has provided the security is unable to fulfil some or all of its obligations, or the arrested ship or the security previously provided was released with the claimant's consent acting on reasonable grounds or the claimant could not prevent the release by taking reasonable steps. In the case of art 5(2)(a) of the Arrest Convention 1999, if the value of the ship that was previously arrested is lower than the amount of the claim, the claimant may resort to arrest one or more other ships owned by the defendant in order to obtain adequate security, but, unlike art 5(1)(a) of the Arrest Convention 1999, there is no express requirement that the aggregate amount of security shall not exceed the value of the arrested ship.

Neither the SMPL nor the SPC Interpretation 2015 deals with the issue of 'multiple arrests' in the same manner as art 5(2) of the Arrest Convention 1999. This was been described as an omission.[69] On examining the context of the SMPL, there seems to be no objection to multiple arrests of sister ships in order to ensure adequate security for maritime claims. According to art 76(1) of the SMPL, the first criterion for adequate security is the amount of the credit. If the credit is higher than the ship's value, it would seem reasonable for the claimant to be allowed to arrest more than one ship up to the value of its credit. However, the difficulty is that art 76(1) of the SMPL does not clearly state whether the ship's value as a maximum ceiling on the quantum of security is based on the value of one ship or multiple ships.

[68] Berlingieri (n 12) vol 2 para 9.09.
[69] Zhang (n 31) 121.

Taking into consideration the fact that the main purpose of ship arrest is to preserve maritime claims, in my view there should be no difference between the arrest of the ship concerned and the arrest of one (or more) sister ships – the fundamental purpose of ship arrest is to provide adequate security for the maritime claimant. It would therefore be fair to adopt the stipulations of art 5(2) of the Arrest Convention 1999 into Chinese maritime law and practice, so that a claimant can arrest multiple ships owned by the same defendant to get sufficient security for its maritime claims. This is particularly so because, as mentioned above, maritime claims in China are actually brought against the defendant shipowner or bareboat charterer rather than against the ship in rem. In that context, limiting security to the value of (one) arrested res does not make any sense.

However, there is another meaning of 'multiple arrest' introduced in the SPC Interpretation 2015, which concerns multiple arrests of the same ship by different claimants. Article 103 of the Civil Procedure Law prohibits multiple seizures, freezing or attachments in respect of the same property. Prior to the SPC Interpretation 2015, if a ship was already arrested, a party other than the first claimant had to wait until the first arrest was officially lifted by the Chinese court before a second arrest could be executed on the same ship.[70] This prohibition obviously caused difficulties for maritime claimants. First, in terms of art 28 of the Maritime Code, a maritime lien is enforced by the court by arresting the ship concerned. Without the timely execution of a ship arrest, a maritime lien will be extinguished, even though the claimant entitled to the maritime lien has registered as a creditor during the judicial sale of the ship arrested for another party. Further, it is common in practice for maritime incidents to give rise to various claims and claimants, but the value of the ship is higher than any one of the claims. Thus, allowing multiple claimants to arrest the same ship is far more reasonable than adopting a 'first in first served' approach.

In China, the Maritime Courts had already introduced some exceptions to the prohibition of multiple arrests, particularly in the context of maritime liens. A claimant alleging a maritime lien could also apply to arrest the vessel to satisfy that maritime lien, even if the vessel had already been arrested by another claimant, and when the ship was released it could immediately be rearrested in favour of the claimant exercising its maritime lien, which would have priority in repayment over any other claims.

Article 2 of the SPC Interpretation 2015 allows multiple claimants to arrest the same ship as security for their respective claims. This article further provides that, if a claimant arrests the ship but does not apply for an auction within the time limit, a subsequent claimant may apply for judicial sale pursuant to art 29 of the SMPL.[71]

However, it is not clear from the SPC Interpretation 2015 whether, and how much, each claimant is required to provide in the way of counter-security in the event of multiple arrests. A prudent view would be that the current provisions and requirements regarding counter-security should apply equally to all claimants in multiple arrest cases.[72] Since the Chinese courts have a broad discretion in deciding the amounts of counter-security, there is no standardised practice. Previously, in different courts, the amounts could be equal to that

[70] Ince & Co Shanghai, 'China: New Judicial Interpretation on the Arrest and Judicial Sale of Ships' *Ince & Co E-Brief* (Spring 2015) 14, 15.

[71] See Deng (n 42) 312.

[72] Ince & Co Shanghai (n 70) 14.

of a maritime claim, or the approximate value of the arrested ship or the loss of 30 days of hire. The SPC Interpretation 2015 tries to provide some guidance. Article 5 stipulates that the amount of counter-security should cover the maintenance costs of the ship during the arrest, losses incurred due to loss of use of the ship and the costs incurred by the defendant in relation to providing security in exchange for release of the ship.[73] Nevertheless, the meaning of loss of use of the ship will still need to be clarified on a case-by-case basis.

iii. 'Live' Arrest and Restraint Measures

The SMPL has created a unique form of non-physical ship arrest in China, which is informally called 'live' arrest or 'active' arrest. According to art 27 of the SMPL, after an order to preserve a ship, the Maritime Court may with the consent of the maritime claimant allow the ship to continue its operation by way of restraining the disposition or mortgaging of the ship. So, 'live' arrest is an alternative measure imposed on ships with the claimant's consent.

The Arrest Convention 1999 only stipulates for the physical arrest or removal of ships. This innovation of 'live' arrest in China originated from the SPC's Interpretations on the Application of the Civil Procedure Law of the PRC in 1992.[74] Pursuant to art 101 of this Interpretation:

> Preservation measures against real properties and some specific movable properties (such as vehicles, ships) can be a deposition of the certificate of such property with serving a notice to the relevant Ship Registry to forbid the transfer of the property. A physical seizure or freezing of the property can also be enforced when necessary.

Even before the enactment of the SMPL, the Chinese Maritime Courts had begun to put this type of 'live' arrest into practice. In November 1994, the *MV Nan Hang You 2* and the *MV Xiang You 11* collided in the Pearl River. As a result of this collision, oil carried by the *MV Nan Hang You 2* leaked into the river. The oil pollution caused significant losses to local fisheries, and the Fishery Association of Guangdong lodged a lawsuit against the shipowners of the two offending ships before the Guangzhou Maritime Court and applied for the two ships to be arrested. Since the liability of the two ships for the collision was unclear, the Maritime Court approved their arrest, but held that the shipowners could remain in possession and control of their ships, but were not allowed to transfer, mortgage or otherwise dispose of them. In addition, the court required the two shipowners to provide cash security and informed the registration authorities about the restraint on these two ships. After the trial, the two shipowners indemnified the claimant and the 'live' arrest and restraint on the two ships was removed as a consequence.[75]

Following the coming into effect of the SMPL, if the defendant is unable to provide security on an application for ship arrest, the ship may nonetheless be released and continue its operations provided the claimant agrees to this. The notice of such preservation (not literally 'arrest') will be sent to the registry of the ship concerned and the local MSA to forbid any transfers of ownership of the vessel or the registration of any mortgages on the vessel. The purpose of such 'live' arrest is to improve the defendant shipowner's or bareboat charterer's

[73] See text at n 40 above.
[74] This document was replaced and repealed by the new Civil Procedure Law in 2012.
[75] Jin Zhengjia (ed), *Chinese Typical Maritime Cases* (Beijing, Law Press–China, 1998) 652–55.

financial prospects of providing security or satisfaction of the maritime claim by keeping the vessel operating. However, the disadvantages of 'live' arrest are quite obvious. Allowing the vessel to operate will expose it to more risks during the period of operation, such as partial or total loss of the res, or the attachment of new maritime liens to the vessel. The court and claimant do not have effective control over a ship under 'live' arrest.[76]

In order to reduce these risks, art 29 of the SPC Interpretation 2003 of the SMPL limits the application of art 27 of the SMPL to the completion of the current voyage on domestic routes. This limitation to domestic voyages and the co-operation required with other local maritime authorities mean that a 'live' arrest can be ordered in respect of Chinese-flagged ships only.

With such limitations placed on the 'live' arrest concept, it is impossible to achieve the underlying purpose of improving the financial status of the defendant shipowner or bareboat charterer by maintaining the continuous operation of the ship. This provides scant motivation for claimants to agree to 'live' arrests. Some practitioners have commented that the advantage of the 'live' arrest system can only be seen when the value of the vessel itself is far less than the amount claimed.[77] In practice, some courts may allow ships under 'live' arrest to operate for more than one voyage.

The 'live' arrest concept has given rise to some problems and confusion in practice. Can a pure 'live' arrest be applied for without a physical arrest? Can 'live' arrest be exercised only for maritime claims or for other civil claims as well? Is 'live' arrest within the exclusive jurisdiction of the Maritime Courts or can other courts order 'live' arrests of ships too? Should the claimants provide counter-security for a 'live' arrest? May a physical arrest applied for by another claimant occur simultaneously with a 'live' arrest? If so, which one takes priority?[78] The practices adopted by the courts are not unified.

It has been said that art 1(1) of the SPC Interpretation 2015 supplements and improves on the previous system of 'live' arrest.[79] In my view, however, the preservation orders confirmed by art 1(1) of the SPC Interpretation 2015 are not intended to supplement so-called 'live' arrest, but rather to supplement full maritime preservations. The traditional 'live' arrest in China is an alternative to physical arrest of ships. 'Live' arrest is ordered on the arrest application and with the consent of the claimant. It falls within the scheme of the SMPL. However, the order 'restraining disposal or mortgage and other preservation measures against a vessel' referred to in art 1(1) of the SPC Interpretation 2015 is distinct from physical or 'live' ship arrest under the SMPL. Article 1(1) provides that the relevant

[76] See Zhao and Li (n 4) para 18.24: 'Therefore, it is submitted that a maritime claimant should be extremely cautious before giving any consent [to a 'live' arrest], and should make preparations if planning to take on such risks.'

[77] See Margot C R Luo, 'Laws and Practice of Ship Arrest in PRC Maritime Courts' *CMI Yearbook 2013: Beijing II Documents of the Conference* (Antwerp, CMI, 2013) 526, 529.

[78] This question arose from a Chinese case involving concurrent and competing physical and 'live' arrests of the same ship. In 2011 a vessel was physically arrested and auctioned off by the Qingdao Maritime Court. However, this vessel was restrained by another Maritime Court from transfer, disposal or mortgaging, and was so recorded in its registry authority, MSA Wenzhou. Initially, the purchaser of the vessel in the judicial auction could not register its ownership because MSA Wenzhou refused to effect transfer until the 'live' arrest had been lifted. This conflict was finally resolved by discussion and co-operation between the two Maritime Courts that led to the 'live' arrest being removed. See Lan Lu'an & Zheng Lei, 'A Study on Several Issues about the "Live Arrest" of Ships Under the Supreme People's Court's Interpretation on Arrest and Auction of Ships' (2015) 4 *Maritime China* 76, 79.

[79] ibid 77.

Maritime Court 'may render a ruling to approve such application and notify the relevant vessel registration authority to provide assistance for enforcement pursuant to provisions of the Civil Procedure Law'. Further, art 1(2) provides that '[p]reservation measures prescribed in the preceding Paragraph shall not affect the applications by other maritime claimants for arrest of the vessel'.[80]

According to the Civil Procedure Law, restraint preservation orders over property can be applied for in all kinds of civil claims, not only maritime claims, although the SPC Interpretation 2015 does not point this out. Furthermore, on its face, art 1(1) of the SPC Interpretation 2015 allows a Chinese Maritime Court to order restraint of transfer of ownership or the mortgages over not just Chinese-flagged vessels, but also foreign-flagged ships. Nonetheless, it is difficult to see how such an order would have extra-territorial effect in respect of foreign-flagged ships, because its execution would depend on the co-operation of ship registries or other authorities at the place of foreign registration.

As to competing claims involving restraint orders on the title of a ship and physical arrests, the judicial sale by auction of the physically arrested ship should break the restraint on the transfer, disposition or mortgaging of the ship. Articles 28 and 30 of the SPC's Rules on Impounding, Seizure and Freezing of Properties provide that, when a court disposes of any property, previously executed impounding, seizure or freezing of that property is null and void. So, if the ship has been sold by auction, the previous restraint order on the ship should also be null and void.

Article 1(1) of the SPC Interpretation 2015 regarding restraint measures provides an alternative method for maritime claimants to protect and enforce their security interests in the ship, but it should not affect the operation of physical or 'live' arrests under the SMPL and its implementation rules. Nevertheless, art 1(1) is not detailed enough. Some questions, particularly in respect of provision of counter-security and the competing jurisdictions of different Maritime Courts, remain. These require further exploration and clarification.

iv. Wrongful Arrests

Article 6 of the Arrest Convention 1999 allows (but does not require) courts to require claimants to provide counter-security as a condition for allowing or maintaining ship arrest in order to indemnify the losses or damages that the defendant may incur in consequence of '(a) the arrest having been wrongful or unjustified; or (b) excessive security having been demanded and provided'. Thus, the purpose of counter-security in this context is to provide compensation for the defendant's losses resulting from a wrongful arrest. However, the Arrest Convention 1999 does not define a 'wrongful' or 'unjustified' arrest. The determination of this issue is left to the lex fori.

Similarly, the SMPL and its interpretations do not contain any definition of 'wrongful' or 'unjustified' arrest or offer any standard or guidelines for deciding this issue. But art 24 of the SPC Interpretation 2003 and art 5 of the SPC Interpretation 2015 set out in general terms the scope of the losses and damages caused by wrongful arrest.

[80] So too Deng (n 42) 312, who describes this as '[a]nother preservative measure other than arrest against a ship'.

a. Basis of Wrongful Arrests

There are no uniform criteria for defining a wrongful arrest in Chinese judicial practice. Generally, a ship arrest may be regarded as 'wrongful' in the following three situations,[81] some of which warrant further examination:

(1) *Arresting the wrong ship*. As elaborated in art 23 of the SMPL, only the ship concerned, or a sister ship may be arrested for a maritime claim. Arresting any other ship is, by definition, a wrongful arrest. In the event of such a wrongful arrest, the owner or the charterer of the ship is entitled to raise an objection against the arrest. If this objection is successful, the arrest will not be approved, or will be lifted if the ship has already been arrested. The claimant may be responsible for the losses incurred by the innocent third party resulting from this wrongful arrest. For instance, after a collision between the *MV 236* and another vessel, the *MV 235* was arrested together with the *MV 236* in Pakistan. It was ascertained that the *MV 235* was owned by an innocent third party. The owner of the *MV 235* sued for indemnification for the wrongful arrest. The Xiamen Maritime Court supported the claim.

(2) *Arrest not properly based on a maritime claim*. In China, when the claim for which the ship is arrested is not a maritime claim listed in art 21 of the SMPL – for example, a claim under a loan agreement with no relation to a ship mortgage, or a dispute arising under a freight-forwarding agreement – this could, on its face, be regarded as a wrongful arrest. However, such cases will not automatically amount to wrongful arrests. It will depend on the court's examination of the basis for the arrest or the nature of the defendant's objection.

More often than not, however, if a claimant is judged not to have been entitled to have arrested the ship on its alleged claim in the case on the merits, the arrest will be regarded as having been wrongful. If the defendants are found not liable for any of the claims secured by the ship arrest, or the claimant failed in its case on the merits, the claimant will usually be liable for the losses incurred by the defendant caused by such an arrest.[82]

In the author's view, this sets the threshold for wrongful arrest too low, and may place an unreasonable burden on claimants bringing difficult, novel or test cases in good faith. In determining whether the claimant is liable for wrongful arrest, the subjective intention of the claimant should be considered, with a higher threshold of bad faith, malice or gross negligence (crassa negligentia) being applied, in line with the *Evangelismos* test applied in English law.[83]

Although a requirement of bad faith, malice or gross negligence has not been cited directly by the Chinese Maritime Courts, some courts have taken the subjective intention of the claimant into consideration in determining whether ship arrests are wrongful. In the *MV Jingcheng* case heard by the Xiamen Maritime Court, the ship was arrested for unpaid bunkering charges owed to a company, CJ. After the ship was arrested, the owner proved that the ship had been time chartered out. The ship was then released upon security being provided by the time charterer. Subsequently, in the litigation between CJ and the shipowner on the bunkering charges, the Court held that the shipowner was not responsible for

[81] Xiang (n 5) 218–21; Zhang (n 30) 129–34.
[82] Zhang (n 30) 130.
[83] See further ch 6; Yang Liangyi, *Maritime Law*, (Dalian, Dalian University Press, 1999) 66–9.

the bunkering charges since the ship was under a time charter. Therefore, the shipowner brought another suit against CJ claiming for losses suffered from wrongful arrest. After reviewing the facts and the evidence, the Court concluded that the claimant had applied for the ship arrest honestly and decided that the arrest application based on the ship's stamp appearing on both the bunkering order and the receipt was 'with good reason' and 'could be considered as excusable'.[84] In my view, this is a fair and reasonable decision.

Some academics and judges, however, advocate for determination of wrongful arrest to be based merely on the objective result, regardless of the subjective intention of the claimant. They worry about the abuse of the right of ship arrest if subjective factors are introduced because the 'consequences to a wrongful arrest is so serious'.[85] With such differing views on the legal test for wrongful ship arrest in China, we are likely to see inconsistent and conflicting cases on this issue until it is settled by judicial interpretation or legislative reform.

(3) *Excessive security has been demanded.* Under the SMPL, primarily, the amount, type and nature of the security to be provided by the defendant is agreed on through negotiations between the claimant and the defendant. If the parties fail to agree, art 75 of the SMPL provides that the court will decide the issue. Further, the security demanded by the claimant may not exceed the amount of the maritime claim. Therefore, a demand for excessive security by the claimant is included as an extended category of wrongful arrest. It is regarded as an abuse of the right of ship arrest, because it may result in the ship being sold because of the defendant's failure or inability to provide the excessive security;[86] or the defendant may suffer an undue burden in providing such security. In certain cases, the claimant has had to indemnify the defendant for requiring excessive security which caused the judicial sale of the ship due to the defendant's failure to provide sufficient security.[87]

However, in consideration of fairness and reasonableness, the author suggests that the subjective intention of the claimant should also be taken into account to determine a wrongful arrest in the context of demands for excessive security. In other words, only where the claimant demands excessive security in bad faith, or is grossly negligent in doing so, should this conduct be regarded as amounting to a wrongful arrest.

b. Compensation for Wrongful Arrests

Article 6(2) of the Arrest Convention 1999 leaves it to the forum arresti to determine the extent of the liability of the claimant for a wrongful arrest or excessive security having been demanded and provided.

In the early stages after the coming into effect of the SMPL, some of the Chinese Maritime Courts were not particularly proficient in deciding the extent and amount of the losses and damages caused by wrongful arrests. However, under the guidance provided by art 24 of the SPC Interpretation 2003, the admissible damages caused by the wrongful arrest of ship are comprised of the maintenance expenses of the ship, the losses incurred by loss of use of the ship during its arrest and the expenses for providing security to release

[84] Civil Judgment of Xiamen Maritime Court, No (2011) Xia-Hai-Fa-Shi-Chu-Zi-80.
[85] Zhang (n 30) 139–40.
[86] ibid 132.
[87] ibid 134.

the ship. Moreover, whether the defendant took reasonable and timely steps to mitigate the damage by providing security will also be examined. Normally 30 days will be considered as a reasonable period by the court. If the time taken to arrange security far exceeds a reasonable period, the court may not be willing to support the defendant's claim for the alleged damages incurred beyond that period.[88]

Article 5(1) of the SPC Interpretation 2015 stipulates similar factors for ascertaining the amount of counter-security to be provided by a claimant to cover potential losses for wrongful arrest. These articles in the two Interpretations are related. Moreover, art 5(2) of the SPC Interpretation 2015 provides that, 'once counter-security has been provided, the owners of the arrested ship may apply for additional counter-security to be posted if they can demonstrate that the initial counter-security is insufficient to cover their likely losses'[89] if the arrest is later held to be wrongful.

These types of rules of counter-security and wrongful arrest are applied in most of the Civil Law countries, including China, but are rarely found in Common Law countries, such as the UK. The cumulative effect of the strict conditions placed on applications for ship arrest and the provision of counter-security in China, together with the relative ease of applying for damages for wrongful arrests, may make China a not particularly inviting venue for ship arrest.[90]

V. Conclusion

In summary, Chinese legislation and practices of ship arrest are transplanted from the substantive framework of the Arrest Convention 1999. Most of the essential stipulations of the Arrest Convention 1999 are codified in the SMPL.

Even on those issues where the Arrest Convention 1999 sets up guidelines but leaves the issue to the courts of its States Parties, Chinese courts have – despite the fact that China is not a State Party to that Convention – adhered closely to the Convention's provisions: for instance, with regard to the provision of counter-security in order to protect the shipowner in the event of wrongful arrest; and to the court's power of jurisdiction over the case on the merits being triggered by the ordering of ship arrest.

Nevertheless, despite such wholesale transplantation of the principles of the Arrest Convention 1999, China has made its own adjustments: for example, in the implicit prohibition on multiple arrest of sister ships; the development of 'live' arrest; the arrest of ships to enforce judgments and arbitral awards; and so on.

However, the rigid interpretation and application of some of the stipulations in China, such as the rules determining wrongful arrest and counter-security, may deter claimants from applying for ship arrest in China.[91]

[88] Luo Congrui, 'Arrest of Vessels in China' (Young CMI Forum, Beijing, 19 October 2012) 6.
[89] Ince & Co Shanghai (n 70) 15.
[90] ibid.
[91] See Deng (n 42) 314: 'The implementation of the new Regulations certainly will not turn China into one of the most arrest-friendly jurisdictions in the world, owing to the fact that a fair amount of court security is still required and claimants remain responsible for unjustified arrests effected erroneously without proper legal foundation but not motivated by bad faith or gross negligence, which can protect ship interests from vicious arrest.'

Furthermore, in those areas that the Arrest Convention 1999 does not touch upon, China has established its own national rules. The SMPL and its Interpretations have established a clear framework governing the procedures of ship arrest, the judicial sale of arrested ships, the priority of maritime claims, and distributions of proceeds among the creditors after a ship is sold. This has made the arrest and judicial sale of ships in China relatively systematic and clear.

However, in practice, there are still some issues that need to be clarified or tweaked, such as the scope of the definition of the party liable for the ship concerned, which arguably needs to be extended to cover non-traditional categories of ship managers, operators and shipping arrangements; and the list of maritime claims for ship arrest in the SMPL, which would benefit from a general definition or catch-all clause in addition to the current closed list, because the current closed list is too inflexible to cope with novel forms of contracts, operations or disputes arising in the shipping industry. Meanwhile, recent circumstances have thrown up new issues that are not dealt with under current legislation, such as the problems of ship arrest and judicial sale in the event of a cross-border insolvency, such as occurred with Hanjin Shipping;[92] and issues relating to the recognition of foreign judicial sales, which the CMI's Beijing Draft is seeking to address.[93]

Given the fact that most Chinese ports operate as international hubs in terms of cargo throughput, the demand for resolving maritime disputes and arresting ships in China is likely to continue to rise.[94] Therefore, if the vision of developing into a leading regional and international maritime law centre is to be realised, China must continually review its legal systems of ship arrest and judicial sale, and must periodically adjust them to improve the legal framework, to adapt to new developments in shipping practices and new problems, and to achieve a better balance between providing an attractive venue for ship arrest and preventing parties from abusing their procedural or substantive rights of ship arrest.

[92] See eg Xiaolin Zeng, 'More Hanjin ships arrested in China' *Fairplay*, 26 September 2016.

[93] The Beijing Draft refers to the CMI Draft International Convention of Foreign Judicial Sales of Ships and their Recognition. The Beijing Draft was approved at the 41st International Meeting of CMI on 17 June 2014. China has been leading the CMI drafting team: see Li Hai, 'The Most Recent Procedure of Comité Maritime International: the Beijing Draft' (2014) 3 *Chinese Journal of Maritime Law* 22. At the time of writing, UNCITRAL has agreed to add the issue of judicial sale of ships to its work programme: see UNCITRAL, 'Report of the United Nations Commission on International Trade Law: Fifty-first session (25 June–13 July 2018)' (31 July 2018) UN Doc A/73/17 para 252.

[94] Official statistics released by the SPC indicate that the 10 Chinese Maritime Courts have made 7,744 arrests and conducted 623 ship auctions between 1984 and 2013: see Deng (n 42) 309.

12

National Translations of the Arrest Conventions: Anglo-Common Law Jurisdictions

BEVAN MARTEN*

I. Introduction

In his magisterial work on the Arrest Conventions 1952 and 1999,[1] Berlingieri details a wide range of ways in which States of all stripes, from Algeria to the Republic of Mauritius, have implemented these somewhat obscure maritime instruments.[2] This Chapter looks at the position taken in respect of these instruments by one group of closely-related jurisdictions, namely England and Wales, Australia, Canada, Hong Kong, India, Ireland, New Zealand and Singapore. However, it will soon become apparent that in most cases this has been a question of how Anglo-Common Law jurisdictions have engaged with English admiralty legislation, as opposed to adhering to the international position represented by the Arrest Convention 1952.

Rather than providing a technical, line-by-line analysis of the differences between the Arrest Convention 1952 and the various domestic enactments that have followed, the Chapter focuses on some broader questions. First, what was the position of the Common Law countries on the arrest of vessels prior to the Arrest Convention 1952, and what role did they play in the treaty's development? Secondly, what are some of the key characteristics of the Common Law countries' current 'translations' of the Arrest Conventions 1952 and 1999, both as compared with the Conventions and with each other? Thirdly, how have the courts in Common Law countries approached the interpretation of their domestic legislation translating and implementing the Arrest Conventions? Fourthly, why has the Arrest Convention 1999, with one remarkable exception, failed to gain any traction in Anglo-Common Law jurisdictions?

* Senior Lecturer, Faculty of Law, Victoria University of Wellington; Partner, Izard Weston, Wellington, New Zealand.

[1] International Convention Relating to the Arrest of Sea-going Ships (adopted 10 May 1952, entered into force 24 February 1956) 439 UNTS 193; and International Convention on the Arrest of Ships (adopted 12 March 1999, entered into force 14 September 2011) 2797 UNTS 3 respectively.

[2] Francesco Berlingieri, *Berlingieri on the Arrest of Ships*, 6th edn (Abingdon, Informa Law from Routledge, 2017) vol 1 (commentary on the Arrest Convention 1952) and vol 2 (commentary on the Arrest Convention 1999).

II. The Common Law Jurisdictions before 1952

The Common Law jurisdictions certainly did not provide the impetus for the 1952 Arrest Convention. For England and its colonies (or former colonies) the practice of arresting a vessel had long been tied to the admiralty jurisdiction, which enabled a proceeding in rem against a vessel in relation to a limited number of maritime claims. While the claims falling within this jurisdiction had expanded and contracted over the centuries, the essential ingredients of admiralty jurisdiction in rem and the ability to arrest the res as security for a claim were not in doubt in the decades leading up to 1952. And in England the Supreme Court of Judicature (Consolidation) Act 1925 (UK) had recently brought together a range of nineteenth and early twentieth-century developments, placing the admiralty jurisdiction on a clear footing.

Such clarity had not yet been achieved elsewhere in the Common Law world, as the 1925 UK consolidation had not taken effect in those countries still governed by the Colonial Courts of Admiralty Act 1890 (CCAA 1890), which included Australia, Hong Kong, India, New Zealand and Singapore. This imperial legislation provided that the colony's court would perform the role of a court of admiralty, with the same admiralty jurisdiction as the High Court in England.[3] However, while a welcome replacement of the older system of imperial Vice-Admiralty Courts,[4] this legislation did not enable a country's admiralty jurisdiction to evolve in step with that of England. So, even for countries like Australia and New Zealand, which had become independent of the United Kingdom before 1952, life under the CCAA 1890 meant working with an admiralty jurisdiction frozen in 1890.[5]

Canada had already taken a step beyond the nineteenth century. Although it had adopted the CCAA 1890 on its own initiative in 1891,[6] it 're-adopted' English admiralty jurisdiction in 1934,[7] following the passage of the Statute of Westminster.[8] Meanwhile Ireland, although having achieved its independence, was still relying on the Court of Admiralty (Ireland) Act 1867 (UK) to define its admiralty jurisdiction.[9]

Accordingly, at the time discussions surrounding the possibility of a Convention on the arrest of ships began, the Common Law countries were all drawing – as could be expected – on the English model of admiralty jurisdiction. Furthermore, they would not have discussed the issues that the international community was about to address in terms of arrest. In a colloquial sense lawyers then and now might speak of arrest as founding admiralty jurisdiction, but only because it generally represents the more dramatic accompaniment of the filing of a proceeding in rem. Once matters turned technical, as they were to do at the

[3] Colonial Courts of Admiralty Act 1890, 53 & 54 Vic c 27 (UK), s 2(2).

[4] See Bevan Marten, 'Constitutional Irregularities in the British Imperial Courts of Vice Admiralty during the Mid-Nineteenth Century' (2016) 37 *J Legal History* 215.

[5] See CW O'Hare, 'Admiralty Jurisdiction (Part 1)' (1979) 6 *Monash U L Rev* 91; CA Ying, 'Colonial and Federal Admiralty Jurisdiction' (1981) 12 *Fed L Rev* 236.

[6] Admiralty Act 1891 (Canada) SC 15-16 Geo V c 49.

[7] Admiralty Act 1934 (Canada) SC 1934 c 31. See William Tetley and Robert C Wilkins, *Maritime Liens and Claims* 2nd edn (Montreal, International Shipping Publications Blais, 1998).

[8] Statute of Westminster 1931 (UK).

[9] Court of Admiralty (Ireland) Act 1867, 30 & 31 Vict c 114 (UK); see also Court of Admiralty (Ireland) Amendment Act 1876, 39 & 40 Vict c 27 (UK); Supreme Court of Judicature (Ireland) Act 1877, 40 & 41 Vict c 57 (UK) (this allocated admiralty jurisdiction to the High Court of Justice in Ireland, mirroring the English Judicature Acts). On the early historical development of Irish admiralty jurisdiction see Kevin Costello, *The Court of Admiralty of Ireland 1575–1893*, Irish Legal History Society Series 20 (Dublin, Four Courts, 2011).

Comité Maritime International's 1933 Oslo conference, a major conceptual gulf between the Civil Law and Common Law systems would quickly emerge.

III. Common Law Contributions to the Arrest Convention 1952

English law had long singled out ships (and to a lesser extent other maritime property) as subjects worthy of a distinctive jurisdiction, with its own rules, courts, and procedures. In contrast, at least at the start of the twentieth century, the Civil Law jurisdictions did not connect vessel arrest with a narrowly defined admiralty jurisdiction. Instead, arrest formed just one aspect of the enforcement of claims against a debtor's assets.[10] For example, under German law the claim in relation to which arrest was sought did not have to be connected to the ship. Instead, the German Maritime Law Association explained, 'German law only allows provisional arrest when the Judgment to be obtained is to be enforced abroad or when, without such arrest, the enforcing would prove appreciably more difficult or even inefficient.'[11]

Although Civil Law jurisdictions did not place restrictions on the types of claims for which arrest could be sought, arrest was nonetheless an uncommon practice on the continent. Unlike in England, where arrest could be ordered by a Registrar following the filing of proceedings, arrest in Civil Law countries would require convincing a judge to make such an order. Another difference was that the threshold for liability for wrongful arrest was much higher in England than in Civil Law systems, making it less of a financial risk for a claimant to arrest a vessel in an English port.[12]

Against this background, it was Civilian States such as France, Germany and Italy that provided the impetus behind the Arrest Convention 1952, seeking a unified approach to their broadly-framed powers of arrest. The relative lack of success of the Maritime Liens and Mortgages Convention of 1926, for example, was perceived as being linked to the lack of international uniformity on this subject.[13] However, limiting the types of claims that would justify a vessel's arrest in the English manner was not at first seen as the way to achieve this. An early draft of the Convention, by France's Leopold Dor simply provided that 'Any creditor of the Owner of a ship … may operate the provisional arrest of that ship', and otherwise focused on the provision of security to release the vessel.[14]

This 1933 proposal received no support from the two Common Law countries then involved in the CMI's discussions.[15] The British Maritime Committee viewed a general right

[10] See CMI, *Oslo Conference 1933* (Bulletin No 96, JE Buschmann, Antwerp, 1934), 20–21 (Germany), 40 (Italy), 86 (Belgium) (CMI Oslo).

[11] ibid 21.

[12] ibid 442–43. See further ch 10.

[13] See Berlingieri (n 2) vol 1 paras 1.01–04. The International Convention for the Unification of Certain Rules Relating to Maritime Liens and Mortgages (adopted 10 April 1926, entered into force 2 June 1931) 120 UNTS 187 has never attracted widespread support.

[14] CMI Oslo (n 10) 182. Compare the early draft of Germany's Alfred Sieveking, which included the restriction (at 9) that 'A ship can be arrested only for the claims attaching to the vessel or for claims relating to the voyages of the ship whose arrest is sought.'

[15] ibid 184–85.

to arrest any ship belonging to a debtor, as proposed in the Dor draft, as an unnecessary restriction on the free movement of shipping.[16] The Maritime Law Association of the United States noted that, as in England, claimants in the United States relied on the availability of an action in rem to commence maritime proceedings. It decided to take no position on what its members saw as a Convention of interest only to the Continental countries.[17]

Following World War II it became apparent that, for an Arrest Convention to have any success, it would be necessary to bridge the conceptual and procedural divide between the Common Law and Civil Law jurisdictions. The new proposal was to adopt an English-style list of maritime claims that would justify arrest, based on the Supreme Court of Judicature (Consolidation) Act 1925 (UK), but to include the Civil Law ability to arrest ships in common ownership.[18] This was not a unilateral diplomatic victory for England: parties such as the Norwegian Shipowners' Association had spoken in support of limiting the availability of arrest along English lines in order to protect shipowners' commercial interests.[19]

Now that it could be described as an instrument whose purpose was to restrict the right of arrest to specific maritime claims, the British Maritime Law Association was prepared to support the draft Convention.[20] However, the United States remained unmoved, noting that the draft Convention did not distinguish between arrest in a proceeding in rem, and the attachment of a vessel in a proceeding against its owner. Furthermore, the list of maritime claims did not align with those claims giving rise to maritime liens recognised under United States law.[21] Having made its brief appearance, the United States drops out of the narrative at this point, making room for the slightly more enthusiastic reception the Convention received elsewhere in the Common Law world.

IV. Common Law Reception of the Arrest Conventions

A. The Early Adopter: United Kingdom

In light of the background outlined above, it is not surprising that the United Kingdom was a signatory of the Arrest Convention 1952, and the first of the Common Law countries to ratify it. The international community had essentially vindicated the English approach to maritime claims and ducked the question of wrongful arrest,[22] while enlarging the availability of arrest in a manner that would hardly threaten the pragmatic sensibilities of a lawyer trained in the Common Law.

The Administration of Justice Act 1956 (AJA 1956) was used to implement the Convention in domestic law for England and Wales,[23] as well as Scotland[24] and Northern Ireland.[25]

[16] ibid 200–01.
[17] ibid 217.
[18] CMI, *Naples Conference 1951* (Bulletin No 105, JE Buschmann, Antwerp, 1952) 2–3; 6 (CMI Naples).
[19] CMI Oslo (n 10), 450–51.
[20] CMI Naples (n 18) 41.
[21] ibid 11–14.
[22] Article 6 of the Arrest Convention 1952 makes this a matter for the lex fori. See further ch 6.
[23] AJA 1956, ss 1–8.
[24] ibid ss 45–50.
[25] ibid sch 1.

This was done, not by giving the text of the Arrest Convention 1952 the force of law, but rather by adapting its key provisions into sections of the Act. This practice was continued in the Senior Courts Act 1981 (SCA 1981), which introduced some refinements to the implementation of the Arrest Convention 1952 (discussed below).[26] The AJA 1956 and the SCA 1981 have since served as models, to a greater or lesser extent, for the admiralty legislation of Australia, Canada, Hong Kong, New Zealand and Singapore.

B. The Fast Followers: Hong Kong and Singapore

Both Hong Kong and Singapore received their first post-1890 Act admiralty legislation during their respective periods as British colonies. For Singapore this initially came in the form of the Courts (Admiralty Jurisdiction) Ordinance 1961,[27] which was essentially a facsimile of the AJA 1956. The legislation has since been renamed the High Court (Admiralty Jurisdiction) Act.[28] The Act was updated in 2004 to insert one narrow change directly modelled on s 21(4) of the SCA 1981, namely the extension of the relevant person link in s 4(4) to allow arrest of demise-chartered ships.[29] Apart from that single provision, the Singapore Act remains in identical terms to the AJA 1956.

Unlike Singapore, which has never become a party to the Arrest Convention 1952, the United Kingdom extended the territorial application of the Arrest Convention 1952 to include Hong Kong in 1963. Hong Kong then received its version of the AJA 1956 by way of the Application of English Law Ordinance 1966. Unlike the Singapore Act, the High Court Ordinance (HK)[30] has since been amended numerous times and follows the wording of the SCA 1981 far more assiduously.

C. The Late Bloomers: Canada, New Zealand, Australia

Canada, New Zealand and Australia did not deal with the reform of admiralty jurisdiction until after achieving sovereign nation status. Canada had been content to adopt English admiralty law in 1934, but came up with a rather idiosyncratic group of jurisdictional provisions in the Federal Court Act 1970[31] (now found in the Federal Courts Act 1985).[32]

[26] See text at nn 64, 115, 117 below.

[27] Ordinance 32 of 1961, in force from 15 January 1962 via SI 10/1962.

[28] Act no 24 of 1969, in force from 9 January 1970; became cap 6, 1970 rev edn, then became cap 123 of the 1985 rev edn. It is now cap 123 of the 2001 rev edn. (HCAJA) Prior to this the relevant legislation was Malaysia's Courts of Judicature Act 1964. See Toh Kian Sing, *Admiralty Law and Practice*, 3rd edn (Singapore, LexisNexis, 2017) 6–9; Damien Cremean, *Admiralty Jurisdiction Law and Practice: Australia, New Zealand, Singapore, Hong Kong, Malaysia*, 4th edn (Annandale, The Federation Press, 2015) 6–7.

[29] See the High Court (Admiralty Jurisdiction) (Amendment) Act (No 2 of 2004); Law Reform and Revision Division, Attorney-General's Chambers, *Admiralty Jurisdiction of the High Court: Arrest of Ships on Demise Charter to Secure the Obligations of the Demise Charterer* (Singapore, AGC Consultation Paper, 2004).

[30] See the High Court Ordinance, cap 4, ss 12A–12E (HK) (amended in 1989, 1990, 1993, 1995, 1997, 1998, 2005, 2009, 2010 and 2017).

[31] Federal Court Act 1970 (Canada), RSC 1970 c 10 (2nd Supp).

[32] Federal Courts Act 1985 (Canada), RSC 1985 c F-7.

New Zealand did not cast off its colonial-era jurisdiction until the passage of the Admiralty Act 1973,[33] while Australia was even slower off the mark with the Admiralty Act 1988.[34]

In each of these cases the countries borrowed, to a greater or lesser extent, from the United Kingdom legislation of the time, but did not ratify the Arrest Convention 1952. For example, the Australian Law Reform Commission in its Report on Civil Admiralty Jurisdiction (ALRC 33) declined to recommend using the Arrest Convention 1952 even as Australia's sole source of 'what is internationally acceptable' in admiralty legislation on the basis that it was 'difficult to reconcile with other, more recent, maritime conventions' and was undergoing revision at the time of the report.[35]

These three countries therefore have law that is based, to varying degrees, indirectly on the Arrest Convention 1952, and more directly on the English legislation that implemented that Convention, without taking on any international obligations in relation to the Arrest Convention 1952. As discussed below,[36] this 'second-hand' reception of elements of the Arrest Convention 1952 via the English statutory model has enabled each of these countries to depart from these precedents in relation to the scope and exercise of their respective admiralty jurisdictions.

D. The Internationalist: Ireland

Ireland was the penultimate jurisdiction in this group to reform its admiralty jurisdiction, and adopted a more principled approach. Following the establishment of its Department of Marine in 1987, Ireland undertook a number of maritime law reform projects, one of which led to the Jurisdiction of Courts (Maritime Conventions) Act 1989.[37] This gives the Arrest Convention 1952, along with the Collision Convention 1952, the force of law in Ireland.[38]

E. The Outlier: India

Despite the fact that India gained its independence in 1947, the colonial admiralty regime of the CCAA 1890 astonishingly persisted in that country until 2017.[39] This caused significant jurisprudential and practical headaches. Despite several draft Bills being prepared to

[33] See Special Law Reform Committee on Admiralty Jurisdiction, *Admiralty Jurisdiction* (Wellington, 1972).

[34] See Australian Law Reform Commission, *Civil Admiralty Jurisdiction* (ALRC 33, 1986) (ALRC Report); Cremean (n 28) 5–8.

[35] ALRC Report (n 34) para 94. The more recent Conventions cited were the Salvage Convention (then in a draft form from 1981) and the Athens Convention on the Carriage of Passengers and their Luggage by Sea 1974.

[36] See Part VI below.

[37] Entered into force on 17 April 1990: see Jurisdiction of Courts (Maritime Conventions) Act 1989 (Commencement) Order (SI 332/89) (Ireland).

[38] Jurisdiction of Courts (Maritime Conventions) Act 1989 (Ireland), s 4.

[39] For the history of the Indian admiralty jurisdiction see Shyam D Nandan, 'Admiralty Jurisdiction Pre and Post *Elizabeth* [sic]' (2007) 49 *Journal of the Indian Law Institute* 81, 84ff. See also Dyutimoy Mukherjee, Arka Majumdar and Anunoy Basu, 'Ship Arrest in India' (2007) 13 *JIML* 289; Shatadru Chakraborty and Shivendra Singh, 'Maritime Liens in India' (2007) 13 *JIML* 440.

amend and update India's admiralty legislation, legislative reform efforts came to naught.[40] Eventually the Indian Supreme Court in the landmark decision of *The MV Elisabeth*[41] held that the admiralty jurisdiction of Indian courts was not constrained by the bounds of its colonial statutory framework. Instead, the Court turned to broad-brush (and some might say highly unorthodox) public international law principles to unfetter India's admiralty jurisdiction:[42]

> All persons and things within the waters of a State fall within its jurisdiction unless specifically curtailed or regulated by rules of international law. The power to arrest a foreign vessel, while in the waters of a coastal State, in respect of a maritime claim, wherever arising, is a demonstrable manifestation and an essential attribute of territorial sovereignty. This power is recognised by several international conventions. These conventions contain the unified rules of law drawn from different legal systems. Although many of these conventions have yet to be ratified by India, they embody principles of law recognised by the generality of maritime States, and can therefore be regarded as part of our common law. The want of ratification of these conventions is apparently not because of any policy disagreement, as is clear from active and fruitful Indian participation in the formulation of rules adopted by the conventions, but perhaps because of other circumstances, such as lack of an adequate and specialised machinery for implementation of the various international conventions by co-ordinating for the purpose the concerned Departments of the Government. Such a specialised body of legal and technical experts can facilitate adoption of international unified rules by national legislation. It is appropriate that sufficient attention is paid to this aspect of the matter by the concerned authorities. Perhaps the Law Commission of India, endowed as it ought to be with sufficient authority, status and independence, as is the position in England, can render valuable help in this regard. Delay in the adoption of international conventions which are intended to facilitate trade hinders the economic growth of the nation.

This controversial and innovative decision allowed Indian courts to borrow freely from the full smorgasbord of available international maritime law Conventions, with no regard as to whether these had been signed up to or implemented by India. In terms of ship arrest, this meant a direct judicial adoption into Indian law of the principles of the Arrest Convention 1999, as that Convention was seen to be the most up-to-date (even if not the most widely adopted) international instrument in the area.[43] Despite the Supreme Court's call in *The MV Elisabeth* for statutory reform, it would only arrive nearly quarter of a century later in the form of the Admiralty (Jurisdiction and Settlement of Maritime Claims) Act 2017, which finally entered into force on 1 April 2018.[44] Perhaps unsurprisingly, given the judicial intervention in *The MV Elisabeth* and its aftermath, the Act embodies most of the key aspects of the Arrest Convention 1999, despite India not being a State Party to that Convention. This will be discussed in more detail below.[45]

[40] Nandan (n 39) 90 ff.

[41] *MV Elisabeth v Harwan Investment & Trading Pvt Ltd* 1993 AIR 1993 SC 1014, 1993 Supp (2) SCC 433.

[42] ibid [90] (citations omitted). See also *Liverpool & London SP&I Association Ltd v MV Sea Success I* [2003] Supp (5) SCR 851, (2004) 9 SCC 5 12.

[43] So, eg, a search of the Manupatra database indicates that the Arrest Convention 1999 was cited or applied in at least 62 cases decided after *The Elisabeth* (n 41).

[44] Notification No SO767(E) dated 22 February 2018.

[45] See Part VII below.

V. Analysis of the Translations

As the outline above demonstrates, most of the Common Law countries examined here were influenced more directly by the United Kingdom's AJA 1956 and SCA 1981 than by the Arrest Convention 1952. Only Ireland ignored English developments and used the 'untranslated' text of the Arrest Convention 1952 as its starting point. Therefore, in order to analyse the Common Law jurisdictions' translations of the Arrest Convention 1952, it is necessary to start with the English legislation and the challenges of implementing the Arrest Convention 1952 within a Common Law system. Next, this part of the Chapter will comment on how closely the other countries have kept to the English template, and where they have introduced their own innovations. The focus here is on substantive changes, as opposed to the many cosmetic re-phrasings that appear across the different national enactments.

A. The Maritime Claims

The list of maritime claims in art 1 of the Arrest Convention 1952 may have adopted the English approach to delimiting the admiralty jurisdiction, but the Common Law world has certainly not accepted it verbatim. Without exception, each jurisdiction has adjusted the claims' descriptions to sit more comfortably within its own domestic legal system.

i. The English Model

As one would hope, given that it was intended to implement international obligations, the claims listed in s 1 of the AJA 1956 and s 20 of the SCA 1981 are in most cases substantively equivalent to those in art 1 of the Arrest Convention 1952. The precise wording of the Convention is almost never adopted, but even the more significant departures appear to be within its spirit. For example, 'title to or ownership' in art 1(1)(o) of the Arrest Convention 1952 becomes 'possession or ownership',[46] better reflecting the common law approach to property.[47] This was something even Ireland saw the need to address in its more 'internationalist' approach, including the provision that 'Article 1(1)(o) shall be construed as including disputes as to possession of a ship'.[48]

In contrast, while art 1(1)(q) of the Arrest Convention 1952 refers only to 'the mortgage or hypothecation of any ship', claims for the mortgage *of a share in a ship* have been added by all Common Law countries.[49] This adjustment goes a step further than the possession

[46] AJA 1956, s 1(1)(a); SCA 1981, s 20(2)(a).

[47] The British Maritime Law Association had noted that: 'Nearly all actions in which the ownership of a ship is in dispute originate by one of the claimants claiming possession of the ship and arresting her.' See British Maritime Law Association, 'Arrest of Ships: Memorandum Upon Jurisdiction ("Competence") of the English Admiralty Court', CMI Naples (n 18) 36. See similarly the introduction of 'beneficial ownership': AJA 1956, s 3(4); SCA 1981, s 21(4).

[48] Jurisdiction of Courts (Maritime Conventions) Act 1989 (Ireland), s 2(2)(a).

[49] See eg AJA 1956, s 1(1)(c); SCA 1981, s 20(2)(c); Jurisdiction of Courts (Maritime Conventions) Act 1989 (Ireland), s 2(2)(b).

example above, which merely introduces familiar common law terminology to the description of a claim, but arguably clarifies the law's application to an alternative business arrangement that is still encompassed by the Convention's original wording.

Another approach taken by the English legislature is the adoption of the basic term employed by the Convention, followed by a provision that 'augments' the claim in question by partially defining its scope. For example, the SCA 1981 provides that claims for 'damage done by a ship' extend to oil pollution damage claims,[50] and also augments the term salvage.[51] Drafting of this kind can provide clarity by taking into account developments in the law, without attempting to constrain the terms drawn from the Convention. For example, a reference to claims under the Salvage Convention 1989 has since been added to the SCA 1981,[52] which the drafters of the Arrest Convention 1952 would not have envisaged when they used the unvarnished term 'salvage',[53] but which comfortably falls within the spirit of the earlier instrument.

This drafting approach is also helpful in signalling to readers any domestic provisions that may relate to an issue such as wages. For example, the enactment of the SCA 1981 updated the wording around wages claims to reflect legislative developments in marine employment law. This is an issue faced by all the jurisdictions examined here – the Arrest Convention 1952 simply refers to 'wages of Masters, Officers, or crew',[54] but most jurisdictions have specialist employment legislation that has required some form of tweaking for this heading.[55] The English legislation extends to 'any sum allotted out of wages or adjudged by a superintendent to be due by way of wages'.[56]

A greater tension arises in relation to personal injury claims, where the Arrest Convention 1952's straightforward 'loss of life or personal injury caused by any ship or occurring in connexion with the operation of any ship' in art 1(1)(b) is replaced with a complex paragraph of over 100 words in s 20(2)(f) of the SCA 1981. This attempts to carve out from personal injury claims the kind of injury 'in which the ship is merely the *passive* cause, such as where a stevedore falls down the hold of a ship'.[57] This narrower wording drawing on older English law appears to be an inadequate implementation of the treaty. Instead of clarifying the scope of a claim in an inclusive way, that is, without limiting its availability to claimants in general (as in the examples discussed above), this appears to be an attempt to restrict the wording of a broadly-framed claim, and to rely on terms that have evolved in response to domestic case law.[58]

In a few cases the English legislation includes claims that do not appear in the Arrest Convention 1952. In the case of claims arising from the forfeiture, condemnation and seizure of ships, along with droits of admiralty,[59] this is excusable. Article 2 of

[50] SCA 1981, ss 20(2)(e) and 20(5).
[51] ibid ss 20(2)(j) and 20(6).
[52] ibid s 20(2)(j)(i).
[53] Arrest Convention 1952, art 1(1)(c).
[54] ibid art 1(1)(m).
[55] See eg Admiralty Act 1973 (NZ), s 4(1)(o); HCAJA, s 3(1)(n).
[56] SCA 1981, s 20(2)(o).
[57] British Maritime Law Association, 'Arrest of Ships: Memorandum Upon Jurisdiction ("Competence") of the English Admiralty Court', CMI Naples (n 18) 37.
[58] See further ch 8.
[59] AJA 1956, s 1(1)(s); SCA 1981, s 20(2)(s).

the Arrest Convention 1952 expressly acknowledged that public law claims of this kind would continue to be exercised by State Parties. However, there is also the example of 'damage received by a ship',[60] which is paired with 'damage done by a ship' and traditionally connected with admiralty jurisdiction over collisions.[61] The value of this heading is questionable. First, such damage will usually be caused by another ship, in which case the accompanying 'damage done' provision will apply, or by a shore-based object such as a pier or crane where a claim in admiralty will be of little assistance. Australia saw no need to include this heading in its legislation.[62] Secondly, as was observed in *The Eschersheim*, such a claim does not work in the in rem context given the damaged ship would not itself be the subject of the proceedings.[63] As a consequence, this head of jurisdiction has now been removed from the list of claims that may be enforced by an action in rem in the SCA 1981,[64] which means that it attracts in personam liability only.[65] It is, however, still to be found on the statute books of those Anglo-Common Law jurisdictions whose laws are largely modelled on the AJA 1956.[66] So, while in becoming a party to the Arrest Convention 1952 the United Kingdom promised to arrest vessels 'in respect of no other claim' than those listed in art 1,[67] the 'damage received' provision is unlikely to give rise to any international incidents.[68]

A potential issue could also arise from the 'catch-all' or 'sweeping-up' provision that England and several other Common Law countries have included in their admiralty legislation, continuing the existence of 'any other Admiralty jurisdiction which [the High Court] had immediately before the commencement of this Act'.[69] Although the general consensus seems to be that these provisions are of little practical relevance, there remains the outside chance that a party could unearth a reason for proceeding in rem and arresting a vessel of a Contracting State to the Arrest Convention 1952, despite the absence of their claim from the list of 'maritime claims' in art 1 of the Convention, as translated into national legislation.[70]

[60] AJA 1956, s 1(1)(e); SCA 1981, s 20(2)(d).

[61] British Maritime Law Association, 'Arrest of Ships: Memorandum Upon Jurisdiction ("Competence") of the English Admiralty Court', CMI Naples (n 18) 36.

[62] Its inclusion was recommended by the ALRC Report (n 34) para 172.

[63] *The Eschersheim* [1976] 2 Lloyd's Rep 1 (HL). A similar difficulty may also arise in respect of claims for goods or materials supplied 'to a ship', where it is the recipient ship that has suffered the damage: see *The Alexandrea* [2002] SGHC 82, [2002] 1 SLR(R) 812.

[64] SCA 1981, s 21(4) now provides that an action in rem may be brought in the case of 'any such claim as is mentioned in section (20(2)(e) to (r)'. The 'damage received by a ship' head of jurisdiction is listed in s 20(2)(d).

[65] SCA 1981, s 21(1).

[66] See, eg, Admiralty Act 1973 (NZ), s 4(1)(e) read with s 5(2)(b); HCAJA, s 3(1)(e) read with s 4(4).

[67] Arrest Convention 1952, art 2.

[68] A New Zealand court did permit a 'damage received' claim in a case involving a sister-ship arrest, but the case was at first instance only and has been subject to a great deal of criticism: *Reef Shipping Co Ltd v The Ship Fua Kavenga* [1987] 1 NZLR 550; not followed in *The Catur Samudra* [2010] SGHC 18, [2010] 2 SLR 518.

[69] SCA 1981, s 20(1)(c); see similarly Admiralty Act 1973 (NZ), s 4(2); HCAJA, s 3(1).

[70] For an interesting example, see *The Ocean Jade* [1991] SGHC 33, [1991] 1 SLR(R) 354: unsuccessful attempt to argue a maritime lien over unpaid freight, extra expenses, return freight and extra services on the basis that this had been recognised under the CCAA 1890 and earlier admiralty jurisdiction. Karthigesu J rejected this argument out of hand and seemed unconvinced that the words together with any other jurisdiction connected with ships or aircraft which may be vested in the Court apart from this Section' at the end of s 3(1) of the HCAJA should be read as a historical 'sweeping-up' provision. On the face of it, the provision does seem to refer to jurisdiction under current cognate maritime statutes, rather than to historical statutory jurisdiction prior to 15 January 1962. If this analysis is correct, the Singapore legislation is a closed code, at least in respect of those historical heads of statutory

ii. Drawing on the English Model

Hong Kong and Singapore's respective enactments are virtually identical to versions of the English template, with Hong Kong adopting the SCA 1981 wording with its updated references to salvage and wages claims.[71] By contrast Singapore, which is not yet a party to the Salvage Convention 1989,[72] has included some additional material of its own devising in relation to salvage.[73] This includes a provision that the Act describes as requiring salvage disputes to be determined summarily where the claim or property involved is worth less than $50,000, but in fact the use of this procedure is dependent on the parties' consent.[74] The Merchant Shipping (Miscellaneous Amendments) Bill 2018, which will implement the Salvage Convention 1989 into Singapore law, does not appear to include any consequential amendments to the salvage head of jurisdiction in its admiralty legislation, which will be necessary to avoid uncertainty regarding the ambit of the consequentially enlarged admiralty jurisdiction, particularly in respect of special compensation under art 14 of the Salvage Convention 1989 for preventing or minimising environmental harm, which is arguably not 'in the nature of salvage' as traditionally understood.

New Zealand's legislation can also be grouped with these two jurisdictions, as it opted for a statute whose list of claims is essentially a copy of the AJA 1956.[75] This approach was chosen with the goal of preserving uniformity among Commonwealth jurisdictions,[76] and at the time was even seen as 'the forerunner of a new approach to admiralty jurisdiction' and a potential precedent for other states to adopt as they too moved beyond the colonial admiralty era represented by the CCAA 1890.[77]

By comparison, Canada and Australia have each taken a more independent approach to defining the scope of their respective admiralty jurisdictions, with lists of claims drawing on both the Arrest Convention 1952 and the AJA 1956.[78] Taking the Canadian list for example, the damage done by a ship and the loss or damage to goods provisions mirror the Arrest Convention 1952 wording,[79] while those relating to co-owners' disputes and personal injury reflect the AJA 1956.[80] Canada's legislation also refers to the concept of 'Canadian maritime law',[81] which is a catch-all provision potentially of more substance

jurisdiction that were not carried across into the current statute. But see dicta in *The Vinalines Pioneer* [2015] SGHC 278, [2016] 1 SLR 448 [17] (Belinda Ang J) to the effect that this phraseology in HCAJA, s 3(1) does amount to a historical 'sweeping-up' provision.

[71] High Court Ordinance, cap 4 (HK), s 12A(2)(i) and (n).

[72] International Convention on Salvage 1989 (adopted on 28 April 1989, entered into force on 14 July 1996) 1953 UNTS 165.

[73] HCAJA, ss 3(1)(i) and 3(3).

[74] Merchant Shipping Act, cap 179, 1996 rev edn (Singapore), s 168.

[75] Admiralty Act 1973 (NZ), s 4(1).

[76] Special Law Reform Committee on Admiralty Jurisdiction (n 33) 2, 12; (14 March 1973) 382 *NZPD* 797; (18 July 1973) 384 *NZPD* 2460.

[77] (18 July 1973) 384 *NZPD* 2463.

[78] Federal Courts Act 1985 (Canada), s 22; Admiralty Act 1988 (Cth), s 4.

[79] Federal Courts Act 1985 (Canada), ss 22(2)(d) and 22(2)(h); compare Arrest Convention 1952, arts 1(1)(a) and 1(1)(f).

[80] Federal Courts Act 1985 (Canada), ss 22(2)(b) and 22(2)(g); compare AJA 1956, ss 1(1)(b) and 1(1)(f).

[81] Federal Courts Act 1985 (Canada), s 22(1); see also s 2(1) for the definition of 'Canadian maritime law'. See *ITO-International Terminal Operators v Miida Electronics* [1986] 1 SCR 752, 28 DLR (4th) 641; *Canadian National Railway Company v Hanjin Shipping Co Ltd* 2017 FC 198. See William Tetley *International Maritime and Admiralty Law* (Montreal, Editions Yvon Blais, 2002) 434–35.

than the equivalent English 'sweeping-up' provision,[82] although its precise scope remains uncertain.[83]

iii. Innovations

Free from the constraints of the Arrest Convention 1952, Australia, Canada and New Zealand have also included claims within their respective admiralty jurisdictions that appear neither in that international agreement nor the AJA 1956. These include ship-related claims arising out of:

(1) Services, such as stevedoring services (Australia, Canada, New Zealand).[84]
(2) Insurance contracts (Australia, Canada).[85]
(3) Through bills of lading (Canada).[86]
(4) Arbitration awards (Australia).[87]
(5) Interest on claims (Australia).[88]

Of these additional claims the Arrest Convention 1999 includes the first two,[89] but not the last three. None of these Common Law countries has seen the need to introduce express provisions for other claims introduced by the Arrest Convention 1999, such as those relating to wreck removal, brokers' fees, or ship sales – although this is not to suggest that existing provisions could not be interpreted to encompass some of them. For example, a ship sale could give rise to questions of ownership or possession, while a wreck situation might involve a claim 'in the nature of salvage' or perhaps damage done by a ship.[90] Furthermore, in the case of Canada, the list of claims is non-exhaustive.[91]

An aspect of Hong Kong's legislation that looks significant at first is a pollution-related claim at the bottom of its list. However, this is in fact very narrow in scope, relating only to claims against the government for unreasonable costs incurred in responding to a pollution event on official instructions connected with the Intervention Convention 1969.[92] Some jurisdictions, such as Australia, have included specific reference to pollution-related claims in their admiralty legislation,[93] while others have been content to include this expressly

[82] Compare SCA 1981, s 20(1)(c).

[83] See eg William Tetley, 'A definition of Canadian maritime law' (1996) 30 *UBC Law Rev* 137; Arthur J Stone, 'Canada's Admiralty Court in the Twentieth Century' (2002) 47 *McGill LJ* 511, 535–536. John G O'Connor, 'Expanding Admiralty Jurisdiction in Canada's Federal Courts' (2013) 44 *J Mar L & Com* 291, 293ff.

[84] Admiralty Act 1988 (Cth), s 4(3)(m); Federal Courts Act 1985 (Canada), s 22(1)(m); Admiralty Act 1973 (NZ), s 4(1)(l).

[85] Admiralty Act 1988 (Cth), s 4(3)(s); Federal Courts Act 1985 (Canada), s 22(1)(r).

[86] Federal Courts Act 1985 (Canada), s 22(1)(f).

[87] Admiralty Act 1988 (Cth), s 4(3)(u).

[88] Admiralty Act 1988 (Cth), s 4(3)(w).

[89] Arrest Convention 1999, arts 1(1)(l) and 1(1)(q).

[90] SCA 1981, ss 20(1)(a), 20(1)(d) and 20(1)(j).

[91] Federal Courts Act 1985 (Canada), s 22(2).

[92] International Convention relating to Intervention on the High Seas in Cases of Oil Pollution Casualties (adopted 29 November 1969, entered into force 6 May 1975) 970 UNTS 211 (Intervention Convention 1969). See High Court Ordinance, cap 4 (HK), ss 12A(2)(s) and 12A(3)(b); Merchant Shipping (Prevention and Control of Pollution) Ordinance, cap 413 (HK), s 7.

[93] Admiralty Act 1988 (Cth), ss 4(3)(b) and 4(3)(ba); Maritime Transport Act 1994 (NZ), s 368(1) (referring to s 4(1)(d) of the Admiralty Act 1973 (NZ)).

within the scope of 'damage done by a ship' in their admiralty legislation,[94] or in cognate maritime legislation.[95]

B. Exercise of the In Rem Jurisdiction

If art 1 of the Arrest Convention 1952 was intended to reflect the English practice of specifying certain claims falling within the admiralty jurisdiction, art 3 was supposed to reflect the Civil Law approach of permitting the arrest of other vessels owned by a defendant.[96] The implementation of art 3 has led to some rather painful drafting in different Common Law jurisdictions at different times, as well as significant litigation over the precise nature of ownership that will enable in rem proceedings against a 'sister ship'.[97]

i. *The English Model*

From a Common Law perspective, the Arrest Convention 1952 is concerned with in rem claims. A statute could list many additional in personam claims and this would not impact upon a Contracting State's obligations under that agreement, as there would be no additional rights of arrest. For example, the SCA 1981 refers not only to admiralty jurisdiction over the 'questions and claims' listed in s 20(2) that may lead to in rem proceedings, but also to 'proceedings' set out in s 20(3), which includes collision actions and claims under various Merchant Shipping Acts. The equivalent provision is even more comprehensive in Hong Kong, where a long list of safety and environmental legislation is set out.[98] However, in both cases these 'proceedings' cannot be commenced in rem;[99] the provisions are merely allocating the workload of a specialist court division.

Turning next to the various in rem claims, those involving proprietary actions against a particular ship are straightforward, as both the Arrest Convention 1952 and the English legislation permit these to be taken only against that particular ship.[100] Claims relying on maritime liens or other charges may also be brought only against the particular ship affected,[101] which could have created problems had England and the other jurisdictions discussed here taken an expansive approach to maritime liens. However, the limited number

[94] SCA 1981, s 20(5); High Court Ordinance, cap 4 (HK), s 12A(5). See further ch 8.

[95] eg, the Federal Courts Act 1985 (Canada) and the HCAJA make no specific reference to pollution damage. However, s 79(1) of the Marine Liability Act, SC 2001 c 6 (Canada) provides that the 'Admiralty Court has jurisdiction with respect to claims for compensation brought in Canada under any convention under Division 1 [which includes all the international marine pollution Conventions that have the force of law in Canada] and claims for compensation under Division 2 [which covers other forms of marine pollution not covered by the Conventions listed in Division 1]'. Section 16(1) of the Merchant Shipping (Civil Liability and Compensation for Oil Pollution) Act, cap 180, 1999 rev edn (Singapore) provides that 'damage done by a ship' (s 3(1)(d) of the HCAJA) shall be construed as extending to any claim in respect of liability incurred by the shipowner under Part II of the Act.

[96] *Owners of the Monte Ulia v Owners of the Banco (The Banco)* [1971] P 137, 151 (Lord Denning).

[97] See text at nn 103ff below.

[98] High Court Ordinance, cap 4 (HK), s 12A(3).

[99] SCA 1981, s 21; High Court Ordinance, cap 4 (HK), s 12B.

[100] Arrest Convention 1952, art 3(1); AJA 1956, s 3(2); SCA 1981, s 21(2).

[101] SCA 1981, s 21(3).

of liens recognised under English law – as opposed to United States law for example – means that all potentially relevant subjects are covered by the list of maritime claims provided in the Arrest Convention 1952.[102]

This leaves situations where a statutory claim in rem may be taken against either the 'particular ship' or a 'sister ship' as per art 3(1) of the Arrest Convention:[103]

> [A] claimant may arrest either the particular ship in respect of which the maritime claim arose, or any other ship which is owned by the person who was, at the time when the maritime claim arose, the owner of the particular ship.

By contrast, s 21(4) of the SCA 1981 provides as follows:

> In the case of any such claim as is mentioned in section 20(2)(e) to (r), where —
>
> (a) the claim arises in connection with a ship; and
>
> (b) the person who would be liable on the claim in an action in personam ('the relevant person') was, when the cause of action arose, the owner or charterer of, or in possession or in control of, the ship,
>
> an action in rem may (whether or not the claim gives rise to a maritime lien on that ship) be brought in the High Court against —
>
> (i) that ship, if at the time when the action is brought the relevant person is either the beneficial owner of that ship as respects all the shares in it or the charterer of it under a charter by demise; or
>
> (ii) any other ship of which, at the time when the action is brought, the relevant person is the beneficial owner as respects all the shares in it.

An immediately evident Common Law touch when compared with the international source material is the inclusion of 'beneficial ownership' to account for equitable doctrines (this is also found in Ireland's legislation giving effect to the Arrest Convention 1952).[104] Like the inclusion of 'possession' in the list of maritime claims, this embellishment of the Arrest Convention 1952's wording is arguably necessary for it to function in a Common Law jurisdiction where legal ownership is not always the only relevant form of ownership in a legal dispute.[105]

However, one cannot ignore the fact that the inclusion of this term has led to a significant amount of litigation, as plaintiff after plaintiff has attempted to argue for an expanded definition of 'beneficial'. To date the soundest statement remains that of Goff J (as he then was)

[102] See Sarah C Derrington and James M Turner, *The Law and Practice of Admiralty Matters*, 2nd edn (Oxford, Oxford University Press, 2016) ch 4.

[103] Note that art 3(4) provides the additional right of arrest in respect of demise-chartered vessels. The New Zealand legislation takes this one step further: see discussion at nn 118–19 below.

[104] Jurisdiction of Courts (Maritime Conventions) Act 1989 (Ireland), s 2(3)(b). Another aspect that Ireland decided to emulate was the clarification as to the relevant point in time for assessing ownership of the sister ship: s 2(3)(a).

[105] But see the Admiralty Act 1988 (Cth), ss 17–19, which simply refer to the 'owner' of the relevant or surrogate ship. The Australian courts have, however, interpreted this to mean 'beneficial ownership', in line with the common law approach: see eg *Malaysia Shipyard v Iron Shortland as Surrogate for the Ship Newcastle Pride* (1995) 131 ALR 738, 747–8; *Kent v SS Maria Luisa (No 2)* [2003] FCAFC 93, (2003) 130 FCR 12 [17]; *Shagang Shipping Co Ltd v Ship Bulk Peace* [2014] FCAFC 48, (2014) 314 ALR 230 [20]; *Korea Shipping Corp v Lord Energy SA* [2018] FCAFC 201.

that the word beneficial was included 'to allow for the peculiar English institution of the trust'.[106] This allows the term to extend to situations where a Common Law system would recognise equitable ownership, such as the position of a purchaser who is awaiting formal transfer of the vessel's registration into their name,[107] but no further. Nonetheless, doomed arguments have been raised for the inclusion of the parent company of two one-ship companies,[108] the managing company of a group of limited partnerships,[109] a joint stock company operating state-owned vessels,[110] and so on over the years.

Another aspect that stands out when compared with art 3 of the Arrest Convention 1952 is reference to the relevant person being the owner, charterer,[111] or in possession or control of,[112] the particular ship.[113] The Arrest Convention 1952 does not focus on a defendant's status in relation to the particular ship, instead it simply permits the arrest of that ship. This additional factor reflects the common law approach to the admiralty jurisdiction whereby – with the exception of a maritime lien claim – an in personam defendant is contemplated as being relevant to the proceedings.[114] In a rare case this wording could give a claimant in England a more limited chance of recovery than the Arrest Convention 1952 would permit, as it inserts the concept of a defendant with a relationship to the ship between the maritime claim and the ship to be arrested.

Finally, the English provision quoted above permits the arrest of a ship even though it is under demise charter, as permitted by art 3(4) of the Arrest Convention 1952, and the arrest of a 'sister ship' in the same ownership, as permitted by art 3(1). It is noteworthy that the reference to ships under demise charter was not included in the AJA 1956.[115] This omission led to some difficult points of interpretation before the law was amended in the SCA 1981 to give effect to this aspect of the Convention.[116]

[106] *I Congreso del Partido* [1978] QB 500, 539; and see *International Transportation Service Inc v The Owners and/or Demise Charterers of the Ship or Vessel Convenience Container (The Convenience Container)* [2006] HKCFI 553, [2006] 4 HKC 435 [22] (and authorities cited therein).

[107] *Vostok Shipping Co Ltd v Confederation Ltd* [2000] 1 NZLR 37 (CA).

[108] *The Evpo Agnic* [1988] 2 Lloyd's Rep 411 (EWCA).

[109] *Ssangyong Australia Pty Ltd v Looiersgracht (The)* (1994) 85 FTR 265, [1995] 2 Lloyd's Rep 411.

[110] *The Nazym Khikmet* [1996] 2 Lloyd's Rep 362 (CA).

[111] The interpretation of 'owner' and 'charterer' gave rise to an ongoing interpretation battle, with a narrower interpretation arguably more closely aligned with the Arrest Convention 1952 being followed in *The Andrea Ursula* [1973] QB 265; *The Eschersheim* (n 63); *Antaios Compania Naviera v The Owners of the Ship Ledesco Uno (Philippine Flag) (The Ledesco Uno)* [1977] HKCFI 64, [1977] HKLR 490; *The Maritime Trader* [1981] 2 Lloyd's Rep 153; *The Evpo Agnic* (n 108). This approach increasingly gave way to a broad, plain language interpretation, particularly in those Anglo-Common Law jurisdictions that had adopted the English model, but had not signed up to the Arrest Convention: see eg *The St Merriel* [1963] P 247; *I Congreso del Partido* (n 106); *The Permina 108* [1976] SGCA 12, [1974–1976] SLR(R) 850; *The Father Thames* [1979] 2 Lloyd's Rep 364; *The Span Terza* [1982] 1 Lloyd's Rep 225 (CA); *The Sextum* [1982] 2 Lloyd's Rep 532; *Societe Anonyme des Petroles Mory and The Owners of the Ship or Vessel Union Darwin (Panamanian Flag)* [1983] HKCFI 136, [1983] HKLR 248; *The Fua Kavenga* (n 68); *Laemthong International Lines v BPS Shipping Ltd* [1997] HCA 55, (1997) 190 CLR 181; *The Tychy* [1999] 2 Lloyd's Rep 11 (CA).

[112] This connecting factor is not mentioned in the Arrest Convention 1952 at all, and was introduced very late in the drafting of the AJA 1956: see Paul Myburgh, '"Possession" and "Control" of Ships: On the Outskirts of Admiralty' [2014] *JBL* 667. It has given rise to differing interpretations in Australia, New Zealand, Hong Kong and Singapore: see ibid, 674ff.

[113] See also AJA 1956, s 3(4).

[114] *Republic of India v India Steamship Co Ltd (No 2) (The Indian Grace)* [1998] AC 878 (HL).

[115] AJA 1956, s 3(4)(a).

[116] See eg *The Maritime Trader* (n 111) 156; for reform see *The Giuseppe di Vittorio* [1998] 1 Lloyd's Rep 136, 142–43; discussion in text at n 29 above for the reform in Singapore.

ii. Drawing on the English Model

As is the case in relation to the list of maritime claims, the Singapore and Hong Kong legislation is substantively identical to the equivalent English provisions of the AJA 1956 as updated by the SCA 1981.[117] By comparison, the New Zealand legislation, which is also closely modelled on the AJA 1956, does include the demise charter provision that was missing from that enactment (thereby predating the SCA 1981 reform in this regard), but inexplicably also extends it to the arrest of a sister ship that the in personam defendant has demise chartered.[118] While New Zealand is not a party to the Arrest Convention 1952 and does therefore not have any international obligation in this respect, this unusual extension, which is not discussed in any relevant Parliamentary or law reform materials, has been singled out for criticism as an unjustifiable extension of the admiralty jurisdiction.[119]

iii. Innovations

Canada has not copied the phrasing of the English legislation on the exercise of in rem jurisdiction, although most of the substance remains the same. Proceedings may be taken in rem against a vessel, regardless of its current ownership, in respect of ownership or proprietary claims, general average, harbour dues and related public law claims, as well as claims of damage done by a ship, salvage and wages (all three of which are connected with maritime liens in the Anglo-Common Law tradition).[120] For all remaining claims, such as personal injury or contractual disputes, proceedings can only be taken in rem against a ship if its current beneficial owner was also the beneficial owner at the time the cause of action arose.[121] Next, under the heading of 'arrest', in rem jurisdiction for all maritime claims is extended to 'any ship that, at the time the action is brought, is owned by the beneficial owner of the ship that is the subject of the action'.[122] This last subsection appears to expand the ability to arrest a sister ship in situations where the English model would only permit a claim against the particular ship – such as an ownership or proprietary dispute.

Australia's Admiralty Act 1988 teases out each in rem option into separate sections, rather than trying to jam everything into a single dense provision as the other Common Law countries have done. Accordingly, there are provisions on in rem claims relying on maritime liens, proprietary claims, and general maritime claims. The third category is

[117] High Court Ordinance, cap 4 (HK), s 12B(4); HCAJA, s 4(4) (since 2004).

[118] Admiralty Act 1973 (NZ), s 5(2)(b)(ii): '[I]n questions and claims specified in paragraphs (d) to (r) of subsection (1) of section 4 arising in connection with a ship where the person who would be liable on the claim in an action in personam was, when the cause of action arose, the owner or charterer of, or in possession or in control of, the ship, the jurisdiction of the High Court may (whether the claim gives rise to a maritime lien on the ship or not) be invoked by an action in rem against … *any other ship* which, at the time when the action is brought, is beneficially owned or *on charter by demise* as aforesaid.' (emphasis added)

[119] Paul Myburgh, 'New Zealand' in *Kluwer Law International Encyclopedia of Transport Law* (Deventer, Kluwer Law, 2002) 110; Paul Myburgh, *Extending New Zealand's Admiralty Jurisdiction: A Modest Proposal for Reform* (Maritime Law Association of Australia and New Zealand, March 2004) para 4.9; Bevan Marten, *Maritime Law in New Zealand* (Wellington, Thomson Reuters, 2016) 236.

[120] Federal Courts Act 1985 (Canada), s 43(2).

[121] ibid s 43(3).

[122] ibid s 43(8).

further divided into claims involving owners' and demise charterers' liabilities, as well as proceedings against a surrogate ship (the term given to a ship in the same ownership).[123]

Finally, it is important to note that, while Singapore's substantive law may emulate England's, that country has become an innovator in the field of procedural law. Singapore now requires a significant degree of disclosure from applicants for arrest. In *The Bunga Melati 5* the Singapore Court of Appeal confirmed that a court registrar in Singapore will play a more active screening role than in other Common Law jurisdictions, checking whether sufficient evidence has been provided, for example, of a connection between the 'relevant person' and the alleged defendant, before issuing a warrant for arrest.[124]

C. Substantive Jurisdiction

An aspect of the Arrest Convention 1952 that is rarely discussed under the English model is that of jurisdiction over the substance of a dispute. Article 7(1) of the Arrest Convention 1952 provides that the country in which the arrest was made shall have jurisdiction to determine the case upon its merits if that country's domestic law gives its courts jurisdiction. The remaining paragraphs of the article, providing for substantive jurisdiction in cases such as where the claim has arisen in the arresting State, are therefore easily overlooked. There is also art 8 stating that the Arrest Convention 1952 will apply 'to any vessel flying the flag of a Contracting State in the jurisdiction of any Contracting State', but that the ships of non-Contracting States can be arrested for any claim listed in the Convention, and may also be denied the benefits of the Convention.[125]

The English model does not engage in any fine distinctions of this kind: the admiralty jurisdiction with which most lawyers trained in the Common Law system will be familiar is that found in the SCA 1981 (and equivalent legislation elsewhere) providing for admiralty jurisdiction over all ships, regardless of nationality, in relation to all claims, wherever arising.[126] If necessary, a forum non conveniens analysis will weed out any claims that do not belong.[127] This can be compared with the position in Ireland, for example, where the 1867 Act could still be applicable in relation to the vessels of a non-Contracting State.[128]

VI. Interpretations of the Translations

The jurisdictions examined here confront four different possibilities when interpreting their admiralty legislation. First, Ireland can proceed on the basis of art 31 of the Vienna

123 Admiralty Act 1988 (Cth), ss 15–19.

124 *The Bunga Melati 5* [2012] SGCA 46, [2012] 4 SLR 546 [113]–[117]. See further ch 6.

125 See eg *Common Market Fertilizer SA v Owners and All Persons Claiming an Interest in the MV Sonata* [2007] IEHC 109 (arrest of a Dominican-flagged vessel in Ireland).

126 SCA 1981, ss 20(7)(a) and 20(7)(b).

127 See Cremean (n 28) 132–37.

128 Catherine Duffy, Vincent Power and Eileen Roberts, 'Ireland' in James Gosling and Tessa Huzarski (eds), *The Shipping Law Review*, 2nd edn (London, Law Business Research Ltd, 2015) 304. See too Helen Noble, 'Arrest of Ships in Ireland' (2007) 13 *JIML* 56.

Convention on the Law of Treaties 1969,[129] giving effect to 'the ordinary meaning to be given to the terms of the treaty in their context and in light of its object and purpose'. This is where its approach to implementing the Convention pays dividends, as there can be no doubt as to the Irish legislature's intentions, namely, to promote international uniformity in the ship arrest sphere. Despite this, the temptation to approach the Irish statute in the light of developments in the courts of other Common Law jurisdictions shows through in a case like *The Von Rocks*, where the definition of 'ship' was at issue, and extensive reliance is placed on such authorities.[130]

Next, the English and Hong Kong admiralty legislation should also be interpreted against the background of international obligations,[131] with reference to the travaux préparatoires if necessary,[132] but the mode of implementing the Arrest Convention 1952 into the English and Hong Kong legislation makes this slightly more difficult than in Ireland's case. When an Act gives effect to a treaty without giving its text the 'force of law', or at least borrowing extensively from its wording, it will not always be easy to determine whether that legislature has deliberately departed from the text of the Convention to achieve a different meaning, or whether the words used should be stretched to accommodate the intention behind the Convention.[133] An example like the inclusion of 'beneficial ownership', discussed above,[134] may be explained by the specific needs of a Common Law jurisdiction, but other departures could simply be grounded in domestic policy.[135]

This sometimes means that the focus is placed exclusively on the wording of the national legislation and the Arrest Convention 1952 origins of that legislation are eclipsed. So, for example, in *The Alas*[136] the plaintiff arrested a ship in Hong Kong, essentially to enforce a previous unsatisfied arbitration award in London, although the writ was carefully framed with reference to the underlying cause of action which had already been determined by the London arbitration. The first argument raised for the defendant shipowner was that the proceedings amounted to an abuse of process and ought to be set aside as there was no head of admiralty jurisdiction in Hong Kong for the enforcement of foreign judgments or arbitration awards.[137] The second argument was that ship arrest is not available once a plaintiff's claim has crystallised in a judgment or arbitration award:[138]

> This is because inter alia in Article 1(2) of the International Convention for the Unification of Certain Rules Relating to the Arrest of Sea-Going Ships 1952 ('1952 Convention'), 'arrest' means 'the detention of a ship by judicial process to secure a maritime claim, but does not include the

[129] Vienna Convention on the Law of Treaties (adopted on 22 May 1969, entered into force 27 January 1980) 1155 UNTS 331.
[130] *The Von Rocks* [1998] 2 Lloyd's Rep 198 (SC).
[131] See eg *The Eschersheim* (n 63); *Gatoil International Inc v Arkwright-Boston Manufacturers Mutual Insurance Co (The Sandrina)* [1985] AC 255 (HL); *The River Rima* [1988] 1 WLR 758 (HL).
[132] *The Sandrina* (n 131) 183–84 (Lord Wilberforce).
[133] See for example *The Span Terza* (n 111) 227.
[134] *The Permina 108* (n 111).
[135] See *The Maritime Trader* (n 111) 156.
[136] *Handytankers KS v The Owners and/or Demise Charterers of the Ship or Vessel M/V Alas Subsequently Renamed as Kombos (The Alas)* [2014] HKCFI 1281, [2014] 6 HKC 239 (Ng J).
[137] ibid [8] referring to *The Chong Bong* [1997] HKCFI 306, [1997] 3 HKC 579; *The Bumbesti* [2000] QB 559.
[138] ibid [9].

> seizure of a ship in execution or satisfaction of a judgment'. Mr Alder urged this court to construe section 12A(2) of the Ordinance consistently with Article 1 of the 1952 Convention.

This second argument was summarily dismissed by Ng J, without any reference in his reasoning to the Arrest Convention 1952.[139]

In the years since the enactment of the SCA 1981, which gave more accurate effect to art 3 of the Arrest Convention 1952, this kind of argument has been less likely to arise in England. Nonetheless, room for argument exists. For example, the description of each maritime claim in art 1 of the Arrest Convention 1952 is preceded by the phrase 'arising out of'.[140] Does the absence of this phrase in all the paras except (h), (q), and (r) of section 20(2) of the SCA 1981 reflect an intention to narrow the scope of the remaining claims listed?[141] Arguing against the legislative background of giving effect to the Convention, the scope of the claims in the SCA 1981 should be the same as its international source, regardless of the introductory words used. But the risk of such arguments arising and being litigated exists any time a Convention is 'paraphrased' in this manner.

While Singapore and New Zealand have no obligations under international law to interpret their admiralty legislation in accordance with the Arrest Convention 1952,[142] a definite sense of promoting international uniformity emerges from both legislature and judiciary when dealing with those statutes.[143] However, this is in more of a 'common law family' than an 'international community' sense. The legislation in these countries closely mirrors the English model so that, where possible, the courts should interpret national statutory provisions in a manner that promotes this type of uniformity. However, without any formal international obligations in relation to the Arrest Convention 1952, there is less constraint on the courts if, as in the case of New Zealand's 'sister ship under demise charter' provision,[144] Parliament has made a deliberate departure from the English model. The Singapore Court of Appeal in 1976 went so far as to express the view that, where there is no ambiguity in the national admiralty legislation, it would be wrong to look to the Arrest Convention 1952:[145]

> In our opinion the terms of s 4(4) of the Act, giving them their plain and ordinary meaning are free of any ambiguity and are not reasonably capable of more than one meaning. It follows that it is unnecessary and indeed it would be wrong to look at the International Convention Relating to the Arrest of Seagoing Ships signed at Brussels in 1952 to arrive at the proper construction of our subsection … . Furthermore, Singapore, even when it was a colony of the United Kingdom, was not one of the colonies to which the United Kingdom had under Art 18 extended the Convention and since independence Singapore has not acceded under Art 15 to the Convention.

139 ibid [24]. The Arrest Convention 1952 also did not feature in the Hong Kong Court of Appeal's subsequent dismissal of the defendant shipowner's appeal application: see *Handytankers KS v The Owners and/or Demise Charterers of the Ship or Vessel M/V Alas Subsequently Renamed as Kombos (The Alas)* [2015] HKCA 691, [2015] 6 HKC 557.

140 Arrest Convention 1952, art 1(1): '"Maritime Claim" means a claim arising out of one or more of the following …'.

141 See further ch 8 on the narrowing down of the 'damage' head of jurisdiction in the SCA 1981.

142 See *The Permina 108* (n 111) [10]; *The Fua Kavenga* (n 68) 556, 564.

143 See Marten (n 119) 222–25.

144 Admiralty Act 1973 (NZ), s 5(2)(b)(ii) discussed above at n 118.

145 *The Permina 108* (n 111) [10].

More recent Singapore decisions suggest that the courts are more willing to have regard to material relating to the Arrest Convention 1952,[146] but the starting point still seems to be that these may only be called in aid where the national statute is ambiguous.[147]

Finally, in the case of Australia and Canada, courts can look to other jurisdictions for guidance in some cases, but with the knowledge that their respective Parliaments were not looking to emulate precisely other jurisdictions. Instead, they have what one Canadian judge described as 'parallel legislation',[148] representing attempts to reform the law to best suit domestic needs, even if the Arrest Convention 1952 has been 'deeply influential'.[149] Much case law from other Common Law jurisdictions will still be applicable – many similarities remain – but the drive for uniformity may not be quite the same as in New Zealand or Singapore.[150] For example, the Australian Law Reform Commission report that led to the Admiralty Act 1988 will be a particularly relevant source to guide statutory interpretation in that country.[151] In *Patrick Stevedores No 2 Pty Ltd v MV Skulptor Konenkov* Sheppard J stated that

> it is not only permissible, but essential, to look at what the Law Reform Commission has said about particular provisions in the bill and thus the Act and about the reasons for the absence from the bill of other provisions which, on a different view of matters, might have been included.[152]

Nonetheless, the High Court of Australia has noted that the Admiralty Act 1988 brought that country 'more closely into line with [the jurisdiction] conferred by the UK [1981] Act and, thus, more closely into line with the practice and principles adopted in the Arrest Convention'.[153] And the Canadian Federal Court of Appeal has similarly indicated that it will require clear evidence of Parliamentary intent to break rank with other Anglo-Common Law jurisdictions before departing from the international consensus:[154]

> Until the adoption of the Arrest Convention 1952 and its incorporation into domestic law, it was not possible in most countries, including the UK and Canada, to arrest a ship other than the offending ship. In the UK, the law now allows for the arrest of only one ship, either the offending ship or a sister ship …
>
> Subsection 43(8) came into force in Canada in February of 1992. The provision only deals with the arrest of sister ships. It does not say whether a sister ship can be arrested in addition to the offending ship. Until that enactment, arrests were restricted to the arrest of the offending ship. By enacting subsection 43(8) did Parliament intend to break rank with those countries, like the UK, which either adopted the Arrest Convention 1952 or incorporated its provisions within their domestic legislation? I do not believe Parliament so intended.

[146] See *The Jarguh Sawit* [1995] SGHC 194, [1995] 2 SLR(R) 913; [15]ff (legal opinions from 16 foreign maritime lawyers on the application of the Arrest Convention 1952 considered by the Court).

[147] ibid [27]–[30].

[148] *The Looiersgracht* (n 109) 413.

[149] *The Ship Sam Hawk v Reiter Petroleum Inc* [2016] FCAFC 26, 246 FCR 337 [47] (Allsop CJ and Edelman J).

[150] See ALRC Report (n 34) para 95.

[151] Cremean (n 28) 9.

[152] *Patrick Stevedores No 2 Pty Ltd v MV Skulptor Konenkov* (1996) 64 FCR 223, 239F.

[153] *The Owners of the Ship Shin Kobe Maru v Empire Shipping Inc* [1994] HCA 59, (1994) 181 CLR 404, 420. See also *El Greco (Australia) Pty Ltd v Mediterranean Shipping Co SA* [2004] FCAFC 202, (2004) 140 FCR 296 [139]–[148]; *Tisand Pty Ltd v Owners of the Ship MV Cape Moreton (Ex Freya)* [2005] FCAFC 68, 143 FCR 43 [64]–[65], [87], [104]–[106].

[154] *Westshore Terminals Limited Partnership v Leo Ocean SA* 2014 FCA 231, (2014) 378 DLR (4th) 220 [72]–[75].

My view is that Parliament, in enacting subsection 43(8), intended to confer upon claimants in Canada the right to arrest a sister ship in lieu of the offending ship. Thus, where a claimant is unable to arrest the offending ship under subsection 43(2) because that ship is not available for arrest in Canada or if that ship's value is insufficient to properly secure its claim, the claimant may resort to subsection 43(8) and arrest a sister ship of the offending ship. By enacting subsection 43(8) Parliament conferred a true benefit to claimants, a benefit which was unavailable prior to the enactment of the provision.

In other words, Parliament did not, in my view, intend for the Federal Court to exercise its jurisdiction in rem under both subsections 43(2) and 43(8) for the same claim. Although the word 'or' does not appear in section 43, I cannot see how the provisions can be read otherwise. The fact that Canada did not adopt the Arrest Convention 1952 does not, as the appellants suggest, militate in favour of concluding that Canada intended to go its separate way with regard to ship arrests.

VII. Common Law Countries and the Arrest Convention 1999

Despite rallying cries in the name of uniformity,[155] with the notable exception of India, the Common Law world has almost completely failed to engage with the Arrest Convention 1999.[156] None of the jurisdictions discussed here are party to it, and of all the Common Law jurisdictions, only Pakistan has gone so far as to even sign it (that was in 2000, and the country has not followed through with ratification). This lack of enthusiasm is not due to any grand, principled stance by the Common Law countries. Instead it is linked to what Gaskell and Shaw described as 'its lack of political sex-appeal';[157] which could just as aptly describe the lack of legislative priority that is given to admiralty matters generally – as similarly demonstrated in relation to the relative lack of success of the three Maritime Liens and Mortgages Conventions.[158] Of the three key areas addressed by international maritime Conventions, regulation (especially safety and environmental regulation) and liability have seen significant success, but procedural law and jurisdictional questions have largely fallen by the wayside.[159]

As discussed above,[160] India has very recently updated its admiralty jurisdiction through the enactment of the Admiralty (Jurisdiction and Settlement of Maritime Claims) Act 2017. Although some formal elements of the 2017 Act are reminiscent of the SCA 1981, the substantive provisions of the Act are modelled squarely on the Arrest Convention 1999 rather than on the Arrest Convention 1952.

So, for example, the definition of 'arrest' in s 2(1)(c) of the 2017 Act mirrors art 1(2) of the Arrest Convention 1999 in including 'detention or restriction for removal of a vessel by order of a High Court', which extends the concept of ship arrest explicitly to include,

[155] William Tetley, 'Arrest, Attachment, and Related Maritime Law Procedures' (1999) 73 *Tul LR* 1895, 1972.

[156] For background to the Arrest Convention 1999 see Nick Gaskell and Richard Shaw, 'The Arrest Convention 1999' [1999] *LMCLQ* 470.

[157] ibid 485.

[158] See nn 172–74 below.

[159] Bevan Marten, 'Maritime Law (Uniform Law)' in J Basedow et al (eds), *Encyclopedia of Private International Law* (Edward Elgar, 2017) vol 2 pp 1210, 1213–17.

[160] See Part IV(E) above.

for example, freezing orders and documentary arrests.[161] Interestingly, the Act goes even further than the Arrest Convention 1999 to expressly include in its definition of arrest 'seizure of a vessel in execution or satisfaction of a judgment or order'.

The list of maritime claims in s 4(1) of the 2017 Act has been reordered to more closely resemble the familiar English list in s 20(2) of the SCA 1981, but in substance the claims listed in the 2017 Act are almost identical to the expanded list of maritime claims contained in art 1(1) of the Arrest Convention 1999. All maritime claims are prefaced, as in the Arrest Convention 1999, with the inclusive wording 'arising out of any …'. Notable statutory expansions to the modern Indian admiralty jurisdiction brought about by the 2017 Act include:

(1) loss or damage to or in connection with any goods (s 4(1)(f), which goes even further than art 1(1)(h) of the Arrest Convention 1999, which refers to goods 'carried on board the ship');[162]
(2) salvage services, including, if applicable, special compensation relating to salvage services in respect of a vessel which by itself or its cargo threatens damage to the environment (s 4(1)(i)), which mirrors art 1(1)(c) of the Arrest Convention 1999 in referring expressly to special compensation for preventing or minimising environmental harm awarded under art 14 of the Salvage Convention 1989);
(3) goods, materials, perishable or non-perishable provisions, bunker fuel, equipment (including containers), supplied or services rendered to the vessel for its operation, management, preservation or maintenance including any fee payable or leviable (s 4(1)(l) – the references to 'perishable provisions' and 'bunker fuel' are not in the equivalent art 1(1)(l) of the Arrest Convention 1999, and may have been included with reference to the recent international OW Bunker disputes);[163]
(4) claim by a master or member of the crew of a vessel or their heirs and dependents for wages or any sum due out of wages or adjudged to be due which may be recoverable as wages or cost of repatriation or social insurance contribution payable on their behalf or any amount an employer is under an obligation to pay to a person as an employee, whether the obligation arose out of a contract of employment or by operation of a law (including operation of a law of any country) for the time being in force, and includes any claim arising under a manning and crew agreement relating to a vessel (s 4(1)(o), which goes beyond the ambit of the equivalent art 1(1)(o) of the Arrest Convention 1999 in explicitly including employment obligations that are based in statute or national awards as opposed to employment contracts, as well as more generic crewing agreements, which have caused difficulties of interpretation);[164]
(5) disputes arising out of a contract for the sale of a vessel (s 4(1)(r), mirroring art 1(1)(v) of the Arrest Convention 1999);
(6) insurance premiums (including mutual insurance calls) (s 4(1)(s), mirroring art 1(1)(q) of the Arrest Convention 1999);

[161] Berlingieri (n 2) vol 2 paras 4.01–02.

[162] See the broad definition of 'goods' in s 2(1)(d) of the 2017 Act, which includes 'live animals, containers, pallets or such other articles of transport or packaging or luggage irrespective of the fact whether such property is carried, on or under the deck of a vessel'.

[163] See *PST Energy 7 Shipping LLC v OW Bunker Malta Ltd (The Res Cogitans)* [2016] UKSC 23, [2016] AC 1034.

[164] See eg *Mobil Oil New Zealand Ltd v The Ship Rangiora (No 2)* [2000] 1 NZLR 82.

(7) commission, brokerage or agency fees (s 4(1)(t), mirroring art 1(1)(r) of the Arrest Convention 1999);
(8) damage or threat of damage caused by the vessel to the environment, coastline or related interests; measures taken to prevent, minimise, or remove such damage; compensation for such damage; costs of reasonable measures for the restoration of the environment actually undertaken or to be undertaken; loss incurred or likely to be incurred by third parties in connection with such damage; or any other damage, costs, or loss of a similar nature to those identified in this clause (s 4(1)(u), mirroring the new general environmental damage provision in art 1(1)(d) of the Arrest Convention 1999); and
(9) costs or expenses relating to raising, removal, recovery, destruction or the rendering harmless of a vessel which is sunk, wrecked, stranded or abandoned, including anything that is or has been on board such vessel, and costs or expenses relating to the preservation of an abandoned vessel and maintenance of its crew (s 4(1)(v), mirroring art 1(1)(e) of the Arrest Convention 1999).

It is obvious from the above that the list of maritime claims giving rise to an action in rem under the 2017 Act is considerably broader than the subject-matter jurisdiction of comparable Anglo-Common Law countries. It will be interesting to see whether this translates into India becoming widely known as a more 'arrest-friendly' jurisdiction.

The other key provisions of the 2017 Act also track those of the Arrest Convention 1999. Section 5, which sets out which vessels may be arrested, mirrors art 3 of the Arrest Convention 1999 faithfully. This means that prominence is given to 'when the arrest is effected' – as opposed to other Anglo-Common Law jurisdictions which, on the English model, focus on 'when the action is brought' – to determine whether the link between the owner or charterer and the ship is satisfied.[165] Section 11(1) of the Act also tracks art 6 of the Arrest Convention 1999, which provides that the court may require the claimant to provide a damages undertaking as a condition of ship arrest or maintenance of ship arrest to cover loss or damage arising from wrongful or unjustified arrest or the demanding or providing of excessive security. In the enactment of this provision, India diverges significantly from the traditional Anglo-Common Law position, which is not to require claimants arresting ships to provide counter-security.[166]

Finally, the Act goes further than the Arrest Convention 1999 and takes a leaf out of the South African statute book in attempting to codify the priorities of maritime liens and other claims in ss 9–10. It also provides in s 8 that, following a judicial vessel sale under the Act, 'the vessel shall vest in the purchaser free from all encumbrances, liens, attachments, registered mortgages and charges of the same nature on the vessel'.

Interestingly, however, the Act has not implemented an equivalent provision to art 7 of the Arrest Convention 1999, which provides for retention of security arrests in support of foreign litigation or arbitration. The High Court of Bombay in *Siem Offshore Redri AS v Altus Uber*[167] nonetheless recently confirmed that security arrests in support of foreign

[165] See the Indian Supreme Court decision in *Chrisomar Corp v MJR Steels Private Ltd* AIR 2017 SC 5530 [26]–[28].
[166] On which see *Natwest Markets plc (Formerly known as the Royal Bank of Scotland plc) v Stallion Eight Shipping Co SA (The MV Alkyon)* [2018] EWHC 2033 (Admlty), [2018] Lloyd's Rep Plus 93; *Stallion Eight Shipping Co SA v Natwest Markets plc* [2018] EWCA Civ 2760; ch 6.
[167] *Siem Offshore Redri AS v Altus Uber* 2018 (6) ABR 361.

arbitration are still permissible in India. Although the 2017 Act does not expressly include an equivalent of art 7 of the Arrest Convention 1999, it does not exclude its application either. The 2017 Act should not be regarded as a code, as it is silent on the procedures following the arrest of the ship.[168] It appears, therefore, that the interpretation principle enunciated in *The MV Elisabeth*, which holds that the relevant international maritime law Convention principles form part of the Indian common law, survives the 2017 Act.[169] Similarly, the 2017 Act has not included a domestic equivalent of art 5 of the Arrest Convention 1999 on rights of rearrest and multiple arrest, but there too, the Indian courts still seem willing to consider the unenacted provisions of the Arrest Convention 1999 as part of their very broad and contextual interpretation of the 2017 Act.[170]

VIII. Conclusions

The history of the Common Law jurisdictions shows that it can take up to a century for a legislature to turn its attention to improving the admiralty jurisdiction. The differences between the Arrest Conventions 1952 and 1999 are not so radical that they are likely to convince a government to prioritise the required international and domestic efforts in this context,[171] with major reform such as the introduction of a broader 'associated ship' arrest not being adopted,[172] and the current law is seen as performing adequately in the meantime. The three Maritime Liens and Mortgages Conventions of 1926,[173] 1967[174] and 1993[175] have failed to achieve significant success in the Common Law world for similar reasons.

If the United Kingdom were to ratify or otherwise implement the Arrest Convention 1999, that might eventually spur other Common Law countries into action, such as Hong Kong, Singapore and New Zealand, in the interests of continuing uniformity. However, the United Kingdom's membership of the European Union has presented one barrier to this due to the need for the collective accession of all Member States to international instruments setting out international jurisdiction and recognition and enforcement of judgment rules.[176] In the meantime, there is perhaps a slight chance of achieving minor

[168] ibid [32].

[169] This open-ended interpretation approach to the 2017 Act has also been adopted by the Indian Supreme Court in *Chrisomar* (n 165).

[170] See *Praxis Energy Agents SA v MT Pratibha Neera* 2018 (4) ABR 148, 2018 (5) Bom CR 154 (application for multiple ship arrest) [55]ff; and see further ch 5.

[171] See Tetley (n 154) 1962–72. A comparison of the two Arrest Conventions is set out in appendix II of Berlingieri (n 2) vol 2 151ff.

[172] Derrington and Turner (n 102) 351.

[173] See n 13 above.

[174] International Convention for the Unification of Certain Rules relating to Maritime Liens and Mortgages (adopted 27 May 1967, not yet in force): see UNCITRAL, *Register of Texts of Conventions and Other Instruments concerning International Trade Law* (UN, New York, 1973) vol II 179.

[175] International Convention on Maritime Liens and Mortgages (adopted 6 May 1993, entered into force 5 September 2004) UN Doc A/CONF. 162/7, 33 ILM 353.

[176] This is because the European Union has exclusive legislative competence in jurisdictional matters covered by the Brussels I Regulation (Recast) (see EUCJ Opinion No 1/03 of 7 February 2006). However, the position is even more complicated in respect of the Arrest Convention 1999 which lays down both international jurisdiction rules (which do fall within the scope of the Brussels I Regulation Recast) and uniform substantive rules

admiralty reforms outside of the international context in countries such as New Zealand and Singapore, for example by adding to the list of claims, than by approaching the matter as one requiring treaty action. Countries like Australia or Canada that have never been party to the Arrest Convention 1952, and which have their own legislation that already extends to insurance-related claims and other aspects covered by the Arrest Convention 1999, would appear to have even less incentive. At face value, it would seem more likely that Ireland would update its law, given the model it chose for implementing the Arrest Convention 1952. It will also be interesting to see whether India's very recent statutory implementation of most of the principles and provisions of the Arrest Convention 1999 has any impact beyond its shores.

(which do not, and would therefore fall within the legislative competence of EU Member States). Laura Carballo Piñeiro, *International Maritime Labour Law*, Hamburg Studies on Maritime Affairs 34 (Berlin, Springer, 2015) 130–31 argues that this 'complex dilemma … can only be resolved if the EU as a whole and individual member states ratify the Convention'.

13

The Future of Ship Arrest

MARTIN DAVIES*

I. Introduction

Albert Einstein once said: 'I never think of the future – it comes soon enough.'[1] Anyone who is tempted to predict the future eventually looks like a farseeing prophet or a credulous fool, as the future comes along soon enough to prove the prediction right or wrong. As a result, any prognosticator is wise to be cautious, and not merely cautious, but also to be aware of the phenomenon that psychologists call 'desirability bias', which is more commonly known as 'wishful thinking'.[2] With characteristic bluntness, George Orwell wrote as follows about that phenomenon: 'People can foresee the future only when it coincides with their own wishes.'[3]

This Chapter, which considers the possibility that courts may become more prepared to probe the reality of corporate structures of ship ownership, rather than simply accepting the face value of separate corporate personality, admittedly indulges in a considerable amount of 'desirability bias'. It is not entirely made up of wishful thinking, however; there are some concrete grounds for believing that some change in this regard may possibly occur. Nevertheless, it must be acknowledged that there is as much advocacy as prediction in what follows, because otherwise there would be very little to say. In other respects, the future of ship arrest looks very much like its long past. It is doubtful that much, if anything, will change about the law of ship arrest in the near to mid-term future. There is no concerted lobby of commercial interests urging change at the level of national legislation or existing international Conventions. It seems unlikely that the law of ship arrest will need to change

* Admiralty Law Institute Professor of Maritime Law, Tulane University School of Law; Director, Tulane Maritime Law Center.

[1] Einstein actually said: 'Ich denke niemals an die Zukunft. Es kommt bald genug.' This quotation, sometimes thought to be apocryphal, was part of an interview with Einstein conducted in German by the International News Service reporter David Sentner on 11 December 1930 upon Einstein's arrival in New York on the liner *Belgenland*. A translation of the interview appeared in the *Clearfield Progress* on 12 December 1930 under the headline: 'Would Take Three Days to Make Simple Explanation of Theories, Says Einstein'.

[2] Zlatan Krizan and Paul Windschitl, 'Wishful Thinking about the Future: Does Desire Impact Optimism?' (2009) 3 *Social and Personality Psychology Compass* 227; Paul Windschitl et al, 'The Desirability Bias in Predictions: Going Optimistic without Leaving Realism' (2010) 111 *Organizational Behavior and Human Decision Processes* 33; William von Hippel and Robert Trivers, 'The Evolution and Psychology of Self-Deception' (2011) 34 *Behavioral and Brain Sciences* 1.

[3] George Orwell, 'London Letter' in *Partisan Review* (Winter 1945), reprinted in Sonia Orwell and Ian Angus (eds), *The Collected Essays, Journalism and Letters of George Orwell: As I Please, 1943–1946* (Boston, DR Godine, 2000) vol 3 293, 297.

in order to accommodate impending technological changes, such as the development of autonomous ships, which will presumably be subject to arrest or attachment in exactly the same way as their present-day crewed counterparts. Nothing seems particularly broken; nothing seems particularly in need of a fix, except for the ease with which ship operators can render their maritime assets immune from arrest. For that reason, this Chapter focuses on one-ship companies and the courts' continued infatuation with the corporate veil.

II. One-ship Companies and the Corporate Veil

The Arrest Convention 1952[4] acknowledged the possibility of surrogate ship arrest,[5] providing for the possibility of arresting a ship in the same ownership as the ship in relation to which the plaintiff's claim arose.[6] Many countries have adopted a version of the surrogate ship procedure, whether or not they are party to the Convention.

Common Law jurisdictions other than the United States and South Africa are generally very reluctant to look beyond the separate corporate personality of a one-ship company when it comes to considering whether to permit surrogate ship arrest. In courts following the English legal tradition, it has been said that one-ship companies are a legitimate device, so that the court will not lift (or pierce, depending on one's preferred terminology)[7] the corporate veil except in exceptional circumstances.[8] In the English tradition, the special circumstances that justify lifting the corporate veil are confined to cases where the one-ship subsidiary company has been set up as a façade or sham to deceive or defraud, with the result that the veil is seldom (if ever) lifted when the one-ship company was already in existence before the plaintiff's claim arose.[9] The mere existence of a one-ship subsidiary company is not regarded as providing sufficient evidence of a general intention to deceive potential creditors.[10] The Singapore Court of Appeal has said that use of the one-ship

[4] International Convention Relating to the Arrest of Sea-going Ships (adopted 10 May 1952, entered into force 24 February 1956) 439 UNTS 193.

[5] Although the procedure is often called 'sister ship arrest', that terminology is eschewed here for two reasons: (1) it is unnecessarily gendered; and (2) it is inaccurate, in that 'sister ships' are, if anything, ships of the same design and structure, not ships of the same ownership.

[6] Arrest Convention 1952, art 3(1).

[7] Courts that follow the English tradition usually refer to 'lifting' the corporate veil; American courts usually refer to 'piercing' it. In an interesting judgment that is considered further below (see text at n 60ff), Staughton LJ distinguished between 'lifting' and 'piercing' the corporate veil, saying that 'piercing' should be reserved for treating the activities of a company as those of its shareholders, whereas 'lifting' should refer to cases where the court has regard to the shareholding in the company for some legal purpose: see *Atlas Maritime Co SA v Avalon Maritime Ltd (The Coral Rose)* [1991] 1 Lloyd's Rep 563, 571. Other, rather less standard, metaphors employed by courts include 'looking behind', 'pulling off', 'drawing aside', 'pulling aside' and 'tearing away' the corporate veil: see Francis Rose, 'Raising the Corporate Sail' [2013] *LMCLQ* 566, 581 fn 71.

[8] See, eg, *The Skaw Prince* [1994] SGHC 18, [1994] 3 SLR(R) 146 [19] (Amarjeet Singh JC); *Simgood Pte Ltd v MLC Shipbuilding Sdn Bhd* [2015] SGHC 303, [2016] 1 SLR 1129 [195] (Vinodh Coomaraswamy J: '[I]t is entirely legitimate for the ultimate economic owner of a number of ships to insulate himself from liability arising from ownership of those ships and to insulate each ship from liability arising from the other ships by holding each ship through a series of one-ship companies'. See also ch 9 Sections VII and VIII.

[9] *The Maritime Trader* [1981] 2 Lloyd's Rep 153, 157 (Sheen J); *The Evpo Agnic* [1988] 2 Lloyd's Rep 411, 415 (Lord Donaldson MR); *The Andres Bonifacio* [1993] SGCA 70, [1993] 3 SLR(R) 71 [41] (Lai Kew Chai J delivering the judgment of the Court); *The Skaw Prince* (n 8) [19] (Amarjeet Singh JC).

[10] *Bakri Bunker Trading Co Ltd v The Owners of and Other Persons Interested in the Ship Neptune (The Neptune)* [1985] HKCFI 236, [1986] HKLR 345; *The Skaw Prince* (n 8).

company structure as a means of evading debts is insufficient in itself to warrant lifting of the corporate veil.[11]

It is sometimes thought that the device of the one-ship company was invented after the Arrest Convention 1952, as a deliberate, albeit obvious, attempt to avoid the effect of the Convention's provisions on surrogate ship arrest. That is far from being the case, however. The device of using individual corporations to own individual ships in a fleet first came into use in the early 1860s, as a result of the passage in the United Kingdom of the Companies Act of 1862. A brief examination of the history of one-ship companies helps to show how inappropriate it is for present-day courts to continue to accept the corporate personality of a one-ship company at face value, without further inquiry.

The Companies Act 1862 (UK) was the culmination of a series of changes that removed all obstacles to incorporation of joint stock companies, and thus profoundly changed the behaviour of entrepreneurs.[12] In the late eighteenth and early nineteenth centuries, the legal environment for the development of joint stock companies in the UK was severely impaired by memories of the South Sea Bubble of 1720, which led politicians to regard joint stock companies as dubious and suspect by nature.[13] The growth of the railways in the 1830s led to an easing of the conditions for establishing joint stock companies because of the need to encourage capital investment.[14] However, until the corporate law reforms that began in the UK in the 1850s, the investors in a company were still held to be jointly and severally liable for all of the company's debts.[15] In contrast, as is now second nature to contemporary readers, limited liability limits the investor's capital exposure to the value of his or her individual share subscription. Although it may now seem as though limited liability is an intrinsic part of the notion of corporate responsibility, it was not fully implemented in English law until the reforms that culminated in the Companies Act of 1862.[16]

As soon as the Act of 1862 was passed, there was an explosive growth in the number of limited-liability companies established in England.[17] Shipowners were quick to take advantage of the new legal model, which enabled them to attract capital investment to finance the construction and operation of individual ships. So much is apparent from evidence given by a man named John Dent to a long-running *Royal Commission on Loss of Life at Sea*, which conducted hearings from 1886 to 1887, and which finally reported in 1887.[18] Dent described himself to the Royal Commissioners as a shipowner and shipbroker from Newcastle-upon-Tyne, giving evidence on behalf of the North of England Steamship Owners' Association.[19] He said that he had owned and managed about 25 ships altogether.[20] Although the Royal Commission was principally concerned, as its name suggests, with safety of life at sea,

[11] *The Andres Bonifacio* (n 9) [41].

[12] David Foucaud, 'The Impact of the *Companies Act* of 1862 Extending Limited Liability to the Banking and Financial Sector in the English Crisis of 1866' (2011) 62 *Revue Économique* 867, 868.

[13] ibid 869.

[14] ibid 870.

[15] ibid.

[16] ibid 871.

[17] ibid 872–4, with charts showing the rapid growth in the number of companies and capital investment.

[18] *Final Report of the Royal Commission on Loss of Life at Sea, with Minutes of Evidence, Appendix, and Digest of the Evidence* (C 5227 (Pt 1), C 5227–I (Pt 2), C 5227–II (Pt 3), 1887).

[19] ibid 300, Questions 20,027–8. Dent gave evidence on the 67th day of the Commission, 25 May 1886, which explains why more than 20,000 questions had been asked before the Commissioners arrived at his testimony.

[20] ibid, Question 20,029.

the Royal Commissioners' examination of Dent also extended to the phenomenon of, and the reasons for, single-ship companies. Dent's testimony about the use of single-ship companies clearly indicates that the Companies Act of 1862 was the trigger for their development. The following exchange took place before the Royal Commission in 1886:[21]

> 20,111. The single ship company has been a recent invention, has it not? – I do not think so.
>
> 20,112. Can you recall when there were no single ship companies? – Yes, I can.
>
> 20,113. How long ago is that? – That is, I should say, 23 years ago [ie, in 1863]. It is not to my knowledge that there were any at that time.

Why did the Companies Act 1862 (UK) stimulate the development of one-ship companies as the owners of the ships they operated? John Dent answered with disarming frankness:[22]

> 20,100. Therefore, as I say, one result of these single ship companies is to evade liability? – Undoubtedly.
>
> 20,101. And that is the object? – The object is to limit your liability to the amount of your investment, that is the plain way of putting it.

Dent's rather defiant answer is very revealing for present purposes. The purpose of having one-ship companies was to encourage investment by limiting the amount of each individual investor's liability to the amount of his or her investment, in place of the pre-1862 system of making investors jointly and severally liable for all liabilities incurred by the ship. Dent explained the pre-1862 system to the Commissioners by telling them the story of one of the part-owners of what he described as 'a 64th ship'[23] being sued for a cargo claimant's entire loss of £14,000.[24] In contrast, the post-1862 system protected individual capital investors:[25]

> 20,064. What is the object of establishing those single ship companies? – My first inducement was that under the old system an owner was called upon to pay the debts of his ship after he had paid his share of them when the ship was wound up.
>
> 20,065. Then a single ship company has the advantage that the shareholder is practically relieved from the payment of the debts of his ship, after the capital is paid up? – Yes.
>
> 20,066. And that is the main advantage? – Yes, that is the main advantage.

Similarly, in the United States, the imposition of limited liability was perceived as a means of encouraging the small-scale entrepreneur, and of keeping entry into business markets competitive and democratic.[26]

[21] ibid 302.

[22] ibid.

[23] The Registration of Vessels Act 1823 (UK) formalised the traditional British practice of dividing ownership of a ship into 64 shares: see Martin Davies and Anthony Dickey, *Shipping Law*, 4th edn (Pyrmont, Lawbook Co, 2016) 94. Many reasons are given for this tradition, none of them reliably accurate: see Howard Alexander, 'How it Was that Ships Came to be Owned in 64 Parts' in MWD White and Aladin Rahemtula (eds), *Table Talk of the Selden Society in Queensland: Papers Delivered at the Annual General Meetings of the Selden Society Brisbane, 1989–2004* (Brisbane, Supreme Court of Queensland Library, 2005) ch 4.

[24] *Royal Commission on Loss of Life at Sea* (n 18) 302, Questions 20,093–5.

[25] ibid 301.

[26] Stephen B Presser, *Piercing the Corporate Veil* (New York, Thomson Reuters Westlaw, 2016 update) § 1.3.

Thus, the traditional reluctance to look behind the fact of corporate personality stemmed originally from the desire to promote investment by protecting individual investors. That being so, why should the reluctance to look behind corporate personality necessarily extend to the situation where all of the shares in a one-ship company are owned by one person, whether natural or itself corporate? That person's liability may be limited in amount by virtue of the concept of limited liability, but why does it follow that the person who owns 100 per cent of the shares should not be regarded as the true owner of the assets of the company?

It is often said, as if in answer to this question, that the shareholders of a company are not the owners of the company's assets.[27] That is simply not good enough in terms of principle: it is no more than a repetition of the rule, rather than a reasoned justification of it.

In the context of ship arrest in general, and surrogate ship arrest in particular, one of the central legal questions is whether the person who would be liable in personam (called the 'relevant person' in the legislation of many countries) is the *beneficial* owner of the ship to be arrested.[28] It seems to be well accepted that the beneficial owner of a ship is the person who has the right to sell, dispose of or alienate all the shares in that ship,[29] also described as the person who has the power to have and dispose of dominion, possession and enjoyment of the ship.[30] Why should that not include a person who has no need to call a shareholders' meeting to get the shipowning company to exercise the right or power of dominion to sell, dispose of or alienate the shares of the ship, because it owns all of the shares in that company? The owner of all the shares in a company has complete dominion over the assets of that company, because it can direct the company to do whatever it wants with those assets. Is it not taking the fiction of corporate personality too far to say that the sole shareholder's 'dominion' does not amount to beneficial ownership of the assets?

The American doctrine of personification regards the ship itself as a separate legal personality, capable of acquiring legal obligations even when its owner would not be personally liable.[31] That aspect of the doctrine is often criticised, even within the United States, as taking the fiction of the separate legal personality of the ship too far.[32] Those who deride the idea that a ship can be liable as an independent person, separate from its owner,

[27] *Macaura v Northern Assurance Co Ltd* [1925] AC 619.

[28] See, eg, Senior Courts Act 1981 (UK), s 21(4) ('beneficial owner'); High Court (Admiralty Jurisdiction) Act (Singapore), cap 123, 2001 rev edn, s 4(4) ('beneficial owner'); High Court Ordinance (HK), cap 4, s 12B(4) ('beneficial owner'); Admiralty Act 1973 (NZ), s 5(2)(b) ('beneficially owned as respects all shares therein'). The Australian legislation refers simply to 'owner' (see Admiralty Act 1988 (Cth), ss 17(b), 19(b)), but it has been held that 'owner' in this context means 'beneficial owner': *Malaysia Shipyard and Engineering SDN BHD v Iron Shortland as the Surrogate for the Ship Newcastle Pride* [1995] FCA 1565, (1995) 59 FCR 535, 546–47 (Sheppard J); *Kent v SS Maria Luisa (No 2)* [2003] FCAFC 93, (2003) 130 FCR 12 [17] (Tamberlin and Hely JJ); *Shagang Shipping Co Ltd v Ship Bulk Peace* [2014] FCAFC 48, (2014) 314 ALR 230 [20] (Allsop CJ).

[29] *The Pangkalan Susu/Permina 3001* [1977] SGCA 5, [1977–8] SLR(R) 105 [9]; *The Ohm Mariana ex Peony* [1993] SGCA 43, [1993] 2 SLR(R) 698 [35]; *The Min Rui* [2016] SGHC 183, [2016] 5 SLR 667 [52] (Belinda Ang Saw Ean J); *The SS Maria Luisa (No 2)* (n 28) [61] (Tamberlin and Hely JJ); *The Ship Gem of Safaga v Euroceanica (UK) Ltd* [2010] FCAFC 14, (2010) 182 FCR 27 [15] (Besanko J); *The Bulk Peace* (n 28) [20] (Allsop CJ).

[30] *Tisand Pty Ltd v Owners of Ship MV Cape Moreton (ex Freya)* [2005] FCAFC 68, (2005) 143 FCR 43 [119] (Ryan and Allsop JJ).

[31] See Martin Davies, 'In Defense of Unpopular Virtues: Personification and Ratification' (2000) 75 *Tul L Rev* 337.

[32] See, eg, Grant Gilmore & Charles L Black, *The Law of Admiralty*, 2nd edn (Brooklyn, The Foundation Press Inc, 1975) §9-18, 615–16 and fn 75; David M Collins, 'Comments on the American Rule of In Rem Liability' (1985) 10 *Maritime Lawyer* 71, 90; George K Walker, 'The Personification of the Vessel in United States Civil In Rem Actions and the International Law Context' (1991) 15 *Tul Mar LJ* 177, 243.

really should not defend the doctrine of corporate personality when it comes to wholly-owned subsidiaries. It is much less absurd to regard a ship, which can itself cause great physical and economic harm, as a legal person separate from its owner (even a sole owner) than it is to regard the mental abstraction that is a corporation as a legal person separate from the person (corporate or natural) who owns it.[33] The English legal tradition insists that the action in rem against a ship is, in truth, an action against the ship's owner.[34] Why, then, does it not also insist that an action against a wholly-owned company is, in truth, an action against that company's sole owner?

Of course, not every wholly-owned subsidiary is set up in order to shield the sole owner from liability. There may be sound business or operational reasons for establishing a wholly-owned subsidiary, even a one-ship company. For example, it seems fairly obvious that the one-ship companies operated by John Dent had their own managers, because Dent assured the Royal Commissioners that the managers of single-ship companies paid just as much attention to safety concerns as did the managers under the 'ordinary system' of fleet ownership.[35] However, where the one-ship company has no separate operational management, it begins to look more like a mere device to shield the owner of the shares in the company from the consequences of ownership.

Courts in the United States often engage in a thorough analysis of the reality of corporate holdings when considering whether one company is the alter ego of another. That kind of inquiry is undertaken in many different contexts, but its significance for present purposes lies in the way in which it is undertaken in Rule B attachment cases. The Rule B attachment procedure is similar in some ways to ship arrest, but it is different in several important respects, not least because it is not, strictly speaking, arrest at all.

It should first be observed that there is no surrogate ship arrest in the United States. That is one consequence of the doctrine of personification. Only the wrongdoing ship itself can be sued in rem and arrested under Rule C of the Supplemental Rules for Certain Admiralty and Maritime Claims of the Federal Rules of Civil Procedure as the personified defendant; no other ship can be held responsible for the wrongdoing ship's liabilities. However, if the shipowner is sued in personam, then *any* of its property, 'tangible or intangible', that is found within the federal judicial district can be attached under Rule B of the Supplemental Rules for Certain Admiralty and Maritime Claims if the shipowner itself cannot be found within that district. In recent years, there have been many cases in which claimants have sought to argue that one company is the alter ego of another, so that the property of the alter ego can be attached under Rule B. That question rose to prominence during the era of attachment of electronic funds transfers in New York City, but it existed before that era began and it has continued after that era came to an end.[36] The American courts' alter ego jurisprudence suggests a sensible, more realistic future for ship arrest when combined with a recent development in English law that will be considered shortly.

[33] See Davies (n 31) 340–41.

[34] *Republic of India v India Steamship Co Ltd (The Indian Grace) (No 2)* [1998] AC 878.

[35] *Royal Commission on Loss of Life at Sea* (n 18) 302, Questions 20,119–21.

[36] The attachment of EFTs was held to be permissible by the decision in *Winter Storm Shipping Ltd v TPI*, 310 F3d 263, 2002 AMC 2705 (2d Cir 2002). *Winter Storm* was overruled by *Shipping Corp of India Ltd v Jaldhi Overseas Pte Ltd*, 585 F3d 58, 2009 AMC 2409 (2d Cir 2009).

Courts in the United States ostensibly display the same reluctance to pierce the corporate veil as their English counterparts have traditionally done. American courts often state that treating one company as the alter ego of another should be done 'reluctantly and cautiously',[37] only in 'extraordinary circumstances'.[38] In substance, however, they are considerably more willing to engage in a thorough, fact-specific, inquiry into the circumstances of corporate ownership and operations. American courts investigate many factors in making the decision about alter ego status. The Fourth Circuit uses the following factors:[39]

> These factors include gross undercapitalization, insolvency, siphoning of funds, failure to observe corporate formalities and maintain proper corporate records, non-functioning of officers, control by a dominant stockholder, and injustice or fundamental unfairness.

The Second Circuit uses a similar, but even more extensive, list:[40]

> (1) disregard of corporate formalities; (2) inadequate capitalization; (3) intermingling of funds; (4) overlap in ownership, officers, directors, and personnel; (5) common office space, address and telephone numbers of corporate entities; (6) the degree of discretion shown by the allegedly dominated corporation; (7) whether the dealings between the entities are at arms' length; (8) whether the corporations are treated as independent profit centers; (9) payment or guarantee of the corporation's debts by the dominating entity, and (10) intermingling of property between the entities.

The Fifth Circuit's list is longer still, and is expressed to be 'non-exhaustive':[41]

> (1) the parent and subsidiary have common stock ownership; (2) the parent and subsidiary have common directors or officers; (3) the parent and subsidiary have common business departments; (4) the parent and subsidiary file consolidated financial statements; (5) the parent finances the subsidiary; (6) the parent caused the incorporation of the subsidiary; (7) the subsidiary operated with grossly inadequate capital; (8) the parent pays salaries and other expenses of subsidiary; (9) the subsidiary receives no business except that given by the parent; (10) the parent uses the subsidiary's property as its own; (11) the daily operations of the two corporations are not kept separate; (12) the subsidiary does not observe corporate formalities.

It is important to note, however, that even if these tests indicate complete domination of one corporation by another, that is not enough in itself to justify a finding of alter ego status.[42] It must also be established that the corporate form has been used to perpetrate a fraud *or* that the corporation is being used to transact the defendant owner's business rather than its own corporate business.[43] It is in the latter alternative that the US courts go beyond

[37] *In re County Green Ltd Partnership*, 604 F2d 289, 292 (4th Cir 1979).

[38] *Vitol v Primerose Shipping Co Ltd*, 708 F3d 527, 2013 AMC 648 (4th Cir 2013).

[39] *Ost-West-Handel Bruno Bischoff GmbH v Project Asia Line, Inc*, 160 F3d 170, 174, 1999 AMC 380 (4th Cir 1999).

[40] *Freeman v Complex Computing Co*, 119 F3d 1044, 1053 (2d Cir 1997).

[41] *Oxford Capital Corp v US*, 211 F3d 280, 284 n 2 (5th Cir 2000).

[42] *Wm Passalacqua Builders, Inc v Resnick Developers South, Inc*, 933 F2d 131, 138 (2d Cir 1991).

[43] *Itel Containers International Corp v Atlanttrafik Express Service Ltd*, 909 F2d 698, 704, 1990 AMC 1817 (2d Cir 1990).

their English counterparts, recognising that some (but not all) wholly-owned subsidiaries are merely vehicles for their owners' business, in which case the corporate veil will be pierced even in the absence of fraud. As the US Court of Appeals for the Fourth Circuit said recently:[44]

> The standard for piercing the corporate veil is high, but its purpose is to achieve an equitable result by focusing on reality and not form, on how the corporation operated and the individual defendant's relationship to that operation.

It is worth repeating at this point that not all one-ship companies are set up to act as a front behind which the real controllers can hide. It is also worth repeating that many are. It is only possible to discern the difference by engaging in the kind of fact-specific inquiry that US courts undertake in alter ego cases. To require evidence of fraud before going beyond the façade of corporate personality is to concede an enormous amount of leeway to the deliberate manipulation of legal structures by canny businesspeople.

The US approach to alter ego status in Rule B attachment cases shares some features with the South African inquiry into 'associated ship' status, which also mandates an inquiry into the underlying realities of the organization of corporate groups. The South African Admiralty Jurisdiction Regulation Act 1983 allows arrest of another ship that is owned, at the time when the action is commenced, by a person who controlled the company that owned the ship concerned when the maritime claim arose,[45] or a ship that is owned by a company that is controlled by a person who owned the ship concerned or controlled the company which owned the ship concerned when the maritime claim arose.[46] Put more simply (although perhaps only a little more simply), if Ship A is the ship in relation to which the claim arose, Ship B can be arrested as an 'associated ship' if:

(1) Ship B is owned at the time of arrest by the person (including a juristic person such as another company) who controlled the company that owned Ship A at the time the cause of action arose;
(2) Ship A was owned at the time the cause of action arose by the person who controls the company that owns Ship B at the time of arrest; or, perhaps most significantly,
(3) Ship A and Ship B are owned by companies that are controlled by the same person – Ship A at the time the cause of action arose, and Ship B at the time of the arrest. Persons (including juristic persons such as companies) are deemed to control a company if they have power, directly or indirectly, to control that company.[47]

South Africa adopted the 'associated ship' procedure in 1983 because of the ease with which the surrogate ship procedure envisaged by the Arrest Convention 1952 could be circumvented by the device of the one-ship company,[48] and it amended the legislation in 1992 to plug gaps in order to make the procedure work even more effectively.[49] As is well known,

[44] *Flame, SA v Freight Bulk Pte Ltd*, 807 F3d 572, 587, 2015 AMC 2705 (4th Cir 2015), quoting *Vitol* (n 38) (internal quotation marks omitted).
[45] Admiralty Jurisdiction Regulation Act 1983 (SA), s 3(7)(a)(ii).
[46] ibid, s 3(7)(a)(iii).
[47] ibid, s 3(7)(b)(ii).
[48] John Hare, *Shipping Law and Admiralty Jurisdiction in South Africa*, 2nd edn (Kenwyn, Juta, 2009), § 2-2.6.
[49] The 1992 reforms are considered in Hilton Staniland, '*Ex Africa Semper Aliquid Novi*: Associated Ship Arrest in South Africa' [1995] *LMCLQ* 561.

the South African legislation goes further than any of the other systems considered so far. As Hilton Staniland pointed out after the 1992 amendments, the South African notion of surrogate ship arrest does not merely look behind the corporate veil if that veil is being used as 'a device, stratagem or a sham to mask the effective carrying on of a business', but rather it 'shred[s] the veil in all cases',[50] because it is not concerned with the detailed questions about control, capitalisation and operations that typify the US alter ego inquiry, but merely assumes that where there is smoke, there is fire.

The South African approach has long been regarded as an outlier, an extreme, perhaps aberrant, example of impatience with the supposedly eternal verities of the doctrine of corporate personality. Nevertheless, it serves to remind us of how far the law has come since the invention of one-ship companies in the 1860s. If the company is genuinely a vehicle for investment by multiple investors, its separate identity should be respected for the reasons John Dent explained to the Royal Commissioners as long ago as 1886. If not, there are sound grounds for at least suspecting that corporate personality is being used as a device to avoid liability, a suspicion that the South African legislature enshrined as a presumption.

By now, the reader may have concluded that this section of the Chapter has long since departed even from the province of wishful thinking and has wandered off into the territory of advocacy. That would be fair comment, perhaps, and it certainly prompts a question that returns both reader and writer to the major theme of this Chapter, which is supposed to be a prophecy about the future. How likely is it that countries other than South Africa and the United States will engage in a more thoroughgoing focus 'on reality and not form' (to use the words of the US Court of Appeals for the Fourth Circuit)[51] when considering ship arrest cases? It is certainly very unlikely that there will ever be a Protocol to the Arrest Convention 1952 or that the Arrest Convention 1999[52] will attract widespread support among countries with a significant maritime trade.[53] What prospect is there that, without some change in the basic legislative structure, courts in countries other than South Africa and the United States will begin to ask themselves which one-ship companies are created for genuine operational purposes and which are simply vehicles for avoidance of liability?

A seed in the wind may be found in the recent decision of the UK Supreme Court in *Prest v Petrodel Resources Ltd*.[54] Actually, *Prest* may prove to be much more than a seed in the wind. Several writers have called *Prest* the most significant decision about corporate personality in UK law since the foundational case of *Salomon v Salomon*.[55]

Prest was a family law case concerned with the distribution of assets after divorce. Mrs Prest contended that her ex-husband's wealth was much greater than he claimed,

[50] ibid 570. See further ch 2.

[51] See text at n 44 above.

[52] International Convention on the Arrest of Ships (adopted 12 March 1999, entered into force 14 September 2011) 2797 UNTS 3.

[53] At the time of writing, the only countries party to the Arrest Convention 1999 are Albania, Algeria, Benin, Bulgaria, Congo, Ecuador, Estonia, Latvia, Liberia, Spain and Syria: see treaties.un.org/Pages/ViewDetails.aspx?src=IND&mtdsg_no=XII-8&chapter=12&clang=_en. The UK delegation at the Conference drafting the Arrest Convention 1999 proposed an associated ship provision which would have explicitly authorised courts to determine whether a ship is 'effectively controlled' by a person, but this was not adopted in the final text: see Francesco Berlingieri, *Berlingieri on Arrest of Ships*, 6th edn (Abingdon, Informa Law from Routledge, 2017) vol 2 paras 8.57–8, 8.70–4, appendix IV 274ff.

[54] *Prest v Petrodel Resources Ltd* [2013] 2 AC 415.

[55] *Salomon v Salomon* [1897] AC 22.

because he wholly owned and controlled several companies that owned substantial assets. Mrs Prest argued that the assets of those companies were, in reality, her ex-husband's assets. She argued that the family court had power to pierce the corporate veil by virtue of the Matrimonial Causes Act 1973 (UK), s 24(1)(a). The case was eventually decided by the UK Supreme Court on the fairly narrow basis that s 24(1)(a) did indeed confer on the court the power to order the ex-husband's companies to convey the properties to Mrs Prest. The principal interest of the case, however, has been in the Supreme Court's broader comments about the corporate veil and the *Salomon* principle.

The leading judgment in the UK Supreme Court was delivered by Lord Sumption JSC. Lord Sumption began with the proposition that a court is justified in piercing the corporate veil if a company's separate legal personality is being abused for the purpose of some wrongdoing.[56] The difficulty, he said, lies in identifying what amounts to wrongdoing for these purposes:[57]

> References to a 'façade' or 'sham' beg too many questions to provide a satisfactory answer. It seems to me that two distinct principles lie behind these protean terms, and that much confusion has been caused by failing to distinguish between them. They can conveniently be called the concealment principle and the evasion principle. The concealment principle is legally banal and does not involve piercing the corporate veil at all. It is that the interposition of a company or perhaps several companies so as to conceal the identity of the real actors will not deter the courts from identifying them, assuming that their identity is legally relevant. In these cases the court is not disregarding the 'façade', but only looking behind it to discover the facts which the corporate structure is concealing. The evasion principle is different. It is that the court may disregard the corporate veil if there is a legal right against the person in control of it which exists independently of the company's involvement, and a company is interposed so that the separate legal personality of the company will defeat the right or frustrate its enforcement. Many cases will fall into both categories, but in some circumstances the difference between them may be critical.[58]

Applying this distinction and this terminology to the situation presently under consideration, one can say that the use of one-ship companies is not obviously or always an example of the evasion principle, but it may very often be an example of the concealment principle.

It is fairly easy to put the evasion principle to one side in this context. A maritime claimant does not have any legal right against the sole owner of a one-ship company that exists independently of the company's involvement. It may well be true, however, that the company has been interposed to conceal the identity of the real actor, which is legally relevant because beneficial ownership of the ship is the central issue in determining whether arrest of the ship is permitted. Understood in Lord Sumption's terms in *Prest*, the question of 'true' or 'beneficial' ownership in a surrogate arrest situation is not one of piercing the corporate veil at all.[59] The relevant legal question is not whether the sole owner of a one-ship company is (or ought to be) liable for the claimant's claim, but whether the owner beneficially owns the supposed surrogate that the claimant seeks to arrest.

[56] *Prest* (n 54) [27].
[57] ibid [28].
[58] ibid [29].
[59] Lord Neuberger PSC made this point (but not about surrogate ships, obviously) when expressing his agreement with Lord Sumption in *Prest* about the concealment principle: see ibid [61]: 'I also agree that cases concerned with concealment do not involve piercing the corporate veil at all.'

Prest certainly does not answer all possible questions about corporate personality, and it is not clear how large an inroad, if any, it makes into the *Salomon* principle. At the very least, however, it urges courts to eschew the metaphors of 'façade' and 'sham' and to focus on the real question. In concealment cases, that question is whether the corporate structure is concealing the true facts about beneficial ownership, 'dominion', control, and the unfettered right to dispose of the asset of the ship. That may or may not be 'banal', as Lord Sumption suggested, but it has certainly been done before, even under the English approach to the sanctity of the corporate veil. For example, in *Atlas Maritime Co SA v Avalon Maritime Ltd (The Coral Rose)*,[60] the defendant company agreed to sell the *Coral Rose* to the plaintiff, but then allegedly repudiated the contract. The plaintiff obtained a worldwide Mareva injunction (now called a freezing order) restraining the defendant or its agents from dealing with any of their assets up to the value of $3 million. The defendant then sold the ship to another purchaser. The sale proceeds, less the sum of $3 million, were paid over to Marc Rich & Co, which wholly owned a Liberian company, which was the beneficial owner of the defendant company. The defendant applied to the court for permission to pay the remaining $3 million to Marc Rich & Co, on the basis that it was the repayment of a loan made to purchase the *Coral Rose* in the first place. The English Court of Appeal affirmed the order of Hobhouse J at first instance that the injunction should not be varied in the manner sought by the defendant. Staughton LJ said:[61]

> In this case I can see no justification for piercing the corporate veil, so as to treat the liabilities of [the defendant] as liabilities of Marc Rich, its ultimate parent. We were referred to *Re A Company* (1985) B.L.C.C. 333 … as an authority for adopting that course. But as Mr. Justice Hobhouse said, that was an exceptional case involving allegations of fraud and the manipulation of corporate structures. I would not regard it as relevant to the determination of the present appeal.
>
> Nor, in my judgment, is it necessary to pierce the corporate veil in order to uphold the decision which the Judge reached; it is enough to lift it or look behind it, so as to ascertain that Marc Rich is as to 100 per cent the ultimate parent of [the defendant] … In my judgment, it is wholly proper, in deciding whether to permit payment by [the defendant] at this stage of the moneys claimed by Marc Rich, to have regard to the fact that Marc Rich is the ultimate parent of [the defendant] as to 100 per cent.

It should be obvious how similar Staughton LJ's distinction between 'lifting' the corporate veil and 'piercing' the veil is to Lord Sumption's distinction in *Prest* between the concealment principle and the evasion principle. There was no evidence of fraud in *The Coral Rose*, no evasion in the *Prest* sense, so there was no justification for piercing the corporate veil to hold that the person really liable was Marc Rich & Co. There was, however, sufficient evidence that the corporate structure was being used to conceal the fact that Marc Rich & Co was the true owner of the defendant, and it was not necessary to pierce the corporate veil to come to that conclusion, but merely to 'look behind' the veil. But for the terminology, this approach is entirely consistent with the view recently adopted by the UK Supreme Court in *Prest*, and it is suggestive of how *Prest* principles might operate in the future in the context of surrogate ship arrest.

[60] *The Coral Rose* (n 7).
[61] ibid 571.

If it is properly the concealment principle that should be applied in relation to one-ship companies, rather than the evasion principle that requires a genuine piercing of the corporate veil, then it will become necessary to determine whether the one-ship company is a genuine business, like John Dent's one-ship companies on the Tyne, or merely a shell interposed 'to conceal the identity of the real actors', like the Liberian company in *The Coral Rose*. Making that determination can only be done by considering factors very like those used in the United States in alter ego cases.

It is worth noting in this context that the English Court of Appeal in *The Coral Rose* said that, although Marc Rich & Co was the true owner of the defendant company, it was not the true owner of the ship *Coral Rose*. That conclusion was based on consideration of at least one of the circumstances that an American court would regard as significant in an alter ego inquiry, namely that Marc Rich & Co and the defendant appeared to operate as independent profit centres.[62] Staughton LJ said:[63]

> I cannot at present see any evidence of an agreement that the beneficial owner of *Coral Rose* should in reality be Marc Rich, and that [the defendant] should act as agents. Indeed, such an agreement would have defeated two objects which the parties most probably had in mind – that Marc Rich should not be liable for the debts of [the defendant], and that profits from the venture should be taxable (if at all) as the income of [the defendant] and not of Marc Rich. Of course the profits might eventually reach Marc Rich in the form of dividends if the venture was successful, or a distribution on the winding up of [the defendant]. But that might be postponed for many a day.

The contrast between the English Court of Appeal's decision in *The Coral Rose* and the decision of the High Court of Singapore in *The Skaw Prince*[64] may help to illustrate the possible significance of the UK Supreme Court's decision in *Prest* in future surrogate ship arrest cases in countries following the English tradition. In *The Skaw Prince*, two ships, *Skaw Prince* and *Skaw Princess*, were each owned by a Liberian company: *Skaw Prince* by Corsair and *Skaw Princess* by Filey.[65] Corsair and Filey each issued only one bearer share; both shares (and, thus, both companies) were owned by a Norwegian company named Pontina. Pontina was in turn wholly owned by a Swedish company named Skaw Shipping A/B. The two ships were mortgaged to a Norwegian bank under a mortgage agreement under which Skaw Shipping A/B was the borrower. The loan agreement between Skaw Shipping A/B and the mortgagee bank was signed on behalf of Skaw Shipping A/B, Corsair and Filey by one Per Olav Karlsen, who was a director of all three companies. Karlsen 'was involved in every level of control in Corsair, Filey, Pontina, Skaw Shipping A/B and [the ships' manager]'.[66] There was no evidence that Corsair, Filey or Pontina participated in any financial or operational decisions in relation to *Skaw Prince* and *Skaw Princess*.

In the High Court of Singapore, Amarjeet Singh JC held that the *Skaw Prince* could not be arrested as a surrogate for the *Skaw Princess* on the basis that Skaw Shipping A/B was the beneficial owner of both ships. Amarjeet Singh JC refused to lift (or pierce) the corporate veil, largely because:[67]

[62] See text at n 40 above: factor (8) on the Second Circuit's list.
[63] *The Coral Rose* (n 7) 570–71.
[64] *The Skaw Prince* (n 8).
[65] The description of the shipowning arrangements in this and subsequent sentences is taken from ibid [7], [9].
[66] ibid [9](e).
[67] ibid [17].

> [T]he legal structure of the Skaw group of companies was all already in place long before the charterparty was entered into by the [plaintiffs] with Corsair. Any argument by the [plaintiffs] of the fact of the *Skaw Princess* and *Skaw Prince* being in the registered ownership of Corsair and Filey as not precluding the court from applying the principles of equity and trust on the evidence in this case and coming to the conclusion that Corsair and Filey were in reality the trustees of the two ships for the benefit of Skaw Shipping A/B of necessity meant nothing more than an invitation that I should lift the corporate veil, embark on a wide ranging inquiry by examining the structure and arrangements of the various existing companies under the Skaw group.

In other words, Amarjeet Singh JC quite rightly did not see the evasion principle at work in *The Skaw Prince*, because the structure of corporate holdings had not been set up to defraud any particular claimants, and in particular not the plaintiffs, whose claim arose long after the structure had been created. But how would this case look as an example of the post-*Prest* concealment principle? It looks very much as though the registered owners Corsair and Filey, and their common owner Pontina, effectively did nothing except to interpose various levels of corporate personality to conceal the identity of the real actor, Skaw Shipping (or perhaps even Karlsen). Without 'a wide ranging inquiry … examining the structure and arrangements of the various existing companies', that suspicion could not be confirmed conclusively. Amerjeet Singh JC was unwilling to undertake that inquiry in *The Skaw Prince*, because he was looking at the case through the lens of what, after *Prest*, would now be called the evasion principle, rather than the concealment principle. That was most probably the right thing to do at the time *The Skaw Prince* was decided. It is not at all clear that it would still be the right thing to do after *Prest*. The key question in relation to surrogate ship arrest is not whether the owner of the shares of the shipowning company should properly be held liable to the plaintiff, but merely whether it is the 'beneficial owner' of the ship that is owned by the company. To refuse to look behind the corporate veil except in cases of fraud is to confuse the evasion principle with the concealment principle. In this context, the difference is 'critical', to use the word Lord Sumption used in *Prest*.[68]

III. Conclusion

It is wearyingly routine for academic writing about ship arrest to refer to the very long history of the practice. In order to spare the reader from a reprise of the usual historical references,[69] it is sufficient merely to observe that something very like the modern procedure of ship arrest has been in place in many countries of the world for centuries.[70]

[68] *Prest* (n 54) [29].

[69] The author confesses to having as little patience for references to the Rhodian Sea Law and the Rolls of Oléron as Hermann Göring supposedly did for culture. The Göring quotation in question is generally given as: 'When I hear the word "culture", I reach for my revolver.' Unlike the quotation from Einstein with which this Chapter began (see text at n 1 above), this quotation is both apocryphal and mistranslated. It is also occasionally attributed to Heinrich Himmler or Joseph Goebbels, but if any of them ever said it, it was only by way of quotation. It is a line from Act 1, Scene 1 of Hanns Johst's pro-Nazi play *Schlageter*, written in 1933, delivered by the character Friedrich Thiemann. The exact quotation is: 'Wenn ich Kultur höre … entsichere ich meinen Browning!' ('When I hear the word "culture", I remove the safety catch on my Browning!').

[70] A well-known survey of the debates about the history of ship arrest and a comparison of Common Law and Civil Law procedures is: William Tetley, 'Arrest, Attachment and Related Maritime Law Procedures' (1999) 73 *Tul L Rev* 1895.

Little has changed; little seems likely to change. Ship arrest has always had the purpose of providing local claimants with an effective means of redress in relation to a peripatetic asset that may be owned and operated by a distant defendant. That purpose is supposedly furthered and enhanced by the provisions for surrogate ship arrest in the international Conventions, but it is thwarted by courts' insistence on not looking beyond the corporate personality of one-ship companies (except in South Africa and the United States). Even in countries that are reluctant (except in cases of fraud) to 'pierce' the corporate veil to attribute liability to the owner of the company, it should be possible to 'lift' the veil, or to look behind it, to answer the question that is central to ship arrest legislation in many Common Law countries, namely that of identifying the 'beneficial owner' of the ship to be arrested.

INDEX

Abbreviations used in the index

AA (Cth) (Admiralty Act 1988 (Commonwealth of Australia))
AA (NZ) (Admiralty Act 1973 (New Zealand))
AC (Arrest Convention[s])
Note: 'AC' is used without a date when reference is intended to both Conventions without distinction or when the main heading indicates which Convention is under discussion. 'AC (1952)' and 'AC (1999)' are used when it is necessary to differentiate.
AJA (Administration of Justice Act 1956 (UK))
AJRA (Admiralty Jurisdiction Regulation Act 1983 (South Africa))
AJSMCA (Admiralty (Jurisdiction and Settlement of Maritime Claims) Act 2017 (India))
ALRC (Australian Law Reform Commission)
BC (Brussels Convention on Jurisdiction and the Enforcement of Judgments in Civil and Commercial Matters (1968))
BR/Brussels I Regulation (Recast) (on jurisdiction and the recognition and enforcement of judgments in civil and commercial matters (recast))
CCAA (Colonial Courts of Admiralty Act 1890 (UK))
CCP (Code of Civil Procedure (Greece))
CJJA (Civil Jurisdiction and Judgments Act 1982 (UK))
CLC (International Convention[s] for Civil Liability of Oil Pollution (1992)/(1969))
CMI (Comité Maritime International)
CPR (Civil Procedure Rules (UK))
EAPO (European Account Preservation Order)
ELD (EU Environmental Liability Directive (2004))
FCA (Federal Courts Act (Canada))
HCAJA (High Court (Admiralty Jurisdiction) Act 2001 (Singapore))
HNS (Hazardous and Noxious Substances Convention (2010))
IAA (International Arbitration Act 2002 (Singapore))
IPRED (EU Intellectual Property Rights Enforcement Directive)
IWG (International Working Group)
JIN (Judicial Insolvency Network)
MARPOL (International Convention for the Prevention of Pollution from Ships (1973) as modified by the Protocol (1978))
MSA (Merchant Shipping Act 1995 (UK))
SALRC (South African Law Reform Commission)
SCA (Senior Courts Act 1981 (UK))
SMPL (Special Maritime Procedure Law (China))
SPC (Supreme People's Court (China))
UNCLOS (UN Convention on the Law of the Sea (1982))
VCLT (Vienna Convention on the Law of Treaties (1980))

www.ingramcontent.com/pod-product-compliance
Ingram Content Group UK Ltd.
Pitfield, Milton Keynes, MK11 3LW, UK
UKHW050943290926
15470UKWH00005B/1611

9 781509 928309